contents

Teaching notes

Student notes

acknowledgements

The authors would like to thank the following people who have been instrumental in the preparation of this book: Mike Gilbert, Rosemarie Griffiths, Richard Holt, Barbara Jones, Jon Moore, Roger Petheram, Anita Sherwood, Nic Spicer and Patsy Spicer.

Osborne Books is grateful to the following organisations for their assistance and for giving permission, where appropriate, to use original material: Biz/ed, The Body Shop International Plc, Brintons Carpets, British Broadcasting Corporation, British Franchise Association, Broadheath Stores, Cadbury Schweppes Plc, Co-operative Retail Services Limited, Co-operative Wholesale Services, Department of Trade and Industry, Ericsson, The Guardian, The Independent, J Walter Thompson, Ledbury Welding and Engineering Limited, LloydsTSB Plc, London Metal Exchange, The Mail on Sunday, Marketing, Marketing Week, McDonald's, Morgan Cars, National Westminster Bank Plc, Nissan Sunderland, The Observer, Office for National Statistics, One-on-One Fitness Centre, Personnel Today, The Post Office, Prontaprint Plc, Raleigh Bikes, The Royal Mail (Warndon Sorting Office), Sage Plc, The Sunday Telegraph, Tesco Plc, Thomson Travel Group Plc, TPG Communications, Transport for London, Unilever Plc, Vauxhall Motors UK, Worcestershire County Council, World Cancer Research Fund.

Lastly, Osborne Books would like to thank QCA and the Awarding Bodies for their invaluable help and advice during the preparation of this text.

the text

Advanced Business has been produced to cover the compulsory Units of what is variously known at the time of going to press as the 'Advanced Vocational Certificate of Education' and the 'Vocational A Level' in Business. This book is suitable for both the double and the single award. The text follows closely the final versions of the Curriculum 2000 specifications produced by the Awarding Bodies. Osborne Books is grateful to the Awarding Bodies for making these available before this book went to press.

tutor pack

A teacher's Tutor Pack has been compiled to accompany this book. It contains assessment guidance, answers to a number of the Activities, sample external test papers and photocopiable material. If you would like to find out more about this Pack, please contact the Osborne Books Sales Office on 01905 748071.

text running order

Advanced Business is presented in Unit order and as far as possible the individual chapters reflect the subject sections within the 'What you need to learn' sections of the unit specifications. This order is for the sake of convenience and familiarity; it is not necessarily the order in which the subject matter should be covered. Most centres will be running units in parallel.

The unit specifications have been interpreted as widely and fully as possible. The aim has been to provide the student with a broad knowledge base, with plenty of Case Studies and activities to develop learning. Specific material for student assessment is contained in the Tutor Pack which complements this book (see above for details).

internal assessment and student activities

Advanced Business recommends that students should compile a Portfolio for all Units, including those that are externally assessed.

The planning of the chapters and Activities in this book have been based very much around the draft 'assessment grids' published by the Awarding Bodies. It is important that students understand the grading structure and what they have to do to achieve the various grades.

The Tutor Pack which complements this book contains further guidance and student activities designed to produce appropriate Portfolio assessment evidence.

external testing and revision

At the time of writing, external tests are the means of assessment for 'The Competitive Business Environment' and 'Business Finance' units for the twelve Unit Award.

Although at the time of writing there was no 'question bank' of past papers, the type of questions provisionally suggested by the Awarding Bodies have been reproduced in this text – and this should prove helpful to students.

The Tutor Pack which accompanies this book contains practice tests and gives guidance on preparation for external testing.

Key Skills 2000

One of the changes in Curriculum 2000 has been to 'decouple' Key Skills from the mainstream vocational units which constitute the Business Awards. The Key Skills are no longer compulsory, but they do form the basis of the Key Skills Qualification which many centres are offering.

Osborne Books has responded to this by publishing a series of photocopiable packs at all three levels – **Business Key Skills**. These sets of assignments, presented in business scenarios, are ideal for the Key Skills qualification. For further details please access www.osbornebooks.co.uk or contact the Osborne Books Sales Office on 01905 748071.

resources for courses

The need for access to a wide range of resources is mentioned in the 'Student Notes' section which follows. As more and more information becomes available on-line, students should be encouraged to access real businesses and also to make use of the excellent facilities offered by educational websites such as www.bized.ac.uk .

feedback

Osborne Books welcomes your feedback on this book. We appreciate both positive and negative comments which originate from teachers and from students. Please let us know by mail, e-mail (books@osbornebooks.co.uk) and telephone (01905 748071) and we will take note of everything you have to say, and will respond.

Michael Fardon, Frank Adcock, Ian Birth, David Cox, Michael Matchan, Sean O'Byrne, John Prokopiw.

May 2000

what is a Vocational course?

The word 'Vocational' means that the qualification relates to an area of work – in your case the business world. In the course that you will be doing you will be given the knowledge and skills you will need in a variety of business careers. The qualification means being able to 'do' a job as well as 'knowing' about it. It provides skills that employers value. Your qualification will also enable you to progress to higher education, which in turn will open up many possibilities for careers in business.

what is a Unit?

Units are areas of study which make up the course. Some are compulsory, some are optional. This book contains all the Compulsory Units you will need to cover.

The Units in this book cover all the essentials of the way businesses work:

1   **Business at work**

    This Unit presents an overview of the different types and sizes of business you will be investigating. It explains what they aim to do and how they work.

2   **The competitive business environment**

    This Unit shows how businesses compete with each other nationally and internationally. It also introduces you to the concept of 'markets' and explains the part the Government plays in ensuring that competition is fair.

3   **Marketing**

    This Unit contains extended Case Studies which illustrate the way in which businesses find out about what their customers need and how they promote their goods and services.

4   **Human resources**

    Employees are an important business resource. This Unit explains the way in which businesses plan for, recruit, train and manage their employees – and how they motivate them to work well.

5   **Business finance**

    Finance is essential to all businesses. This Unit investigates the way in which businesses manage their finances and shows how financial information can be interpreted to provide a picture of their financial 'health'.

6   **Business planning**

    This Unit takes a practical look at the way in which a business plan is drawn up, incorporating a sales and marketing plan, a production and resources plan and a financial plan.

Unit portfolios

Two thirds of the Units you cover are assessed through your coursework which is presented in a Portfolio – a folder containing your work which is known as Assessment Evidence. This is the work you have collected together so that you can be graded by your Assessor.

The grades you can get range from A to E.

Unit external tests

One third of the Units you cover are assessed by an External Test set by your Awarding Body. There is a separate test for each unit.

If you are doing the twelve Unit award, these Units are 'The Competitive Business Environment' and 'Business Finance'.

These tests are likely to contain a combination of short answer questions and Case Study work. You will be given plenty of practice in doing these tests.

how the chapters are organised

All the chapters in this book begin with an introduction which tells you what the chapter is about and what you will learn from it.

The chapters finish with a summary and key terms telling you what you should have learnt. Do not skip these sections – they are there to help you. The chapters also contain Activities for classwork and for investigation. These are Activities which will help build up Assessment Evidence for your Portfolio or give you practice for the external tests.

The chapters also contain Case Studies – most of them based on real businesses. When you read these through, try to relate them to situations that you have encountered in businesses that you have investigated, visited on work experience or worked for.

information – paper based

In your Advanced Business course you will do a great deal of investigation. You will have to find out about at least one medium-sized or large business and see how it is organised, how it markets its products and how it deals with its employees.

Sometimes it will not always be possible to investigate a business at first hand. You may need to read newspaper articles, magazine articles or textbooks. There are a number of published Case Studies of Business, including 'The Times 100' which your school or college should have in its library or resources centre.

information – the internet

One of the best and most comprehensive sources of up-to-date business information is the internet. The problem is really that there is almost too much information available. You need to be selective in what you find and print out.

You can access business websites direct, or can do a search on a particular word, for example 'co-operative' to find out about specific types of business. A good search engines can be found on www.yahoo.co.uk .

As a start, for a useful and informative site which contains a wealth of information about a wide range of businesses, try Biz/ed, the educational website:

www.bized.ac.uk

'good surfing' guide

We set out below a subject guide to useful websites. The addresses were correct when this book went to press. They can sometimes change, so if an address does not work, try doing a search on the name.

Company sites:

www.virgin.com   www.cadburyschweppes.com

www.gner.co.uk   www.tesco.co.uk

www.manutd.com   www.halifaxplc.com

www.toysrus.co.uk   www.lloydstsb.co.uk

www.adventureworld.co.uk   www.raleighbikes.com

Co-operative site:

www.co-op.co.uk

Franchise sites:

www.prontaprint.com   www.british-franchise.org.uk

Public Corporation site:

www.bbc.co.uk

Multinational sites:

www.unilever.com   www.mcdonalds.com

Ethically aware site:

www.the-body-shop.com

Charity sites:

www.nspcc.org.uk   www.oxfam.org.uk

Sites useful for marketing studies:

www.acnielsen.com   www.asa.org.uk

Consumer issues and market competition site:

www.oft.gov.uk

Human resources sites:

www.stepstone.co.uk   www.totaljobs.com

Business finance and planning:

www.barclays.co.uk   www.hsbc.co.uk

www.dti.gov.uk   www.hm-treasury.gov.uk

Try these sites for statistics and business news:

www.ons.gov.uk   www.bbc.co.uk/news

For the European Union:

www.europa.eu.int

Lastly, if you need blank financial documents for the 'Business Finance' Unit, access our website (Resources Section), download the file and then print out your documents. The address is:

www.osbornebooks.co.uk

Surf creatively!

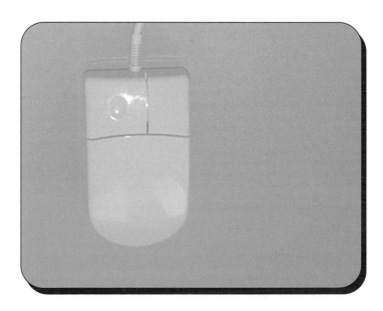

Business objectives

introduction

Businesses are able to exist because customers buy the goods and services that they produce. Businesses adopt a variety of objectives (goals) which include making a profit, providing quality products, helping society and caring for the environment, all of which combine in the overall business aim – its 'mission'. A business needs to make sure that its workforce works together to achieve its objectives. In providing goods and services a business is answerable to groups of people known as 'stakeholders'; these include customers, owners, employees and society at large, all of whom in one way or another are affected by the business and influence the way it operates.

what you will learn from this chapter

● the overall aim of a business is set out in a mission statement

● the objectives of a business are the goals it sets to enable it to achieve its aim

● a stakeholder of a business is an individual or group that has an interest in the business; stakeholders can be:
  - *internal:* managers, employees, owners
  - *external:* customers, suppliers, investors (shareholders), lenders, the local community, environmental pressure groups

● the objectives of a business – which include profit, growth, quality, helping the community, environmental protection – satisfy the needs of stakeholders but can sometimes conflict with each other

● the 'culture' of a business describes the 'way of thinking' within the business, eg the workforce 'thinking' total quality, customer focus, sales maximisation; this culture will affect the way different objectives are perceived and achieved by the business

what is a business?

common factors in business

If you ask the 'person in the street' what a business is, you are a likely to be given an example: W H Smith, Tesco, the local leisure centre, Virgin Trains, the window-cleaner, and so on. All these examples of 'businesses' have factors in common:

- they provide products in the form of goods or services – books, food, fitness training, travel, clean windows
- some businesses provide products which customers need – for example basic food and clothing
- some businesses provide products which customers can be persuaded to want through advertising – for example luxury food, fashion clothing, a holiday

A business may therefore be defined as:

an organisation which provides goods or services which satisfy customer needs and wants

Activity 1.1

Classification of businesses

The following organisations can be classed as businesses. Decide in each case (through individual work or class discussion)

- whether they provide a need or a want (or both)
- whether they provide goods or services (or both)

1   Tesco

2   BMW

3   BBC

4   Coca Cola

5   A local fitness centre

6   A local 'posh' restaurant

7   McDonalds

8   Mothercare

9   Direct Line Motor Insurance

10   Virgin Trains

business aims

business aims and the Mission Statement

An aim is what you set out to do.

An aim for a business is the overall direction in which the management wish it to develop over a period of time. Examples include:

> *"I want this company to be the biggest supplier of building materials in the area."*
>
> *"I want this travel agency to provide the best level of customer service in the town."*

The small business owner is likely to have a reasonably clear idea of the main aim of the business and will work hard to achieve it. The management structure of a larger business will be more complex and will have to deal with many more staff. It is the job of management to identify a common aim and to motivate the employees to work together to achieve that aim – the business 'vision' to maximise sales, to provide the best service, and so on.

A business will often set out its aims in a published 'statement'. This can take the form of a brief 'Vision Statement' – which is how a business sees itself – or a 'Mission Statement' which is normally longer and more detailed. This how Boots the Chemists sees itself – concentrating on its customers:

> Our vision is to be the world's leading retailer of products and services that help make our customers look good and feel good.

Activity 1.2

Mission statements

1   Use the internet and other sources such as company reports from resource centres to research Mission Statements. Try the useful company information section on the educational website www.bized.ac.uk

2   Comment on how brief or long the statements are and how successful they are in telling you what the aim of the business actually is (some Mission Statements are very bland and vague).

3   Make up a Mission Statement for your school or college.

business objectives

An **aim** expresses in general terms what the business sets out to do in the long term.

An **objective** is a goal the business wishes to achieve.

A business will succeed in its aim through the achievement of a variety of objectives, including profitability, growth, quality and social responsibility. As you will see, some of these objectives can conflict with each other.

making a profit and covering costs

All businesses, whether they are large companies like Tesco or state-owned corporations like the BBC, need to make a profit or a surplus. Profit is what is left from sales income after expenses have been paid. Profit provides money for further growth and for rewarding the owners.

The extract from the Tesco Annual Review and Summary Financial Statement shown below illustrates this point. But businesses are wary of adopting profit as their main objective. Profit has in some circles become a 'dirty' word – associated with overpaid 'fat cat' directors and the exploitation of cheap overseas labour.

Tesco – a growth business

In the UK, Tesco is the leading food retailer with 639 stores. We aim to increase food sales while developing our non-food business, offering the convenience of one-stop shopping to our customers.

Outside the UK, we currently have 182 stores. In the last financial year, we acquired the largest food retailing business in Ireland and we are expanding our hypermarket businesses in Central Europe and Asia.

By understanding customer needs better than anyone, we aim to increase value for customers, earning their lifetime loyalty and to enhance returns to shareholders.

Financial highlights

- Group sales   up **6.3%**
- Group operating profit*   up **7.8%**
- Earnings per share   up **7.7%**
- Dividend per share   up **6.5%**

---

growth – increasing sales and market share

For some businesses, beating the competition is one of the main objectives because the survival of the business often depends upon it. A weak business can be a prime target for a take-over by another business. Beating the competition can be achieved in a number of ways:

- growth – a policy of expansion to increase sales and market share (market share is the percentage of the market taken by the products of a business)
- price cutting

Activity 1.3

Survival of the fittest

A number of types of business are cutting prices (and consequently profits) in order to increase sales and market share. These include supermarkets, airlines, on-line retailers.

1   Find out the lowest price of a sliced loaf of white bread from a supermarket and the price charged by a local 'corner' shop?

What is the difference?

Why is there this difference?

What might happen to the businesses as a result of this difference in price?

2   Can you think of any other businesses which carry out price cutting like this? What are these businesses aiming to do?

providing quality

A business which provides a quality product and quality customer service keeps its customers. Quality products – which can be manufactured items or services – are often the result of a policy of quality which extends to every person and procedure within the business. This policy is known as Total Quality Management (see page 114). Some businesses apply for and are granted a quality certificate in line with ISO 9000, an international standard for quality systems (see page 118).

If a business adopts quality as a major objective – particularly if it is charging a high price for its products – it will ensure that the whole workforce is involved in the quality process. It will implement stringent standards of quality control if it is a manufacturer; each stage in the production process will treat the next stage in the process as if it were a customer of the business.

a skilled workforce

Another objective of a business is to build up a skilled workforce. This often goes hand in hand with the issue of quality. A quality manufactured product or service can only be provided by employees who are trained in the necessary skills. Car plants like the Nissan plant featured below often adopt 'teamworking' which gives responsibility and a 'say' to all employees involved in the production process. Businesses which offer a service, financial services companies, for example, need to ensure that their employees are fully trained and qualified to give informed advice.

Activity 1.4

Quality at Nissan, Sunderland

COMPANY PHILOSOPHY

Nissan's Sunderland plant aims to build profitably the highest quality cars sold in Europe, to achieve the maximum possible customer satisfaction and thus ensure the prosperity of the company and its staff.

To assist in this we aim for mutual trust and co-operation between all people within the plant. We believe in **teamworking** wherein we encourage and value the contribution of all individuals who are working together towards a common objective and who continuously seek to improve every aspect of our business. We aim for **flexibility** in the sense of expanding the role of all staff to the maximum extent possible and we put quality consciousness as the key responsibility above all. We genuinely build in **quality** rather than inspect and rectify.

Achievement of these tough targets is assisted by the fact that we give common terms and conditions of employment to all our staff. For example, everyone is salaried, there are no time clocks, and the sickness benefit scheme, private medical insurance, performance appraisal system and canteen are the same for all.

All of this means that we believe that **high calibre**, well **trained** and **motivated** people are the key to success.

Read through the text and answer the following questions:

1   What term can you use to describe the first paragraph of the Company Philosophy?

2   What objectives are built into the first paragraph?

3   What is the key responsibility of all staff working at the plant?

4   How is this responsibility put into action at the plant?

5   What is the key responsibility of all staff working at the plant?

6   What does Nissan see as the key to successful quality production?

7   How does Nissan achieve this?

serving the community

A further business objective is to support the local community. Many businesses provide active support by giving to national and local charities, sponsoring local events, helping with community projects and providing resources for education. The Tesco 'Computers for Schools' tokens are a well-known example, as the 1999 Annual Review points out:

> **Tesco is helping to create a better life for everyone, taking practical steps to protect the environment, and support projects which make a real difference at local level to the communities in which we work.**

> This has been the eighth year of Tesco Computers for Schools which, to date, has put £44m-worth of computer equipment into schools across the UK. It is one of the most successful national cause-related marketing programmes ever.

Why do businesses support the local community? A business that is seen to be socially responsible will retain the respect of customers. A business that advertises its good works is likely to gain new customers.

caring for the environment

It is common knowledge that the earth's resources are being depleted and damaged by business on a worldwide scale. Not only are resources running out, but it is likely that pollution is damaging the balance of gases in the atmosphere, leading to global warming. It is claimed that the production of genetically modified food is also disturbing the balance of nature.

Businesses are under increasing pressure from governments and pressure groups such as Greenpeace to carry out a policy of *sustainability*. This means adopting objectives such as:

- cutting down on pollution
- not wasting natural resources
- using recycled materials wherever possible
- using energy efficiently

Businesses like to be seen to be helping to save the environment. If they are thought to be socially responsible, consumers are more likely to think the better of them and therefore more likely to buy their products. The ban in some supermarkets of the sale of genetically modified food is a case in point. Also, savings on the use of resources such as energy use can mean savings in costs; this directly helps to boost profits.

Activity 1.5

Caring for the environment

Sustainable development

We aim to develop our business in a way that will allow us to remain prosperous in the long term. As stated in our environmental report, in our contribution to sustainable development, we focus on three areas that are directly relevant to our business. These are fish conservation, clean water stewardship and sustainable agriculture.

☐ **Fish conservation** We continue working towards sourcing all fish from certified fisheries by 2005. The first products to carry the on-pack logo of the Marine Stewardship Council are due to be on sale in 1999. This will give consumers the opportunity to show their support for sustainable fishing.

☐ **Clean water stewardship** Clean water is necessary for the consumption of many of our products: from cooking food to personal hygiene. During the year, we initiated a number of projects to help safeguard this vital resource. In June, for example, we launched our three-year sponsorship of the Global Nature Fund's Living Lakes initiative. By sharing our in-house expertise, as part of this initiative, we are helping communities in different continents to better manage their local lakes and wetlands.

☐ **Sustainable agriculture** We launched pilot projects focusing on our strategic crops: ranging from tea in Kenya to tomatoes in Australia. These projects will help us establish sustainability indicators, as a step to defining, and contributing towards, soil health and productivity.

As public interest in biotechnology increased, our companies in Europe took a lead in labelling products with genetically modified ingredients. We believe biotechnology has an important role to play in meeting the everyday needs of people. Confidence in the technology will only be fostered through understanding and we think that society should be involved in the debate on the issue. We therefore support the establishment of clear and comprehensive regulations and the provision of information on the application of genetic modification technology to consumer products.

The extract on this page is taken from the Report and Accounts of Unilever, a large public limited company which operates worldwide and produces many leading brands, including Persil, Lynx, Birds Eye and 'I Can't Believe it's not Butter'.

1   What is Unilever doing to help sustainability?

2   What is Unilever's view on genetically modified foods?

3   Do you think this is a view shared by all businesses?

stakeholders and objectives

stakeholders

You will have seen that business objectives involve different individuals and groups of people – customers, employees, the local community, for example. These people are often referred to as 'stakeholders'. A stakeholder has an interest – a 'stake' – in the business. It matters to a stakeholder what the business does and it matters to the business what the stakeholder does or thinks. Some stakeholders are external and independent of the business, some are internal – they work for the business and share the business 'culture'. It is the task of the management of a business to prioritise business objectives – some of which will be conflicting – to keep the majority of the stakeholders happy for the majority of the time.

external stakeholders

customers and suppliers

Many businesses are **customer**-focused – in other words they aim to keep their customers happy by looking after them, listening to their views and meeting their needs. With businesses in keen competition, a customer that is ignored is a customer that is lost.

Suppliers are also important to businesses because they provide the quality goods and materials which customers demand. A business needs to build up a long-term relationship with its suppliers to ensure continuity and quality in the supply chain. Look at the importance that Tesco gives to both customers and suppliers in its Annual Review:

> **We give customers genuine choice and variety in food. Tesco selects, prepares and packages everyday products in dozens of different ways – from fresh to frozen, from value packs to gourmet treats, from raw ingredients to ready meals.**

> **The Supply Chain covers suppliers, buyers, distribution, stores and office support, aiming to give stores what they need to serve customers better.** Supply Chain improvements have continued to deliver savings in line with our target of £100m between 1997 and 2000. Last year, we saved £60m to spend on our customers. For example, continuous replenishment systems are now in place and a new scanning system has been installed in every store.

shareholders and lenders

External **shareholders** who invest in a business, but do not take part in its day-to-day management, are stakeholders because they have a money stake in a company and look for a return. **Lenders**, such as banks, also have an interest in a business: they need to be able to get their money back. A business will need to be profitable to satisfy both groups of stakeholders.

pressure groups, the local community, the government

The environmental and non-profit making objectives of a business are driven by **pressure groups** which represent public opinion about issues such as the environment. Greenpeace, for example, protested when Shell Oil planned to sink an old oil platform, which may have polluted the Atlantic. The public boycotted Shell petrol stations until the company changed its mind.

The **local community** has an interest in local business for a number of reasons. The local community needs full employment, a clean environment and support for local events and charities. Local pressure groups can often have significant influence on business decisions – blocking planning for new business projects, for example.

The **government** has an interest in and influence over business. Laws cover areas such as planning, environmental hazards and the ways employees are treated. Taxation through the Inland Revenue raises money for government spending on areas such as transport, education and healthcare.

Activity 1.6

Conflicting business objectives

The external stakeholders of a business often place conflicting demands on what a business does. The management of a business has to decide which objectives take priority. What potential conflicts of interest can you see in the following situations? What stakeholders may be affected, and in what way?

1   A supermarket is forced to slash its prices on many best-selling lines as part of a price war.

2   A supermarket is forced by public opinion to ban the sale of genetically modified foods.

3   A pressure group launches an attack on a manufacturer of brand name trainers for importing footwear which has been made overseas using cheap child labour.

4   A tobacco company invests money in a marketing campaign to sell cigarettes to a Third World country where the health risks are less well-known.

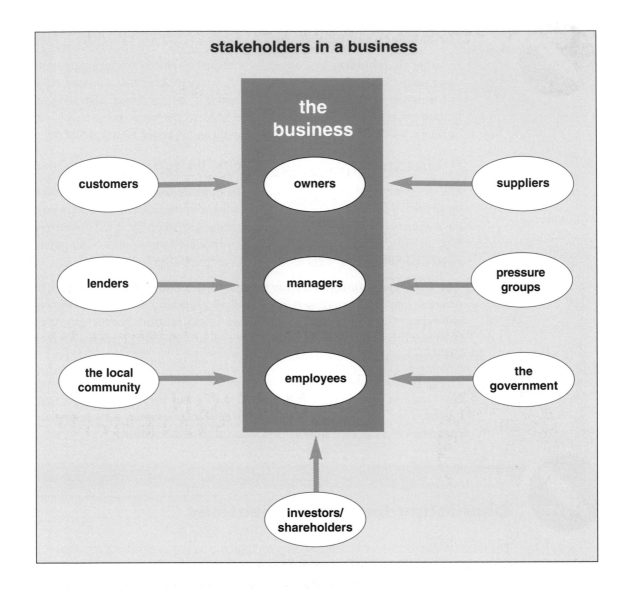

internal stakeholders

owners, managers and employees

The **owner** of a business is a stakeholder who looks for a return on the capital (money) put into the business. In the case of a small business the owner is often also the management and a member of the workforce. In a larger business, such as a limited company, there is a distinction between the owners, the management and the employees. **Managers** and **employees** are stakeholders in a business because the success of the business in terms of making a profit and the employees working together with the same aim (see 'culture' on page 25) ensures job security and job satisfaction.

Activity 1.7

Identifying business objectives

Set out below are the Mission Statements (or equivalents) of The Body Shop International PLC, Unilever PLC and the BBC.

1   Find out what these businesses do and what type of businesses they are.

2   Summarise the business objectives of each business.

3   Identify what you think is the main objective of each business.

4   State what stakeholder groups are targeted by each business.

5   Identify any areas in each statement where you consider there may be a conflict between business objectives.

6   Write a conclusion emphasising the differences between the three businesses.

MISSION STATEMENT

OUR REASON FOR BEING

- To dedicate our business to the pursuit of social and environmental change.

- To creatively balance the financial and human needs of our stakeholders: employees, franchisees, customers, suppliers and shareholders.

- To courageously ensure that our business is ecologically sustainable: meeting the needs of the present without compromising the future.

- To meaningfully contribute to local, national and international communities in which we trade, by adopting a code of conduct which ensures care, honesty, fairness and respect.

- To passionately campaign for the protection of the environment, human and civil rights, and against animal testing within the cosmetics and toiletries industry.

- To tirelessly work to narrow the gap between principle and practice, whilst making fun, passion and care part of our daily lives.

We aim to be the world's most creative and trusted broadcaster and programme maker, seeking to satisfy all our audiences in the UK with services that inform, educate and entertain and that enrich their lives in ways that the market alone will not. We aim to be guided by our public purposes; to encourage the UK's most innovative talents; to act independently of all interests; to aspire to the highest ethical standards; to offer the best value for money; to be accountable to our licence payers; to endeavour to be the world's leading international broadcaster; and to be the best – or to learn from the best – in everything we do.

The BBC Beyond 2000

Unilever's Corporate Purpose

Our purpose in Unilever is to meet the everyday needs of people everywhere – to anticipate the aspirations of our consumers and customers and to respond creatively and competitively with branded products and services which raise the quality of life.

Our deep roots in local cultures and markets around the world are our unparalleled inheritance and the foundation for our future growth. We will bring our wealth of knowledge and international expertise to the service of local consumers – a truly multi-local multinational.

Our long-term success requires a total commitment to exceptional standards of performance and productivity, to working together effectively and to a willingness to embrace new ideas and learn continuously.

We believe that to succeed requires the highest standards of corporate behaviour towards our employees, consumers and the societies and world in which we live.

This is Unilever's road to sustainable, profitable growth for our business and long-term value creation for our shareholders and employees.

culture

achieving business objectives

The management of business sets objectives such as customer care, quality and environmental responsibility to satisfy the needs of external stakeholders. But there is little point in doing this if the whole workforce is not dedicated to achieving these objectives. If you go into a shop and find the sales staff indifferent and the goods in poor condition the business is failing in its objectives because the employees and the internal systems are not geared up to a common aim. The attitude to work is all wrong. The business lacks a 'culture' (also known as 'corporate culture').

corporate culture

The word 'corporate' means 'belonging to a body' – in this context 'relating to a business'. 'Culture' means 'a way of doing things.' Corporate culture may be defined as:

the attitudes, values and beliefs that are shared by the people in a business

If a business is to succeed in achieving its objectives, it is vital that its people (owners, managers, employees) share a belief in those objectives. It is up to the management of a business to instill that belief in the employees – to promote a common 'vision' involving:

- the business objectives
- a common code of behaviour for the employees

different types of culture

There are a number of different influences which dictate how a culture will evolve. In your studies you will get a 'feel' of a business when you deal with it as a customer, get a part-time job or do work experience. Some businesses will see sales performance and profit as a major objective, other businesses may give product quality priority, others may be more concerned with environmental and ethical issues. The influences on culture may be summarised as:

- **economic** influences – the need to make a profit and be efficient
- **social** influences – the need to serve local communities and society as a whole
- **environmental** influences – the need to conserve energy and sustain natural resources
- **ethical** influences – the need to help and not to exploit developing economies (which may be a major source of supply)

management styles and culture

The way in which a business is structured and managed can affect the implementation of a culture within a business. For example if a business organisation is based on teamwork (see the Nissan example on page 17), a common culture can easily be adopted and adapted. If, on the other hand, a business is managed very much 'from the top', the workforce may be less cooperative in adopting a culture which it has dictated to it. These issues are covered more fully on page 66.

Activity 1.8

Business culture and objectives

The following extracts are from the Annual Reports of The Body Shop International PLC and Unilever PLC. For further information about the companies try and get hold of the Reports yourself, or access the websites:

www.the-body-shop.com **and** www.unilever.com

- To meaningfully contribute to local, national and international communities in which we trade, by adopting a code of conduct which ensures care, honesty, fairness and respect.

- To passionately campaign for the protection of the environment, human and civil rights, and against animal testing within the cosmetics and toiletries industry.

- To tirelessly work to narrow the gap between principle and practice, whilst making fun, passion and care part of our daily lives.

Responsible Corporate Behaviour

How we conduct our business
Unilever's commitment to responsible corporate behaviour is fundamental to our operating tradition.

Dedicated to meeting the everyday needs of people everywhere, it is essential for our business success that Unilever people stay close to and understand evolving consumer needs and values. With a decentralised operating structure local companies have maximum opportunity to be closely in touch with local consumers. Local companies are predominantly run by local people in tune with their local societies. By the very nature of our business we are an integral part of the societies in which we operate.

The principles and values which guide Unilever's corporate behaviour are set out for all employees in our Corporate Purpose and Code of Business Principles. To frame this corporate behaviour we have worldwide operational standards which are central to the way we do business. These standards are set to ensure the quality and safety of Unilever's products and services, the health and safety of Unilever people at work and to minimise the environmental impact of our operations, wherever they are in the world. Every company chairman is required to give positive assurance on an annual basis of their company's adherence to these policies and to the broader principles set out in the Code of Business Principles. Company performance is regularly audited.

Best practice in responsible corporate behaviour, as in other areas of business management, is constantly developing and has again become a matter of public debate. We are reviewing the policies which guide our actions and the processes through which we evaluate them in order that we can meet transparently society's evolving expectations of corporate behaviour.

We believe that outstanding business performance must be underpinned by the highest standards of corporate behaviour towards our employees, consumers and the societies and world in which we live.

The Body Shop International PLC

1   What are the four key features of the Body Shop code of conduct? What evidence do you see of these features in any Body Shop premises?

2   What three aspects of the working lives of Body Shop staff will help to narrow the gap between principle and practice?

3   Summarise the corporate culture of The Body Shop.

Unilever PLC

4   How do Unilever people 'stay close to and understand evolving consumer needs and values'?

5   What document sets out the culture of Unilever?

6   What are the aims set out in this document?

7   What stakeholders are targeted by the Unilever culture?

Conclusion

8   What differences can you identify in the cultures of The Body Shop and Unilever?

CHAPTER SUMMARY

- A business is an organisation which provides goods and services that customers need and can be persuaded to want.

- The aim of a business – what it sets out to do in the long term – is often summarised in a Mission Statement.

- Business objectives are goals that the business sets out to achieve as part of its overall aim. They include:

  - making a profit

  - survival – beating the competition

  - increasing sales and market share

  - providing quality goods and services

  - developing a skilled workforce

  - helping society both locally and on a wider scale

  - caring for the environment

- Business objectives can conflict.

- A stakeholder of a business is an individual or a group that has an interest in the business.

  Internal stakeholders include owners, managers and employees.

  External stakeholders include investors, customers, suppliers, lenders, the local community, the government and pressure groups.

- Stakeholders are directly affected by the objectives adopted by the business because they are influenced by what the business does.

- Businesses must balance the demands of its stakeholders in its adoption of business objectives.

- The 'culture' of a business – often referred to as 'corporate culture' describes the 'way of thinking' within the business, for example the workforce 'thinking' total quality, customer focus, social responsibility.

- If a business is to succeed in achieving its objectives it is essential that these are built into its culture – they must be adopted by the entire workforce – which is a task for the management of the business.

KEY TERMS

business	an organisation which provides goods or services which satisfy customer needs and wants
aim	an aim is what a business sets out to do
objective	a goal which a business aims to achieve, for example profitability, growth in market share
Mission Statement	a written statement setting out the aim of a business – sometimes it also lists business objectives
TQM	Total Quality Management (TQM) is a policy which aims to ensure a high level of quality in an organisation's products and procedures
ISO 9000	an international standard for the certification of quality in organisations
sustainability	a policy of conserving natural resources and preserving the environment
stakeholder	an individual or group which has an interest in a business and is affected by what the business does
shareholder	someone who has an ownership stake in a limited company business
culture	the attitudes, values and beliefs that are shared by people in a business
corporate culture	another term for 'culture' – 'corporate' meaning 'belonging to a body', in this case a business

2

Types of business

introduction

The last chapter looked at the aims of a wide range of businesses. In this chapter we look in detail at the different types and sizes of business: how they are owned, how they are set up and how they change as they expand.

what you will learn from this chapter

- businesses can be classified according to 'sector':
  - public sector businesses which are wholly or partly state-owned
  - private sector businesses which are owned by individuals
  - voluntary sector – 'businesses' such as charities

- businesses can be also classified according to ownership:
  - sole trader – a 'one person' business
  - partnership – a business owned by a group of individuals
  - limited company – a separate body owned by shareholders (either the smaller 'private' company or the larger 'public limited company' whose shares can be traded on the stock markets)
  - co-operative – a business owned and run by its members
  - franchise – a licence to use a well-known business name
  - charity – a business set up to help society rather than to make a profit

- the type of ownership of a business will largely dictate the size of the business

- businesses may need to change ownership type as they expand; this is likely to affect factors such as finance, control, profit allocation and the legal liability of the owners

business sectors

Businesses have traditionally been divided into what is termed the private sector and the public sector. In addition to these there are the charities which form the voluntary sector.

the public sector

This sector comprises government-owned or government-controlled bodies including:

- public corporations such as the Post Office and the BBC
- Government Departments (the Civil Service)
- local authorities such as County, Metropolitan or District Councils

Some local businesses are public sector. Your local leisure centre may well be owned by the Council and either run by the Council itself, or run by an independent company which has tendered for the business.

the private sector

This sector comprises businesses which are directly or indirectly in private ownership. This sector accounts for most businesses operating within the UK. Private sector businesses include:

- sole traders (one person businesses)
- partnerships (groups of people in business)
- limited companies (a limited company is a body owned by shareholders, set up to do business)
- co-operatives (groups of people 'clubbing' together for a specific purpose - eg a farmers co-operative set up for producing and selling grain)
- franchise operations (where a trader can 'buy' a name and set up a business which is already established and used by other independent operators, eg Thorntons and Dynarod)

Privatisation is a process whereby public sector operations have been 'sold off' by the Government, in order to raise money, to private sector shareholders. British Telecom (BT) is a well-known example.

charities – the voluntary sector

Charities are independent bodies in what is known as the voluntary sector. They include registered 'do good' charities such as Oxfam and Scope, and educational and arts organisations such as many independent schools and the National Trust. See page 264 for a Case Study on the operations of Cancer Research.

sole traders and partnerships

sole trader

A sole trader is an individual trading in his or her name, or under a suitable trading name.

The sole trader is the most common form of business. There are approximately 3.6 million businesses in the UK; of these over 2 million are sole traders.

If you set up in business, you may do so for a number of reasons: redundancy, dissatisfaction with your present job, or developing a hobby or interest into a business. The majority of people setting up in this way do so on their own. If you decide to do so, you become a sole trader.

unlimited liability

In law a sole trader is an individual who is liable for all the debts of the business. He or she is personally responsible for repaying those debts. This is known as 'unlimited liability'.

advantages of being a sole trader

There are a number of advantages of being a sole trader:

- freedom – you are your own boss
- simplicity – there are no legal formalities required before you can start trading – there is less form-filling than there is, for instance, for limited companies, and the book-keeping should be less complex
- savings on fees – there are none of the legal costs of drawing up partnership agreements or limited company documentation

disadvantages of being a sole trader

There are also disadvantages of being a sole trader:

- risk – you are on your own, with no-one to share the responsibilities of running the business or taking over if you are ill or on holiday
- time – you may need to work long hours to meet tight deadlines
- expertise – you may have limited skills in areas such as finance
- you may not be able to raise capital so easily

the bankruptcy risk

Another risk of being a sole trader is bankruptcy. Sole traders run the risk of going 'bust' – or, in technical terms, being made a 'bankrupt' by the court. If you are bankrupt it means that the money you owe is more than the money you have, and also that you cannot repay your debts on the due dates. Someone can make you bankrupt by demanding money that is owed and you failing to pay; they can then take you to court to try and recover the money for themselves and other creditors. If a sole trader is declared bankrupt he or she may have to sell his or her personal belongings to pay off those debts.

It is clear that setting up in business as a sole trader involves total commitment in terms of capital, time, and the risk involved. If you are starting your business with other people or need to raise substantial capital, you may consider establishing a partnership or a limited company.

partnership

A partnership is a group of individuals working together in business with a view to making a profit.

A partnership is simple to establish and involves two or more people running a business together. In legal terms, the partners are the business. Examples of partnerships include groups of doctors, dentists, accountants, and solicitors. A partnership – often known as a 'firm' – can either trade in the name of the partners, or under a suitable trading name. For example if M Smith & G Jones set up a glazing business, they could call themselves 'Smith and Jones & Co.' or adopt a more catchy name such as 'Classy Glass Merchants'.

unlimited liability or limited liability

The essential legal point about a traditional partnership is that each partner is liable for the whole debt of the partnership. This means that if one partner runs up a big debt, each of the other partners will be liable for all of it. It therefore pays to take care whom you admit as a co-partner in your business. A partner therefore, like a sole trader has unlimited liability for the business. The only exception to this rule is the limited liability partner (see next page).

limited liability partnership

At the time of writing legislation was being passed through Parliament which will in due course become the Limited Liability Partnership Act. This will enable newly formed partnerships in a trade or profession to have the flexibility of a partnership but it will also give the partners limited liability.

Partnership Agreement

Partnerships are currently regulated by the Partnership Act 1890.

Most partnerships will operate according to the terms of a Partnership Agreement, a document usually drawn up by a solicitor (see the extract shown on the next page). This document will normally set out:

- the amount of capital contributed (money invested) by each partner
- the sharing out of profit (and losses) by the partners
- the procedure in the case of partnership disputes (these are unfortunately common)
- the procedures for new partners coming in and old partners retiring – this is not shown in the extract here

It must be stressed that a partnership does not have to draw up a Partnership Agreement; it is just that a written document sets out clearly each partner's rights and obligations, a useful factor in the case of a dispute. In the absence of a written agreement, the Partnership Act 1890 sets out certain terms and conditions relating to partners' rights and obligations. If there were a dispute, these terms would be recognised in a court of law.

advantages of a partnership

- there is the potential to raise more capital than a sole trader is able to – there are more individuals to contribute funds
- there is more potential for expertise and specialisation – one partner may be a technical expert, another a salesperson, another a financial expert
- there is cover for holidays and sickness
- unlike a limited company (see next page), a partnership does not have to make its accounts available to the public

disadvantages of a partnership

- unlimited liability – each partner is liable for the whole debt of the partnership, to the extent that he or she may be made personally bankrupt if the business fails
- each partner is also liable for the business deals of the other partners (this could be a problem if a deal went badly wrong)
- disagreements can and do occur amongst partners – occasionally this can lead to the break-up of the partnership and the business

PARTNERSHIP AGREEMENT
(extract)

MADE on 30 June 2000

BETWEEN Solomon King of 45 Park Gardens, Ormskirk

AND Gloria Maisey of Flat 7, Parkway Mansions, Maghull

IT IS HEREBY AGREED AS FOLLOWS

1. Solomon King and Gloria Maisey will become and remain partners for a period of five years from the date of this Agreement.

2. The Partners shall practise in partnership in the firm name of Solomon & Maisey & Co at the address Equity House, 191 High Street, Ormskirk.

3. The initial capital of the partnership shall be in the sum of £100,000, to be contributed by the partners in equal shares.

4. The partners shall be entitled to the net profits arising from the business in equal shares, or such other shares as may from time to time be agreed by the partners.

5. Each partner shall be entitled to five weeks holiday in each year.

6. Should any dispute arise at any time between the partners with regard to this agreement or in respect of the rights, duties and liabilities of the partners in the conduct of partnership business, then an independent Arbitrator shall be appointed. The ruling of the independent Arbitrator shall be accepted by both Partners.

Signed by
Solomon King of 45 Park Gardens, Ormskirk

Solomon King

in the presence of Henry Purcell, 45 Melody Gardens, Birkenhead

Henry Purcell

Signed by
Gloria Maisey of Flat 7, Parkway Mansions, Maghull

Gloria Maisey

in the presence of Henry Purcell, 45 Melody Gardens, Birkenhead

Henry Purcell

Activity 2.1

sole traders and partnerships

Stan is a plumber and central heating engineer who has been made redundant. He has been in the trade for fifteen years and has a number of customers for whom he can do work. He has redundancy money which he can use to set himself up in business. He likes the idea of being his own boss, but has heard that a large number of new start-up businesses fail in the first year of trading.

Answer these questions for Stan.

1   *"People say it is risky going into business on your own. What do you reckon? What could I lose?"*

2   *"What do I need to do to set up on my own?"*

Stan has a mate, Olly, who sometimes works with him. Olly wants to go into partnership with Stan, but Stan is not so sure. Answer these questions for Stan.

3   *"What do I stand to gain if I let Olly come into business with me? He is not the most reliable of people and seems to get caught up in some shady deals."*

4   *"What paperwork do I need if I set up in partnership? Is it worth it?"*

limited company

If a group of people wants to set up a business, another option is the formation of a limited company.

A limited company is a business
— owned by shareholders
— run by directors
— set up as a body which is separate from its owners (the shareholders)

A limited company is very different from a sole trader or partnership business. The sole trader or partner is the business; if the business goes 'bust' then so does the owner. The shareholder owner of a limited company stands apart from the business, which is a body in its own right. If the company goes 'bust' the shareholder is protected by limited liability and does not lose all his or her money – just the money invested.

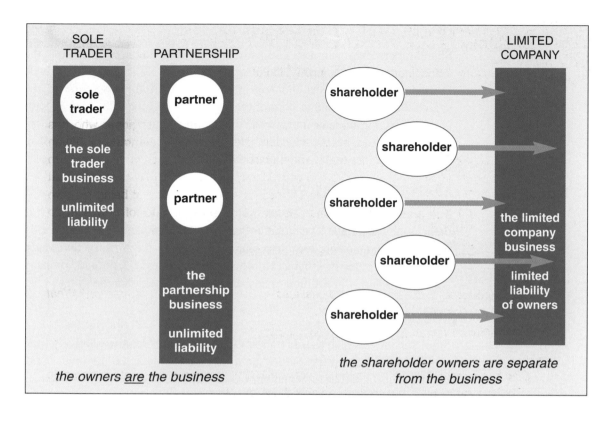

the owners <u>are</u> the business

the shareholder owners are separate
from the business

private and public limited companies

A limited company will either be:

• a **private limited company** (abbreviated to Ltd), or

• a **public limited company** (abbreviated to Plc)

Most small or medium-sized businesses which decide to incorporate (become a company) become private limited companies; they are often family businesses with the shares held by the members of the family.

Private companies cannot offer their shares for sale to the public at large, and so their ability to raise money may be limited.

A private company may, however, become and trade as a public limited company if it has a share capital of at least £50,000 and is issued with a Trading Certificate issued by Companies House. It must also have the words 'public limited company' or 'plc' in its name.

A public limited company can offer its shares for sale on the Stock Market in order to raise finance, but not all plc's take this step. When a business offers its shares for sale to the public it will employ a merchant bank to manage the operation, which is known as a 'flotation'. The cost of a flotation can be high, sometimes running into millions of pounds for the largest issues.

the control of limited companies

Shareholders own a limited company and appoint directors to control the management of the company and plan for its future. In the case of a private limited company, the shareholders often are just the directors, and so the shareholders can be said to control the company directly. The chief director is the managing director. In the case of a public limited company, directors often hold shares, but there are likely to be many more shareholders who take no part in the day-to-day running of the company.

sharing company profits

Sole traders and partners can take profit straight out of the business – it is their money, after all. The situation with limited companies is more strictly regulated: shareholders receive a share of profit in the form of dividends, normally twice yearly. Directors – who are employees of a limited company – are paid salaries in addition to any dividends on their shareholdings.

documentation

Small businesses such as sole traders and partnerships require relatively little in the way of paperwork. Setting up a limited company, on the other hand, requires substantial documentation. Companies are regulated by Companies House, a government-owned agency. All companies have to register with Companies House and are issued with the company equivalent of a birth certificate – the Certificate of Incorporation. In addition, a company will also need two further documents:

• the Memorandum of Association – which states what the company can do

• the Articles of Association – the internal 'rulebook' of the company

MEMORANDUM OF ASSOCIATION

sets out what activities the company can carry out

ARTICLES OF ASSOCIATION

'rule book' for internal running of company – sets out what directors can and cannot do

CERTIFICATE OF INCORPORATION OF A PRIVATE LIMITED COMPANY

No.   2126859

I hereby certify that

EFFORTSENIOR LIMITED

is this day incorporated under the Companies Act 1985 as a private company and that the Company is limited.

Given under my hand at the Companies Registration Office, Cardiff the   29TH APRIL 1987

'birth certificate' of a limited company

D. G. BLACKSTOCK
an authorised officer

Activity 2.2

Pilgrim Computing Limited
a new company

A group of ten people in the computing business are setting up a new software company to be called Pilgrim Computing Limited. They will all become directors.

The company will be a private limited company to start with, but if it grows according to plan, the directors hope it will convert into a public limited company within five years so that it can raise further finance on the Stock Market.

The directors will also be shareholders as they are contributing £50,000 each to form the share capital of the new business. The directors have also negotiated a £75,000 business loan from the bank.

They have placed all the paperwork of starting the business in the hands of their Accountants.

Answer the questions set out below

Information for the answers can be found in the text above and on pages 36 to 38.

1   What type of company will Pilgrim Computing Limited be initially? What is the main restriction placed on this type of company?

2   How will the directors take their share of profits out of the company? How does this differ from a partnership?

3   What type of company will Pilgrim Computing Limited possibly convert to in five years time? Why should it do this? What are the benefits and costs of doing so? How will it affect the directors' control of the company?

4   What is the share capital of the new private company?

5   What type of liability will each shareholder director have, and what money amount can each director stand to lose?

6   What are the documents that their Accountants will have to arrange, and what is the function of those documents?

7   Why do you think Pilgrim Computing Limited is not being set up as a sole trader or partnership business?

co-operatives

The term 'co-operative' refers to two types of business:

- a retail Co-operative Society – which sell goods and services to the public
- co-operative – a group of people 'clubbing' together to produce goods or to provide a service

We will deal with each of these in turn.

retail Co-operative Societies – the background

Retail Co-operative Societies date back to 1844 when a group of twenty eight Rochdale weavers, suffering from the effects of high food prices and low pay, set up a society to buy food wholesale, ie at the same price as it was sold to the shops. This food was then sold to the members at prices lower than the shop prices, and the profits distributed to the members in what was known as a dividend, the level of which depended on the amount of food they had bought. These self-help co-operatives grew in number during the nineteenth century, but declined in the later twentieth century, largely because of competition from the 'big name' retailers such as Tesco, Sainsbury and Asda.

the Co-op today

A well-known example of a retail co-operative is the Co-operative Wholesale Society (CWS), which took over the operations of Co-operative Retail Services in April 2000. This group of companies is generally known as 'the Co-op'. It operates a wide range of businesses, including 1100 food stores, the UK's largest funeral business, car dealerships, travel services and opticians. It also incorporates the insurance company CIS and the Co-operative Bank.

The Co-operative Wholesale Society operates a number of on-line services, including on-line banking.

Visit www.co-op.co.uk for full details of this group of companies.

who owns the Co-op?

A retail Co-operative Society is owned by its members. You can become a member by filling in a form obtainable from your local Co-op store and buying a share, normally for £1. As a member you have voting rights (one vote per member) and can often obtain discounts at the Society's retail shops and the use of other facilities such as funeral services.

other co-operative ventures

The term 'co-operative' also applies more loosely to co-operative ventures. At the time of writing there are around two thousand co-operatives which fulfil a number of different functions:

trading co-operatives

Groups of individuals, such as farmers, who do not have the resources in terms of capital and time to carry out their own promotion, selling and distribution, may 'club' together to store and distribute their produce. They may also set up co-operative ventures to purchase machinery and equipment.

workers co-operatives

A workers co-operative may often be found where the management of a business is not succeeding and a shut-down is proposed. The 'workers' step in, with the consent of the management, and take over the ownership and running of the business with the aim of 'making a go of it' and at the same time safeguarding their jobs.

co-operatives on the internet

For an up-to-date view of co-operative ventures carry out a UK search on the internet through www.yahoo.co.uk using the word 'co-operative'.

franchises

The franchise system was first established in the USA and is now a rapidly growing business sector in the UK. A franchise is an established business name – eg Burger King or Prontaprint – which is 'sold' to someone setting up in business. A number (but not all) of McDonald's are franchises.

The two people involved in the deal are:

• the **franchisor**, the person who has developed a certain line of business, such as clothes retailing, hamburgers, drain clearing, and has made the trading name well-known

• the **franchisee**, the person who buys the right to trade under the well-known trading name

In return for an initial fee the person setting up (the franchisee) receives full advice and in some cases the necessary equipment. As the business trades a 'royalty' percentage of takings is paid to the franchisor.

advantages of a franchise

- you are entering into a business which has been tried and tested in the market
- your business may well have a household name such as Burger King
- you are more likely to be able to raise finance from a bank for a franchise
- you should receive training, and in some cases, be provided with tried and tested equipment

disadvantages of a franchise

- the initial cost of going into the franchise – the payment to the franchisor
- a proportion of your takings also go to the franchisor
- you are less independent in that you cannot develop the business as you wish – you cannot change the name or change the method of doing business

Franchises – UK facts and figures

total franchisors	568
total franchisees	29,100
total annual sales from franchises	£7 billion

who does what? – some examples

business	franchisees
Building services	1080
Catering and hotels	3675
Cleaning services	1775
Direct selling	3995
Parcels and taxis	1520
Quick Printing	600
Retailing	4785
Vehicle services	2035

Source: British Franchise Association www.british-franchise.org.uk

Activity 2.3

Franchising

The extracts shown on this page have been reproduced by kind permission of Prontaprint, a leading UK 'on demand' printing franchise. You can find further details at www.prontaprint.com. Look also at the statistics on the previous page.

1   What is an 'on demand' (quick print) printing business?
2   What percentage of franchisees in the UK are in a 'quick print' business?
3   What are the risk factors for starting up a franchised business?
4   List the benefits of taking up a franchise with a franchisor such as Prontaprint.

REDUCING THE RISK

Starting a new business is daunting. Starting a business which is based upon an established and successful formula is much less so.
A Prontaprint franchise offers the opportunity to enter into an exciting and rewarding market, offering customers a proven high quality product with unparalleled levels of service. As part of an established and highly successful nationwide network of modern business service centres, the risks associated with a typical new business are significantly reduced.

Businesses still working after 3-years

60% New start-up

94% Franchise

SOURCE: BFA Guide to Franchising

DIP A TOE IN THE WATER?

To summarise:

The Print-on-Demand Market
■ Is dynamic and poised for significant UK, European and global growth.
■ Is developing based upon a regional, national and international "distribute and print" model, which will be satisfied by an integrated and high quality Print-on-Demand network. Prontaprint is that network.

Prontaprint
■ Is part of the largest Print-on-Demand network in the world, with a strategic alliance with the US-based Sir Speedy and its affiliates, covering the USA, South America, Australia, South East Asia, Canada and Europe.
■ Offers expert business planning to assist new franchisees achieve business objectives.
■ Provides close links with major clearing banks for investment assistance.

Network Support Centre providing:
■ Intensive induction training.
■ Training in key services; digital design, print, copying, sales and marketing and IT.
■ Structured support from field-based Business Development Managers.
■ New Franchisee Support Team for on-site, hands-on assistance.
■ On-going training and support programme.
■ Expert assistance from technical, IT and purchasing teams.
■ Legal and estates advice.
■ Centralised Prontaprint brand marketing.

publicly owned businesses

private and public sectors

Businesses are either:

- private sector businesses or
- public sector businesses

The private sector includes businesses which are directly or indirectly owned by private individuals. Most businesses in the UK are in the private sector. They include all the businesses covered so far in this chapter, from one person businesses to large companies.

Public sector organisations, on the other hand, are directly or indirectly controlled by the government. They include:

- Public Corporations
- Local Authority enterprises

public corporations

Public corporations are bodies established by Act of Parliament, and owned and financed by the State, for example the Post Office, the Bank of England and the BBC.

Public corporations are run by a Board of Management headed by a chairperson appointed by the Government. There used to be more public corporations, but in the 1980s and 1990s a number of them were privatised. In

other words they were sold off to the public by the government, which turned them into public limited companies, enabling the public to buy their shares.

British Gas, BT and BA are examples of privatisations.

local authority enterprise

'Local Authority' is a term applied to local governing councils which operate both in the county areas and also in city areas. Local Authorities have a wide range of services to administer. These include education, environmental health, planning, refuse collection, social services, transport, fire services, libraries and leisure facilities. They finance these from Central Government Grants, local taxation (currently the Council Tax) and income from local authority enterprise.

Local authority enterprises include a wide variety of commercial activities, including, for example:

- leisure – swimming pools, sports centres, golf courses
- transport – local bus services
- car parks
- local lotteries

Local Authorities now often use outside businesses for supplying services such as waste collection and catering and also for running leisure facilities. This gives private enterprise new opportunities, but it can also mean that the local community may end up getting the cheapest service rather than the best service!

non-profit making organisations

There are a number of types of organisations which employ business methods but which do not aim to make a profit for the organisers' benefit. These include:

- charities – both national and local which raise money for humanitarian and social needs; these include well-established international charities (Red Cross), national charities (Mencap, Cancer Research), local charities (the local hospital scanner appeal) or 'one-off' events (Comic Relief)
- Arts Associations – national foundations, local dramatics, operatics and choral societies
- Sports Associations – national associations and local clubs
- pressure groups – examples include Friends of the Earth and Greenpeace

Activity 2.4

Public sector businesses

1   Investigate a public corporation, for example the BBC. Find out where its income comes from, if it makes a profit and who its competitors are. Would you class the corporation as a business? If so, why?

To find out information, try out the corporations's website: www.bbc.co.uk

2   Investigate a local authority enterprise, for example a local swimming pool or the catering in your school or college. Who runs the enterprise? How do you rate it compared with similar enterprises in the private sector?

business size

When you investigate the range of businesses in your area you will see that they range from the small one-person business to the national and international names seen in the High Street. The most common methods of classification by size are by the number of employees and by the amount of annual sales – by 'turnover'.

classification by size and turnover

The government divides businesses into three classifications by employee:

small business	up to 50 employees
medium-sized business	50 to 249 employees
large business	250 or more employees

A common classification term is 'SME' which stands for Small & Medium-sized Enterprises; this includes the first two categories listed above.

Another way of looking at the size of a business is to compare it with other businesses in terms of its annual sales figure: the sales turnover. One classification range is up to £100,000, £100,000 to £499,999, £500,000 to £999,999, £1,000,000 to £4,999,999, £5,000,000 and over.

Activity 2.5

Business size – some statistics

THE NUMBER OF UK BUSINESSES – BY EMPLOYEE		
size (employees)	type	number of businesses
0-49	(small business)	3,626,620
50-249	(medium-sized business)	24,610
250 and over	(large)	6,660
TOTAL		3,657,890

Source: DTI statistics published by the Government Statistical Service

Small businesses account for a higher proportion of employment in agriculture and construction.

Large businesses dominate electricity, gas, water supply, mining and manufacturing businesses.

Source: DTI statistics published by the Government Statistical Service

1   Which is the most common size of business, and why? What types of business are likely to be represented in this sector?

2   What percentage of the total is this sector?

3   What types of business are represented in the remaining sectors?

4   What percentage of the total do these represent?

5   Draw up a pie chart or bar chart showing the three size categories in the table. If you can, draw up the figures on a spreadsheet and use the computer to generate the chart. Make sure all your labelling is clear.

6   Why do you think agriculture and construction account for so many small businesses?

7   Why do you think electricity, gas, water supply, mining and manufacturing account for the majority of large businesses?

geographical spread – multinationals

Some of the largest businesses – multinationals – operate worldwide.

A multinational is a business which manufactures or provides services in countries outside its 'base' country.

An example is Ford Motors, based in the USA, but manufacturing 'Fords' in Europe and also other brands of cars through companies it owns such as Jaguar in the UK, Mazda in Japan and Volvo in Sweden.

Unilever is one of the world's largest multinationals, producing well-known products such as Persil, Lipton's Tea, Solero ice lollies, Flora, Lynx and Domestos. The profile below gives an idea of how large the group is.

Unilever profile

Unilever is one of Europe's largest multinationals. Based in Rotterdam, the Netherlands and London, UK, it has more than 500 subsidiary companies in 90 countries worldwide. It is larger than Coca-Cola and Sony with annual sales of approximately £27 billion and annual profits before tax of £1.8 billion. Unilever is the world leader in ice cream, margarine and tea-based drinks and deodorants. It leads the European markets for frozen foods and the North American markets for skin care and meal sauce. It also has a substantial market share in fabric cleaners and hair care.

www.unilever.com

CHAPTER SUMMARY

- The public sector comprises government-owned or government-controlled bodies. Many of these are run on business lines, including public corporations such as the BBC and local authority enterprises.

- The private sector comprises businesses which are owned by private individuals and organisations.

- The voluntary sector comprises bodies such as charities and Arts organisations which aim to be 'non profit-making' but which use business techniques to promote themselves and raise money.

- Small businesses employing up to 50 employees account for most of the businesses in the UK – they are predominantly sole traders, partnerships, franchises and private limited companies.

- Medium-sized businesses, employing from 50 up to 250 employees mostly comprise large partnerships and private limited companies.

- Large businesses (250 employees and over) are predominantly public limited companies which operate nationally.

- The largest companies are multinationals which are based in one part of the world but operate worldwide in the production of goods and services.

- Business owners who are sole traders or partners in an unlimited partnership have unlimited liability for the debts of their business.

- Business owners who are limited partners in a limited partnership or shareholders in a limited company have limited liability for the debts of their business.

- The burden of documentation required of business owners increases with the size of the business. Sole traders, apart from the normal business stationery, do not need documentation to set the business up. Partners often have a Partnership Agreement to establish the rights of the partners. Limited companies are strictly regulated by Companies House; they need a Certificate of Incorporation and Memorandum and Articles of Association.

- Co-operatives are businesses which were originally 'self-help' societies which were set up for the mutual benefit of their members. Some have now grown and amalgamated to form the retail 'Co-op'. Other co-operatives exist on a smaller scale either as groups of traders or as workers co-operatives.

- The franchise arrangement, which originated in the USA, allows a franchisee to trade under a trading name developed by the franchisor. In return for a fee and a share of profits the franchisee receives training and, in some cases, equipment.

KEY TERMS

public sector	businesses that are controlled or owned by the government
public corporation	a government-owned business
private sector	businesses that are in private ownership
voluntary sector	non profit-making organisations run on business lines
sole trader	an individual setting up in business on his or her own
partnership	a group of individuals working together in business in order to make a profit
limited partnership	a partnership set up by the Limited Partnership Act which allows partners to have limited liability
partnership agreement	a document which sets out the rights and duties of partners, including capital invested, share of profits, and the procedure in the case of a dispute
unlimited liability	the obligation to repay all the debts of the business if the need arises
limited liability	the obligation to repay all the debts of the business restricted to a certain amount – normally the amount of the investment
limited company	a business owned by shareholders and run by directors set up as a body separate from its owners
private limited company	a limited company whose shares are held by the directors and are not for public issue, it must have 'limited' in the name
public limited company	a limited company with a share capital of at least £50,000 which can be issued for sale to the public; it must have 'PLC' in the name
franchisor	the owner of a business idea and name
franchisee	a person who buys the right to use a business idea and name
SME	Small and Medium-sized Enterprise – a business which has from 1 up to 250 people working in it
multinational	a business which manufactures or provides services in countries outside its 'base' country

Business functions and structures

introduction

When a business manufactures a product or provides a service it uses resources in different ways, for example in production, marketing, and administration. These are 'functions' which enable it to achieve its objectives. Whether a business is successful or not in achieving its objectives depends on how the business is organised and run – the way it is structured and managed.

what you will learn from this chapter

- businesses use resources such as buildings, machinery and manpower – 'factors of production' – to enable them to produce goods or services

- businesses combine these factors of production in a number of different functions: finance, production, human resources, marketing, research and development

- business functions need to operate efficiently together in order to achieve the objectives of the business, for example growth or profit

- businesses are structured in different ways with different levels of management – some have many layers of management, others have very few; these structures are likely to vary according to the type of market each business is operating in

- the current trend is for fewer levels of management – for what are known as 'flatter' structures which allow more decision-making for people lower down in the organisation

- each business will have its own management 'style', largely dependent on its structure; this will reflect the way of thinking – the 'culture' of the organisation

the factors of production

A business employs a variety of resources when it produces goods or services. These resources are normally divided into categories and are known as the 'factors of production':

land

This includes everything on or under the earth's surface such as coal and other mineral deposits. It also includes rivers, lakes, seas and all other natural resources.

labour

This refers to the services of unskilled and skilled workers – from labourers to craftsmen and keyboard operators to managers.

capital

Anything that is not wanted for its own sake but for the contribution it makes to the production of other goods and services comes under the heading of capital. It includes factories, offices and all the machinery used in the production process. It also includes raw materials used in the production process. It does not, however, include money; this is only useful to the extent that it can be used to buy capital.

enterprise

It is possible to distinguish a further factor of production – enterprise. Enterprise comes from people who have the ideas, are willing to take the risks and who bring together the other factors of production. Enterprise can be seen as a division of the factor of labour or it can be seen as a factor in its own right. In either case production could not take place without it.

the cost of the factors of production

As it is impossible to produce anything without using some of each of the factors of production they are also responsible for the main costs of production. The costs of employing the factors of production are:

labour	=	wages
land	=	rent paid
capital	=	interest paid on finance raised to buy capital
enterprise	=	profit (as a reward)

Activity 3.1

Classifying the factors of production

Classify the resources listed below that might be used in the production of cars, in terms of the four factors of production (land, labour, capital and enterprise).

assembly line workers	sheet steel
tyres	body press plant
company directors	designers
paint	administration buildings
car sales reps	computers
factory site	engine components

combining the factors of production

A business manufacturing a product such as cars can in theory choose from a wide range of methods of production. It can employ many workers and make the cars by hand (as some small sports car manufacturers do) or it can make more use of modern robotic machinery and employ fewer workers per car. The manufacturer that chooses the first of these alternatives is opting for a 'labour intensive' production method while the manufacturer who chooses the second alternative is opting for a 'capital intensive' method. The combination chosen will also depend on the level of demand; products such as canned drinks, for which there is an extremely high demand, will tend to be mass produced using large amounts of modern machinery.

Morgan Cars UK – labour intensive production

Vauxhall Motors UK – capital intensive production

functions in business

the functions

Whatever the size of the business – whether it is a sole trader or a public limited company – or whatever the product, the factors of production are combined in a variety of functions. These include:

- **production** – using the factors of production (resources) to produce a manufactured product (eg a canned drink or car) or a service (eg a holiday, a haircut) – it is the basic function of any business
- **research and development** (R&D) – investigating new products and new ways of producing existing products
- **finance** – the control of money and the recording and reporting of money transactions – a central function in any business
- **marketing and sales** – finding out what customers need; promoting and selling the products
- **human resources** – the management of people in the business
- **administration** (also known as facilities management) – providing all the back-up needed by the business, for example catering, office machine maintenance, security, reprographics (photocopying and printing)

the management

All the functions listed above have to be co-ordinated by the management of the business to achieve the objectives of the business. For example:

- the type of products that are to be sold and to whom
- the amount of finance that will be needed
- the resources that will be needed – premises, people, equipment

This all requires careful operational planning. The success of the business will largely be determined by the quality of the planning and the way the management co-ordinates the way the functions work together.

Remember that these principles apply equally to any size of business – a sole trader or a large company. The sole trader will have to carry out most of the functions him/herself and so will need to be highly organised and focused. The management of a larger business will need to ensure that all the functions operate smoothly and in a co-ordinated way to achieve the business objectives. We will look at the effectiveness of management styles later in this chapter (see pages 65 to 66). First we will examine in more detail the business functions and see how they inter-relate.

business functions

functions and departments

Business functions remain the same, whatever the size of the business – sole trader or PLC. In the descriptions which follow we look in more detail at the functions carried out by departments in a typical limited company. The range of activities carried out by the departments will, of course, vary according to the type of business. The descriptions here are fairly typical, but you will find variations in your investigations.

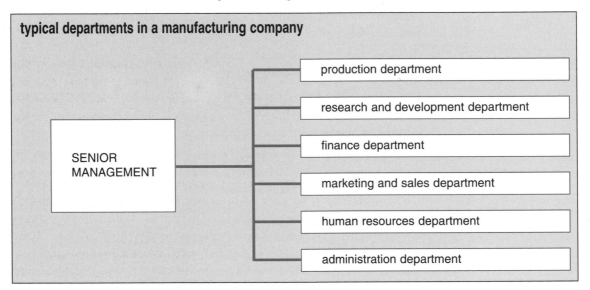

typical departments in a manufacturing company

SENIOR MANAGEMENT

- production department
- research and development department
- finance department
- marketing and sales department
- human resources department
- administration department

the production function

If a business is manufacturing a product, the manufacturing process will have to be strictly controlled in order to maintain quality and keep to production targets. The business must also monitor the efficiency of production methods and research and develop new techniques in line with modern technology (see R&D below). The purchasing function must ensure that it obtains raw materials from the right supplier, at the right price, at the right time, and of the appropriate quality. If the business is providing a service, the role of the production department will be taken by an operations department.

research and development function

As you will appreciate when you study marketing, a business that does not develop new products or revamp existing products will soon lose out to its competitors. Research and development (R&D) is an essential function, particularly where the business is technology based. In the pharmaceuticals industry, for example, the success of a company is based on the drugs it researches and develops; ICI has reaped the rewards for developing the best-selling anaesthetic, Diprovan. The R&D function forms an integral part of production and is sometimes included as part of a production department.

the finance function

The finance department of a business is responsible for financial record keeping. This involves keeping records – either in manual form, or on computer file – of money received and paid out. The financial records maintained will be used to produce the financial statements of the business (see Chapter 21), which in the case of limited companies are required by law. The finance department normally also oversees the payment of wages and the handling of cash by the cashier. The finance department is also responsible for the management accounts of the business. These are figures produced for the management of a business showing how well the company is performing in terms of income and expenditure in comparison with budgets prepared in advance. The finance department will also be closely involved in the planning process as it is responsible for raising the finance needed by the business.

the marketing and sales function

Marketing is involved with satisfying customers' needs at the right price. It means researching what the customer wants, and investigating how the business can satisfy that need. Selling, on the other hand, involves persuading the customer to buy the products the business has already produced. The sales function will co-ordinate the selling programme, using a variety of techniques – travelling sales representatives, telephone sales, mailshots and a follow-up schedule. Often in an organisation the marketing and selling functions are closely linked. Many businesses now have a customer services section (or department) which answers customer enquiries and deals with customer complaints.

Once a product has been sold it will have to be delivered. This is carried out by 'distribution'. Efficient distribution ensures that the customer gets the product on time and in perfect condition. Distribution involves warehousing and storage, packing, despatch and transport. Businesses will vary in their distribution methods, but the most successful businesses will always monitor the quality of their distribution. Many businesses use outside distributors.

the human resources function

The human resources or personnel function fulfils a number of needs. It is responsible for the hiring and firing of employees, for staff training and development, and for dealing with matters relating to industrial relations. See Chapters 15 to 17 for a fuller discussion of this function.

administration (facilities management)

The administration and support services are essential in keeping the 'wheels' of the business turning. They include maintenance of the business premises and equipment, reprographics, in-house printing (forms, stationery, newsletters), catering and computer services, mail handling and data storage. The department which provides these services is traditionally known as the administration department. Larger businesses are increasingly turning to specialist businesses to carry out a number of these functions, a process known as 'outsourcing'.

co-ordinating the functions

A successful business knows how to co-ordinate its functions/departments so that it runs efficiently and achieves its objectives. This co-ordination is a result of good management and good communications. Read through the Case Study and carry out the Activity which follows.

Case Study

Zephyr PLC
Tornado 201 – a quality problem

Zephyr PLC manufactures vacuum cleaners in Bristol. During the course of the year it encounters a quality problem with one of its new products, the Tornado 201. A large number of customers have complained about its tendency to drop dust when the power is turned off. A feature about the problem has appeared on a TV consumer programme and sales have started to decline.

How do the functions within the business communicate together to deal with the problem?

marketing & sales	receives complaints from customers
marketing & sales	makes note of adverse TV report
finance	records decline in sales
	problem passed to senior management
SENIOR MANAGEMENT	meeting held to discuss problem

continued on next page

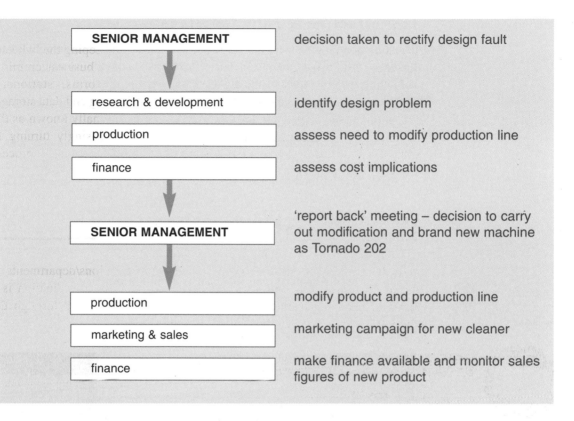

SENIOR MANAGEMENT	decision taken to rectify design fault
research & development	identify design problem
production	assess need to modify production line
finance	assess cost implications
SENIOR MANAGEMENT	'report back' meeting – decision to carry out modification and brand new machine as Tornado 202
production	modify product and production line
marketing & sales	marketing campaign for new cleaner
finance	make finance available and monitor sales figures of new product

Activity 3.2

Co-ordinating business functions

A number of different business functions will be involved in any business activity. Identify the functions which are likely to be involved in the following situations, and explain how they connect with each other.

1   A customer returns a carton of double cream to a supermarket. The cream has gone 'off' before the expiry date on the carton. He wants a refund.

2   Sales of petrol at a local independent petrol station have declined sharply. Customers have been heard to say that petrol is cheaper at the supermarket round the corner and also that you cannot get sandwiches and drinks there.

3   A window cleaner wants to expand his 'round' to another area as he has heard that the local window cleaner there is going to retire to the Algarve.

4   An expanding firm of accountants want to open up a new office in a town five miles from its main office.

how effective are the functions?

The functions of business will operate as well as the management of the business will allow them to. The effectiveness of the management in achieving the objectives of the business will depend on three factors:

- the structure of the business – how well management can control and communicate with employees
- the style of management – the attitude taken by the management to employees
- the culture of the business – the way of thinking of the whole workforce

organisational structures

In the study of organisational theory it is common practice to illustrate the organisation by means of a structure chart. Look at the structure of a family – the most basic of organisations – set out below. In this family there are two parents and five children. Note in particular:

- the routes of communication between different parts of the organisation
- the levels of control and authority within the organisation

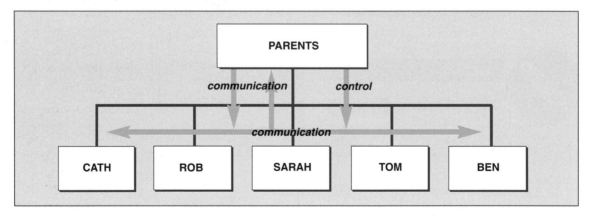

- the parents are at the top of the diagram as they are responsible for, and control, the family
- communication flows both horizontally and vertically

If you then compare the family with a business (as some Japanese companies do) you will see how an organisation should function, and can go wrong. Any failure in communication routes or in control could result in serious problems and inefficiencies – just as it does in a family.

We will now look at how these principles work in different 'shapes' of business structure.

hierarchical structures

A hierarchy is a series of levels of people, each level controlled by the level above it.

Large organisations, public limited companies or Civil Service Departments, for example, may have thousands of employees. They are likely to have a more elaborate and 'tall' organisational structure which has:

• a number of levels of hierarchy

• division into functional areas such as sales, finance, human resources

The structure chart below is that of a manufacturing company.

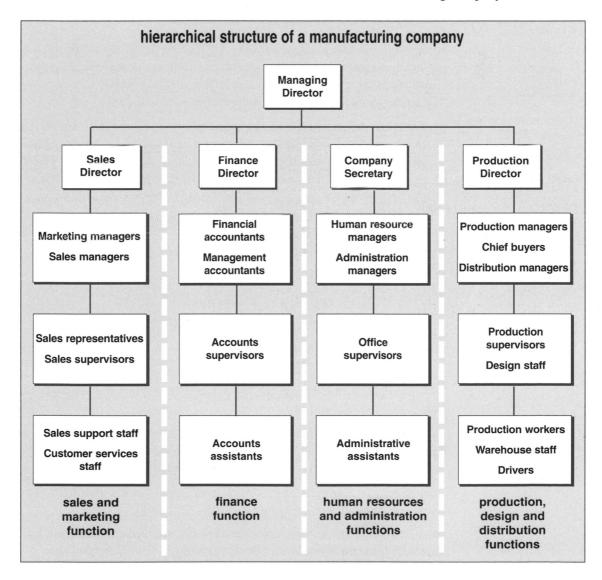

hierarchical structure of a manufacturing company

Managing Director

Sales Director	Finance Director	Company Secretary	Production Director
Marketing managers Sales managers	Financial accountants Management accountants	Human resource managers Administration managers	Production managers Chief buyers Distribution managers
Sales representatives Sales supervisors	Accounts supervisors	Office supervisors	Production supervisors Design staff
Sales support staff Customer services staff	Accounts assistants	Administrative assistants	Production workers Warehouse staff Drivers
sales and marketing function	finance function	human resources and administration functions	production, design and distribution functions

points to note from the structure chart

You should note that the chart set out on the previous page represents a manufacturing company. The levels of hierarchy and functions (sales etc) are only illustrated as an example of a hierarchical structure. The essential point to remember is that the basic pyramidal or tall shape of the hierarchical structure will remain the same, no matter how the functions or levels of authority change.

management levels

Each horizontal level represents a step in the level of importance and responsibility of the staff:

- the managing director is responsible for communicating company policy and making sure it is carried out

- the other directors are responsible for making decisions affecting their function areas (eg sales, finance, production) and communicating those decisions to the people working in the function areas; the company secretary is the director responsible for the administration of the company

- managers are in charge of the departments; they are responsible for carrying out or delegating the directors' decisions, their role is to organise their staff, to motivate them and to ensure that their staff know what is going on in the organisation – managers must be good communicators!

- supervisors are in charge of the day-to-day running of the departments and normally work alongside the production and administrative staff; sales representatives and design staff are also on this level

- production, administrative and support staff carry out the day-to-day work of the company

responsibility, authority and delegation

Each level of the hierarchy has **responsibility** for the actions of the people in the levels below it. The person at the top has overall responsibility for the whole organisation.

Each level has **authority** over the levels below it. Without this authority the organisation would not function properly – it would be anarchy!

Each level can, however, **delegate** its powers to a lower level; a manager on holiday may delegate to a supervisor. A doctor may delegate by getting a nurse to see more routine medical cases and so save his or her time.

up and down the hierarchy

Communications pass up and down the hierarchy; instructions are passed down, problems and complaints are passed up, discipline is exercised by a higher level over a lower level. Good communication is important here.

flat structure

A simple horizontal or 'flat' structure is in complete contrast to the 'tall' hierarchical structure. Here there are few layers in the organisation. The example shown below shows the simple flat structure of a sole trader shop which employs four assistants: three in the shop and one in the stock room.

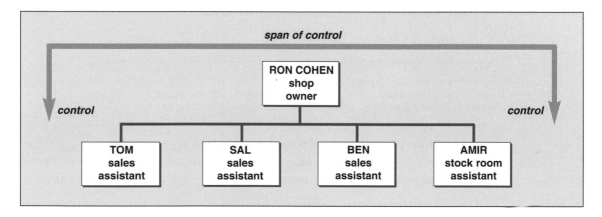

You will see from this diagram that:

- the structure is flat in shape; there is only one level of command – Ron himself tells the assistants what to do

- Ron has a span of control which extends over the four assistants; if he had more assistants, it would extend over those as well

- Ron presumably carries out the main functions of the business – finance, administration, human resources, marketing; his assistants do the selling

The flat structure is not confined to sole traders. Your own class is a flat structure with many students and one tutor in charge. Your school or college is also likely to have a flat structure.

divisional structures

The flat structure is also seen in what is known as the more complex 'divisional' structure, where separate independent divisions of an organisation operate under the overall 'umbrella' control of the higher management. Many large companies have reorganised themselves into groups of smaller operating companies in this way. Divisions can be by:

- function – eg manufacturing division, research division, sales division

- product – eg cars, trucks, buses, bikes

- geographical location – eg a national company (UK North, UK South) or a multinational (groups of companies which operate worldwide)

Activity 3.3

Identifying divisional structures

What type of business divisions do these structure charts illustrate? What are the benefits of organising the structure in this way?

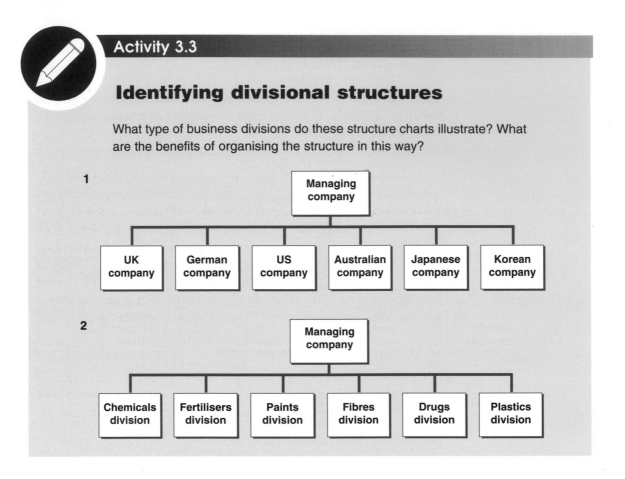

divisional structure and the size of the business

These structure charts all show large organisations – manufacturers and multinationals, but it should be noted that the divisional structure can be adopted on a much smaller scale. For example a sole trader owner of shops in four towns may decide to make the individual shop managers completely responsible for their own shop. Each shop will then become a 'division'.

advantages and disadvantages: divisional structures

advantages

- there can be specialisation in the separate parts of the organisation, eg different products, different geographical areas, different functions (eg sales, production, finance, marketing)

- there is more motivation for the management of the individual units, who are rid of the bureaucracy of a hierarchical structure, and are able to take more decisions without reference to a higher level

disadvantages

- poor communications across the organisation – the 'left hand' not knowing what the 'right hand' is doing
- weakened control from the top management which has a greater span of control to sustain and a wider spread of resources to manage

decentralisation

The trend for creating divisional structures – for 'flattening' organisations – is popular. The management of large hierarchical organisations are finding that it is advantageous to make functions, product divisions and geographical areas more independent of the senior management. They are in effect turning a centralised organisation into a decentralised organisation. A centralised organisation does all its major decision making at higher levels of management – 'from the top'. A decentralised organisation is a collection of independent operating units which ultimately answer to top management – decision-making has been delegated to lower levels of management.

'delayering' and 'downsizing'

This process of decentralisation often involves 'stripping out' layers of management from a hierarchy to save money and to open up the lines of communication from senior management to line staff. This can have its advantages (efficiency and cost savings) but also its disadvantages:

- the middle management are often made redundant or retire early in the process
- the top management end up doing more junior tasks in what has become known in management jargon as 'downsizing'

Activity 3.4

Decentralisation and delayering

1   With help from your teacher/lecturer, draw up a structure chart of your school or college, including all the layers of the hierarchy.

Discuss in general terms the advantages and disadvantages of:

- Decentralisation – for example making all the subject departments completely independent of each other.
- Delayering – for example removing the deputy head/deputy principal from the hierarchy.

2   List examples of businesses that you know which might benefit from decentralisation and delayering. What would the benefits be?

matrix structure

Another form of structure which needs to be examined is the matrix or 'project team' structure. The word 'matrix' (as in the American film) means a grid which operates in two directions.

Sometimes in an organisation it is necessary to take people out of their specific function areas – finance, sales, production – to form teams to work on specific projects. The project team or 'matrix' concept originated in the aerospace industry where new projects were essential to keep manufacturers in business. Project teams needed to work quickly in order to launch a new product first, before competing businesses brought out their version.

The matrix concept involves a different form of organisational structure chart. Look at the example below which sets out a traditional functional structure extended to staff two project teams. The 'matrix' operates in two directions – to the project management and to the departmental management.

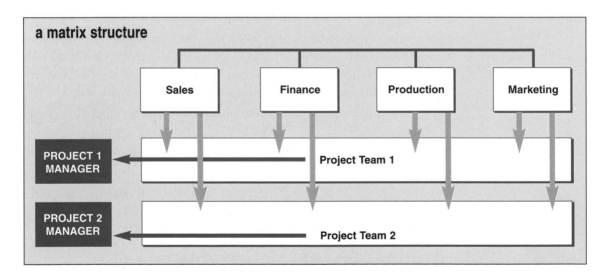

a matrix structure

Activity 3.5

Matrix structures

Hurricane Aerospace PLC manufacturers military aircraft. It wants to set up a project team for a new design of fighter, the Raven. The company needs to use staff from the research and development, marketing, finance and production departments.

Draw a suitable matrix structure chart showing how the project team could be set up.

management functions

It is generally recognised that there are four main functions of management:

1 planning

Planning involves the setting of objectives and making plans that will achieve those targets within set timescales. Plans include projections such as manpower planning, production budgets, cash budgets, sales targets.

2 organising

The role of management is also to set up structures and procedures within the business which will enable the objectives to be achieved. For example, the factors of production will need to be organised and chains of command will need to be established. A manufacturer will need to organise the production line, the sales force, the financial control, distribution and quality systems, all of which you will recognise as the functions of business.

3 directing

Once the functions within a business have been established, it is the job of management to co-ordinate the workforce and direct what they are doing, often through delegating tasks. Co-ordination may mean reconciling conflicting interests in different functions of the business in order to achieve the objectives of business. It is through directing staff that management can also motivate them.

4 controlling

Management must control the activities that they are directing. This means that they must monitor and measure what is being achieved. For example, sales performance or cash flow must be measured against budget. If anything is going amiss, corrective action must be taken. Management is a dynamic role which requires people 'to think on their feet'.

management styles

The success of management in motivating employees to meet the business objectives they have set is largely based on the management style they adopt. There are three main management styles ranging in a wide spectrum from the dictatorial to the 'oh, let them get on with it' attitude. The style adopted by a manager will fall somewhere within this spectrum. The three styles are as shown in the diagram which follows and explained in the text below.

the spectrum of management styles ➡

autocratic style	**democratic style**	**'laissez faire' style**
The manager makes the decisions.	The manager makes the decisions, but can 'consult' in the process.	The manager lets the employees 'get on with it'.
They are obeyed.	Employees tend to be far more motivated.	Employees tend to be unproductive.
Employees tend to be less motivated.	Suited to flatter structures.	Suited to small team structures.
Suited to hierarchical structures.		

autocratic style

The autocratic manager is the main decision maker. He or she sets objectives, allocates tasks and expects the workforce to do exactly as required. This does not normally make for a happy or motivated workforce. It does however, work well in a hierarchical organisation in which discipline is important, for example the armed forces and the police force.

democratic style

The democratic manager allows the employees to take part in decision making. They are consulted and made to feel part of the final decision-making process. This helps to motivate the workforce and also ensures that they are well aware of the objectives of the business and will work hard to achieve them. This style of management means that managers have to be good communicators. This style obviously suits a flatter business structure which is geared up to team working rather than a hierarchical structure which has many layers through which communications have to pass. When looking at a democratic style in action it is important to distinguish between:

- the manager who has probably made up his/her mind about the course of action to be taken anyway but involves the workforce in discussion to motivate them and make them feel part of the decision-making process

- the manager who genuinely consults the workforce in the decision-making process and is influenced by their views – this style of management is known as a 'consultative' style

'laissez faire'

The manager here allows the workforce to get on with whatever has to be done and has little input in the way of direction or control. This can work well in a small team 'flat' business such as a group of software developers where all are equal and are well motivated. In a larger, hierarchical business this style can be a recipe for disaster, encouraging laziness and apathy.

organisational culture

An organisational culture (see page 25) is reflected in the way that individuals in the organisation carry out their tasks. It combines the beliefs and values of the individuals and the extent to which they rely on the organisation's rules and procedures. There are four main styles of culture:

- **role culture** – best suited to a hierarchical structure where every employee plays a set 'role' and acts according to the rules and regulations
- **task culture** – a team working on a specific project – a matrix structure
- **power culture** – an organisation based around a central powerful figure
- **person culture** – administrative back-up for an individual

Different types of culture are suited to different types of organisational structure as the table below shows.

type of culture	what it involves	what businesses it suits
ROLE CULTURE	- reliance on rules and procedures - tasks are clearly defined - a clear chain of command	hierarchical structures
TASK CULTURE	- task or project based - no formal hierarchy	matrix structures (team project work)
POWER CULTURE	- strong central figure - decisions taken at the top	company with dominant chairman
PERSON CULTURE	- no formal structure at all - back-up for an individual	professionals, eg architects, entertainment 'stars'

Activity 3.6

Management styles and cultures

Discuss the management styles, organisational structures and cultures you might find in the following enterprises:

1   The Virgin group of businesses

2   A 'star' such as Robbie Williams

3   A research team working in a pharmaceutical company

4   A regional police force

How well do these factors help the organisations to perform and achieve their objectives?

CHAPTER SUMMARY

- A business combines a number of 'factors of production' when it produces goods or services. These are:
  - land – natural resources
  - labour – people working in business
  - capital – buildings, machinery, raw materials – items used in production
  - enterprise – the ideas contributed by people who run the business

- A business combines the factors of production in a variety of functions which include: production, research and development, finance, marketing and sales, human resources, administration.

- A successful business will co-ordinate these functions so that it runs efficiently and achieves its objectives.

- Businesses are structured in different ways with different levels of management – some have many layers of management, others have very few; these structures are likely to vary according to the type of market each business is operating in.

- A hierarchical structure involves many levels of management and is likely to be divided into separate functional areas (departments). It relies on a strong chain of command from top to bottom and good communication channels.

- A flat structure involves fewer levels of management, but the span of control of the top management is likely to be wide.

- A divisional structure is flat in shape and applies to independent divisions of an organisation, for example functional, product and geographical divisions. These structures are often the result of decentralisation and 'delayering'.

- A matrix structure is a 'project team' flat structure which operates in two directions – to the functional management and to the project team management.

- The role of management in a business involves four main functions: planning, organising, directing and controlling.

- There are three main management styles:
  - autocratic – the manager is the main decision maker
  - democratic – the manager consults the workforce when making decisions
  - laissez faire – the manager inputs little in the way of direction or control

- Organisational culture is reflected in the way that employees carry out their tasks and rely on rules and procedures. Cultures can be role culture (best for a hierarchical structure), task culture (matrix structure), power culture (a strong central figure in charge of a business) and person culture (back-up for an individual).

KEY TERMS

factors of production	the resources (eg land and labour) used when a business produces goods or services
function of business	an area of activity within a business
outsourcing	using an outside supplier to provide goods or services used within the business
span of control	the people or areas of responsibility over which a person in a business structure has control
hierarchical structure	an organisational structure characterised by a series of levels of people and command (a hierarchy)
flat structure	an organisational structure which is flat in shape – it has few (possibly only one) layers of management
divisional structure	a flat structure representing independent operating 'divisions' – which are 'decentralised'
delayering	the process of stripping out layers of management from a hierarchical structure in order to improve efficiency
matrix structure	an organisational structure which is based on a matrix grid and which operates both horizontally (eg to project management) and vertically (to function management)
autocratic style	a style of management where the manager is the main decision maker, telling people what to do
democratic style	a style of management where the manager allows the employees to have their say in the decision-making process
consultative style	a style of management where the manager actively encourages the employees to take part in the decision-making process
'laissez faire' style	a style of management where the manager has little input in the way of direction or control – the workforce is left to get on with the job
organisational culture	the way in which people working in an organisation carry out their work and the extent to which they rely on rules and procedures

Communication in business

introduction

Businesses need to communicate effectively – both internally and with outsiders such as customers and suppliers. Effective communication is needed if the business is to be successful in achieving its objectives. The means of communication have changed dramatically with the introduction of new information and communication technology (ICT); a business must make the most of the advantages of these new developments.

what you will learn from this chapter

● the communication process is more than just sending a message – it means being understood and the message being acted upon

● the communication process helps a business work efficiently and achieve its objectives; its functions include:
  - providing information
  - giving instructions and receiving feedback
  - negotiation with staff and with customers and suppliers

● communication channels can therefore be:
  - internal or external (with people inside or outside the business)
  - up and down and across the business hierarchy
  - formal or informal (a specific communication or 'the grapevine')
  - open or restricted (a question of who is to receive the information)

● communication can be written (eg memo, letter, e-mail) or oral (eg face-to-face discussion, telephone, voicemail)

● developments in communications technology – including networks, the internet, mobile phones – means the modern business has greater power to communicate than ever before; this has its advantages and disadvantages

communication in business

communicating to achieve objectives

All the people involved in a business need to have access to suitable information in order to do their jobs effectively and to achieve the objectives of that business – for example to maximise sales potential.

A business needs to be co-ordinated so that the right things happen at the right time. Good communications are necessary for effective co-ordination between people. Listed below is just a small sample of things that people need to know in an organisation. Even in a small business, there will be the need for far more information transfer than this.

people	example of what they need to know
accounts staff	sales figures on invoices
managers	how profitable certain lines are
order clerks	what is being ordered
personnel	details of new employees
sales staff	what products are being promoted at the moment
shareholders	how well the company is performing

For purely practical purposes, it is clearly essential that people are kept 'in the know', they cannot do their jobs without relevant information. As far as information is concerned, it is not a case of 'the more the better'. Too much information can obscure the main issues. Getting information provision right is one of the most important considerations in any organisation.

what is communication?

If you ask what communicating is, you will probably get a variety of responses:

> *"Passing on a message."*
>
> *"Telephoning someone or sending an email."*
>
> *"Getting the message across."*
>
> *"Making sure that they understand me."*

The first two responses show only part of the process: a message is sent. The second two show an understanding of the full process: the message is understood.

The process of communicating may be broken down into several distinct stages:

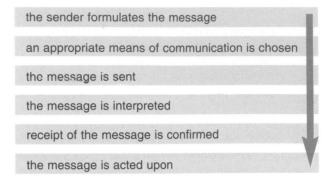

the sender formulates the message

an appropriate means of communication is chosen

the message is sent

the message is interpreted

receipt of the message is confirmed

the message is acted upon

Here the communication process involves:

- formulating the message, ie deciding what you want to say – this is a critical stage, and too often one where communication problems start – "I am sorry, I didn't mean that" . . . "Is that what I said?" . . . "You can read into it what you like. I meant . . ."
- choosing the appropriate means – would an e-mail be better than a letter? would it be easier and quicker to send a fax showing the route map?
- the message is sent and interpreted – an area where misunderstandings can arise – a message should be read or listened to carefully
- the message is confirmed – it is essential in business that a communication is confirmed – letters should be acknowledged, faxes will automatically produce a correct transmission report
- the message is acted upon – this final stage confirms the success of the communication

You should note that these principles apply equally to oral (word of mouth) communication as to written communications.

objectives of communication

So far in this chapter we have explained what communication is. We will now look at what communication aims to achieve – its objectives.

providing information

A successful organisation is one that enables its employees and customers to have access to up-to-date, relevant and correct information. Successful communication means getting the right message across. You will no doubt be able to think of situations where the wrong message was given!

giving instructions

Communication in an organisation sometimes requires instructions to be transmitted from one person or department to another. So that activities are co-ordinated, each member of an organisation will have to carry out certain functions at an appropriate time. For example, a sales person needs to receive a list of clients to visit or leads to follow up; production staff need to be informed regarding what to produce, how much and when.

making checks and receiving feedback

Management staff at various levels need to keep an eye on and check on areas of work for which they are responsible. Feedback from the relevant areas will need to be sent to managers so that they can make decisions on future courses of action.

negotiation

Human resources managers will need to negotiate job descriptions with staff. Sales staff might want to discuss the sales targets or the rate of commission that they are given. In cases like these, face to face discussions will be the most likely to produce an acceptable and amicable solution.

confirmation

In some cases, replies need to be sent in response to memos or emails so that the originator knows that the message has got through and that a course of action is in fact going to occur. A departmental manager might need to confirm to colleagues that he has booked a hotel conference suite for a meeting so that they all know to keep that date free.

channels of communication

There are a number of different 'channels' of communication:
- internal or external – with people inside or outside the business
- up and down and across the business hierarchy
- formal or informal – (an official method of communication or reliance on 'the grapevine')
- open or restricted – a question of everyone receiving the information or just an selected few

internal communications

Much of the communication which takes place in an organisation is designed solely for use within the organisation itself. This includes:

- information which is confidential such as payroll data or certain development plans
- information which is of no interest outside the organisation such as when departmental meetings are planned

Internal communications are typically carried out by means of face-to-face contact, memos, internal telephone calls or internal e-mail. Internal and external communications can also be classified according to whether they are oral (word of mouth) paper-based (eg a letter) or electronically based (eg electronic mail).

external communications

External communications are used when an organisation needs to interact with other organisations or individuals. Examples of external communications include:

- a letter to a customer promoting a new product
- a sales brochure, a sales invoice
- a job advert in a local paper

vertical and lateral communication

If you study the diagram on the next page you will see that communication within a business can be downwards, upwards or lateral (from side to side). You will recognise here a hierarchical structure (see page 59) and realise that an appreciation of organisational structure and communication are an integral part of understanding how a business 'works' to achieve its objectives.

downwards communication

The most important role of 'downwards' communication is that of management providing information and giving instructions about decisions that have already been made. The 'culture' of the organisation (see page 66) will largely determine how this is done: in an autocratic culture, for example, these 'downwards' communications will be orders!

upwards communication

This type of communication is critical because feedback, ideas and complaints from the workforce are needed and valued by management which has to monitor to what extent business objectives are being achieved.

lateral communication

Departments and functions within a business must communicate together and co-ordinate their activities to ensure that the business works effectively.

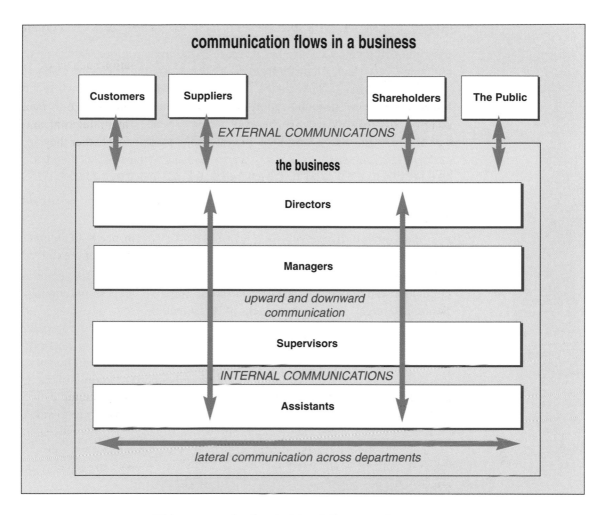

This communication is lateral, for example:

- the Human Resources Department providing the Finance Department with payroll details of a new employee
- the Finance Department telling Sales Department about 'blacklisted' customers who do not pay their invoices

formal and informal communications

Businesses within a formal structure (such as the one illustrated above) will have formal and informal ways of communicating.

formal communications

There are a number of situations where formal channels of communication are necessary. For example, disciplinary procedure has to follow formal guidelines, or it may be ineffective. Business information, sales figures for example, is reported formally because it will be involved in budgeting.

informal communications

Informal communication also has its place in the organisation. Management and employees can learn much from each other from 'the grapevine'. This is often no more than a conversation in a corridor, over coffee or down at the pub. This type of communication can be more informative than formal channels – management can learn about problems with people and processes, and act on them, if they have their 'finger on the pulse'.

restricted and open channels of communication

Communication in an organisation can either flow through restricted channels or through open channels.

restricted channels

Restricted channels are when the communication is not for general circulation and is aimed at only one person or a small number of individuals. Examples might include a speech or presentation from a manager to members of the board, a memo sent to a small group of staff or a computer system which only channels information to certain users on a network. Electronic mail, as we shall see later, can be placed in specific mail boxes so that the only people who receive it are those with a need to know.

The reasons why information flow may be restricted could be because of issues of confidentiality or more often, because it is simply inefficient and unnecessary to broadcast information to people who do not need it. This would waste time and effort. It is far more effective if the sender of information can filter it as far as possible so that it only goes where it is really needed.

open channels

Open channels are routes of information flow where information is placed where anyone can have access to it. This is useful when it is not certain who needs the information or where it is assumed that most people will find the information of interest. Open channels can be traditional or electronic. A notice board or a newsletter will potentially reach all the members of an organisation. Announcing the launch of a new product will be of concern to all and carry no security risk. Such open methods are suitable when the message is the same for all.

Computer Management Information Systems (MIS) can also be tailored to send information to all users. For example, messages can be broadcast to all the users of a computer network so that everyone logging on will see them. Likewise, data which is of use to all the employees, such as the availability of stock , can be made available across a network to all users. This is covered more fully in the Case Study which starts on page 85.

Activity 4.1

Infinity Software Limited
channels of communication

Read through the following situations which occur in a software development company, and state in each case whether the communication that takes place is:

- internal or external

If the communication is internal, also state whether the communication is:

- downwards, upwards or lateral
- formal or informal
- restricted or open

Also comment on how effective the communication method is. Would you have approached the situation in any other way?

1   A research assistant complains loudly to her supervisor that she has not had enough time off for her lunch.

2   The supervisor asks some assistants in the coffee room if, in their honest opinion, the lunch break is long enough.

3   A business sends a promotional brochure to a customer.

4   The business places an advert for a job in the local Employment Gazette.

5   The Human Resources Manager asks a new employee for her banking details so that her pay can be sent direct to her bank account.

6   The Human Resources Manager faxes the new employee's banking details to the Finance Department Manager so that they can be input into the computer ready for the payroll run at the end of the month.

7   The company directors have a meeting to discuss the new year's operating plans.

8   The Company Secretary drafts an article for the company newsletter telling all the staff about the plans for the business for the forthcoming year.

9   The Company Secretary and Marketing Director send out a press release about the company's results for the last year and the prospects for the future.

10   The Managing Director goes to a staff social at the local pub and while chatting finds out from the sales staff about some of the problem customers they have.

11   The Managing Director emails one of the customers suggesting a lunch meeting to iron out any problems.

12   The Software Research Manager calls in one of the researchers to give a verbal warning about spending time surfing the net in company time. This problem has been picked up on the company's on-line usage log.

written communications

Each business is likely to have its own printed stationery and 'house style' of writing letters and internal communications. The increasing use of e-mail both for internal and external communications is leading to a greater informality, with greetings such as 'Hi Robbie' rather than 'Dear Mr Williams' becoming more common.

Set out below are some of the more common form of written communications.

MEMORANDUM   the memo

To   K Roach, Finance Manager

From   Tim Blake, Sales Manager   **Ref** KR/AC/1098

Copies to Departmental Managers   **Date** 23 June 2000

Subject   Product A163 Launch SuperSucker cleaner

Please attend a presentation of our new A163 SuperSucker cleaner on 24 July in the Ground Floor Conference Room. Details of the new product are attached and a fully working model will be demonstrated on the 24th.

enc

Osborne Electronics Limited   the fax

Unit 4 Everoak Estate, Bromyard Road
St Johns, Worcester WR2 5HN
tel 01905 748043 fax 01905 748911

facsimile transmission header

To: Jamie Milne, Buying Office, Zippo Computers

Fax number: 01350 525504

Number of pages including this header: 1   Date: 10 October 2000

message
Jamie
Just to let you know that the consignment you called about this morning was despatched last Thursday (5 October) and should be with you soon.
Regards, Jon Smart, Despatch Dept.

the letter

Wyvern Double Glazing Contractors
107 High Street
Mereford
MR1 9SZ
Tel 01605 675365 Fax 01605 765576

reference → Ref DH/SB/69

date → 14 December 2000

name and address of recipient →
J D Sutton Esq
23 Windermere Close
Crofters Green
Mereford MR6 7ER

salutation → Dear Mr Sutton

heading → Double Glazing of 23 Windermere Close

body of the letter →
Thank you for your letter of enquiry dated 11 December.

We are pleased to enclose a brochure with details of our double glazing units, all of which comply with the most up-to-date building regulations.

We will be happy to give you a quotation for glazing your new extension. In order to do this we will need to send our surveyor to measure up your property. We shall be grateful if you will kindly telephone us to arrange a visit at a convenient time.

We look forward to hearing from you.

complimentary close → Yours sincerely

signature → *D M Hunt*

name and job title →
Derek Hunt
Sales Manager

enclosures → enc

verbal communication

Verbal (sometimes called 'oral') communications are by word of mouth and include face-to-face conversations, telephone calls, meetings and presentations.

discussions and meetings

Some face-to-face discussions are restricted to two individuals such as in disciplinary matters or when a particular specialist is being questioned about matters relating to his particular area of concern.

Meetings involve a number of participants, and the objectives can include:

* passing on information (eg briefings)
* obtaining information and feedback (eg a sales representatives meeting)
* negotiation (employer/trades union meeting)

presentations

Presentations are useful when a single topic is communicated to a group with a particular end in mind. They can be external: a sales representative can make a sales presentation to interested customers. They can also be internal: a sales director might make a presentation to management in which the sales figures for various products are explained. It is common to use visual aids such as slides and handouts in presentations. You will have to make presentations as part of your coursework.

a meeting in progress

communications technology

Businesses rely more and more upon modern technology to communicate. This is because new methods make communication:

- more reliable
- more targeted
- quicker
- more convenient
- more versatile

The technology of communication is changing so rapidly that individuals and businesses are often faced with solutions before they even know they have problems! They then have to act quickly in order to make the best use of new methods before their competitors do. There are many opportunities in the new methods of communication if only businesses can find them. There are new ways of advertising, selling, conducting market research and providing information to customers and business partners.

web technology and the Internet

The Internet is a world-wide network of computer networks. Any computer connected to the Internet can communicate with any other. This powerful concept has become possible because of the widespread availability of cheap computers and the global adoption of common standards. The ways in which computers communicate across the Internet follow a standard set of rules or protocol. The rules are known as TCP/IP (transmission control protocol/ Internet protocol) and underpin the most important aspects of the Internet.

Computers may be connected to the Internet in a variety of ways:

- The connection may be a telephone dial-up connection such as many people have from their home computers. A modem is required to match the computer signals to the telephone system. Such a connection may be quite slow. This is acceptable for the occasional sending of e-mails or a limited amount of web page browsing.

- Most businesses have their own internal computer networks that are connected by a router to the Internet. This sort of connection may be a quick ISDN line (Integrated Services Digital Network) which is dialled up when needed.

- Large organisations usually have a special dedicated line that is connected all the time and can be very fast indeed.

Businesses are making increasing use of the Internet for communicating messages and information.

e-mail

This is the sending and receiving of electronic messages by means of computer. Apart from a connected computer, an e-mail account is necessary. The account may be held by an Internet Service Provider (ISP), or held locally by the company itself. To keep the mail reasonably secure, a user identity and a password are required to access the account.

When someone wants to check an e-mail account, it is necessary to log in. A list of messages is displayed. The user can read them or delete them. When a message is read, it is easy to reply to it. The original message re-appears and comments can be added to the original. If a message is of interest to someone else, it can be forwarded.

Special mailing software is required. This is usually installed on the user's own computer, but many companies provide users with on-line e-mail software which can be accessed from any computer connected to the Internet.

When composing an e-mail, a screen such as the one illustrated below is used.

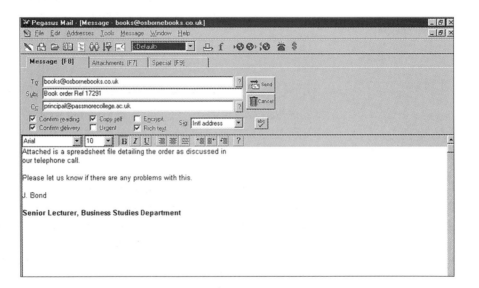

It can be seen that there is:

- space for the message
- a place to type in the e-mail address of where the e-mail has to go
- a box to summarise the content of the e-mail - useful so that the person reading a message list knows which ones are the most important
- a CC (carbon copy) box so that a copy of the e-mail can be sent to anyone else who needs to know about the message.

It is easy to send attachments. These can be any computer files at all. So a spreadsheet can be sent, or a word-processed document or even digitally recorded music!

Mailing software provides various utilities such as automatically including a message with every e-mail. This could be your name, address and telephone number, or a sales message. Mailing lists can be set up so that, for example, certain messages always get sent to all members of the sales team in a particular area.

When the message is complete, clicking on the send button gets the message on its way and it will be delivered very quickly.

advantages of e-mail

For many people, e-mail is now the preferred method of business communication. Messages can be checked at a time which suits the individual. E-mails are more convenient than telephone calls because there is no waiting around for someone to be found. Replying to an e-mail is quick and efficient so information is sent to where it has to go straight away. With paper memos, it is an effort to reply and very tempting to put off responding. E-mails are delivered cheaply anywhere in the world. Time differences do not matter.

disadvantages of e-mail

Some people cannot be reached by e-mail. Sometimes a misunderstanding can happen if a quick message is dashed off with little thought.

world-wide web

The world-wide web is a huge collection of pages of information stored on hundreds of thousands of computer servers throughout the world. This is what comes to mind when most people think of the Internet. Millions of pages of information are now available on websites all over the world. Web pages can be displayed on a computer by using software called a web-browser. It does not matter what sort of computer is used, there will be a browser written for it and it will be able to display the pages, wherever they come from. All web pages are written in the same way, using a special coding system called HTML (Hypertext Mark Up Language).

Anyone can publish anything on the world-wide web, so anybody with an Internet connection can see it. This poses a real problem, as often you cannot be sure that what you are reading has any authority. Also, there is so much rubbish on websites that unless you know where to look, it can be difficult to find what you want. Some companies have set up search engines to help find what you need, but there is an increasing problem of too much information being too easily available.

Businesses use websites for all sorts of purposes. Most now advertise on websites. Many also conduct their business on the web, taking orders from customers. The web page below describes goods offered and also has a link to an on-line order service provided by the company.

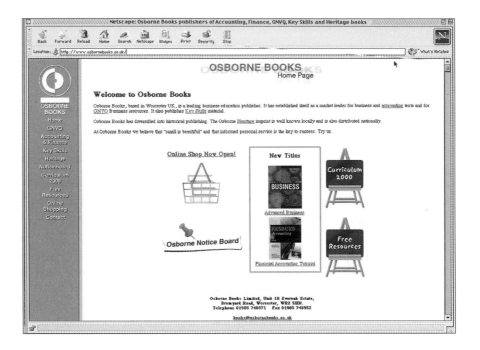

file transfer

The Internet makes it easy to send computer files from one place to another. This can be useful to a business in many ways. Documents can be downloaded from remote computers. Files can be backed up onto remote file servers. This makes it easy to safeguard important files off site, so if a disaster occurs and data is lost, another copy is safely stored somewhere else. The server can be anywhere in the world. This part of the book has been written in Worcestershire and backed up on a server in San Francisco!

intranets

Many companies have their own private, internal websites. They behave exactly like Internet websites and rely on exactly the same technology. The difference is, they are not accessible to the world. They are called intranets and in many ways are far more significant than the more widely available Internet. They can be totally customised to serve the interests of the company and can be directed to help employees perform their tasks more efficiently.

Case Study

Astra Electronics
intranet and Internet

the business

Astra Electronics plc is a large manufacturing company which makes consumer electronic goods. It occupies three sites in the UK. One site specialises in product design, another in assembly. The third site is the head office, where administration and sales departments are located.

the problem

It recently became apparent that communications between departments and more especially sites was not as efficient as desired and people did not always have the up-to-date knowledge necessary for them to perform their jobs efficiently.

For example, at Head Office, Val, the receptionist receives telephone calls and visits. These can be about a wide variety of matters. Last year, Astra launched an innovatory hi-fi system and invested a lot in promotion and advertising. There was much press interest and Val received many enquiries. It was difficult to find all the relevant information and Val had to do a lot of looking up to answer all the various questions put to her by the reporters. This took a lot of time and stopped her doing all the other jobs she needed to do.

Sometimes people who want a job at Astra call in and ask questions about the company. Again, they want to know a variety of things and the printed handouts often ran out.

Jack is the Operations Manager in the workshops. He has to allocate work to the various teams. He always needs to know the stage that a job has reached so that he can arrange for the delivery of the correct parts. He used to have to go around the workshops and check the forms that were filled in by the foremen. Sometimes a rush job came in and had to take precedence over existing work. It often took a long time to find out from all the foremen, which jobs were currently in progress.

When Jack needed parts for a particular job, he had to look them up in the catalogue and telephone the supplies department. He had to enquire about availability and sometimes he did not know the part number of the component required. The Spares Manager then had to look this up.

Recently, the company installed an enterprise-wide computer network. This linked up all three sites. The idea was to enable all the workers to be able to interact with a company-wide database. Everyone would then always have access to the latest information, whether it concerned parts availability, sales figures, orders or even social events.

The trouble with this was it was difficult to use. Complicated instructions had to be given to the database software in order to get at the information that people needed. Most staff had to go on expensive training courses and when they came back, they still did not know how to make the database provide information in the ways they needed.

the solution

The managers of Astra called in a firm of consultants who told them that the data could be made accessible through an ordinary Internet web browser with an intranet. With this, anyone could just click on links to get the information they needed. Requests for information could be submitted via on-line forms. When people were in difficulties, they could even ask the experts questions on-line. Astra implemented the intranet and soon discovered all sorts of advantages.

Val was pleased that she could now look up commonly asked questions with a few mouse clicks. The information was always up-to-date as well. Old handouts were no longer a problem as enquirers could be given a printout of the latest news.

This is what Val could use on her computer workstation.

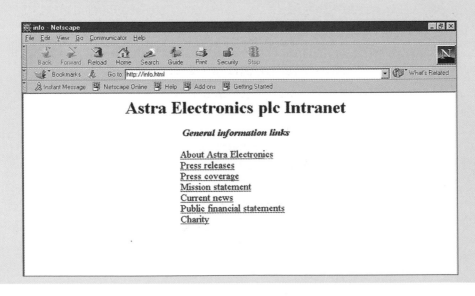

Jack was pleased too. He had no trouble in keeping up with the progress of jobs any more. The allocation of work was easy to check. Rush jobs could be posted for him to see at regular intervals.

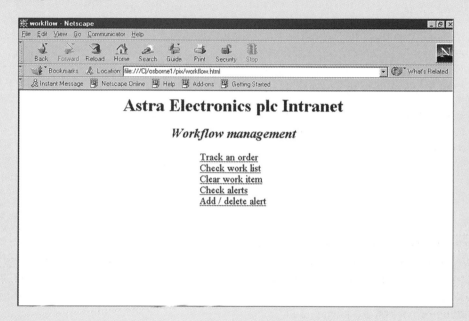

When Jack needs to check on the availability of parts or order them, he can now check on the stock database by a few clicks, using the intranet.

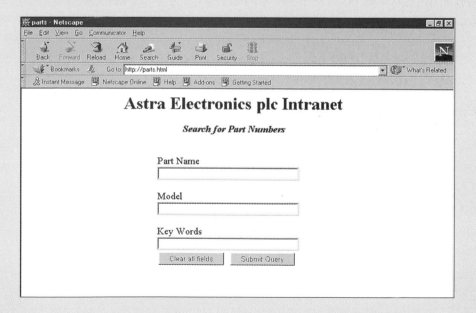

Astra soon realised that the intranet had far more potential than they ever anticipated. They now use it to provide on-line training for their workforce. Interactive learning courses have been written and anyone can use them without having to learn any extra computer skills. They all know how to use a web browser and it works for all the intranet functions. When new software is installed, or when new procedures are adopted, staff can be trained immediately by using new courses available on the intranet.

When any equipment goes wrong, there is a facility for reporting faults on the intranet, so nothing gets forgotten. Support staff always have up-to-date information to help them plan their work. All the telephone extensions are listed on the intranet so no one loses paper-based directories.

The IT staff at Astra are also pleased. The intranet is totally independent of computer platform. The Head Office uses ordinary PCs, but the design people use workstations connected to a mini computer. All of them can run web browsers so can access the company intranet.

The design department now maintains a library of parts designs so they can share their work among themselves. This reduces the amount of duplicated effort.

When new jobs become available in Astra, they are posted on the intranet and staff can see them immediately.

video-conferencing

Managers at Astra Electronics travel a great deal to attend meetings with colleagues within the company and with associates throughout the world. The director was becoming increasingly concerned that their time was not being used as productively as it could be. The managers were also getting fed up with all the frustrations of driving along crowded roads and waiting at airports. They spent many nights away from home and they felt that their family lives were suffering.

The director asked for some research to be done and was surprised to find:

"The typical manager driving to and from work and on business spends nearly 11 hours behind the wheel each week – two of them stuck in traffic jams – to travel 232 miles."

"It is estimated that today's technology could replace 7% of business travel and that video-conferencing could replace 20% by 2007."

"The average business traveller makes 21 trips a year and spends on average 37 nights in hotels."

"Around a quarter of all miles driven by car or van are work journeys, and this has a major impact on congestion and air quality."

"Nearly two-thirds of top executives say they suffer serious physical symptoms from business trips of 100 miles or more."

Because of this, Astra Electronics has started to make use of video-conferencing. Everyone at Astra can now make use of their network connections to have immediate sound and vision contact with anyone else. All they need is a microphone and small camera connected to their desk top PCs plus freely available software.

Sometimes, only a few minutes are needed for two or three managers to discuss some small point for a decision to be made. At other times, a larger meeting is required and groups of staff gather in video-conferencing rooms at the different locations.

When there is a lot of information to show around, they often use two monitors per person. On one of them it is possible to see the person you are speaking to and on the other, spreadsheet tables and charts can be displayed. With their ISDN links, they get good quality pictures.

It is now much easier to get a number of managers together for a video conference than it used to be. Video meetings tend to be much better prepared, come to the point quickly and are more decisive. Astra has found that they facilitate and speed up the making of management decisions.

The move towards video-conferencing does have its drawbacks. A video link carries enormous amounts of information. The moving pictures have to be updated regularly so that the human brain does not detect any flicker. The system needs a great deal of bandwidth, in other words, the capacity to send and receive a great deal of data.

There is a human cost too. Some managers now feel that they are keyed up all the time, with no chance of ever relaxing or having an informal chat with colleagues. In a conversation, one of them said "It's all well and good having video meetings arranged at the drop of a hat, but I can find out far more about what is really going on by having lunch with colleagues or chatting to the workforce".

mobile communications

Astra sales staff and engineers have long used mobile telephones to keep in touch with their offices. Increasingly, they want to be able to have access to their normal data while on the move. Many of them now have a Digital Personal Assistant. This is a small hand-held computer, which can act as an organiser as well as communicating with the office via a mobile telephone.

Mobile phones are able to access the Internet and also Astra's intranet by making use of a communications method called WAP (Wireless Application Protocol).

Some executives use a specially adapted phone to access web pages that have been simplified to make the best use of the phone's small screen.

When on the move, some of Astra's staff like to use their mobile computing capabilities in order to find a good restaurant!

e-commerce

Increasingly, business is being conducted by using modern methods in Information Technology. This is often called e-commerce.

E-commerce has been around for a long time. For example, EDI (Electronic Data Interchange) has allowed Astra to send business information to its partners over private computer networks. Orders to regular suppliers have long been conducted this way, with the progress of orders being communicated from the supplier's computer system to the customer's.

Payment for goods has also long been possible using computer networks. Astra pays many of its bills electronically by moving funds from their bank account to that of their supplier. This is called Electronic Funds Transfer.

Increasingly, Astra is using Internet technologies to conduct business. This is attractive because it reduces costs. For example, the company that provides Astra Head Office with supplies has been allowed to put an ordering page on Astra's intranet. This makes it much simpler for the office manager to make purchases and saves a lot of time and paper work.

This works both ways. Astra has set up a website so that its customers can look at what products and services they have on offer and if necessary, order on-line.

It has been hard work developing the e-commerce aspect of their business. This is because they had no computer staff who were experienced in developing such applications. They found that they needed to appoint a technical director who understood the business they were in as well as what could be achieved with e-commerce. The technical director runs a small team of web developers who make sure that the whole site has a coherent "look and feel" and is regularly updated.

Some directors were worried that the public nature of the Internet would allow hackers to access their orders and their data, but any sensitive information is encrypted before being transmitted. Also, Astra has installed a firewall between its network and the Internet, which gives control over who is allowed in and what is allowed out.

Astra has taken time to adapt to the new ways of working, but customers are pleased with how easy it is to do business with them.

Activity 4.2

Astra Electronics intranet and Internet

Read the Astra Electronics Case Study and then answer the following questions:

1   What were the problems faced by Val and Jack before the intranet was installed?

2   What are the advantages of the intranet to Val and Jack?

3   What other uses does the intranet have?

4   Why were Astra's managers not working efficiently before video-conferencing was installed?

5   What are the advantages and disadvantages of using a video-conferencing system in an organisation?

6   What are the advantages of using mobile telephones?

7   To what extent (if any) has mobile telephone technology changed since the Case Study was compiled? What new features have been introduced?

8   What opportunities has e-commerce opened up for Astra?

9   What is the reaction of Astra's customers to e-commerce? Do you think this is typical of the public's reaction to e-commerce.

CHAPTER SUMMARY

- Good communication in a business organisation is essential – it enables the business to achieve its objectives.

- Communication is more than just sending a message – it means being understood and ensuring that the message is acted upon.

- The communication process helps a business work efficiently and achieve its objectives:
  - providing information
  - giving instructions
  - making checks and receiving feedback
  - negotiation with staff and with customers and suppliers
  - confirmation of the communication

- Communication channels can be internal or external (with people inside or outside the business)

- Communication can be:
  - up and down the business (vertical)
  - across the business (lateral)
  - formal or informal (a specific communication or 'the grapevine')
  - open or restricted (a question of who is to receive the information)

- Communication can be written (eg memo, letter, e-mail) or oral (eg face-to-face discussion, telephone, voicemail)

- Communications technology is increasingly used by businesses; this means that the modern business has greater power to communicate than ever before. This has its advantages and disadvantages.

- The internet is used for
  - sending e-mail
  - accessing websites
  - file transfer

- An intranet is used for
  - accessing data in an organisation
  - sending internal e-mail
  - in-house training

- video-conferencing helps make management more efficient, although it can reduce the amount of social interaction and informal communication.

- Mobile telephones provide great flexibility, particularly when they are linked up to the Internet.

KEY TERMS

communication channels the ways in which communication travels in an organisation

lateral communication communication which travels from side-to-side in a business

vertical communication communication which travels through the different levels of a business hierarchy

formal communication communication which is passed in a set-down and official way

informal communication communication which is passed informally, for example on 'the grapevine'

restricted communication communication which is not for general circulation

open communication communication of information which is available to all

verbal communication word of mouth communication – including telephone calls, discussions, meetings, presentations

memorandum an internal formal communication

fax an electronic method of scanning and sending an image down the telephone line

intranet a computer communication network within a business

Internet a worldwide computer network linked by telephone lines and other dedicated communication channels

world wide web information stored on pages on computers worldwide

e-mail 'electronic mail' sent between computers

website a computer file set up on the internet allowing 24 hour access – a 'shop window' for the business

video-conferencing the linking of cameras (often with computers) at different locations, enabling the users at either end to see and hear each other on-screen

e-commerce business conducted through computer links with business suppliers and customers

5

Production and quality

introduction

Production is the process by which businesses produce goods and services. This process involves 'adding value' to the factors of production such as labour and materials so that the finished product can be sold at a profit to meet the needs of customers. The quality of a product is an important requirement for customers. Businesses need to have systems in place to ensure that the production process and the product itself are of a consistently high quality.

what you will learn from this chapter

- the production process adds value by converting inputs into outputs

- the productivity of any process is the ratio of output produced to input required

- the objective of capital investment is to improve productivity

- production planning aims to maximise productivity and control the production process

- quality is all the features and characteristics of a product or service which affects its ability to satisfy the needs of customers

- quality control implies making sure faulty items are removed before products are delivered to customers

- quality assurance aims to make sure that faulty items are never produced in the first place

production

The term **production** is taken to mean the process by which businesses provide the goods and services, which meet the needs of their customers.

Production involves changing a range of **inputs** into the required **outputs** and can be represented by the following diagram . . .

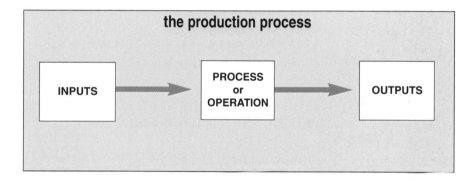

the production process

INPUTS → PROCESS or OPERATION → OUTPUTS

The inputs used are all the various resources needed to produce the goods and services required – the output.

question
Suppose you run a small business repairing bicycles for your friends. What inputs are needed? Think about this before referring to the answer at the bottom of the page.

inputs

For all businesses the inputs will be some combination of:

- people's work
- materials used
- equipment used
- a place to do the work
- the information needed (know-how)

These are often referred to as the factors of production and are defined as (see next page):

answer Your time, somewhere to do work, equipment, parts, your experience of bicycle repairs.

- **land** – natural resources
- **labour** – people's work, their time, ideas, their energy, their imagination and enthusiasm (also known as 'enterprise')
- **capital** – capital equipment (machinery, tools) and other long-term investments (factory, office, workshop)

outputs

These are products (goods) or services or some combination of the two. For example:

- in a car plant the output will be finished cars
- in a hairdressing salon the output will be styled hair – haircuts, hair tints
- in a restaurant the output will be prepared food and drink

Products are physical things and can be referred to as 'artefacts' while services are 'intangibles' – you cannot actually touch a good holiday, but you know when you have had one!

question
What are the outputs of the bicycle repair business you run for your friends (see previous page)? Think about this before referring to the answer at the bottom of the page.

process or operation

The process or **operation** is concerned with all activities involved in making a product or providing a service. It is responsible for the transformation of various kinds of inputs into useful outputs. Look at the diagrams which follow.

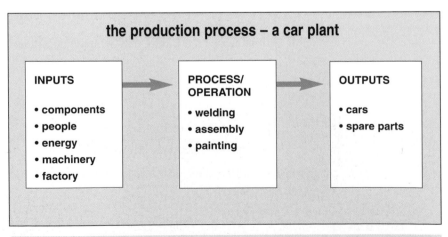

the production process – a car plant

INPUTS	PROCESS/ OPERATION	OUTPUTS
• components • people • energy • machinery • factory	• welding • assembly • painting	• cars • spare parts

answer Working bicycles, satisfied customers.

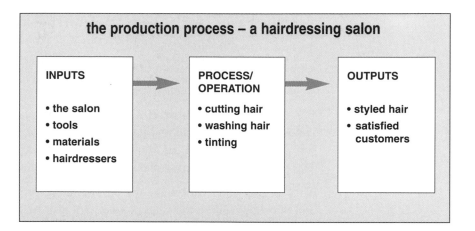

the production process – a hairdressing salon

INPUTS	PROCESS/ OPERATION	OUTPUTS
• the salon	• cutting hair	• styled hair
• tools	• washing hair	• satisfied
• materials	• tinting	customers
• hairdressers		

Activity 5.1

Inputs and outputs

Identify the inputs, processes/operations and outputs involved in

1   farming

2   a hospital

3   a night club

4   another business with which you are familiar

adding value in the production process

The aim of the production process is to 'add value' to the goods or services being supplied so that they can be sold at a profit.

For example, iron ore is extracted from the ground, processed into steel, pressed into sheet steel, used to manufacture cars which are then sold by dealers. At each stage value is added and a business aims to make a profit.

adding value in the production process

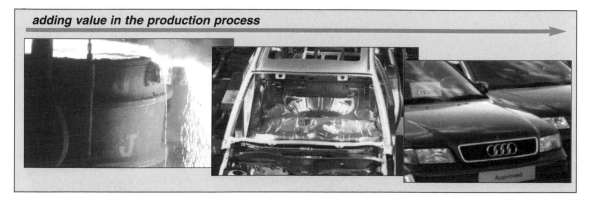

adding value for profit and marketability

The work done to 'add value' may:

- make the product more profitable for the business
- improve its marketability (make it more attractive to the customer).

For example, there is a trend nowadays in supermarkets to sell vegetables sorted, prepared, washed and packaged – ready for cooking. The price they will sell for may be 70p per kilo instead of 30p per kilo for the loose product. The processes of preparing and packaging the product has 'added value'.

This 'added value' will make the product more profitable for the producer and the supermarket; the final product will also be more convenient for the busy shopper – its marketability is improved.

adding value for survival

Added value strategies can often provide a survival lifeline when businesses are having difficulties. For example, for a number of years UK farming has been experiencing one problem after another – salmonella in chickens and eggs, BSE, the strong value of the UK pound. In this very demanding climate some farmers have 'added value' by retailing their produce direct to the public via farm shops, or on the internet. Others have gone into areas such as cheese and yoghurt production or the provision of leisure and educational facilities such as horse riding and farm 'zoos' for children.

UK businesses also find it difficult to compete with the lower labour costs of overseas producers. As a result many UK businesses are seeing their profits decline. The answer is an increase in the number of businesses with much higher added values such as financial services, computer software and consultancy which rely on a high level of skill from a trained workforce.

Activity 5.2

Adding value to products

Discuss in class how the following products make good use of added value in achieving profitability and marketability for the business which produces them:

1   A frozen 'convenience' meal.

2   An exclusive sports car which costs £150,000.

3   Selling mail order up-market leisure clothes which are imported cheaply from overseas.

4   A sea fisherman who runs 'seal spotting' and mackerel trips for the public on his boat during the summer months.

efficiency and productivity

efficiency – average cost

A process is efficient if you achieve the maximum result from the minimum cost. No matter what the business does, or in what sector of the economy it operates, the aim will always be to organise production in the most efficient way possible.

Efficiency is achieved where the unit cost is at its lowest. Unit cost is the average cost of producing one unit – an item or a service. Average cost is simply cost divided by output. If, for example, it costs £40,000 for a manufacturer to produce 500 TV sets then:

average cost $= \dfrac{£40,000}{500} = £80$ per TV set

If a business can reduce the unit cost to a minimum, it is efficient. It will be able to maximise added value and increase its profitability.

productivity – inputs and outputs

Efficiency relates to costs and to profits, but businesses also find it useful to relate output to specific inputs – the factors of production – such as the number of employees used (labour), the raw materials consumed, the capital investment of the business in machinery. The relation between these inputs and output is **productivity**.

Productivity relates inputs and outputs directly together. In other words, the greater the output in relation to input, the greater the productivity. The formula used is:

$$\textbf{productivity} = \dfrac{\textbf{output}}{\textbf{input}}$$

increasing productivity

Looking at the relationship between input and output in this formula we can see that productivity will increase if:

- output increases while input remains the same
- output remains the same while input falls
- output rises proportionately more that input, for example output increases by 20% while input rises by only 10%

Now carry out the Activity which follows. It looks at productivity at a night club. Here the output is clients, inputs are the cost of labour, drinks, music and so on.

Zone 999 Night Club
measuring productivity

read the explanation below and then answer the questions that follow . . .

You own and manage Zone999, a warehouse night club that is regularly full to bursting with 250 customers by 11.00 each evening and you are turning away a substantial number of potential clients. How can you tackle this problem?

One solution suggested is that you might be able to double the floor size by opening up another floor in the warehouse you are renting. You would pipe the music to the additional area so you would only require the one DJ. You could also open another bar and increase bar staff by 50%. You will still only have one entrance so you only need the same number of bouncers. Your nightly 'input' cost would go up from £250 to £375.

By this approach your output (the number of satisfied clients) might double while your inputs will only rise by 50%. As a result your business will be significantly more productive.

EXISTING PRODUCTIVITY = $\dfrac{\text{output: 250 clients}}{\text{inputs: £250 per night}}$ = 1 client per £1 of inputs

NEW PRODUCTIVITY = $\dfrac{\text{output: 500 clients}}{\text{inputs: £375 per night}}$ = 1.33 clients per £1 of inputs

questions

Calculate the productivity in terms of clients per £1 of inputs for Zone 999 if the expansion plans went ahead and:

1   the number of clients doubled and the input costs rose by 75%

2   the number of clients rose by 300% and the input costs doubled

Would you be happier with the higher rate of productivity? Can you foresee any practical problems with an increase of this size?

other ways of measuring productivity

So far in this chapter we have expressed productivity in terms of items of output – night club clients, for example – and costs of inputs. It is important to appreciate that productivity is a very flexible measure. You could look at the productivity of the night club in terms of the number of employees, or the cost of the drinks, or the cost of the music equipment.

These are all 'factors of production' and the management of the business will need to look regularly at how effectively they are being used. He (or she) may face questions such as:

"Is it worth investing in new lighting and music equipment? Is it worth putting lasers on the roof? All this might attract more clients. Will productivity increase?"

"Am I getting the best deal from my drinks suppliers? If I cut costs will my productivity go up?"

It is therefore necessary to relate productivity to the various factors of production. Here are some typical measures of productivity . . .

---

worked example

The following information relates to a week's production in a factory.

Number of units sold	40,000
Income from units sold	£80,000
Cost of raw materials	£16,000
Labour employed in production	50 workers
Cost of labour	£10,000
Other costs	£30,000
Estimated value of Capital Equipment	£1,000,000

---

labour productivity

Labour productivity is measured by dividing the output achieved over a given period by the number of workers employed.

$$\textbf{Labour productivity} \ = \ \frac{\text{output}}{\text{number of workers}} \ = \ \frac{40{,}000}{50}$$

$$= \ \text{800 units per week per person}$$

material productivity

Material productivity is measured by dividing the output achieved by the cost of raw materials used.

$$\textbf{Material productivity} \ = \ \frac{\text{output}}{\text{cost of raw materials}} \ = \ \frac{40{,}000}{£16{,}000}$$

$$= \ \text{2.5 items output for every £1 of raw materials used}$$

capital productivity

Capital productivity is measured by dividing the value of the output by the value of the capital investment.

Capital productivity $=\dfrac{\text{output}}{\text{capital investment}}=\dfrac{40{,}000}{£1{,}000{,}000}$

$= 0.04$ of an item each week for every £1 invested

overall productivity

Overall productivity is measured by dividing the output by the value of the input.

The value of the output (the items sold) is £80,000 per week.

The value of the input is £16,000 + £10,000 + £30,000 = £56,000 per week.

Overall productivity $=\dfrac{\text{output value}}{\text{input value}}=\dfrac{£80{,}000}{£16{,}000 + £10{,}000 + £30{,}000}$

$=\dfrac{£80{,}000}{£56{,}000}$

$= £1.43$ of output was produced for every £1 of input

Activity 5.4

Measures of productivity

This activity is partly based on the data set out above.

As a consequence of increasing demand for its products the management negotiated with the workforce to increase production the following year. Comparable information was collected for one week and it showed:

Number of units sold	60,000
Income from units sold	£120,000
Cost of raw materials	£24,000
Labour employed in production	65 workers
Cost of labour	£13,000
Other costs	£30,000
Estimated value of Capital Equipment	£1,000,000

Use the productivity indicators shown on the previous page and draw up a table comparing the figures for the two years. Comment on the changes in productivity.

productivity and capital investment

Improvements in productivity are often the result of capital investment in plant and machinery. These investments often occur because increases of output are needed to meet sales growth and one solution is to mechanise significant parts of the production process. Also, as the cost of labour rises it becomes increasingly cost effective to replace people with machinery.

The Case Study which follows explains how the Royal Mail has dealt with the need for improving the efficiency of handling an increasing volume of mail in the Worcester area. Read it and then do the Activity on the next page.

Case Study

Royal Mail sorting and delivery
productivity and capital investment

The Royal Mail sorting and delivery office at Warndon, Worcester, is a typical example of the modern methods and techniques currently used by the Royal Mail. Worcester is one of eighty mail processing centres in the UK which are supported by an infrastructure of air, road and rail distribution networks. The Worcester office sorts mail for Herefordshire and Worcestershire. This covers an area of over 1,500 square miles and a population of about 650,000.

Before this modernisation took place letters and cards would arrive in big sacks at the sorting office.They were first sorted by hand into local delivery areas and then the individual postmen would organise them for their own 'walk'. This process at the sub-postal offices was very labour intensive and time consuming.

Nowadays the majority of this sorting operation for the 'WR' and 'HR' postcode areas is done at the main Worcester sorting office. The postmen working out of the sub-offices receive all their mail for delivery pre-sorted in the correct order for their individual 'walk'. This saves much work at the sub-offices but it also means that the main sorting office has much larger volumes of mail to sort.

If this sorting was still done manually the main office at Worcester would struggle to cope with the volumes involved and there would be little overall gain in productivity. However, the Royal Mail has had the foresight to invest in electronic Integrated Mail Processors at their main sorting offices – Worcester has two such installations. They cost over £1 million each but can sort 30,000 items of mail per hour. Four staff are still required to support the Integrated Mail Processors (the process is not entirely automated). But this compares very favourably with the 40 staff who would have been required to sort this volume of mail manually (manually about 17 items per minute per person), with about 50% of the mail requiring double sorting.

It is clear that the capital investment has resulted in a big improvement in labour productivity and overall there has been a significant rise in the total productivity. Other benefits include an improved ability to deal with unexpected increases in local demand and the capacity to deal with mail diversions from other sorting offices.

Activity 5.5

Productivity from capital investment

Answer the following questions using the data from the Case Study.

1   What is the labour productivity in sorted items per person per hour following the installation of the integrated mail processors? You should measure labour productivity by dividing the number of items sorted per hour by the number of staff doing the sorting.

2   What was the labour productivity in sorted items per hour before the mail processors were installed? Use the figure of 40 staff for your calculation.

3   What is the increase in labour productivity?

4   Why was the labour productivity figure you worked out in Question 2 not the same as the 17 items per minute per person quoted in the Case Study?

other productivity considerations

As we saw in the Case Study, capital investment will often improve productivity. Also, since capital equipment can be very expensive it is often necessary to keep the equipment in use for more than 8 hours a day, 5 days a week. If you have invested £1,000,000 on some automatic machinery you want to keep it working for as long as possible. That is one of the reasons modern factories often work 2 or even 3 shifts 7 days a week.

For example, modern printing presses can cost more than £1,000 per hour whether they are operating or not. So, if you want to keep them operating for as long as possible you may need an extra machine engineer available at, say, £10 per hour in case of emergency. The result of this will be a fall in labour productivity but a rise in overall productivity.

techniques to improve productivity – work study

An important technique used to improve productivity is known as Work Study. This consists of two aspects; method study and work measurement. Their relationship to productivity is shown in the following diagram.

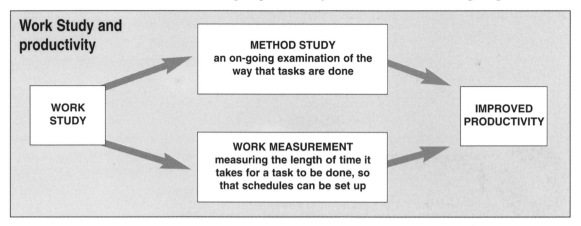

Work Study and productivity

WORK STUDY

METHOD STUDY
an on-going examination of the way that tasks are done

WORK MEASUREMENT
measuring the length of time it takes for a task to be done, so that schedules can be set up

IMPROVED PRODUCTIVITY

Method study is essentially a critical examination of everything that is done with a view to ensuring that if a job really does need to be done it is done in the best possible way and as efficiently as possible.

Work measurement involves measuring the time it takes for a skilled worker to complete a particular task. This enables the business to schedule work effectively and to cost it out accurately.

Remember that these techniques apply equally to a service business as to a manufacturing business. Tasks to be 'studied' can include haircuts and meals served as well as operations on the production line.

production planning

producing for external customers

High levels of productivity are normally the result of careful planning. Effective production management is rarely just a case of producing as much as you can in as short a time as possible. This could only ever be possible if you had a one product business, but even then customer demand would need to be continuous and more than you could meet. If demand fluctuated then producing 'flat out' would just mean that at times you had far more stock than needed and would incur all the costs that holding stock involves.

The reality for most businesses is that you have a range of products and a number of possible production processes able to do different jobs. For example, in a light engineering company one job might need machining, assembly and packing. Another might require drilling, painting, drying, assembly and packing. Yet another might need the same drilling and machinery work done but with different tooling.

Further complications arise because you should be trying to meet a range of customer demands for varying quantities of different products – and customers have been known to change their mind at the last minute! Also, you can only maintain the production process if you have adequate supplies of raw materials.

It is not unknown for a well planned and highly productive schedule for a week to be thrown into total chaos because a tiny component is not available. Alternatively, similar chaos can be caused trying to meet the sudden change of requirement of a very important customer.

producing for 'internal customers'

In this context the component supplier or customer who provides a 'challenge' for the production manager might be internal. In other words different sections in the factory are providing components you need and you yourself are providing parts to another section. This concept of internal customers is also an important part of the quality process.

production planning and control

The objective of production planning and control is to try to ensure that the available resources (people, machinery, materials) are used efficiently to meet the needs of the customer. Generally speaking a balance has to be struck between the conflicting demands placed on the production process for high productivity on one hand and meeting customer needs on the other and a plan prepared which satisfies both.

Simple planning processes involve scheduling using bar charts. The information input to this process would be data on machine/line capacities, resource availability, specific customer demand for the product range and whether any of this demand can be supplied from stock and are stock levels to be built up or reduced.

Production schedules will typically be for a week (though they could be for any length of time) and will normally be produced on the preceding Thursday or Friday. A typical schedule is shown on the next page, the horizontal form of the bar chart is known as a GANTT chart (after a Work Study engineer Henry Gantt). Once the planning information is available it is often convenient to computerise the planning process.

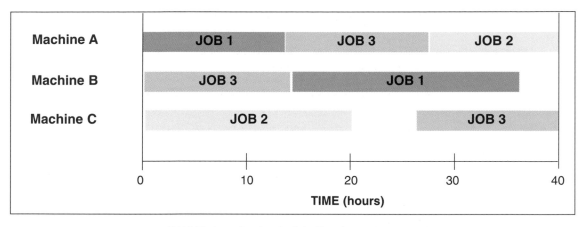

a GANNT chart showing the job allocation to three machines

As can be seen in this diagram, machine B and machine C have spare capacity, so there are opportunities for productivity improvement. Part of the planning and control function is to adjust production to use this spare capacity whenever possible. This chart may well represent the plan on Friday evening but by Tuesday lunch time things may be different. Perhaps machine A has had a breakdown. The production control function should manage these problems so as to minimise the disruption to the schedule and obtain efficient utilisation of the resources which are available. At the same time customers' needs should still be met. On the rare occasion when delivery times need modification the customer needs to be advised. This will often involve some negotiation. Customers are not unreasonable and usually recognise the realities of production schedules. Provided problems do not occur too often and every effort is made to identify and satisfy customer needs, a good working relationship can be maintained.

Now read through the Case Study which follows.

Case Study

Ledbury Welding and Engineering
production planning in action

the product

Ledbury Welding and Engineering Limited manufactures fuel storage tanks of up to 135,000 litre capacity.

These tanks can be set up above ground, or buried below ground level. For example, petrol for service stations is stored in tanks below ground while diesel for companies involved in distribution (such as Royal Mail, Co-Op Creameries, Railtrack) is normally stored in tanks above ground.

the logistics of production

The design and production procedure is typically as follows. An enquiry is received leading to design and quotation. When an order is received and delivery has been agreed the job will be given a contract number and scheduled into production. Steel already cut to size, pumps, valves etc will be ordered specifically for that job. The job order will be sent to the production supervisor and will include drawings, specifications, delivery dates, quality checks to be conducted and so on.

The supervisor will then organise actual fabrication according to the schedule, space on the production floor and work team availability. Space on the floor is an important planning consideration because the tanks are typically 10 metres long, 3 metres wide and 2 metres high, although on occasions they can be nearly 3 times as big!

They are completely built at one location with the welding team working round them. Ideally they are only moved when they are ready for finishing (shot-blasting, painting) and delivery to the customer. Typically a tank takes a month to six weeks to make and there will be 15 - 20 tanks at various stages of build on the shop floor at any one time.

the planning process

Production planning meetings are held weekly to review progress and agree the detail of the production schedule. In addition, weekly customer contract meetings are also held when changes in customer requirements are notified or difficulties in organising distribution can be identified (cranes needed, police notification of heavy load etc). Clearly production planning and customer contact need to work well together because they are dependent on each other for providing good quality service to the customer.

the planning schedule

Part of a production schedule is shown below and you can see that the planning is based on the number of hours of work available. The schedule also shows that the company had a full workload for about 7 weeks at that time. This is typical of 'jobbing' production (making jobs to a customer's specific order).

LEDBURY WELDING & ENGINEERING PRODUCTION SCHEDULE — 17-Feb

Drawing Required (21, 22) · Drawing Approval (23, 24, 25, 26) · Drawing Complete (27, 28, 29, 30)

Cont. No.	Customer	Description	Date Reqd.	our	W/C 14/02	W/C 21/02	W/C 28/02	W/C 06/03	W/C 13/03	W/C 20/03	W/C 27/03	W/C 03/04	W/C 10/04	W/C 17/04
6139	Swansea Yacht Club	2,000 g Basic	TBA	25						25	P	*		
6399	Damar Engineering	2,800 ltr T/E D/P	10/01	48						48	Pp	Painting		
6401	Glen Moor Garage	8,000 g H/C S/S	TBA	37						37	*			
6479	Broadcrown	2,500 ltr NTL type	29/11	3	3									
6489	Hutton Construction	5,000 g T/E D/P & Equip Cabinet	hold	45			45	*						
6494	Broadcrown	12,500 ltr A/G H/C	17/01	C&Z p	p	*								
520-	F.I.S.	8,000 g T/E D/P	14/02	Fab' p*	p*									
6521	John Sisk	2,700 ltr T/E L/I	21/02	Fab' p	p	*'								
6522	Stradform	Equipment Cabinet	07/02	50	50		P	*						
6525	Specialist Wheel Services	1,500 g T/E D/P	28/02	Fab' P	P		*							
6527	Argyll & Bute	8,000 ltr Basic 2 Comp	21/02	Fab' P	P	*								
533-	Forecourt Eng	10,000 g T/E Avtur Unit	07/02	Fab' Paint	Paint	*								
6537	Phillips Petroleum	90,000 Ltr T/E Truckstop	21/02	196		100	96	PP			*			
6538	Interpan	45,000 Ltr T/E D/P	28/02	94						94	P	*		
6541	South Northants C.C.	15,000 ltr T/E D/P	21/02	Fab' P	P	*								
6542	Broadcrown	26,000 ltr Rect	07/02	40	40									
6545	Dairy Crest Transport	9,000 g T/E D/P	21/02	85	85	P*								
6547	Trebor Bassett	1,000 g T/E L/I	28/02	24	24	p	*							
6555	Argyll & Bute	8,000 ltr Basic 2 Comp	06/03	33	33		*							
6556	F.I.S.	15,000 Ltr Basic 2 Comp	14/02	Fab' Pp	Pp	*								
6557	Independent Pumps	1,000 g Basic	06/03	Fab'd			P	*						
6558	Independent Pumps	45,000 ltr T/E D/P 2 Comp	06/03	102	102		Pp	*						
6631	East Riding of Yorksh..e Coun	40,000 ltr T/E D/P 2 Comp	27/03	93						93	PPP	*		
6632	Cummins Power Gen..tion	26,000 ltr Basic	11/04	50							50	P		
6633	Cummins Power Gen..tion	4,040 ltr T/E D/P	31/03	28						28	P	*		
6636	Macob	Equipment Cabinet		50							50	P	*	
7283	C.M. Downton	80,000 ltr Truckstop		175					135	40	PP	*		
	Broadcrown	2*10,000 & 1*7,200 NTL Basics		93						62	31	PPP	*	
7813	Stagecoach	55,000 ltr T/E D/P		110						110	P	*		
	Irish Pump & Tank/Spondrad	13,368 ltr Basic		28						28	P	*		
	Irish Pump & Tank/Mick McQ	45,000 ltr T/E D/P		94						94	P	*		
	NFC Hebburn	60,000 g Truckstop		196							156	200	PP	*
	Highcross	Tesco Modcourt 4 * 10000g		200							200	*		
	TOTAL HOURS				779	492	511	692	495	701	498	133	60	16
	HOURS AVAILABLE				642	591	591	591	591	591	591	591	591	591
0	BALANCE				-137	99	80	-101	96	-110	93	458	531	575
0	CUMULATIVE				-137	-38	43	-58	38	-71	22	480	1012	1587
	MAX HOURS PER WEEK				43	39	39	39	39	39	39	39	39	39

Activity 5.6

Ledbury Welding and Engineering

This activity is based on the Case Study on the previous three pages.

1   Suppose the work load of the company – the orders waiting to be processed – suddenly increased substantially from 7 weeks in hand to 26 weeks. This is potentially good news for the company, but it could cause problems . . .

   (a)   what might the customers waiting for work to be done be concerned about?

   (b)   what could the company do in order to cope with the extra work load and speed up the order processing?

2   At a production meeting it is realised that a tank promised for delivery in 4 weeks may not be ready for 8 weeks. What should the company do?

quality

The concept of the quality of a product or service seems straightforward but it is often not as obvious as it appears. Quality is not just what is 'best' but what is most 'suitable'. To illustrate some of the difficulties, imagine someone was choosing a car for a journey and had a choice between a sports car and a four wheel drive vehicle. A young person might well choose the glamour of the sports car, a farmer is more likely to choose the four wheel drive vehicle. If it was then discovered that the journey was to be off-road across the Sahara Desert both drivers would be likely to choose the four wheel drive.

Quality can be defined as:

'all the features and characteristics of a product or service which affect its ability to satisfy the needs of customers'

So, quality is a mix of customer expectation and the suitability of the product or service to do the job required. A simpler definition is that *'quality is fitness for purpose'*.

further aspects of quality

price paid

Price or cost can't be ignored in any sensible consideration of quality. You cannot expect the standards of five star hotel accommodation if you only pay bed and breakfast rates.

service

Quality has a number of dimensions. For example, if you go out for a meal and the food is a good standard but the service is poor you will probably rate the quality as poor and not go again.

setting standards

We expect trains and buses to be clean, on time and staff to be courteous. If you are ordering goods you expect to receive what you order in due time and an undamaged condition. It is important to make sure that you meet your promises. The golden rule is not to promise what you can't deliver.

Public service businesses such as the rail companies issue 'Customer Charters' under the terms of which they undertake to maintain standards of service. If they breach these terms, the customer may be entitled to compensation. Read through the London Underground Charter shown below.

Our Customer Charter

Our commitment

London Underground aims to deliver the best possible service for all its customers. You want a quick, frequent and reliable train service, a safe, clean and welcoming station environment with up-to-date information and helpful, courteous staff. This means a continuous, demanding programme of improvements to meet rising expectations.

Our targets

To drive and measure these improvements, performance targets covering many aspects of our service have been agreed with Government as part of the Citizen's Charter programme. If you would like to know more, please contact our Customer Service Centre, which is open between 0830 and 1730, Mondays to Fridays, on 0171-918 4040. We regularly publish our performance against the targets. Train service performance information is posted at every station and details of other targets are available from the ticket office.

Our refund pledge

If you are delayed more than 15 minutes because of our failure, we will give you a refund voucher to the value of the delayed journey. Please claim by filling in this form. We cannot give refunds in circumstances which prevent us from safely running trains such as a security alert, freak weather or because of action by a third party; nor when we have publicised in advance an alternative route, for example because of planned engineering works. Special conditions apply if we have an industrial dispute. Extra claim forms are available from any station or the Customer Service Centre.

Your feedback

If you have any complaints or suggestions on how we can improve our service, please contact your local manager. The address and telephone number are displayed in the ticket hall.

Improving Service

performance and durability

The product should perform as would be expected under certain conditions. A four wheel drive vehicle would be expected to tackle off-road conditions with ease, a sports car would be expected to accelerate rapidly and reach high speeds.

The product should last as would be expected for the price and specification. You would be unlikely to use paper cups more than once but would expect china mugs to survive for a great deal longer.

quality and competition

We explained earlier the usefulness of added value as a strategy for making a business more competitive. Producing a product with better quality than the competition can be a very effective added value strategy. This approach has been very effectively adopted by the Japanese, whose products in the middle of the last century were renowned for being shoddy and 'plastic'. Their reputation is now for high levels of quality.

quality and profitability

The view used to be taken that improving quality would cost money and reduce profitability. An alternative view is that improving quality will increase profitability because:

- good quality will attract and retain customers and so increase sales – a good reputation is worth a great deal
- good quality in a manufactured item will mean less maintenance and fewer returned products

It is clear therefore that while it can cost more to produce better quality goods and services, it can also save money as well.

Activity 5.7

Measures of quality

1   Collect an example of a Customer Charter from a local services provider.

2   Do these services meet their targets? If they do not, what are the problems?

3   Can you think of ways of improving the quality of those services?

4   One of the companies in the Volkswagen car manufacturing group is Skoda, based in the Czech Republic. The quality of manufacture of a Skoda is as good as any Volkswagen (they share many of the same parts, both in the engine and in the cabin). The public seem reluctant to buy Skodas in preference to Volkswagens. Why is this? How is this view reflected in the pricing of the two types of car?

quality control and quality assurance

Quality control and quality assurance are very different even though their ultimate objective is the same – to provide a guarantee of product quality to to the end user. The difference is perhaps best illustrated by showing how attitudes to quality have changed.

quality control

Businesses in the past accepted that you could not guarantee quality; there were bound to be some mistakes. In recent years, however, customers have grown to expect a higher degree of quality – defects are no longer acceptable. So, as the producer what do you do? Initially the strategy for manufacturers was to adopt very rigorous inspection procedures to ensure that defective products did not leave the factory. This is what quality control is all about.

self-checking and inspection

Quality control involves inspection of output to ensure that it meets the quality standard with satisfactory output being passed, unsatisfactory output being rejected and, if possible, re-worked or just scrapped. While this approach may result in customers receiving satisfactory products there are a number of disadvantages:

human error

Inspection is most unlikely to find all the faulty items because the normal inspection procedure is to sample say 10% of the output. If the 10% is satisfactory the rest is assumed to be. Obviously, if you sample, you can never be 100% sure the rest are satisfactory. And even if you do check every item (100% inspection – which is expensive) faults will still slip through.

Activity 5.8

Quality control and human error

The paragraph below contains a jumble of letters. Count how many times the letter A appears. Only run through the letters once – if you repeat the exercise you would be carrying out 200 per cent inspection!

```
W A Q R A Q W S F A W T A S A D G D A F F C H A S A D A F Y
T Q A A G A D T A S A R A G F A W H H A J A A H F A D R E A D
E E A A W W S F G A J R T D A R E R A F A R W T Q A E R H N
U A A T G F Y T A R E T T F G A F A G H H G A W D U A Y A R
D A E T E T A G D K A C A H K H A J A W K A R U P A C O X O
Q A S H W R R T Q A G D H R J E L A E A D Z A D A S A F R E
```

The correct answer is that the letter A appears 51 times. By concentrating hard, you may have got it right, but most people will have miscounted by one or two. If you asked an inspector to carry out such routine detailed work for a long period of time, you could certainly expect many mistakes to be made.

potential staff conflict

We have already identified the cost of 100% inspection being very high. But even sample inspection tends to be expensive. If a company has an inspection procedure as described it will normally have a quality control section or department whose main job is testing output. So there is the cost of that operation. Further, there can be disagreements and friction between quality control and production because of an apparent conflict of interest. Any rejected work will not count towards the workers' bonus payments. You can imagine some of the working relationship problems that can develop!

Despite all the disadvantages explained above, quality control is suitable for simple processes where faults can be easily identified and inexpensively rectified, for example in a restuarant.

quality assurance

Quality Assurance is based on the idea that quality is everybody's responsibility. There is a saying that you 'can't inspect quality into a product.' You may be able to inspect faults out, but you can't inspect quality in. This is the starting point of quality assurance.

The emphasis is on trying to ensure goods and services are produced free of faults. Quality Assurance is based on the belief that if everybody involved in the production of that product or service is really committed to ensuring faults are eliminated, they can be. So you do not try to inspect faults out; you make sure they are not there in the first place. The involvement of everybody in the organisation is crucial; quality is not just the responsibility of the quality control department – it is everybody's.

This idea is embodied in TQM (see below).

Total Quality Management (TQM)

The concept of total quality was developed in the 1950's (by Deming) and enthusiastically followed by the Japanese who, as we discussed earlier, were having quality problems at that time. It is generally agreed that the whole-hearted endorsement of this technique (and other quality measures) has been largely responsible for the transformation of Japanese quality and the current high reputation of Japanese goods.

Studies in the late twentieth century showed that air conditioners made in the USA had 70 times as many faults on average as air conditioners made in Japan and Japanese-made television sets averaged 0.5 faults per 100 sets while American made television sets averaged 150 faults per 100 sets.

TQM is a way of managing to improve effectiveness, flexibility and competitiveness of business as a whole. For a business to be truly effective every part must work together because every person and every activity affects and is in turn affected by every other. The effectiveness of TQM depends on total team working.

TQM and team working

The essentials of the TQM approach is that workers on production processes have a personal responsibility for passing on to following operations only products of perfect quality. This is quality at source and it is passed down a 'chain of quality'. Each work team checks the quality of its own products often known as self checking. So operators must be capable of doing and understanding the statistical quality analyses. The results are displayed (often on a board hanging from the ceiling) so everyone knows how the work team is doing. Anybody can stop the production process if they are unhappy about quality until the reason for the problem is found and resolved.

the advantages of TQM and team working

The benefits of TQM are that everyone is committed to improving the quality of the goods or services provided to the customer and accepts responsibility for this. It can result in high levels of motivation and involvement, leading to better quality standards, lower levels of waste and generally higher productivity.

the disadvantages of TQM and team working

TQM is a total management system. Workers who are committed and involved expect management to listen to their views and act on suggestions. Management cannot just choose the bits of TQM it likes and ignore the others! To be effective TQM requires a well trained, committed, competent workforce capable of identifying and analysing problems. It needs the time and total commitment of everyone in the organisation. If management is unable or unwilling to devote the time and effort to enable TQM to work properly then the system may end up creating more problems than it solves.

Formal TQM systems tend to be most appropriate for larger organisations, although it can be argued that in small companies TQM occurs naturally because everybody knows what is going on and is involved as a 'team'. It might be said that TQM is a way of getting small company values and culture adopted by larger organisations.

quality circles

For team working to be successful, it relies on a competent responsible workforce who want to improve quality. Their ideas for improvement can be discussed at regular meetings – quality circles. This is a management philosophy rather than just a quality improvement technique (in spite of the title). A quality circle is a group of workers who meet voluntarily at frequent and regular intervals to discuss problems encountered in their work with a view to discovering solutions.

The problems studied may relate to safety, productivity, cost reduction, improving the working environment as well as quality; the solution is likely to impact on all areas. For quality circles to be effective a business needs a well educated and trained workforce capable of receiving, analysing and solving problems.

advantages of quality circles

Quality circles include everyone directly involved in a problem. If they are properly managed they will encourage and motivate the work team to take pride in its work and accept responsibility for output.

disadvantages of quality circles

Quality circles require a well-trained workforce and committed management if they are to work effectively. Quality circles can fail if:

- managers hand over their responsibility for quality to the quality circle

- it is assumed that quality circles are able to solve all problems

- managers ignore what the quality circles recommend

Activity 5.9

A quality circle in the classroom

Discuss the possibility of running a quality circle for your class – involving students and a teacher (or teachers).

What do you think the advantages and disadvantages of this arrangement would be?

training and development – Investors in People

INVESTOR IN PEOPLE

All techniques designed to improve quality standards depend entirely on the people who work with them. If a business is to be truly quality focused it depends on everybody being involved as we have seen when looking at TQM and Quality Circles. If the whole workforce is to be involved and effective then everybody needs to be properly trained. The company needs to invest in its people.

A business that is effective in training and developing its workforce can apply to be an 'Investor in People'. Investors in People (IIP) is a government initiative that recognises businesses that train and develop their workforce effectively by awarding them an IIP kitemark.

benchmarking

The motivation for continuous improvement by the company and its workforce must often be the recognition that 'we are not the best.' If others are doing better, then so can we. Benchmarking involves a number of stages:

1 to decide what in the business needs benchmarking – production time? delivery time? after sales service?
2 to choose another business for standards of excellence to benchmark against
3 gathering information about the standards of excellence
4 setting standards and making sure everyone in the business knows about them

An example of benchmarking is the Government's publication of national league tables for schools and colleges. The basic idea is that those schools that are doing less well than the standard or benchmark will strive to improve. Furthermore, schools that are doing well will work to improve still further. By this process a culture of continuous improvement is encouraged.

advantage of benchmarking

The advantage of benchmarking is that it is a very simple concept and gives the business a target at which to aim.

disadvantages of benchmarking

The main disadvantage is that benchmarking only works if suitable benchmark data is available and the comparison is valid – in other words, like is being compared with like. Another criticism of benchmarking is that the approach is rather simplistic and does not help a business resolve quality problems.

Quality Certification - BS EN ISO 9000

For many businesses quality certification through national standards is the benchmark. BS EN ISO 9000 is a set of international standards. For all the activities involved in the business it sets down rigorous standards covering:

- supply of goods
- quality control
- training
- internal documentation
- after sales service
- procedures for dealing with faults
- management of the system

These all ensure that the finished product will be of a standard that will meet customer requirements. The certification process is very demanding but businesses are increasingly finding achievement of the quality 'kitemark' (see opposite page) worthwhile because benefits include:

- marketing necessity – because many 'big' customers require suppliers to be quality certified
- saving in costs – because internal procedures will be soundly based and efficient
- fewer complaints, fewer problems
- reduction of waste in internal processes

Activity 5.10

Comparing quality systems

Read through the following description of the quality systems used at McDonald's and then answer the questions that follow.

A dedicated Quality Assurance team in the UK is responsible for monitoring the quality of McDonald's food products, both in the restaurants and at the suppliers at all stages of production. This involves a continuous round of visits and inspections at McDonald's production facilities, distribution centres and restaurants. It even extends to the farms which sow the seeds and provide the food in the first place.

In the restaurants no delivery is accepted until a series of quality and safety checks are completed. All restaurant staff receive training in food safety and hygiene and food preparation procedures. All restaurants complete a Daily Product Safety Checklist to ensure that the food served is of the highest quality.

Reproduced by kind permission of McDonald's and www.bized.ac.uk

1   What types of quality systems are used by McDonald's in the complete production process?

What are the advantages and disadvantages of these systems?

2   Suppose you were starting up a fast food business in your area.

(a) How could you involve your staff in ensuring that quality was maintained?

(b) How could you find out from your customers about the levels of quality?

CHAPTER SUMMARY

- Production converts inputs into useful outputs which customers need; it adds value in the process.

- Productivity is the efficient use of resources and relates outputs to inputs.

- Productivity can also be related to the factors of production:
  - labour
  - materials
  - capital

- Work study is a technique which is used to improve productivity.

- Production planning is used to help businesses to:
  - achieve high levels of productivity
  - meet the needs of customers
  - control the production process

- The added value resulting from the production process may:
  - make the product more profitable
  - improve the marketability of the product
  - help the business survive

- Quality is a mix of customer expectation and the suitability of the product or service to do the job required.

- Quality control aims to ensure that customers do not receive substandard products; quality assurance aims to ensure that faulty products are not produced in the first place.

- There are a number of quality systems available including:
  - Total Quality Management (TQM)
  - quality circles
  - inspection
  - benchmarking
  - quality certification

KEY TERMS

inputs	the various resources needed to produce the goods and services required
outputs	the goods and services provided
added value	the production process adding value to inputs by converting them to outputs
productivity	a measure of the efficiency of the production process – the ratio of outputs to inputs
efficiency	achieving the maximum result in a process from the minimum effort
GANNT chart	a horizontal bar chart used in scheduling
quality	all the features and characteristics of a product or service which affects its ability to satisfy the needs of customers
quality control	preventing substandard products from reaching the customer
quality assurance	preventing substandard products from being produced in the first place
TQM	Total Quality Management (TQM) is a way of managing to improve effectiveness, flexibility and competitiveness of the business as a whole
ISO 9000	a set of international standards for the certification of quality in organisations
quality circle	a group of employees who meet voluntarily at frequent and regular intervals to discuss problems encountered in their work with the aim of finding solutions
inspection	examining the output to ensure that substandard products are rejected
benchmarking	comparing your business with a business known for best practice – bringing your business up to the quality standard of the other business

Competition and markets

introduction

An economy can be examined in terms of markets. There are several types of market but they all perform the same basic function. Some businesses operate in very competitive market structures where there are many businesses competing for customers. At the opposite end of the spectrum some businesses operate in markets where they are the only business and competition is non-existent. Other businesses operate in markets that fall somewhere between these two extremes.

what you will learn from this chapter

● there are numerous types of market, the most common of which are those for consumer goods, services, commodities and capital goods

● the most competitive market structures exist where there are many individual businesses trying to sell virtually identical goods and services to many independent buyers; these markets are comparatively rare

● in reality there may be lots of individual sellers but each one tries to make its customers believe that its product is in some way better than that of its competitors

● in some markets there is only one seller so there is no competition at all; in these circumstances the business has the power to sell at very high prices and make equally large profits

● nowadays many markets are dominated by a few very large businesses so that there is some degree of competition between businesses, but often not in terms of price

the structure of the UK economy

The structure of an economy is usually discussed in terms of its component parts, often called sectors. These can be defined in various ways but the three widest and most commonly used definitions used are: primary, secondary and tertiary.

the primary sector

This involves activities directly related to natural resources, eg farming, mining and fishing.

the secondary sector

This covers all the other goods produced in the economy by manufacturing; it also includes gas, water and electricity (the 'utilities').

the tertiary sector

This includes all services, for example transport, distribution, financial services and leisure.

the changing structure of the UK economy

In 1750, at the beginning of the industrial revolution, almost all business activity was in the primary sector. The overwhelming majority of the workforce was employed in agriculture which at that time was a very labour intensive industry. However, the industrial revolution witnessed an enormous expansion of the manufacturing and the hence the secondary sector of the economy. This, in turn led to the relative decline in importance of the primary sector. This trend continued until the early to mid-twentieth century when manufacturing output peaked and the tertiary sector began to account for a relatively larger share of the total output of the British economy. In the second half of the twentieth century there was further growth in the service sector's importance, but a decline in the secondary sector – and manufacturing in particular. Over the same period the position of the primary sector remained relatively stable.

The Activity on the next page asks you to comment on the relative importance of the three sectors in the British economy for selected years from 1964 to 1998. The percentages shown reflect the value of output of each sector in comparison with the total output of the economy.

Activity 6.1

Trends in the industrial sectors

The table below shows the percentage share of output of each of the three UK industrial sectors. You are to:

1 Draw a line graph or bar chart showing the trends from 1964 to 1998. Use a computer spreadsheet to handle the data if you can.

2 Comment on the trends you see. Back up your comments with examples of growing and declining businesses in your local area.

industrial sectors:
percentage shares of the sectors of the economy

	1964	1979	1990	1998
	%	%	%	%
Primary Sector	6	7	4	3
Secondary Sector	41	37	32	20
Tertiary Sector	53	56	64	77

The most significant features you will have seen from this Activity are the decline in the importance of manufacturing industry and the steadily increasing importance of the tertiary sector. This trend, which is a common feature of a post-industrial society, is likely to continue into the forseeable future. When a country's wealth increases beyond a given level and much of its material needs are satisfied then people increasingly demand more and better services. The 1970s and 1980s saw the rapid expansion of the financial services sector of the economy while the 1990s were associated with the boom in leisure. As consumers' incomes have increased they have spent more on holidays, eating out and getting fitter.

the development of markets

In the early days of man's existence communities were self-sufficient. They produced all the goods they needed – such as food, clothing and shelter – for themselves. In these circumstances the need for markets did not exist. However, over time it was realised that it was better for people to concentrate on producing the goods they were best at (specialisation) and then trade their surpluses for the surpluses produced by others. It was from this desire to trade (exchange) that markets were born.

the benefits of markets

Without markets people who wanted to sell, say wheat, would have to go to enormous lengths to find other people who wanted to buy wheat. This might include advertising, haggling over price and transportation. All these activities could be very time consuming and also very expensive. Markets that work well (efficiently) make it easier for people to buy and sell. It is said that they reduce the transaction costs of exchange. Low transaction costs are good for everyone involved. It means that producers can retain a greater share of the selling price in the form of profit which gives them an incentive to produce more. Similarly buyers will pay less for the things they purchase which in turn means that consumers – ordinary people buying food, cars clothing and all the other things they want – get things as cheaply as possible.

types of market

If asked to explain the meaning of the term 'market' most people would probably describe their local car boot sale, or an area of their local town which is used by stall holders selling everything from second hand CDs to Manchester United football shirts. If they happen to live in a more rural part of the country they may consider a market to be a place where local farmers go if they wish to sell their sheep, cattle and other livestock. Markets like these are in precisely defined places. When, however someone is talking about the 'oil market' he or she is referring to virtually the whole world. This is because oil is produced in many different places on the globe and the people who need to buy it are situated in almost every part of every country in the world.

In reality there are thousands, even millions of markets all over the world exchanging everything from cotton to coal, but they all have one thing in common. They are all points where buyers and sellers meet so that goods and services can be exchanged.

consumer markets – goods and services

The markets that are most familiar to us are the markets for consumer goods and services. The term 'goods' simply refers to products such as computers, cars, carpets – anything in fact that is produced by businesses that can be seen and touched comes under this heading. Items produced in this way are also known as **end-products**. Services on the other hand are 'intangibles', – things that we cannot touch such as cleaning and health care. Consumer goods and services are needed by people to be able to survive and improve their lives. We buy cars because they make it easier for us to travel around. We buy books to increase our knowledge and we have bank accounts because they make it easier for us to manage our financial affairs.

commodity markets

There are also **commodity markets** which deal in raw or semi-raw materials. Commodities are materials that can be graded and stored for long periods of time without deteriorating. Most commodity markets deal with trading in commodity futures – that is trading at a fixed price for delivery several months ahead. Major commodity markets exist in Chicago, Tokyo and London. Although there are some highly specialised markets such as the market for silkworm cocoons in Tokyo, most trade is in cereals and metals. 'Softs' is the term for commodities other than metals.

Case Study

Commodity markets
the London Metal Exchange

The centre of the world's trading in base metals is the London Metal Exchange where each day Ring Dealing broker firms meet to trade the main industrially used non-ferrous metals – copper, primary aluminium, aluminium alloy, lead, nickel, zinc, tin and silver. These periods of floor trading, where deals are made through the medium of the spoken word, provide the focus of the day's business. To meet world demand, the broking member firms of the LME span the time zones by operating 24-hour trading services. The resultant trade is enormous and is currently valued at $10 billion per day.

The Exchange which has a virtual world monopoly in many commodities, is able to reflect changes in supply and demand for non-ferrous metals, and to allow various interests in the trade – from mines to merchant banks – to establish prices and by such means as hedging (dealing forward) to protect themselves against price fluctuations. For further information log onto www.lme.co.uk

Activity 6.2

Commodity markets and competition

Study the 'Commodities' section in the financial pages of the press or log on to commodity prices on the internet.

1 What range of commodities are shown?

2 Where do you think the buyers and sellers come from? What industrial sectors do they represent?

3 Do you think producers of commodities can easily compete by cutting their prices?

industrial markets and capital goods

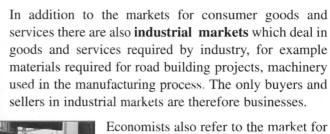

In addition to the markets for consumer goods and services there are also **industrial markets** which deal in goods and services required by industry, for example materials required for road building projects, machinery used in the manufacturing process. The only buyers and sellers in industrial markets are therefore businesses.

Economists also refer to the market for **capital goods**. These are goods wanted by businesses not for their own sake but for the contribution as 'factors of production' that they make to the production of other goods and services. Businesses need to buy specialised machinery and equipment which will be used to make other goods and will not be needed by consumers.

internal markets

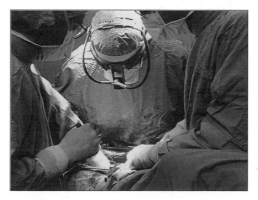

In some areas of the economy artificial markets – sometimes known as **internal markets** – are created, for example, in the public sector where in the past goods and services often did not have 'prices' and so it was not previously possible to make rational decisions about how best to use scarce resources. Internal markets are designed to help organisations such as the National Health Service, some sections of which supply services at artificially set prices to other sections – for example the 'sale' of heart bypass surgery carried out by a NHS hospital trust to a Primary Care Trust (a group of GPs).

Activity 6.3

Identifying types of market

1 Match up the numbered list of businesses or activities given below with the lettered list of markets.

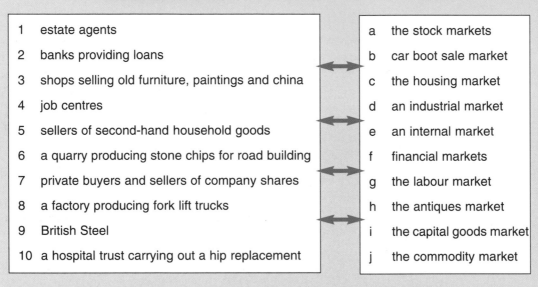

1 estate agents	a the stock markets
2 banks providing loans	b car boot sale market
3 shops selling old furniture, paintings and china	c the housing market
4 job centres	d an industrial market
5 sellers of second-hand household goods	e an internal market
6 a quarry producing stone chips for road building	f financial markets
7 private buyers and sellers of company shares	g the labour market
8 a factory producing fork lift trucks	h the antiques market
9 British Steel	i the capital goods market
10 a hospital trust carrying out a hip replacement	j the commodity market

2 If the market involves transactions carried out with consumers, state in each case whether the market is for goods or for services.

3 If you can, think of another example of a business operating in each of the types of market listed on the right.

market economies

Economies that rely predominantly on markets to allocate resources are known as **market economies**. Many economists and politicians nowadays regard markets and the market mechanism (the way in which markets work) as the best system for allocating resources. It is indeed tempting to conclude that the market mechanism does work extremely well. After all most people in Britain today can obtain all the goods and services they need to achieve a reasonable standard of living. Visitors to Britain from, for example, Russia where the market mechanism is less fully developed, are often amazed by the range of goods on display on the shelves of our supermarkets. Possible benefits to societies where the market mechanism plays an important role include:

a wide range of goods and services

In market economies businesses are free to provide whatever goods and services they like. In practice businesses know what to produce from the spending patterns of consumers and other businesses. If there is a demand for it businesses will be willing to supply whatever it is that people want providing they can make a profit from doing so.

command economy – the avoidance of surpluses and deficits

The alternative to the market economy is the command economy where resources are allocated by the state. An example of a twenty-first century command economy is Cuba. If the state is able to know what people really want this can have some potential benefits but in practice countries that operated on this basis found there were severe shortages of many essential goods while simultaneously there were surpluses of others that few people seemed to want.

the mixed economy

While countries like the UK, France, Germany, Japan and the USA are often referred to as market economics they are more accurately described as mixed economies. Although they depend heavily upon the market mechanism for the allocation of much of their resources they recognise that markets do not always work perfectly, for example in the areas of healthcare and education. To try and overcome these imperfections other methods of resources allocation such as those used in a command economy are employed by the Government.

markets and competition

Some businesses operate in very competitive market structures where there are many businesses competing for customers. At the opposite end of the spectrum (shown below) some businesses operate in markets where they are the only business and competition is non-existent. Other businesses operate in markets that fall somewhere between these two extremes. In each case the consequences for businesses and their customers will vary.

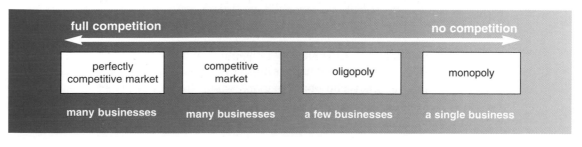

perfectly competitive markets

Markets work well when producers get a worthwhile return for their efforts while at the same time buyers can obtain the goods and services they want at a reasonable price. It is generally believed that this is most likely to happen where the market for a particular good or service is highly competitive.

Consider the market for vegetables. If you were to visit your local town centre you would probably find that the price of, say, carrots, would be virtually the same in every shop. This is because there are so many independent sellers that no one seller can have an influence on market price. If one seller tried to raise the price of carrots above that of other local shops then consumers, who know the price being charged by other shops (they can walk around and see the prices for themselves) will simply buy their carrots elsewhere. Similarly no single buyer of carrots is big enough to influence the price. If one household decided that they needed three times as many carrots this week as they did last it would have no impact on the price of carrots. Each buyer accounts for such a tiny share of the total demand that individually any change in the amount they buy is insignificant.

Markets that are extremely competitive are known as **perfectly competitive** markets. Perfectly competitive markets tend to have the following features:

a large number of businesses
– each business is so small that on their own they cannot affect the market price (as described above)

perfect customer knowledge
– all buyers and sellers know the quality and the price being offered by other businesses – this ensures that no one will buy or sell above or below the going (market) price

there is no consumer loyalty
– consumers do not normally care where they buy their carrots from – they simply look for the lowest price

businesses can enter and leave the market easily
– if the demand for the good or service rises new businesses can set up relatively easily

In reality perfect markets are rare, although the market for carrots and many other agricultural products is close to the definition. They may also exist in some currency and share markets where the development of information technology has meant that millions of buyers and sellers are linked through computers. They have virtually perfect knowledge of all prices in the market.

the consequences of perfectly competitive markets

price

Businesses in perfectly competitive markets have no control over the price of the good or service they are selling and so they must employ competitive pricing strategies. In the same way that a new shop selling carrots would have to sell then at the 'going' (market) price, a dealer offering US dollars must accept the market selling price for dollars. A business that tried to sell above the market price would find that it would have no customers as they would have all gone to other sellers offering better deals. Businesses would not sell for less than the market price because they would not be able to make enough profit to survive.

the need to drive down costs

Businesses in perfectly competitive markets have a big incentive to cut costs and produce goods and services as cheaply (efficiently) as possible. Producers that can do this successfully will be able to make larger profits for themselves. In the long term this tends to force prices down as businesses will try to out do each other in an attempt to become more efficient than their rivals.

perfectly competitive markets – a conclusion

Businesses in competitive markets have no power to influence price and so have little choice but to price their goods and services at the same level as every other business. Such businesses effectively compete in terms of costs.

Consumers have little choice but this does not matter if they regard all products in the market as identical and they do not care who they buy from. Their only concern is price which, due to the intense levels of competition, is kept at a minimum.

Activity 6.4

Perfectly competitive markets

You are interested in setting up a service station selling fuel to motorists.

1   Explain the likely pricing strategy you might adopt for the fuel you want to sell.

2   In the light of your answer to question one explain why it will be important for you to minimise your costs.

3   Petrol and diesel might be considered to be 'homogenous' products. Find out what this means and suggest other goods that might be similarly defined.

4   To what extent do you consider petrol retailing to be a perfectly competitive market? How easy, for example, would it be to enter the market?

competitive markets

While examples of perfectly competitive markets are extremely rare there are other markets that are slightly less competitive but where the level of competition amongst businesses is still very high. These are known simply as **competitive markets**.

Clothes retailing is one example of such a market. In a typical town in the UK there are a large number of shops selling clothes. These will range from famous high street names such as Next, Benetton and Marks & Spencer, to smaller locally owned independent retailers.

the consequences of competitive markets

The consequences for businesses and consumers of competitive markets are:

product differentiation

In an attempt to gain customers some businesses will attempt to product differentiate – make themselves a little different from their competitors. Some shops might try to cater for the needs of teenagers; others might try to provide for the needs of young working people who may have a lot more money to spend and are therefore willing to pay much higher prices for better quality garments. Some will orientate themselves towards the needs of older people who may have very different tastes.

Product differentiation may also mean that some businesses will try to create perceived differences between themselves and their competitors. Some of these differences may be real but others may be in the minds of consumers. In other words they will be trying to make consumers believe that they are the best through attractive advertising, window displays, merchandising (displays of goods at the point of sale) and eye-catching posters.

From the consumer's point of view product differentiation means that they have a wide choice of shops, selling a wide range of clothes at varying prices. Choice is good news for consumers as it makes it more likely that they will be able to find the item they are looking for.

quality

In competitive markets the rivalry between businesses is so fierce that each one knows that they will not succeed by selling poor quality goods and services. Every clothes retailer will be well aware of the importance of their reputation amongst consumers and the need to ensure that customers will return. For these reasons each retailer will strive hard to be able to offer the best quality clothes they can within the price range that their customers are willing to pay.

Businesses which operate in competitive markets also provide a number of obvious benefits for consumers . . .

competitive pricing

The price of clothes will depend upon the quality of the goods and the segment of the market each business is trying to reach (see market segmentation in Chapter 11). Consumers will be willing to pay more for the clothes on sale in some shops if they believe that the product is superior in some way. However, shops within any particular segment of the market cannot charge any price they may wish. They have to ensure that their prices are similar to those charged by similar shops selling similar quality clothes. If they try to sell their clothes at a significantly higher price shoppers can simply go elsewhere. Businesses in this situation will normally adopt a strategy of competitive pricing.

penetration pricing

When a new business is trying to break into an established market it may employ penetration pricing by setting a price below that of its major competitors, and then raising it once it has gained an acceptable market share. Look at the markets for mobile telephones and for internet connection – they are all fiercely competitive. There are many new entrants into the market and prices have fallen – all to the benefit of the consumer.

becoming more competitive – adding value

All businesses aim to make money and become more competitive by adding value to their products and making them more attractive.

The clothes retailer adds value to his or her stock by packing and displaying them in an attractive way. Supermarkets add value to fresh vegetables by washing them and packing them ready for cooking – and, of course, charging more for them. The greater the value added the higher the price the business can justify charging and thus the larger their profits.

Businesses are constantly looking for new ways to add value to the good or service they produce. Drug companies are looking for new ways of combining what can often be relatively cheap ingredients to produce pills than can relieve symptoms or even cure disease. Think how much a pharmaceutical producer could charge for a pill that could cure cancer. At one time banks were simply places for depositing money. Today banks offer a wide range of services to their customers including mortgages, currency dealing services, share dealing and advice, to mention just a few. This allows them to increase their income for what they do and it enables them to attract more customers. The search for new ways to add value gives businesses the opportunity to make greater profits and become more competitive.

the need to cut costs

Businesses in competitive markets have a big incentive to cut costs and become more efficient. Lower costs means a greater added value and thus higher profits. From the consumer's perspective greater efficiency is good because lower costs means that prices will be lower than might otherwise be the case.

competitive markets – a conclusion

Businesses in competitive markets constantly need to find ways of making themselves look better than their competitors. At the same time they need to keep costs low and ensure that their prices are kept in line with those of their competitors. Consumers benefit from having a very wide choice of goods and services at reasonably low prices.

Activity 6.5

Competitive markets

You are considering setting up a business as a hairdresser in a local town or city.

Write down the answers to these questions individually . . .

1 Define a 'competitive market'. To what extent would you consider hairdressers to operate in a competitive market?

2 Why might you wish to differentiate your business from your competitors?

3 Why is it important for businesses to add value to the good or service they provide?

Now divide into small groups and discuss the following questions. Appoint a group member to write down your findings and to report back to the class.

4 Explain the various strategies you might employ to differentiate the service your business provides.

5 Make a list of the ways in which you might add value in your business.

6 Draw up a list of other businesses in your area that operate in competitive markets.

7 To what extent do you think that competitive markets are good for consumers?

no competition in the market – monopoly

At the opposite end of the competition spectrum from perfectly competitive markets is **monopoly** – the type of market which is characterised by the complete absence of competition. In a 'pure' monopoly like this there will be a large number of buyers but only one supplier of a good or service.

In the same way that perfectly competitive markets are very rare and may only exist in the pages of economic textbooks, it is very hard to find real world examples of pure monopoly. The best examples are probably from the past, in the days when major industries such as coal mining, steel and public transport were all largely owned and controlled by the state. These former nationalised industries, which today have largely been sold off to the private sector (privatised), became monopolies because no other businesses were allowed to compete with them.

Up until 1984 the company now known as BT had a virtual monopoly in the telecommunications market. Businesses and households who wanted to make use of the telephone had no choice but to use British Telecom, as they were then known. As you will appreciate, the telephone market is now very different.

the consequences of monopoly

The absence of competition has a number of consequences for businesses and consumers.

very high barriers to entry

In perfectly competitive and competitive markets new businesses can enter the market without too much difficulty – a clothes store in the local high street, for example. The exact opposite applies to 'pure' monopoly where barriers to entry may mean that other businesses are denied the opportunity to compete. This is very rare, however. When the coal industry in Britain was nationalised (owned and controlled by the state) no other businesses were permitted to mine and sell coal except for the National Coal Board.

price

Businesses that are monopolists can virtually choose the price at which they wish to sell their products. They can set price at the maximum level that the market will bear. As there is only one supplier customers have no alternative but to pay the price the monopolist demands. Either they buy or go without.

For consumers this may not matter too much if the market for china dolls is dominated by a price setting monopolist. However, if markets which supply essential products such as water, gas, electricity and food are controlled by monopolists then there may be serious cause for concern. They are forced to pay much higher prices than would be the case in more competitive markets.

quality

Businesses that are monopolists sometimes neglect the quality of their products because consumers have to accept what they are offered. Customers have no alternative, except that in the long run they may turn to alternative products. Before competition came into the telecommunications market consumers who wanted to have a telephone line installed by BT (the sole supplier) often had to wait several months. Today it may take less than a week. There are therefore no real quality benefits in monopolies.

efficiency

Competition forces firms to be efficient and to minimise their production costs. In monopoly, however, producers have little incentive to be efficient and keep costs low. To maintain profits an inefficient monopolist can simply raise prices to deal with rising costs. This may not be an option in a more competitive market.

Consumers under monopoly often pay higher prices because goods and services are inefficiently produced and businesses have high costs. The introduction of competition in the markets for gas and electricity, both of which were previously controlled by monopolies, has forced suppliers to cut costs, causing prices to fall.

lack of innovation

Businesses in competitive markets need to introduce new products and refine existing ones to be competitive. The incentive to innovate in monopoly is much less as there is no need to worry about being competitive – there is no competition. Consumers have to put up with the same old thing.

high profits

As they can charge high prices for their products monopolists have the potential to make very large profits indeed. High profits are bad news for consumers as they are made at their expense. If, however, a monopoly uses its profits to finance research into the development of new and better products then there are potential benefits for consumers.

monopoly – a conclusion

For businesses monopolies offer the prospect of high prices and high profits for relatively little effort. Consumers may suffer from high prices and poor quality goods and services that are inefficiently produced. But, as we will see in Chapter 9, the Government does intervene to protect the consumer through the Competition Act and the Competition Commission.

Activity 6.6

the Microsoft Monopoly

Read through the report below and answer the questions that follow.

Gates on the ropes

It's official. Microsoft is a monopoly. This was the conclusion of the judgement delivered by US district court judge Thomas Penfield Jackson in November 1999. The court found that the company operated a monopoly, abused that monopoly and harmed the consumer by restricting competition and innovation.

The US government's case against Microsoft, focused on the software giant's dominant position in the industry. It was argued that Microsoft used its power in operating system software to force its rivals out of the market.

Microsoft, headed by the world's richest man Bill Gates, enjoyed monopoly power in the market for Intel-based PC operating systems. In this sector of the market the kind of PCs most users have at home or work – Windows had up to 95 per cent of the market. There was no real alternative.

Microsoft demonstrated that it had used its prodigious market power and immense profits to harm any firm that insisted on pursuing initiatives that could intensify competition against one of Microsoft's core products. The judge said: 'Microsoft largely succeeded in exiling (Netscape's) Navigator from the crucial OEM (original equipment manufacturer) distribution channel.' In other words it bounced Netscape out of the market by bundling its own Internet browser, Internet Explorer, with its software.

Source: *The Observer*, 7 November 1999

1   In what area did Microsoft have a monopoly?

2   How did Microsoft make it difficult for Netscape to compete?

3   In what sense was this unfair?

4   Why was the US government so concerned about Microsoft's monopoly?

competition amongst the few – oligopoly

At the monopoly end of the competition spectrum (see page 129) lies **oligopoly** – which means literally 'the rule of the few'. In oligopolistic markets there is a degree of competition but in reality the market is dominated by a few very large firms. Examples of this kind of market are numerous. The grocery (food) market contains many small independent shops but they are insignificant compared with the big supermarket chains – Tesco, Sainsbury, Safeway, Asda and Morrisons – who between them have 75% of the total market. The same position exists in the car market, which is dominated by large manufacturing conglomerates (including General Motors and Ford) and also in the UK banking industry.

the consequences of oligopoly

high barriers to entry

It is difficult for new firms to enter the market due to high entry barriers. These might include high sunk costs. These are costs, such as advertising expenditure, that are unrecoverable should the business fail. The risk of losing such large sums might deter new entrants. Existing firms may benefit from economies of scale – very low costs that arise from large scale production – which make it virtually impossible for new firms to compete with well established businesses. Some businesses have developed a special product, design or process which is protected by a patent (a way of making it illegal for firms to copy the idea).

Barriers to entry tend to work against the interests of consumers as they make competition less likely.

price

Businesses in oligopoly have to keep a very careful eye on the actions and reactions of their competitors. If, for example, Ford were to cut the prices of their entire range of cars tomorrow all other car manufacturers would eventually be forced to do the same. This is clearly of no long term benefit to Ford. They may be able to increase sales and profits for a while but eventually they would find themselves in a position where sales returned to their previous levels but profits were lower.

 If, on the other hand, Ford were to raise their prices above those of all other car manufacturers they would find that their sales would fall as consumers switched to the products of their competitors. For these reasons strictly oligopolistic markets – where there are genuinely very few players in the market – are noted for the absence of competition in terms of price. Where there are more players in the market, price wars can and do break out

price wars

In some market situations however, price competition amongst oligopolists can become intense resulting in what are known as price wars. Price wars often happen in markets where there are too many suppliers and where profits in the industry are low. In an attempt to drive out one or more of their rivals, the biggest player (the one with the largest profits) will sometimes lower prices to levels where other firms simply cannot compete and are thus forced out of the market. Once one or two of their rivals have left the scene they will raise their prices to previous levels but they will benefit from greater sales and profits because there are fewer competitors. Such tactics are known as price predation or destructive pricing.

Activity 6.7

Oligopoly and price wars

Read through the two Case Studies shown below and then answer the questions that follow.

Newspaper price wars

In the early 1990s price wars broke out within the newspaper industry. In July 1993 *The Sun* reduced its price from 25p to 20p and a month or two later the price of *The Times* fell from 45p to 30p. Both newspapers were owned by the same company, News International, controlled by the Australian media magnate, Rupert Murdoch. As a result sales of *The Times* increased significantly, by around 145,000 copies per day. For a while the other quality newspapers - *The Daily Telegraph*, *The Independent* and *The Guardian* - held their prices but falling circulation figures led *The Daily Telegraph* to reduce its price from 48p to 30p. The next day *The Times* responded by cutting its price by a further 10p. After months of intense competition *Today*, one of the smaller players in the market, was forced to close as it was unable to compete with the aggressive tactics of its rivals. *The Guardian* and *The Independent* have remained but only by the skin of their teeth. Eventually *The Guardian* was rescued by The Mirror Group and *The Independent* has come close to collapse on at least two separate occasions.

Asda turns the screw

ASDA, the Leeds based supermarket chain owned by Wal-Mart of the USA, yesterday posted a fresh round of aggressive price cuts aimed at luring customers away from the UK's top food retailers such as Sainsbury's and Tesco.

As part of a £200m-a-year 'rollback' programme aimed at reducing prices to US levels, ASDA said it would spend £30m cutting the prices of 200 food products, including households brands such as Pot Noodle and Birds Eye beef burgers, by up to one-third. A spokesman said: "If our competitors were hoping we would take our foot off the pedal in 2000, they're going to be very disappointed."

Yesterday's move follows a recent £45m promotion to reduce the cost of 2,000 home and leisure items in ASDA stores. The UK group has promised to bring 10,000 prices into line with Wal-Mart's discount levels by the end of the year.

Source: Lucy Baker in *The Independent*, 7 January 2000

1 Explain why Rupert Murdoch in the early 1990s and, more recently ASDA, might have decided to employ such aggressive pricing strategies.

2 Why are businesses in oligopolistic markets often reluctant to engage in price cutting strategies?

3 Suggest alternative strategies that businesses in oligopolistic markets might employ to compete more effectively.

4 To what extent do you consider that oligopolistic markets are good for:
   • the businesses themselves?
   • consumers?

Try to use examples from oligopolistic markets with which you are familiar to illustrate your answers.

oligopoly – cartels and collusion

Such are the pressures on firms in oligopolistic markets not to compete in terms of price that they sometimes get together and enter into formal and informal agreements on price. These arrangements are known as **cartels**. Perhaps one of the best known examples is that of OPEC (Organisation of Petroleum Exporting Countries). This is a group of countries including Saudi Arabia and Kuwait that works together to restrict the supply of crude oil onto the market in order to maintain artificially higher prices. During the 1970s OPEC was extremely successful in achieving its objectives and managed to raise the price of crude oil by over 400 per cent.

Collusion ('getting together') stifles competition and usually results in higher prices for consumers.

oligopoly – competition through advertising

Businesses that cannot readily compete in terms of price must look to other ways to attract customers. Advertising plays a particularly important role in oligopolistic markets. It helps to increase general customer awareness about a good or service and it also helps to make customers believe that one product is superior to that of the competitors.

Advertisements for mobile phones, for example, have helped to make consumers aware of the benefits of having a mobile phone – it can be used to contact the emergency services in the event of an accident, it can help business communications, it can help a boyfriend contact a girlfriend – and vice versa!

Informative advertising is helpful for consumers, but persuasive advertising often has to be paid for in the form of higher prices. Advertising may also be used as a form of barrier to entry to deter competitors. Potential rivals may find it impossible to afford to promote their products on the same scale.

competition – services and accessibility

Oligopolists may also compete in terms of the number of outlets provided – these make it easier for customers to gain access to the goods or services on offer. At one time banks used to try to outdo each other by claiming that they had more branches than their competitors. Nowadays they tend to compete by offering the best internet or telephone access – because, in fact, they are cutting down the number of branches.

Customers can obviously benefit from this form of competition.

oligopoly – a conclusion

Businesses in oligopoly face relatively little competition because there are high barriers to entry. Sometimes price competition is non-existent and so businesses compete using non-price methods such as advertising and service. Consumers have a reasonable choice of products but may have to pay higher prices than would be the case in more competitive markets.

CHAPTER SUMMARY

- The UK economy is normally divided into three main sectors: the primary sector (fishing, mining and agriculture), the secondary (manufacturing) sector, the tertiary (services) sector. The current trend is for growth in the tertiary sector and decline in the secondary sector.

- The main function of markets is to bring buyers and sellers together to facilitate the exchange of goods and services. There are numerous types of market. The most widely accepted categories are – consumer goods and services, capital goods, commodity markets, internal markets.

- Perfectly competitive markets exist where there are a large number of businesses selling a virtually identical product. Competition is so intense that prices are driven down to such a low level that businesses make only just enough profit to survive. In reality perfectly competitive markets are rare.

- In competitive markets there are a large number of businesses selling the same basic product, but each tries to make customers believe that its product is in some way superior to that offered by its competitors.

- Where there is only one seller in a market a business is said to have a monopoly. The absence of competition often means that businesses can exploit their dominant position by charging very high prices which enables then to make very high profits. In practice monopolies are very rare.

- An oligopoly is a market which is dominated by a few large businesses. Businesses in oligopoly face relatively little competition because there are high barriers to entry. Businesses often compete in oligopolies using non-price methods such as advertising and service.

- The 'spectrum' of types of market can be summarised as follows:

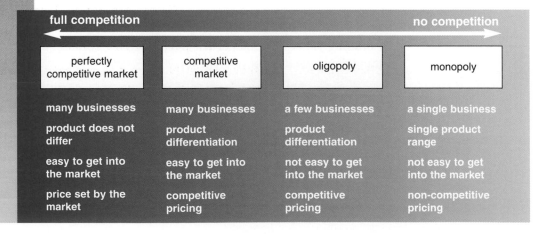

full competition			no competition
perfectly competitive market	competitive market	oligopoly	monopoly
many businesses	many businesses	a few businesses	a single business
product does not differ	product differentiation	product differentiation	single product range
easy to get into the market	easy to get into the market	not easy to get into the market	not easy to get into the market
price set by the market	competitive pricing	competitive pricing	non-competitive pricing

KEY TERMS

primary sector	businesses involved at the first stage of the production process such as mining, fishing and agriculture
secondary sector	businesses involved at the second stage of the production process – the manufacturing sector
tertiary sector	businesses involved in the supply of services such as retailing and banking
market	a place, although not necessarily a defined area, where buyers and sellers meet to trade
consumer market	markets which provide goods and services which are purchased by private individuals and households
end-products	complete or finished goods
commodity market	markets which deal in raw or semi-raw materials
industrial market	markets which deal in goods and services required by industry
capital goods	goods such as tools and machinery that are wanted not for their own sake but for the contribution they make to the production of other goods and services
internal market	artificial markets such as those created within the NHS to help decision makers make more informed judgements on the best use of resources
market economy	an economy where most of the key economic decisions (what to produce, how to produce them and for whom they should be produced) are made through the price mechanism
perfect competition	markets for undifferentiated goods where the level of competition is so intense that prices and profits tend towards their lowest possible levels
competitive markets	markets where there are a large number of producers supplying differentiated goods and services
monopoly	a market in which there is only one supplier
oligopoly	a market structure where a few large businesses are dominant
product differentiation	strategies employed by businesses to enable them to accentuate real or imaginary differences between goods and services

Competition and pricing

Unit 2 The competitive business environment
How competition in the market affects business

introduction

Market prices are determined by the forces of demand and supply. Changes in demand and supply can lead to changes in market prices which businesses need to respond to. Businesses like to be able to anticipate possible changes in market prices and to do this they must be able to understand how changes in market conditions will affect demand and supply. It is possible to develop an understanding of the way in which prices are determined on a common sense level, but it is also helpful to adopt a more scientific approach through the use of simple demand and supply diagrams.

what you will learn from this chapter

- a key function of markets is to help determine price; businesses need to understand and respond to changes in market prices

- market forces involve demand factors and supply factors

- the level of demand is influenced by the age distribution of the population, incomes, tastes and fashions, the influence of marketing, changes in the price of related products, expected price changes and the price and availability of credit

- the level of supply is influenced by the costs of production, technology, the physical conditions in which production takes place and by taxes and subsidies

- the law of demand can be represented as a downward sloping line known as a demand curve while the law of supply can be represented as an upward sloping line known as a supply curve

- the point where the demand and supply curves cross is known as equilibrium price; shifts in demand and supply curves cause the equilibrium price to change

the importance of market price

The key function of markets is to make trade easier, but in addition to this they play a vital role in helping to determine the price of the good or service traded. Economists commonly use the term **market price**. Essentially this is the name given to the price that is a compromise between how much sellers are willing to sell for and how much buyers are willing to pay for the good or service in question.

Market price is important because price changes send signals to producers which tells them whether they should produce more or less of their good or service. If the price of a product is rising this is a sign that producers need to supply more. Producers will respond to this signal because, in general, higher prices lead to higher rewards for producers (profits) and so they have an incentive to work harder and increase production. Falling prices, on the other hand, generally lead to falling profits and this is the way that the market signals to producers that they should produce less.

Activity 7.1

BSE – changing the market price

Read the following extract taken from an article in *The Sunday Telegraph* (24 October 1999) and then answer the questions set out on the next page.

Businessman ruined by BSE turns his crisis into a drama

BSE, a disease which affected thousands of cattle forcing many of them to be destroyed as consumers stopped buying beef, has led a man whose multi-million pound business was destroyed as a result of the crisis to turn his bitter experience into a satirical comedy, producing a novel and television drama about "mad-cow" disease.

Mark Frankland, 38, wrote One Man's Meat - a quirky book with a plot centred on the British Beef crisis - after his family's £18 million agricultural feed company ran into trouble in 1996.

"When the world wide beef ban was imposed huge numbers of animals became surplus," Mr. Frankland said. "Suddenly all the animals for which we sold feed were being slaughtered."

"Within twelve months the family company - which had grown over twelve years to employ 70 people - was in deep trouble. Our customer base had collapsed and we couldn't meet all our financial commitments. All this over a badly-handled crisis."

His story is now to be shown to a wider film audience. Crescent Film Productions, an independent film company has picked up the work and is having talks with Channel 4 over the production of a two-part drama-documentary.

Read the article on the previous page and then answer the following questions:

1   Explain what you think would have happened to the market price of cows following the BSE crisis.

2   Explain what you think would have happened to the price of animal feed following the crisis.

3   What was the message contained in the signals being sent by the market to animal feed businesses such as the one owned by Mr. Frankland's family?

4   Explain in terms of prices and markets, why Mark Frankland may have moved out of the animal feed business and become an author/playwright.

the market mechanism

The process described earlier and examined in the article above, whereby thousands and even billions of sellers and buyers both determine market prices and react to changes in market prices is known as the price or **market mechanism**. It is through the market mechanism that buyers are able to send signals to producers about what goods and services they want. These signals tell producers both what and how much to produce.

changes in market prices

For any business person price is probably the most important factor that influences their decision making. There is little incentive to produce goods or services that have a very low market price, whereas goods and services that command very high prices are often more attractive to produce as profits are often (though not always) correspondingly greater.

Many crucial decisions will depend on what business people think will happen to price in the future and so it is very important for them to understand how market prices will react to changing market conditions. To make this easier to understand economists divide the main changes in market conditions into two groups:

*   demand
*   supply

demand

Demand simply means the amount of a good or service that people wish to buy over a defined period of time, eg 10,000 tins of baked beans a week.

There are a number of factors that can cause demand to change . . .

the influence of price on demand

The price of a good or service is obviously one of the main factors that influences how much we buy of it. The general rule is that:

the higher the price of a good or service the less we will buy of it

the lower the price of a good or service the more we will buy of it

This rule is known as the law of demand.

The factors that cause the level of demand to change are explained below. The general rule is:

an increase in demand leads to a rise in price

a decrease in demand leads to a fall in price

changes in income

Most people gain an income from working in the form of wages and salaries. However, people can gain an income from a number of other sources. These are summarised in the table below:

source of income	form of income
employment	wages, salaries, bonuses
savings	interest
retirement pension	pensions
state benefits	job seekers allowance, child benefit
property ownership	rent
share ownership	dividends
business (entrepreneurship)	profit

It is clear that the greater the level of people's income the greater the level of demand. It also follows from this that the higher the level of demand the higher the market price. Obviously this logic can also be applied the other way around – lower incomes lead to lower demand and lower market prices.

It is helpful to appreciate that the actual amount of money that people have to spend – better known as disposable income – is dependent on how much is taken from people's wages and salaries in the form of taxes, national insurance and pension contributions (superannuation). An increase in pension contributions, for example, will cause people's disposable income to fall. Similarly a fall in taxes on incomes will produce a rise in disposable incomes. The amount that people spend each month on their mortgage will also cause disposable income to change. A change in interest rates will usually force lenders to charge borrowers more or less each month for their mortgage repayments and this will cause disposable incomes to rise or fall. This in turn will lead to a change in the level of demand for a wide range of goods and services.

changes in the age distribution of the population

The age distribution of the population refers to the number of people in the various age ranges:

0 - 4	pre-school children
5 - 16	children in compulsory education
17 - 65	those who are potentially available for employment – sometimes known as the working population
65 +	those eligible to claim state retirement benefit and generally not available for work

People in each of the different age groups have quite different tastes and they demand widely varying goods and services. Over the next twenty years or so the number of people reaching retirement age will increase while the number of people available for employment will decline. This will almost certainly lead to an increase in the demand for health care, nursing homes and a variety of other goods and services that tend to be consumed by older people. At the same time the demand for goods and services most associated with a younger population is likely to fall. Businesses will need to respond to these different patterns of demand, and change production and marketing efforts to meet the needs of these customers.

changes in tastes and fashion

Over time consumers' tastes change – goods and services which were subject to heavy demand in the past may no longer be regarded as desirable. Styles of clothing, for example, which at one time were considered to be 'in vogue' or 'cool' can be easily be viewed as out of date or 'uncool'. Changes in tastes and fashion can have positive and negative effects on demand.

the influence of marketing

Goods can be made fashionable by effective marketing. A successful advertising and promotional campaign for consumer goods such as cars, clothes, watches and cosmetics can substantially increase the level of demand among status-conscious consumers. This is probably the most significant area in which businesses can influence demand for products.

changes in the price of related products

If there was a sudden and steep fall in the price of new cars so that people bought significantly more of them it would not surprise many people if in the near future the demand for petrol also increased. Similarly a decrease in the price of PCs might well lead to increase in demand for computer games and other software.

Goods which are related in this way are known as **complementary goods**.

It there was a sudden and steep fall in the price of train fares then it could well lead to a significant fall in the demand for buses. A rise in the price of fresh chicken might lead to a rise in the demand for turkey.

Goods which are related in this way are known as **substitute goods**.

Activity 7.2

changes in demand

How will demand for products be affected in the following situations? Explain the reasons in each case.

1   the effect of a fall in the birth rate on the market for disposable nappies

2   a reduction in income tax and consumer spending on holidays

3   the effect of bad publicity about under-age drinking and the sale of alcopops (alcoholic drinks which are packaged in the style of non-alcoholic drinks)

4   the effect of a fall in price of internet access on the market for PCs

Then . . .

5   give examples of successful advertising campaigns which have increased the demand for specific consumer goods

expected price changes

If the price of wine was expected to rise in a month's time as a result of an anticipated increase in duty on alcohol, then many people who like wine might well ensure that they stocked up on wine before the increase in taxation came into effect. People who behave in this way are effectively bringing their purchases forward in the hope that it will save them money. It will also lead to a temporary increase in demand for wine.

If the price of domestic appliances was expected to fall in a few months time then many people might well postpone their purchase of a fridge or microwave in the hope of buying more cheaply in the near future. In this example an expected price fall can lead to an actual fall in the current demand for the product in question. Now read the Case Study on the next page which shows what can happen if people delay in buying a car.

Case Study

Expecting car prices to fall
a fall in demand

CAR PRICES PLUMMET
Dealers and consumers wait for report

Manufacturers reacted angrily after it was announced that the Government decision on new car prices will be delayed until at least the spring of 2000. This follows the news that the Competition Commission's report into vehicle pricing will be delivered to the Secretary of State for Trade and Industry at least six weeks later than planned.

The enquiry was called into the pricing of new cars, which consumer groups claim can lead motorists paying up to 50 per cent more in Britain than mainland Europe, an argument dismissed by manufacturers.

The motor companies have pressed for an early decision because they claim that motorists, expecting prices to come down, might delay buying new cars until after ministers make the announcement.

In November 1999 vehicles up to a year old, on average cost 13.5 per cent less than they had a year previously, while new car prices declined by a modest 1.9 per cent.

A report by Charterhouse Securities suggests makers have lost £100m in sales because of motorists' fears about prices. The report urged manufacturers to lower prices immediately and not wait for the outcome of the Competition Commission report. Charterhouse estimates a 14 per cent reduction in prices could lift car sales by 350,000 a year. As many as 75,000 new vehicle purchases may have been deferred in the September-December 1999 period while would-be buyers wait for prices to fall.

discussion points

1   Has the position over car prices and car purchasing patterns changed since this book went to press? Explain the reasons for any changes.

2   Try and find examples of other markets for products which suffer from the same problems as the car market in the report printed here.

the price and availability of credit

The price of some goods and services that people wish to buy can often be so high that they find it difficult to afford them out of one month's income. In this case people sometimes find it more convenient to borrow the money they need to buy a new car or foreign holiday. This is known as buying on credit. If the cost of obtaining credit falls because of a fall in interest rates or, because a new and better credit card becomes available then this tends to lead to an increase in the demand for many goods that are commonly bought using borrowed funds. Similarly a rise in interest rates, or tighter restrictions on the amount of credit that lenders are willing to offer tends to reduce the demand for many goods and services.

The large rise in house prices that was experienced in many parts of the country at the beginning of the millennium was in part due to the fact that interest rates were at record lows. Mortgage lenders were able to reduce the monthly repayment cost of taking out a mortgage to equally historically low levels. This, combined with the fact that banks and building societies were willing to lend larger sums than had often been the case in the past, helped fuel the demand for houses. Now read the report below.

Highest growth in personal borrowing for eight years

The Bank of England's Monetary Policy Committee is expected to come under intense pressure to increase interest rates next month after figures, due this week, are expected to show the highest growth in personal borrowing for eight years.

The rise in expenditure is putting upward pressure on prices as the demand for a wide range of consumer goods from cars to carpets increases. The Bank of England is becoming increasingly concerned that the a possible increases in the prices of consumer goods could jeopardise the Government's target for inflation.

discussion point

How is the current trend in interest rates affecting demand?

Activity 7.3

Factors affecting the price of new cars

The table below shows a list of factors that can influence the demand and the market price of new cars. In each case state whether demand and price will rise or fall.

Factor change	Effect on demand *rise/fall*	Effect on market price *rise/fall*
a major advertising campaign by car manufacturers		
an increase in the cost of borrowing		
an increase in the size of the working population		
a fall in the cost of public transport		
bicycles becoming more fashionable		
an increase in the price of petrol		
an increase in income tax		
a decrease in household mortgage repayments		

supply

Supply means the amount of a good or service that businesses wish to produce over a defined period of time, eg 50,000 cars each week.

There are a number of factors that can cause supply to change . . .

the importance of price

As was the case with demand, the price of a good or service is obviously one of the main factors that influences how much we buy of it. The general rule is that:

the higher the price of a good or service the more businesses will want to produce

the lower the price of a good or service the less businesses will want to produce

This is the law of supply.

The law of supply is a little harder to understand then the law of demand but if it is accepted that the greater the level of reward (profit) the harder businesses will work then it is also possible to accept that higher prices generally mean higher profits and thus businesses are willing to supply more.

The factors that cause the level of supply to change, and hence the market price of goods and services to alter, are explained below.

The general rule is:

an increase in supply leads to a fall in price

a decrease in supply leads to a rise in price

changes in the cost of production

A rise in business costs will often lead to a fall in profit levels and so firms will lose some of their incentive to produce. If the majority of firms in the industry are affected in the same way then there will be a fall in supply.

Similarly a fall in business costs tends to increase profit levels and they have an incentive to produce more. If most firms in the industry respond in the same way then there will be an increase in supply.

Business costs might change because of a change in the cost of employing people (wages and salaries). A change in raw material costs or the cost of transporting goods may also change the costs of production. There are numerous other factors that might cause business costs to change.

Now carry out the Activity on the next page.

Activity 7.4

changes in the supply of computers

Computer prices soar after Taiwan earthquake

Computer prices are about to rise sharply because component suppliers were affected by last month's earthquake in Taiwan.

The cost of computer memory chips, known as RAM, has increased by as much as 50 per cent over the last few weeks, and the prices of computers on sale in the high street chains are expected to rise by hundreds of pounds.

There has been a spate of panic buying of computer parts since the earthquake on September 21, which killed more than 2,000. "These memory chips are now like gold dust," said a salesman at Notino computers. "We had no inkling that this could happen".

Several manufacturers have already increased their catalogue prices. A Notino desk top computer that was selling at £939 at the time of the earthquake has now been repriced at £1,093, and is expected to go up even more.

An Evesham Voyager portable computer that was on the market for £1,385 at the beginning of October now costs £1,408. It will cost £1,440 by the end of the month and is likely to rise further. Shops are still selling computers from stock at lower prices, but they have been warned by suppliers that new orders are going to be delayed and will have increased in price.

"Prices will be around £50 higher than they might otherwise have been on a standard computer. We've been able to cushion ourselves against the memory crisis, but some of the smaller suppliers will be hit much harder. They're going to be in trouble."

Source: *The Sunday Telegraph*, October 24 1999

Read the article above and then answer the following questions based on your understanding of the theory of supply

1 Explain why the price of computer chips has soared.

2 Explain why the supply of computers on the market is likely to have fallen.

3 Can you think of any other examples where the price of a product has risen because of an increase in costs, resulting in a fall in supply of the product?

improvements in technology

Most of us tend to accept the fact that we live in a world of rapid technological change. Changes in technology have had a significant effect on the way in which we work. They have often led to the introduction of bigger, faster and more powerful machines which have in turn helped to reduce production costs.

Improvements in technology, therefore tend to increase supply of the goods and services affected.

Recent developments in health care such as micro-surgery, have meant that patients receiving treatment for numerous conditions only need stay in hospital for a few hours whereas previously they may have needed to stay for several days. This has enabled hospitals to treat more people every year increasing the supply of health care.

physical conditions

At the beginning of the industrial revolution manufacturers cared very little about the physical conditions of their workers. Factories were commonly dirty, noisy, dangerous and generally miserable places to work in. Nowadays employers have a much more enlightened approach and they have come to understand that the quality of the working environment can have a significant impact on how well and hard people can work.

Improvements in physical conditions generally leads to an increase in supply.

taxation

In addition to taxing people's incomes (income tax) and the goods and services that people buy (VAT, fuel duty, alcohol duty) governments also impose taxes on businesses. As taxes on businesses tend to reduce their profits they lose the incentive to produce as much. Occasionally the government lowers the level of business taxation to help them to invest to increase their profits and so to produce more.

An increase in business taxes tends to reduce supply while a decrease in taxes on firms has the opposite effect and supply will increase.

subsidies

Some businesses receive money in the form of subsidies which are intended to help them overcome the effects of a temporary fall in profits. Some farmers in the EU receive government subsidies where production is very difficult, for example hill sheep farmers in Scotland and Wales. Without these subsidies many farmers in these areas would not be able to survive.

The giving of subsidies to business tends to increase supply while a decrease in subsidies has the opposite effect and supply will fall.

Activity 7.5

Factors affecting the supply of new cars

The table below shows a list of factors that can influence the supply and the market price of new cars. In each case state whether supply and price will rise or fall.

Factor change	Effect on supply rise/fall	Effect on market price rise/fall
a rise in car manufacturing wage costs		
an improvement in car manufacturing technology		
a fall in business taxation		
an increase in subsidies to car manufacturers		
a fall in the price of steel		
an improvement in working conditions		

Activity 7.6

Factors affecting the market price of potatoes

Now see if you can put your knowledge and understanding of the laws of supply and demand together to see how changes in market conditions can affect price. The table below shows a list of factors that can influence the supply and demand and thus the market price of potatoes (which can be bought as an alternative to rice). In each case state how supply and demand will be affected and the likely effect they will have on market price.

Change in market conditions in the country which grows potatoes	Effect on supply rise/fall	Effect on demand rise/fall	Effect on market price rise/fall/unchanged
bad weather conditions and a rise in the price of rice			
a fall in the price of fertiliser and a fall in the price of rice			
good weather and a rise in income tax paid by consumers			
an increase in farm workers' wages and potatoes being seen as healthy			
a fall in rents paid by farmers and a highly successful advertising campaign by potato growers			

the determination of prices – using diagrams

While it is possible to develop an understanding of the way in which prices are determined on a common sense level it is helpful to adopt a more scientific approach through the use of simple demand and supply diagrams. Such diagrams are used by economists to make it easier to see how changes in demand and supply factors lead to changes in prices and ultimately how the market mechanism works.

the demand curve

According to the law of demand the higher the price of a good or service the less will be bought of it. This simple but fundamental idea is shown in the diagram below in the form of a **demand curve**.

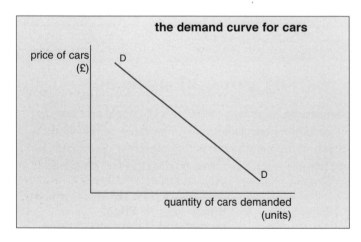

the demand curve for cars

price of cars (£)

quantity of cars demanded (units)

the demand curve

The vertical axis of the diagram represents the price of cars while the horizontal axis represents the amount of cars demanded in a year. The demand curve (line DD) is said to be downward sloping. This kind of demand curve is also known as a normal demand curve and it represents the basic law of demand.

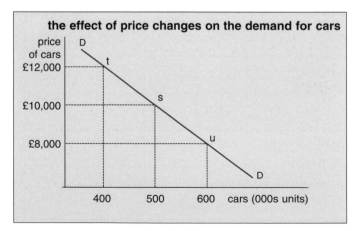

the effect of price changes on the demand for cars

price of cars
£12,000
£10,000
£8,000

400   500   600   cars (000s units)

the effect of a change in price

Here the effect of a price change can be seen. To start with assume that when the price of the typical car is £10,000 the quantity of cars demanded each year is 500,000. When the price rises to £12,000 the quantity of cars sold drops to 400,000. Similarly if the price falls to £8,000 the quantity of cars sold each year rises to 600,000.

It is important to notice that changes in prices cause a movement along the demand curve. At the initial price of £10,000 this is at point 's' but as the price rises there is a movement up to 't' and when the price falls there is a movement down the curve to point 'u'. Changes in prices are said to cause a change in quantity demanded as opposed to a change in demand itself. The rule is therefore:

a rise in price causes a fall in quantity demanded

a fall in price causes a rise in quantity demanded

the effect of a change in demand

A change in any of the influences on demand (such as income) causes the whole demand curve to shift. A fall in demand is shown by a shift of the demand curve to the left while a rise is represented by a shift to the right. Both these effects can be seen in the diagram below:

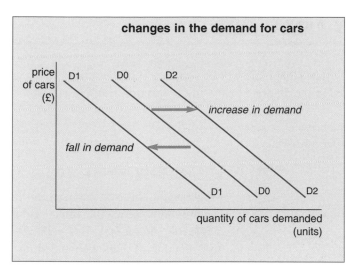

The original demand curve is (D0D0) but a fall in demand is shown by a movement of the whole curve to the left (D1D1) and a rise in demand by a movement of the whole curve to the right (D2D2).

Remember that this diagram shows changes in the demand for cars, not changes in price. These shifts in demand could be brought about by changes in the amount of income people have to spend or the changing cost of alternative forms of transport.

Activity 7.7

changes in demand

The table on the next page shows a list of factors that can affect the demand for various goods and services. In each case state whether the demand curve for the good or service in question will shift to the right, left or if there will simply be a movement along the demand curve.

See pages 147 to 151 for an explanation of what can cause demand to change.

good or service	change	effect on the demand curve *shift to left/shift to right*
potatoes	a rise in the demand for chips	
new cars	a rise in the price of new cars	
houses	a fall in mortgage payments	
beef	a fall in the price of pork	
compact discs	an expected fall in the price of CDs	
bus and coach services	a rise in train fares	

the supply curve

The law of supply states that more will be supplied at higher prices. This too can be represented in the diagram below in the form of a supply curve.

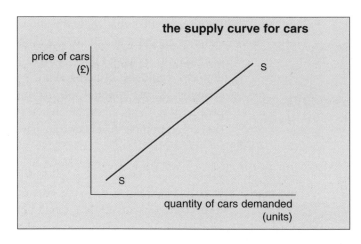

the supply curve for cars

price of cars (£)

S

S

quantity of cars demanded (units)

the supply curve

Once again the vertical axis of the diagram represents the price of cars while the horizontal axis represents the amount of cars demanded in a year. The supply curve (SS) – a straight line – is said to be upward sloping.

the effect of a change in price

In the diagram on the top of the next page the effect of a price change can be seen. To start with assume that when the price of the typical car is £10,000 the quantity of cars supplied each year is 500,000. When, however the price rises to £12,000 the quantity of cars supplied rises to 700,000. Similarly if the price falls to £8,000 the quantity of cars supplied each year falls to 300,000.

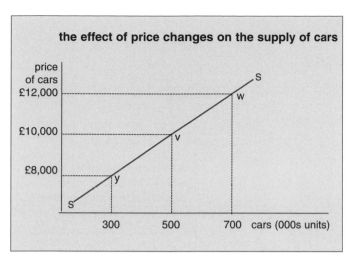

It can be seen that changes in price cause a movement along the supply curve. Point 'v' represents the initial price of £10,000 but as the price rises there is a movement to 'w' and when the price falls there is a movement down the curve to point 'y'.

Changes in prices are said to cause a change in quantity supplied. Note that change can also be brought about by a factor not related to prices – for example the cost of production – which causes a change in supply.

The rule is:

a rise in price causes a rise in quantity supplied

a fall in price causes a fall in quantity supplied

the effect of a change in supply

A change in a factor other than price which influences supply – for example the cost of production – causes the whole supply curve to shift. A fall in supply is shown by a shift of the supply curve to the left while a rise is represented by a shift to the right. Both these effects can be seen in the diagram below.

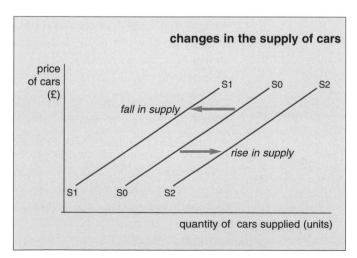

The original supply curve is (S0S0).

A fall in supply (a rise in the cost of production, for example) is shown by a movement of the whole curve to the left (S1S1).

A rise in supply (a fall in the cost of production, for example) is shown by a movement of the whole curve to the right (S2S2).

Activity 7.8

changes in supply

The table below shows a list of factors that can affect the supply for various goods and services. In each case state whether the supply curve for the good or service in question will shift to the right, left or if there will simply be a movement along the supply curve. See pages 152 to 154 for an explanation of changes in supply.

good or service	change	effect on the supply curve shift to left/shift to right/ shift along the supply curve
new cars	a rise in the cost of sheet steel	
new cars	a fall in tax on businesses	
compact discs	a fall in the price of CDs	
train services	an increase in subsidies to train operators	
computers	a development in technology making it cheaper to produce	
new houses	a fall in the cost of building materials	

the determination of prices

In competitive markets price is determined by the interaction of the forces of demand and supply. Diagrammatically this can be shown by combining demand and supply curves as has been done in the diagram to the left which shows how the price of new cars is determined.

Demand is represented by the line (D0D0) and supply by the line (S0S0). The price 'p0' is determined by drawing a horizontal line from the point where the demand and supply curves meet to the price axis. Notice that at this price the quantity demanded is exactly equal to the quantity supplied (q0).

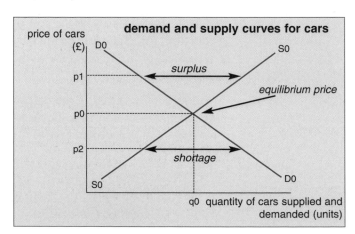

demand and supply curves for cars

equilibrium price

Economists refer to the situation in the diagram at the bottom of the previous page as *equilibrium price*. This simply means the price where there is no tendency for change.

The reason for this is that if car manufacturers tried to set the price of cars above 'p0' at 'p1' then the quantity demanded would be less than the quantity supplied. In other words there would be a surplus or excess supply of cars and in order for the market to 'clear' the price would naturally tend to fall to the equilibrium level.

If, on the other hand the price was set at 'p2' there would be a shortage or excess demand of cars and in order for the market to 'clear' the price of cars would naturally tend to rise to the equilibrium level.

changes in demand and supply

Having seen how demand and supply curves can be used to show how prices are determined it is now possible to consider how price responds to changes in demand and supply.

an increase in demand

The diagram below illustrates the effect of an increase in the demand for new cars. This could happen, for example, if there is an increase in the income of consumers.

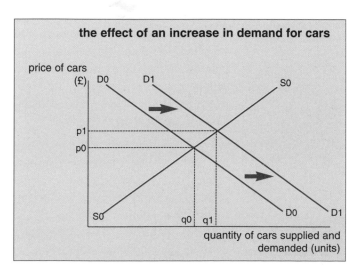

the effect of an increase in demand for cars

price of cars (£)

p1
p0

S0

D0
D1

q0 q1

quantity of cars supplied and demanded (units)

The original price is 'p0' with 'q0' being the quantity demanded and supplied. If there now follows an increase in demand for new cars the demand curve will shift to the right from D0D0 to D1D1. The supply curve is unchanged at S0S0.

For a while the price will not change and there will be a temporary shortage of new cars. Over time, however the price of cars will naturally tend to rise to the new equilibrium level of 'p1' with 'q1' being the new and greater quantity demanded and supplied.

a fall in demand

The diagram below illustrates the effect of a fall in the demand for new cars. This could happen, for example, if consumers expected the price of cars to fall and so delayed purchasing (look at the Case Study on page 150).

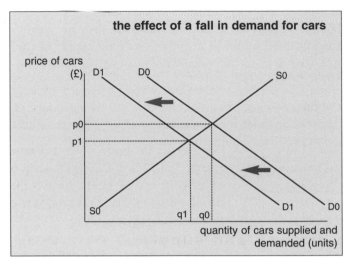

The effect of a fall in demand for cars

The original price is 'p0' with 'q0' being the quantities demanded and supplied. If there now follows a decrease in the demand of new cars the demand curve will shift to the left from D0D0 to D1D1. The supply curve is unchanged at S0S0.

For a while the price will not change and there will be a temporary surplus of new cars. Over time, however the price of cars will naturally tend to fall to the new equilibrium level of 'p1' with 'q1' being the new and lower quantity demanded and supplied.

an increase in supply

The diagram below illustrates the effect of an increase in the supply of new cars. This might be caused, for example, by improvements in technology leading to more efficient production methods.

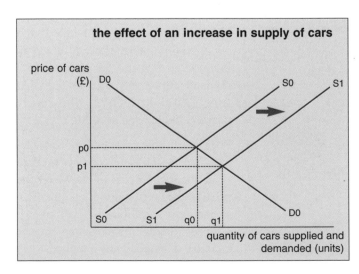

The effect of an increase in supply of cars

The original price is 'p0' with 'q0' being the quantities demanded and supplied. If there now follows an increase in the supply of new cars the supply curve will shift to the right from S0S0 to S1S1. The demand curve in unchanged at D0D0.

For a while the price will not change and there will be a temporary surplus of new cars. Over time, however the price of cars will naturally tend to fall to the new equilibrium level of 'p1' with 'q1' being the new and greater quantity demanded and supplied.

a fall in supply

The diagram below illustrates the effect of a fall in the supply of new cars. This might be caused by a factor such as the rising costs of production.

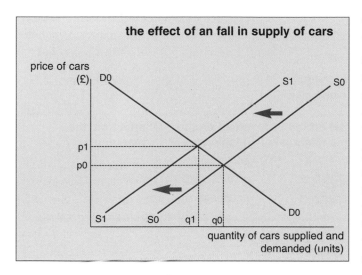

the effect of an fall in supply of cars

The original price is 'p0' with 'q0' being the quantities demanded and supplied. If there now follows a decrease in the supply of new cars the supply curve will shift to the left from S0S0 to S1S1. The demand curve is unchanged at D0D0.

For a while the price will not change and there will be a temporary surplus of new cars. Over time, however the price of cars will naturally tend to rise to the new equilibrium level of 'p1' with 'q1' being the new and smaller quantity demanded and supplied.

DEMAND AND SUPPLY – A SUMMARY

● **an increase in demand** leads to a rise in price and an increase in the quantities demanded and supplied

● **an increase in supply** leads to a fall in price and a rise in the quantities demanded and supplied

● **a decrease in demand** leads to a fall in price and a decrease in the quantities demanded and supplied

● **a decrease in supply** leads to a rise in price and decrease in the quantities demanded and supplied

Activity 7.9

the effects of changes in demand and supply

Now see if you can put your knowledge and understanding of demand and supply diagrams together to explain the effect of changes in demand and supply on various markets.

In each case illustrate the change with a demand and supply diagram and then complete the boxes as shown below.

change	effect on the demand curve? shift to left? shift to right? unchanged?	effect on the supply curve? shift to left? shift to right? unchanged?	effect on the market price? rise? fall?
the effect on the new car market of a rise in consumer incomes			
the effect on the European wheat market of a decrease in government subsidies to farmers			
The effect on the market for new houses of a significant fall in building costs			
the effect on the market for steel of a world wide slump in orders			
the effect on the market for computers of a shortage of silicon chips			
the effect on the market for rice following the news that potatoes help to prolong human life			

Activity 7.10

A study in house prices

Read the report below and answer the questions at the bottom of the page.

House prices set to go through the roof?

Recent house price data from a number of different influential groups has shown continued growth in prices with more forecast for the market into 2000. October saw the highest monthly rise since the summer of 1988, with the average price of a home breaking through the £80,000 barrier for the first time, according to figures from the Halifax. The survey said that prices went up by 2.8 per cent in October, pushing annual house price inflation to 10.8 per cent.

A shortage of property is helping to fuel the increase particularly in areas such as the South-East. According to the Nationwide the data shows that Greater London saw prices rise by more than 15 per cent in the third quarter of 1999, with some London boroughs such as Kensington and Chelsea seeing prices rising by more than 20 per cent. The lack of property on the market, the general good health of the economy, rising consumer incomes and the relatively cheap cost of home loans are all helping to push prices upwards.

Elsewhere, rises of between five and ten per cent were report in regions such as Yorkshire and Humberside, East Anglia and the South West. These regions have particular hot spots such as Cambridge and Leeds, where there has been a boom in service sector jobs, and that has meant far higher demand and prices.

The current boom is not being experienced in all regions of the country. Nationwide figures show that across Scotland the annual growth in house prices has been only 0.8 per cent, while in Wales they have risen by just 2.9 per cent.

---

1 With the aid of demand and supply diagrams explain why property prices are rising strongly in areas like the South East but less so in Scotland and Wales.

2 Identify
   • the demand factors
   • the supply factors
   that determine the price of houses.

CHAPTER SUMMARY

● Markets play a key role in determining the price of goods and services; it is through changes in market prices that businesses know what goods and services to produce and in what quantities.

● Market price is determined by the forces of demand and supply.

● The law of demand states that more of a good will be bought as the price of the product falls.

● The level of demand is determined by factors such as: income, the age distribution of the population, tastes and fashion, changes in the price of related products, expected price changes and the price and availability of products.

● The law of supply states that more of a good will be produced as the price of the good rises.

● The level of supply is determined by factors such as: the cost of production, improvements in technology, physical conditions, taxes and subsidies.

● Demand and supply curves can be drawn on a diagram with price on the vertical axis and quantity along the horizontal axis.

● A change in price will cause a movement along the demand/supply curve and a corresponding change in the quantity demanded/supplied.

● Changes in other factors relating to demand and supply cause the demand/supply curve to shift. Increases in demand/supply are shown by shifts of the curves to the right while decreases are shown by shifts of the curves to the left.

● The point on a diagram where the demand and supply curves cross is known as equilibrium price. At a price higher than the equilibrium point there will unsold goods and services and price will tend to fall back to the equilibrium level. At a price below the equilibrium point there will be a shortage of goods and services and price will tend to rise back to the equilibrium level.

● A change in the level of demand/supply will cause the demand/supply curve to shift and a new equilibrium price will be established. An increase in demand can be seen to cause price to rise while a decrease in demand can be seen to cause price to fall. On the other hand an increase in supply can be seen to cause prices to fall while a decrease in supply can be seen to cause prices to rise.

KEY TERMS

market price	the price prevailing in the market at any given time and determined by the forces of demand and supply
demand	the amount of a good that buyers wish to purchase over a given period of time
supply	the amount of a good that businesses are willing to produce over a given period of time
complementary goods	goods that are linked together in such a way that as more of one good is demanded more of the related good will also be demanded, eg cars and fuel
substitute goods	goods that are related in such a way that as more of one good is demanded less of the other good is wanted, eg bus and taxi travel
demand curve	a line that shows the relationship between price and the quantity of a good purchased over a given period of time
supply curve	a line that shows the relationship between price and the quantity of a good business are willing to produce over a given period of time
a movement along the demand curve	a change in quantity demanded of a good caused by a change in price
a movement along the supply curve	a change in quantity supplied of a good caused by a change in price
a shift in the demand curve	a movement of the whole demand curve caused by a change in the level of demand
a shift in the supply curve	a movement of the whole supply curve caused by a change in the level of demand
equilibrium price	a price, often known as market price, which has been determined by demand and supply – the price will remain at this level unless there is a change in the level of demand or supply

National and international competition

> **Unit 2 The competitive business environment**
> **How competition in the market affects business**
> **How businesses are affected by international competitors**

introduction

Businesses need to grow to increase market share and profitability. They can expand their scale of operations on a national scale through internal growth and also by merger and takeovers. Business growth is also increasingly becoming international as businesses seek a 'global' presence. Businesses therefore clearly need to be aware of the factors that affect their competitiveness in international markets.

what you will learn from this chapter

● the desire to make larger profits gives businesses the incentive to expand – this can be achieved by producing more of existing products, diversifying into new areas, and also by buying and taking-over existing businesses

● businesses can grow in a variety of ways – they can buy other businesses at the same stage of the production process as themselves; they can also move either towards their market outlets or towards the source of their supplies

● nowadays many businesses are so large that if they wish to expand further they have to look beyond their national boundaries

● a number of factors affect the competitiveness of businesses in international markets:

- exchange rates can move to benefit or to damage competitiveness

- barriers to trade such as trading blocks, tariffs and quotas can restrict competitiveness

- the World Trade Organisation, European Union and European Monetary Union have broken down many of the barriers to competition

the benefits of size

There are a number of reasons why very large businesses tend to compete more effectively and so become more profitable than smaller businesses.

monopoly power

Larger businesses gain greater market power (monopoly power). This means that they have the potential to restrict the supply of their products onto the market and are thus able to increase prices.

lower unit costs

Businesses with lower costs are usually able to make higher profits. Larger businesses have the potential to benefit from economies of scale – reductions in unit (average) costs resulting from increasing their scale of production. The sources of economies of scale are varied:

- **spreading overheads**: as businesses grow, their fixed costs (see Chapter 23) are spread over a larger output and their unit costs are reduced

- **financial economies**: banks and other lenders tend to see large businesses as less risky investments than smaller businesses and so charge them lower interest rates and lower fees – this reduces their financial costs

- **capital costs**: some items of capital equipment (machinery) are very large and cannot be adapted for small scale operations – eg robotic production lines used in the car industry

- **the benefits of increased specialisation**: in small businesses workers may have to perform several roles – the owner of a small business may find himself/herself acting as secretary, accountant, sales and marketing manager; as businesses grow they are able to employ more productive specialists to fill these roles – which reduces costs overall

- **increased dimensions**: engineers have what is known as a 'rule of two-thirds' – the cost of building a new factory or machine only rises by two thirds as much as the output or capacity increases; this rule helps to explain the reason for the existence of very large oil tankers which help to reduce the unit costs of transporting oil – only large firms are able to benefit from this rule

- **managerial economies**: the size of a business may double but this does not mean that it is necessary to employ twice as many marketing, or human resources managers; managerial and administration costs do not rise in the same proportion as output and so the unit costs of larger businesses may fall

Activity 8.1

Big business and small business

An MP representing a rural constituency is very concerned about the decline in the number of small village shops. Many of them are finding it difficult to compete with large supermarkets situated on the outskirts of major towns and cities. The owner of a local store at a village three miles outside a large town has complained to her at a constituency 'clinic' about the planning of a large 'out-of-town' supermarket only two miles away. The owner says "We can't compete with their prices – I don't know how they dare to do it. These supermarket chains seem to get bigger and bigger – we will soon all be driven out of business!"

questions

1   Explain the reasons why supermarket chains are able to expand as they do and why they are able to compete on price.

2   Suggest some ways in which small stores could have a competitive advantage over the supermarket chains – how can they appeal to local and passing customers?

how businesses grow – the urge to merge

internal or external growth?

Some businesses may find that they are able to grow by simply expanding their scale of operations. A business producing electrical products for consumers can grow by simply producing more washing machines, fridges etc. They can also try to expand through diversification – developing new products or moving into new markets. This is known as internal growth. In practice, however businesses may find that the opportunities for internal expansion are very limited and businesses may look outwards and aim for external growth whereby they attempt to merge (join forces) with existing businesses.

horizontal mergers

The majority of mergers in the UK (around 80 per cent) occur between businesses at the same stage of the production process. These kind of mergers are described as being **horizontal.** An example is the Ford Motor Company's acquisition of Jaguar and Volvo.

This type of merger helps a business to compete because a wider range of products can be offered to the consumer – eg Fords, Jaguars and Volvos. Consumers see these as different 'makes' of car. There are also economies of scale – the different makes of car can share certain components and design features.

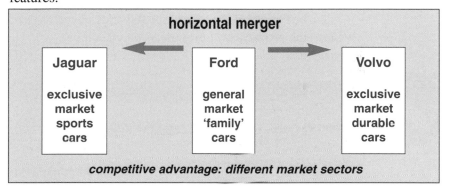

horizontal merger

Jaguar	Ford	Volvo
exclusive market sports cars	general market 'family' cars	exclusive market durable cars

competitive advantage: different market sectors

vertical mergers

Some mergers (about five per cent) are, however predominantly **vertical** in nature. For example Associated British Foods, a multinational food company based in the UK acquired Gregg and Company which manufactures glass jars and bottles used in food packaging. Mergers – such as this one – often take place between firms at different stages of the production process.

This type of merger helps a business to compete because the costs of production can be cut and stabilised, and profitability increased.

vertical merger

Associated British Foods

food products – sales of over £4 billion

Gregg & Co

a Yorkshire glass packaging company

competitive advantage: a stable and cheaper supply

backwards and forwards mergers

In addition, vertical mergers can be described as **backwards**: when a business moves towards its source of supplies, eg a supermarket taking over a food manufacturer or a tyre manufacturer taking over a rubber plantation. In this case the aim is to achieve security of supplies.

Mergers may also be **forward** in nature: when a business moves towards the retail end of the industry, eg a brewery taking over a group of pubs, or an oil refiner taking over a group of petrol retailers. In this case the purpose of the acquisition is to obtain a guaranteed outlet for the product.

These types of merger again make the business more competitive. Costs can be cut and in the case of the forwards merger a guaranteed market found for the products of, for example, an oil company.

Activity 8.2

Mergers and competition

State whether the following acquisitions by a major car company are

- horizontal or vertical?
- backwards or forwards?

In each case state what competitive advantages the company will gain by the merger. The car company in question manufactures family cars in volume for the mainstream market.

1   It buys a manufacturing company which specialises in off-road vehicles.

2   It buys a company which makes plastic mouldings used in the car manufacturing process.

3   It buys an e-commerce company which will sell its cars on-line.

conglomerate mergers

Mergers that cannot easily be classified as predominantly horizontal or vertical are described as being **conglomerate** mergers, a conglomerate being a group that is 'lumped' together. The former British American Tobacco has transformed itself into BAT Industries which includes Allied Dunbar and Eagle Star – two well known names in the investment and insurance markets. The rationale of conglomerate mergers is found in the saying 'don't put all your eggs in one basket'. Businesses which have interests in a variety of markets are less likely to suffer as badly if there is a downturn in one area.

Activity 8.3

Competitive advantages of conglomerates

Read through the profile of Daewoo of Korea and answer the questions that follow.

DAEWOO

"the leading general trading company in Korea"

Founded: 1967

Total Sales in 1998: $30.6 billion

Exports in 1998: $17.6 billion

Heavy Industries

Machinery, equipment and defence manufacturing, shipbuilding and offshore platforms.

Construction

Roads, housing and industrial plants including nuclear and hydro power.

Motor vehicles

Aims to manufacture a total of 2.5 million cars by 2000 in Korean and overseas plants.

Electronics and telecommunications

Consumer electronics and home appliances for domestic and overseas markets. Also involved in telephone systems, satellite communications and personal computers.

Finance and services

In investment banking it has a growing securities division trading in international markets and a commercial banking arm.

1   Access the website www.daewoo.com to gain a fuller picture of Daewoo's activities. Have they changed since this book was published?

2   What are the benefits to Daewoo of being involved in such a wide variety of activities?

3   How does the size of Daewoo enable it to compete effectively in UK markets?

4   Are there any dangers to Daewoo of being involved in a large number of different activities?

5   Investigate these issues as they affect other conglomerates by using the internet. Try . . .   www.gm.com   www.unilever.com   www.cadburyschweppes.com

take-overs

There are two different types of company take-over. A business may make a take-over bid for another business by offering to buy out the shareholders of a second business 'over the heads' of the company management. The managers of the business being taken over are unlikely to welcome such an offer as they may lose their jobs. This is referred to as a **hostile bid**.

In other cases the managers of the second business may agree that by linking up there may be substantial benefits to both businesses and agree to the **merger** – the voluntary linking-up of two businesses. They will recommend to the shareholders that they accept the offer.

Mergers hit record levels in 1999

UK take-over activity has broken all records in 1999. Two hundred publicly quoted firms worth a total of £72 billion have already fallen to predators. As bid fever sweeps banking, telecoms and high streets, the total value of bids amounts to a staggering £168bn.

Examples of take-overs are not hard to find. The financial services industry has experienced a wave of mergers over the last decade. These include HSBC's take-over of Midland Bank and the Royal Bank of Scotland's 'hostile' take-over of National Westminster Bank. The Halifax Building society also went on the acquisition trail, merging with the Leeds Building Society, becoming a PLC and taking over the Midshires Building Society.

competitive advantages

economies of scale

In the case of the Halifax-Leeds bid the Halifax were hoping to benefit from substantially greater economies of scale. It was anticipated that the Halifax-Leeds merger would enable the newly formed company to close a number of outlets and avoid unnecessary duplication of staff and branch resources. This would mean that the unit costs of administering mortgages and savings accounts would fall. Secondly the Halifax were clearly trying to achieve greater monopoly power. The new Halifax PLC is now one of the five or six most powerful players in this industry, enabling it to play a much greater role in setting the market price of financial services.

brands

Another competitive advantage gained from merger concerns the importance of brands. Whitbread, which most people tend to associate with brewing, is a business which in the mid 1990s launched a series of take-over bids based on the acquisition of a range of brands in the hotel, restaurant and leisure industries. In 1996 Whitbread acquired the Pelican Group of companies which included a number of well known restaurant brands such as Dôme and

Café Rouge chains. Whitbread's acquisitions have also included other reputable brands such as T.F.I. Friday's and Marriott hotels. Stella Artois and Heineken are also brand names in the Whitbread portfolio.

Activity 8.4

Take-overs

Investigate examples of current take-over bids. Use sources such as the financial pages of the newspapers (you may be able to find them on CD ROM) and the internet (news releases on the company sites). Photocopy or print out details.

Why is the business on the acquisition trail trying to buy the other business? What competitive advantages will it gain? Is it a hostile bid, or is the target company happy with the proposed deal?

globalisation

Since the mid 1900s businesses have increasingly looked beyond their national geographical borders towards markets in other countries. This in turn has led to a rapid expansion in world trade – a phenomenon now commonly referred to as **globalisation**. When businesses expand their global operations they also invest in production and distribution facilities in other countries. The decisions by Honda, Nissan and Toyota to start producing in the UK are obvious examples of foreign motor manufacturers extending their production base beyond that of their country of origin.

The growth in world trade is, however, just one side of the story. The other side concerns the rapid growth in capital movements (movements of money) between nations which is associated with this 'globalisation'.

the growth of international competition

The need for businesses to extend their operations overseas is prompted by the same reasons which drive businesses to expand nationally – essentially profitability and growth in market share:

* the need for increased sales and revenues
* the achievement of further economies of scale
* pressure from shareholders to maintain profit and dividend growth
* increased security from the risks of being taken over
* diversification – the wish to avoid over-dependence on a single market
* the opportunity to move into growing markets

exploitation of new markets

A business may find that its home market is saturated so that it is impossible to expand its sales further. Businesses producing, for example, white goods (fridges, washing machines etc) could find that virtually all households in their country of origin possess these products and they are only able to sell replacement purchases when they come to the end of their life cycle. The way out of this problem is to move into a market where the opportunity for new business is likely to be much greater. The newly industrialised countries (NICs) of South East Asia are areas where the potential for market expansion is considerable.

global brands

Businesses like Coca-Cola are able to sell their product world-wide largely due to the fact that they have created a global brand. In other words it is a product that appeals to people everywhere. Global brands offer businesses the opportunity to sell standardised products – they are identical in all markets. The alternative strategy is to alter the product to suit the particular tastes of the market. Beer in the North of England is often brewed to a different recipe compared to beer designed for markets in the South. The same principle applies when selling in foreign markets and involves businesses in conducting extensive market research to discover what consumers really want.

. . . but local production

Global businesses also need to make decisions about where their products might be manufactured. In the case of Coca-Cola they have little choice but to ensure that it is bottled close to its market. The option of bottling in the US and then exporting it to the rest of the world would not make economic sense as the costs of transporting filled bottles would be greater than their value. In the case of high value electronic products it is possible to set up plants in areas of the world where costs are low and then to move the products to where ever they are required.

global communications

Rapid developments in communications are revolutionising the way in which global businesses organise their production. Under their 'Ford 2000' plan, Ford's European and North American businesses have changed from a two company organisation into a single combined organisation, enabling it to make substantial cost savings by avoiding expensive duplication of management and production resources. The business is now being organised on a product as opposed to a geographical basis. Video-conferencing and state-of-the-art computer links enable workers separated by distance to work together on the same car project.

globalisation – some facts

The trend towards globalisation is such that the importance of large corporations is now enormous. According to the American economist and author David Korten, 50 of the world's 100 largest economies are now corporations. The sales of the world's largest companies exceeds the GNP of the world's 100 smallest countries. The leading 50 industrial corporations control up to 25 per cent of the world's economic output. The combined assets of the world's 50 largest banks and financial companies control 60 percent of the world's global capital. In 1970, there were approximately 7,000 corporations operating internationally; today there are more than 50,000.

Case Study

Unilever PLC
a multinational and competition

Read through the material on the next two pages and answer the questions at the end of the Case Study.

Unilever

www.unilever.com

Unilever is a multinational company based in the UK and the Netherlands.

Its products are well-known household food and Personal Care brands, including Lipton, Ragú, Solero, Domestos, Dove, and Elizabeth Arden.

Unilever's sales in 1999 were £26,994,000 in its five geographical regions:

Europe (46%), North America (22%), Africa & Middle East (6%), Asia and Pacific (16%), Latin America (10%)

A truly multi-local multinational

Unilever is dedicated to meeting the everyday needs of people everywhere. Around the world our Foods and Home & Personal Care brands are chosen by many millions of individual consumers each day. Earning their trust, anticipating their aspirations and meeting their daily needs are the tasks of our local companies. They bring to the service of their consumers the best in brands and both our international and local expertise.

Source: *Unilever Annual Review 1999*

The path to growth

In February 2000 we announced a series of linked initiatives to align our entire organisation behind ambitious plans for accelerating growth and expanding margins. By 2004 we will increase annual top line growth to 5% and operating margins to 15%, underpinning our commitment to double digit earnings growth.

The principal components of the plans are:

Brands We will concentrate product innovation and brand development on a focused portfolio of 400 leading brands. These have been chosen both on the basis of the strength of their current consumer appeal and their prospects for sustained growth. They include familiar brands such as *Dove, Lux, Lipton, Magnum,* and *Calvin Klein* fragrances. We will invest a total of £1 billion in additional marketing support over five years and by 2004, we expect this investment to have driven growth rates in the focused portfolio to at least 6% per annum.

E-Business E-business is directly relevant to our growth plans in the areas of brand communication and building direct relationships with consumers. The development of online selling will be pioneered by the recently announced venture with iVillage. Alliances with AOL, Microsoft, Excite@Home and Wowgo are in place to support brand communication and build consumer understanding. E-business also offers significant opportunities in business-to-business transactions throughout the supply chain and we will be rolling out a global e-procurement system over the next two years. We are intent on achieving a rapid expansion of e-business and have committed £130 million to these initiatives in 2000 and this will grow.

Source: *Unilever Annual Review 1999*

Supply chain Our local businesses will be involved in developing plans to reorder our manufacturing activities into integrated regional networks in support of our brands. Our target is a world-class supply chain based on some 150 key sites plus a number producing principally for local markets. As a consequence we expect there will be a substantial reduction in the number of manufacturing sites, probably by around 100.

Simplification Concentrating on 400 brands will give us the opportunity to focus resources where they can be most effective, reduce overheads and streamline the Corporate Centre. Central to the plans will be revised knowledge and information systems to support our leading brands and the redesigned supply chain.

Source: *Unilever Annual Review 1999*

questions

Use the data on these two pages or data from the Unilever website www.unilever.com

1 What are the annual sales of the Unilever group?

2 Calculate the regional sales of the Unilever group and use a spreadsheet to present your figures in the form of a pie chart.

3 What are the target annual growth rates of Unilever PLC?

4 What regional markets do you think offer
   (a) the greatest competition for Unilever?
   (b) the greatest potential for future growth?

5 What is the brand policy of Unilever? How will this enable the company to compete in its regional markets?

6 What competitive advantages will e-commerce bring to Unilever?

7 How is Unilever restructuring its supply chain to make it more competitive and profitable?

international trade

The increasing trend towards globalisation means that international trade is even more important for businesses today than it has ever been and businesses need to be aware of the factors that might affect their competitiveness in international markets.

the importance of exchange rates

The exchange rate is the price of one currency in terms of another. It is usually expressed in terms of how much of a foreign currency can be bought with £1.00. If the Sterling/US Dollar exchange rate is 1.65 it means that you can buy $1.65 with £1.

The market for foreign currency is a freely competitive market and so exchange rates fluctuate daily. This can bring an element of uncertainty for businesses which trade internationally.

If there is a rise in the exchange rate then £1.00 will buy more foreign currency; if there is a fall it will buy less.

The fluctuations can also cause a problem for a business which wants its products to be competitively priced: if your own currency is appreciating (the exchange rate is going up) it means that foreign buyers will find your goods effectively going up in price. This is bad news for exporters.

exchange rates and exports and imports

The table below illustrates the effect of a change in the exchange rate on the price of a car made in the UK but sold in the USA. Notice that as the exchange rate rises from £1.00 = $1.80 to £1.00 = $2.00, the price of the car in the USA rises. When the exchange rate falls from £1.00 = $2.00 to £1.00 = $1.50, the price of the car in the USA falls. This type of fluctuation can make a significant difference to the competitiveness of cars such as Jaguars, which are popular exports from the UK to the USA.

The effect of a change in the exchange rate on the price of UK exports to the USA

Price of car in the UK (£) x	Exchange Rate =	Price of car in USA (US$)
£20,000	£1.00 = $1.80	$36,000
£20,000	£1.00 = $2.00	$40,000
£20,000	£1.00 = $1.50	$30,000

The table below shows the situation if the exchange rates move the same way but now an American car is imported from the USA to the UK. This time exactly the opposite occurs: as the exchange rate rises, from £1.00 = $1.80 to £1.00 = $2.00, the price of the car imported into the UK falls. When the exchange rate falls from £1.00 = $2.00 to £1.00 = $1.50, the price of the car imported into the UK rises.

The effect of a change in the exchange rate on the price of UK imports from the USA

Price of car in the USA ($) ÷	Exchange Rate	=	Price of car in UK (£)
$30,000	£1.00 = $1.80		£16,667
$30,000	£1.00 = $2.00		£15,000
$30,000	£1.00 = $1.50		£20,000

rules to follow . . .

1   When converting from £ to $, **multiply** the £ amount by the exchange rate

2   When converting from $ to £, **divide** the $ amount by the exchange rate

3   For **exporters** a rise in the exchange rate means that exports become more expensive abroad – which is bad news – your goods become less competitive and more difficult to sell

4   For **importers** a rise in the exchange rate means that imports become cheaper – which is good news – your imports become more competitive and easier to sell

fluctuating exchange rates and competitiveness

As you can see from the tables above a rise in the exchange rate can have a major affect on the competitiveness of UK businesses. In some cases a rise in the price of UK goods sold abroad may cause a significant fall in sales. This is most likely to be the case in markets where there is intense competition. However, in other markets a product may face little competition or have such strong brand loyalty that sales may fall only slightly. Similarly a business may be operating with such a large profit margin that it can afford to reduce prices in order to remain competitive. Businesses operating with much lower margins will not have this flexibility and may suffer considerably.

Businesses that import a large quantity of raw materials to be used in their production process may be adversely affected by a fall in the exchange rate as this will raise their costs and reduce profitability. In some cases it may be possible to buy raw materials from a country where the exchange rate is more favourable but often this is not the case.

Activity 8.5

exchange rates and competitiveness

Complete the tables below by filling in the appropriate prices in the spaces provided.

The effect of a change in the exchange rate on the price of UK exports to France

Price of Car in the UK (£)	Exchange Rate	Price of car in France (Fr)
1 £15,000	£1.00 = 10.00 Fr	Fr...............................
2 £15,000	£1.00 = 12.00 Fr	Fr...............................
3 £15,000	£1.00 = 8.00 Fr	Fr...............................

The effect of a change in the exchange rate on the price of French imports into the UK

Price of Car in France (Fr)	Exchange Rate	Price of car in the UK (£)
4 Fr 150,000	£1.00 = 10.00 Fr	£...............................
5 Fr 150,000	£1.00 = 12.00 Fr	£...............................
6 Fr 150,000	£1.00 = 8.00 Fr	£...............................

7   Complete the sentence below by filling in the missing words.

A rise in the exchange rate causes the price of exports to .... and the price of imports to .... , whereas a fall in the exchange rate causes the price of exports to .... while the price of imports will ....

8   A business which makes furniture is exporting its goods to Germany. What effect would a rise in the value of the £ against the DM have on the competitiveness of its goods in Germany if the furniture was (a) mass market furniture which is sensitive to price? (b) high-priced luxury market furniture?

9   The UK furniture business imports much of its timber from Norway. What effect would a fall in the value of the £ against the Norwegian Kroner have on the ability of the business to be profitable and competitive in the UK market?

10 Explain each of the following three statements:

(a) Early in 2000 the German car manufacturer BMW declared its intention to sell off its UK subsidiary Rover. One of the reasons given was that the high value of the pound made it very difficult for Rover to sell its cars in Europe.

(b) At the same time the head of Nissan UK, which manufactures Nissan cars in Sunderland, Tyne & Wear, declared that the high value of the pound against European currencies was putting thousands of car workers jobs at risk because labour was cheaper elsewhere.

(c) At the same time exports from countries which had adopted the Euro were booming due to the low value of the currency against other currencies.

In April 2000 approximate exchange rates for the pound were: £1= $1.58; £1=3.2Dm; £1=10.8Fr; £1=1.7Euros. Look up the current value of the pound against the Euro, US Dollar, French Franc and Deutschmark. Has the value of the pound changed since early 2000, and if so what are the likely consequences for UK trade with countries who use those currencies?

european monetary union (EMU)

On 1st January 1999 eleven of the fifteen members of the EU including Belgium, France, Germany, Eire, and Italy (but not the UK) permanently fixed their exchange rates against each other in the first step towards full Monetary Union. In doing so they effectively abolished exchange rates between member nations.

The second stage, which should be achieved by 1st July 2001 involves the replacement of national currencies such as the Deutschmark and the Franc with a Single European Currency – the Euro. To achieve this, member countries have also set up the European Central Bank which is responsible for monetary policy including the determination of interest rates.

the benefits of a single currency

- problems caused to business through fluctuations in the exchange rate are eliminated
- the costs to business resulting from buying foreign currencies in order to trade are removed
- it requires member states to exercise strict control over their economies – which has helped to lower interest rates in member countries – which is good for businesses

- it encourages greater international trade between member countries as the establishment of a single currency would remove the last of the major barriers to trade between member nations

the disadvantages of a single currency

- the strict control imposed on the economies of member states can lead to higher unemployment

- the European Central Bank removes some element of economic independence and there is concern that the interest rate level cannot be set to please all member states all of the time – this argument is often described in terms of the loss of national sovereignty

At the time of writing the attitude of the British Government to the adoption of a single currency is unclear. Prime Minister Blair is on the record as stating that we will join when it is in the national interest to do so.

the benefits of international trade

At one time the benefits of international trade were seen purely in terms of the amount of money that individuals, businesses and nations could gain through selling abroad the goods and services they produced. Gradually, however, it came to be understood that the more international trade there was the more all nations could benefit whether they were buyers or sellers of goods and services.

Economists and politicians often talked in terms of the benefits of free trade – a situation where no barriers are placed on trade between countries. The main advantages of international trade are summarised below.

wider choice

Businesses and consumers can chose from a wider range of goods and services than would other wise be the case. The greater the choice, the more likely it is that buyers can obtain the goods and services they really want.

increased competition

Nowadays businesses have to compete with each other on a world-wide basis. This means businesses producing sub-standard products or operating inefficiently are much less likely to survive and are forced to improve or go under. This has obvious benefits to consumers who find that over time prices should fall and the quality of goods and services should increase. Increased competition can be bad news for inefficient businesses but the best will learn from their competitors how to improve and outperform them in the future.

more and larger markets

Domestic businesses find that international trade increases their access to new and larger markets, making it possible to expand, reduce unit costs and increase profitability.

increased specialisation

International trade encourages countries to concentrate on producing the goods and services in which they excel – this in turn helps to raise standards.

Case Study

Rover Cars
a victim of international competition

In the late 1960s and early 1970s Rover, then known by a variety of names such as BMC and British Leyland, were synonymous with poor quality. Their range included models such as the Maxi, Marina and Allegro which despite selling in reasonably large numbers at home were much less successful abroad.

Eventually domestic sales also began to fall as buyers began to switch from British to foreign manufacturers in increasingly large numbers. A particular cause of concern in the early to mid- seventies was the increasing market share being achieved by Japanese producers – a previously unknown source of competition. Their cars quickly gained a reputation for reliability and innovation, against which much of Rover's output compared unfavourably.

The net effect of all this was that Rover, along with all British car makers were forced to improve the quality of the vehicles they were producing. Vauxhall linked up with Peugeot of France and were eventually taken over by General Motors from the United States. Vast amounts of money were injected by Ford into its British offshoot through the modernisation of its factory in Dagenham. In an attempt to shake off its second-rate image Rover joined forces with Honda – a move that led to the introduction of the Rover 200 series and one which, in the short term at least, helped it to restore its faltering reputation.

Eventually this relationship collapsed when BMW took control in 1996. Then in 2000 – after disappointing sales and ever-increasing costs of production – BMW announced its decision to sell out. The rest is history.

questions

1   Why were Rover cars poor sellers abroad in the 1960s and 1970s?

2   Why did the domestic market for Rover also collapse?

3   Why were Rover's overseas owners unable to get the company fully back on its feet again?

4   How have consumers in the UK benefited from increased competition in car manufacture?

barriers to trade

restricting competition from overseas

While the principle of free trade still holds true there is the problem that its widespread benefits are often taken for granted and not fully understood. In the short-term countries can gain an advantage by flouting the rules of free trade and imposing barriers or restrictions on the amount of goods they buy from abroad. Inefficient businesses are often keen to persuade governments that they should be protected from the effects of increased competition to prevent unemployment and a fall in their profits.

The situation is similar to the principle of the rule of law. All the citizens of a country are better off if everyone obeys the law. However, any individual can gain an advantage over others by breaking the law. One person might be able to obtain more goods by stealing instead of earning the money and buying them, but if everyone were to break the rules and steal from each other everyone would lose out.

In an attempt to gain short term advantage nations have imposed a number of restrictions or **barriers to trade**. These protectionist measures often take the form of:

tariffs

Tariffs are taxes on imports of goods and services which artificially raise their price, making them uncompetitive in the home country's market.

quotas

These are limits, either in terms of value or quantity, on the amount of goods and services that one country will buy from another and are usually set at a level below which is currently traded.

exchange controls

Governments can reduce the amount of imports into their country simply by imposing restrictions on the amount of foreign currency that individuals and businesses can buy. The ability to buy foreign currency is essential to international trade (except in the case of a single currency) as sellers naturally insist on being paid in their own currency

bogus safety measures

Some countries refuse to import goods on the grounds that they are unsafe, or that they break strict environmental rules. While there may be legitimate reasons for imposing such bans they have often been used as a pretext for simply restricting the amount of imports into a country. These kind of restrictions are very difficult to break down as it is difficult to distinguish between bans that are genuine and those that are not.

Businesses often find that because of differences in culture and language, breaking into international markets is often extremely difficult; but when they also have to overcome some of the protectionist measures described above, it can be virtually impossible.

removing barriers to trade – GATT and WTO

In an attempt to encourage international trade and remove barriers to trade an organisation known as the GATT (General Agreement on Tariffs and Trade) was established. In recent years this has developed into the WTO (World Trade Organisation). Although GATT and the WTO have met with considerable success in reducing tariff barriers on goods, recent meetings, such as the one held in Seattle in 1999, have made little progress.

Increasing concern is being expressed that the decisions made are too often of benefit to countries such as the USA and other leading exporters (see table opposite) at the expense of smaller developing countries. For example, the motion proposed by the USA to ban products made with the help of child labour may at first sight seem to be morally responsible. However, those countries that employ child labour argue that this is simply a move to help protect US markets from much cheaper foreign imports.

Activity 8.6

Barriers to international competition

The table on the top of the next page shows the value of exports from the world's most successful exporters. Study the table and discuss the following points . . .

1   What do the economies represented in the table have in common?

   Do you think this league table may change in the future?

   Can you suggest any new countries that might be coming in?

2   If the WTO places a ban on the import of goods produced as a result of child or very low-paid labour, who will be affected?

   How could this be a barrier to free competition?

Top world exporters

Annual value of exports ($billions)

US	682	Germany	540
Japan	388	France	305
UK	272	Italy	242
Canada	214	Netherlands	199
China	184	Belgium	177

trading blocs

In an attempt to avoid the damaging effects of trade barriers, groups of countries have sometimes joined together as a trading bloc. Examples include LAFTA/LAIA and CACM centred around Latin America; the Asian Free Trade Area (AFTA); the Economic Community of West African States (ECOWAS); the North American Free Trade Agreement (NAFTA), which includes the USA, Canada and Mexico – and the European Union (EU).

These 'blocs' encourage trade between members but, on the other hand, set up barriers to trade against non-members.

Trading blocs can have a number of characteristics:

free trade areas

Member countries reduce or abolish restrictions on trade between each other while retaining trade barriers against non-member countries.

customs unions

Barriers to trade between member countries are abolished but a common or identical tariff is applied by all members to imports from non-members.

common markets

The customs barriers between members are removed to include the free movement of labour and capital as well as products.

economic union

In addition to creating common markets, member countries also seek to harmonise national economic policies.

advantages of trading blocs

- trade between member countries increases, which leads to an increase in living standards throughout the bloc
- consumers and businesses can buy cheaper products due to the absence of tariff barriers
- businesses have access to larger markets which encourages them to expand and gain increased benefits from economies of scale – this makes them more competitive with businesses in non-member countries
- nations which organise themselves into trading blocs have greater power than individual nations to negotiate lower trade barriers with other trading blocs
- trading blocs help to harmonise taxes and trading standards – making international trade easier
- greater trading links between nations reduces the likelihood of political conflicts

disadvantages of trading blocs

- high tariff barriers imposed on non-members often reduces the volume of external trade – which depresses living standards
- member countries may suffer from being forced to buy products from other members rather than cheaper external sources; when it joined the EU the UK was forced to reduce its trading links with Australia and New Zealand and to buy more expensive products from inside the EU
- the formation of a trading bloc encourages other countries to form further trading blocs – this increases the level of protectionism and discourages trade between non-member nations

the European Union

The European Union and World Trade				
	EU	*US*	*Japan*	*Rest of the World*
	%	%	%	%
Goods	19.2	18.1	9.6	53.1
Services	26.1	23.2	7.1	43.6

For further information about the EU and world trade: www.europa.eu.int/comm/dg01

The European Union (EU) was originally known as the European Economic Community (EEC) and was a customs union which allowed the free movement of goods between member states. On 1st January 1993 all barriers to the free movement of labour and capital were removed to create the Single European Market. For holiday makers from the UK to mainland Europe the most obvious effect has been that they can bring back as much wine, beer and cigarettes (providing they can show that it is for their individual consumption) as they can carry. For businesses it has meant:

- the harmonisation of technical standards so that, for example, the rules governing safety standards in the UK also apply across the rest of the EU

- it is illegal for governments to favour local suppliers in awarding contracts (you may find that your water is provided and your refuse collected by a French-controlled company)

- border controls have virtually disappeared between many countries (but this is not true of the UK)

- trade barriers in services such as banking and insurance have been eliminated

future developments

Without doubt the most significant development on the horizon is enlargement. The EU has already agreed to accept Turkey as a full member and there are moves afoot to extend the list of member countries to Poland, Albania and other underdeveloped Eastern European nations. In the long term the potential benefits to business in terms of the opportunity to sell to new and expanding markets is enormous. However, in the short term taxes throughout EU may have to rise to help pay for the much needed industrial and social infrastructure that must be put in place before such opportunities can be realised.

Activity 8.7

Competing in the European Union

A friend of yours runs a web-based mail order business selling bed linen in the UK. She wants to expand her operations into the EU because she knows her website is getting 'hits' from all over Europe. But she is concerned about dealing with customers overseas. Answer these questions for her:

1   "What are the advantages of selling within the EU rather than to the USA?"

2   "Should I price my goods in pounds sterling? Are there any advantages of pricing my goods in Euros? I need to be able to compete in terms of price."

3   "Is there any chance of selling to countries in Europe which are not currently in the EU? Do you think my goods would be competitive in Eastern European states?"

CHAPTER SUMMARY

- Larger businesses can often compete more effectively than smaller businesses due to greater monopoly power and lower unit (average) costs which derive from economies of scale.

- Businesses can grow internally by expanding their existing operations but it is often easier for them to grow externally by merging or taking over other existing businesses.

- The majority of mergers are horizontal in nature and occur between businesses at the same stage of the production process; others are described as being vertical and occur between business at different stages of the production process.

- Limited room for expansion in domestic markets has led many businesses to look abroad to increase the scale of their operations. International competition is such that many businesses not only sell across the world but also take advantage of the availability of natural resources to base their production and distribution facilities in other countries – a phenomenon known as globalisation.

- Businesses that compete internationally need to be aware of the way in which changes in exchange rates can affect their international competitiveness. A depreciation in a business's domestic currency will usually make its goods and services more competitive abroad while an appreciation will make it less competitive.

- To avoid the risks associated within varying exchange rates and the costs of exchange the majority of members of the EU have permanently fixed their rates of exchange in a move towards monetary union and the establishment of a Single European Currency – the Euro.

- Increased competition and international trade have many benefits but businesses that are unable to respond by increasing their efficiency, reducing prices and improving the quality of their goods and services may not be able to survive without help. Such businesses may be able to persuade their governments to impose trade barriers such as tariffs and quotas in order to remain competitive internationally.

- Barriers to trade are damaging as they inhibit competition and reduce the level of international trade. It is the responsibility of the World Trade Organisation (previously known as the GATT) to try to reduce barriers to trade.

- Some countries have joined together to form trading blocs. There are several types of trading blocs including free trade areas, customs unions, common markets and economic unions like the EU, of which Britain is a member.

KEY TERMS

monopoly power	the ability of a business to restrict output and raise price to make larger profits
economies of scale	reductions in unit costs arising from the growth of a business
internal growth	when a business expands the size of its existing operations
external growth	when a business grows by merging with or taking over other businesses
horizontal mergers	mergers between businesses at the same stage of the production process
vertical mergers	mergers between businesses at different stages of the production process
backward mergers	a business merges with another business closer to the supply end of the production process
forward mergers	a business merges with another business closer to the retail end of the production process
conglomerates	mergers between businesses producing unrelated and diversified products
exchange rate	the amount of a foreign country's currency that can be obtained with a unit of domestic currency
EMU	European Monetary Union is the process whereby certain member countries of the EU scrap their national currencies in favour of a common currency
single currency	the existence of a common currency between members of a trading bloc, eg the Euro, enabling countries to avoid the risks from trading arising from changes in foreign exchange rates
barriers to trade	restrictions such as tariffs, subsidies and exchange controls which protect domestic businesses from the effects of foreign competition and thereby reduce the level of international trade
trading bloc	a group of countries that join together to encourage trade between them

Government policy and business

introduction

It is generally recognised that a free market economy, if left to itself, would not allocate resources fairly. Competition would result in smaller businesses being driven out of the market, consumers and suppliers being taken advantage of and the environment polluted. It is the role of the Government to intervene in the market through legislation and other measures to protect these 'stakeholders' and to provide a healthy economy in which businesses can prosper.

what you will learn from this chapter

- the demands of business stakeholders sometimes run contrary to the need for businesses to be profitable and competitive

- some markets – such as health and education – need an element of state control in order that they can receive the necessary resources

- the Government intervenes in the market to protect consumers – largely through legislation and through the setting up of regulatory bodies

- the Competition Commission has been set up under the Competition Act and acts as a regulatory 'policeman' to prevent large businesses abusing their competitive position to the disadvantage of consumers and suppliers

- employees – another stakeholder group – are protected by legislation and also through the influence of the EU Social Chapter

- the interests of the environmental lobby – another stakeholder group – are protected by UK legislation and EU directives

- the Government also regulates demand in the market through its monetary policy (which aims to regulate interest rates) and its fiscal policy (announced in the Budget) which regulates taxation and spending

the importance of stakeholders

A stakeholder is:

any person, organisation, interest group or other body which has an interest in the business

While most people would probably accept that competition between businesses often produces many benefits it is also useful to recognise that there may also be some undesirable consequences. These negative aspects often affect not just the owners, managers and employees of a business – their internal stakeholders – but a wide range of interested groups – external stakeholders.

stakeholders - internal and external

The main internal and external stakeholder are shown below. For a further discussion of stakeholders see pages 20 to 22.

internal stakeholders	external stakeholders
owners	shareholders
managers	customers
employees	suppliers and lenders
	the government
	pressure groups
	the local and wider communities

negative aspects of competition

the need to cut costs – unemployment

When a business is expanding, the interests of shareholders and employees coincide. However, shareholders who expect to see rising share prices and dividends may react to intense competition in an industry by putting managers under pressure to reduce costs. In the short-term this can often be most easily achieved by reducing the size of the workforce leading to possible unemployment.

pollution of the local environment

The desire to cut costs and the fact that businesses only consider the private consequences of their decisions may lead to possible conflict with stakeholders in the local community. It may be cheaper for a business to get rid of their waste products by dumping noxious chemicals in the local river as opposed to having it treated and disposed of elsewhere. Similarly the cost of installing a filter to reduce unpleasant odours that occur as an indirect consequence of the production process may be seen by the business as unjustifiably expensive.

social and ethical issues

The trend towards globalisation has led some businesses to move their production source outside of the country of origin to countries where labour costs are much lower. In recent years Nike, the sport products manufacturer, has moved its production to the Philippines and Indonesia. This has brought it into conflict with some child welfare groups who accuse companies like Nike of taking advantage of lax employment legislation in these countries to exploit child labour. Monsanto, a company strongly linked with research into Genetically Modified (GM) crops, has recently found itself in considerable conflict with consumer groups who are concerned about the long-term health risks of eating GM foods.

government protection of stakeholders

As we will see later in the chapter, the government intervenes in the market to protect stakeholders – both business owners and consumers. It does this through legislation and by regulating the economy. First, however, we need to look at markets which have traditionally been under state control.

the need for government intervention

In Chapter 6 we looked at the advantages of a market economy, where nations rely on markets to ensure the efficient allocation of resources. In reality, however most countries recognise that markets do not always work as well as they might. In an attempt to overcome some of the inadequacies of markets the state often took on the responsibility for allocating significant amounts of resources and took control of areas such as education, health and transport, which became 'nationalised'.

the creation of markets in education and health

In the 1980s and 1990s there were a number of privatisations. A privatisation is the 'sell-off' of a state-owned business to the private sector. British Rail, for example, was nationalised in 1948 and 'privatised' in the late 1990s.

There are some areas, however, where government ownership and control looks likely to continue for the foreseeable future. This is particularly true in the case of education and health. It is widely accepted that both these 'industries' should be made available to everyone regardless of their ability to pay. Currently these services (with the exception of dental health and some prescriptions) are provided free and paid for through general taxation.

It is possible to argue that activities such as education and health that are run by the state and not exposed to the natural forces of competition are in danger of operating inefficiently. Potentially the public could receive relatively poor quality services at a higher cost than would be the case if they were privately owned and controlled. On the other hand, supporters of the National Health Service and state education argue that wholesale privatisation would deprive many people who cannot afford to pay the true cost of the services they receive of the opportunity to benefit from them. In an attempt to get the best of both worlds successive governments have attempted to retain ownership of these areas but then to create internal markets and introduce an element of competition where none previously existed.

Activity 9.1

A marketplace in school education?

> Most schools now control their own budgets which has given them the right to spend the money they receive in the way they see fit. Previously schools were under Local Education Authority (LEA) control and many important decisions including how many teachers they wanted to employ, were made by the LEA. Freedom from LEA control has also encouraged schools to compete with each other for pupils. Parents have also been given a much greater say than used to be the case about which school they can send their children to. This in turn has led to a degree of product differentiation as schools have attempted to make themselves appear better than their competitors by offering a slightly differentiated product. In effect there is something resembling a market place within the state education sector which many will argue has created a number of benefits both to parents and schools.

1   Why has education come under state control in the first place?

2   Why was education not privatised?

3   What elements of the free market has been given by the government to schools?

4   What are the benefits of these freedoms to the schools?

5   What are the benefits of these freedoms to the customers of the schools – the students and their parents?

6   Why do you think some people still send their children to private schools? What do you think the Government should do about private schools?

competition in healthcare

Before 1990 doctors and hospitals worked together under the control of their Local Area Health Authority. A family doctor (GP) might refer a patient to his or her local hospital for treatment but would have no idea how much this might cost. Even the Local Area Health Authority might not know. Money was simply allocated to the different departments within the health service as people thought appropriate.

The reforms in the National Health Service (NHS) that started in 1990 have placed an increased emphasis on the role of markets and competition. In particular a clear effort has been made to separate the purchasers of healthcare products from providers. By separating providers and purchasers the government has created an internal market in healthcare. The purchasers – groups of 'Primary Care' GPs – behave like ordinary consumers in that they need to ensure that they get the most from their limited resources.

Activity 9.2

A true marketplace in healthcare?

> GPs are organised in groups known as Primary Care Groups (or Primary Care 'Trusts'). These groups use the money they are allocated to spend to maximise patient welfare, ie spend it in a way that gives their patients the maximum possible benefit. This means that, for example, the benefit a patient might receive from being prescribed a drug such as Viagra has to be balanced against the benefit a patient with cancer might receive from expensive new treatment. The choice is partly an ethical one.
>
> This new system also means that Primary Care Groups (GPs) can buy treatments such as heart surgery operations from any provider (hospital or clinic) they choose, although in practice they tend to use the local group of hospitals (the 'Hospital Trust'). The Hospital Trusts in turn can price their operations and courses of treatment at a level which enables them to cover their costs. This can lead to regional variations in pricing.

Carry out research into current methods of healthcare provision. Talk to friends and family about their experiences of healthcare, operation waiting lists and so on.

1   Why has the Government decided to introduce an element of competition into the state provision of healthcare? Who are the consumers in this market?

2   What are the benefits of these reforms?

3   What are the disadvantages to the patients of this competitive system?

4   Is healthcare a freely competitive market? How would you categorise it?

consumer protection

the consumer

One type of stakeholder – the customer – is always in the public eye because the public **is** the customer or 'consumer'.

Strictly speaking the 'customer' buys goods and services, the 'consumer' uses them. The parent who buys disposable nappies is the customer, the baby is the consumer – a distinction which is probably lost on the baby.

Consumer protection has therefore become a topical issue – kept very much in the minds of the public by 'watchdog' programs on TV and radio.

consumer legislation

Since the middle of the twentieth century a number of important changes have taken place in the market for consumer goods:

*   their complexity has increased: it is unreasonable to expect the average person to understand how computers, cars and microwaves work in anything but the broadest of detail
*   goods are often packaged in such a way that it is difficult to inspect them
*   goods are increasingly ordered by phone or electronically which makes inspection impossible

For these reasons the balance of power in consumer contracts lies with retailers who potentially have the ability to exploit the consumer. In recognition of this governments have sought to redress the imbalance by passing a series of Acts of Parliament, including:

> The Trade Descriptions Act (1987)
>
> The Consumer Protection Act (1987)
>
> The Sale of Goods Act (1979 & 1994)
>
> The Supply of Goods and Services Act (1984)

Details of consumer protection can be found on the excellent website of the government's Office of Fair Trading (OFT): www.oft.gov.uk to which we will refer again later.

the impact of consumer legislation on business

Consumer legislation has laid down minimum standards for the quality of goods and services supplied and, if something goes wrong, businesses must also accept a much greater responsibility for the consequences of their actions than was formerly the case. This has unquestionably led to an increase in business costs although in most cases these have been passed on to the consumer in the form of higher prices. It is also interesting to note that competition has helped to push standards even higher. It is, for example, commonplace amongst retailers to give cash refunds on returned items even though there is no basis in law to do so.

Activity 9.3

Consumer protection and competition

1 What are your rights in consumer law if you buy some clothing which is faulty? Refer to statute law (Acts of Parliament) to support your answer.

2 Investigate returns policies operated by two clothing retailers, eg a 'High Street' store and a mail order firm. Do they meet with the legal requirements, or do they go further? Why should they go further than the minimum legal requirement?

regulating monopolies

the regulation of privatised businesses

One of the dangers of privatisation was that in returning the vast majority of state owned monopolies to the private sector the government were simply creating several new private monopolies with all the potential dangers that this entailed. Whilst these industries were under public ownership their monopoly power was not an issue. There was no danger of a state owned industry that was run for the benefit of society as a whole abusing its power and exploiting consumers through, for example, charging unreasonably high prices. Once these industries returned to private ownership, however, the potential dangers were very real. In an attempt to prevent the possible exploitation of consumers the government has acted in two main ways:

1 a number of regulatory bodies or watchdogs were set up to monitor the performance of the gas, water, electricity, telecommunication, railway and other public services –a selection of these bodies is shown below

2 the setting up of the Competition Commission

the regulatory bodies

Financial Services Authority (FSA)

The FSA is a new regulatory body for the whole of the financial services industry.

National Lottery Commission

The current regulatory body replaced OFLOT in April 1999 and is responsible for ensuring that the Lottery is run with sufficient care to protect the interests of players and to maximise the money raised for good causes.

Office of Gas and Electricity Markets (OFGEM)

The regulatory body for gas and electricity following the merger of the Office of Gas Supply (OFGAS) and the Office of Electricity Regulation (OFFER). The Office is responsible for regulating the gas and electricity markets, protecting consumers' interests and encouraging competition, as you will appreciate from the 1999 report printed below . . . .

OFGEM wants to see more competition between electricity generators

OFGEM, the merged gas and electricity power regulator, is restricting price increases made by Britain's leading electricity generators to prevent them from abusing their market power.

The energy regulator intends to introduce a "good behaviour" condition to the licences of seven generators: National Power, Power Gen, Eastern Mission, Energy, AES, Nuclear Electric and Magnox Electric.

The generators are being reigned in after Ofgem's inquiry into extraordinary moves in wholesale power prices last June. Generators raised prices, leading to an 80 per cent increase in pool prices in the first week of July compared with the previous year.

Callum McCarthy, Director general of Ofgem, said he was determined to see more competition and lower electricity prices.

Ofgem has no power to impose penalties on generators that breach their licence but new powers to be introduced under the Competition Act next March will enable Ofgem to impose fines of up to 10 per cent of turnover.

Office of the Rail Regulator (ORR)

The ORR aims to create a better railway for passengers and freight customers, and better value for public funding authorities, through effective regulation.

Office of Telecommunications (OFTEL)

The duties of the Office include protecting the interests of consumers, promoting competition in fixed and mobile telephone markets, ensuring that telephone and cable companies meet their licence obligations, regulating access to digital television services (UK).

Office of Water Services (OFWAT)

This body monitors the activities of companies appointed as water and sewerage undertakings, regulates prices, promotes economy and efficiency, protects customers' interests and facilitates competition in England and Wales.

the Competition Commission

the Competition Commission

The body responsible for policing anti-competitive behaviour in the UK is the Competition Commission which replaced the Monopolies and Mergers Commission (MMC) in 1999. The Competition Commission is granted powers under the Competition Act 1998 and has cases referred to it by it the Office of Fair Trading (OFT).

The Competition Commission deals with areas such as mergers, monopolies, and anti-competitive practices. In addition the Commission is responsible for hearing appeals by businesses which have been caught by the EU's regulations on the control of mergers. EU law prohibits all agreements and practices which may affect trade between member states and which are designed to prevent, restrict or distort competition.

The Competition Commission is a watchdog with strong teeth. The mere threat of being referred to the Commission is often a sufficient deterrence to mergers. The preparation needed for defending a proposed merger can be such that as to tie up a large quantity of senior executives' time, a cost that many businesses seem to find unacceptable. Businesses that wish to avoid the attention of the Commission and the Office of Fair Trading will often moderate their behaviour by ensuring that their prices and profits are not so high as to attract attention.

the Competition Act

The Competition Act gives the Office of Fair Trading substantial powers to investigate anti-competitive abuses and to hand out large fines. The previous legislation was essentially administrative without much in the way of pro-active powers or penalties, but under the new rules it will be more worthwhile for people to complain or sue over anti-competitive behaviour as offending businesses will face tough fines if they are found out.

The Act is split into two parts. The first prohibits anti-competitive agreements, such as price fixing, market sharing, imposing minimum resale prices or bid rigging, between businesses or trade associations. The second part forbids companies with a dominant market share of usually more than forty per cent from abusing their position, for example by predatory pricing or cutting out rival suppliers.

The Act gives the OFT and the other regulatory bodies the power to launch dawn raids, search offices, demand documents and answers to questions if they have reasonable grounds for suspecting that the Act is being infringed. Full details of the Act and its powers can be found on www.oft.gov.uk

THE COMPETITION ACT 1998

the rules

The Act includes competition rules which prohibit anti-competitive agreements and abuse of a dominant position in the market, for example by

- price fixing

- limiting or controlling production, markets, technical development or investment

- applying different trading conditions to equivalent transactions which will put some parties at a competitive disadvantage

- making contracts subject to unrelated supplementary conditions

enforcement

The Director General of Fair Trading has wide-ranging powers to investigate suspected breaches – his officials can enter premises and demand relevant documents, and even get a warrant to make a search.

penalties

Businesses can be fined up to 10 per cent of their UK turnover. Prohibited agreements will be void and unenforceable, and any third party harmed by an agreement or conduct may be able to sue for damages.

how to start an investigation

The OFT welcomes complaints from anyone who suspect that the rules are being broken and has appropriate evidence. You can complain in writing or by telephone and your identity will be protected. A formal investigation may be launched if there are reasonable grounds for suspecting that the rules are being or have been broken.

Activity 9.4

The Competition Commission at work

SUPERMARKETS IN THE CLEAR

Customers not suffering from abuse of monopoly, says Competition Commission

UK supermarket chains each belong to at least one monopoly but have been largely cleared of abusing their position and profiteering at the expense of shoppers and suppliers.

The watchdog that was asked to investigate the £90bn market after an inquiry by the Office of Fair Trading, cleared 19 of the biggest chains, including Marks & Spencer, Waitrose and Lidl, of operating against the public interest.

After a nine month enquiry the Competition Commission said in its preliminary report that food prices were rising at a slower pace than both general retail prices and European food prices. In fact shoppers reported "high levels of consumer satisfaction" with local outlets. The Commission could find no evidence of "excessive profitability".

Over the past year the supermarkets' squeaky clean image has been under attack. Consumers groups demanded to know why shoppers appeared to pay more for food in the UK than Europe. While farmers claimed that supermarkets were driving them to the brink of bankruptcy by paying them ridiculously low rates for their produce.

Yesterday the grocery groups which began a round of price promotions when the inquiry started last year, seized the watchdog's report as evidence that there is no such thing as "rip-off Britain".

There were suggestions that the watchdogs might order store sell-offs, relax planning rules to allow more stores to be built, encouraging competition, or ban supermarkets from selling below cost price for promotional purposes.

The commission said that that there were two complex monopolies: one in relation to pricing of groceries and the other deriving form the relationship between grocers and suppliers, but they were not automatically operating against the public interest.

Source: *The Guardian*, 2 February 2000

1 What two groups of stakeholders felt threatened by the supermarket chains?

2 What was the complaint against the supermarkets?

3 What were the findings of the Commission?

4 What two 'monopolies' were identified by the Commission?

5 Have there been any changes in this situation since this book was published? If there have been changes, what are they, and how have they come about?

other stakeholder issues

UK employee protection – European influence

Employees – important internal stakeholders – are protected by a series of Acts of Parliament, explained in detail in the Human Resources Unit (pages 382 to 385). The issues covered by this legislation include:

- discrimination at work on the grounds of race, disability and sex
- minimum pay
- maximum working hours
- redundancy payments
- health and safety at work

the Social Chapter

You should also note that many measures protecting employees have been influenced by European directives. The milestone here is The Social Chapter, which forms part of the Maastricht Treaty. The 'Chapter' includes coverage of the following areas:

- the right to equal treatment for men and women
- the right to a minimum wage
- a maximum working week of 48 hours
- a minimum of four weeks paid holiday a year
- the right to join a Trade Union
- the right to take industrial action

the effect on competition

Clearly these measures add to the labour costs of business, a trend which reduces profit and is reflected in higher consumer prices. This in turn has a negative effect on the competitiveness of a business. It is evident that many UK manufacturing businesses are turning to source products from countries where the cost of labour is lower.

Activity 9.5

Stakeholder conflicts

A well-known clothing store has announced that its has been forced to source its products from low-cost overseas producers because of the high cost of UK labour. Is this a case of employment protection by Government legislation scoring an 'own goal'? What stakeholder interests are involved in a decision like this?

pressure groups – the environmental issue

Pressure groups acting on behalf of the community at large form another powerful stakeholder lobby. Legislation in the UK and environmental directives from Europe ensure that their interests are well served.

In the UK laws such as the Clean Air Act and the Environmental Protection Act regulate the amount of pollution allowed – for example the quantities of specified gases businesses can release into the atmosphere.

The EU in the Treaty of Amsterdam embodies the principle of sustainable development as one of the European Community's aims. It has adopted a policy of encouraging reduction in pollution in a number of areas: industry, energy, tourism, transport and agriculture.

One visible sign of the EU's commitment to environmental protection is 'eco-labelling' which can be used on products (excluding food and drink) which have a reduced impact on the environment during their life cycle.

The eco-label symbol is reproduced on the left.

The EU also encourages the use of environmental taxes (the 'polluter pays' principle).

Full information about the European Union and its environmental policies can be found by logging onto www.europa.eu.int – and then carrying out a word search on the site on the word 'environment'.

Activity 9.6

Environmental measures, profit and competition

Find examples of businesses (by looking at advertising and websites) which make a marketing point of their environmentally friendly policies – eg car manufacturers using recyclable materials, food supermarkets selling organic produce.

What effect do you think this has on

1   their profits?

2   their position in a competitive marketplace?

business and government policy

creating a healthy business environment

Most of the factors that make for a successful business, eg a sound marketing strategy, are the responsibility of its managers. There are however other factors, external to the business, that are equally important but over which managers have no influence at all. These external factors make for a healthy environment within which the business can compete grow and be profitable.

There are four key characteristics of a healthy business environment which governments now assume at least some responsibility for:

- low inflation
- high employment
- a stable exchange rate
- high and sustainable economic growth

We will look at these in turn.

low inflation

Inflation is the term used to describe the rate at which prices are rising. The 1970s and 1980s were times of high inflation in Britain but in the latter part of the 1990s inflation rates have been very low by historical standards. High inflation causes a number of difficulties:

- businesses need to devote time and energy to re-pricing their goods; mail order businesses that rely on sales through catalogues might incur considerable costs from the need to reprint their literature to accommodate their constantly changing prices
- consumers tend to lose confidence in, for example, their ability to remain in employment and so tend to save a larger proportion of their existing incomes causing sales to fall
- businesses also become uncertain about the future and tend to cut back on investment in new plant and machinery which can harm their long-term competitiveness
- in the past British businesses have become uncompetitive as their prices raced ahead of the prices of their overseas competitors

high employment

A high level of employment is obviously good for workers but it is good for business too. It is always going to be easier to sell goods and services in times when more people are in work and incomes are high.

a stable exchange rate

The exchange rate is important because it determines the price of UK goods abroad and the price of goods from abroad sold in the UK. As we saw in the last chapter, changes in the exchange rate can have an adverse effect on the competitiveness of UK businesses – making their products more expensive at home and abroad. Businesses that sell a lot of their goods abroad prefer the exchange rate to be low while business that buy a lot of goods from abroad prefer a high exchange rate.

a high and sustainable level of economic growth

Economic growth is a term used by economists to describe the rate at which the output of the economy – the amount of goods and services produced by a nation in one year – has changed compared to the previous year. Economic growth is a crude measure of how quickly the wealth of a nation is increasing. The general expectation in Britain and most developed economies, is that economic growth will be positive. There have, however, been occasions when growth has been negative, suggesting that the output of the economy is falling. Periods of negative economic growth are often described as periods of recession.

From the consumer's perspective positive economic growth means they are more likely to be able to afford more goods and services. For businesses it means that there are greater opportunities to:

• launch new products

• increase sales volumes

• make greater profits

• expand

government control of the economy

The ideal economic position for businesses and consumers would be:

• a low rate of inflation

• a steady rate of economic growth

• low unemployment

• a stable exchange rate

It is a principal aim of the government to provide these conditions. It does so mainly by controlling the level of demand in the economy.

There are two main weapons that the government can use to achieve a healthy and competitive business environment: monetary policy and fiscal policy.

- **monetary policy** involves using changes in interest rates and the supply of money to affect levels of borrowing, savings and the exchange rate
- **fiscal policy** involves adjusting the levels of government income and expenditure – changes normally announced in the Chancellor's Budget

monetary policy: the cost and supply of money

The cost of money is another way of talking about of the rate of interest or the cost of borrowing money. The supply of money refers to the total amount of money in circulation in the economy. The government influences the level of interest rates through the Bank of England's Monetary Policy Committee.

the consequences of a change in interest rates

A rise in interest rates will cause demand to fall while a fall in interest rates will have the opposite effect. Interest rates are a very important tool for controlling the general level of demand in the economy because they can affect all of the following:

the level of borrowing

A rise in interest rates will raise the cost of borrowing money. This will affect consumers who might think twice before deciding to finance Christmas or a summer holiday by borrowing on credit card or taking out a personal loan for a new car. It will also affect businesses that are contemplating building a new factory or buying an expensive piece of machinery.

the level of saving

A rise in interest rates might encourage individuals and businesses to save more of their incomes rather than spend it.

monthly mortgage repayments

A rise in interest rates will, for many people, increase the size of the monthly mortgage payment they make to their bank or building society, effectively causing their incomes to fall. This can often have a major affect on business as the demand for many consumer products will fall as a result.

the exchange rate

A rise in interest rates in Britain will tend to attract in large amounts of money from abroad because foreign investors will switch from other currencies to sterling accounts which pay high rates of interest. This will raise the value of the pound sterling on the foreign exchange markets, making the price of exports rise and the price of imports fall. This is bad news for UK businesses – it will make UK exports more expensive and less competitive and foreign imports less expensive and more competitive.

The effects of monetary policy on business

the effect of a change in UK interest rates		
	a rise in UK interest rates	**a fall in UK interest rates**
borrowing	it is more expensive to borrow - borrowing tends to fall - consumers have less to spend	it is less expensive to borrow - borrowing tends to rise - consumers have more to spend
savings	a better return on savings - savings tend to rise - consumers spend less	a poorer return on savings - savings tend to fall - consumers spend more
mortgages	repayments become more expensive - consumers spend less	repayments become less expensive - consumers have more to spend
exchange rate	the £ rises against other currencies - exports are more expensive - imported goods are cheaper	the £ falls against other currencies - exports are less expensive - imported goods are dearer

Study the table above and answer the following questions, using the appropriate factors in the left-hand column to justify your answers.

1   What is the effect of a rise in interest rates on a business selling consumer goods in a competitive market the UK? Would a fall in interest rates have the opposite effect?

2   What is the effect of a fall in interest rates on a business selling industrial goods overseas? Would a rise in interest rates have the opposite effect?

3   If the effect of a fall in interest rates is so significant, what is to stop the Bank of England's Monetary Policy Committee dropping rates to a very low level to keep everybody happy? What are the disadvantages? If you are not sure about this, take a look at changes in mortgage rates and house prices.

changing interest rates

At the time of writing, the level of UK interest rates is fixed by the Bank of England's Monetary Policy Committee. They meet regularly to discuss the state of the economy – price levels, exchange rates, the level of economic growth. They attempt to fine tune the economy by fixing a Base Rate (a rate to which all interest rates are related) which will balance growth in the economy with inflation, for example with growth at 2% and inflation at 2.5%.

The Monetary Policy Committee is not a government body, but acts completely independently.

Activity 9.8

Monetary policy at work

MARKETS BRACED FOR NEW YEAR RATE RISE

Financial markets on both side of the Atlantic were today bracing themselves for new year interest rate rises after fresh data showed consumer confidence surging in Britain and the United States.

With shops and stores in Britain reporting bumper post-Christmas sales, new data published today showed that consumers were shrugging off the small increase in the cost of borrowing last month and instead gearing up for a spending spree.

This followed evidence from the US yesterday indicating that the three increases in interest rates have so far failed to put the brakes on America's booming economy, in which confidence is standing at its highest for 31 years.

Michael Saunders, economist at Salmon, Smith Barney, said the Bank's monetary policy committee was edging towards a rate rise last month, though it was decided to keep borrowing costs at 5.5%. He is forecasting a half-point rise over the next two months, with rates hitting 6.75% by the end of 2000 and 7% to 8% in 2001.

Source: *The Guardian*, 29 December 1999

---

1   Why should businesses that sell consumer goods be pleased with this press report?

2   What was the trend in interest rates when this article was written?

3   From the evidence in this report does it look like monetary policy is working?

4   What does this report have to say about economies in different parts of the world?

fiscal policy: changing income and expenditure

Governments receive their income from taxation on individuals and businesses. Government expenditure takes many forms including health, education, defence and social benefits such as pensions and child benefit. Changes in government income and expenditure have a significant bearing on the general level of demand in the economy . . .

> To increase demand the government will reduce taxes and increase its expenditure.

> To reduce demand the government will increase taxes and reduce its expenditure.

the Budget

Every March the Chancellor of the Exchequer proposes in the Budget the levels of taxation and spending it would like to see. These measures are later debated in Parliament and eventually enshrined in law as the Finance Act. The Budget – announced in the Chancellor's speech in the House of Commons – covers the following areas:

- targets for **public spending** – health, education, defence, transport, social security, housing, law and order

- money to be raised in **taxes** – income tax and National Insurance, Council tax, business rates and taxes, VAT

The Budget also covers a wide range of other measures, including adjustments to benefits, savings, duties on drink and tobacco, taxes on pollution. Full details of successive budgets can be accessed on the Treasury website: www.hm-treasury.gov.uk

policies for a healthy business environment

In the past governments have made considerable changes to levels of taxation and government expenditure to try to achieve the right balance of inflation, employment, exchange rate level and economic growth,. However such changes often proved to be unsuccessful. The current view is that it is probably better not to make radical changes to fiscal and monetary policy but to concentrate on controlling inflation. At the time of writing the government has set a target for inflation of 2.5% and it is the job of the Bank of England under its monetary policy committee, who are ultimately responsible for setting interest rates, to keep it at this level by making appropriate adjustments to interest rates.

There are no effective short-term measures to raise the level of output of the economy and achieve sustainable and high levels of economic growth. Over the longer term however it is generally recognised that a number of supply-side policies that might be followed. These might include:

reduced taxation

It is generally believed that if you over-tax both individuals and business then they will lose the incentive to work as hard as they might and thus output will fall. This partially explains the trend started by a Conservative government in 1979 and continued up to the present time by the Labour government elected in 1997, of reducing income tax. The basic rate of personal income tax has fallen from 33% to 22% and is likely to fall further in the future.

encouraging small businesses

It is an often quoted saying that 'big trees from little acorns grow'. The hope is that the more new businesses there are the more likely it is that some of them will grow into large companies with high levels of output. To this end successive Chancellors of the Exchequer have attempted to reduce the burden of taxation on small businesses in particular and also to remove some of the red-tape which small businesses have often claimed hamper their efforts to expand.

education and training

There is no clear link between economic growth and expenditure on education and training but recent Conservative and Labour led governments have both adopted improvements in these areas as key planks of their overall economic strategy.

Activity 9.9

The Budget and business

Research details of the last budget. Sources include the press, leaflets produced by firms of accountants, and www.hm-treasury.gov.uk

What measures did the Chancellor introduce to encourage businesses? Possible areas might include:

- capital allowances for investments in equipment (this means that the cost of the equipment can be wholly or partly set off against the business tax bill)
- reductions in business taxation or indirect taxation such as VAT
- reductions in business 'red tape'
- incentives for people who want to invest capital in new companies

How will these measures help provide a healthy business environment and help businesses become more competitive?

CHAPTER SUMMARY

- The Government sometimes intervenes in markets in an attempt to reduce some of the negative aspects of competition on stakeholders.

- In some areas such as health and education government intervention has taken place to encourage competition and the creation of markets where they previously did not exist.

- The Government has introduced a significant amount of legislation to protect consumers. This has helped to improve the quality of goods and services and the level of customer care but has also contributed to an increase in business costs.

- The privatisation of many former state-owned utilities such as gas and electricity has led to the creation of a number of new monopolies. To ensure that these businesses do not exploit consumers, the Government has created a number of regulatory bodies whose role is to monitor their activities and to limit price rises.

- The Competition Commission, set up by the Competition Act, is responsible for monitoring the activities of businesses throughout the UK to ensure that their behaviour is not anti-competitive. Business activities that are regarded as anti-competitive are defined in the Competition Act. Businesses that are found to be breaking the Act can receive substantial fines.

- In the drive to become more efficient and to cut costs businesses may not always act in the best interests of their workers. Employees are protected by UK and European legislation, some of which derives from the Social Chapter.

- Another possible undesirable consequence of business activity is the damage caused from pollution. The environment is protected by both UK and European legislation. Environmental pressure groups are a powerful stakeholder lobby in this area and their influence is significant.

- A key responsibility of government is to help create an environment in which businesses can flourish. The characteristics of this environment are: low inflation, high employment, a stable exchange rate and economic growth.

- The Government aims to create a healthy business environment through a mixture of fiscal and monetary policy. Fiscal policy is concerned with the level of government spending and taxation while monetary policy deals with the supply of money and the level of interest rates.

- The Government's policy is to achieve economic growth through a long-term combination of sound fiscal and monetary policy.

KEY TERMS

stakeholders	a person, organisation, interest group or other body which has an interest in a business
privatisation	the process whereby previously state-owned and state-controlled businesses were returned to private ownership
internal markets	artificial markets created in the public sector and designed to enable managers to gain a better understanding of the cost of the activities under their direction
consumer legislation	laws created to protect consumers from the unfair practices and sub-standard goods and services
regulatory bodies	bodies created by the Government to monitor and report on the activities of businesses, especially the utilities such as gas, water and electricity
Competition Commission	the body responsible for policing anti-competitive business practices
Competition Act	legislation that defines business practices that restrict, reduce or distort competition between businesses
Social Chapter	the part of the Maastricht Treaty which lays down the principles for the conditions of the employment of workers for countries which are members of the EU
fiscal policy	changes in the level of government income (taxation) and expenditure through the control of demand
monetary policy	changes in the total supply of money and level of interest rates in the economy
supply-side policies	policies designed to encourage individuals and businesses to be more productive

What is marketing?

introduction

This chapter explains what marketing is, and discusses some of the principles involved. It outlines the main marketing activities, and offers suggestions as to how they fit together. It suggests a possible departmental (functional) break down for these activities. It also shows the importance of developing and maintaining a good relationship with customers and other stakeholders.

what you will learn from this chapter

- The theory of marketing puts forward a variety of marketing principles. These principles affect the type and substance of the marketing activities undertaken by an organisation and its management.

- All successful organisations accept the need for a strong customer focus. You will note how all definitions of marketing emphasise the importance of the customer to the organisation.

- The needs of organisations will be fulfilled only if they are truly marketing orientated – ie finding out what customers want and delivering a product or service that satisfies those wants.

- An organisation must have a clear set of marketing objectives, and they must be understood by the entire workforce.

- The future of marketing and marketing activities are tied to changes in the marketplaces of the world. These are increasingly technology based, and the speed of change is gathering pace.

- Regardless of these changes, the marketing principles hold firm.

marketing definitions

At this stage you will find it useful to examine the different definitions of the term 'marketing' so that you can identify the common factors.

> 'Marketing is the management process responsible for identifying, anticipating and satisfying customer requirements profitably.' (Chartered Institute of Marketing)

> 'Marketing is a total approach to business that puts the customer at the centre of things.' (Channel 4 and Yorkshire TV's 'The Marketing Mix')

> 'Marketing is selling goods that don't come back, to people who do.' (Baker)

Have you got the message? By now you should be appreciating that organisations do not make products which they then try to sell to customers, but that they research what customers want and then try to make and market a range of those wants. This is the crucial difference between:

- product orientation – putting the product first, and
- market orientation – putting the customer first

Marketing really is about 'getting the right product to the right people at the right price and at the right time.'

marketing principles

There are many priorities within an organisation, but if it is truly marketing orientated, many of the following principles will be high on its agenda. The diagram on page 217 organises the principles that you will have to investigate, plus a few others, into categories. These principles will be explained here, and then developed more fully in later chapters.

customer satisfaction

Market research must establish whether customers' expectations are satisfied by current products or services.

customer perception

What images do customers have of the organisation and its products? Do they perceive value for money, product quality, fashion, reliability etc? Do they themselves feel valued? How do they see the situation? Recent thinking in the Marketing Journal has suggested that 'perception is now marketing's most important 'p'. Certainly over the past few years there has a been a move toward socially conscious communication, environmental awareness, and an acknowledgement of stakeholder, rather than shareholder, value.'

customer needs and expectations

Anticipating the future and forecasting tomorrow's customer needs and expectations is the task of marketing research. This is vital to all organisations.

generating income or profit

This principle clearly states that the need of the organisation is either:

- to be profitable – to generate income for growth and to satisfy shareholders/stakeholders, or
- to generate as much income as possible eg. like a charity

satisfactory growth

This can be achieved by entering new markets or creating new products or both. See the discussion of the theorist Ansoff – page 278. Growth can also occur by expanding in existing markets, or linking with other organisations – mergers, takeovers, joint ventures etc.

coordinating marketing activities

Having a clear plan of action is essential for an organisation, as it is for you when you come to demonstrate your understanding of this unit in your portfolio. Be aware of SWOT analyses – page 257, the Marketing Mix – page 258, the Boston Matrix – page 275, and Ansoff – page 278. The whole emphasis of the planning process is for the organisation to 'think customer' and 'think marketing'.

awareness of change

The PEST analysis examines changes in a marketplace caused by Political, Economic, Social and Technological factors. See page 279. Technology will have a massive impact on all businesses. The Internet is here to stay, as are other interactive ways of doing business. See pages 319 to 320. Any organisation unaware of what is going on in the business world will risk being outmanoeuvred.

awareness of legal constraints

Changes in the law will add to the uncertainties listed above. Statute Laws like the Consumer Protection law, and voluntary agreements like the monitoring of advertising by the Advertising Standards Authority, all require organisations to understand their obligations. See pages 280 to 283. Note that with L for Legal added, the acronym 'PEST' can be rearranged to become the more up-to-date 'SLEPT'. Some have moved on to 'STEEPLE', (adding environment, education).

analysis of the competition

Clearly understanding who the competition are and what benefits they are offering is essential for an organisation. Marketing Research has this role to play as well. What is sometimes less obvious is what the word 'competition' actually means. In its broadest sense, every product competes with every other for the limited resources in your pocket. More specifically, it could be any product satisfying the same customer need.

Note how all the principles we have explained can be arranged into three categories:

- needs of the customer
- needs of the organisation
- influence of the market

Activity 10.1

Marketing basics

The mighty crash when they forget marketing basics

Why does it seem that commercial disaster must strike before great brands can rediscover their marketing strengths?

British Airways, whose recent financial performance has looked more like a nose dive than a gradual descent, is now proffering better branding, communications, relationship marketing and improved service as its solution. The announcement accompanied a disasterous set of trading results in May. It was depressingly close in circumstance and tone to that of another great British brand gone bad: Marks and Spencer.

Both have lost share to smaller rivals that have been quick to take advantage of complacency, both have had to shed jobs when their product is already below par and both are now belatedly reaffirming their commitment to customer needs. M&S is now embracing advertising and is close to appointing a board-level marketing director to reverse its fortunes; the born-again BA has identified its service failures and is now acting to halt the drift of high-value customers to rivals such as Virgin Atlantic.

It is vindication of the marketing-led message, but did it have to happen the hard way?

Source: *Marketing*, 26 August 1999

Read the article shown above.

1 What marketing basics (principles) does the article suggest that BA and Marks & Spencer have forgotten?

2 Collect evidence from the media to show how these firms are tackling or have tackled their problems since the article was written.

marketing functions

Now that we have identified marketing principles (the theory that underlies marketing) we can turn to see how marketing works in practice – its functions, ie what it 'does' in an organisation. This involves looking at

• the type of marketing activities involved

• a possible marketing departmental structure

marketing activities

To consolidate your thoughts on what marketing is, study carefully the many activities of marketing in the diagram below. The marketing process is continuous. Many or all of these activities are occurring at the same time, especially where a product or service already exists. Remember that this process applies equally to the marketing of a manufactured product, and also to a service which is supplied. Note that the diagram is called the 'marketing cycle' because it shows a circular flow of activities in a clockwise direction.

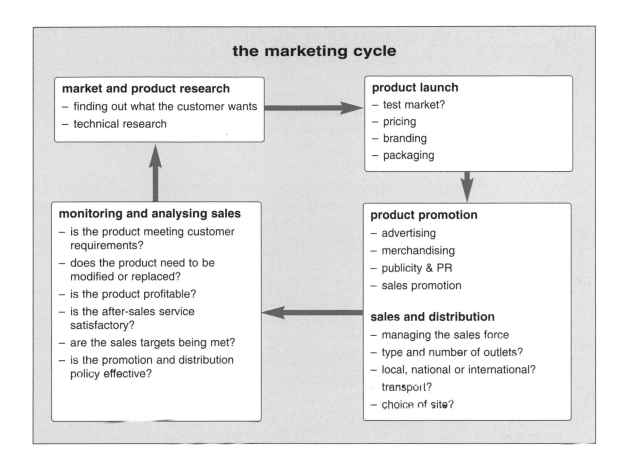

the marketing cycle

market and product research
- finding out what the customer wants
- technical research

product launch
- test market?
- pricing
- branding
- packaging

monitoring and analysing sales
- is the product meeting customer requirements?
- does the product need to be modified or replaced?
- is the product profitable?
- is the after-sales service satisfactory?
- are the sales targets being met?
- is the promotion and distribution policy effective?

product promotion
- advertising
- merchandising
- publicity & PR
- sales promotion

sales and distribution
- managing the sales force
- type and number of outlets?
- local, national or international?
- transport?
- choice of site?

Activity 10.2

identifying marketing activities and functions

Study the diagram shown above and identify on it the marketing activities and functions related to one particular product with which you are familiar, or which you have investigated, for example

- your Young Enterprise or mini-business product (if you are taking part in such a scheme)

- an evening course arranged by a Further Education college

- a new high-profile product being launched nationally, eg a new car, a chocolate bar

Draw up a flow diagram illustrating the marketing cycle for the product you have investigated. Write down notes for each stage, explaining the activities, eg 'advertising on TV', 'sold nationally through shops' . . . and so on.

the organisation of marketing

The way marketing activities are organised in a business will depend on the size of the business. A sole trader is most likely to do all the marketing himself or herself. This can sometimes be the cause of business failure – how often have you seen someone start a shop, for example, because they like the product they sell, rather than see a customer need for it. So often small shops only last a short while because the sole trader sees the business as product orientated rather than customer orientated.

A larger organisation – a limited company, for example – is likely to have a marketing department to plan and carry out marketing activities. Marketing departments can be organised in a variety of ways. A typical function orientated organisation is one which breaks down its activities as in the layout below.

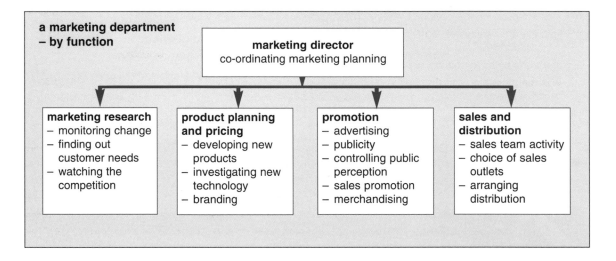

a marketing department – by function

marketing director
co-ordinating marketing planning

marketing research
– monitoring change
– finding out customer needs
– watching the competition

product planning and pricing
– developing new products
– investigating new technology
– branding

promotion
– advertising
– publicity
– controlling public perception
– sales promotion
– merchandising

sales and distribution
– sales team activity
– choice of sales outlets
– arranging distribution

customer focus and organisational needs

We will soon look in practical terms at how an organisation plans and carries out its marketing activities. Before it can plan, however, a business must have objectives – what it aims to achieve.

The marketing objectives of an organisation will be focused in two areas:

- what the customer needs
- what the organisation needs

Many businesses are now stressing what is known as a 'customer focus' – all activities are based on providing the customer with the right product at the right price at the right time in the right place. You should note carefully the following definitions:

product/production orientation

This describes the situation in many organisations when the economy is booming and sales are strong. There is a tendency to be inward looking, focusing management efforts on production capacity and technical research. Customer needs take a back seat. This may be acceptable in the short term but it must *not* detract from the need to maintain high customer service levels, nor limit the amount of marketing research undertaken into future needs. Today's strong demand may be gone by tomorrow.

market/marketing orientation

This describes outward looking organisations that focus on customer needs and satisfactions by planning along the lines of the marketing mix. They can still satisfy their own objectives (see below) but they forget customer satisfaction at their peril. Problems can arise from this philosophy within organisations because the various department managers have different priorities, such as:

productivity – the amount of production achieved per worker

If marketing department ask for variations to products to please consumers, the production process will be slowed down and productivity lowered.

profitability

If the cost of providing a product rises through meeting all the needs of the consumer, the profit level will fall.

accountability

The organisation is accountable to the customer through the law and other constraints (see page 282). These factors may detract from business profit.

marketing objectives

An organisation will set itself one or more objectives, to establish its position in the market place. These could include:

- maximising sales to dominate the market using all available outlets
- being the technical leader in its field
- being a leader in environmentally friendly products
- dominating a sector (niche) of the market
- maximising profits
- maintaining a good relationship with actual and potential customers and other stakeholders ie suppliers, shareholders and employees

All of these would be difficult to achieve at the same time and you can appreciate that some of these objectives will clash. For example, it would be hard to combine profit maximisation whilst concentrating on environmental matters (though see 'cause related marketing' on page 299). Nevertheless, the majority of organisations realise that whichever objectives are chosen, a high level of customer focus is important to attract customers and ensure that they keep coming back.

The American Adventure Theme Park, for example, has a mission statement that conveys a basic proposal to the marketplace as to how the business intends to trade and what can reasonably be expected. It is aspirational in setting high standards for all employees to buy into and to attempt to deliver. The proposal is:

> The American Adventure will entertain a family audience in a fun, exciting and challenging way with high quality rides, shows and attractions; will deliver excellent customer service and will remain accessible, affordable and free from unacceptably long queues.

Activity 10.3

Marketing objectives – customer focus

Identify a local business with which you are familiar, eg a shop, means of transport, leisure centre.

Make a list of marketing objectives which you think is appropriate to this business – particularly in terms of its customer focus – and draft a mission statement in the style of the American Adventure quoted above. Do you consider the business is achieving these objectives?

the future for marketing

Each year the research firm Richmond Events organises a Marketing Forum for nearly 1,000 top marketing people. In the mid-nineties their verdict on 'key marketing issues for the future' stressed consumer behaviour patterns, IT communications development, product development and business to business relationships.

More recently the Marketing Forum has had a running theme, the e-commerce revolution. This does not mean that consumer behaviour patterns have lost importance. It is the very fact that today's consumers are turning to the internet and other ways of doing business that has forced this change of emphasis in marketing. The consumer still leads!

The Marketing Society is an organisation which was set up to enable top marketeers to discuss key issues affecting their profession. The results of a survey of delegates attending a recent conference asked their views of the future. The survey, undertaken by brand consultancy Headlight Vision, identified key areas of concern and provided the following quotes (reproduced from 'Marketing', 18 November 1999):

change

'An organisation's ability to learn and translate that learning into action rapidly is the ultimate competitive advantage.'

stakeholders

'The evidence of research suggests that there is a place for principles and profit.'

consumer watchdogs

'Despite billions of pounds being spent on 'consumer services' by businesses in the past few years, one in two of us complained about products or services bought last year.'

customer involvement in the product

'Toyota encourages customers to design cars using their computer aided design. Not only are the consumers' dreams met, but the results are analysed and impact on future design.'

Activity 10.4

The future of marketing

Collect examples and discuss in class the following areas (or any other areas) which are affecting the way marketing is being carried out.

1   e-commerce

2   rapid change in market conditions (eg in technology)

3   consumer pressure on principles and products (eg organic foods)

4   consumer awareness of quality and consumer rights

5   areas where the consumer is able to play a part in the design of a product

CHAPTER SUMMARY

● The emphasis in marketing definitions is on 'customer focus' and 'marketing orientation'. This means putting the customer at the centre of the organisation's planning.

● The principles of marketing cover the needs of the consumer, the needs of the organisation and the observation of change in the marketplace.

● The marketing cycle diagram suggests a certain order of activities when designing and launching a new product. With existing products, all of these activities are happening at the same time.

● Marketing departments are organised on a functional basis, ie splitting the activities between a number of section managers. The actual structure chosen will differ between firms, according to their individual priorities.

● Marketing objectives must be clear, achievable and understood by all staff, so that everyone is pulling in the same direction.

● The future of marketing lies in technology, but this does not mean that the basic principles will change – only that they will be followed using new techniques.

KEY TERMS

marketing principles   the ideas which the marketing team in an organisation tries to put into practice

marketing activities   the individual areas of activity such as advertising, selling, pricing

marketing functions   the division of marketing activities into manageable sections, for example a market research section

marketing orientation   making sure that all personnel keep the customer in mind

customer focus   the concept of providing the customer with the right product at the right price at the right time and in the right place

customer perception   what the customer thinks of your products and the whole organisation

marketing objectives   how the organisation wishes to position itself in the market place and what it wants to achieve

stakeholders   an organisation's shareholders and employees directly; its suppliers and customers indirectly

the Marketing Society   the organisation that represents the interests of marketing personnel throughout the UK

11 Establishing customer needs

Unit 3 Marketing
Establishing customer needs

introduction

A business has to understand the needs of its customers and be aware of the activities of its competitors before it can develop its marketing strategy. This chapter looks at how organisations rely on marketing research activities to make sound decisions for the future. It examines a variety of research techniques, pointing out some advantages and disadvantages in their use.

what you will learn from this chapter

- the terminology of marketing research and its meaning

- the contribution made by good marketing research information to marketing decision making

- how 'desk' research will provide background information about the market, using existing published data

- how 'field' research may be needed to provide specific and more up to date and new information

- how to select and apply the most appropriate field research methods; the accuracy of the research will depend upon the suitability of the techniques used

- how market segmentation is the key to choosing the right customers to research, in both consumer and industrial research

- how research analyses customer attitude and behaviour towards new and existing products in the market place

- how the construction of databases relies on both desk and field research, and how these databases then make possible further research into lifestyles and buying habits

- it is vital to forecast future demand accurately

the language & methods of marketing research

'marketing' research

We often use the term 'marketing research' rather than 'market research'. Why? 'Marketing research' means not just the various estimates of market size and location and consumer attitudes; it also means research into all of an organisation's marketing activities, such as pricing, advertising, selling and distribution policies. An organisation must do what the market wants.

We will now outline the main terminology of marketing research.

secondary research and primary research

Secondary (Desk) Research is the gathering and analysis of already available information. This is a natural starting point because it is quicker and cheaper, and commercial organisations are always keen to save time and money. The problem is that information already available is already partly out of date. It may not be precisely what is required, either. Always check its collection date and relevance.

Primary (Field or Original) Research is the gathering of fresh information, specifically tailored to the business' own requirements. The problem here is the expense of the survey. Syndicated research is one answer: here the information seekers join together to conduct the research. Alternatively, established research agencies may undertake research and sell their findings to interested organisations.

Field and Desk Research are the most important classifications of marketing research, and the methods of carrying out the research will be covered in greater detail later in the chapter. Other classifications are shown below.

quantitative and qualitative research

Quantitative Research collects numbers: the number of items bought, the price paid, the number of outlets stocking the product, and so on. In such numeric form the information is easy to collect and analyse, often by computer.

Qualitative Research examines opinions. As such it is the growth area of research, as consumer opinions are sought by product and service providers, politicians, town planners and virtually every organisation that exists. The key problem is that of information collation. Open ended questions collecting chatty responses tend to confuse, not assist, the opinion seekers. Therefore opinion research is usually quantified. For the techniques used, see the section on questionnaire construction later in this chapter.

industrial and consumer research

Industrial Research studies data about industrial goods and services: items sold to the trade, not to the private individual. 'Industrial' involves one organisation finding out about other organisations, eg suppliers, retailers and so on.

Consumer Research investigates the end users of consumer goods and services. It looks at the market as a whole but may also divide the general public into different categories (segments); it may assess quantities bought and consumer opinions. It can, in addition, give valuable insight to organisations about competitor activity, eg. market share, distribution patterns and so on.

ad hoc, continuous and omnibus research

Ad hoc means 'one off', a piece of research conducted for a specific 'once only' decision eg the council asking if the public want a bypass to their town.

Continuous means that the same questions are asked at regular time intervals, of the same make up of sample of respondents, to gain an insight into changing trends ie of products bought, views held etc. For instance, market size and market share data is monitored, to become the information used in a Boston matrix analysis. See page 275, and the Nielsen data on page 248. Even the largest organisations use agencies of this type for trend analysis.

Omnibus surveys tend to carry a mix of questions on different subjects from different organisations, usually because the number of questions on any particular topic is small. The J. Walter Thompson survey described on page xx was partly researched by putting a few questions on to a questionnaire carried out by another research firm.

We will now look at the practicalities of desk research and field research.

desk research

Desk research is an essential starting point for any research work: if information is available already, it saves time and money. What a new organisation must do, even before it is set up, is to evaluate all relevant data about the market, from whatever source. Desk research combines:

- an examination of your own organisation's internal records, if you are in business already

- a study of external publications, compiled by experts in various fields

sources of internal data

Much data is available within an organisation which is already trading, for example:

- records of sales to customers: the number of items, frequency, how the goods were purchased (eg whether by mail order or through shops)

- accounts: the sales figures, costing and profit figures for individual items

- regional sales trends

- an analysis of the types of customer

- the life cycle of individual items (how long they stay on the market)

- previous market research

From this data the organisation should be able to assess present trends, and have a starting point for predictions into the future.

sources of market data – external to the firm

Government publications

Government agencies, The Stationery Office and The Office for National Statistics, are important sources of data. These provide statistical publications, including Social Trends, Economic Trends, Annual Abstract of Statistics, Monthly Digest of Statistics, Business Monitor, Family Spending, National Food Survey, Censuses of Production, Population and Distribution, Departmental Journals, National Income Statistics, Import and Export Statistics etc, but the cost is rising. Try your town library if your college cannot stay up to date. The available data is listed on The Stationery Office's website www.tso–online.co.uk

Commercial Organisations, Trade Associations and Professional Bodies

Much useful information can be gathered from organisations and societies which cater for the needs of businesses and particular trades and professions. These include the Confederation of British Industry (CBI), Chambers of Commerce – local and national, Business Clubs – local, the British Institute of Management, the Chartered Institute of Marketing, and Trade Associations. The latter are listed in 'Trade Associations and Professional Bodies of the UK'. There will be a Trade Association relevant to your area of enquiry, but information may cost you.

other useful sources

- Trade journals – for a full list of what exists, consult Willing's Press Guide in any reference library. These are the best up to date sources about each and every industry or trade.

- Directories – first consult the 'Current British Directories' publication to see what exists; other key directories are Kompass, Kelly's and Sells, three excellent publications on products and organisations.

- Banks publish Economic Surveys, Industry Surveys and Country Surveys, but they may only help customers.

- Newspapers – most libraries have subject indices on CD, a very useful research resource. Just feed in your 'key' words.

- The Internet – so many organisations have their own website, each offering selected information about itself and its products.

- Universities and Business Schools regularly undertake research and publish their findings.

- Market Research organisations that undertake surveys of chosen industries on a regular basis – always find out whether Mintel (Market Intelligence), Keynote or Market Research Great Britain have published recently on the required subject; try the library.

- Overseas Information: Government Import and Export Statistics, International Marketing Data and Statistics, OECD publications, banks' Country Surveys

research method

The list of information sources set out above may seem daunting, but it must be stressed that if you are undertaking desk research you will be very selective as to what you read. Desk research of this type may well form part of your project work in Business Studies, if for example you are studying a particular company or industry. It is a good idea before going to your reference library (your school/college library or a city centre public library) to make a list of the key areas you are researching, and check them with your teacher/lecturer. These details will comprise names and terms relating to your project, eg the names of the industry, the companies, the products and so on. You can then consult the index in the library and approach the reference librarian with your list. It is possible that the library has a computer index system and CD Roms which will then highlight the sources you need to consult. Always ask.

One word of warning! Past data is past! Do not assume that an identified trend will continue indefinitely. This is where 'field' research picks up the investigation.

Activity 11.1

Desk research

Look at the information about desk research on the previous pages and visit a reference library. List the sources of information which would be useful if you were conducting desk research into:

1   holidays for the over 50s
2   soft drinks in the UK
3   exporting music CDs to Europe and Japan

field research

As we saw at the beginning of the chapter, the most valuable method of market research is the collection of primary or original data out in the marketplace, ie field research. It is this area of investigation that the 'person in the street' normally identifies with market research.

Field research consists of several stages:

1   clarify the objectives of the research
2   choose a suitable data collection (market research) method
3   construct a questionnaire, if one is thought necessary
4   decide on the sampling techniques (the methods of choosing the people to be surveyed)
5   carry out a sample survey to test the questionnaire
6   brief the interviewers for the main survey
7   collect the data in the field
8   collate, analyse and interpret the data
9   present your findings, with forecasts if required

clarify the objectives of the research

Always ensure that you establish exactly what it is that the person who commissions the research needs to find out. They can all too easily ask for the wrong things and if this happens you will get the blame later. Talk it through! If you are undertaking school or college project work, this means discussing it with your teacher or lecturer.

choosing a data collection method

surveys

These are the core of fieldwork. Using a variety of techniques, questions are put to, or observations made of, a selected sample from the target group. The techniques are discussed below, but first note the following definitions:

population   the total market, or market segment, under review. This may involve people, or businesses, or products eg the UK car or confectionery markets, or services from the banking sector and so on. Nowadays, details of the population relevant to an organisation are likely to be kept on database, either of its own creation, or one bought in from a specialist provider.

sample   a selection taken, randomly or otherwise, from the market being investigated.

respondent   the person/business/product user who answers the questions in a particular survey.

observation

The simplest method, ie merely recording numbers and events, like counting cars passing a certain spot, or noting the 'walk past rate' when assessing the potential of a retail site. The filming of customer behaviour at the point of sale eg eye levels, body language, is increasing. The information recording system and the categories used must be carefully planned beforehand. All researchers understand the phrase 'rubbish in, rubbish out.' It means that if your techniques are faulty, so will be your ultimate recommendations or forecasts. (This applies to all data collection methods.)

telephone research

Telephoning the respondent is one of the fastest methods. It is very useful for industrial research, with firms well scattered; it is intrusive and effective, but the number of questions asked must be kept short. It has become increasingly popular in consumer research, with specialist agencies offering this service to clients. The research tends to be in the evenings/at weekends to catch the respondents in, and to make use of the cheaper telephone rates.

postal research

Questionnaires are sent to respondents, fairly cheaply, and a large geographical area can be covered. Costs increase when reply paid envelopes have to be included, or when reminders and gifts are used to persuade people to respond. It has become very popular to offer 'entry into a competition' as the incentive to respond. Something is necessary because response rates are usually low (20% in consumer research, perhaps 40% with reminders).

Another drawback is that the sample gained may be unrepresentative – it may be comprised only of people interested in the subject, or those with a complaint to register.

face-to-face interviews

The personal interview is usually the best research method. Interviews can be:

Street interviews, which are fast and the results quickly analysed, but the questions must be simple (no time for thought) and their number limited. A quota sample can be taken quickly as 'non-responses' can be rectified immediately. Queries regarding questions can be dealt with.

Home or office interviews, which can take more time to achieve but will reward by gaining more considered answers. More detailed questions can be set, and the number of questions increased. Explanations can cover areas of doubt. The drawbacks include the added cost of making the visits, and the time spent finding the chosen target group.

'In hall'/customer acceptance tests, which give the consumer the opportunity to express opinions on existing or new products by examining them. An extension to the street interview, the consumer is invited into a hall or shop to give a more considered viewpoint. Often a cup of tea or other gift is offered!

Product acceptance tests, which ask existing customers their opinion on the products they have bought, after a period of use.

Focus groups/group research, which are invaluable in gaining qualitative information, especially leading up to the creation of a questionnaire, or the initial trials of a new product concept. Groups are chosen from people who fit the required categorisations ie age, sex, social background etc, and the interview is 'focused' on a particular topic area. The interview may be structured, with specific questions asked, or unstructured, with the group allowed to talk generally around the topic. Discussions are usually taped, for later analysis. The drawback is the unreliability of the small sample size.

panel research

This consists of a carefully selected number – a panel – of respondents, usually working separately. Consumer panels can be discussion groups, but normally panel members just record their individual purchases, as part of a large sample of the population, either in diary form or more recently using electronic recording of purchases using a bar code scanner. With records being kept by the same people over long periods of time, trends in consumption can be monitored for individual brands and whole markets. The problem is the 'drop out' rate as panel members get bored. Elaborate prize incentives try to reverse this.

field trials and test marketing

This involves research into the acceptability of new products, or product variations, usually in small geographical areas of the market. Such pilot projects enable any aspect of the product to be tested, but the key factors usually are product acceptability and price. More than one location or area will be used, with slight variations in the factor being assessed. A test market must be allowed to run long enough to establish whether repeat purchases are made. Many people will try a new product, but only those satisfied with it will buy again.

using telecommunications and technology

Telecommunications and technological developments in marketing research have been made possible by great advances in computer technology. This has led to the creation of databases of customers, market segments, age groups making sampling, ie talking to the right people, much more accurate. Also, it has enabled a greater quantity of information to be handled, leading to an improvement in the quality of marketing decisions.

The information itself is often gathered electronically.

Electronic interviewing relates to the use of interactive systems with a telecommunications network. Questions can be asked of respondents who subscribe to the telephone and television networks. The technique offers high speed responses, and the arrival of digital TV and interactive mobile phones will see rapid development in this area.

Electronic gathering and transmission of data is becoming commonplace with the use of lap top computers at interviews. Answers are recorded by the interviewer on the computer and the information downloaded at the end of the day to a central computer for instant analysis.

Electronic data processing refers to the automatic 'reading' of completed questionnaires by the computer which scans the boxes on the response sheets. This technique cuts out 'input error'.

Electronic point of sale (EPOS) data enables trends in sales within an outlet to be noted and acted upon. Most shops use these for stock control, but also for instant research information for forecasting purposes. Your 'loyalty' card links your purchases to your personal data, collected when you applied for the card. These and other techniques create databases, which if compiled correctly and kept up to date, lead to a much better understanding of an organisation's customer base. See page 246.

the suitability of research techniques

You can appreciate that all of the above techniques are useful under the right conditions. The choice between the research methods depends on the importance of the following factors:

Total cost involved	Personal interviews can be costly.
Total time available	Research often has tight deadlines.
Validity	Do we know who exactly filled in that questionnaire addressed to the managing director?
Reliability	Did the respondent have enough time for a considered answer?
Accessibility	Who are the intended respondents? Are they local, national or international?
Fitness for purpose	Is the sample taken large enough? Is it representative of the population under review?
Number of questions to be asked	These must be limited in the street or on the phone.
Number of personal questions	Would the presence of an interviewer embarrass the respondent?
Degree of explanation needed	Will an interviewer be needed to explain a questionnaire?
Products to be examined?	An interviewer may be needed.

Activity 11.2

Field research

Suggest a best and second-best method of data collection for the following research needs:

1   opinions on new packaging styles – few questions, quick results

2   opinions from industrialists nationwide – detailed answers, no time constraints

3   political survey – a large number of interviewees with a balance between age groups and sexes, in a local area, today!

4   views on a technical subject – businesses to be questioned, London area, many questions

5   instant opinion of the general public on two topical issues for the local paper

6   facts from business people nationally, for a region by region analysis, requiring some confidential information

7   national survey into sex and alcohol related topics, full questionnaire, the general public

In each case use the list of possible data collection methods set out on the previous pages.

constructing a questionnaire

We will now spend time looking at the construction of a questionnaire that can be used in market research. This will be a useful exercise because your Assignment for your Marketing Unit can also incorporate a questionnaire for carrying out market research.

A questionnaire comprises a list of questions which can provide data including:

• factual information

• opinions

• value judgements

The size of the questionnaire will depend on the type of interview used, whether it is postal, face-to-face, or telephoned. The principles of questionnaire construction will, however, remain the same. In essence, it is a 'garbage in, garbage out' situation – the quality of the answers and information gathered will reflect the quality of the questions asked. An example of a self completion questionnaire is illustrated on pages 238 to 240.

structure of the questionnaire

• Tell the respondent who you are and ask for his or her co-operation. Explain the purpose of the survey. Sometimes an incentive (eg an entry into a free draw) may be given to the respondent.

• Keep the questionnaire as short as possible, especially when interviewing in the street or on the telephone. There is always the danger that the respondent will walk away (or put the telephone down).

• Thank the respondent for his or her time and in the case of a street interview record the name and address so that the validity of the interview can be checked out.

construction of the questionnaire

• Include 'Instructions to the interviewer or respondent', eg 'tick the relevant boxes' so that answers are recorded accurately and consistently. This is particularly important if the questionnaire is to be sent through the post.

• The layout and style of the questions asked are of paramount importance.

• Plan a logical sequence so that easy, confidence building questions come first, and the respondent can begin to take an interest.

- Record only as many personal details as are essential for your analysis. If details like 'salary' are required, try leaving this until last and give 'ranges' for their answers. Remember, personal details being asked for can result in the interview being terminated, so take care. If ages are required, give a range and ask them to indicate the relevant one. Common age classes are: under 16, 16 – 24, 25 – 40, 41 – 60, over 60, but you must decide which are relevant. Note, no overlap.

- Try to keep the boxes which record the response over to the right. This allows for easy analysis, although the modern trend is for electronic reading (monitoring) of the completed questionnaires, so this point is not now so important.

- Boxes may be coded (ie given letters or numbers) for easy and rapid analysis after the interview. An analyst records only those box numbers where a mark has been inserted. Again, electronic reading has lessened this need. (Look at the example questions on this and the next page, but then at the specimen questionnaire.)

designing questions

- Keep the language simple.

- Avoid biased or 'loaded' questions.

- Questions should not be leading, ambiguous, too personal or misleading.

- Open ended questions – asking for opinions and comments – should be limited, as they are difficult to record. They are, however, a useful source of qualitative data.

- Use closed questions, to which the answer is a clear 'yes' or 'no'.

- Create questions of a multi-choice nature, giving a good selection of responses without confusing the respondent. These can be factual multiple choice, as shown below.

4.	In what type of accommodation do you live?			
	(tick the relevant box)			
	(a)	lodgings/bedsit	❑	15
	(b)	flat	❑	16
	(c)	terrace/semi-detached house	❑	17
	(d)	detached house	❑	18

- Create questions of a multi-choice nature, even when asking for opinions. A common technique is to use the Likert scale which sets out a range of responses, as in the example below:

5.	The local library is efficient. Do you …	
	(tick the relevant box)	
	(a) agree strongly	☐ 19
	(b) agree	☐ 20
	(c) neither agree nor disagree	☐ 21
	(d) disagree	☐ 22
	(e) disagree strongly	☐ 23

Again, variations occur. The Thomsons market researchers (see below) chose four rather than five responses, and are happy with the results.

This technique is thought to eliminate the middle (neutral) response. They will remain with this format for continuity of analysis.

Now study the questionnaire from Thomson holidays on the next three pages.

Customer Satisfaction Questionnaire

THOMSON

Please ☒ the appropriate box, or write in as requested.

1. Your details

Title   First name   Other initials

Surname

Address

Postcode   Date of birth
/ /
Day Month Year

Today's date   Daytime telephone number
/ /

2. Your holiday details

A Which holiday company are you with?

Thomson .... ☐   Portland Direct .... ☐
Skytours .... ☐
Other ☐ ➡ write in

B The name of your hotel(s)/villa/apartments
(name all accommodation stayed in)

C The name of your resort (s) or the name of your tour/safari/cruise

D Board arrangements:

Bed and breakfast ...... ☐   Self catering .... ☐
Full board .... ☐   Half Board .... ☐
Room only .... ☐
Flexible dining   ☐   All Inclusive   ☐
(combining B/B & H/B)   (all meals, drinks etc. included)

E Number of nights abroad:

6 or less ☐   8 - 13 ☐   15 - 20 ☐
7 ☐   14 ☐   21 or more ☐

F If accommodation not included in your holiday price, was this:

Airfare/flight only ...... ☐   Flydrive .... ☐
(flight & car rental only)

2. Your holiday details cont.

G If accommodation not specified until you arrived in resort, was this a:

Late deal .... ☐   Price Breakers .... ☐

H I am travelling (indicate all that apply):

Alone .... ☐   With other adult(s) of same sex .... ☐

With spouse/partner .... ☐

With other adult(s) of opposite sex .... ☐   With an organised group of 10 or more .... ☐

I Was this a Young at Heart or Magic Moments holiday?

Yes ☐ No ☐

J How many children in each of the following age groups are you travelling with?

	None	Number of children 1	2	3+
a) Under 4 years	☐	☐	☐	☐
b) 4 - 7 years	☐	☐	☐	☐
c) 8 - 12 years	☐	☐	☐	☐
d) 13 - 16 years	☐	☐	☐	☐

3. Flights

	Excellent	Good	Fair	Poor
A UK airport check-in	☐	☐	☐	☐
B Overseas airport check-in	☐	☐	☐	☐
C In-flight comfort	☐	☐	☐	☐
D In-flight food	☐	☐	☐	☐
E Cabin crew: service and assistance ...	☐	☐	☐	☐
F In-flight audio/visual entertainment ...	☐	☐	☐	☐

4. In-resort service

	Excellent	Good	Fair	Poor
A On arrival: assistance at overseas airport	☐	☐	☐	☐
B Transfer journey to and from your accommodation	☐	☐	☐	☐
C On departure: assistance at overseas airport	☐	☐	☐	☐
D Welcome Get-Together: presentation and content	☐	☐	☐	☐
E Excursions: choice	☐	☐	☐	☐
F Excursions: value for money	☐	☐	☐	☐
G Excursions: commentary and knowledge of guide	☐	☐	☐	☐

5. Your accommodation

Please give an average rating of all accommodation stayed in:

	Excellent	Good	Fair	Poor
A Representatives: service and assistance	☐	☐	☐	☐
B Location	☐	☐	☐	☐
C Reception service	☐	☐	☐	☐
D Bar service	☐	☐	☐	☐
E Cleanliness	☐	☐	☐	☐
F Public areas: furnishings and decor ...	☐	☐	☐	☐
G Bedroom comfort	☐	☐	☐	☐
H Food quality	☐	☐	☐	☐
I Waiter service/buffet efficiency	☐	☐	☐	☐
J Daytime activities and leisure facilities	☐	☐	☐	☐
K Evening entertainment	☐	☐	☐	☐
L Villa/Apartment kitchen equipment ...	☐	☐	☐	☐

6. Overall

Taking everything into account:

	Excellent	Good	Fair	Poor
A Flights	☐	☐	☐	☐
B Holiday weather	☐	☐	☐	☐
C Resort	☐	☐	☐	☐
D Accommodation	☐	☐	☐	☐
E Representatives	☐	☐	☐	☐
F Holiday overall	☐	☐	☐	☐
G Holiday company service in resort	☐	☐	☐	☐
H Holiday company overall	☐	☐	☐	☐
I Value for money	☐	☐	☐	☐

7. Other features

Did you yourself:

	Yes	No
A Go to the Welcome Get-Together	☐	☐
B Go on any Thomson company excursions	☐	☐
C Ask your Representative for any help or advice during your holiday	☐	☐

	Excellent	Good	Fair	Poor
D Children's facilities for 0-12 year olds ...	☐	☐	☐	☐
E Children's club for 4-7 year olds	☐	☐	☐	☐
F Children's club for 8-12 year olds	☐	☐	☐	☐
G Children's Representatives	☐	☐	☐	☐

8. Holiday experience

A How accurate was the brochure description of your:

	Excellent	Good	Fair	Poor
a) Accommodation	☐	☐	☐	☐
b) Resort	☐	☐	☐	☐

B Not counting this one, how many holidays abroad have you taken in the last 12 months?

	None taken	1	2	3+
a) With Thomson/Skytours	☐	☐	☐	☐
b) With Portland Direct	☐	☐	☐	☐
c) With other package holiday companies ...	☐	☐	☐	☐

C How likely are you to choose the same Thomson company for your next package holiday? (ie. Thomson, Skytours or Portland Direct)

Definitely .... ☐   Possibly .... ☐

Probably .... ☐   Not likely .... ☐

D With which company did you take your last package holiday abroad?

Thomson .... ☐   Sunset .... ☐
Skytours .... ☐   Sunworld .... ☐
First Choice .... ☐   Virgin .... ☐
Cosmos .... ☐   Inspirations ..... ☐
Unijet .... ☐   Kuoni .... ☐
Eclipse .... ☐   Airtours/Aspro ... ☐
Portland Direct ..... ☐   Direct holidays ... ☐
Other .... ☐

8. Holiday experience cont

E Where did you go for your last package holiday abroad?

Mainland Spain .... ☐   Greece (inc. islands) .... ☐
Majorca .... ☐   Minorca .... ☐
Florida .... ☐   Malta................ ☐
Portugal/Madeira ...... ☐   Morocco/Tunisia/Egypt.... ☐
Ibiza .... ☐   Cyprus.............. ☐
Caribbean .... ☐   Canary Islands .... ☐
Other (Europe) .... ☐   Other (Rest of the world) ... ☐

F Did you go on a Summer package holiday abroad between May and October 1999?

Yes ☐ No ☐

9. Car rental

A Did you rent a car for/during your holiday?

Yes ☐ No ☐

	Excellent	Good	Fair	Poor
B Car rental: value for money	☐	☐	☐	☐
C Car rental: overall	☐	☐	☐	☐

D Which car rental company did you use?

Thomson Car Rental .... ☐   Hertz .... ☐
Dollar .... ☐   Other company ... ☐

E Was the car:

Pre booked via Thomson, Skytours, Portland Direct in the UK ☐
Booked overseas via your Representative .... ☐
Pre-booked independently in the UK .... ☐
Booked independently overseas .... ☐

10. About you

A I am:

Male .... ☐   Female .... ☐

B I am:

Married .... ☐   Single .... ☐
Separated/widowed/divorced .... ☐   Living with partner ☐

C I am:

In full/part time employment .... ☐   A student .... ☐
A full time housewife ... ☐   Retired .... ☐
Self employed .... ☐   Otherwise not employed .... ☐

D If you are in employment, which best describes the type of job you do, or if retired, the last job you did?

Skilled trade/craft .... ☐
Plant and machine operator/driver etc. .... ☐
Foreman/supervisor. .... ☐
Manual worker/factory worker. .... ☐
Service worker (eg. shop assistant/cleaner/catering/caretaker/goods delivery etc) .... ☐
Clerical/secretarial/other office work .... ☐
Technical (eg. programmer/technician/nurse/representative) ☐
Junior management/junior professions/executive .... ☐
Senior and middle management/professions .... ☐
Other (write in) ☐

10. About you cont.

E Age:

Under 16 ☐	16 - 17 ☐
18 - 24 ☐	25 - 34 ☐
35 - 44 ☐	45 - 54 ☐
55 - 64 ☐	65 - 74 ☐
	75+ ☐

F Which Sunday newspaper(s) do you read?

Mail on Sunday ☐ News of the World ☐
Sunday Telegraph ☐ Sunday Mail (Scotland) ☐
Sunday Post (Scotland) ☐ Independent on Sunday ☐
The Observer ☐ Sunday Mirror ☐
The People ☐ Sunday Times ☐
Sunday Express ☐ None of these ☐

G Which of the following credit cards do you use regularly?

Visa (eg.Barclaycard) ☐ Mastercard (eg. Access) ☐
Diners Club ☐ American Express ☐
  Do not have a credit card ☐

H If unwell during your holiday, please specify:

Sunstroke/Sunburn ☐ Infection ☐
Stomach upset (lasting more than 24 hours) ☐ Other ☐

I Return flight number: Seat row   Letter

11. Any other comments and suggestions:

THOMSON

Win Thomson Holiday Vouchers worth £1500
by filling in this questionnaire

Rules: Draw to be made in November 2000. All entries received before 31st October will be included. Draw open to all holidaymakers over 18 who return a fully completed Thomson Customer Satisfaction Questionnaire. Prize not transferable, no cash alternative offered. Details of winner can be obtained by writing to the Market Research Department, at the address given at the end of this questionnaire.

We may from time to time contact you for market research purposes or with information on products and services offered by companies within the Thomson Travel Group plc. If you do not wish to receive details of these, please place a cross in this box. ☐ Thank you.

Thomson or Portland Direct, Customer Service, Greater London House, Hampstead Road, London NW1 7SD

J16000/W99/V1

the pilot survey

It is essential to carry out a pilot survey, to check if the questionnaire works properly. Test the order of questions, identify any ambiguities, ensure that all the areas of information needed are being produced. Re-write the questions if there is any misunderstanding. Keep testing and altering until the questionnaire runs smoothly. Better a few minutes checking than a disaster in the field. Remember, 'rubbish in, rubbish out.'

brief the interviewers (and train them if necessary)

Make sure they understand their areas of responsibility and the limits to which they can go with any prompts; eg the way to record answers like 'did you watch programme x?' if the answer is 'half of it'. Make them clear as to their sample requirements, ie how many interviews and with whom. Give them a time deadline.

a note on sampling techniques

Samples are taken from a population (ie the people or businesses being investigated) to give a 'reasonable' assessment of some value about that population. Accuracy depends upon the choice of sample type, how well it represents the population, and its size. Sampling can be random, and can be taken from a defined group known as a sampling frame. An example of a sampling frame is the Electoral Register, the list of people over 18 living in specific geographical areas. Quasi-random sampling involves the use of some control device over the selection of the items within the sample. Such samples can be:

systematic – taking, say, every tenth item from a list like a telephone directory – a process which gives a measure of 'randomness'

stratified – selecting specific people or businesses to make sure that all market segments are represented in the right proportion – a very precise method

quota – similar to stratified sampling, but interviewees are not specified; the interviewer may be told '10 men, 10 women' and will make the actual choice himself/herself – a very common street interview technique

multi-stage – dividing the country into regions, randomly selecting a few, then subdividing these into even smaller areas for analysis – this technique saves travel time and cost

problems with sampling

Sample errors arise from human error in questionnaire construction, eg failure to ask the right questions (missing the relevant point); asking ambiguous questions that respondents interpret in different ways; asking misleading questions that gather the wrong information. An error in sample size is either choosing one too small to give the required level of 'significance' or 'confidence' in the results, or one too large to be acceptable on a cost basis.

marketing research and marketing decisions

'Marketing research' means not just the various estimates of market size and location, but all research into the firm's marketing activities . . .

- It examines opinions as well as facts.
- It searches for new product ideas.
- It tests new products before the decision to launch.
- It examines the organisation's environment and the success (or otherwise) of its use of the marketing functions in dealing with that environment.
- It will find out whether a price change was successful; which outlets sell most goods; which adverts appeal, etc.
- It looks at product substitution – one product supplanting another in the market place.

In other words, marketing research provides the back-up data for decisions in all areas of the marketing mix.

analysing marketing research information

Research monitors change. Organisations need up to date information on trends. Businesses watch their sales figures, politicians watch opinion polls on voting intentions, non-profit (and all) organisations watch their image. Questions to be asked and answers to be analysed might include:

- Are sales rising or falling?
- Is market share being gained or lost?
- Is profitability being maintained?
- How do prices compare with the competition?
- Do prices fit the product's image in the customers' minds?

The latter point is very important. If the image of the product is portrayed as say 'up market', yet the price appears too low to justify that image, consumers are less likely to buy. 'It can't be any good at that price' is a comment often heard. It means that the organisation is not co-ordinating its marketing mix. Research thus is very important on a continuous basis. A number of market research agencies specialise in supplying market share information to their clients on a month by month, or even week by week basis. One such is A C Nielsen, who have kindly provided the following analysis of the UK Snacks Market. Other providers of different types of regular data on an industry basis are Mintel and Keynote. These two may be available in your library.

Osborne Books gratefully acknowledges A C Nielsen, who have asked that students should *not* approach them directly for actual data. Their general website address is www.acnielsen.com

UK Potato Chips Market

Total Value £M

Brands	52 weeks to 11.7.98	52 weeks to 10.7.99	month to 15.5.99	month to 12.6.99	month to 10.7.99
Golden Wonder	34.9	29.0	1.63	1.63	1.57
Kettle	18.1	20.1	1.72	1.75	1.77
Walkers	397.6	429.1	33.09	35.73	33.83
KP	27.8	28.3	1.96	2.96	2.37
Own Label	196.0	166.3	15.37	12.52	11.88
Other	30.0	31.0	2.25	2.50	3.68
Total	704.4	703.8	56.02	57.09	56.10

UK Potato Chips Market

Total Volume Kg (millions)

Brands	52 weeks to 11.7.98	52 weeks to 10.7.99	month to 15.5.99	month to 12.6.99	month to 10.7.99
Golden Wonder	5.85	6.06	0.31	0.29	0.27
Kettle	1.99	2.21	0.19	0.18	0.19
Walkers	60.92	66.29	4.93	5,67	5.60
KP	4.11	4.56	0.29	0.44	0.40
Own Label	47.37	37.22	3.40	2.80	2.64
Other	5.53	5.33	0.41	0.48	0.63
Total	125.77	121.67	9.53	9.83	9.73

Activity 11.3

the UK Potato Chips market

Examine the data given above. Use a spreadsheet if you can to input and analyse the figures. Answer the following questions.

1   What do the two tables measure? Why do you think both tables are shown?

2   What is meant by the 'own label' brand?

3   Using the Total Value table, draw up a pie chart showing market share of each of the brands in the second year. What conclusions can you draw?

4   Using the Total Volume table, draw up a multiple bar chart showing the market share of each of the brands over the two years. What conclusions can you draw?

5   Divide total value by total volume for each of the brands. What does this tell you about the brands?

The data above provides only a part of the overall picture that Nielsen provides for market analysts. This table refers to just one type of product (potato chips) from the overall 'snacks' market. Other tables would look at other products, by 'individual brand' and by manufacturer. From these, market growth and market share can be monitored.

understanding the market

In the remainder of this chapter we look at the way businesses making marketing decisions analyse 'the market' by getting to understand the customer/consumer. We look at market segmentation, buyer behaviour and preferences, lifestyle and values.

market segmentation

Market segmentation is the process whereby the overall market is divided up into separate sets of customers (segments) who have separate identifiable product needs.

Industrial market segments are categorised according to the type of industry, the location and size of the target business, and the end-use of the product. If for instance you were manufacturing household products, you would distinguish between selling to supermarkets and to corner shops (segment by size). If you manufactured fertilisers, you would sell well in rural areas, but would have limited success in city areas (segment by area).

There are a number of different ways of identifying consumer market segments:

social stratification

A common way of segmenting the market is by social class, although the value of this method is declining. Each group will have its own product needs and pattern of income and expenditure. The UK social classes are divided into letter groupings (A to E) as follows:

Social group	Social class	Occupation type
A	Upper/upper middle class	higher managerial, professional, eg director of a large company, partner in a firm of solicitors
B	Middle class	intermediate managerial, professional, eg commercial manager, salaried accountant
C1	Lower middle class	junior managerial and supervisory, eg insurance clerk, nurse, shop manager
C2	Skilled working class	skilled manual workers, eg electrician, fitter
D	Working class	semi-skilled and unskilled workers, eg warehouseman, driver, shop assistant
E	Subsistence level	the lowest paid and the unemployed

age groups

The age groupings chosen will depend on the research being undertaken eg a 'whole population' survey would subdivide over the 0 to 100 range; a survey of the working population would span the 16 to 65 range; the 'kids views' survey on page 248 only looks at the 7 to 16 age group. Your research may need to think of different subdivisions. To avoid the false analysis of results, keep the sub-sectors as equal in width as possible.

regional groups

Different regions in the UK have different preferences: try selling tripe in Surrey and beer with a frothy head in London!

sex

Products for 'him' and 'her' are clearly different market segments, but note the arrival of unisex.

income groups

This distinction sometimes overrides the social grouping set out above: lower income groups may look for a 'bargain', higher income groups may look for quality or self-consciously expensive products. Note: never ask a respondent 'how much do you earn?' Give ranges of earnings for them to indicate their income. These groups may be researched via 'occupation' type questions.

ethnic groups

Many new religious and racial groups have appeared over the last fifty years, each requiring specialised products and services.

Activity 11.4

market segmentation

Divide into small groups within the class. Discuss what different market segments could be considered by

1   a clothes manufacturer

2   a holiday company

Each group should make as long a list as possible for each type of product and then compare lists in full class session.

understanding customer types & behaviour

In order to appreciate the needs of each market segment, planners must understand buyer behaviour, an area which involves an element of psychology. The first consideration when looking at buyer behaviour is that there are two basic classifications of buyer: the industrial buyer (organisations buying machinery, raw materials, office supplies etc), and the consumer (the private purchaser). In this chapter we will concentrate on the consumer.

consumer preferences

Consumer goods buyers are the subject of regular market and motivational research as to what makes them buy or not buy. The key point to appreciate is that people do not buy products and services: they buy the benefits that such products or services offer to them. Think about this! Why do you buy a particular coat, or car, or chocolate? The reasons are many, but in all cases, they will be a combination of practical and emotive factors, some of which are set out below. Apply these factors to an item of clothing you want to buy:

practical factors	*emotive factors*
price/good value for money?	status (as fashion leader)?
hard wearing?	social acceptance (everyone else has one)?
suitable for work?	high price (to boast of wealth)?
easy to clean?	low price (to boast of bargaining skills)?
warmth?	sexual attraction?

Psychologists have commented at length on buyer behaviour and marketing logic. They understand the basic needs and wants of individuals and groups. Marketing's motivational researchers also seek to understand the reasoning that triggers the buying decision.

Databases list and carry information about the people, or organisations, in any one market. A local supermarket will have a 'list' of its customers if they have applied for a loyalty card. An industrial firm will know its customers, and if they have bought in a list from a professional agency, will know about all the other firms in their line of business. Bought-in lists have become so sophisticated that they are often linked together. Early efforts saw NDL International link their lifestyle database to the specialist financial database of Infolink Decision Services to market 'Portrait', which offered researchers detailed household information at post code level. On a similar line, CACI offer 'Acorn', which stands for 'A Classification Of Residential Neighbourhoods' and the 'Acorn Lifestyle List', which is a demographic overlay of household composition, age, shopping area, TV region and wealth. There are many others, each trying more accurately to explain who and where the potential consumers are, and what they buy. The future is about datafusion and cross tabulation – jargon for the linking of databases to provide ever more accurate market information to improve marketing success – for mailshots, choosing advertising media, siting new stores and so on.

lifestyle databases

Lifestyle databases like the ones described above can be established using a mixture of quantitative and qualitative research techniques. These databases may include details of social class (income potential), cultural background, family data, reference groups, social interests and so on. These can be mixed with information on age, sex, location plus other information on media usage (newspapers read, TV watched, radio heard) to build accurate market segment pictures.

values research

Values Research is a growth area of a similar type to lifestyle analysis, but it focuses on consumer beliefs and motivations more than on income levels and demography. It believes that fashions change even in the way we think, and that the values of say modesty, respect for authority and conformism are views of the past. Today is about excitement, escapism and sexuality. Such research has given us a new style of advertising such as Diet Coke's girls ogling a young male passing their office, and the very provocative Häagen–Dazs ice–cream adverts. The message is 'if you can't think like your target market, you won't sell to it'. First carry out the Activity below on current adverts. Then read the article from 'Marketing' and the associated case material from JWT Insight and answer the questions that follow them.

Activity 11.5

Values research

Discuss in class current TV and other adverts. What consumer 'values' are being assumed by advertisers?

How do they help sell the products?

Case Study

JWT Insight – Kids and Food Study

introduction

JWT Insight is the market research arm of J Walter Thompson, a leading Advertising Agency. Osborne Books is grateful to Judy Harmon, Planning Director, JWT Insight, for writing about the background to their survey on childrens' eating habits and also to 'Marketing' for permission to reproduce the article below which comments on the survey.

JWT survey reveals kids' food views

By Paul Whitfield

Kids like pizza best, think McDonald's is bad for them and don't believe that ads influence what they eat, according to a new survey by JWT Insight.

The survey asked more than 1000 children aged between 7 and 16 to name their favourite food and give their opinions on healthy eating, advertising, peer group influence and genetically modified foods.

The survey also found that more than half of the children were aware of the GM food debate, with 84 per cent of 13 to 16 year-olds surveyed aware of GM ingredients. Of those who knew about GM foods, 87 per cent felt that they should be clearly labelled in the shops, but only one quarter thought GM ingredients were unhealthy.

The findings come at a time when marketers are being criticised for targeting children with foods which are high in salt, fat and sugar.

A total of 18 per cent of kids nominated pizza as their top food, with chips and pasta placed second and third in the survey, on 15 per cent and 12 per cent respectively.

Two-thirds claimed their diet wasn't adversely affected by advertising and more than three-quarters didn't believe peer group pressure played a role in determining their diet. Healthy eating is a big concern among children, with 71 per cent claiming that they tried to eat as much healthy food as possible. Despite this, 53 per cent of boys and 43 per cent of girls surveyed said people make `too much fuss' about healthy eating. When asked which foods were unhealthy, children named specific brands, such as McDonald's and Coke.

However, the youngsters' parents were more suspicious, with more than 50 per cent claiming that both advertising and peer group pressure led children to eat more junk food.

A report released last week, by industry watchdog The Food Commission claimed children's foods manufacturers were representing junk food as healthy through misleading labelling. A survey earlier this year found that British children were among the most obese in Europe.

JWT Insight, the agency's research arm, estimates that the UK children's foods sector is worth £1.2bn and that food marketers, believing children to be a significant influence on food purchasing, are targeting younger consumers.

Source: 'Marketing'

Case Study

JWT Insight –
Marketing Research –
Kids and Food

Case Study written by Judy Harmon,
Planning Director, J Walter Thompson

Objectives

The study was part of a larger project looking at kids' opinions on a range of subjects. The overall aim was for JWT to keep in touch with childrens' attitudes and behaviour on a number of general topics (most of our client research projects are concerned with particular brands, whereas this exercise was for our own better understanding of this market area).

We have monitored childrens' views through our own research for around 10 years, and this has provided input into our understanding of how children use advertising, childrens' relationships with brands, liked and disliked advertising, ownership of durables, heroes and heroines, how fads develop etc.

A section of the latest questionnaire was dedicated to questions about food. We supplemented this with omnibus research, ie we put questions about kids and parents into another firm's survey.

The key objective was to understand more about the dynamics of childrens' food choices, particularly with regard to healthy eating. More specifically 'to monitor any trend changes in the favourite foods of children aged 7 to 16; to assess attitudes to healthy eating; and to assess attitudes to GM and organic foods.' It was partly designed to investigate 'hot' media topics where in reality there was a lack of original child research.

Methodology and Sampling

It began with informal focus groups to get a feel for the areas to be investigated. These used both quantitative and qualitative questions. The resulting questionnaire was pilot tested. This established a possible problem in that the children would exaggerate their intake of healthy foods. As a result a specific question was changed to 'Please write down the names of any fruit and vegetables you ate yesterday.' The mainly quantitative questionnaire went to 1013 primary and secondary school children, split between schools in the north and the south. The surveys were conducted in the same schools two or three times per year, with a mix of repeated and one-off questions. The questionnaire was self completion, with a mix of pre-coded (multi choice) and open ended questions.

The supplementary 'omnibus' questions were put to 401 children aged 7 to 16, and 117 parents of this age group, and commissioned through a BMRB (British Market Research Bureau) Access face-to-face random location sample survey. This involved stratification using 'Acorn' districts to get a sample proportional to the population in terms of social class. The interviewers were sent to specific streets. It was conducted 'in home', using the CAPI system (Computer Assisted Personal Interviewing ie laptop technology).

Desk Research was used at the time of writing the report to provide comparative information on the size of the childrens' meals sector, and weekly expenditure on food.

Activity 11.6

Kids and food survey

1   Why does an advertising agency conduct market research?

2   What was JWT's key objective? To what use might they put the information gained? Why would The Food Commission's views be important to JWT and its clients?

3   Explain the purpose of pilot testing the questionnaire.

4   What evidence is there of continuous and omnibus research, random and stratified sampling, closed questions and the use of technology?

5   Why did some desk research come last on this occasion? What sources would you use for the required information?

buying patterns and competitors

buying patterns

These are analysed to give trends for the future. Firms must be aware of their products' performance. Data can be mapped to give important information on the stage of the product life cycle that each product has reached. In addition, trends suggest new product needs as fashions change, and give retailers vital information that should affect stock policy. Past and present data can be used to predict the future, using averages, graphs, and tables.

sources of information about consumer trends

Two key government agency publications detailing expenditure patterns on product types are:

- National Food Survey (MAFF), which is the annual report of the National Food Survey Committee
- Family Spending, which is a report on the Family Expenditure Survey; this gives details of the size and membership of families, and how they spend their money

competitor activity

Competitors' activity must be monitored, as must their products. Marketing research should ask:

- who are our competitors?
- what markets do they serve and what is their market share?

Changes in competitor profitability can be monitored in the financial press, along with other details of their business activities. Trade and Marketing journals are very useful here, as well as marketing research firms.

product development and market research

Business will constantly be undertaking marketing research using the techniques outlined in this chapter. As a result of marketing research information obtained they will be able to develop new and existing products. Even the most traditional product can be given a surprising 'new look' which can make it appeal to consumers in a new way and sell to new market segments.

Now read the case study that follows and carry out Activity 7.

Case Study

Raleigh Bikes
New Product research

the process starts with intensive market research

Raleigh marketing personnel attend continuously a variety of exhibitions to establish trends in the marketplace. These exhibitions may be specific to the bike trade, where information on competitors, technical progress, design etc. can be gathered. Suppliers of bike parts will also be there – in particular the Japanese producer of 'Shimano' gears, the leader in technical development. Their new ideas will be critical for Raleigh. 'Shimano' gears are often a must for consumers. Alternatively exhibitions can be non-specific to bikes, but relate to lifestyle areas (where bikes offer consumer benefits) eg sport, leisure, health; or motorbike shows that give styling hints to bike designers.

The Product Development team at Raleigh use a variety of other market research methods. Both quantitative and qualitative data is gathered before decisions are made. Nielsen's dealer audits give information from the shops; GFK consumer panels check on current prices, brand sales, sales by outlet; and NDL's database analyses the warranty cards that buyers are asked to fill in after their purchase of a bike. These give valuable 'lifestyle' data. Consumer panels record current thinking about bike purchasing. Mintel surveys are commissioned by the bike industry itself to gather statistics on behalf of all firms in the industry. These will be studied.

product ideas are formed

The research done, the team undertakes 'filter' analysis to sort out the most promising new product ideas. The ones selected go to the technical drawing board with a design brief. Project plans will include costings, visuals and a prototype model to research dealer reaction. The concept might also be put to a consumer focus group for their thoughts. The final product is then refined and ready to go.

product planning takes place

A promotional budget for the launch is set and the launch plan is enacted. First the sales force are informed. Next the Trade receives details of the consumer launch plan, promotional point of sale material and possibly the offer of support for promotion locally, the amount depending on the scale of their current business with Raleigh. Finally the consumer gets to hear of the new product through a variety of promotional activities – advertising, publicity, special offers and of course via the retail display and the store staff.

Market research has the final say as the new product's progress is carefully monitored through the outlets eg warranty cards, consumer and trade opinion etc. The new product will always be considered for

modification as opinion is formed, and new versions of the product will generate interest in the marketplace. Besides, too much money, time and effort has been spent to allow the newcomer to fail.

The launch of the Max Lite (see picture) brand of mountain bikes in September 1998 followed this research process. Already the company is looking forward to the next wave of products even as the 'Max' establishes itself in the marketplace.

Activity 11.7

the 'Max' bike

Read the case study and then answer the questions.

1   Why are 'non-bike' exhibitions of interest to Raleigh?

2   What 'lifestyle' data would warranty cards supply?

3   Explain the value of the other data collection methods mentioned above?

4   For what reasons is a 'prototype' built?

5   What is the logic behind the 'salesforce, dealer, consumer' order of relaying the news about a new product?

6   Why is the company looking to future product development so soon after the launch of the Max?

CHAPTER SUMMARY

- Marketing research provides the essential information for marketing decisions on product, price, promotion and place.

- It may suggest a need or opportunity for a new product, suggest changes to an existing one, or even advise on its eventual replacement. Research is a continuous business activity.

- All research must be objective and technically accurate.

- Desk research is the usual starting point for an information search, unearthing already published information at reasonable cost.

- Field research provides any necessary new information on the market, using an established format of setting objectives, choosing from a variety of data collection methods, surveying samples from the total population and then collecting, collating and analysing the data to enable accurate business decisions to be made.

- Some research is quantitative in that it gathers facts in number form eg. 'how many did you buy?'; 'how often did you go?'; 'how much did you pay?'.

- Much research is qualitative in that it examines opinions, eg 'did you enjoy the holiday?'; 'what do you think of the local bus service?'. Answers are usually graded.

- Markets are segmented so that the behavioural patterns of the various segments can be examined and their needs identified by the product and service producers.

- Competitor activity is monitored and market share established, often through external research agencies.

- Research is becoming dominated by new technology, with databases for accurate sampling; software for the analysis of collected data; and desktop designs for presentations.

- Information from marketing research forms the basis of an organisation's forecast of the future, not just in marketing, but in the purchasing, production, human resources and finance departments as well.

KEY TERMS

marketing research	research into all of an organisation's marketing activities
secondary market data	desk research: investigates published information
primary market data	field research: gathers fresh information about the market
quantitative research	collects numerical values
qualitative research	gathers opinions
ad hoc research	is a 'one-off' investigation
continuous research	asks the same questions in the same market segments at regular time intervals
omnibus research	putting one or two of your questions onto someone else's questionnaire
sample	a selection of respondents from the chosen market sector
population	the total market, or market segment, under review
open questions	giving views/opinions – they do not lead to a selection from given answers
closed questions	ask respondents to choose the best answer from a given selection
sampling methods	ensure that the sample taken is representative of the population under review
pilot survey	a small survey to check that the questionnaire and other aspects of the main survey will work correctly
segmentation	dividing a population into convenient and suitable smaller segments for closer analysis
product substitution	is one product replacing, or doing the same job as another, in the same market
lifestyle research	links the background and the buying habits of customers
values research	studies consumer beliefs and motivations
database	a computerised list of the components of a market
forecasting	gives a calculated expectation of the future

Analysing marketing opportunities

introduction

When you develop your marketing strategy you need to be able to use market information to analyse the competitiveness of your product or service and to gain an understanding of the environment within which the business is operating.

what you will learn from this chapter

● the planning of marketing activity is crucial to the success of the organisation; the planning can take a variety of forms

● SWOT analysis looks at the organisation's strengths, weaknesses, opportunities and threats

● the Marketing Mix organises marketing into four policy areas, known as the '4Ps': product, price, promotion and place

● product policy controls the range of goods or services that an organisation offers to its markets and is based on the Product Life Cycle concept

● market policy decides into which market segments the business will sell its products

● product policy and market policy can be analysed using a number of different models, including the Boston Matrix, Ansoff and PEST analyses

● constraints on marketing activity can be legal, voluntary or ethical

marketing planning

For any organisation to function efficiently and effectively the Marketing Team (often a Marketing Department) must analyse past performance and present trends, and attempt to predict the future in the form of a Marketing Plan. Clearly a Marketing Plan is the result of much careful research, consultation and discussion. No organisation will plan in exactly the same way as another organisation. There are, however, a number of planning techniques and processes which have been successfully tried and tested over the years. These include:

- SWOT analysis
- Marketing Mix
- Boston matrix
- Ansoff strategy
- PEST (or SLEPT) analysis

We will explain each of these in turn. It must be stressed that these are techniques which can be used singly, or, more commonly, in combination.

SWOT analysis

SWOT stands for **S**trengths **W**eaknesses **O**pportunities **T**hreats

SWOT analysis is a technique much used in many general management as well as marketing scenarios. SWOT consists of examining the current activities of the organisation – its Strengths and Weaknesses – and then using this and external research data to set out the Opportunities and Threats that exist. The process can be well illustrated by the practical Activity which follows.

Activity 12.1

SWOT analysis

Take as an example the school or college where you are studying, and make suggestions for each of the four SWOT categories. Some points are already listed to get you started. Your lecturer/teacher/trainer could lead the discussion and add to the list. Make recommendations as to what needs to be done as a result of your findings

strengths:	large catchment area
weaknesses:	old buildings, overcrowding
opportunities:	offering new subjects/courses
threats:	falling numbers of 16 year-olds

the marketing mix

This is a traditional approach to marketing planning which is based on the four Ps:

Product

Price

Promotion

Place

A SWOT analysis, of course, can be used to collect the data required to build the Marketing Mix plan. We will now introduce each of the four Ps in turn.

product policy

'Product' is, in fact, the range of products (goods or services) that the organisation offers to the marketplace. Decisions have to be made about quantities, timing, product variations, associated services, quality, style and even the packaging and branding.

Most organisations have a range of products of different quality for the different market segments. Whatever quality is decided upon for whichever market segment, the quality should remain consistent.

A 'brand name' establishes the product in the consumer's mind, eg Persil, Coke, Adidas. Although branding is an integral part of product policy we will examine it in detail in Chapter 13 as a promotional activity. It will be chosen with the market sector in mind. Note that 'Market policy', (market segmentation, page 244,) is an integral part of Product policy. The two must be planned together.

price policy

'Price' is a vitally important decision area because although it is a 'promotional' tool in many respects, it is the main source of income to the organisation. If prices are lowered for promotional purposes, the cash flow within the company, and its long-term profitability, could be seriously affected.

As with products, there is normally a range of prices. These can vary according to the quantities bought, the importance of the customer, and the market segment. Pricing can be long-term (set at a level for sustained profit-making) and short-term (cut prices for tactical reasons, such as market penetration). Pricing can involve discounts, special offers, allowances, credit, and 'trade-ins'. It is vitally important to get price decisions right.

The concept of pricing will be discussed in the next chapter.

promotion policy

'Promotion' consists of a number of techniques which create awareness of the products and persuade the potential customer to make the buying decision. It involves all communication with actual and potential consumers. The techniques include advertising, branding, packaging, publicity/public relations, sales promotions and merchandising. Each differs from the others but all, or all of them thought relevant to a given situation, will be used to create a unified product image and an image for the organisation, the 'corporate identity'.

Selling – also part of 'promotion' – is a personal activity, with some form of direct contact between buyer and seller. Promotional activity is impersonal, aimed generally at a market segment and with no personal contact. This point is mentioned because of the different emphasis placed on these activities by different organisations. A simple example is the difference between promoting/selling an industrial machine and a chocolate bar. The machine needs expert demonstration by a salesperson. With the machine, marketing would split 80% selling effort, 20% back-up promotion. With the chocolate, 80% promotional effort would be backed by 20% selling, ie gaining retail/wholesale distribution.

The concepts of Promotion and Selling are developed further in Chapter 13 and in Chapter 14.

place policy

A business when planning its marketing will ask a number of questions relating to place ie 'Through which outlets should we sell the product? How do we physically move the product to these chosen outlets? How far afield do we wish to operate (locally, nationally, or internationally)?' Place, or distribution policy, is a massive, complex decision area that incorporates these three problems, and potentially more. See Chapter 14.

the marketing mix – conclusion

The Marketing Mix gives a plan by which to operate to influence and satisfy the buyer/consumer. The four Ps approach is not perfect, and is certainly not intended to cover all of marketing's activities, eg Marketing Research. Research, of course, is the provider of information for the decisions in all of the four P areas, and so your portfolio must show ample evidence of both desk and field research.

Activity 12.2

The marketing mix

Work in small groups within the class

1   Think up an idea for a new product which you think customers need (use a 'brainstorming' session for this).

2   Work out how you are going to implement the marketing mix (the 4 Ps) for the new product.

3   Give a five minute presentation to the rest of the class explaining your ideas.

Note: this Activity could be a useful preparation for your Portfolio assessment evidence.

marketing principles at work

We will now look at two Case Studies of 'businesses' – a carpet manufacturer and a charity – to illustrate marketing principles and functions at work and to see applications of this Marketing Mix.

Case Study

Brintons
Brintons Carpets: 2000

the company

Brintons is a Midlands firm serving a global market. The firm manufactures a range of medium to high quality carpets for both residential and commercial users. The range includes plain and patterned carpets for sale through retail outlets, and customised (made to order) carpets for contractors and end-user individual customers such as hotel groups, large offices, leisure centres and many others.

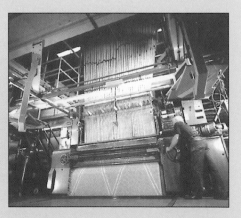

the need for change

The recession of the late 1980s and early 1990s led to a period of major change in the firm's sales and marketing policies. Customer focus has led to a 'total service approach' and the growth of 'relationship marketing' with major customers, ie giving them improved support in the form of technical, design and merchandising back-up. More recent reorganisation has seen the appointment of an overall marketing manager. Internal policy reviews continue to be an annual company exercise.

marketing research

Marketing research indicates continued demand for quality carpets from both residential and commercial users. Whilst the firm's plain carpets range is holding off constant pressure from improving alternative technology and many competing products, demand for its patterned and customised carpets is still expanding. Product development continues to be based on 'customer acceptance', though the technique has changed from 'in hall' tests organised by outside research agencies to 'in store' tests of new designs run by Brintons itself. Customer focus is seen as the key to future success. The customers' perception of the range and its worth is monitored by 'product acceptance tests', ie existing customers commenting on their purchases, and 'product gap' analysis, ie the company examining its own brands against competitor brands.

product

It was decided that the company's product policy would continue to be to service the mid to premium end of the market, maintaining the quality gap between its wool rich 'woven' product and the lower quality 'tufted' competition. Continual quality improvement would be ensured by investment in Research and Development. This already includes 'in house' design, and the design and building of its own looms.

place

Market development continues apace as Brintons aims for a truly global image. This not only relieves pressure on the highly competitive UK market, but it ensures growth and increased profits with which to further even more product and market development. It could be said that by concentrating on the woven sector of the market Brintons is 'niche' marketing, but this sector alone is massive. The current key export areas are Europe and the USA. The firm has bought up a USA producer of woven carpets, to add to its existing manufacturing capabilities in Australia and Portugal. Most recently it has built a new factory in India, which will reduce production costs and help the firm to service new markets.

price

Pricing continues to follow a long term strategy, with a 'value for money' philosophy at the mid to premium end of the market. The lower costs of production in India will allow lower prices so that new 'product area' targets can be attacked. The winning of customised orders means competitive tendering, which requires the pricing of each enquiry, individually. For standard products in the residential market a price list exists, but only for the retailers, not the consumers. Discounts are available for large and 'preferred' customers. Short term tactical pricing is not used in the UK, but 'penetration' pricing might be considered to gain a foothold in a new overseas market.

promotion

Communication with the marketplace is a combination of sales force activity and promotional effort. Overall, because customers are either commercial (large individual firms) or trade (mainly retailers), a mixture of activities is used. In the commercial market the emphasis is on selling (perhaps 60/40%), whereas in the residential markets the main thrust is promotional. The balance is again difficult to quantify and will vary according to circumstances eg new or established product? new market?

Brintons recently reorganised its sales force. It has an established Contract Field Sales Force dealing with the commercial sector, whilst in the residential sector there is a national sales team, with individuals working 'areas' and visiting individual or 'small group' retailers, plus, a key account salesperson who services the head offices of major groups like 'House of Fraser'. The Contract team have the task of identifying the person who will make the buying decision for the customer ie they meet architects, interior designers, flooring contractors and any other people who have an input into the decision 'which carpet?', 'which supplier?' For this reason they are supported by their own design team plus technical back-up.

The residential sales team are supported by strong promotional activity aimed at the trade and (mainly) the end user, with strong merchandising activity at the point of sale. Most promotion is handled internally by Brinton's own marketing department, although outside agencies may be used at the preliminary stages of a campaign.

Advertising is aimed at the trade, (using trade journals), and the end user, (using a variety of middle to up market female orientated consumer magazines, such as 'House Beautiful' and 'Ideal Home'). An earlier campaign featured 'carpet clothes' by Vivienne Westwood, a leading fashion designer. A more recent campaign used photographs by Lord Lichfield, again using eye catching carpet gowns, and the strap (punch) line 'some things in life wear better than others'.

Clearly the message is both factual and emotive, linking experience (trust) with modernity (fashion, status). The basic principle of the advertising is 'one message; don't confuse'. Branding is both family (Brintons) and individual (Bell Twist Woven Wilton), but to this has been added a new logo featuring the Royal Warrant.

Public Relations forms a key part of the overall corporate image, raising public awareness and perception of the firm. Newsletters are circulated to relevant parties in the trade, one of which announcing the major triumph that Brintons had won the 'Queen's Award' for export achievement. This followed an earlier industry award for advertising. These facts become good publicity material for use in the more general media.

Customer and consumer perceptions of the company are further enhanced by careful consideration of the environment. Care is taken that the manufacturing process does not pollute the local area, and even wider concerns are shown in the use of predominantly natural rather than man-made materials in this production process. Such policies generate a desirable and carefully protected corporate image.

For further information, log onto the company's web site www.brintons.net

Activity 12.3

Brintons Carpets

Read through the Brintons Case Study and answer the following questions.

1   What evidence is there of responsiveness to change?

2   At what end of the UK market are the products aimed, and why?

3   In what ways are the markets segmented?

4   What evidence is there of long and short term pricing strategies?

5   On which promotional activities do Brintons place most emphasis?

6   What evidence is there for Brintons' claim to be a 'global concern'?

7   Why is continual marketing research so important to Brintons?

Case Study

Cancer research
World Cancer Research Fund (WCRF)

the charity

WCRF is a non profit making organisation. It is a registered national charity committed to increasing awareness and knowledge of the relationship between food, lifestyle and cancer, and of cancer as a preventable disease. WCRF's primary aim is to prevent cancer in the UK, but it is also part of an international network which has a more extensive mission: to prevent cancer worldwide.

World Cancer
Research Fund

'product'

WCRF does not sell a 'product' – rather it sells positive messages about the long term benefits of healthy eating and living to the public. One of several objectives is to sell the message that 'eating healthily plus staying physically active and maintaining a healthy weight can cut cancer risk by 30-40%, and that this is increased to 60-70% by not smoking.' A wide range of programmes carry this and other messages to the public and to the health professionals they turn to for advice, eg dietitians, doctors, health visitors and practice nurses, who are supplied with materials to assist them in their work. All WCRF education material is available free. Newsletters are sent out to the organisation's supporters, to the public on request, and to medical health and lifestyle conferences. They are available also in schools, doctors' waiting rooms and some hospital receptions. Booklets and leaflets are circulated to help people help themselves.

Products also appear as 'purchases', using the funds raised eg WCRF's Science Department serves the scientific community with programmes of support for laboratory, applied and epidemiological research, involving funds and grants for researchers in UK medical schools, universities and other research centres. Supporters are informed of these 'purchases', that they have made possible, through the WCRF Newsletters, in an attempt to give 'tangibility' to product policy.

the market

The market sectors targeted for donations are many, but in particular they are older charity donors with a particular interest in health. The profile of supporters is currently predominantly female, over 55 years of age and living in the south east of England. Distribution of fund raising efforts is however nationwide and diverse. The HQ in London co-ordinates fundraising activities across the UK, including special events and house to house collections, and is helped by a nationwide team of volunteers. Database lists of helpers are compiled, for the circulation of newsletters and volunteer packs. The market sector for the message is 'all ages', but particular emphasis is being put on the young. 'The Great Grub Club' is for 4 to 7 year olds, with a biannual newsletter. The information given is linked to the national curriculum, so that teachers become interested.

marketing research

Market research questionnaires about eating habits are conducted through the newsletter and as part of direct mail fund raising. Over a period of time results are checked to assess any significant 'changes in behaviour patterns'. The results are released as news items, mainly to journalists associated with health issues. Market research into the acceptability and usefulness of these packs and other promotional materials is conducted once a year.

promotion and place

Promotional activities are many and various. Advertising is extremely limited due to high costs, but special events are covered eg a London Marathon advert. Some specialist publications are used to target older people to encourage legacies, and the Supporter Services team run a legacy programme designed to develop WCRF's relationship with those who have pledged their support. This uses postal and telephone contact.

Public Relations is extremely important. WCRF works with consumer publications such as health and fitness magazines, men's and women's lifestyle magazines and regional and national newspapers to create public interest stories on the benefits of healthy eating and living for the promotion of good health and the prevention of chronic diseases.

Cause Related Marketing (the use of sponsorship) is looked at with care. WCRF are anxious not to be seen to be endorsing directly related manufacturer's products in return for funds. However, educational grants from for example British Telecom are considered acceptable (see below).

The main promotional thrust centres on the distribution of education materials to raise awareness of WCRF's work, and the way that funds are allocated to research. This gives a potential donor something tangible on which to focus. The message is 'Stopping cancer before it starts'. The overall aim and corporate image is 'To make WCRF the intellectual leader in cancer prevention'. With this in mind, a website has been established, with advanced publicity leaflets going to1200 journalists.

Sales activity is organised by representatives, whose brief is to get local volunteer groups motivated into active fund raising. Concerts, sponsored walks, teddy bear sales and so on are the result. Executives of WCRF make visits and offer support and advice, and approach charitable trusts and other organisations for support on particular programmes eg. the BT sponsored website – www.wcrfhealthcheck.org which offers a variety of information for different market sectors.

WCRF attends up to eight conferences per year – a mixture of medical conferences, targeted at health professionals, and consumer conferences, aimed at WCRF supporters and the wider public.

The growth of the organisation depends on high profile activities, good public relations and sound marketing in the increasingly competitive charity sector. WCRF have offices already in the USA and the Netherlands, and new ones are planned for France and Germany. Brochures have been translated for distribution around the world.

Activity 12.4

Cancer research
World Cancer Research Fund

1   What evidence is there of WCRF marketing research activity?

2   What other types of research are mentioned, and why?

3   How does WCRF transform its cause into a tangible product?

4   What is the purpose of targeting children?

5   Who are the 'key people' to reach with the message?

6   Why is public relations seen as more important than advertising?

7   What types of organisation would not be acceptable for sponsorship deals?

8   Why is having a website important?

9   How can the National Lottery be both a good and a bad influence for WCRF?

10 What place decisions have been made by WCRF, both in the UK and worldwide?

product policy

Now we will look at the individual 'mix' items in detail, starting with product policy, before showing price, promotion and place in the next chapters.

Remember, it all starts with Marketing Research, the subject of the last chapter.

The product policy of an organisation sets out the range of products – the product mix – that it will offer to its market(s). Its resources will be used to produce a type (or types) of product, and decisions will be made as to the timing and volume of that production. The range itself will change over a period of time, because markets for products and services are dynamic (constantly changing). An organisation is always researching the next step – tomorrow's needs!

product themes

A successful way of combining a product mix is the development of product themes. This has become increasingly popular in the leisure industry, where theme parks such as 'The American Adventure' present all of their entertainment under a single co-ordinated style. The Danish firm 'Lego' tries to introduce a new product theme each year to ensure continued sales to its regular customers. Such ideas are good for business and keep customer interest alive.

complementary or competitive products

The product planners also have other factors to consider: some products are complementary to one another; others are competitive.

Complementary products sell together. The manufacturer of town clothes may also make leisurewear. Retailers selling sports equipment also sell trainers and sports clothes. Customers for one product might be persuaded to buy some of the other items. In fact, the customer would expect this range and may use only the manufacturer or shop that provides it.

Competitive products, as the name suggests, compete with each other for the buyers' attention. Competitive products may be produced by the same manufacturer. Why? There are several reasons: consumers have different requirements, so a range of soap powders or dog foods is an attempt to catch as many buyers as possible. For example the dogfoods Pal and Pedigree Chum are both made by Pedigree Masterfoods. If a consumer changes from Pal to Pedigree Chum, at least the sale goes to the same company.

updating the product range

An organisation will constantly prune and update its product range and mix. The extent of the mix is another important issue. If there are too few products, there is the danger that one going out of date will seriously harm total sales. If there are too many products, the range becomes difficult to organise and will fragment production too much. Whatever the decision however, never be caught with just one product in just one market. The failure of one product or market could mean the failure of the organisation. Look at the effect on William Baird, a UK clothing manufacturer, when Marks & Spencer changed its purchasing policy late in 1999 and sourced more of its clothing from cheaper overseas producers. William Baird were over-reliant on just one customer.

The product range of a firm is often limited by its area of expertise and by the limits imposed by its size and resources. Most firms adapt, the better ones by anticipating change, the others by reacting to it. Those that fail to adapt will fail to survive.

product substitution

This can mean one of two things

- the replacement of one product or product model by another within your own range, as above, or
- the decision by consumers to change from one brand to another – in this event it is important to understand how 'close' your own, or a competitor's, alternative substitute product is to your original.

new product development

The above sections point to the need for innovation, creativity and insight in identifying strategies for changing market position and for new product development. There must be a policy to bring through new ideas, and executive time should be allocated to brainstorming and 'think tank' activities. This further emphasises the importance of marketing research, technical research and the need to study the current positions of products and markets. See stage 1 of the product life cycle below.

product life cycle

'In the long term we are all dead'. (J M Keynes)

Marketing people have accepted a slight variation of this principle when referring to each and every product or service ever placed before the consumer, ie 'In the long term all of our existing products and services are dead'. More concisely, 'Nothing lasts for ever'. An example of this is the replacement of the Ford Cortina (a highly successful car) by the Ford Sierra, the replacement of the Sierra by the Ford Mondeo and the replacement of the old Mondeo by a new Mondeo in 2001. Just as each of us is conceived, is born, grows, matures and dies, so in the commercial marketplace products and services are created, launched and withdrawn, in a process known as the product life cycle. The graph on the next page shows the product life cycle (PLC) as a series of five stages. It plots the money value of sales (the upper line) and the profit on those sales (the lower line) against the five stages, which we will explain in turn.

Stage 1: development

No product or service is dreamed up on the Monday and produced and sold on the Tuesday. Each new product idea has to be researched, designed and tested. This may take a few weeks or, in the case of hi-tech products, many months or years. All of this requires funding, so it is important to calculate the extent of such costs when making the decision to develop a product. Costs include:

- market research, to establish whether the intended customers like the idea in this form
- technical research, to bring the product from the drawing board, through Research and Development, to test market condition
- test market (a limited trial run), where many aspects of the new product are tried out, but in particular the acceptability of the product itself and the price
- executive time, to co-ordinate the research work and make decisions on 'go ahead' or 'discontinue'

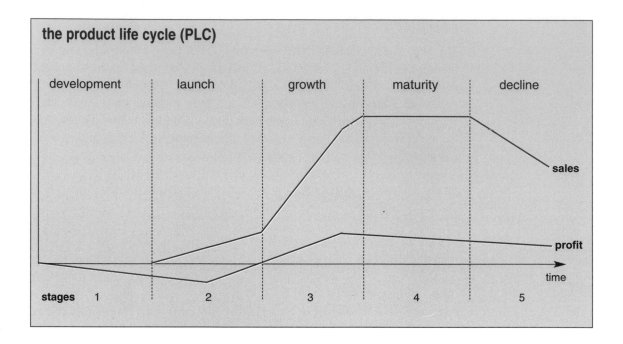

Note that the 'development' stage shows on the graph as a loss on the 'profits' line; this stresses the importance of a successful launch to recover the development expenses.

Stage 2: the launch

The go-ahead has been given and the new product is introduced to the market place. This is a nerve-testing time in business. The failure rate of new products is remarkably high, despite all of the research and testing undertaken. Test markets often do well because consumers are curious people. They will try anything once. The real test for the new product is 'will they buy it again, and again, and again?'

The diagram shows a slow sales uptake and an even deeper trough in the 'profits' curve – why? – think what costs a product launch entails:

- the product must be made available both to the trade and to the public; the costs of distribution are high

- no-one is aware of the new product, so it must be promoted and sold to the trade and the public; promotional costs are high and sales teams are expensive

The timing of the product launch needs careful thought. It also needs nerve if uptake is slower than expected, but herein lies the real problem. Just how long can it be given? How much more money can be risked to recoup the development costs? There are no easy answers here.

Stage 3: growth

The launch is successful, consumers take to the product and sales take off. An exciting time for the company, especially as the 'profits' line really does mean profits. Depending upon the uniqueness and originality of the new product, profitability should be strong. Vigorous promotion and/or sales force activity will take the product into all the required outlets and sales to the final consumer will be influenced by the 'newness' factor.

Inevitably, the fast rising sales curve will begin to level off as the new product excitement is lost and the competition reacts to your success. Sales continue to rise but new customers are harder to find. It is here also that the profits curve reaches its peak. Why should this be so if sales are still rising? The additional costs of promotion and sales force effort in keeping the sales curve rising may be large, especially in warding off your competitors' attack. Their own new products will be attracting attention and perhaps even taking your customers away. It may even be time to review your own 'new' product with a view to redesign, repositioning, and so on. Remember, nothing lasts for ever, and change is always influencing your market position.

Stage 4: maturity

This stage is more of a plateau than a curve, and its length varies from six months to six or sixty years. Once a product reaches this stage it is in the interests of the company to keep it there as long as profitably possible. Once distribution has been (expensively) achieved, the company will battle to maintain customer loyalty. Certain products seem to go on for ever, eg Cornflakes and the Mars bar – and these will be very valuable to the producer. Throughout this stage it is essential to watch the profitability level. Probably it will be in decline but it still represents the company's principal source of the revenue needed for new product development and the long-term survival of the company. Products at this stage are often referred to as 'cash cows', being milked for the benefit of the company. Products – eg cars and chocolate bars – can be 'revamped' during maturity (see next page).

Stage 5: decline

Inevitably the product or service will reach the end of its commercial usefulness. Sales will fall as newer, technically improved or more fashionable ideas appear in the market place. The decision to 'drop' a product is an extremely difficult one. Managements often argue, quite persuasively, for its retention. Are the newer products in the range established yet? Will important customers be upset by its removal from the range? Is the drop in sales purely temporary? Usually, however, the decision to drop the product has to be made, for sound reasons: it makes the business appear out of date; another product is planned to take its place; it is not economical to produce in small production runs.

recycling:

The revamping/repositioning of a product is a commonplace occurrence at any stage of the product life cycle. As a result of research data analysis there may appear the need/opportunity to make changes to an existing product. These changes eg. product redesign, new packaging can take place at any point in the product life cycle. Some common examples are:

• during growth, if a wider market is identified

• during maturity, if the competition is gaining

• from decline, if your latest new product launch is failing and you need to keep the old one going until a replacement can be developed

the product portfolio

The product life cycle concept offers organisations a blueprint for the present and for the future. It is not enough for firms to say 'we must have a range of products to offer the market(s)'. They must have both a range of products and a range of time scales for product development, ie something in most of the stages of the product life cycle. This is known as the product portfolio, shown below.

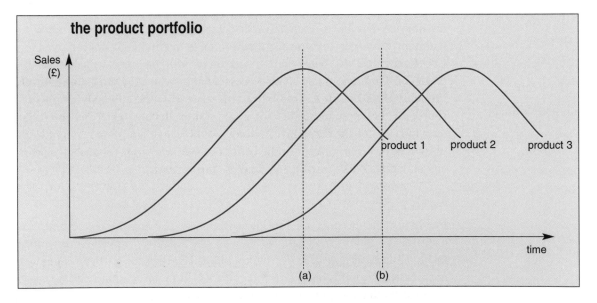

You will see from this diagram how the product life cycles for individual products overlap in terms of time scale, providing the business with a steady source of income and profit.

Now do the Student Activity on the next page.

Activity 12.5

The product portfolio

1 Look at the product portfolio diagram on the previous page and identify the position that each product has reached in its life cycle at point (a) and at point (b)

2 What should the business be doing at point (b) as part of its product policy?

marketing of services

If your choice for your portfolio is a service rather than a product, the marketing activities remain the same but there are a few additional difficulties, as shown below . . .

intangibility

This means something that cannot be touched. A service cannot be picked up, examined or tried out before it is purchased. Therefore, the reputation of the provider is most important. It is possible to talk to an earlier recipient of the service ie a holiday, a show, but there is always more of an element of risk in the purchase than with a product. Also note . . .

heterogeneity

This means the difficulty of making the service you are selling exactly the same as the one before. To the buyer, the next Mars bar will be identical to the one bought previously, but the seller of a service can never guarantee that the next visit to the same theatre, or the next ride home from college on the same bus, will be identical to the previous one eg the lack of atmosphere in a half-empty theatre, the discomfort of a full bus on a wet day, and so on. Quality control and customer satisfaction cannot be guaranteed, and there will be disappointments.

perishability

Consumer durables, such as TVs, have a long 'shelf life'. If not sold today they can be sold tomorrow. Some food products have a limited life, made more problematic by 'sell by' dates. Services are instantly perishable. If a show starts or a train leaves the station and a seat is empty, that sale is lost for ever. The costs of production stay the same, but the revenue from the empty seat on that day is lost. Note in this situation how the seller will try to sell at lower prices at the last minute. Half price is better than no money at all.

distribution

Distribution (or inseparability) problems occur because the customer is required to travel to the seller for a service, in most cases ie to actually make the effort to travel to Greece for the holiday, to the theatre to see the show. Here, extra time and money is being used up by the customer, which may influence the decision to buy. Note how sales can be encouraged by making the booking procedure as easy as possible – eg on the Internet.

ownership

When a product is bought, you own a physical item, ie a TV, a car, that may be kept by yourself and shown to others. With a service, an experience is enjoyed but at the end there is nothing physical to show for it or to show others. Here it is important for the provider to make mementos available – a brochure about the show, Disneyland merchandise, and so on.

Activity 12.6

The marketing of services

Divide into groups. Discuss the difficulties related to marketing services identified above and on the previous page. List the specific problems of marketing a leisure centre, a railway company, bank services, a plumbing service and a foreign holiday.

market policy (segmentation)

market strategies

Another aspect of marketing planning is deciding which market segment(s) you are targeting. A market segment is a 'type' of customer, or industry or region. There are therefore different strategies for approaching different market segments. If you are launching a product, do you aim at one segment, or do you aim at all of them? The choice may depend on the breadth of the product's appeal, or the size of the business promoting the product(s). A large concern can afford to promote a wide range of products to different segments; many small businesses, on the other hand, have successfully exploited a gap in the market by what is known as niche marketing of a single product ('niche' means 'gap'). The traditional classification of strategies is:

undifferentiated marketing

This type of marketing (also known as mass marketing) is where a product is launched at all sectors. This strategy can be expensive and wasteful, but can be successful where the product suits all markets, eg Coca Cola, the Mars Bar. Note now the influence of the Internet, enabling small firms to reach potentially large markets merely by having a website.

concentrated marketing

This is highly defined marketing, whereby a product is launched at a specific market segment, for example National Savings Childrens Bonds, 'singles' holidays; this technique is useful for small businesses which may prefer to rely on niche marketing (see above).

differentiated marketing

This form of market strategy promotes a range of different products, each designed specifically for a different market segment. It is costly in terms of promotion and production expenses, but it can be highly effective. Examples include different types of bank account, and different types of car (compare the small family run-about with the four-wheel drive off-road vehicle).

Market segmentation is a very important marketing principle. It was described in detail in Chapter 11 but is also a vital factor in 'marketing communication' (talking to the right people), the subject of Chapter 13. Customer behaviour and buying patterns were also covered in Chapter 11.

There are several ways of combining the analysis of product and market policies. Two of the best known are the Boston matrix and the Ansoff strategy. These are internal analyses and it is thus often difficult to get organisations to discuss them because they relate to current policy and planning. The techniques involved are as follows . . .

Boston matrix – showing product/market share

Look at the matrix diagram on the next page. Products are positioned on the diagram according to each one's share of the relevant market. The markets themselves are also analysed for growth rates. Note carefully how this diagram shows high values to the left of the horizontal axis. This is unusual, but this matrix has always been shown in this way. This base line shows the market share of a product relative to its major competitor. For example a value of 0.1 indicates that your product has only one tenth of the market share of its leading competitor, whereas a value of 10 indicates a market share of ten times more than its leading rival. The value 1 shows that you have the same market share as your major competitor.

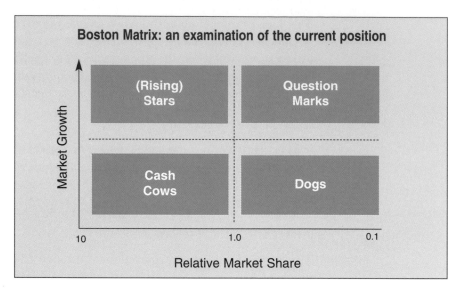

Note how the names given to the broad categories in the diagram could be seen as similar to the stages of the product life cycle . . .

Question Marks

These are low market share in a growing market – possibly a new product in a promising market, or perhaps a product that is having difficulty in getting established.

Stars

These are often associated with the (strong) growth stage of the cycle (hence they are sometimes called 'rising' stars). Sales are good, with the potential for market leadership. The market itself is expanding.

Cash Cows

These sell strongly with good market share, but in a mature market ie low growth. These products provide current profits and cash for the development of new products and/or shareholder dividends.

Dogs

These may be associated with the decline stage of the product life cycle, and may be discarded if profitability declines further. Low market share may suggest falling appeal, or never having come up to expectations in the first place. Firms are often reluctant to talk openly about these, so information gathering may be difficult.

The firms themselves can acquire data of market share and market growth from research firms which provide 'continuous research' data of this type. See the crisps data from the researchers A.C.Nielsen on page 242. All products in the portfolio must be monitored on a regular basis. Do 'question marks' fail to make it? Do 'rising stars' fail to mature into long term money makers ('cash cows')? Should 'dogs' be put down?

growth of organisations

A product successfully marketed will cause the producer to grow – whether financially, or in terms of sales or market share, or in the perception of the consumer. Present day success stories – like Bodyshop and Virgin – are the result of a single minded entrepreneur marketing a range of products in expanding markets.

reasons for growth

Why should a business grow? Very often it has little choice – it is market led – unless the management has a conscious policy of slowing down activity. There are a number of compelling reasons for growth:

- to increase income and/or profitability
- to dominate the market and beat the competition
- to safeguard the organisation's future
- to exploit opportunities and new markets
- to gain the advantage of market leadership
- to improve performance overall
- to achieve economies of scale (cost per unit)
- to gain prestige

types of growth

Natural growth over time is the result of increased marketing effort, achieving higher sales levels. These efforts will expand the customer base by selling to new customers and markets, whilst ensuring the continued satisfaction of existing customers. New products for new markets should ensure steady growth, whilst an increased share in existing markets is always a priority.

Product development, following market research, results in growth through technological breakthroughs – these enable entirely new product concepts to be developed and introduced. The Internet, for example, is revolutionising home entertainment, retailing and education. It is providing immense opportunities and growth prospects for high technology UK firms.

Artificial growth occurs through mergers and/or takeovers. The merger is the agreed linking together of two organisations, neither taking overall control of the other. The takeover is the purchase of the ordinary shares of another organisation, thus gaining control. This form of growth can be marketing linked in that takeovers often increase market share. Let us look at a model of growth strategy . . .

Ansoff's Growth Matrix

This is a further method of analysing product and market policies.

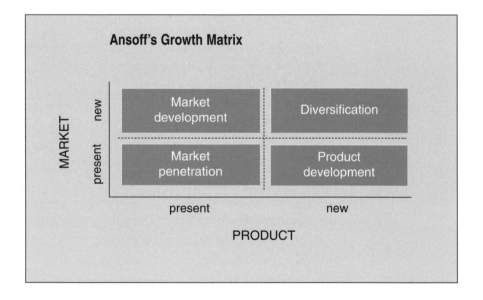

Market penetration is the basic growth area, ie continuing with existing products to gain a larger share of existing markets. Growth is unlikely to be great.

Product development means coming up with ideas for new products for existing markets.

Market development means searching for new markets for existing products.

Diversification means developing new products with which to attack markets that are also new to the organisation. This is the most risky if the competition is well established, but if the product type or market is new, it can have the greatest potential for long term growth eg internet-related ventures.

causes of change

PEST

You must appreciate that marketing is the management of change. The adequate manager notices that change is happening; the good manager anticipates it via market research; the top notch manager causes change, leading the market into new areas. A mnemonic used to summarise the areas which create change is 'PEST'.

P Political change, from one party to another in control – for example the rise in private healthcare and privatisations under Conservative governments.

E Economic change, for example a recession creating increased activity at the lower ends of product price ranges. Rate of interest rises depressing business and causing redundancies and lower spending levels.

S Social change involves changing attitudes and lifestyles. The increasing number of women going out to work, for example, led to the need for time-saving products for the home.

T Technological change - as we have seen - creates opportunities for new products and product improvements and of course new marketing techniques- the Internet, e-commerce.

SLEPT

A more recent mnemonic is SLEPT. This covers the four categories above plus L for **Legal**. Legal change such as the introduction of the breathalyser saw brewery firms turn to non-alcoholic drinks and the greater provision of pub meals – a threat turned into an opportunity. This is good marketing!

In today's world the legal constraints on marketing activities are numerous. They may be statute law (such as the Trades Description Act), or voluntary within an industry (the Advertising Standards Authority) or come from pressure groups in society at large (environmental issues like the introduction of genetically modified food).

Activity 12.7

Causes of change

Collect examples of the causes of change relating to a specific industry (eg banking, brewing, motor transport, fast food, the internet) for discussion in class. Back up with current press articles where possible. Which 'Slept' factor seems dominant? How are firms within these sectors reacting?

constraints on marketing

control of advertising

It is generally agreed that some adverts are 'near the mark' or should not be seen. Advertising which offends, is unsuitable for children, or which is plainly misleading or untrue needs an element of control. This control is firstly attempted by:

- the Advertising Standards Authority. The ASA monitors press and poster advertisements for legality, decency, honesty and truthfulness

- the British Code of Advertising Practice, which is a voluntary agreement by advertisers supervised by the ASA

- adverts which are broadcast are controlled by three statutory bodies – the Broadcast Complaints Commission, the Broadcasting Standards Council and the Independent Television Commission

- the Broadcast Advertising Clearance Centre 'vets' all advertising copy before it can be screened

Despite (or perhaps because of) this number of controlling bodies, confusion can arise. In an attempt to clarify its position, the Committee of Advertising Practice issued a new Code of Advertising Practice (CAP) in February 1995. The rules specifically covered alcohol, children, motoring, environmental claims, health and beauty, slimming, financial services and sales promotions. There were also special rules on distance selling, database usage and the offering of employment/business opportunities.

In 1999 the rules were revised, and became operational on 31 January 2000. The only changes of substance were new rules on political advertising, prices and protection of privacy, but in November, 1999 the majority of UK Web advertising fell under the control of the ASA, after the Internet Advertising Bureau announced it had signed up to the industry's self-regulatory system (see the Marketing Journal, 2/12/99).

It is well worth asking the ASA for a college or school copy of the latest review. See also more cases on their website www.asa.org.uk

complaints to the Advertising Standards Authority

The ASA monitors some 10,000 complaints in a year, 90% of these coming from members of the public, and 10% from competitors or pressure groups. Recent examples are shown on the next page.

Read the articles and carry out the Activity on page 282.

ASA rules against misleading Asda comparative price ads

Asda's attempts to portray itself as the best value supermarket in the UK have suffered a setback after the Advertising Standards Authority (ASA) ruled that one of its comparative price ads was misleading.

The ASA upheld a complaint by Tesco that accused Asda of exaggerating the 'representative nature' of a promotion comparing the price of an Asda customer's shopping basket with those of its four main competitors - Sainsbury's, Tesco, Safeway and Morrisons.

The ads, which came under Asda's 'low price guarantee'

banner and support its much-vaunted 'rollback' price cuts, displayed price differences between equivalent items in a randomly selected customer's shopping basket.

The ASA says problems in finding equivalent items at all four supermarkets meant the comparisons were not representative enough of the chosen shopper's original choices. The authority says the ads could miss significant categories, such as dairy products, because of problems with availability.

The decision comes three weeks after Asda chief executive

Allan Leighton revealed the chain would cut prices - by as much as 20 per cent - to levels similar to those of its US parent Wal-Mart within 18 months.

In the wake of the price cuts, the ASA has issued a warning to supermarkets that claims made in comparative ads must be substantiated to avoid censure.

An ASA spokesman says: 'Competitors will be scrutinising companies' ads, and they have to ensure they have the evidence to back up claims. Otherwise competitors will complain and, where they can not back it up, the ASA will uphold the complaint.'

Source: Marketing Week, November 4 1999

ASA cracks down on Stern posters

Religious and community organisations were among more than 220 complainants who contacted the Advertising Standards Authority (ASA) over a poster and print ad campaign for shock jock Howard Stern's TV chat show on cable TV channel Bravo.

The ASA has upheld a series of complaints against Bravo in its latest monthly report on the basis that lines featured in the £1m ad campaign for The Howard Stern Show were likely to cause serious or widespread offence.

Created by Mother, both print and posters featured quotes from the show, including: 'It's OK for a man to commit adultery if his

wife is ugly.'

Bravo will now have to submit future poster campaigns for pre-vetting.

The ASA has also upheld a complaint against press ads for the Honda Civic which claim the car is made in Swindon, on the grounds that all models of the car are not manufactured in the UK.

Honda is refusing demands by the ASA to change the wording of the press campaign created by CDP.

It claims that copy was submitted to the Committee of Advertising Practice for advice prior to the launch of the £15m press, poster and TV campaign which centres around the Swindon theme.

Crispin Reed, director of the Honda account at CDP, says: 'Honda's policy is to pre-submit all advertising to the ASA and no fault was found with the ads at the time. Honda and CDP are both talking to the ASA about this.'

The complaint came from a member of the public in the West Midlands.

The ASA also upheld a complaint against Whitbread over a poster for its Source vodka drink, which showed a waiter floating face-down in a swimming pool with his back being used as a table for bottles of the drink. The ASA said the ad was likely to cause offence because it trivialised death.

Source: Marketing Week, October 14 1999

Activity 12.8

Advertising control

Read the articles on the previous page and answer the following questions.

1   Why do firms monitor, and sometimes complain about, the advertisements of their competitors?

2   Why have the advertisements in the article about Bravo caused complaints? Who has made the complaints?

3   Visit the ASA website   www.asa-org.uk   and discuss in class the types of complaints made.

legal constraints

The Sale of Goods Act 1979 and **Sale and Supply of Goods Act 1994** regulate contracts for the sale of goods. They imply the following terms:

*   the seller must have the legal right to sell the goods ie he is the legal owner
*   the goods sold are 'as described' eg the stated size
*   the goods are of 'satisfactory quality' and 'fit for the purpose'

Note that the term 'satisfactory quality' was introduced by the Sale and Supply of Goods Act 1994 which amended the 1979 Act. This means that the goods must meet the standard that a 'reasonable' person would regard as satisfactory, taking account of any description of the goods, the price if relevant, and all other relevant circumstances eg if a new car is scratched it is still 'merchantable,' but it is hardly 'satisfactory.' If there is a sale by sample then the goods sold should be the same as the ones sampled. If any of these conditions is broken, the buyer is entitled to a refund of the purchase price from the seller, and perhaps compensation for damage or injury. Also note that the seller cannot exclude responsibility by putting up notices or declaring on the receipt such statements as 'no refunds given.'

The Supply of Goods and Services Act 1982 gave the same protection to consumers who purchase a 'service'.

the **Trade Descriptions Act** states that it is a criminal act

*   to apply a false trade description to any goods, or to supply or offer to supply, any goods to which a false trade description is applied
*   to give a false indication as to price (see Consumer Protection Act 1987)
*   to make a false statement knowingly or recklessly as to the provision of a service eg 'TVs in all rooms' if this is not so

- to give a misleading indication that goods have been offered at a higher price, as in a shop sale, when this is not the case

The **Competition Act 1998** operates through the Competition Commission (which replaced the Monopolies and Mergers Commission). This body can now investigate any firms in dominant market positions to see if they are acting 'against the public interest'. Equally, attention has turned to 'predatory pricing', whereby a firm tries to run competitors out of business by long term, sometimes loss making, prices, to establish a monopoly.

the ethical picture

Marketing has a major impact on the conflicts between businesses and social issues, and it is important that marketing people understand the criticisms that they may receive. The problem centres around the need to increase sales or cut costs, but being seen to be doing this in a socially unacceptable manner. Note the clash of interests in businesses amongst its stakeholders: the shareholders, management and workers may approve measures which increase profits and wages, but that as private individuals they might condemn. A variety of pressure groups monitor business activities, such as Friends of the Earth and the Consumers' Association (the 'Which' magazine). An early environmental conflict saw thousands of plastic bottles being dumped outside the factory which manufactured soft drinks after the firm switched from returnable glass bottles to plastic ones to cut costs. More recently the testing of products on animals has made bad PR for some firms. Social marketing is a key current issue, ie the concept of materialism modified by the need to care. The Stock Market now offers 'ethical' investment trusts/unit trusts for investors who wish to make a 'social' point.

Activity 12.9

Trading ethics

1   Give examples of organisations that are under pressure for ethical reasons at the present time, What are their reactions to the charges? Which pressure groups are involved?

2   Are they 'customer focused' in their response? How are their Marketing departments (in particular their PR people) reacting?

3   Give examples of organisations that you recognise as being socially aware or environmentally friendly. How are you made aware of their policy?

CHAPTER SUMMARY

● Planning of marketing can be achieved in a number of recognised ways, eg SWOT (Strengths, Weaknesses, Opportunities, Threats) and the Marketing Mix (Product, Price, Promotion and Place).

● Product policy and Market policy are closely linked. Product policy decides which products to make and sell. Market policy decides which products each chosen market sector should want to buy.

● The Boston matrix plots individual product's market share, and market growth; the Ansoff strategy examines the markets available for expansion; Market strategy decides how wide a market to aim for; PEST analyses changes in the marketplace that will affect the organisation. These are all tools for the product and market policy makers.

● The product life cycle concept applies to each and every product and service on sale today.

● The product portfolio examines the timing of new products and the life stage of existing ones.

● The marketing of services has special problems relating to intangibility, heterogeneity, distribution, perishability and ownership.

● The growth of an organisation can be by natural expansion (product and market development) or by merger or takeover.

● Constraints on marketing activity include statute law, which is legally binding; voluntary agreements, which involve the organisations in a market agreeing to a code of practice; and ethical considerations which try to ensure that the community at large is not offended or disadvantaged in any way.

KEY TERMS

SWOT	an approach to planning which takes into consideration an organisation's Strengths and Weaknesses, and the Threats and Opportunities with which it is presented
product policy	decides the type and range of products to supply to the marketplace
product life cycle	describes the length of time, from launch to removal from the range, that a particular type of product is available for purchase
product substitution	the replacing of an existing model of your own, or a change by consumers to a different brand
competitor	another organisation providing products that satisfy the same needs as do your own
market policy	deciding to which markets to sell
market position/share	a share of a particular market held by a business
market segment	a section of a total market with specified characteristics eg an age group, a region
Boston matrix	examines the products in a product range relative to growth and market share
Ansoff strategy	examines possibilities for growth via new products and/or new markets
PEST	analyses change from the political, economic, social and technological standpoints.
Code of Advertising Practice Committee	sets out the rules to be observed by the advertising industry
Advertising Standards Authority	investigates complaints from firms and individuals about any advertisement's legality, decency or honesty, based on the Code of Advertising Practice
Competition Act	set up a Commission to establish whether firms with large market shares were acting against the public interest
Trade Descriptions Act	makes giving a false description of a product or service a criminal act
business stakeholders	people and organisations who have an interest in what the business does
pressure groups	bodies that try to influence business policies in a specific area, ie animal rights, the environment

Marketing strategies – pricing and promotion

introduction

This chapter and the next look at the creation of strategies that meet customer needs. You must understand the need for a coherent 'mix' of strategies. This chapter concentrates on the choices involved in ensuring that the 'price is right', and how the many promotional activities function together.

what you will learn from this chapter

● pricing is a mixture of both long and short term influences

● there is a variety of communication techniques used by businesses to inform and influence their target audience

● advertising uses a wide variety of media and messages

● branding and logos are a key element in consumer loyalty

● packaging relates to both product protection and presentation

● public relations involves promoting a precise image of the business and its products to the public; publicity involves the business and its products or personnel being newsworthy

● sponsorship is an important advertising medium

● sales promotions – eg competitions, special offers – are used to promote products 'in the short term'

● product presentation is a mixture of design, branding, merchandising and putting your outlet in the right place, combining to create the desired corporate image

● direct marketing uses adverts that stimulate immediate orders by giving the seller's address, telephone number or website address

pricing

Price is an important element of the marketing mix. The price charged for a product can determine whether a consumer will buy it, and the level of sales achieved can determine whether or not the business will make a profit. The question is – what price to charge? The accountant's view of pricing is cost plus, ie the cost of the product plus a profit margin. Price is also affected by factors such as the state of the economy, what competitors are charging, the stage reached in the product's life cycle, and above all else, what price the market will bear. From the marketing point of view, this is what matters. Think what you pay for a can of Coke in the nearby shop. Now, how much are you charged at a club for the same quantity? A simple explanation, but a crucial one.

There are a number of pricing strategies which can be used:

long term objectives

These will depend upon how the organisation wishes to position itself in the market place, or how it wishes to establish itself financially. Here are some examples:

*   making a profit, for the stakeholders and for future investment
*   pricing to keep competitors out
*   pricing which positions the company at the premium end of the market
*   pricing to maximise sales and become the market leader

Choose carefully. It is difficult to change once underway.

short term objectives

These are tactical, as in promotion and selling. Here are some examples:

*   **skimming** – charging high prices for new products that at first have no competition, eg today's new technology; this helps to recover development costs
*   **penetration pricing** – a low price to penetrate an existing market
*   **destruction pricing** – knocking out the competitors by cutting prices, a process commonly known as 'price wars'
*   **promotion pricing** – the special offers or 'sale' pricing
*   **loss leaders** that get people into the shop. Beware the law here. If the rest of your prices are above average, you are liable for prosecution.
*   **psychological pricing** – the study of what motivates a consumer. Is it possible to price too high? Of course it is. Is it possible to price too low? Surprisingly, yes. Consumers have a perception of value. Have you ever heard someone say "it can't be any good at that price". So, put up the

price and sell more! Think fashion – are you guilty of paying too much for a 'name'? See the extract from Marketing Week on the next page.

Another aspect of psychological pricing is its appearance. We are all used to seeing £0.99, £9.99, £995 etc. So why are these still used? They don't fool people, but the first figure catches the eye – especially in the above. Why?

Activity 13.1

'technology breaks chains . . .'

Read the article from 'Marketing Week' shown on the opposite page and explain the quotations that follow and answer the additional questions.

1   *'An item's price is pregnant with meaning and symbolism'.*

'High prices can also imply status.'
What is the significance of high and low prices?

2   *'Technology-driven price disruption.'*

'The information age is generating the mother-of-all price disruptions.'
What up-to-date examples can you add to the illustrations given in the article?

3   *'Growing consumer doubts as to what is fair and reasonable'*
What other examples can you give of apparent 'give-aways'?

4   *'The notion of a fixed price list is a relic.'*
How is the internet changing the notion of a fixed price?

5   *'. . . the quality of the relationship between marketer and consumer'*
What evidence can you find in the UK of consumers becoming 'smart'?

advertising

Advertising is defined by the Institute of the Practitioners in Advertising (the IPA) as:

the most persuasive possible selling message to the right prospects (markets) for the product or service at the lowest possible cost

Advertising has its critics and its supporters. Its critics would say that it is expensive and pushes up the price of the product, it can offend people and persuade consumers to buy products which they cannot afford. Its supporters on the other hand claim that it increases demand, stimulates competition and lowers prices. Both points of view can be true. The control of advertising by law and by public bodies was discussed at the end of the previous chapter.

Technology breaks chain linking price with value

In the 'Information Age', consumers do not want price cuts, they want value for money. The marketer's priority is proving a product's true worth. **By Alan Mitchell.**

The Encyclopaedia Britannica used to sell for £1,500 or more. Today, its content is available free on the Internet. Like a twist in the plot at the end of a thriller, it makes you question your previous judgements about value and value for money. It makes you sceptical; it forces you to reassess your beliefs.

As we hurtle helter-skelter into the information age, a tidal wave of such reassessments will confront us, both from consumers and marketers. Much of it will be agonising.

Marketers have always known that price is not the product of a pure, cold rational economic equation. An item's price is pregnant with meaning and symbolism. A relatively high price can signify quality and reassurance, for example, whereas low priced products are often assumed to be shoddy.

High prices can also imply status: "The mere fact that I paid so much for this tells the world how successful I am, or how much I love you."

The other side of the coin is that people - especially certain segments of the population - love a bargain. For them, there is something tremendously exciting about getting things cheaper.

Signals like these are unlikely to go away soon. But four hugely powerful forces are transforming the context in which they work. The way consumers and marketers think about prices is changing.

The first force is technology-driven price disruption. There is nothing new here. As new technologies transform the cost of making something, so previous price expectations are disrupted. The information age is generating the mother-of-all price disruptions.

When first introduced in 1915, a domestic fridge cost the average worker 3,162 hours labour. By 1997, they could buy it for 66 hours' work. Thanks to industrial age technologies and economies of scale, the price has fallen by 98 per cent over 80 years. Thanks to information age technologies, however, the price of a cellular phone has fallen more dramatically than that, in just 15 years.

Information processing now accounts for more than 50 per cent of all economic activity in modern societies. And, thanks to Moore's Law (that the price of computing will halve every 18 months or so), information processing costs will plummet forever. Yesterday we had the known value item, which created a sort of pricing standard for consumers. Today, they are being taught to expect continuing price reductions - or "roll back" as Asda calls it.

Secondly, growing consumer doubts as to what is a "fair" or reasonable price are being compounded by the emergence of new business models that make a point of giving away, or at least selling below cost, what was once an expensive core product.

Britannica.com hopes that by giving away its core product it will attract enough eyeballs to become a major advertising site. Buy.com does the same with physical goods, selling them at zero or negative margins and making its money on ad sales. A message to the consumer: why buy at the "full" price when you can get it at a massive discount?

But - and this is the third point - the information age pricing revolution does not stop there. The notion of a fixed list price is a relic of a fading industrial age which depends on standardised prices to make its system of mass production, distribution and advertising work. Everything about the modern era - from mass customisation and life-time customer value-driven marketing strategies to the emergence of auctions, reverse auctions and buying clubs - points in the opposite direction.

Prices are set by markets, not marketers. When companies issue stock on the stock market, they know the market, rather than the marketer, will control the price at which it trades.

Slowly, painfully, we are moving in the same direction in the market for goods and services.

The fourth mega-force is a product of the first three. As old assumptions about price are challenged, so the emotional connotations of different pricing strategies are beginning to change. For example, a certain price not only says something about the quality of the item but also the quality of the relationship between marketer and consumer. Are these people taking me for a ride? Or are they on my side, acting for me, in my interests?

In Germany, many of the cars parked outside deep-discounting Aldi stores are Mercedes and BMWs. These people are not poor and they do not see themselves as mean either. What they hate, however, is anyone treating them like a fool, or a mug. Shopping at Aldi is a sign that you are a smart shopper. Likewise, in the US it is getting to the stage where anyone who buys at list price is seen as a loser. Now, stung by the excesses of the designer label years, British consumers are adopting the same mentality. Hence the great "rip-off Britain" debate.

the advertising campaign

The stages in the advertising campaign set out set out at the bottom of this page are in a recommended order. Some organisations may adopt a different procedure. It should be obvious, however, that certain decisions must precede others. The campaign described may be carried out by an advertising agency for a large organisation. A small business may not use an agency because of the expense, but nevertheless the principles described are still relevant for the smaller business. The important starting point is to have clear objectives as to what is to be achieved. See the section on page 303 on product performance and marketing communications.

identify the right markets

The advertiser must be aware which markets, or market segments, are being targeted. This is a straight-forward market segmentation exercise. With consumer goods, the choice might be age, sex, socio-economic grouping, occupation, race, religion, or region. The choice is increasingly associated with lifestyle categorisations (see page 247). With industrial goods, the choice might be the channel of distribution used, the type of industry, the region, or a public/private sector split. Segments must be identified or the wrong media will be chosen.

identify the right media

How are you going to put the message across?

How would you best attract and influence the chosen target group(s), given the type of product or service? The choice of media is large, and rapidly expanding as more TV channels and the new technology of the Internet add to the choice. Selection is therefore critical and must be based on the following:

* Is the cover to be local, regional or national?
* Does the overall cost rule out any medium?
* How many people are reached and at what cost per person?
* Which social group(s) does the medium reach?
* How often can the message be put over – hourly, daily. weekly etc.
* Can the message be detailed/how long a life will it have?
* What is the image/status/prestige of the medium?
* How important are sound, movement, colour, size?
* Will the results be measurable eg. replies to one advertisement?

These are the key questions to be asked when selecting suitable media.

The lists in the boxes in the diagram on the next page have been drawn up in categories in order to help answer these questions.

Vision & sound TV Radio Cinema Video	**Paper-based text** National papers Local papers Free papers Magazines Trade directories	**Leaflets &** **Catalogues** mailed door-to-door inserts
Electronic teletext Internet TV shopping	**advertising media**	**Sponsorship** individuals teams events
Transport related own vehicle buses, trains roadside posters	**Exhibitions** national shows local shows in-store on the street	**Giveaways** diaries T shirts bags pens

Activity 13.2

Choosing the advertising media

Discuss or write a list of the media you would choose to advertise . . .

- a new brand of bicycle
- a revamped chocolate bar
- 18/30 holidays
- your second hand car
- new computers
- a local clothing shop
- a range of cosmetics
- a multiplex cinema

Activity 13.3

Targeting mini consumers

Read the article from the Marketing Week shown below and answer these questions:

1   Why is 'pester power' of importance to advertisers?

2   What is the current problem in reaching 'mini consumers'?

3   What must media planners do to remain effective?

4   Discuss in class your own exposure to and knowledge of 'electronic advertising'.

To target 'mini' consumers you must play their game

The new breed of techno children is a growing consumer group. To keep pace with their 'electronic' lives, advertisers need to get online. **Dean Weller** reports

I have recently been studying and interviewing a group of children who are best described by American Doug Tapscott in his book Growing Up Digital as "Netgeners" or "generation Y". They are the progeny of parents whose own mothers and fathers were products of the "post-War baby boom."

They are 3 to 15 year old children who are "frighteningly" comfortable using technology and have electronic theme park bedrooms crammed full of "stuff". They eat on their own, watch their own TV sets, play video games on their PC, have a video games console and surf the Internet on BT's "Home highway".

These children live in ABC1 households of "moneyed" parents and are of particular interest to advertisers who want to stimulate the now common vernacular "pester power".

The older ones - 10 plus - are viewed by mobile phone companies as potential pre-pay callers. Car companies see them as influencing mum and dad's choice of vehicle.

This growing band of mini - but mature - consumers are, not surprisingly, popping up all over the place in ads. The best example of this is the BT commercial where a father plays an intercontinental game of chess against his pre-teen (tween) son using fax, e-mail, mobile telephone and, of course, a regular phone. The son manages to upstage his dad and win.

For marketers, the problem with this valuable target audience is that it is becoming harder to reach using traditional media. By that, I mean TV.

While these tweens spend as much as 22 hours a week watching screens, "live" TV programming is taking an increasingly smaller share. On average, "we" are losing an hour's TV viewing by children every week of every year. And there are indications that this is accelerating, especially in ABC1 households.

Children in C2DE households who do not have PCs and modems - and form the stable core of child and youth TV viewing - still have games consoles, and this is where the big changes are going to occur.

The new Sega Dreamcast system is Net-ready, as will be PlayStation 2. These machines will be realistically priced and provide a true democracy of the Net, especially as we move to a truly "free to enter" Web.

The problem with new media audience measurement and analysis is that many practitioners are applying the planning and buying techniques they were using years ago. The new game is not which ads are being shown to children but one where a communication solution stimulates a long-term, measurable and accountable response.

Maybe we need a few full-time "Netgener" employees to provide the insight and technical solutions to how we should measure effectiveness in our brave new market. Maybe I should recruit some of my interviewees.

Dean Weller is managing director of The First Age! Media Company, which specialises in children's, youth and family communication solutions.

Marketing Week, October 21 1999

create the right message – stress the benefits!

The 'right' message is one that appeals to the market segment identified, and suits the type of media chosen. Advertisers in particular, and the marketing team in general, are always searching for a USP – a Unique Selling Point or Proposition. Many messages work so well that they become part of the language, for example, "I bet he drinks ....". Not all approaches work. You will no doubt have experienced an advert and then thought "What was that all about?"

What makes a successful message? Messages generally fall into one of two types, both of which set out the benefits to be gained by purchasing the product. The types are

- factual messages
- emotive messages

For example, we have a new car to advertise. What possible features might we stress? What benefits does it have?

factual	emotive
price and value	status – must be rich or important to own one
economy of performance	sex appeal – attracting a partner
acceleration	family comfort and safety – the caring parent
body strength (anti-rust)	personality – lost youth – sports car
safety record	comfort – arrived relaxed for the meeting
reliability	health – of others – runs on lead-free petrol

Activity 13.4

Getting the message across

Discuss one or more products which are widely used and write down the factual and emotive benefits which could be used when advertising them. Products could include . . . a pair of jeans, a drink, a deodorant, a magazine for the under-18s.

psychological factors in the message

When you consider the emotive content of a message you will see that there are certain basic drives which relate to and affect the behaviour of us all. When you study Human Resources you will encounter Maslow (page 408).

Advertisers base much of their logic on his 'Hierarchy', as they realised that his motivational factors could be taken advantage of when offering 'benefits' to consumers . . .

a need for basic necessities	To breathe, to stay alive, to eat and drink. Surely these are guaranteed in our society? But can we create doubts in the buyer's mind? Of course we can.
the fear of death	Does our car have good tyres or air bags? Do we have adequate insurance?
a safe drink	Is tap water safe? Perhaps bottled water is better?
safe food	Is our food safe? Look at the additive content and the sell by date.
sex	The suggestion is that wearing this, smelling of that, or buying a box of this will enable us to attract the partner we want.
love	When not connected with sex, love can involve family and animals: mothers are persuaded to buy for children, animals soften our feelings towards products.
achievement at work	we strive for success, promotion- will the new suit improve our image? At home we take pride in our surroundings – will that new DIY tool improve our home?
self indulgence	the top of Maslow's triangle. Purchases for yourself alone – "L'Oréal – because I'm worth it."

Activity 13.5

the advertising message

Record on video a number of TV adverts at random. Make a note of when the adverts are screened. Watch the tape, preferably as a class exercise, and answer the following questions:

1   In what other media have you seen the product advertised?

2   At what market segment(s) is the advertisement aimed?

3   Is the timing of the advert (eg morning, early evening, late evening) significant?

4   Is there a specific message? Does it work? Is it mainly factual or emotive?

5   What psychological factors can you identify in the advertisement?

identify the right timing

Timing of the advertising is crucial. Too soon before the event, and the customers forget; too late and they have bought something else. Seasonal markets need careful timing. A Media Expenditure Plan should be drawn up, detailing at what stages of the campaign the money should be spent, and on which media ie the Trade need to be informed first so that stocks will be in the shops when consumers get to hear about it. Clearly an initial burst would accompany the launch of a new product. After that it would be a matter of choice.

A media expenditure plan is a table that lists months across the top and the chosen media down the left hand side. Expenditures are placed in this spreadsheet as thought fit.

calculate the cost of the campaign

This area is one where marketing personnel and accountants sometimes disagree. It is obviously desirable that costs are covered by sales, but marketing personnel may want a boost to the advertising budget if sales are unsatisfactory, whereas the accountant may argue for a reduction. Costs can be found in BRAD (British Rate and Data). Your tutor may be able to get a slightly dated copy from a local agency (they are very expensive). Alternatively and in more simple form ask your local newspaper or radio station head office for a 'rate card'. Collect a varied set of cost information between you.

branding

Branding is a method of identifying one product or service from another by creating a name, term, design or symbol (logo) which is unique to that product or service in your line of business. It creates an image which differentiates the product in the consumers' minds from the products of competitors.

advantages of branding

The establishment of a brand name will save on future advertising costs. The product has become 'known'. To the consumer a brand name represents a known quality of product, the next one bought being the same as the previous ones. To the manufacturer branding allows a range of products to be offered, to different market segments. It also allows brand loyalty to be established, ie some consumers always specify and buy the same 'name'. They have a perception of the product which satisfies their needs.

types of brand

- **Individual Brands** are those which stand alone, with no reference to the maker's name, eg Persil.

- **Family Brands** often carry the name of the company, eg Heinz, Boots, as a guarantee of quality. A family brand allows new products to be established more easily but should one product gain a bad reputation it may drag down all the rest.

- **Multibrand Strategy** – this involves the use of more than one brand in the same market segment to increase the chances of a company product being selected, eg different soap powders manufactured by the same firm.

- **House branding** – 'own' brands, eg Marks & Spencer, Tesco, Sainsbury all have their own version of consumer goods made especially for them and they sell under the retailer's own name or a chosen alternative. Once a house brand name has been established, it is customary to maintain the chosen quality or 'good value' image.

Activity 13.6

branding of products

Write four lists of as many brand names as you can think of – one list for each of the categories explained above. If you can, investigate examples of multibrand strategy by looking at the shop shelves – eg petfood, magazines, drinks.

When the lists are compiled, hold a class session where a member of the class (or the tutor) writes the names of the brands on the board in the four categories. Discuss the findings in class and come to some group decisions about branding.

packaging

This often used to appear as part of 'product policy', but over the years it has become a major aid to promotion and 'product presentation'. Note the following play on words:

- **Packing** is for Protection – it saves the product from damage/decay
- **Packaging** is for Promotion – it attracts the shopper's attention, especially at the 'point of sale'

Packing protects against breakage, pilferage, bacteria, chemical change (such as shrinkage, discolouration, rust), explosions and so on, all of which can create the marketing problems of lost reputation, lost orders and customer complaints.

Packaging enhances appearance using colour, shape and size. It carries the brand's name, product photographs and information re product use. It may allow the product to be seen whilst keeping it clean (meat), offer 'ease of use' advantages and continue to have marketing value even after the product has been used eg biscuit tins and coffee jars are kept for general storage purposes (but will continue to bear your brand name). A change to a product's pack can even increase sales and product life cycle.

Don't forget that packaging has other meanings – in the tourist industry you may buy a packaged holiday (transport, accommodation, tour guide, insurance etc); the banks may package financial products (mortgages, insurance and pensions).

Activity 13.7

Packaging today

1   List the ways in which packaging can attract attention.

2   List the ways in which packaging may lose sales.

3   Why is packaging criticised by environmentalists?

4   Why may lawyers and consumer groups study packaging?

publicity

Publicity is gained by being 'newsworthy'. As such it is never quite under the control of the marketing team. It depends upon what others say about the product or organisation. Kotler says that publicity is the

"non-personal stimulation of demand for a product, service or business unit by planting commercially significant news about it in a published medium or obtaining favourable presentation of it upon radio, television or stage that is not paid for by the sponsor"

The significant differences between advertising and publicity are:

*   Advertising is a known cost for an agreed amount of contact with the market. Publicity tends to be non-controllable, often unplanned.

*   Publicity has far greater impact in that it appears to come from a third person, and is thus more believable. If the press favourably review this book, it will sell more than any advert could achieve. A bad review may curtail sales!

*   Publicity catches readers off guard, whereas when they read an advert they know they are being sold to.

*   Advertising allows the repetition of the message several times, whereas publicity has the limited life of a news story.

*   Both advertising and publicity can dramatise the product to create interest.

public relations (PR)

"If I had one last marketing dollar, I'd spend it on PR." Bill Gates, Microsoft.

Public relations (PR) aims to safeguard and promote the image of the whole organisation, as well as its individual products. In the political world is has become known as 'spin'. It is an extension of the publicity approach in that it tries to co-ordinate the effort. It may consist of press releases about the organisation's achievements, whether they be new product concepts, technological breakthroughs or environmental concerns. Other approaches may involve appearances on radio and TV in relevant programmes or in the news; open days for the public at the factory or showroom; distribution of printed material (leaflets) and even internal channels eg house magazines for the staff. Sponsorship is another important area of PR.

Activity 13.8

public relations at work

Investigate examples of publicity gained by firms in the local and national press which are the result of a public relations team at work. These may be:

* good publicity – eg sponsorship

* bad publicity – eg examples of bad press, where a product has injured a user, or the firm has polluted the environment

In the case of good publicity and bad publicity what should the public relations function in the organisation do? Discuss each item within your class.

sponsorship and cause-related marketing

Although technically this is an advertising medium, recent changes in approach have linked it very firmly with PR. Originally used in advertising by supporting an individual athlete, football team, or event, it developed in the 1990s into other areas such as TV programme sponsorship.

More recently we have seen many organisations wish to position themselves as caring members of the community in which they exist. Community relations exercises linking firms with local schools, environmental care, and sponsorship of local sports teams are commonplace.

At present 'Cause Related Marketing' (CRM) is very fashionable as companies sponsor good causes. Examples include 'Tesco Computers for Schools', Persil's 'Go Red for Comic Relief', and Cadbury's 'Strollerthon'.

"Call it ethics, call it corporate philanthropy, call it CRM – but there is little doubt that the business of being seen to be good is a growth one."

(Laura Mazur, 'Marketing')

Activity 13.9

Cause Related Marketing (CRM)

Investigate other examples of CRM. Is there a real link between sponsor and recipient, as when 'Center Parcs' linked itself with 'wild flower conservation', or when the manufacturers of 'Andrex' linked with the 'Guide Dogs for the Blind Association'. Discuss the advantages and disadvantages of CRM to the sponsor and the sponsored.

sales promotion methods

A sales promotion may be defined as 'an attempt to create interest in and stimulate sales of a product or service by a non-standard activity in a limited period of time, or with a controlled amount of product ('while stocks last').'

In many ways, a sales promotion is a link between advertising and direct selling. It gives the advertiser an extra benefit to draw to the consumers' attention, persuading them to go to the shops, and it allows the manufacturer's sales person to revitalise the interest of the retailer by having something new to discuss or offer. Many, but not all, sales promotions generate activity at the point of sale, ie the shop. There are two types of promotion:

- trade promotions – manufacturers promoting to retailers and wholesalers
- consumer promotions – manufacturers and/or retailers promoting to the final consumer

trade promotions

The object of a trade promotion is to get the retailer to stock a product, or more of a product, or to stay loyal to the manufacturer. Types of trade promotion include:

- quantity discounts – if more than a stated number of items per period are ordered by the buyer, a discount or prize will be given
- tailor-made promotions linked to one store, ie the manufacturer puts on a special display free of charge in the shop. See Case Study on page 252

Trade promotions are easily targeted as the manufacturer knows which outlets do, or might, stock the product. Note that many trade promotions run at the same time as consumer ones. It is however increasingly difficult to get retailers to 'make space'.

consumer promotions

The object of a consumer promotion is for the seller to raise the long term level of sales by offering some added value to the purchase of a product in the short term. A few examples are:

- money off this or the next purchase, or two for the price of one
- coupons or samples delivered through the door
- competitions, with attention-gaining prizes
- free gifts
- loyalty incentives (eg points cards) that reward regular customers

Activity 13.10

Consumer sales promotions

Visit retailers or read the press to find evidence of consumer promotions. Note the type of promotion and the product involved. Talk to independent retailers about recent trade promotions. Gather evidence for discussion in class. How successful do you think they are? Is there a particular type popular at the moment?

merchandising at the point of sale

In a retail outlet, the merchandiser is in charge of the presentation of the products and of the store itself. His or her job involves making the environment so attractive that the consumer wants to make a purchase and to call again. A merchandiser or salesperson employed by a manufacturer visits retailers to offer advice on presentation of his own company's product eg to set up displays – see the Cadbury case study on page 309.

Modern merchandising leans heavily on the psychology of advertising in its research into what motivates the consumer. Factual and/or emotive messages, package design, brand names, publicity, short-term promotions all influence the consumer. It should be fairly obvious, therefore, that factors such as shop layout, lighting, outer and inner appearance, will also affect the buying decision. Most people can recall an 'impulse' purchase. Why? Was it previously seen advertising? The known brand name? The appearance of the package? Or was it the general 'feel' of the shop that inspired the additional buy, or the change from the usual brand? If it was the latter, the merchandiser has been successful.

product presentation

This has a variety of meanings, all of marketing significance:
*   the design of the product, researched early on and possibly revamped during its life cycle
*   the packaging and logo design as seen in the store
*   the merchandising and the product's position in the store
*   the type of outlet, suited to the product's image
*   the site of the store in which it appears – the right 'area'

The first three of these points are covered in the article by Marcus Gibson in 'The Mail on Sunday', reproduced on the next page. Read the article and then carry out the Activity which follows it. The other points are developed in Chapter 14.

Stores set to make millions in space race

That annoying habit stores have of moving your favourite products around is about to get worse.

A virtual-reality program that helps retailers put the right product in the right place at the right time is to blame.

The Retail Focus program produced by Advanced Visual Technology is used by Tesco, Comet, Marks & Spencer and Waitrose to work out the exact location and display for every product in their hundreds of stores.

But it is not designed just to confuse shoppers. Every square foot of space saved is worth an extra £100,000 a year revenue, says Comet.

The money-spinning space is found by using a 3D viewer to model a store's layout.

Planners can tell every store in their group where to position fresh food as it comes into season and can see how well specific items sell in each store.

AVT's marketing director Bernard Barnett, based in Nottingham, says the software helps most when a new store is being planned.

A task that used to take six weeks can now be done in less than 48 hours. Where teams of planners once produced thousands of drawings, Retail Focus performs the entire operation on screen and individual managers can log on to get the whole picture.

Head offices issue `planograms' dictating how much selling space to allocate daily to each item. Few stores within a group have identical layouts, but the program allows managers to adapt the plan to fit their stores.

An architectural diagram of each store is also loaded into Retail Focus so head office managers can calculate the best overall layout for each store.

Waitrose has linked Retail Focus to its own computer system to create one of the most detailed store management networks.

Tesco uses the program to make certain that all the goods allocated to each store will fit inside. Barnett says: `If calculations are even 1 per cent out it can be very costly.'

David Weavers, Tesco's head of space planning, says: `With this system we can streamline our planning process and continuously improve our working practices.'

Mothercare has used Retail Focus to put its 340 stores on to one database. `When Christmas comes, the system remembers those successful seasonal layouts from last year,' says Barnett.

Putting one product next to a complementary one to boost sales - for example, tomato sauce bottles next to sausages - is a well-known ploy of retailers.

AVT's program allows retailers to test this idea, known in the trade as `adjacency'.

`One retailer saw sales soar when it used our program to re-site ice cream,' says Barnett.

AVT is now selling the system to US and France, and its first-year sales of £1 million are expected to double this year.

`We spotted a gap in the market for visual systems that linked goods with shelf space,' says Barnett. `There is no comparable software in America.'

Interior design has not been overlooked. If signs designed for a promotion block the view of other products, the program will identify the flaw before the signs are ordered.

The program enables managers and planners to see the store through a child's eyes, showing which items would remain in sight when placed on certain shelves.

Health regulations have also been built into the database. If, by mistake, eggs are allocated to a freezer, or chilled meat to a room temperature display unit, the system will trigger an alarm.

The AVT program also handles in-store safety. Wal-Mart recently faced court action by customers hit by bicycles that fell off shelves.

The program alerts managers to potential problems such as shelving that is unable to support bricks at a DIY store.

Office planners, too, are beating a path to AVT's door to squeeze maximum value out of expensive space.

Clifford Chance, the UK's biggest law practice, plans to use the software to optimise the layout, check inventory and boost the efficiency of facilities for the 1,200 staff at its 600,000 square foot London office.

Source: *The Mail on Sunday,* 5 September, 1999

Activity 13.11

merchandising

Read the article on the previous page. In groups or general class discussion, build a list the factors you have discovered.

Then arrange with the manager of local stores for you to visit, in small groups, to study 'in store appeal', ie the use of space, special promotions, colour schemes, lighting, ventilation, use of music, availability of customer facilities like lifts, 'coffee shops', product positioning etc.

product performance & marketing communications

The ultimate aims of all marketing communications are:

- To stress the benefits that the customer will gain by buying the product (or subscribing to the charity) – be aware that sellers sell benefits, not products, ie a reason for buying the product must be communicated.

- To improve awareness of a product or organisation – this is critical when the product is in the early (launch) stage of its life cycle – customers must be made aware of its existence.

- To improve product performance in terms of sales levels, by volume, value and profitability – the approach to this will depend again on the stage reached in the product's life cycle. In its launch and growth stages, large increases can be achieved, but in maturity, small market share increases are usually the best that can be gained. Nevertheless, communications with the customer must continue, to retain market share. (A detailed account of product life cycles can be found on pages 269 to 271).

- To increase income, as in the case of a charity or a political party.

- To improve an image, as with a political party, to gain votes. In fact, all organisations work hard on their image these days. It is very important, especially where many of the products sold are very similar. This goes for manufacturers, service providers, charities, retail outlets and so on. Sales and income depend upon it. Refer to the section on PR on page 298.

- To achieve brand loyalty and gain repeat sales from existing customers.

- To find new customers.

corporate image

Corporate image is literally the 'image of the company' – the ways consumers 'see' it. As we noted in the first chapter of this book, The Body Shop promotes a corporate image of caring for the community and the environment. Sir Richard Branson and his 'Virgin' enterprises have given off mostly good 'vibes' for giving customers value for money.

All of the communications activities explained in this chapter must be chosen with care, and co-ordinated to suit the required corporate image. If the organisation has an 'up-market' image, every communication with its public must carry that image through. Take, for example, the car manufacturer Rolls Royce. It wishes to be perceived as the provider of motor cars to 'top' people. It does not offer price reductions – one of the points of owning one is to display one's wealth or position in society. It does not advertise in down-market papers or magazines. Even the purchase of a Rolls Royce could be classed as difficult – dealers are not to be found everywhere.

Activity 13.12

product performance and the life cycle

Examine current advertising campaigns for examples of:

(a) the launch of a new product

(b) the promotion of a corporate image, eg Boots, Abbey National

(c) an attempt to change the image of a product to improve sales and market share, eg in the motor industry – the sporting image given to Volvo cars, or the association of the Skoda name with Volkswagen

In each case write down

•   the specific aims of the marketing communications

•   the techniques used to improve (or achieve) product performance through marketing communications

direct marketing

Direct Marketing combines the art of advertising with the need to get the person who sees it (or hears it) to take immediate action.

The term **AIDCA** stands for Attention, Interest, Desire, Conviction and Action. Direct Marketing uses an advert to gain attention, interest and desire, and then, if the customer is convinced, tries to ensure that action is taken immediately. Direct Marketing takes a number of forms.

direct mail

Direct mail uses the postal service to contact prospects (prospective customers) directly with advertising material linked to 'fill in response forms'. These should be targeted with great accuracy, using up to date databases. The phrase 'junk mail' is often used by recipients, but if material is targeted correctly, it should be relevant, not junk!

off-screen selling

Selling off-screen uses an advert on a TV screen which gives a telephone number to ring or a website address to contact to place an immediate order. It combines this technology with the credit card facility to make the payment instantly. Many holidays are booked in this way, especially at short notice. 0800 telephone numbers pass the cost of the call to the seller. Other organisations may charge only at local area rate.

selling off-page

The technique of selling off-page has traditionally used an advert that contains a cut out response box for easy ordering, but today it may carry a direct call telephone number. Both techniques rely on a well designed advert that will convince consumers to act straight away.

telemarketing

The growth of direct marketing has come about partly because of the revolution in telemarketing capacities. Telemarketing is the provision of a telephone number in an advert to stimulate an immediate enquiry or order. Telephone bureaux are needed to receive the rush of calls that follow a convincing advertisement. Even now, the technology is stretched, but this is a solvable problem. The future is bright for direct marketing, and the E-commerce technology revolution is pushing it forward at speed.

Activity 13.13

Direct response to TV advertising (DRTV)

1   Watch a set number of TV ads and count the number of times the telephone number is given. In 1994 the figure was 17%. What is the percentage now?

2   Is this an effective form of marketing? Ask a sample of friends and relatives, and collect their thoughts in the form of 'the advantages and disadvantages of DRTV'.

3   Why is it forecast that direct marketing is set to grow? Investigate different examples and analyse how new technology such as websites is making growth possible.

Case Study

Raleigh Industries
price, promotion and sales strategy

As you would expect from your reading so far, this is a mixture of promotional techniques and sales force activity, because although a bike is a consumer product, it is quite technical in make up and is often sold via specialist retailers. The budget for this strategy is split therefore about 70% on promotion (mainly directed at the final consumer), and 30% on sales activity (mainly directed at 'the trade'). The 30% does not include sales force salaries, cars etc, so the probable overall split would be nearer 60/40. This is fairly typical for a consumer durable.

pricing

This depends on the sector of the market being targeted, but the overall aim is for long term profitability, shareholder satisfaction and the funding of continued growth. A careful eye is kept on the cost of production, the competition, and what the market will bear. This relates to both product types and user categories, both home and overseas. Tactical pricing is not often used.

promotion to the Trade

• Point of sale material is distributed to outlets, to help them 'sell out'.

• Newsletters keep outlets up to date and promote the Raleigh name.

• 'Co-operative' advertising jointly between the Raleigh and the local outlets

advertising to the Consumer

• TV (limited by overall cost)

• radio (local dealers like this and often drive it themselves)

• literature (leaflets, brochures, dealer price lists)

• national press, by readership types, eg The Sun, Daily Mail and The Times

• magazines (specialist and general, eg womens' fashion, health)

• posters (general and roadside)

• electronic (Raleigh web site and electronic brochure, E-commerce is a growth area – log on www.raleighbikes.com)

• sponsorship (the Raleigh racing team was funded partly by the company and partly by outside sponsors)

The message concentrates on the benefits to the consumer, and varies according to the target audience. Both factual and emotive benefits of the product are stressed.

Branding

Corporate or 'Family' branding is now the priority as the cost of individual branding grows with the product range. However, 'Raleigh Special Products' covers the more specialist types of machine on offer.

Packaging

Designed to protect the product, particularly in transit. Strong cardboard protects paintwork and gears to avoid retailer and consumer dissatisfaction. The packaging carries the company name.

PR and Publicity

Events are sponsored and media publicity gained. Stories, some self generated, are offered to the press. These might concern charity rides, personnel in the news.

The environmental friendliness of the bike is promoted.

Exhibition stands are taken at non-bike events, on a non-selling basis, to promote the Raleigh name eg The Motor Show, race meetings, Ideal Homes exhibitions. These stands may be linked to dealers as part of the 'cooperative' policy.

Editorial reviews in the specialist press are vitally important for credibility eg the launch of the Max Lite brand drew the following comment from the specialist magazine 'Mountain Biker International' – "Raleigh's suspension designs have come a long way since the Activator, and this year's range have confirmed that they're once again back in the game."

Sales Promotions

These may be linked to key retailers, or to large non-bike organisations where bikes are the prizes on offer in a competition. Kelloggs and Raleigh have combined in this way.

Trade promotions used to offer prizes eg holidays, to retailers who sell the most Raleigh bikes in a given time period although these have been dropped in favour of enhanced margins instead.

Merchandising

This is always a problem as a bike is bulky and takes up valuable retail floor space. It is also difficult to display interestingly. It is usually a balance between displaying a few models that reflect the stocks held, and using point of sale material to show the product in use. It is difficult to balance between the 'cluttered' effect and showing enough to generate consumer interest. Advice on best practice is offered to retailers by Raleigh, using specialist consultants. Specially designed point of sale stands are also used to assist in effective display, and product leaflets are made available.

Sales Team

The national team is divided into north and south divisions, each with an area manager and four salespersons. The latter cover all dealers within their territory, supported by the area manager at 'key account' level. Customers include Halfords, JJB Multi Sports, John Lewis, and the Mail Order firms.

Activity 13.14

Raleigh strategies

1   What is meant by 'cooperative' advertising?

2   What do you understand by 'The Trade'? What examples are given?

3   Which media would you choose for the Max Lite mountain bike?

4   What benefits could be offered for the Max Lite mountain bike?

5   What are 'key accounts' and why would the regional sales managers get involved?

Case Study

Cadbury
Promotion and sales strategy: Yowie UK

The launch of Cadbury Land Yowie in the UK in April 1999 was associated with a promotional campaign aimed at both the trade and the consumer. The mix in this case saw a greater spend on promotional activities than on the sales activity as you would expect. Although considerable effort from Cadbury's own sales force was involved in introducing the product to the trade, the bulk of the budget went on advertising and PR to both the trade and the final consumer. As with all fast moving consumer goods (FMCG), the main thrust is to make the public aware of the product and to persuade them to buy. The trade is happy when it sees a big consumer 'push'.

promotion to the Trade

The Cadbury sales force was briefed late in 1998, and they, supported by trade advertising, approached trade outlets in December 1998 and January 1999. Even here there was an order of priority. The large supermarkets were informed first, so that they could inform, and order for, their own outlets. 'Key account' salespersons take this responsibility, along with responsibility for redistributive retailers ie the cash and carry and the wholesale chains who are important in getting to the 'symbol' outlets like 'Spar' and many of the independent accounts. These are a large part of the confectionery business. The rest of the sales team cover other 'independents', smaller shops who have one or just a few outlets. The sales team is organised on a regional basis.

The sales team overall have the task of explaining to the trade how the launch will run; the objectives, the support that the retailers can expect and the amount of promotion that will take place to get the consumers into the shops. This is designed to obtain orders from the trade. Included in their job role is the merchandising activity of creating displays within the shops ready for the launch.

Promotion to the consumer: advertising media

- Television – a major launch campaign aimed to create impact, awareness of the product and briefly to stress key benefits. TV is not a medium for long messages because air time is expensive.

- Direct mail – 100,000 households with children of the relevant age received a mailshot containing a covering letter for the parents and a Yowie Power pack for the children. The pack contained fun stickers, a handbook explaining the Yowie concept, and a map of the Yowie kingdom with a detailed reverse side giving facts about the (real) wildlife that live there – with spaces to stick the collected wildlife pictures. It is worth noting here that the database used for the mailing was built up by Cadbury Ltd., but in conjunction with two other major (non confectionery) UK firms. An interesting collaboration exercise.

- Website – www.yowie.co.uk offers games and information. Note how even the newest generation is being assumed to be going 'on line'. In the event nearly half a million visits to the site were logged in the first 4 weeks.

- Word of mouth – the recipients of the handbook get a ' tell your friends' message.

The advertising message concentrates on appeals to the kids . . .

- Yowie Power! Be part of what your friends are into! Play together!

- Collect a set of pictures to swop with your friends

- Learn how to protect the environment (this has parent appeal as well; it is important to gain the support of the people who buy the product for the kids)

Branding

The decision to stay with the Australian scenario and its Yowie names gives an idea as to just how global marketing has become. Research suggested that these names would be acceptable in the UK. (The overall Cadbury strategy uses both Family and Individual brands).

Packaging

Using fun character shapes and colourful packaging was seen as important in approaching this age group, especially in the multi coloured background at the point of sale. The emphasis is on packaging, not packing!

Publicity/PR

This was a major activity at the launch. Press releases went to the trade press, eg the Grocer journal, with examples of the product to 'key' journalists. The general press also received these releases. The Marketing Director of Cadbury was invited to give an interview on local radio. In addition, a special exclusive 10 week link up with the 'Funday' Times attracted much interest. Media coverage outside of pure advertising is such a valuable form of communication.

Sales Promotion

The Cadbury Roadshow attracted attention, and competitions used the product as prizes. This activity also was linked to The Sunday Times.

Merchandising

Attractive displays in shops create interest for parents or other donors to purchase for the children. There is a clear link here with packaging and product presentation. The Cadbury field sales force talk to retailers and help them 'sell out' from the shop by creating eye catching displays.

Activity 13.15

Cadbury Yowie

1   What estimate would you give to the ratio of expenditure on promotion to sales a) at launch? and b) after the product has become established?

2   What priorities are observed by the sales team?

3   The Yowie advertising campaign relies heavily on which two media? What are the advantages and disadvantages of this approach?

4   Suggest alternative strategies using a different media mix. Justify your ideas.

5   What factual and emotive benefits are suggested to the consumer?

6   Why are branding and packaging so important to the Yowie campaign?

7   Why is the interest of the media so important?

8   What factors go towards a successful merchandising display?

9   What is the meaning of the phrase 'salesmen sell in, merchandisers sell out'?

CHAPTER SUMMARY

● This chapter has examined two of the four parts of the marketing mix – price and promotion. You should appreciate that they, together with product (Chapter 12) and place (Chapter 14), must be part of an integrated strategy.

● Product pricing will have long and short term policies; in the long term profitability must be achieved; in the short term pricing can be tactical.

● Pricing must allow for 'what the market will bear', as well as achieving the desired profit level.

● Organisations must communicate with their prospective customers (prospects) in order to become known, but in a way that establishes the right corporate image.

● Organisations must make their products or services known to the right audiences if they wish to sell.

● Promotional communication methods consist of advertising, sponsorship, branding, packaging, publicity, public relations, sales promotions and merchandising. They must not offer conflicting messages.

● Product presentation is important at the point of sale, being a mixture of branding, packaging, merchandising and as will be explained in Chapter 14, in the choice of 'where' to sell the product.

● Advertising media must be chosen for its ability to reach the right market segments.

● Advertising messages must stress the 'benefits' that the purchaser will enjoy.

● The performance of a product in the marketplace will depend on the successful integration of the other three P's – price, promotion and place.

● The effectiveness of pricing and promotion in achieving product growth is also linked to the product's life cycle, eg its newness, or its established image etc.

● Direct marketing involves the prospect responding instantly to a marketing communication, either by telephone, post or Internet. Watch for new methods. The distinction between direct marketing (communicating with the customer) and direct selling is becoming blurred.

KEY TERMS

pricing policy	the decision as to the price or price range in which to place a product
advertising	communicating a product message through one or a selection of media channels in the hope of instigating a purchase
benefits	reasons why a potential customer should make the decision to buy
target audience	the sector of the market the seller has chosen to approach
branding	the name or logo that identifies the product
packaging	the physical wrapping around a product that attracts consumer attention at the point of sale, or the 'bundling' of services that sell together
publicity	promotion achieved for a product through news coverage not paid for by the producer
public relations	techniques used by an organisation to safeguard and promote its image and the image of its products
sponsorship	associating a firm with a person, team, event or good cause
sales promotion	techniques for creating an interest in a product and for stimulating sales in the short term
merchandising	displaying the product or the outlet itself attractively, to encourage the customer to buy
product presentation	combining the skills of packaging, display, merchandising and choice of site
corporate image	the overall image of the organisation in the eyes of the consumer
direct marketing	persuading the customer to respond by telephone or post immediately and directly after seeing or hearing an advertisement

14 Marketing strategies – sales and distribution

introduction

This chapter looks firstly at the sales function; that part of the promotional 'p' where the seller has personal contact in some form (face to face, by telephone etc) with the prospect or customer. It looks at the logistics of moving the product around the market (distribution) to outlets convenient to the customer. It also looks at the provision of services at places which the customers find convenient – at home, the office, or at leisure facilities.

what you will learn from this chapter

- organisations can sell direct to the customer, or indirectly, using intermediaries such as agents and retailers

- in the selling process organisations must balance the needs of their customers (eg providing full and clear product information, after-sales service) with their own needs (eg making a profit, increasing market share)

- a sales campaign will involve informing and co-ordinating the sales force; a number of different channels of communication can be used – letters, memos, meetings, conferences

- a sales person has a number of responsibilities – including product knowledge, awareness of legal issues; a sales person also has to be able to communicate effectively

- the sales function in an organisation can only work efficiently if there is an effective sales administration system in operation

- a distribution policy is needed by product manufacturers to make their products available in the right places

- a place (site) policy is needed by service providers to attract customers to their place of business

selling and distribution policies

The producer of a manufactured item or a service can sell to the customer in two very different ways:

indirect sales

Selling by indirect methods means using an intermediary (middle-person), such as a retailer or agent. In other words, the goods are sent through national (and even international) distribution channels before they reach the consumer.

direct sales

Sales can be made direct from the producer to the customer – helped by the direct marketing methods described in the last chapter (selling through direct response advertising) or employing direct personal contact (eg telesales, door-to-door selling, sales force activity or setting up an internet website).

We will look first at indirect sales methods.

indirect sales methods

As we have just seen, selling by indirect methods means using an intermediary (middle-person), such as a retailer or agent. Look at the diagram below. You will see that the black arrow represents the traditional selling route where the goods pass through a number of parties, each making a profit on the transaction. The blue arrows show the situation where the consumer 'cuts out' one or more of the intermediaries. Obviously the seller makes more profit here, and the consumer hopefully will also make a saving.

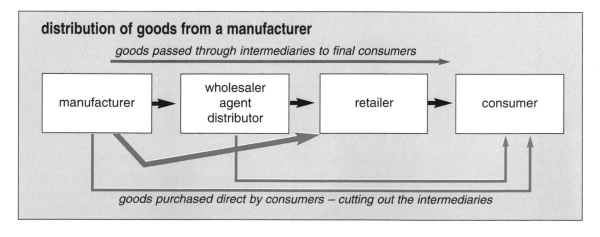

We will now look at some chains of supply to the consumer:

manufacturer – wholesaler – retailer – consumer

This is the traditional route, with gradual dispersion of the goods from bulk down to small quantities. All make small profit margins and the consumer gets a very local service, possibly 'open all hours', but at a higher price.

manufacturer – retailer – consumer

The growth of massive retail chains led to direct distribution to these retailers. This is convenient for manufacturers, though it actually puts them under price pressure. Consumers gain wide choice at lower prices from these large outlets – a point currently being disputed. Some retailers have formed co-operatives in order to have more buying 'clout' – in other words they can negotiate a better price if they negotiate as a group, eg Spar shops. Some retailers are franchises, in which case their supply is direct from the manufacturer/franchisor. Mail order companies such as Kays, the catalogue company, are also retailers that buy direct from the manufacturer.

manufacturer – wholesaler – consumer

This is technically impossible in that wholesalers supply 'the trade', but given the threat above, some managed to make their 'trade card' available to local firms and societies for use by their employees/members. Consumers obtain trade prices.

manufacturer – agent/distributor – retail store – consumer

Some times a manufacturer will use an nominated agent or distributor to distribute goods to the retail stores or to the final consumer. This can happen

- on a national scale if the manufacturer does not have the resources (or the inclination) to warehouse and distribute its goods
- on an international scale – an exporter of goods will use an agent in another country to organise the distribution of the exported goods

Other alternatives for an exporter of goods range between

- delivering the goods abroad using their own transport
- establishing a subsidiary company in the importing country to distribute the goods (a common arrangement with car exporters)

service provider – agent – customer

In our service oriented society we use travel firms, theatres and occasionally need the services of the plumber or an insurance company. Whilst we often deal directly with these businesses, many have made themselves more available through high street agencies or service collectives.

Activity 14.1

Indirect sales methods

Find an example of all the types of distribution in your area. Set out in short note form:

(a) the advantages and disadvantages to the customer in each case

(b) the advantages and disadvantages for the manufacturer

direct sales methods

Direct sales involve the producer of the goods or service selling direct to the consumer. We discussed the use of 'direct marketing' in the last chapter. It is worth bearing in mind the distinction between the two:

- direct marketing is advertising which stimulates an immediate response from the consumer, eg coupons in newspapers, phone numbers on TV

- direct selling is the active process of the seller approaching the consumer direct by a variety of means – calling at the door, party selling

Direct selling is a major growth area as it benefits both producer and consumer and often makes use of new technology.

Examples of direct selling include:

direct mail – catalogue selling

Here the manufacturer sends a catalogue to the chosen market segments or on request of the customer with details of the product and price, and details of how to order. Garden centres, charity gift catalogues, sports equipment manufacturers and many others use this method. Direct mail is sometimes referred to as 'junk mail' as much of it is binned. This will only happen if it is badly targeted! Accurate databases should avoid this.

door-to-door sales

This is the earliest form of selling, with 'travellers' and 'hawkers' knocking on doors. It is still used for 'cold calls' by traders such as double glazers and roof insulators. You may have heard of the Avon cosmetics organisation, or Betterware. They use commission-only salespersons, each working their area on a regular and reliable time pattern. Catalogues are hand delivered at the first call, orders being taken at the return visit.

party selling

Party selling is a very effective way of utilising amateur sales persons, supervised by a few full time area organisers. Selling parties are held in private homes, with friends of the home owner invited. Product demonstration is followed by order taking, with the 'guests' often feeling obliged to buy. Many products are sold in this way – clothing, jewellery, art products, perfume, childrens' books, all following the example of the originator of this policy – Tupperware.

network selling

Network, or multi-level marketing, became fashionable in the 1990s, based on an earlier idea known as 'pyramid selling' which fell into disrepute. Network selling involves an individual making an agreement to sell the product, whilst taking the opportunity to recruit new salespersons into the organisation, who then also recruit new members. Commission and rewards (such as holidays) are paid both on direct sales and also on the sales of the people recruited, and the sales of the people recruited by the people recruited! You can soon see that the person who starts the business will become very well off at the expense of the new recruits.

telesales

Selling by telephoning the prospective customer direct – telesales – has become big business, particularly as databases have become available which pinpoint the type of customer who might be interested in the product concerned (see section below on the use of technology). Telephone calls can either be made to existing customers or to new customers ('cold calling').

Telesales were traditionally carried out by businesses such as double glazing firms, but are now used to great effect by larger organisations such as banks and insurance companies telephoning their customers for repeat or additional business. Businesses have to take care when cold calling because it is illegal to cold call people who have indicated that they do not want to receive calls.

direct selling – the 'pros' and 'cons'

Consumers gain the feeling of security by dealing directly with the producer and often a known representative; they also enjoy the benefits of armchair shopping. However the profusion of junk mail, sales calls by phone or at the door, and friends exerting sales pressure could eventually prove bad for business.

Manufacturers gain by cutting out all intermediaries, thus keeping control over pricing, products and after sales service. Using representatives means that they can provide personal customer service.

the growth of technology – e·commerce

Direct selling owes its growth in part to the major technological advances in the field of communications. In addition, the personal computer has allowed the build up of huge databases so that accurate targeting may take place (see the Cadbury case study on page 309). Now, these two are joined together via the Internet – a communication and selling facility which is changing the face of marketing, especially on the High Street.

Other technological developments include smart cards, online ads, touchscreen shopping/banking, TV shopping and video catalogues from the mail order firms. No wonder the retailer feels threatened. E-commerce is undoubtedly the future, although there will always be those who prefer a day out at the shops and the ability to see what they are buying.

Activity 14.2

the threat of e·commerce

Read the articles below and discuss for any given product type the advantages and disadvantages of buying and selling on the internet. Products to be discussed could be clothes, cars, jewellery, foodstuffs and services such as holidays.

Internet threat to town centres

By Anita Howarth

Town centres, already hammered by out-of-town developments, face a devastating new attack from home shopping on the internet, according to a top retail boss.

Barry Gibson, chief executive of mail-order and pools firm Littlewoods, says towns will have to reinvent themselves as places for leisure and entertainment rather than shopping centres if they are to survive.

Though the government has closed the planning doors that allowed out-of-town superstores, it is encouraging the growth of internet shopping.

Gibson says this will tear the heart out of many town centres, just as superstore developments have done.

He believes that 'e-tailing' could be the straw that breaks the back of many shopping districts. Some have already suffered up to a 3 per cent fall in turnover because of out-of-town retailing.

The e-tail revolution could snatch between 2 per cent and 5 per cent of their remaining customers, Gibson believes.

He revealed his gloomy view to a conference of the British Council of Shopping Centres last week.

He admitted that the drop in custom might not sound much to many people.

But with retailers having already driven down costs, any 'further reduction in turnover could have a disproportionate impact on profits'.

It could become a landslide, he added.

Leading retailers are already looking for ways to cut back on their outlets in towns, concentrating on the largest regional centres and on the most profitable retail pitches there.

Source: *The Mail on Sunday*, October 31 1999

SHOPPING HABITS

A study into the nation's shopping habits carried out by MORI on behalf of Kesslers International revealed that the public still views in-store shopping as having key advantages over the internet.

- Customers are concerned about credit card fraud over the internet and like to interact with products before making the final decision to buy. Two-thirds of consumers are `unlikely' or `certain not to' buy from the internet in the future.

- 53% believe displays would prompt them to buy on impulse and 74 % said displays alert their attention to new or improved products in-store.

- 94% of consumers are keen to see information accompanying products on display stands.

- The products most likely to be bought as an impulse purchase in-store are food and drink (30%), videos (27%), sunglasses (21%) and make-up (19%).

- Two-thirds of shoppers say they always stop and look at special displays when they are shopping and 70% buy, or consider buying, on impulse as a result of seeing products displayed.

- Women are more likely than men both to stop and look at special displays (76% compared with 52% men) and to be interested in seeing the other products on display (93% compared with 76%).

- 49% of respondents believe that the whole shopping experience will become more exciting as shops and displays introduce new technologies.

Source: *Marketing*, October 28 1999

sales policy

the sales campaign

A sales campaign may be defined as:

'a range of selling activities taking place within a specified time period (a year, or a short period) to achieve a specific objective'

the sales campaign and the marketing plan

In reality, you should appreciate that the campaign would be a co-ordinated part of the overall marketing plan. The campaign would be controlled by a sales manager or director, or a marketing director. The campaign would need the organised involvement of all sales personnel, and efficient communication with all outside parties. The organisation's distributors, such as agents and dealers, wholesalers and retailers, must be consulted and made aware of the campaign. This can be achieved by a combination of sales letters, memos and the issue of promotional material to the chosen outlets. Other methods of communication include telephone, telex, fax and networked systems using computer links. The 'Extranet' is an extension of internal communications to include selected outside firms eg suppliers.

sales organisation

internal sales force

The sales force within a retail or leisure outlet could be organised on a simple departmental basis. Communication would be via internal memos and regular sales meetings, often in the time before the store opens for the day. Much communication will be face-to-face. Training days will ensure that staff are updated on procedures. Communication from a Head Office would be with local management, to be passed on to staff as relevant. See the McDonald's case study on page 326 and the table below.

HOW TO BOOST PRODUCTIVITY IN-STORE

What measures are most likely to boost productivity?

On-going training	30 %
Training combined with product briefings	30 %
Better technical and pre-sales support	15 %
Sales incentive schemes	15 %
Others (e.g. customer incentives)	10 %

Poll of IT and consumer electronics sales staff and managers. Source: EMSChiara 1999.

Source: *Marketing*, September 30 1999

field sales force

The sales force working for a manufacturer, wholesaler or service provider could be organised in a variety of ways:

- regionally, by 'territory', by far the most common method
- by type of product, or type of customer (market)
- by key accounts, ie senior sales staff selling to key customers, like the head offices of major firms

You will realise that many salespersons work from home, ie they are not office based. Head office communication with the team must therefore be efficient in time and cost. Internal memos, price and product review lists and possibly newsletters are all needed by the team members. The telephone, fax and networked computer links are now common in car and/or home, and e-mail is rapidly becoming the most used communication method in business. It is both fast and cheap – two priorities in business.

A sales team meeting can disseminate much information and save paperwork, but you will appreciate that this also takes the team away from its main duty – selling!

A sales conference is part information dissemination, part morale boosting. You can appreciate that a sales representative works alone for most of the time. Bringing these individuals together and including a social element, at a pleasant venue, can stimulate the team to greater effort.

The telephone operator at your office is part of the sales team. This particular communication link is often the customer's first impression of your organisation's customer care programme. This link must be right. The training of this member of staff is just as important as that of a salesperson. Give some thought also to the modern phenomenon of using a standardised recorded message to greet callers. Does it help or does it annoy?

the selling process

Selling involves specific skills, and a sales force trained in the right skills is essential for a successful sales campaign. Selling involves a number of stages:

1 researching for and making contact with the customer
2 establishing the customer's needs
3 presenting the product, explaining features, but most of all, stressing the benefits that will accrue to the customer
4 answering questions and overcoming doubts
5 assessing whether the customer is ready to make a decision
6 closing the sale – asking for and getting the order

Activity 14.3

Effective sales campaigns

1   Agree a product or service with your tutor. Research the real competition. Make a sales presentation to a buyer (your tutor or a member of your group). The rest of the class should observe and make comments on the performance.

2   Draft out a sales campaign for a new soft drink in cans for a new manufacturer. The firm will use a sales team and a variety of intermediaries for distribution. The sales team will work away from the office. Outline your sales and distribution plan for the first year.

Note: it would be helpful for these tasks (and also for the Assignment at the end of the chapter) to make contact with the Sales Department of a business. Talk to the sales staff about how a sales campaign and a sales presentation are conducted in practice.

effective customer service

the needs of organisations

You should appreciate that, whether the organisation is profit motivated or income maximising, its relationship with its clients/customers must be such that the latter keep coming back. The achievement of customer satisfaction must be a major objective of the organisation, or the other objectives will not themselves be achieved. Marketing orientation is not just thinking about customer satisfaction, it is about achieving it. A customer-orientated organisation with the right products in the right place and at the right prices will soon achieve an increase in market share. The only problem might be the increased cost of customer service provision. In most organisations however, this cost should be absorbed by increased sales and profits because the customers stay loyal. Note also the growth of loyalty cards.

the right image

Impressions of organisations may actually begin with stories in the press or on television (publicity) that influence whether the public bother to visit you at all. If they do come, remember that first impressions count. If prospective customers don't like what they see (and this could be the scruffy staff or a dirty or badly laid out shop/office) you may still never get a chance to communicate with them, let alone make a sale. See the section on Merchandising (page 301).

needs of customers – customer care

Most people entering a shop, or contacting a firm by letter or telephone, have suggested by this action that they have a need. It is the sales person's responsibility to try to turn that initial contact into a sale. Some contacts initially seek only information. They may be uncertain as to their precise requirements, or wish to be made aware of the options, or need to examine items that advertising has told them are available. Whichever it is, their interest suggests a potential sale, so they must be treated and advised accordingly. Advice must be accurate. It is easy to make a 'one-off' sale, but the duty of the salesperson is to convert that enquirer into a regular customer, not try desperately for a sale at any cost.

point of sale service – staff training

Sales training should enable the salesperson to find out what the customer wants from the salesperson and the organisation in addition to the product or service offered. Time may be a crucial factor, in which case quick and easy purchasing systems must exist. In a retail outlet this will entail clear signs as to product location and till availability. Clear and accurate information must be evident in the form of signs, product brochures and helpful, well-informed staff. If a refund is needed, or goods need exchanging, help must be available with the minimum of fuss. The law may give the customer such a right, but even if this is not so, a clear policy statement is necessary on this for the benefit of both customers and staff. Occasionally, customer complaints may arise: this too must be part of the customer service policy. Whatever the need, the salesperson's attitude is a key factor. He or she must be genuinely helpful rather than just 'go through the motions'. Read through the following article by Tom Peters.

Tom Peters – on excellence

I'm 52, I've been around, and when it comes to service, I am some kind of a fanatic (not just a demanding customer, but often a real pain in the neck). The truth is, however, that I could probably count on the fingers of one hand the number of times that I've sent a meal back to a restaurant kitchen.

Well, I sent one back the other night, at a place that normally serves fine food. (I had ordered the vegetarian plate, and it had turned out to be merely a lump of bland pasta topped with a glob of nondescript cheese. It made one of those instant microwave meals seem like haute cuisine). Anyway, I sent it back, and I learned something in the process.

The owner of the restaurant was on hand - which was to her credit - and quickly came to the table. But the first words out of her mouth were about money. To wit: she would remove the meal from our tab.

Well, that's fine - but ....

I was still left with a sour taste in my mouth, and it wasn't just from the food. The issue wasn't the money.

The truth is, the $16 (£10.25) tab wasn't going to significantly alter my bank balance (nor would it for most of the people who dined there).

There was something else that was missing - and that something showed up spontaneously the next time our waitress stopped by the table. She said she had worked for another restaurant that was always toying with its nightly vegetarian entree. Her casual remark triggered a five-minute conversation about vegetarian cooking and the like.

What she provided was worth 100 times the $16. She offered attentiveness. Is this the most powerful force in the universe? Perhaps.

point of sales service – clinching the sale

Point of sale service is often the key to finalising a deal. Everything must ensure that a decision to buy does not get reversed at the last moment. A careless last word from a sales person, the lack of a till free from queues, the positioning of a till, the poor attitude of a tired till operator – all may lose the sale. The organisation must be such that the sale is completed quickly and efficiently – enough tills, plenty of carrier bags, help in packing the bags, many ways of making the payment – cash or card.

product knowledge

The salesperson's knowledge of the organisation's product range, or main aims (as in a charity) are crucial. Knowledge of competitor products is also important. It is not your task to 'rubbish' the opposition. Customers are suspicious of this. They need to be given reasons why your product offers more of the benefits that they seek. By listening rather than talking all of the time, you establish what their needs are. Customer satisfaction is achieved when a purchase solves the buyer's needs. Product knowledge could result in customer satisfaction and a sale made, if combined with customer care.

good sales administration

A business must make sure that the administration system works and is customer or user friendly. Excessive bureaucracy and complicated paperwork can lose the sale even at this stage. The sales function in a business needs efficient administration if customer service is to live up to its name. Imagine the situation if wrong goods are delivered, or if they are delivered late and to the wrong address. Customers would soon go elsewhere for the product.

after-sales service

After-sales service is an essential element of customer service in any type of organisation. In the retail situation it may involve a maintenance contract for a durable product, eg a television. This might be an insurance contract whereby for an extra payment the goods are serviced or repaired over a stipulated period of time. After-sales policy may cover faulty goods, refunds, exchange of goods, complaints about goods, service and hygiene. It may require the salesperson to be aware of aspects of the relevant laws on sale of goods (see page 282).

When selling industrial goods and services a business must ensure adequate back up services to cover things such as spare parts, servicing, technical advice, replacement of faulty equipment and so on. Any business which does not offer this support will quickly lose out to the competition. After-sales service may be crucial to gaining the business in the first place. It may be part of the product promotion and the sales promise.

Many firms establish Customer Service Departments to deal with queries, thus taking the stress away from sales personnel. Regardless of this, sales persons must be trained how to respond to all of the above situations, politely and efficiently, even if their only action is to pass the customer on to a colleague. Good after-sales service can ensure that the customer is not lost, even if temporarily unhappy.

Activity 14.4

After-sales service

Compare the after-sales service that may be necessary in the following businesses. Account for any differences. In the case of example 4, what additional pressure is there to maintain the quality of after-sales service?

1   a garage selling new cars from one manufacturer

2   a second-hand car firm

3   an electrical appliance store

4   a business with a large market share, eg British Gas, BT

communicating effectively with customers

The art of communicating with customers is vitally important for success in both customer service generally and 'customer care' campaigns. As you will know from your development of the Core Skill of Communication, it is possible to make an impression through body language (facial expressions and gestures) and through tone of voice. You know that you can sense the shop assistant who is bored (yawns, looks into the distance when talking to you) and the telephonist who chirps a message in a mechanical and totally uninterested way.

Case Study

McDonald's
2000 – 'the year of service'

The service experience clearly begins with the well-branded signage attracting and directing customers to a familiar place.

At McDonald's there are two distinct styles of service, at the counter or at the 'drive thru' window. With the counter service, on entering the restaurant, the counter is clearly visible, allowing the customer instant access to the ordering facility. There will always be a member of staff facing the customer as he or she walks towards the counter. The information regarding prices and menu items is displayed in a variety of ways. Behind the counter is a menu board depicting names of menu items and their prices. There are also 'translites', illuminated pictures of particular food. These will usually display items that are either new or seasonally-based items that the regular customer will not be familiar with. The majority of restaurants have 'till-toppers', small pictures above the tills showing one line of the menu.

McDonald's relies heavily on serving staff knowing the range of items provided. This is enhanced by the staff being trained specifically in the art of how to serve customers with speed and efficiency in a friendly manner. This training is constantly updated as new products come into being and also to ensure that they are maintaining the standard of service we expect.

McDonald's is very much a 'hands on' management company and therefore all the managers in the restaurant are trained in every aspect of a regular team members job, and are also trained to be on the restaurant floor as much as possible, running the business from the 'sharp' end. This enables them to ensure the food that is being served is of the highest quality and that the service being provided is first class. It also gives them the chance to address any customer complaints immediately they return to the counter.

Some minor complaints will be dealt with by team members themselves, some are referred to the manager. Managers are trained to do as much as possible to help customer requests. Managers are clearly discernible with a particular uniform whilst team members have name badges. There will usually be a board up on the wall displaying the name of the shift manager at the time and every restaurant has customer comment cards for the customer to make a record of their experience.

McDonald's also have trained staff who work in the dining area to find seats for customers in busy times as part of their customer care managers' role. On a more general basis, staff will maintain the cleanliness of the area, talk to customers and provide children with a small gift such as a balloon, hat or flag. These staff are trained to replace any items of food with which the customer may not be happy, and answer any questions they may have about the restaurant.

The drive-thru service is different in so far as the customer usually requires a faster service. The drive-thru system is clearly indicated both by low level signage in the car park and a distinctive coloured road that leads to the service window. Once again there is a menu board giving price and pictorial information of menu items, illuminated for night time. The drive-thru till system is computerised so that as the order is keyed in to the till at the ordering window it automatically appears on a screen at the pick-up window so that the order can be collected and given to the customer in the quickest and most efficient way.

The mainstay of McDonald's service policy is a clear definition of what is being sold, high standards of recruitment and training and precise standards of service constantly monitored by all levels of managers at all times.

Osborne Books is grateful to McDonald's for providing this Case Study

Activity 14.5

McDonald's

Read the Case Study (and also visit your local McDonald's to support your investigation), and then answer the questions.

1 How does McDonald's attract customers to the counter when they enter the restaurant?

2 How are the staff trained to help customers and make them feel welcome once they are in the restaurant?

3 What aspects of managerial training and managerial style ensure that standards of customer service are maintained?

4 What type of 'brand image' is offered to customers at McDonald's?

place (or 'distribution') policy

This is the fourth 'P' of the marketing mix. The reason for the alternative headings is that there are different problems here:

• the manufacturer of a product has to physically move it to where it is convenient for the customer ie to shops around the country. Would you travel to the Cadbury factory in Birmingham for a bar of chocolate? Obviously a distribution policy is required.

• The provider of a service usually requires the customer to come to him ie the retailer, the leisure centre or cinema manager, the hotelier etc. So, a place (choice of site) policy is required.

• The charity fund raiser has both needs – to have a physical presence in the high street eg Oxfam shops, and a 'site' address to where donations can be sent.

distribution policy – effective logistics

To some extent we have covered this topic in the preceding pages under direct and indirect selling. There we looked at the need or otherwise for intermediaries to sell our products. There is more to distribution however:

- **The number of outlets**. Should we be exclusive, selective or aim to saturate the market? The decision is important. Rolls Royce, an exclusive product, has a very limited number of outlets. Other types of car are more widely available, but there will still be only one retail outlet in a given area. This is selective distribution. Finally, the chocolate manufacturer tries to saturate the market, selling through every conceivable outlet.

- **The area to be covered**. Should we stay local, or go national or even international? The logistics may depend on the newness of the firm, or its size, the location of its customers or the extent of the ambition of the management. The Internet is increasingly important here, enabling the small manufacturer to 'stay at home' but still sell over a wide area (but note possible distribution constraints).

- **Transport.** How best should your products be moved? The standard alternatives are road, rail, sea or air, but there are choices within these eg should we own our own lorries, or lease them, or simply call a carrier firm to deliver for us?

place or 'site' policy – the physical environment

In the past this would be an important decision for a manufacturer in placing a factory, but with vastly improved transport and communications, and government development grants, this is less so. To the service provider who deals with the customer face-to-face, on the other hand, this decision is vital. Once the leisure facility or hotel has been built it is not going to be moved. Here are some considerations for the choice of site:

- The physical environment. Can you be reached, by customers, suppliers and your workforce? A mountain top hotel might sound attractive, but can it be serviced?

- The 'right' part of town. Is it fashionable? Is it safe for customers to come to you, especially after dark?

- The right neighbours. A fashion boutique next to a curry house might find its products smelling less than sweet.

- The competition. Do you want to be close to them or well away? There are advantages in either – people go to the jewellery quarter in Birmingham, or head for the 'best' shops on Oxford Street. Alternatively, being the only one puts you in control, providing the customers come at all.

- Your building. Is it suitable for your image? What type of promotional window space does it offer?

- Your accessibility. Can customers park? Is there public transport? Are you too far out of town?

- Your pavement image. Does the entrance look inviting, (particularly important for a hotel or restaurant)? Is there scope for improvement, space to expand?

- The 'walk past' rate. The high street shop is seen by many, but the rent and rates will be high. The backstreet shop will be cheaper but may cost a fortune for you to advertise the fact that you are there.

Activity 14.6

Business appearances

As a group, analyse a local retail outlet, hotel or fast food establishment in terms of the points mentioned in the text above. What strengths and weaknesses have you observed ? From first impressions would it be (a) easy or (b) desirable to do business with this organisation?
Make notes of your impressions and discuss them in class.

Case Study

The American Adventure
place decisions

The American Adventure Theme Park site was originally an open cast mine. When mining finished, a small natural lake was left in a large open 'brownfield' site. Initially, as the land settled, the lake was allowed to expand over 32 acres and the whole area became part of Shipley Country Park. Eventually, the Derbyshire County Council looked to a group of businessmen to help them develop an attraction on the site. Britannia Park, a memorial to British Industrial achievement, opened in 1985, and closed 12 weeks later. The site was then acquired by Park Hall Leisure who, in conjunction with the Granada Group plc, opened the American Adventure in June, 1987. At the present time, the Park occupies 189 acres of the 345 acres available.

To build a theme park in the present day, you would need a huge financial backing, and would need the approval of the local planning authority. The park would have to fit into the local plans of the district and county councils, and fit the Department of the Environment's planning guidelines. Various issues come into play, for example, is the proposed park on 'Green Belt' land? A number of studies would

www.americanadventure.com

have to be undertaken. These would involve traffic flow and parking surveys, services provision, noise implications, rights of way, landscaping suggestions and the likely impact on local businesses.

External influences, including the weather and the seasonal nature of the business, would influence opening times (months and weeks) and cause internal staffing difficulties. The nature of the business means large numbers of part time staff are required. Are they available in the months specified?

Like all site decisions, the future must be considered. Is there space to grow? Other considerations include:

Is the transport infrastructure adequate and convenient?

Is there a sizeable local population base for the provision of both customers and a part time workforce?

Is skilled labour available, or is there a pool of trainable workers already available in the vicinity?

Osborne Books is grateful to the American Adventure for helping with this Case Study.

Activity 14.7

The American Adventure

points for class discussion

1   Examine the diagram of the site and comment on its geographical suitability and the transport infrastructure.

2   What factors would have encouraged Park Hall Leisure to take on this site, despite the failure of the Britannia Park project?

3   What structural unemployment was occurring locally that might have provided the required 'pool of trainable labour'?

4   Market research into Guest Profiles revealed that 80% visit by car; 66% live within one hour's travelling time; 70% have previously visited the park. What do these facts suggest to management about the site, and what do they suggest might need to be looked at for future expansion?

5   Build these and other points into a SWOT analysis of the site.

CHAPTER SUMMARY

● A product producer needs to get his products to the customer in ways efficient for the firm, but convenient for the customer ie in the right place (outlet), at the right time.

● A service provider needs to make his services available to the customer at the customer's home, or place of work, or at some place easy and convenient for the customer to get to, eg a fast food outlet.

● Sales distribution channels vary from the indirect, using wholesalers and retailers or some combination of these, to the direct, ie producer to end user. The latter methods might include door to door, manufacturer's catalogue, telesales etc.

● Note carefully the growth of the new technology (the Internet) for both direct and indirect sales.

● The organisation of sales policy includes the sales campaign, sales force management and the training of sales staff.

● An organisation's sales staff, whether internal or external, must be customer-orientated, with the right attitude backed by good training and an effective system.

● After sales service is crucial to retaining customers. It may be important also in making a sale in the first place, eg offering computer installation and back-up service.

● Effective customer service cannot be achieved without an efficient back-up administration system, whether it relates to a sales team out in the field, or at the point of sale eg a shop.

● Efficient communication systems must exist for internal message relaying (especially when the sales team is scattered), and for external communication with suppliers and customers.

● Distribution policy requires effective logistics to get the manufacturer's products to its customers and/or outlets at the right time.

● Place policy requires service providers to think very carefully about their choice of site – its convenience for customers to drive to or to reach via public transport.

KEY TERMS

distribution channels	the use of intermediaries, or otherwise, to make available products and services from producers to prospective customers
logistics	plans the whereabouts of outlets, the types and number of outlets, and the transport methods needed to service them.
direct selling	supplying directly to the customer without using intermediaries
indirect selling	supplying the customer using intermediaries such as wholesalers, agents, distributors and retailers
e-commerce	the use of electronic communication in business – at the point of sale (Epos}, databases of customers, online advertising, purchasing of products via home computers
sales policy	the organisation of the selling function and its relationship with other promotional activities
sales campaign	the organisation of the selling activity over a specified time period
internal sales force	personnel who deal mainly with customers in for example a retail outlet or a hotel
field sales force	personnel who go out to visit prospective customers at their place of work, or home
selling process	the skills and routine acquired by sales personnel
customer service	ensuring that customers gain maximum satisfaction of their needs in their dealings with the firm
after sales service	the provision of back-up services, eg guarantees and maintenance contracts, or simply the offering of refunds or replacements
sales administration	processes for ensuring the efficient working of the sales function, eg creating simple sales procedures, delivering goods carefully and on time
place	examination of the physical environment and the overall suitability of the site and the premises

15 Planning the workforce

introduction

This chapter examines the way organisations decide on the size and structure of their workforce. It also looks at the importance of having a workforce that is flexible in what it does and when it does it.

what you will learn from this chapter

● Human resources (HR) planning is concerned with making sure that the organisation has the right number of employees and of the right quality.

● The main problems for the HR planner are skill shortages, competition for employees and labour turnover.

● HR planners have to devise techniques to measure and reduce labour turnover.

● Organisations try to keep sickness and accidents as low as possible by the use of effective health and safety policies and good occupational health services.

● Succession planning must be used to ensure that the organisation has a steady supply of new managers available to fill posts left by resignation or retirement.

● In many organisations HR planners operate a flexible workforce. This is a workforce that has numerical, financial and functional flexibility.

● A flexible workforce is composed of core and peripheral employees with differing pay levels, conditions of service and job security.

● The purpose of a flexible workforce is to create a more competitive organisation which has a better long term future for all of its employees.

human resources planning

Human resources planning used to be called manpower planning. It has been defined as:

> *'the activity of management which is aimed at coordinating the requirements for and the availability of different types of employee'*

the reasons for human resources planning

There are four main reasons for human resources planning:

1 It encourages employers to develop clear links between their business plans and their HR plans so that they can integrate the two more effectively, for all concerned.

2 Organisations can control staff costs and numbers employed far more effectively.

3 Employers can build up a skill profile for each of their employees. This makes it easier to give them work where they are most value to the organisation.

4 It creates a profile of staff (related to gender, race, disability) which is necessary for the operation of an Equal Opportunities policy.

If HR planning works properly the outcomes will be . . .

* staff employed are fully-utilised to the benefit of the organisation

* staff do challenging work which motivates and stimulates them

* overtime is only done when vitally necessary

* staff are properly qualified to do the job allotted to them

the process of human resources planning

Essentially there are four key stages involved

* stock taking

* forecasting the supply of labour

* forecasting demand for employees

* implementation and review

We will deal with each of these in turn.

stock taking

This asks the question 'what is the quantity and quality of staff available in this organisation?' It uses the following techniques:

jobs analysis

This means gathering together all the information available about all the jobs in the organisation. What are the duties in each job and what are the skills required to do each job? The most important tools to do this are the job description and the person specification for each job. These are dealt with in Chapter 16 (pages 360 to 364).

skills audit

This is a survey of the skills, qualifications and experience of all existing staff.

performance review

This involves looking at the performance of all employees in order to:

*   identify staff potential
    and to
*   identify where staff have more training needs

forecasting supply

This asks the question 'how many employees will we have in the future?' It therefore means looking at internal and external sources of labour.

When looking at the total supply of labour in the organisation it is very important to look at labour turnover.

There are three main ways to calculate employee turnover.

annual labour turnover index

$$= \frac{\text{leavers in a year}}{\text{average number of staff employed during the year}}$$

This is sometimes called the 'percentage wastage rate'. It tells you what percentage of the workforce left in a year.

The two main problems with this method are:

- It tells you nothing about the length of service of the people who left. Some could have left after four weeks and others could have retired.

- It also does not tell you if, for example, ten people left the same job or ten people left ten different jobs. Obviously the action needed to deal with these two situations would be completely different.

stability index

$$= \frac{\text{Number of staff employed with one year's service on a certain date}}{\text{Number of staff employed exactly one year before}}$$

This is a more useful indicator. It gives a good idea of how long employees are staying with the organisation. If employees are not staying very long in certain departments this can be pinpointed and investigated.

This method still does not deal with the second problem listed above.

Bowey's stability index

$$= \frac{\text{Length of service in months over a two year period of all current staff added together}}{\text{Length of service in months over a two year period if all staff had worked for the full two years}}$$

This looks at actual length of service and calculates a stability percentage.

For example if there are 50 staff they could have worked a total of 1,200 months (ie 50 x 24 months = 1,200).

Suppose one woman left during the two years. She is excluded from the data because she is no longer 'current'.

The 49 remaining staff have service as follows:

40 with 24 months each*

2 with 18 months

4 with 10 months

2 with 3 months

1 with 1 month

* Note that some of the 40 could have been there far longer but we only count the last two years' service.

The total service is 1,043 months so the formula becomes:

$$\frac{1,043}{1,200} \quad \text{x} \quad 100 = 87\% \text{ stability (ie a very stable workforce)}.$$

cohort analysis

A cohort is a homogeneous group of staff who join at the same time such as a group of apprentices or graduate trainees. They can be followed throughout, say, a two year period to find out what happens to them and, hopefully, the reasons for any problems.

For example, university graduate turnover is often quite high. In many organisations perhaps half of a cohort of graduates will leave soon after appointment due to disillusionment or because they have a better offer elsewhere. By contrast, due to the shrinking manufacturing sector most of a cohort of apprentices may stay with a particular employer for most of their lives.

other influences on the internal supply of labour

sickness

A high level of sickness absence affects the supply of labour very badly. If it is all genuine (eg a flu' epidemic) then there is not much that can be done in the short term.

In reality quite a lot of sickness is bogus. If it is not tackled it causes poor morale amongst the employees who are coming to work. They will, understandably, feel that the managers are 'wimps' for letting people get away with it.

Sickness absence needs monitoring against:

- performance in the previous year
- trends in other organisations in the same industrial sector
- national sickness absence figures

Ways of controlling and monitoring sickness and bogus sickness include:

- keeping proper records of sickness for all staff
- a policy of 'sick visiting' by the personnel manager or by the company nurse
- return to work interviews after one day of absence; this puts pressure on people who regularly have the odd day off 'ill' but do not want the embarrassment of an interview each time.
- a clear statement to staff that regular periods of unexplained sickness could lead to a disciplinary procedure or even dismissal

accidents

Better health and safety procedures and the use of EU regulations (eg on lifting and manual handling) have reduced the level of accidents in the workplace. A big factor has been the closure of many unsafe, old fashioned factories, steelworks and coal mines.

skills and training

This is covered fully in the next chapter.

succession planning

This really only applies to employees at supervisor/line manager level and above.

A proper system of succession planning should include:

• an estimate of what managerial jobs will be available in the future

• an analysis of what skills and other abilities those jobs will require

• a review of the strengths and weaknesses of existing staff who might fill some of those jobs

This enables the organisation to ensure that staff with potential to fill top jobs are given extra training or wider experience so that when the time comes they will be able to fill those positions. This is dealt with in the next chapter. Showing this kind of interest in employees will improve their motivation and morale.

If there is no succession planning then good employees will leave for better opportunities elsewhere. This will make it harder to fill gaps in the organisation at a later date.

external sources of employees

These factors can provide fresh sources of labour:

• Closures of other workplaces locally. If a large manufacturer or services company closes down, other local companies will find it easier to recruit skilled people from the redundancies that occur.

• Transport developments – eg when new high speed train links open more people are prepared to travel longer distances to work (there are now even 'Eurostar' train commuters to and from Paris every day.)

• The 'output' from the education system. Schools will provide local supplies of employees and universities will provide them from further away.

using local and national statistical resources

When planning its workforce and operations a business may need to look at the local area or it may be faced with a choice of location. It might want to move out of London, it might want to open up a new office or factory for a new product. The choice of location will depend on a number of factors, but the cost of labour will be an important one. The cost of labour can be found from local and national statistics.

Local statistics can be obtained from the relevant Local Authority and Chamber of Commerce who undertake employment surveys in the area.

The 'Economic Assessment' published on a regular basis by Worcestershire County Council, for example, compares local and national data such as:

- employment by occupation – which shows, for example, that employment in manufacturing businesses is higher than the national average
- employment by gender – there are more females in employment than the national average
- average earnings levels – which are lower than the national average

National Statistics are available from the 'Labour Force Survey', carried out by the Office for National Statistics (www.ons.gov.uk) and published by the Stationery Office.

Useful figures include unemployment levels and average earnings in the regions. Some sample figures for earnings are shown below.

Average weekly full-time earnings in the UK regions (1999)

	male £	female £
North East	352	265
North West	365	274
Yorkshire & Humberside	376	277
East Midlands	397	279
West Midlands	367	266
East of England	443	309
London	514	383
South East	458	315
South West	378	267
Wales	334	269
Scotland	382	282
Northern Ireland	307	246

Activity 15.1

Labour planning problems

Read the article on the next page.

1   What are the benefits to an airline of retaining seasonally-contracted pilots throughout the whole year?

2   How does British Airways 'call the shots'?

3   How does the business you are studying for your Portfolio deal with labour planning problems?

Airlines suffer from shortage of pilots

by David Arminas

Airlines are stepping up recruitment and retention drives amid a growing pilot shortage. Increased competition with the emergence of new carriers is making recruitment of experienced pilots more difficult.

"It has been building in the past 12 months," said Virgin Express pilot trainer Paul Skellon. "We are using every means possible to recruit. A lot of younger pilots are interested in looking at the Internet."

Earlier this month Virgin Express said a pilot shortage will affect the bottom line.

Qualified Boeing 737 pilots and first officers are needed most. "The relief will come at the end of the summer holiday season, which will hopefully put a few people on the market," Skellon said.

But not all airlines are releasing their seasonally contracted pilots. "Now airlines are holding onto these pilots throughout the year," said John O'Shea, director of consultancy Parc Aviation.

Last February British Airways launched its largest ever recruitment drive, seeking 2,500 pilots over the next 10 years partly to replace an estimated 1,500 pilots scheduled to retire.

"BA really calls the shots," according to Hilary Shaw, group personnel manager of air-cargo company Channel Express. "It will take from people like British Midland and then they take from people like us."

To boost retention, Channel Express has created the position of air crew manager whose job will be to handle all personnel functions for their 120 pilots, from rostering and training to welfare needs when staying away from base.

Parc Aviation said the boom in both passenger and freight business has meant that pilots, particularly younger ones, have more options for advancement.

forecasting demand for employees

This means asking the question 'How many people will we need? Today? In five years?'

This is the most difficult question of all in human resources planning. Managers have to look at factors such as the following when forecasting demand for employees:

* the organisation's trading and production patterns
* demand for their products
* technological and administrative changes
* capital investment plans
* acquisitions, divestments and mergers
* product diversification

For example, new technology often means fewer jobs need filling but there will be more demand for skilled people. Mergers will mean that many head office jobs are made redundant, but if the merged company is now more efficient there may be new jobs in other areas.

The skills factor

Skills gap worries engineers

A third of engineering companies are seriously concerned about a gap between their staff's skills and those needed to meet business objectives, according to a major survey out this month.

Engineering firms are also suffering recruitment difficulties because applicants lack the qualifications and skills as well as relevant work experience.

The 1998 Labour Market Survey for the Engineering Industry, from the Engineering and Maritime Training Authority, is one of the largest surveys of the sector. It covers 4,200 sites employing about a quarter of the industry's 1.65 million staff.

The shortages are compounded by the fact that 53 per cent of companies believe skills needs are rising for their staff. Aerospace and electronics firms are most concerned.

Practical skills are most lacking, 63 per cent of respondents say. "This is quite a broad brush - from the ability to operate a basic PC to welding a box together," EMTA research manager Andrew Birnie said. Lack of computer literacy was noted by 35 per cent.

The hardest vacancies to fill are for craftspeople, according to 44 per cent of respondents. Next hardest are operator positions, say 28 per cent.

"The biggest surprise was the number of firms reporting recruitment problems," Birnie said.

The EMTA identified 337,000 women in engineering, up by 30,000 since 1993. The positive side is that women now make up 21 per cent of engineering employees, up from 18 per cent in 1993, Birnie said.

Reproduced by kind permission of *'Personnel Today'*

1   Why would a human resource planner in the engineering industry be concerned about the points raised in this article? What type of skills are lacking?

2   What particular skills are needed for employees in the business you are studying for your Portfolio? Does the business have any problems in recruiting people with these skills. Are any of the skills predominantly provided by men or women? If so, why is this the case?

implementation and review

Organisations must undertake regular reviews to ensure that their human resources planning process is effective. For example, has a new recruitment drive been effective in recruiting the right number and right quality of people?

The organisation must also look at all the various environmental factors which might affect the supply and demand for labour. This involves collecting information on social, political, industrial, legal and technological changes. It also means finding out what their competitors are doing. A good example of legal and political change is the 48 hour maximum working week. As this limits the amount of overtime an employee can work organisations may have to reorganise work rotas and employ more people.

the flexible workforce

In simple terms this means that many employers now use their employees in a 'flexible' way so that they can get the most value from them. Employers argue that without this flexible approach their businesses would close down.

In the UK, employment practices have traditionally been inflexible and this has made employers inefficient and uncompetitive compared with businesses in other countries.

Examples of inflexibility include:

* permanent contracts of employment for most staff
* full-time contracts of employment for all staff
* no flexibility in working hours
* Union opposition to employees doing anything outside their contract of employment – eg an electrician does electrical work and nothing else
* Union opposition to 'distancing' (see below for an explanation of 'distancing')

'the flexible firm'

Atkinson (1984) devised the 'flexible firm' model. His argument was that organisations need several types of employee flexibility to be really efficient.

He based his findings on how businesses were beginning to change in the early 1980s. Since then his flexible approach has become extremely common and, whereas it only used to be found in private companies, it is used a great deal in the public sector as well (eg in local government) in order to save money.

* **Numerical flexibility**

  'the ability to adjust the level of labour inputs to meet fluctuations in output'

  This means either altering hours worked or changing the total number of staff.

* **Functional flexibility**

  'the firms ability to adjust and deploy the skills of its employees to match the tasks required by its changing workload, production methods or technology'

* **Financial flexibility**

  This means that the employer can increase or decrease levels of spending on HR as business conditions require.

- **Distancing** (another form of numerical flexibility)

  This means that more and more services inside an organisation are carried out by other companies in return for fees. These other companies employ their own staff to carry out these services.

  The most common examples these days are catering, cleaning and security – some very large sub-contracting firms, such as Rentokil Plc and Group 4, can offer several of these services as one complete package. The aim of this strategy is to cut costs because the sub-contractors can usually do the jobs more cheaply than the organisation can. This offers extra numerical flexibility.

core and peripheral workforces

Atkinson goes on to explain that this flexibility means the workforce is broken up into two distinct groups:

the core workers

These are highly paid workers who offer 'firm-specific' skills which are hard to acquire from anywhere else. Often such skills will have been acquired within the organisation itself. They provide functional flexibility because they do a range of tasks. Because they are so 'firm-specific' they have high job security.

peripheral workers

There are two types of these:

- **First peripheral group**

  These are quite well looked after but less so than with core workers. They have reasonable security since they carry out skilled jobs, and are therefore sought after by many employers, but the key difference is that they do not have 'firm specific' skills. Good examples would be typing and word processing or a wide range of computer-related skills.

- **Second peripheral group**

  This group mainly provides 'numerical' flexibility. They are easily hired and fired as required. They will be on lower pay rates, usually have poorer working conditions and job insecurity.

Some of them may be very highly skilled but are unable to get better jobs, perhaps because of family commitments.

Second peripheral group workers include

- full-timers on short contracts
- part-time workers
- teleworkers and other kinds of home workers

- people employed on government schemes
- sub-contractors for cleaning, security etc
- agency temps

Apart from the financial and numerical flexibilities noted above there are other real benefits too:

- Because the workforce is broken up into several groups it becomes harder for them to unite in a common cause against management. On the one hand, 'core' workers are well looked after and, on the other, many peripheral workers will not cause trouble because of fear of losing their contracts or because they hope to get a 'core' job in the future.

- Human Resources and Accounts departments have less work to do because many staff are no longer the organisation's own employees.

- If the core workforce is well looked after, it will be highly motivated and will increase its output.

Many organisations are now adopting flexible firm policies to some degree and the number of part-time workers and temps has increased dramatically (witness the big increase in the number of temp agencies for example). Sub contracting has increased as well – some of these (eg Group 4, Rentokil, Sketchley, Compass Catering) are now far bigger than many of the organisations for which they provide services.

methods of flexible working

annualised hours

This means that an employee has a contract to work so many hours per year. The way that they are spread across that year depends on the needs of the business. This arrangement is only valuable where an organisation has a fluctuating demand for their products or services.

The employee gets the same weekly or monthly salary throughout the year but hours per week could be, for example, up to 55 or down to 25.

This means that employees are only at work when they are really needed. In a traditional business with standard weekly hours employees can sit around doing very little at certain times of the year but they still get paid. When they are busy at other times they get generously paid overtime. In contrast annualised hours reduces much of the overtime bill. Not surprisingly it is not popular with employees, although they do get more days off at certain times of the year.

zero hours contracts

This is where the employee is 'on call' to come into work whenever they are needed. If they are not needed they earn no money. This is not unusual in retailing where staff requirements vary during a week or even within one day.

Some employees like it because it gives them flexibility as well – after all, if they do not want to come in on a particular day they need not do so. However, for people wanting a secure job with reliable weekly pay it is not ideal. The fact that it has become fairly common is because high unemployment for most of the 1980s and 1990s forced many people to take whatever work they could get, however unreliable it was.

job sharing

This means that two employees share a job. This could be a divided week or a divided day. The advantage is that the employer has an extra source of labour from people who could not work full-time. Job share requires that the sharers work well together because they have to overlap to pass ongoing work between them and to discuss any problems arising from that work. Even very senior management jobs can be 'shared'.

teleworking and telecottaging

Increasing numbers of people work at least part of their time from home or, increasingly, from a telecottage or telecentre.

The introduction of the lap-top computer and, more importantly, the advent of e-mail and the Internet, has made teleworking very easy in practical terms.

For example, salespeople can e-mail their sales direct to the office and receive e-mailed instructions directly from there. Reports can be written in Aberdeen and e-mailed directly to the office in London or New York. The Internet provides a vast range of material which would only be available in a library 10 years ago.

Working at home for part of the week has big advantages in terms of the reduction in travel time and travel costs. There is also the reduced stress and the ability to work at the best time of the day to suit the person involved.

However, employees can feel cut off from the workplace and therefore forgotten by their managers. This could affect their promotion prospects. Also telework can be an intrusion into the employee's private life with computers and paperwork tying up spare bedrooms or even the living room.

Telecottaging, where employees meet at a dedicated telecottage with proper computer links and office facilities a few miles from home, is a better alternative because it separates 'work' from 'home'.

Activity 15.3

The problems of teleworking

Logging on for the morning news

Bass Brewers has stopped homeworkers from getting lonely by installing high speed ISDN telephone lines in their homes and automatically downloading company news and views each morning.

Before the 900 odd home based salespeople and pump maintainers go on pub visits they log onto "Brewnet", the company intranet, which includes details of internal news, press reports about Bass with the corporate reaction to it, and updated customer information.

The Collinson Grant survey found that more than one in four employers use teleworkers and half of them, like Bass, are trying to prevent staff getting socially isolated at their home. Being primed with information has helped Bass's sales staff adjust to their new roles as account managers as well as selling beer and other drinks.

If a pub or club manager wants a loan from the brewery, the salesperson can work out a repayment plan on the spot using their laptop computer without having to refer the request to a commercial regional manager. Salespeople now also have the power to decide whether to sponsor promotions or music nights, for example.

By spring, Bass hopes to have 99 per cent of its 4,400 staff connected to Brewnet, which includes a daily news service any employee can contribute to via an intranet manager, and an unrestricted question and answers page which staff can contribute to anonymously.

"We thought that people would not necessarily ask their line manager all the questions they would really like to ask - such as why some people get bigger bonuses than others," explains Maryon. "When we started they were all anonymous; now people are putting their names to it."

Brewnet enables Bass to beat the rumour mill by preparing a

Homeworkers get all the gen via the Bass intranet

tabloid version of the company results overnight to post on Brewnet to get an hour's head start on the morning radio and TV news.

"Now we can get our company's point of view across ahead of the media. Our results go to the Stock Exchange at 7.30am and our people view it at the same time."

Maryon gives a real example of how bad communication makes managers look stupid. Staff in a canning factory were briefed by managers that they had a top priority project to produce certain cans of beer. "Within 24 hours they suddenly find they are turned away from the job to do something else. They might ask a supervisor, "What is going on, why aren't we doing the important job?"

"We use the intranet to give an electronic notice from the planning department that says the cans have not arrived from the supplier so we are going to use your time on something else while we wait. That has happened a couple of times."

Reproduced by kind permission of *'Personnel Today'*

1   What were the problems faced by homeworkers employed by Bass Brewers?

2   How is Bass Brewers using communications technology to overcome these problems? Do you think this will solve all the problems of a teleworker?

3   To what extent is the business you are investigating for your Portfolio dependent on teleworking? What steps is it taking to avoid similar problems?

the problems of flexible working

More enlightened employers are unhappy about some aspects of operating 'flexibly'. They feel that:

- the use of short-term contract employees actually increases costs because new people are being recruited very frequently and this increases the amount of basic training required

- if unemployment is very low, flexible contracts will look less attractive and employees will look for something more secure and better paid – this will increase staff turnover

- treating employees differently clashes with the harmonisation of conditions (harmonisation means that all employees have to have the same basic conditions of service)

- many employers want to get 'Investor in People' status (see page 117) and this requires that employees are treated properly on a long-term basis

Activity 15.4

Agency nursing – a flexible alternative

Trusts forced into shifts U-turn

By Helen Rowe

Use of agency nurses in the NHS has led to lower efficiency after changes to shift patterns.

The claims come from personnel directors and Unison as the Government announced pay rises to help recruitment and retention.

Trusts are now reverting to traditional shift patterns and more family-friendly policies.

John Adsett, head of personnel at Basildon and Thurrock General Hospital Trust, said there had been too much emphasis on the use of nurses supplied by agencies.

He said, "At one time we were all being preached at that you have to have a core workforce and a peripheral workforce.

"It was a fashionable theory for a while. It was at a time when we were told that what was good for industry was good for the NHS."

He added, "Part of the problem was that you had staff to whom the organisation was not particularly loyal because we only asked them in when there was a crisis. Consequently you do not get the loyalty.

"There are a lot of trusts that have had a long, hard look at things like working patterns and are trying to be as flexible as possible now."

Unison's head of nursing Karen Jennings said many nurses left for agencies because they were forced to work a full range of shifts under the internal rotation system introduced in 1995-6. They found

agencies offered them more flexibility.

"For example many had previously chosen to work night shifts only, because it suited them. But with internal rotation everybody had to work all types of shifts." Last week's pay rises for nursing staff range from 3.4 per cent for a nursing assistant to 7.8 per cent for an experienced staff nurse.

In 1995-6, health regions in England spent £163m on agency staff. The figure rose to £191m in 1996-7 and £216m in 1997-8.

Jennings added, "Agencies are part of nursing now, so if hospitals want nurses back, it is all about offering good career development, understanding their domestic arrangements and not being dogmatic about internal rotation."

Reproduced by kind permission of 'Personnel Today'

1   What are the advantages and disadvantages for hospitals of relying on 'agency nurses'?

2   What is the 'U-turn' being taken, and what incentives are being offered for recruitment?

flexible working and employment contracts

It is quite easy for employers to build flexibility into their contracts of employment. Unless there is effective trade union opposition employers can require employees to carry out a wider range of duties or change their hours of work. Employers can also offer people fixed term and temporary contracts which give the employee very little security. In the case of temporary contracts these are often based on just one weeks notice by either party. In addition, until 1999, any employee could be employed for up to two years and be dismissed without any reason being given at all (however, see below).

Since 1997 a number of new laws have made it harder for organisations to operate 'flexibly'. Most of these come from the European Union in Brussels.

the Working Time Directive

This limits employees to work no more than 48 hours per week averaged over a 17 week period. This makes it harder to operate annualised hours arrangements. However, employees can opt out of this rule if they wish to. Employers cannot force them to although it may be in the employer's interests to encourage them to do so.

the Parental Leave directive

This gives both parents the right to take unpaid time off work to look after their children up to the child's fifth birthday.

Transfer of Undertakings regulations

Where an organisation takes over the employees from another organisation those employees are entitled to keep the conditions of service they had with their previous employer. For example, if a business wants a private caterer to take over its staff restaurant facilities, the private caterer would usually aim to save money through lower pay rates and increases in working hours. This obviously would not be to the advantage of the existing catering workers. These regulations make it more difficult to do this.

changes in unfair dismissal rules

Employees are now protected from unfair dismissal after one year's service (until 1999 employees could be dismissed without a good reason up to two years after appointment).

the Minimum Wage

All employees must be paid a legal minimum wage. This makes 'distancing' (as in the private catering example above) less attractive to organisations than it used to be.

CHAPTER SUMMARY

● Businesses have to plan carefully to ensure that they have the right number and right quality of employees to meet their requirements.

● Human resource planning is affected by factors such as employment trends, skill shortages and competition for labour.

● Employers should take note of local or national employment statistics when human resource planning.

● Managers need to know how to measure labour turnover using wastage and stability rates.

● Organisations need good occupational health services and health and safety systems to keep accident and sickness levels as low as possible.

● Proper succession planning will ensure that the organisation always has the right people at the right time to fill vacant posts.

● A flexible workforce must be recruited in order for a business to remain competitive.

● Whilst it is chiefly for the employers' benefit, flexible working also suits many employees who could not work under any other arrangement.

● There is a wide range of flexible working options available to suit different organisations in different situations.

● It is relatively easy to introduce flexible contracts of employment.

● There are a number of laws and regulations which protect employees' rights in employment contracts and make it more difficult for employers to impose total flexibility. These include:

  - the Working Time Directive, which restricts the number of working hours that can be imposed

  - the Parental Leave Directive which gives both parents the right to take leave to look after young children

  - Transfer of Undertakings Regulations which protect the rights of employees when a business changes hands

KEY TERMS

human resource planning
how to ensure that the organisation always has the right number and the right quality of employees

labour turnover
a measure of the recruitment into and the resignations from an organisation

stock taking
finding out the quantity and quality of staff available in an organisation

the annual wastage rate and the stability index
formulas that are used to calculate labour turnover

jobs analysis
an analysis of the duties involved and skills required for every job in an organisation

flexible workforce
a workforce unrestricted by permanent contracts, full-time working, fixed hours – a workforce that can adapt to changing conditions in workflow

skills audit
a survey of the skills held by all employees in an organisation

succession planning
a process of ensuring that vacant posts can be filled with the minimum of difficulty

core workers
the key employees in an organisation with the best pay and conditions and the highest level of job security

peripheral workers
groups of employees who are employed under a range of contracts with differing terms, pay rates and job security

job sharing
where the same job is divided between two people

zero hours working
where the employee is only called into work when the organisation really needs him/her

annual hours working
hours worked are spread across the year according to the needs of the organisation and can therefore vary considerably from week to week

Recruitment and selection

Unit 4 Human resources
Recruitment and selection

introduction

One of the most important jobs for the human resources manager is recruiting and selecting new employees. Without the right employees the organisation will be unable to operate efficiently or serve its customers properly or make any profits. With the proper recruitment and selection techniques, organisations can make as sure as possible that they can achieve these objectives.

what you will learn from this chapter

● the ways in which recruitment procedures are used to attract good quality job applicants

● how job descriptions and person specifications match applicants with vacancies

● how to produce and evaluate letters of application for clarity and quality of presentation

● how to produce and evaluate a curriculum vitae for clarity and quality of presentation

● how to practise and appraise interviewer techniques

● how to practise and appraise interviewee techniques

● there are a number of important legal considerations to take into account in the recruitment process

the process of recruitment

filling a vacancy

Vacancies for jobs exist in organisations for one of several reasons:

- A new job is available because of the expansion of the organisation.

  When the economy is growing and people are becoming better off organisations take advantage of that and expand their operations. To do this they may take on extra employees. This is more likely if they believe the economy is going to continue to grow for some time. If they expect economic growth to be short-lived they are less likely to create new jobs, preferring instead to use other methods listed below under 'Alternatives to filling a vacancy'.

- Someone in the organisation has retired.

- Someone has been dismissed.

- Internal promotion(s) have occurred – the vacancy arises because the previous holder has been given a better job either in the same establishment or the same organisation. This is dealt with below under 'Filling the vacancy – internal candidates'.

- Someone has died – sadly there are some employees who die during their working lives and with increased stress and the growing incidence of heart disease this is becoming more common.

- There is a restructuring of the business, which means there are gaps to be filled in the organisation.

- Someone has left because they do not like the job or have found a better job elsewhere.

alternatives to filling a vacancy

Human Resources Management departments are under constant pressure to justify the filling of a vacancy because it will save the organisation money if they do not. There are several alternatives to filling a vacancy, all with benefits and all with disadvantages too:

- overtime by the remaining employees
- restructuring of the work
- employing part-time staff
- more use of machinery/technology

At this stage it is important that the Human Resources Manager looks critically at the job description and person specification for this vacancy. From these documents (examined later in this chapter) it will be possible to assess how far it is practical to rely on these options instead of filling the vacancy.

filling the vacancy – finding the applicants

If the Human Resources Manager, after consideration of alternatives examined above, decides that the vacancy will need filling, then the next stage will be where to look for candidates. There are only two sources of candidate – internal and external.

internal candidates

Unless a vacancy is for the lowest grade job possible, there will be internal candidates who are interested in the vacancy for promotion.

Internal promotion is an important method of motivating employees and is identified by several writers as a feature of a 'best practice' employer (ie a 'good' employer who tries to do everything properly).

the main benefits to the employer of internal appointments

- an organisation with a reputation for internal advancement will find it easier to motivate staff, whereas in organisations where internal advancement is rare, staff will be less committed to the work and may be preoccupied with external job applications
- the organisation will attract better candidates if they see there is a future career in it
- many candidates will be local people who have bought homes there, have children at local schools and husbands/wives in other local jobs
- internal candidates know the business and what will be expected of them, and they can become effective in the new job very quickly
- although there is bound to be bitterness from other internal applicants who do not get the job, they will at least feel that there will be other career opportunities in the organisation and that they will get promotion later on
- the organisation will not need to rely upon external references when choosing from internal applicants – accurate information will be available from departmental heads and other colleagues

the disadvantages of appointing internally

- the successful candidates may suffer role conflict in that they are now senior to people with whom they worked with as equals – there may be a problem for them in asserting their authority
- a person promoted internally may be expected to pick up the new job in an unreasonably short space of time
- filling a vacancy internally leaves another vacancy to fill

Note also that where an employer is practising 'equal opportunity' policies (see below) they cannot favour internal candidates when filling vacancies. Moreover, internal candidates must be required to carry out exactly the same recruitment procedures as external ones.

Activity 16.1

Internal recruitment by Asda

Asda saves money by promoting junior staff

SUPERMARKET CHAIN Asda has saved thousands of pounds in recruitment costs by introducing a scheme to promote junior staff to management posts.

Nearly 150 managerial positions have been filled by internal candidates who completed the programme last year.

The company, which has only four layers between the shop floor and the board, found that some staff were leaving because they felt there were few promotion opportunities. "We felt that if it was right to take these positions out in the first place we should not re-layer and put them back in," said head of development and resourcing Sue Newton.

Some Asda staff say promotion opportunities are limited

"But people were becoming dissatisfied and some were leaving because they believed we were not prepared to promote them. We had to do something."

The aim of the scheme, called "So you want to be...", was to retain promising staff. But saving recruitment costs has been a hidden bonus. Asda has calculated that it costs up to £15,000 to recruit a general store manager from outside.

Personnel, general and department managers have been recruited in the first batch.

Reproduced by kind permission of 'Personnel Today'

1   What are the benefits to Asda of internal recruitment?

2   What are the benefits to Asda's existing employees of internal recruitment?

3   Identify examples of internal recruitment in the business you are investigating for your Portfolio. Who stands to benefit in these cases?

recruiting external candidates

There are clear **advantages** from recruiting external candidates to fill a vacancy. These benefits are :

- a much wider range of people from which to choose
- newcomers to the organisation will bring in new ideas
- newcomers are not associated with the old policies of the organisation – for this reason it is always a good idea to bring in people from outside if a change in the organisational culture is planned
- newcomers are likely to be more mobile than existing staff and in a multi-site business this can be very useful to the organisation
- newcomers may bring skills and management techniques from their former employers which your organisation might also adopt

There are also **disadvantages** of filling a vacancy with an external candidate:

- it is far more expensive than internal recruitment
- it takes time for a newcomer to get used to his or her new employer, and therefore the newcomer will not be performing effectively for the initial period
- people who move between jobs have a better idea of their market value than people who stay with the same organisation for a long time, and they make the best use they can of this by threatening to leave unless they get high pay rises or rapid promotion
- employers have to rely heavily on the references of other employers, and in reality these can be quite unreliable – people are sometimes given good references by their employers simply to help to get rid of them!

sources of external candidates

Assuming that the advantages of external recruitment are judged more important than the disadvantages, where would an organisation go to find external applicants? It will depend on the type of job an employer is trying to fill. The main sources and the particular jobs they specialise in are as follows:

- **School Careers Services**

  These provide school leavers for a wide range of jobs and traineeships such as the government-financed 'New Deal'.

- **Job Centres**

  These provide a wide range of jobs but chiefly semi-skilled, unskilled and clerical workers.

- **University Career Services**

  These provide graduates and postgraduates (eg people with further degrees).

- **Employment Agencies**

  They will find applicants in virtually all areas of work although their busiest areas are clerical, secretarial and unskilled manual employees

  Agencies also employ their own staff and hire them to organisations on a weekly (or even daily) fee basis – this is mainly for short term unskilled manual and basic clerical work

- **Recruitment Consultants and Executive Search Agencies**

  These are the 'head hunters' for people to fill senior management and professional jobs

high tech options for finding external candidates

- **Internet CVs**

  Jobseekers are now using private, portable and updatable CVs that they can send to employers by e-mail. Organisations such as recruitment agencies can also register CVs from a group of job hunters (eg a group of graduates) and individuals on-line and make them available to employers, also on-line.

  Try www.stepstone.co.uk and www.employdirect.co.uk

- **Voice recognition shortlisting**

  More and more organisations are using this as a way of short listing when they need to recruit large numbers of staff (eg retailing and hospitality) Potential applicants ring an 0800 number and are told what vacancies are available. If they wish to continue they then answer a set of questions. A computer scores the answers, based on a series of criteria, then automatically prints out a letter of rejection or an invitation to a job interview within a few hours of the telephone call.

  Try www.resumix.com

- **CD-Rom CVs**

  The job applicant is filmed with a digital camera whilst answering questions set by a potential employer. In one example Budget Rent a Car did an initial telephone screening (see student activity on the next page) and then invited 100 promising applicants to use this CD-Rom technique. Managers then viewed all 100 applicants on the CD-Rom. This took a far shorter time than the usual 'first interviews' would have taken. Final short-listed candidates are then interviewed in the traditional manner.

Activity 16.2

Telephone interviewing

When a telephone becomes an interviewer

There are two main types of computerised recruitment – telephone screening, which is catching on in the UK, and online screening, still confined to the US. Telephone screening is ideal for low-level bulk recruitment, such as staff call centres.

There are two rival suppliers in the UK – SHL, which markets the computer aided telephone screening system (CAPS), and Gallup, whose product is GATSI.

An applicant calls the freephone number day or night and keys in their unique personal identification number, which automatically sets up a file for them on the employer's HR system.

During the interview, typically lasting 15 minutes, the candidate answers multiple-choice questions using their telephone keypad.

The computer scores and weights their answers, and automatically sends them an application form or schedules a face-to-face interview if they are successful. The system then e-mails the hiring manager an interview schedule.

Where more detailed answers are required, online interviewing is preferable, but the snag is applicants need Internet access or to be within travelling distance of the employer's offices. The computer compares their answers with those for a control group of top-performing staff in the relevant job. Such online assessment may soon be supplemented by virtual personality tests, accessed on an employer's website. PA Consulting plans to launch an Internet based psychometrics service in January.

Reproduced by kind permission of *'Personnel Today'*

List and discuss the advantages and disadvantages to a job applicant of being interviewed over the phone in the manner described here.

In a typical organisation with a mixture of jobs – skilled and unskilled, secretarial and clerical, professional and managerial there will be a need to call on most of the above services at some time. Agencies can find staff to fill short-term contracts and can supply ready-made work teams to organisations for as little as one week (or even one day) for a fixed fee (this means the employees do not go onto the organisation's own payroll, thus saving administrative work).

Apart from the Careers Service and the Job Centres, which are both free, the other services are quite expensive. Using an Executive Search Consultant to fill a senior management job can cost the equivalent of 20 to 30% of the first year salary for that manager. Agencies supplying short term labour will charge hourly rates that are far higher than the standard pay rates offered by an organisation. Convenience costs money!

Other sources available include notices on premises (such as supermarkets), newspaper and radio advertising and word of mouth. These all take a lot of departmental time to sort through to find the few good applicants. High-tech options mentioned above are far quicker and more effective although they are probably unappealing to older job enquirers.

Activity 16.3

Web recruitment

ICL slashes costs with DIY website

John Robinson

Computer firm ICL has slashed its graduate recruitment costs by training personnel staff to write world-wide web pages. Two members of the HR team created a new graduate recruitment section on the company's website at a cost of £7,000. The pages will go live later this year.

Graduate recruitment manager Anna Ruewell said the Internet will become ICL's main tool for recruiting 300 graduates per year. "There is a perception that web design is the domain of technical people," said Ruewell, "but anyone who can use Microsoft Office can do what we have done."

All of ICL's graduate recruitment marketing will point students towards the web site and the company will replace its graduate brochure with less expensive fliers.

Ruewell said cost savings would also spring from not using external help to update the site and on-line application forms. Applicants will be able to set up interviews with existing ICL graduates via the web.

However, survey director of consultants High Fliers Research Martin Birchall warned the Internet is not as effective as traditional graduate recruitment tools, although it is much less expensive.

"If you compare the cost of putting together a web site with a 64 page brochure and visiting 30 universities, the Internet is much cheaper," Birchall said. "But our research shows it is not effective on its own."

The company estimates the average cost of recruiting a single graduate is between £9,000 and £22,000.

The Internet will become ICL's main graduate recruiting tool

What are the benefits of switching to Web advertising for:

1   the employer, ICL?
2   the graduate job applicants?

Is it likely to replace traditional methods of recruitment?

job descriptions and person specifications

Before an organisation goes any further in the recruitment process it needs to examine the job description and the person specification for the post.

We will now examine what these two documents contain.

job description

A job description lists the main tasks required in a job. More and more organisations have job descriptions for every job they have – from the caretaker to the managing director.

In drawing up a job description the personnel department has a number of alternatives. These are:

(a)   the line manager can draw up a description of what the job entails

(b)   the existing job holder can do it

(c)   the Human Resources Manager can interview the job holder and the line manager to find out what the job involves

In most cases it is probably best to combine approaches.

Clearly approach (b) may produce a biased view of what the job involves. After all, most people are likely to exaggerate the importance of what they do and the effort and ability that is required to do it. Moreover, the job holder may over emphasise those duties they prefer to do rather than their most important duties. Also, since they are leaving they may not bother to do a very thorough job of it anyway.

On the other hand, in approach (a) the line manager will probably miss out many little but important tasks which are only obvious to the job holder.

The aim of the exercise is to itemise all the tasks involved in a job and to try to allocate a proportion of the working week to each task. The list of tasks, and the relative importance of each one, is vitally important for several reasons:

- In carrying out appraisals of employees – a manager cannot appraise his employees if he/she does not know what the job involves.
- When analysing the job for training needs the manager must be able to see what tasks a job involves so that he/she can determine what training may be required.
- In planning the size of the workforce for the future, it will be necessary to know exactly what tasks each job involves in case the re-allocation of tasks between jobs is required, eg three people may be required to share the work of a fourth post which is being made redundant – this cannot be

done fairly without a detailed knowledge of the tasks involved in the fourth post.

- For pay determination – analysis of, and comparisons between, job descriptions means that each job can then be allocated a pay rate. This process is known as 'job evaluation'. A simple example is where clerical jobs which include the responsibility for handling money get a higher ranking, and therefore higher pay, than clerical jobs which do not.

Clearly, none of this is possible without good quality and detailed job descriptions.

drafting the job description

From all the information collected, by whichever method is chosen, it will then be necessary to draw up the document itself. Most people applying for jobs will be sent a job description along with an application form and a person specification (explained below).

The main features of a job description are:

1. the job title
2. the location of the job
3. a brief outline of what the employing organisation does
4. the main purpose of the job
5. a detailed list of the main tasks required in the job
6. the standards that the job holder will be required to achieve
7. pay and other benefits
8. promotion prospects
9. the person to whom the job holder reports
10. the person(s) who report(s) to the job holder

Nowadays employees are expected to be more flexible and to be able to do a wider range of work. This means that job titles (point 1) tend to be broader than they used to be. Point 3 is important in that a go-ahead, successful, organisation will find it easier to attract applicants of an above average quality. Points 4, 5 and 6 are the essentials of the job description, so that anyone interested in applying will know what they would be required to do if offered the job. Points 7 and 8 are needed as attractions to draw in good quality applicants. Finally, points 9 and 10 give the applicant a clear idea of the position of the job within the organisation.

In summary, the job description has a number of roles, not least of which is to turn enquiries from capable people into real job applications. Therefore, presentation of the job description is very important, although, regrettably, this is often forgotten by many employers in the selection process.

an example of a job description

THREE VALLEYS DISTRICT COUNCIL

PERSONNEL DEPARTMENT

Job Title	Personnel Assistant
Post Reference	43/789
Section	Personnel Department
Employer	Three Valleys District Council is a 'second tier' authority in Wiltshire. Apart from the main town, Wereford, it is mainly rural and is an attractive area in which to live and work.
Grade	Scale 1 (spinal column pay points 1-10). The successful applicant will be placed on the point appropriate to his/her previous experience and qualifications.

Aim and purpose of the job

To carry out a wide range of personnel administration work in a busy department consisting of three personnel assistants, two personnel officers and a personnel manager. This role is chiefly involved with personnel issues in the Council's Finance and Legal departments (employing a total of 97 staff). The postholder may be expected to carry out other duties when required (eg cover for colleagues on holiday).

Responsible to	Personnel Officer (Legal and Finance)
Duties	To assist the Personnel Officer (Legal and Finance) in a wide range of personnel work.
	Administration of recruitment and selection processes/organisation of job interviews.
	Organisation of induction programmes for new staff.
	Appraisals administration.
	Maintenance of absence and holiday records.
	Administration of employee training programmes.
	Liason with finance department on pay/benefits.
	Handling general enquiries from staff in the two departments.

continued on next page

Job prospects	This is a compact department which offers ample opportunity to gain a wide range of personnel experience. This will provide a firm foundation for a successful career in local government personnel management.
	The Authority will encourage, and support financially, the postholder to acquire professional personnel management qualifications (CIPD) through study at Wereford Technical College.
Contact	Mrs Fiona Mellor, Personnel Manager, The Personnel Department, Three Valleys District Council, Hardy Street, Wereford WR1 3HN.
	Direct line – 01876-567345
	For an informal chat about this post ring Sue Stephens, Personnel Officer (Finance and Legal departments) on 01876-567333
Application deadline	Application forms must reach the Authority (address shown above) by March 15, 2001.

person specifications

A person specification sets out the qualities of an ideal candidate whereas a job description defines the duties and responsibilities of the job.

The best-known method of drawing up person specifications is called the 'seven-point plan' originally devised by Alec Rodger. This bases the person specification upon seven separate groups of characteristics:

1 **Physique, health and appearance** – this includes grooming, looks, dress sense, voice, hearing and eyesight as well as general health matters.

2 **Attainments** – this includes educational qualifications such as GCSEs, GNVQs, A levels and degrees and vocational qualifications such as NVQs and job experience.

3 **General intelligence** – this is estimated by IQ tests and by assessment of general reasoning ability.

4 **Special aptitudes** – what special skills does a person have? These include skills with words, with numbers, with musical instruments, with artistic technique and with mechanical equipment.

5 **Interests** – are they intellectual or practical or social or a mixture of them all?

6 **Disposition** – this is an assessment of the person's acceptability by other people, leadership qualities, the person's emotional stability and self-reliance.

7 **Circumstances** – factors such as age, whether single or married, whether mobile or not.

Rodger's Seven Point Plan usually requires managers to distinguish between essential and desirable qualities under each of the seven headings. For example, five GCSEs at grade C or above might be an essential 'Attainment' to do a particular job whereas two GCE 'A' levels might be desirable but not essential.

Activity 16.4

Person specifications

Draw up a person specification for the job advertised by the Three Valleys District Council (see previous page). Use Rodger's Seven Point plan, remembering to identify essential and desirable characteristics.

Now examine the Job Description below. It is for a job as a Personal Assistant at Chorospan Ltd, a company in the pharmaceutical industry.

CHOROSPAN LIMITED
Job description

Job Title Personal Assistant

Further information Sylvia Marples, Personnel Manager (01675 453421 x 564)

Responsible to The Managing Director, Andrew Jackson

Responsible for Two Clerical Assistants

Job location Chorospan Ltd, Head Office, Reginald Road, Chester CH2 7KB

Duties Acting as Secretary at business meetings

Producing Agenda and Minutes of meetings

Making travel arrangements for the Managing Director and for other Executive Directors.

Accompanying Mr Jackson on business appointments in the UK and abroad.

Organising hospitality/accommodation for business visitors to Chorospan Ltd.

Supervision of duties of the Clerical Assistants.

Previous experience   Good secretarial and P/A experience at a senior managerial level is essential.

The Organisation   Chorospan Limited is a medium-sized manufacturer of products for the retail pharmaceutical industry specialising in cough syrups, throat lozenges and paracetamol-based pain relief tablets. They sell 30% of their products to the French and Spanish markets. Apart from two factories in Chester and Blackpool they also have a distribution centre in Calais, France.

Pay and Conditions   Working hours 09.00 to 17.00 Monday to Friday.

Salary is negotiable.

There is a generous company pension scheme.

Because the nature of the job involves foreign trips a travel allowance is paid.

General comments   This job calls for organisational abilities and personal qualities of a very high order.

Activity 16.5

Job descriptions and person specifications

1   Compare the Chorospan job description with that for the Personnel Assistant in Three Valleys District Council.

In what respects are the job descriptions similar?

How do they differ?

2   How does the Chorospan example meet the key requirement which is to attract 'good quality' applicants?

3   Draw up a person specification for one of the two jobs. Refer to qualifications and experience and the kinds of personal characteristics you think would be most appropriate.

advertising the job

Unless an organisation pays a recruitment consultancy or an executive search consultant to find potential recruits, it will have to design its own advertisements to attract people. Specialist consultancies have sophisticated advertising departments which place large and expensive adverts in the 'quality' press such as 'The Times', 'The Guardian', 'The Sunday Times' and 'The Independent'. Most businesses, however, will not have such facilities and they will have to draw up their own advertisements. The newspaper will typeset the final version.

writing the advertisement

Before writing the advertisement the employer must determine exactly what is wanted from the job being advertised. To ensure this the employer must look carefully at the Person Specification – what type of person is required – and the Job Description – what the person will be required to do in the job – before writing the advert.

When drafting the advertisement the key points to consider are:

- **job description**

  The advert should specify what the job requires the person to do. Obviously this can only be fairly general but the key duties do need outlining.

- **type of person**

  The advert should then say what kind of person is required. It is illegal to specify a particular sex or someone of a particular racial origin, except in a few quite rare situations (eg you could advertise for a person of Chinese origin to work as a waiter or waitress in a Chinese restaurant). You will also need to look at issues such as experience and qualifications.

- **pay and conditions**

  Depending on the nature of the job, state what the pay and conditions are, eg holidays, hours and pension arrangements (where appropriate). As the government moves towards restricting rights to State-provided pensions the provision of good private pension schemes by employers becomes more and more attractive to job seekers. Flexible hours ('flexitime') is an attractive feature of a job for some people, whilst for others the opportunity to earn overtime pay will be very appealing.

  Obviously, what to stress most in the advert will vary from job to job – office work jobs might emphasise the good pension or the flexitime, whereas a factory job might stress the chance to earn money from overtime.

- **place of work**

  The job location should be made clear. Some organisations are multi-sited: for example most County and District Councils have offices and workshops all over a County or town, and the location of the job may be awkward for some potential applicants, eg if they have to deliver children to school before 9 am. The advert should also say if travel is required as part of the job, and if so, how it is dealt with financially – is a company car or a mileage allowance provided?

- **how to apply**

  The advertisement should say whether applicants should write in or telephone for an application form. It needs to be borne in mind that it will take up more staff time dealing with telephone requests than dealing with enquiry letters.

- **depth of detail**

  An advertiser should not give too much irrelevant detail on the background of the organisation, although its 'guiding principle' or 'philosophy' could be mentioned if it helps to attract good candidates. For example, Body Shop Plc stresses its commitment to being environmentally friendly, and this will be an appealing feature to many people looking for work.

- **ethics and honesty**

  Be honest about the job being advertised – it is no use giving an over-attractive picture of a job in order to attract very good candidates, because if the job does not measure up to what they expect they will soon leave – remember that very good candidates can find other jobs quite easily.

- **placing the advertisement**

  Finally, where and when is the advert to be placed? This will depend on the type of job, how many vacancies there are, the budget available, and how quickly the job needs filling. For example the government advertises on the television to encourage recruits into the armed forces, teaching and nursing. A factory with a sudden order may need extra people, so an advert in the local evening paper will be essential (and usually over two or three consecutive evenings). If a business needs a chief accountant or a personnel manager, an engineer or a solicitor, then the best place is a specialist magazine for that particular profession. Certain newspapers, notably 'The Guardian' and 'The Daily Telegraph' run specialised job supplements on particular days of the week.

hi-tech options for filling vacancies

Increasingly organisations are using new technologies to help them to short list job applicants. These methods include:

internet job boards

A number of 'job boards' now appear on the Internet. The biggest advertises 2,500 jobs at any one time. Interested net users can enquire about the jobs on-line and send their CVs via e-mail should they wish to do so.

Try www.totaljobs.com

Apparently 20% of 'net' users never read a newspaper so job boards capture a market of job hunters that the newspapers do not reach.

Companies create job boards to fill specific vacancies – Shell Services International used its own job board to advertise for 70 IT specialists and received 600 replies.

In a typical job recruitment exercise using manual systems and traditional advertising, the process from beginning to job offer can take 30-32 days. Some commercial internet recruitment services can give a job applicant a first interview via the job board's on line facility. This is followed up with a 'traditional' interview and job offer – a total of 15-17 days.

letter of application, CVs and references

Having attracted a number of candidates, the next stage will be to reduce them to a small enough number to invite for an interview. For some jobs like the Managing Directorship of BT Plc there will be very few serious candidates and so a lot of time can be spent on investigating all of them. For most jobs, depending on the general economic situation, there are many applicants and a simple quick process is needed to sort them out.

The three main documents assessed in this sorting process are:

• the letter of application
• the curriculum vitae (CV)
• the application form

All organisations ask applicants to send in at least one of these documents. We will now examine all three in turn.

the letter of application

This is simply a letter (written or typed or word-processed) asking for the job and explaining why the writer is suitable for it. The letter will be structured in any way the writer thinks is appropriate, and this very fact makes it a useful selection method. If the letter is badly structured, poorly expressed and full of spelling mistakes, it could indicate that the applicant is not suitable for a clerical or administrative job which requires neat well-structured work and a 'tidy mind'. On the other hand, a poorly-structured letter which is nevertheless imaginative and interesting could indicate that the applicant may be suitable for other jobs.

Human Resources department staff may have to read hundreds of application letters so it is in a writer's interests to pay attention to doing it properly. Key points for the writer to bear in mind include:

- Keep the letter brief.

- Check grammar, punctuation and spelling.

- It should be handwritten, unless the handwriting is hard to read.

- Structure the letter as follows:

  An opening paragraph which explains how the writer found out about the job and why they are applying for it.

  A second paragraph should give the applicant's basic details – but most personal detail should be in the application form or CV

  A third paragraph will give the particular reasons why the applicant wants the job and why they want to work for that organisation.

  A fourth paragraph which says that the writer is available for interview at most times. This will enable the organisation to fix an interview if they are interested in the applicant.

disadvantages of letters of application

The disadvantages of letters of application as an assessment method are that:

- The person taught to write letters well at school will stand out even though their other qualities might not be so good. This applies even more so nowadays since the art of letter writing is rarely taught in schools and is therefore highly valued by some employers.

- The letter writer may miss out information which is important, and conversely is likely to dwell on factors which make them look a more attractive applicant – the only way around this is to ask applicants to supply a curriculum vitae (which is discussed below).

Despite their shortcomings, letters of application are quite often used and increasingly it is specified by employers that they should be handwritten.

The science of graphology (the assessment of a person's character by the analysis of his/her handwriting) is highly regarded in the USA, France and Germany because many personal characteristics are apparent from a close analysis of handwriting. It is less well regarded in the UK, but is becoming more commonly used by recruitment and executive search consultants.

an example of an application letter

23 Trent Road
Mackworth Estate
Derby
DE2 6RG

4 May 2001

Dear Sir or Madam,

I am interested in applying for the job of personnel clerk advertised in last night's 'Derby Evening Telegraph'.

I am presently studying for the Vocational Advanced Level in Business at Derby Technical College, which I will finish at the end of June this year. My qualifications and educational details are in the curriculum vitae attached.

I am very interested in personnel work and I did one week's work experience in the personnel department of Toyota Cars near Derby in November last year. I am also studying a personnel unit on my course.

I am available for an interview at any time convenient for you, apart from the dates of May 11 and May 17.

Yours faithfully

Deborah Smith

Deborah Smith

Activity 16.6

Letter of application

Study the letter shown above.

Give four reasons why you would probably invite Deborah for an interview for this job.

the curriculum vitae

'Curriculum vitae' means the 'course of your life' – the story so far.

The written curriculum vitae (the CV) is a formal description of an applicant's life and achievements.

It will normally accompany a letter of application as an alternative to the application form when the advert asks 'please apply in writing'.

the design of a CV

Unfortunately some people who write their own CVs do it in an unprofessional and untidy manner which does little to impress a possible employer. Such CVs are badly typed (or even written) often on poor quality paper.

Nowadays there are plenty of specialist agencies that can prepare CVs for people in a professional manner. If you have access to a computer and printer you should have no difficulty in producing a well presented CV on a word processing program.

The next question is what goes into a CV?

The simplest rule is to include anything which would normally be asked for in an application form. The basics will therefore be:

- name and address
- telephone number (some people may miss this out for security reasons)
- e-mail address (if there is one)
- date of birth
- marital status
- education & qualifications
- training (where appropriate)
- employment history (school and college leavers should include part-time employment)
- hobbies and interests
- references

When listing employment in chronological order, start with the most recent job. This principle also applies to education and qualifications.

Attached to the letter of application for Deborah Smith on the previous page was her curriculum vitae, shown on the next page.

CURRICULUM VITAE

NAME	Deborah Smith
ADDRESS	23 Trent Road
	Mackworth Estate
	Derby DE2 6RG
TELEPHONE	01332 – 565678
DATE OF BIRTH	3 February 1983
EDUCATION	Mackworth High School, Marlborough Road
	Derby (1994-1999)
	Derby Technical College
	Derby (1999 – present)
QUALIFICATIONS	GCSEs:
	English (A)
	Maths (C)
	History (B)
	Business Studies (C)
	Geography (A)
	German (C)
PRESENTLY STUDYING	Vocational Advanced Level in Business
EMPLOYMENT DETAILS	Store Assistant, Sainsway Superstore,
	Mackworth Centre (since October 1999)
	Saturdays only
	Work experience at Toyota Cars
	(November 2000)
INTERESTS	Foreign travel, music, amateur dramatics with
	college drama group
REFEREES	Mr A Chapman,
	Headmaster, Mackworth School
	Marlborough Road
	Derby DE1 4GH
	Mr T Poole
	Staff Manager
	Sainsway PLC
	Mackworth Centre
	Derby DE1 9DF

Activity 16.7

Job application – some practice

You are required to write an application letter and a curriculum vitae for the job advertised below. Use your own details, existing qualifications and experience (eg part time jobs you may have had). Unless your tutor says anything to the contrary, draft the letter in your own handwriting and then use a word processing package to set out the curriculum vitae.

THE JOB
Chorospan Limited
PERSONNEL ASSISTANT

We are a large producer of throat lozenges and other medical products with two factories in Britain and a distribution centre in France. In fifteen years we have doubled our sales volume and have increased our workforce in our UK factories to approximately 450. Expansion plans will take this to 550 within two years.

Our personnel department, which is based at our head offices in Chester is now seeking another person to help provide our first class personnel service to all staff. Experience in all areas of personnel work will be provided and it may include some travel to our other operating units in the UK and France.

We intend to appoint someone with good experience and qualifications but the most important factor is enthusiasm to do a job which deals mainly with people rather than routine office work. People of all ages are very welcome to apply.
The salary offered will reflect the successful person's experience and qualifications. Other benefits include a contributory pension scheme and BUPA membership plus five weeks holiday.

Please apply in writing to
John Bates,
Personnel Director,
Chorospan Ltd,
Reginald Road,
Chester,
CH2 7KB

---

additional task

Find out from the business you are investigating what method of application they prefer, or whether they use different methods for different jobs. If they use application forms, try and get a copy for your Portfolio.

the application form

This is a far more commonly used method of selection. Consultants devote hours to designing new and better forms which will extract even more accurate information from people. A typical form will require details on addresses, next of kin, education, training, qualifications, work experience, non-work interests and the names of referees from whom the organisation can collect personal recommendations. Look at the example on the next two pages.

BASSETT CONSTRUCTION LIMITED

application for post of _____

personal details

surname	forename(s)
Mr/Mrs/Miss/Ms	date of birth
permanent address	
postcode	telephone number
nationality	marital status

education and training

school/college/university	qualification	grade	date

employment history

employer	job held, duties and responsibilities	dates

additional information

Describe your present state of health.
Please give details of any serious illnesses or operations over the last 10 years.

Do you have a criminal record or criminal charges pending? Yes/No

Do you hold a clean driving licence? Yes/No

Where did you hear of this vacancy?

When are you *not* available for interview?

references

Please give the names and addresses of two referees

name	name
address	address

interests

Please give details of your interests and hobbies, any positions of responsibility held, and any other information which you would like to support this application.

DECLARATION

I declare the information supplied by me in this form is, to the best of my knowledge, correct.

signature of applicant	*date*

benefits to the employer of application forms

The personnel staff will have identified specific requirements from the job and person specifications. They can then compare these with the information on the forms. They need only shortlist for interview those people who have met those requirements, eg a particular qualification.

The forms can act as a framework for the interviewer to use should the applicant get shortlisted. For example the interviewer can query gaps in the employment record, or ask about poor examination results, or about relevant non-work interests.

The organisation can keep all the forms for the shortlisted candidates for the vacancy and draw on them again if another vacancy arises.

The form from the successful applicant will become a very useful part of his/her initial personnel records.

references

For most jobs it is usual for the prospective employer to take up references provided by the job applicant. There are several types of reference:

- **Testimonial** – a letter, usually from a former employer or teacher which will say very positive and kind things about the applicant. As the applicant has been given this letter it is unlikely that the writer will make anything other than positive helpful statements (clearly, if the writer did say something critical the applicant would tear the testimonial up and look around for someone else to write one!)

- **Reference letters** requested by the prospective employer – this is the most usual type of reference. The letters are confidential so that the referee can be completely honest without embarrassment, but it may not tell the prospective employer all he/she needs to know. Employers can learn to 'read between the lines', and often the omission of information can be a telling factor.

- **Reference forms** – some organisations, the Civil Service being a good example, use a structured form which asks specific questions about the applicant. These include assessments of effort and ability, and opinions about their honesty and health.

- **Telephone references** – some organisations telephone the people given as referees. The main benefit is that the recruiter can assess the tone of voice of the referee, and this can often say far more about an applicant than a letter can. They can also question the referee far more searchingly.

- **Medical references** – most employers will carry out some kind of medical check up even if it is only the completion of a form asking a few simple questions about health problems in the past. Such a check is necessary because:

- the employer needs to safeguard the health of other employees
- the job itself may require specific health standards (eg perfect colour vision for a train driver, because of the need to be able to distinguish railway signals)
- if an employee is to join a company pension scheme a medical check-up will be needed (again only the completion of a simple form may be required)
- Medical matters of growing importance – notably the problem of AIDS – may mean that in the future medical checks will have to be far more rigorous, and include blood tests

interviewing

interviewer and interviewee techniques

The final stage in the processs will be an interview, and – increasingly common these days – some form of test or assessment. Interviews are arranged for almost every kind of job. The process of sifting through forms or letters and the examination of references will mean that only a few of the applicants for the job will be interviewed. This is because interviews take up the time of senior managers who have to carry them out, and this will be costly for the business.

interviewing – the employer's viewpoint

Interviewing is sometimes done in a poorly thought out and badly structured manner which gives the organisation a bad image. To avoid this situation only requires the observation of a few simple rules:

planning the interview itself

- The interviewer must ask 'what are my objectives? What am I looking for? How will I phrase the questions I am going to ask?' It may sound obvious, but one key objective is to fill in all the gaps which are left after all the information from the application forms, CVs and references have been assembled. Another objective is to explore in detail and in depth some of the points raised in the application forms which you consider to be of importance.
- Decide if the vacancy requires just one interviewer or two or even a panel of four or five. There are advantages and disadvantages to either approach.

'One to one' interviews put applicants at ease so that they will talk more naturally. The problems are that:

A single interviewer lacks the range and depth of knowledge of a panel of experts.

A single interviewer is more likely to suffer from bias and can be highly prejudiced.

One interviewer is more likely to suffer from:

- mirror imaging – favouring candidates who are like them
- 'halo' effects – favouring candidates who have particularly attractive characteristics even if those characteristics have little bearing on the job applied for
- 'horns' effects – the opposite of 'halo' effects

• If there is more than one interviewer, the panel should ensure that there is a planning meeting beforehand to decide how the questioning will be shared out. Nothing gives a worse image to an interviewee than if the interviewers interrupt or contradict each other or repeat questions.

practical points for interviewers

• Send very clear instructions to applicants with the precise time and venue for the interview. A map and a list of local hotels may be useful for those coming from far away.

• If possible the interviews should be planned so that applicants are interviewed soon after they have arrived and so that they can leave immediately afterwards.

• Decide if there is a need for a test as well. For example, more and more schools and colleges expect applicants for a teaching post to do a practice lesson to assess actual teaching ability. For secretarial posts a test in shorthand/keyboarding may be required. Where tests are needed extra administrative arrangements will have to be made.

• The facilities should be organised well in advance – an interview room and also a comfortable waiting room, with freely available tea and coffee, are important. If the interviews take all day, applicants should also be given lunch.

carrying out the interview

• As a general rule the 'talking split' in a job interview should be around 20% for the interviewer and 80% for the interviewee. The interviewer learns far more from the applicant if he/she listens than if he/she talks! However, 'listening' is not just 'not talking' – listening is the art of conveying to the applicant that you are interested in what they are saying, together with an ability to make the occasional comment which encourages them to say a lot more.

- The interview should always begin with a few friendly questions to put the candidate at ease – ones about the journey or the weather – before asking more detailed questions. Most interviewers will ask a mixture of questions. Some will be about the application form itself, eg asking for more details about work experience or about qualifications. It is usual to follow up with deeper questions such as how the candidate might handle a difficult situation at work.

- Finally, there should be a question asking the candidate if they have any questions.

the use of tests

It is increasingly common for employers to expect job applicants to carry out tests to give a fuller picture of their ability to do the job applied for. These are usually referred to as Aptitude Tests. They are appropriate for manual work where there is some skill involved and also in office work where applicants might be required to take a short typing or word processing test. For professional posts such tests are less usual because it is felt that the candidates qualifications, references and experience are sufficient evidence.

In more recent years new developments in testing have included . . .

psychometric testing

Psychometric tests assess the intelligence and personality of applicants. They are much more sophisticated than aptitude tests and the employer must have properly trained staff to analyse the test results properly. Such tests are particularly valuable when assessing intelligence, interest in the job applied for, motivation and personality. The producers of such tests (there are dozens available) argue that they are completely unbiased and extremely accurate. They are supposed to be particularly good at assessment of personality – for example, they can show if a candidate would work well in a team or would be more effective working alone.

assessment centres

Job applicants are subjected to a wide range of assessments over a whole day or sometimes two days. They are required to participate in group exercises (with all the other applicants), psychometric tests, aptitude tests and traditional interviews. By using a mixture of assessment this process is claimed to produce more accurate resulst. The applicants are given longer to prove themselves and therefore become more relaxed and more 'natural'.

Recent developments now mean that these assessment centre exercises can be videoed and then sent to a team of independent experts to be properly analysed. This reassures the candidates that their performance will be assessed objectively.

Activity 16.8

On the job 'interviewing'

Staff have to be prêt à accepter

John Robinson

SANDWICH CHAIN Prêt à Manger is giving its employees the final say in recruitment decisions.

Candidates are asked to work an eight-hour trial shift at one of the company's 75 outlets. At the end, staff vote whether they will be taken on. Personnel staff still undertake initial screening.

The policy is intended to reduce the number of employees leaving soon after being appointed.

"Much of why some people have not been a success with us was because we did not work hard enough to make them fit in," said recruitment centre manager Steve Carpenter.

"If people are involved in the training and recruitment process they tend to work hard to make sure the new recruit fits in."

Employees get to vote on whether candidates would fit in

So far, about a third of candidates have been rejected by staff. Carpenter said the practice does not conflict with equal opportunities policies. "We are quite wary if a shop has a lot of one nationality. If that was the case we would try to mix it up a bit."

Chairman of recruitment agency Park Human Resources Simon Howard said the practice is a lesson for recruiters in all sectors.

"It is common sense and practical, and they have shown that they are streets ahead of some of the HR conventions," said Howard.

Reproduced by kind permission of 'Personnel Today'

Duscuss the main advantages and disadvantages of this form of 'interviewing' and testing for

1 the employer
2 the job applicants

Would it be suitable for the business you are investigating? If not, why not?

after the interview

After interviewing all candidates and carrying out whatever tests may be necessary, the final stage is to select one or more of them. Interview panels often find it very hard to choose between the final two or three applicants. Although applicants will need to know the outcome within a few days there should be a thorough analysis of all the information that has been collected on each of them. It is fairly easy to devise a list of the key points. These will include:

• attainments

• experience

• disposition

• personal circumstances

• reference letters

• results from the medical check up

• results from any essential tests/assessment centres

• and, finally . . . comments from the interviewers themselves

The job and person specifications make it a lot easier to do the final selection. From these documents a list of selection criteria will have been devised for the job. Every member of the interview panel can then mark each candidate out of 10 for each of these criteria. The panel can then compare their results, see where they have similar marks and where they differ significantly. They then need to discuss the differences and come to a final result. It is important, for the image of the organisation, to be polite and constructive when telling unsuccessful applicants that they have failed to get the job. They may be suitable for different vacancies later on, and a polite, helpful letter may encourage them to apply for such positions.

The successful applicant should be notified first of all. This is because they may be looking for other jobs and if you have thought the applicant suitable to employ there is every chance other organisations will too. It is wisest to wait a day or two before notifying the best of the unsuccessful candidates just in case the successful one does turn down the offer.

induction

The successful applicant should be sent immediately all the details relating to the job. This should include joining instructions (the date of starting work, where to go and who to ask for on arrival) and some details of the social facilities such as canteens, sports clubs, as well as medical care and pension provisions. The applicant is also legally entitled to a Written Statement of the terms and conditions of their employment.

Induction training is dealt with in the next chapter (page 391).

other types of interview

The other types of interview that an organisation is likely to carry out are:

performance reviews

These are dealt with in the next chapter (page 404).

exit interviews

Good employers will always interview employees who are leaving, unless they are being made redundant or are retiring. This is in order to:

- sort out final paperwork and any financial matters
- find out why they are leaving
- find out if there is anything wrong with the job they are leaving. Is it related to pay? conditions? prospects?
- find out if personal relationships in the workplace had caused problems for them
- find out what is so attractive about the organisation they are moving to – again is it pay or conditions or prospects?
- thank them for their service with the organisation

employer legal and ethical responsibilities

Always remember that there are legal obligations and ethical responsibilities which the candidate and the interviewer should abide by throughout the entire recruitment process.

All employees are protected by a variety of laws that have been introduced over the past 25-30 years. Some of the more important ones are described below.

Equal Pay Act 1970

This requires employers to pay the same rate of pay to men and women if they are doing the same job. Prior to this Act many jobs paid lower rates of pay to women.

The chief problem with this Act was that a job where most job holders were women could be badly paid whilst in a similar job where most job holders were men pay rates could be a great deal higher.

For this reason the government introduced the Equal Value Amendment (1983) which requires men and women to be paid the same rates of pay if women can show that their jobs are of 'equal value' to a range of specifically-named jobs held by men.

Sex Discrimination Act 1975

This law states that employers may not discriminate on grounds of gender.

It makes it illegal to discriminate against a particular sex when:

- advertising to fill jobs available
- appointing employees for those jobs
- promoting staff into better jobs
- determining the terms and conditions of the job.
- when offering employees opportunities for training and development

exceptions to the Act

There are a number of examples where the Act does not apply. These include:

- private clubs – for example some of the exclusive 'gentlemens clubs' in London can and do refuse to admit women
- the armed forces – recruitment of women is restricted to specific areas – there are now female personnel on board Royal Navy ships and a number of female fighter pilots
- acting roles

Recent rulings from the European Commission have extended the law in this area. For example, retirement age must now be the same for both sexes (65 years of age) and women in the armed forces cannot now be forced to leave because they are pregnant.

Race Relations Act 1976

The 1976 Race Relations Act makes discrimination on grounds of race illegal in the same areas as described above under the Sex Discrimination Act 1975, ie advertising jobs, appointing staff, promoting staff and providing staff benefits.

Again there are a few exceptions to the Act including:

- ethnic restaurants can specify they want people of a particular race to work as waiters/waitresses to make the restaurant look more authentic
- social work departments can specify they want to appoint staff of a particular race where they have to deal with social problems of people of the same race
- acting roles will sometimes require people of particular races – for example, a Chinese actress is unlikely to make a convincing job of playing the role of Queen Victoria

direct and indirect forms of discrimination

Both the Sex Discrimination and Race Relations Acts state that there are two ways in which employers could break the law:

direct discrimination

This means that there is a positive decision to discriminate either against men or women.

indirect discrimination

Indirect discrimination is where the employer creates certain conditions of employment which make it harder for a particular racial group or for women or men to get the jobs advertised. Such a practice is only legal if the employer can show that the condition was a 'genuine occupational qualification' of the job.

For example a minimum height requirement might make it harder for large numbers of woman (or for certain racial groups) to apply for a job. If there were safety or health reasons for this height limit this would be a 'genuine occupational qualification'. Therefore it would not be indirect discrimination.

the Disability Discrimination Act 1995

This Act updates the protection for disabled persons and places it onto a similar basis as for other forms of discrimination. It does not cover organisations employing under 20 people.

key aspects of the Act

- Employers must not discriminate against disabled people when:
  - advertising jobs and inviting applications
  - offering jobs after interviews have taken place
  - when determining the terms and conditions of the job.

  Once appointed, a disabled person must be treated the same as everyone else when training or promotion or any other benefits are on offer. If five people are applying for a promotion and there is only one post vacant the disabled person cannot expect favourable treatment.

- The employer must take reasonable steps to ensure that a disabled person can work on the premises. This includes making arrangements such as:
  - modifying the buildings (entrances, ramps, lifts etc)
  - changing working hours to suit the disabled person
  - allowing time off for treatment or rehabilitation
  - allowing extra training so the disabled person can carry out the job

- providing a reader or an interpreter

- putting a disabled person in a different more convenient work place (eg the ground floor rather than three floors up)

Employers only have to do what is reasonable. If modifications are very expensive then this would be deemed unreasonable. There is some government financial assistance available for modifications to buildings.

Activity 16.9

Discrimination at work

Here are some examples of adverts for job vacancies and situations which might occur at work. Look at each of them and suggest whether they discriminate against certain people or not.

1   Advert: 'Barman required for Zone999 Club'

2   Advert: 'Young English woman required as live-in Nanny to three children'

3   Advert: 'Indian man required as waiter in Indian Restaurant'

4   Three women have been appointed as supervisors in a factory. The manager explains "there were too many men supervisors – we wanted to even things out between the sexes."

5   Three women take a case against their employer to court complaining that men employed in a similar job by another company are paid more than they are.

evaluation of the recruitment process

The recruitment process should be under constant review. Questions to ask include:

• How many application forms sent to enquirers actually came back?

• How many were sent back incorrectly or incompletely filled in?

• How many job applicants were shortlisted for each interview?

• If only a few good quality candidates bother to apply why is this so?

• What percentage of candidates accepted a job when offered it?

• How many successful candidates were still in the organisation:

    – after the induction period?

    – after 6 months?

Assessment of these factors will enable the organisation to monitor its recruitment and appointment processes and make improvements where necessary.

CHAPTER SUMMARY

● Businesses recruit staff for a number of important reasons – these include business growth, resignations, retirements, dismissals and changes in job roles.

● The basic documents required before recruitment and selection take place are the job description and the person specification for the job concerned.

● Other important documents are the letter of application, the curriculum vitae (CV) and the application form.

● It is vital to plan carefully how and when to advertise jobs.

● Interviews must be carefully planned in order to recruit the right person for the job and to show fairness to all the candidates concerned.

● A variety of tests and exercises, including psychometric tests are often used to give a more accurate picture of the job candidate than an interview can provide on its own.

● Employers must understand that there are legal and ethical responsibilities relating to recruitment and selection of new employees. Important legislation includes:

  - the Equal Pay Act 1970

  - Sex Discrimination Act 1975

  - Race Relations Act 1976

  - Disability Discrimination Act 1995

● Employers must understand that there are legal and ethical responsibilities relating to the recruitment and selection of new employees.

● Good employers use a series of established criteria to evaluate the effectiveness and fairness of their recruitment and selection procedures.

● Other important types of interview used by an employer are for pay reviews and for employees who have decided to leave.

KEY TERMS

job description	this lists the main tasks and responsibilities in a job
person specification	this lists the qualities of an ideal candidate for a job
Rodger's seven point plan	a method of drawing up a person specification, based on seven groups of characteristics
curriculum vitae	usually known as a CV, this gives the career and educational background of a job seeker
testimonial	a supporting letter from a referee which is supplied by the job applicant
Internet job board	an on-line noticeboard provided by employers and web search engines such as Yahoo
psychometric testing	specialist tests which assess the suitability of a job applicant to carry out a job successfully – psychometrics is the systematic measurement of intelligence, aptitudes and personality
exit interviews	these are carried out with any employee who has decided to leave – the aim is to find out the main reasons why they are leaving
assessment centres	a series of exercises which job applicants carry out to give a fuller picture than an interview alone could ever provide
job references	these can be provided in a number of ways – their purpose is to provide more information about a job applicant so the interview panel has a better idea of their experience, ability and character
direct discrimination	preferring one job applicant or employee over another
indirect discrimination	creating conditions of employment or entry to employment which makes it harder for certain groups of people to work or obtain work

Developing and assessing employees

introduction

This chapter examines the reasons why the training and development of employees is vital to the competitiveness of a business. It also looks at the main types of training and development. Finally it examines how employee performance is assessed.

what you will learn from this chapter

● Training and development are vitally important for the overall efficiency and competitiveness of an organisation.

● There are several types of training and development designed to fulfil a variety of organisational needs.

● All training is either 'on the job' or 'off the job' – both are equally important and valuable.

● Some skills and competences learnt in the workplace are non-transferable and others are transferable.

● All organisations must regularly assess the performance of their employees to make sure that they are fulfilling their potential.

● The working environment plays a significant part in the effective performance of employees.

● Employees are motivated by a mixture of financial and non-financial factors in the workplace.

● There are a number of motivation theories which explain how organisations should manage their employees.

training and development

Firstly we will examine the importance of training employees. Secondly we will look at how employees might be developed to increase job satisfaction and, consequently, become of more use to the organisation in the longer run.

training

A general definition of 'training' is:

'the acquisition of a body of knowledge and skills which can be applied to a particular job'

Traditionally, young people left school and found a job which provided them with sufficient initial training to enable them to continue to do the same job indefinitely. This was true whether the job was unskilled or semi-skilled, requiring only very basic training, or skilled where an 'apprenticeship' of several years was required. It was not unusual to be given an apprenticeship in, for example, a shipyard, a coalmine or a newspaper printing works which would provide a steady, secure and well-paid job from the day of joining the company until the day of retirement fifty years later. The training provided in that apprenticeship would be expected to be sufficiently thorough to ensure that very little extra training would ever be required.

Today there are very few 'traditional' apprenticeships, and people can no longer assume that any job will be a 'job for life'. Even people who do keep the same job for a long time are required to update their skills regularly, or face redundancy because their old skills are rapidly made useless by the advance of new technology.

For most people it is now assumed that they will change their jobs several times in a lifetime, often switching to completely different types of work.

The significance of this is that training is much more central to peoples' lives as an ongoing process rather than just something they do at the start of their careers.

training programmes

Nowadays most larger organisations employ professional training officers to run training programmes for employees. In a large manufacturing or services company, for example, the training manager will have teams of training instructors to teach all kinds of courses to employees. Even in small businesses several types of training will still be necessary.

Training can be divided into two main categories: 'on the job' training or 'off the job' training.

'on the job' training

This means that the employee acquires their training or development (see below) in the workplace itself. For many people they enjoy the direct link with their job and can see more clearly how relevant the training or development is to the performance of that job.

'off the job' training

This means attending courses which may be in a college or a training centre away from the workplace (or one situated inside the workplace). This type of training is important to an employee's career development as well as being an integral part of a training programme (see pages 397 to 398).

non-transferable skills and transferable skills

Skills acquired by employees can be either non-transferable or transferable. All the types of training and development described below fall under one or other of these two headings.

non-transferable skills

These are skills that are extremely specific to the job held. They are of little use in any other job. Training to work on a particular machine in a factory may provide the employee with not only a skill that is non-transferable but also one that causes 'negative transfer'.

This means that when the employee switches to a newer machine they have to 'unlearn' the skills acquired on the old one. This takes time, and time costs an employer money.

transferable skills

These are skills that can be used in a wide variety of other jobs later on. In the economy today, where people are changing jobs far more frequently than twenty years ago, non-transferable skills are of little use to a job seeker. In looking around for jobs, people must have a selection of 'transferable skills'. People with transferable skills are more useful to employers because they learn a new job quickly and they are cheaper to train.

This ability to use skills more widely is called positive transfer. An example is the skill of interviewing. This is transferable to a whole range of interviewing situations, eg a disciplinary interview. Key skills such as verbal and written communications, numeracy and IT are transferable to most jobs.

Activity 17.1

Transferable and non-transferable skills

Choose a part time job that you do or someone that you know does. Identify and list those skills required in it that are non-transferable and those that are transferable to other jobs.

types of training

induction training for new employees

Induction is the process of introducing new employees to the organisation and its way of life and 'culture'.

A successful job applicant should be provided with induction training of some kind. As might be expected the larger, well-resourced organisations do this more thoroughly than poorly-resourced, smaller, organisations.

What does an induction programme include? Most will involve:

- a tour of the buildings to show the newcomer all the important areas – the sick room, the canteen, the pay office, toilets, car parking etc – and to introduce them to the important staff such as the pay and personnel clerks and the person in charge of First Aid

- an introduction to their new workplace – the specific office or factory area or shop department – where they will be working

- some background detail about the organisation – the easiest and best way to do this is to show them a video

Activity 17.2

Induction programmes

Work in groups and draw up an induction programme for new entrants to your college/school. Plan it around their first day at the college/school.

Investigate the induction programme (if there is one) of your Portfolio business – it may give you ideas for the programme you are drawing up.

initial training for new employees

This is to ensure that the job is done competently and safely. All new employees must be given training immediately after the induction procedures have been carried out.

updating training

Increasingly employees are required to learn new skills in place of skills that are becoming redundant, eg in the newspaper printing industry the traditional printing skills have virtually been replaced by completely different work requiring completely different skills. Printers either had to learn the new skills or lose their jobs.

Most importantly there is now a 'culture' of training in which employees are increasingly expected to update knowledge and skills on a regular basis.

multi-skilling training

Multi-skilling means that employees are trained to do several jobs rather than just one.

Employers gain from this because:

• an employee can do the work of somebody who is absent through illness or holidays

• employees are more motivated because doing several jobs is usually more interesting than doing just one; where an employee is able to do several jobs it increases their value to the organisation and makes them feel more appreciated and more secure

• the flexibility gained from multi-skilling means the total number of employees can be cut down

open learning centres

Many organisations help to encourage off the job training through the provision of open learning or self learning centres where their employees can study a range of topics in their free time. These can be work-linked topics such as time management or business communications or general interest topics such as 'foreign languages for holidays'.

The aim is to get employees to realise the importance of keeping up-to-date with new developments in industry and in their own particular areas of work.

As the Activity on the next page shows, open learning is not always very successful.

Activity 17.3

Problems with open learning?

Open-learning centre is not too popular

Chemicals manufacturer Zeneca is reviewing its self-learning centre, as few staff are using it. Based at the firm's production site in Macclesfield, the centre was opened in the mid 1990s and contains hundreds of computers, and books on topics such as coaching, time management and self-development.

HR manager David Westbury said the company had great hopes of the centre, but less than 20 per cent of the 1,800 employees at the site are using it. "We thought that an all-singing, all-dancing learning centre would attract significant numbers, but we have not seen it."

Staff are asked to sign a book when they use the centre to monitor numbers.

One possible reason, said Westbury, is the pressures of business. "The centre is at our production plant and it may be that line managers simply cannot spare the time to attend the centre."

Or it could be that the centre has the wrong training packages, or it could be due to lack of staff motivation, he added.

Senior management at Zeneca are asking for the cost of the centre to be justified, and Westbury and his colleagues in the training department are carrying out research to find out why staff are not using it.

Results are expected in the new year.

Reproduced by kind permission of 'Personnel Today'

1   Why does self-learning at Zeneca seem to be a turn off ?

2   List some suggestions for increasing the popularity of the open-learning centre among Zeneca employees.

government training schemes

Since the 1970s the government has financed training programmes to help people find work. Although the emphasis has been on finding young people jobs, older people have also been helped by a series of training programmes.

After the Labour government came to power in May 1997 it introduced its 'New Deal' for the unemployed. This scheme offers out of work 'under 25s' four options (A,B,C,D) to choose from. By March 1999, 247,000 people had signed up for 'New Deal' and there were 44,300 employers participating in the scheme.

A   **The employer option** – an employer taking on an unemployed 'under 25' gets a £60 per week tax rebate for six months.

B   **The voluntary sector option** – this is where employers get financial help to offer 'under 25s' approved in-work training for at least one day per week and for a nationally recognised qualification.

C   **The full-time education option** – young people will be able to keep their DSS benefits if they carry out full time studies to gain a nationally recognised qualification.

D The Environmental task force – young people will carry out environmental projects tied into part time day release study for a nationally recognised qualification.

The controversial aspect of these four options is that all under 25s out of work must choose one of them if they are not otherwise suitably occupied (eg at university). Staying at home and just claiming benefit for nothing will no longer be an option.

These measures cost a lot of money – for the tax rebates, for extra places at colleges of further education and for setting up of appropriate environmental projects. This came partly from the 'Windfall Tax' (paid out of the excess profits of privatised corporations).

a new Youth Training Programme

This was piloted under the previous Conservative government. It is called 'Target 2000' and requires all 'under 18s 'to study for at least a National Vocational Qualification (NVQ) or General National Vocational Qualification (GNVQ) level 2 course for at least one day per week.

There will be a greater duty placed on employers to ensure that their 'under 18' employees actually do this course.

Individual Learning Accounts (ILAs)

The Labour Party has announced its intention to introduce a national voluntary system of individual learning accounts (ILAs). Learning Accounts are a mechanism whereby individuals can save to purchase learning and development whenever they need it. They can get some funding from a Local Skills Council (formerly known as TECs or LECs) provided that they are prepared to top that up with some money of their own.

In the future there are plans to introduce a 'smart card' which individuals will have when they embark on a training programme. These cards will contain details of how much the individual, the employer and the state are paying towards the course fees. The state would put £150 into a person's account for every £25 they contributed themselves.

Many people will like the idea of their own personalised training account which they can contribute to and build up just like a bank account. As they move from job to job they can take their account with them and buy more training whenever they want to.

Investors in People (IIP)

This is known as 'a national standard for effective investment in people'. It sets out a range of targets which employers should achieve. For example, there must be a regular review of the training and development needs of all employees and resources clearly identified for this purpose. All employees should have a clear vision of where the organisation is going and be encouraged to contribute to the achievement of that vision.

Where an organisation achieves the specification laid down by IIP it is given the accreditation of 'an Investor in People'. This is not just a nice certificate to hang on the wall. More and more companies take the view that their suppliers should be IIP accredited since it reflects the fact that the organisation has a committed workforce who do a good job. Not having 'IIP' may therefore mean less business in the future.

National Vocational Qualifications (NVQs)

The aim of NVQs (SVQs in Scotland) is to create a national system of approved competency-based qualifications.

QCA (the Qualifications and Curriculum Authority) and SQA (Scottish Qualifications Authority) are the bodies that accredit NVQs/SVQs set up by the occupational bodies and the industry training organisations. These organisations have established sets of standards or 'competences' which employees need in the workplace to do their jobs properly.

The main principles behind this initiative are these:

- qualifications are workplace-based, reflecting real workplace needs
- workplace requirements are now a far bigger influence on what is taught in further education colleges
- the Single European Market means that these new qualifications will eventually become part of a common system of Euro-qualifications

NVQs/SVQs qualifications are in five bands – NVQ 1 being the lowest level and NVQ 5 being the highest level – associated with managerial skills. The basis of assessment is reaching a performance standard laid down by the industry concerned. Assessment is mainly 'on the job'. There is no time period set to complete any particular NVQ stage. People proceed at the rate which suits them. As long as a person is competent for a particular level NVQ, he or she will gain the appropriate Award. In essence these qualifications are based purely on results, not on how people learn.

GNVQs – a short note

NVQs are workplace based so, obviously, students on full-time courses cannot achieve them. GNVQs were established to meet the needs of these students. The qualifications are basically 'academic' NVQs in the sense that there is academic content combined with a work-based focus to study.

The Vocational A Level is essentially a Level 3 (Advanced Level) GNVQ.

Activity 17.4

NVQs at BP Express

NVQ scheme fuels fall in petrol staff turnover

By Katrina Fox

The course helps BP retain staff in an increasingly competitive market

Petrol retailer BP Express has cut its annual turnover rate of forecourt staff from about 100 per cent to 66 per cent after introducing training for NVQ Level 2 qualifications.

More than 300 staff have qualified with NVQ Level 2 in retailing since the firm became the first oil company to offer NVQs to forecourt staff in January. A further 500 staff are currently on the programme.

Turnover of those on or taking the NVQ is very low, about 6 per cent, a signal that the training is working, according to retail training manager David Burns.

"Historically, people have not placed any real value on working as a forecourt assistant," said Burns. It was a stop-gap rather than a possible career.

It is the same NVQ offered to counter staff by other retailers, such as Marks & Spencer, Burns said, but includes hazard awareness because of petrol products. Subjects include merchandising, customer service and handling complaints.

"Our turnover target is 35 per cent," John Browning, Developing People project manager at BP's training centre, said.

BP is focusing on retaining staff in an increasingly competitive petrol retail market. The number of filling stations has dropped from close to 30,000 in 1988 to about 14,000 now, Browning said.

BP wants to attract people who view forecourt work as good training for future jobs in BP retailing, according to Browning. "Petrol retailing has had a poor record of training."

Some store managers have achieved Level 3 NVQs and the company is considering other NVQ options.

1   Why was employee turnover at BP Express so high?

2   How have NVQs helped to reduce staff turnover?

training courses

We will now examine the main types of training course that organisations may run.

'in house' training courses

This is where employers run courses inside their own organisation. Courses might be held in an ordinary office room or in a smart training centre owned by the organisation. Courses run 'in house' will be ones where it is impractical and unrealistic to offer any other alternative – an obvious example would be the organisations induction programme. Other examples include training staff to use equipment which is specific to that organisation and customer care programmes.

The main benefits of using in-house courses are:

- they are fairly cheap – there is usually no need to employ outside trainers and lecturers
- course content is tailor-made for your organisation
- references and examples to highlight points can be related to your own organisation
- everybody knows one another, so there is no time wasted in having to get to know people

external courses

Sometimes it is necessary to send staff to do courses elsewhere. This may be with another employer or at a specialist training centre or at the factory of an equipment supplier (when an organisation buys new equipment the supplier will usually run training programmes at its own factory to get employees accustomed to using it).

The benefits of using external courses are:

- they bring together specialist trainers/tutors who would never be available to an 'in-house' course chiefly because of the high cost
- course members get together from several organisations, and this enables them to learn more about each other and how their respective organisations operate
- trainers place great value on the benefits of being away from the workplace – the course members are in a comfortable and peaceful environment away from any distractions

External courses are generally quite expensive because they include fairly luxurious accommodation in lavish surroundings and the guest speakers are highly paid. This means employers have to think very seriously about the value of such courses to the organisation and they have to carefully identify which staff would get the most personal benefit.

vocational and professional courses

Internal and external courses often have to be reinforced by courses provided by local colleges and universities. These courses provide the essential knowledge to support what is learnt in the workplace and on internal courses. College courses include vocational courses and professional courses:

vocational courses

These provide training in job-related skills, eg office-skills; the Qualifications and Curriculum Authority (QCA), which took over the role of the National Council for Vocational Qualifications (NCVQ), sets standards for workplace competences which can be assessed both in the workplace and at College by examining bodies such as Edexcel (BTEC), OCR (RSA) and AQA (City & Guilds).

professional courses

All the professions operate professional training schemes which enable people to acquire qualifications for their career development; these include the various Accountancy Institutes, the Law Society, and the Chartered Institute of Personnel and Development; colleges are given permission to run these courses and the students sit exams which are usually set by the professional bodies.

Employers are therefore faced with a very wide range of options to offer their staff. For example a school leaver starting work at 18 with 2 GCE A levels might be encouraged to do a Higher National qualification by part-time study at College. After successful completion (in two years) the employee could then be encouraged to do a professional qualification such as accountancy or personnel management (both taking 3 or 4 years to achieve).

evaluation of training in the organisation

Good employers will continually evaluate the effectiveness of their training programmes to ensure that they are worthwhile. The key points to consider are:

how have trainees reacted to the training given them?

Typically training officers will have a review session at the end of a training course to assess what participants thought about it. A questionnaire asking for individual comments may also be used. It is important to stress that a training course might have been a lot of fun with a great deal of personal interaction between the participants, but in fact they may have learnt very little of direct use to their jobs.

what have they actually learnt – what skills have they acquired?

The simplest way of checking this is through a test. Trainers should stress that the test results are to assess the effectiveness of the training course not to assess how particular individuals have performed.

how has their job performance improved?

Over the first few months after the training the participants work performance could be monitored to see if there has been any improvement.

how has the training benefited the organisation as a whole?

Training is not done just for the employees' benefit. The organisation will aim to achieve specific benefits from running training courses, and if those benefits are not achieved then the training needs looking at again.

A good example are 'customer care' programmes – more and more organisations are training employees how to deal with customers in a more sensitive, helpful and friendly manner. This has obvious benefits in terms of increasing customer loyalty and increasing sales.

Activity 17.5

Course evaluation

Working in groups, make a list of the things you would look at when evaluating how good your own college/school course has been.

employee development

Employee development may be defined as:

'a course of action designed to enable the individual to realise his or her potential for growth in the organisation'

In other words the employer does not just train people for now, but for the future.

How is this done? A good employer will have a system of identifying career potential in an employee. If there is no system to do this, the result will be that employees stay in 'dead end' jobs which may make them frustrated and bitter. Often they will leave for a better job where their potential is more likely to be recognised. This means that the employer will lose people who could have been a very great asset to the organisation, had their potential been realised.

A system to identify potential should include:

- An appraisal system

  This is an analysis of employee performance. It is examined in detail in the next section of this chapter.

- A system of assessment centres

  In simple terms this means that the employer identifies particular staff with potential, using previous work experience etc as a guide, and then arranges a series of practical tests to assess their ability to handle the kind of work which more senior jobs might involve. This is dealt with in more detail in Chapter 16 (Recruitment and Selection).

developing employees with potential

Several techniques can be used to help promising employees to develop their abilities and give management a better idea of exactly where the employees' future may lie:

job rotation

Giving people a range of jobs in rotation widens their experiences and increases their skills.

job enlargement

Giving people extra tasks to do gives management a better idea of the employees true capacity, ability and stamina.

job enrichment

Adding more interesting and more difficult tasks to the job. This might be done with a person of very great potential (often known as a 'high-flier') to see just how capable he or she really is.

understudying

This means that an employee will be attached to a very senior manager to act as an assistant. This gives the employee insight into what senior managers have to do, and is often used to groom very able people to move rapidly into a top job. Many top business people today acted as understudies at some time in their early careers.

mentoring

This means that an experienced senior manager is allocated to a young employee in order to help them to structure their career development within the organisation. The mentor passes on the benefits of their experience, insight and wisdom. They will advise the young employee how to deal with a wide variety of managerial problems but they are not there to help them to improve specific skills. Try www.merryck.com

coaching

This is rather similar to mentoring but the key difference is that coaching involves helping the young employee to acquire high quality skills in a number of specific management areas. Such skills include communication with staff, budgeting, how to appraise staff and how to carry out disciplinary procedures. It is similar to coaching in a sporting sense where, for example, top tennis or golf players are coached to improve particular aspects of their game. Try www.CoachingFutures.co.uk

project work

Giving a promising employee a specific investigative project enables them to get to appreciate many aspects of the organisation and it enables them to get to know senior managers. A typical project might involve the employee devising ways of saving the organisation money by proposing redundancies or by restructuring the workforce. How the employee handles people in this sensitive area will give a accurate picture of their potential to take on a very senior post later in their career.

internal and external courses

Potential managers will be sent on a wide range of courses to help them and the organisation to develop their skills and other abilities. Some courses will give them the detailed knowledge they will need to be able to take on more responsible jobs (eg courses in law and accountancy). A special type of course, which is now extremely popular, is the 'survival weekend' in which a group of managers or potential managers (sometimes from several different organisations) are brought together and given tasks to perform in a hostile environment. Tasks might include building bridges across streams or rock climbing or canoeing – in most cases the aim is to get the participants to work together as a team and to develop leadership skills.

Try www.callofthewild.co.uk

studying for further qualifications

Many employers encourage able employees to study for advanced qualifications. This not only improves their knowledge for use at work, but it also demonstrates they possess the stamina to complete courses which may be two or three years long.

One final point . . .

It is not very useful to encourage employees to carry out any of activities listed above unless it does lead on to improved career prospects in that organisation.

performance management: appraisals

This section examines how and why employees are appraised. The next section looks at how employers carry out performance reviews.

Nowadays the regular and systematic assessment of a person's work performance is commonplace. Contrary to initial worries it is now welcomed both by managers and by employees so long as it is done fairly, managers are properly trained how to do it, and the process is fully explained to everyone concerned.

This is called **Performance Appraisal** and it is normally carried out by the job holder's immediate superior.

The person who appraises is called the 'appraisor' and the person being appraised is the 'appraisee'. The usual procedure is:

Firstly, the appraisor writes an appraisal report of the appraisee.

This can be done in several ways . . .

- use a blank sheet of paper – this gives the appraisor freedom to write what he or she likes
- a form with questions and spaces to complete – this makes sure that all issues are covered
- a rating form – for each heading the appraisor simply gives a mark out of, say, 10 or a grade (A to E)

The best choice is probably a mixture of all three.

The essential features of an appraisal report will be as follows:

- an examination of the strengths of the employee
- an examination of the weaknesses of the employee
- the advice given to the employee in relation to future performance; this should include:

- praise for strengths
- helpful criticisms of the weaknesses the manager has identified
- an action plan for the next few months until the next appraisal; this will list the key objectives which the employee will be expected to have achieved by then.

Secondly, this is discussed with the appraisee at an interview. There are several options available . . .

- **open appraisal** – this is where the appraisee can discuss the appraisal with the manager as the interview takes place
- **two-way appraisal** – some organisations ask the appraisee to do an appraisal of himself/herself – this means that they fill in an identical form to that filled in by the appraisor – the forms are then compared and where there are clear differences there must be more discussion between them; for example if the appraiser rates the appraisee's work effort at 5 out of 10 and the appraisee rates it at 8 out of 10 they need to discuss why there is such a big difference of opinion
- **360 degree appraisal** – this is the most modern approach – it is sometimes called 'peer appraisal'

In **360 degree appraisal** the appraisee is appraised by most of the people they deal with. Therefore a 'middle manager' would get appraised by staff working for them, by fellow managers and by their boss. The opinions of their customers will also be collected (for example through 'customer satisfaction surveys').

This gives an extremely thorough picture of an employee and it pinpoints strengths and weaknesses very well. However, it takes up much staff time. Nevertheless it is increasingly popular.

how often does one get appraised ?

Appraisal normally takes place once or twice a year. In some organisations it happens every three months. The more often it is done the better.

the benefits of performance appraisal

- it helps to identify training needs
- it may reveal other problems – for example, there may be workplace difficulties with other staff (eg it might be caused by sexual or racial harassment)
- it may untap useful new skills
- it improves communications between employees and managers – a few words of encouragement and praise for doing a good job are often highly motivating

- it provides disciplinary documentation – if the employer needs to dismiss somebody, the existence of thorough appraisal records which identify the person's inabilities or lack of effort will be very useful
- it helps to fix pay rises – increasingly people get performance related pay which is based upon the appraisal interview

performance reviews

Every year or every six months managers should interview their staff and review their pay. This gives managers a chance to reward employees and to thank them for doing a good job.

In more recent years reviews have been associated with the system of 'performance related pay'. This means that managers must examine the individual's performance by reference to performance benchmarks (ie what the typical employee can be expected to achieve). This will then enable them to see how far above or below that benchmark an employee is performing. This then determines what pay rise the individual will get.

Some organisations will only give a rise in the individual review for above average performance. Other organisations will give all staff except the poorest performers something in their individual review. This is for morale reasons – after all even those who are only 'adequate' are still making a positive contribution to the organisation.

There is often a problem with managers who try to be kind to everyone so that poor performers get very little less than good ones. This is because the manager sees the employee every day and may not want to create bad feelings that would damage their working relationship.

It is important to note that in many organisations trade unions negotiate a pay deal with the employer. In such cases the pay deal agreed will apply to all employees, except for senior managers. In these organisations individual pay reviews will only apply to senior managers.

Now do the Activity on the opposite page.

employee performance

It is very important that the employee has the right environment in which to work. As the theorist Herzberg pointed out (see page 410) even the most interesting and fulfilling job will not motivate an employee if the 'hygiene' factors are poor.

Activity 17.6

The effect of a clumsy appraisal

Clumsy appraisals start employees on job hunt

By Helen Rowe

A quarter of employees start looking for a new job within two weeks of a bad appraisal, according to new research.

The survey, which examined appraisals on 500 employees, also found 40 per cent had begun a job search within a month.

Paul Jacobs, director of corporate communications at recruitment consultancy Office Angels, which commissioned the survey, said managers need to be aware of the pitfalls.

And he warned that clumsily handled appraisals could send valuable employees straight into the arms of competitors.

"The time spent on the appraisal could mean the difference between motivating their staff or looking for a new candidate."

The research identified common mistakes made by appraising managers, including continuously postponing the appraisal, rushing through it, and taking telephone calls during the meeting.

A badly handled meeting can push staff into joining rival companies

The research also found that a third of employees waited for up to a year at a time for feedback on how their career was progressing.

Russell Martin, global HR director at data services firm Primark, said there is a difference between a badly handled appraisal and a negative one that is fair.

"If you give someone a bad appraisal, then, in a good organisation, that should not be news to that individual. If someone is give a bad appraisal with continuous feedback, and

wishes to leave, then to a certain extent that is a success for the organisation. You should be managing them out."

Primark spends considerable effort training line managers in how to carry out appraisals and give feedback.

P & O head office personnel manager, Ken Windsor, said: "Appraisals have to be done properly and that means with thought and care.

For example, I think a good appraisal will identify training needs. That makes it useful to both employer and employee."

Reproduced by kind permission of 'Personnel Today'

1   What are the characteristics of a poorly-handled appraisal?

2   How does a manager make appraisals effective for everyone involved?

3   What is the appraisal policy of the business you are investigating for your Portfolio?

We have already looked at legislation which makes the working environment more amenable to employees. Other important legislation includes:

the working time directive

This limits a persons weekly working hours to 48 per week. The figure is averaged over 17 weeks so a person could work, say, 10 weeks at 55 hours and 7 at 38 hours (816 in all, ie 48 x 17 weeks). The aim is to put employees under less stress because this makes them ill. Any employee can opt out of this directive if they want to.

the minimum wage

The government now sets a minimum hourly pay rate. The minimum set is not very high (£3.70 per hour in 2000-2001) but it is still a lot higher than some employers had been paying before.

maternity and parental leave

As well as improved maternity leave both parents are now entitled to take time off from work to look after their children (up until the child's fifth birthday). This can be taken as occasional days or in longer periods of up to a total of 13 weeks per child. With three children under 5 a parent could therefore claim a total of 39 weeks parental leave. The catch here is that it is unpaid leave, so many employees will be unable to afford to claim it.

Health and Safety regulations

The Health and Safety at Work Act 1974 states that an employer must have a 'written statement' of its health and safety policy. This must be available for all staff to read – a good employer will give personal copies of it to all new staff when they have their induction.

What will be in this statement?

- an explanation of how all accidents must be reported by staff
- a list of all staff trained in first aid and details of where first aid boxes are located
- a list of all Safety Representatives – their job is to ensure that the employer is carrying out safety policies properly and they are required to carry out full three monthly safety checks
- the name of a senior manager responsible for health and safety policies

As well as the 1974 Act more recent legislation has brought in further protection for employees. For example the C.O.S.H.H. regulations (1988). This stands for '**C**ontrol **O**f **S**ubstances **H**azardous to **H**ealth'. They lays down very strict rules on how dangerous chemicals are to be handled, stored and recorded.

In 1992 a number of new regulations were introduced by the European Union.

- The Health and Safety (Display Screen Equipment) Regulations introduced tight controls on the use of visual display units on word processors and computers. This was due to the problems they were known to cause (particularly eyesight problems). The regulations now require free eye tests for all 'habitual regular users' of VDUs.

- Repetitive strain injury in the arms is now covered by the Workplace (Health, Safety and Welfare) Regulations. This also requires workplaces to be properly lit and ventilated.

- The Manual Handling Operations Regulations – these state that where lifting of items is potentially dangerous the employer must carry out a risk assessment of the task involved and then minimise the danger as far as possible.

- More generally all employers must now carry out 'risk assessments' of all activities carried out in their organisations.

motivation theories

Frederick Taylor and scientific management

Taylor (1856-1915) worked as a factory superintendent in a locomotive axle factory in the USA. From his studies of how people worked making axles he concluded that:

Employees got jobs there because they were friends or relatives of the managers, not because they were any good at the job.

Employees did not work hard because they thought it would throw some of their friends out of work.

Employers paid employees as little as they could get away with.

Employees got very few instructions on how to do their jobs so they did them badly. The amount produced and the quality of output was often poor.

Taylor said that the following ideas would improve matters:
- only money would motivate employees to work hard – therefore they should be paid on a piecework system, ie each item made would earn them a certain amount of money – this would encourage hard work
- properly trained managers should run organisations and supervise employees effectively with firm but fair disciplinary methods
- employees must be properly trained, through what he called 'scientific management', to do specific tasks efficiently – this was the beginning of what we today call Organisations and Methods Study or Work Study

- employees should be properly selected through tests and interviews to make sure they are right for the job; Taylor was one of the first people to see the need to do this
- employees, if motivated by good pay, would work efficiently without questioning what they were required to do

Many organisations still operate Taylorism, even in rich countries, but there has long been a recognition that employees want more from their jobs than job security and good pay. Other writers have developed more complex theories about what motivates people at work.

Abraham Maslow and 'the hierarchy of needs'

Abraham Maslow (1908-1970) said that all motivation comes from meeting unsatisfied needs. He stated that there was a ranking of needs which must be achieved in the correct order – from the bottom to the top of a 'pyramid' (see diagram below). Basic physiological needs (eg food, water) are at the bottom and self actualisation is at the top.

the need . . .	which is achieved by . . .
self actualisation	personal growth and self fulfilment
Esteem	Recognition
	Achievement
	Status
Social needs	Affection/love/friendship
Safety needs	Security
	Freedom from pain and threats
Physiological needs	Food, water, air, rest, sex

Once one need is satisfied it ceases to motivate and the next higher need 'up the pyramid' comes into play. This implies that higher level needs have more value than the ones at the bottom.

Only an unsatisfied need can motivate behaviour, and the dominant need is the prime motivator of behaviour.

From a manager's viewpoint, Maslow is saying that:

- employees need to be paid adequately so they can at least provide their basic physiological and safety needs (paying for food, mortgages, life insurance)
- employees need social contact through friendship with colleagues; working in teams helps to encourage social contact – look at how unhappy many people are who work alone in their own private offices
- esteem can be provided where an organisation offers prospects of promotion; at the very least there should be an opportunity for an

employee to show that they are capable and they are winning the respect of other employees; organisations can raise employees' esteem by giving higher managers better cars, smarter offices, nicer restaurants, more generous pensions

- self actualisation is far harder to achieve – it really means that an employee has the chance to become everything they ever wanted to become – for example the employee might always have dreamt of becoming 'the boss' of the company he/she has worked for all his/her life

Two significant problems arise here . . .

Firstly, an employer simply cannot offer such opportunities to all their employees. That would be unrealistic.

Secondly, writers like Maslow and Herzberg (see below) seemed to think that everybody is self actualised by work. This is not true – many people are self actualised by aspects of their private lives (bringing up their children for example) and work is just a means to pay the bills.

Douglas McGregor and theory X and Y

McGregor (1906-64) said that many managers made sweeping generalisations about the people who worked for them. They would either put all their employees into a theory X category or a theory Y category. They would then manage their organisation using a theory X or a theory Y management style.

theory X

This states that all employees are lazy, unambitious and dislike extra responsibilities. They will always resist change of any kind and are totally uninterested in the future success or otherwise of their employer. They are not interested in how the organisation works and just prefer to be told what to do.

theory Y

This is just the opposite. Employees are interested in their work and want to be asked for their opinions on how to improve things. They want to be given more responsibility and will naturally work hard without having to be told what to do all the time. They are also prepared to accept change because they understand it is in everyone's best interests to move with the times.

The manager who takes a theory X attitude about their employees will need to supervise them very closely and introduce methods to control their behaviour (eg tight controls on absenteeism and lateness). There will be a lot of very specific rules and regulations with serious consequences for employees who break them. Frequent inspections of work will be needed to ensure that output is of adequate quality.

Naturally there will be no attempt to get employee views on how to improve the running of the organisation.

A theory Y manager can be very positive about his or her employees. He/she can leave them to do their jobs virtually unsupervised (which also saves a lot of money) and they can rest assured that the work will all be well done. Again this saves money because quality inspections will not be needed very much. It will be easy to find people who are willing to work over their normal hours, and often for no extra money. They will also be happy to take on more responsibilities because they hope it will improve their long term career prospects. Because absence and lateness will be unusual costly supervision will not be needed.

McGregor's ideas have meant that to this day people will still describe an organisation as 'theory X' or 'theory Y'. The trouble is that no organisation is completely full of theory X people nor of theory Y people.

This means that in theory X organisations many good employees are handled in a way that they do not really deserve and in theory Y organisations many people are getting away with things that they should not. Even inside the same organisation there are theory Y departments where good employees resent the fact that other colleagues can get way with doing very little. By contrast in a theory X department good employees will often leave if they are constantly supervised and not trusted by their managers.

Frederick Herzberg and the Two Factor theory

In 1957 Herzberg (born 1923) devised his 'motivation-hygiene' theory which stated that two groups of factors affect employee motivation.

Herzberg said that certain elements in a job motivate people to work harder. He called these elements **satisfiers**. They include:

achievement, recognition, responsibility, advancement and personal growth . . . and the actual work itself.

Other elements do not motivate people to work harder. These are called **hygiene factors**. They include:

pay and conditions, status in the organisation, job security, benefits (pensions, company cars etc), relationships with fellow employees, the quality of the organisation's managers.

Herzberg's key point was that hygiene factors do not motivate but if they are not very good then the satisfiers will not motivate either.

A simple example will explain this. Even if a job is interesting and gives a person a substantial sense of achievement it will not motivate them properly if they are not earning enough money to live in a reasonable house and cannot feed themselves and their family properly.

some other motivation theories

expectancy theory

This theory states that an employee will only be motivated to work harder if they believe that it will lead to a reward which they feel is worth having. The key point is that if the reward does not match the employee's needs it will not motivate them very well.

equity theory

This means that people are better motivated if they feel they are fairly treated by their bosses and on a par with other employees.

goal theory

Setting employees specific goals motivates them more effectively. If the goals are achieved they get more money or a promotion.

reactance theory

This means that people are motivated by what they think they have achieved. For example, where pay is tied to an employee's performance it motivates them to work far harder. Their achievement has been rewarded.

Activity 17.7

Motivation in the workplace

Design, in groups, a short questionnaire to assess what factors motivate employees.

Write eight questions, based on the writings of the four theorists Taylor, Maslow, McGregor and Herzberg (ie two for each writer). Get your tutor to discuss the questions with you.

Try the questionnaire out at work if you have a part-time job, or at the organisation you are studying for your Portfolio, or at a work placement.

IMPORTANT – you MUST get the permission of the management of the organisation before carrying out the questionnaire.

When you have got the answers to your questionnaire, analyse and write up your findings, making reference to the theories of the four writers in your analysis.

Here are some suggestions for the type of questions you might ask.

"What factor do you consider to be more important in your working life, (a) or (b)?"		
(a) the level of pay	(b) the job itself	(Taylor)
(a) good working conditions	(b) recognition for what you do	(Maslow)
(a) lack of responsibility	(b) having an input into what you do	(McGregor)
(a) job security	(b) promotion prospects	(Herzberg)

CHAPTER SUMMARY

● Proper training and development are essential if an organisation is to retain its employees and remain competitive. An organisation should draw up a co-ordinated training programme for its employees.

● Training can be divided into two categories: 'on the job' (workplace) training and 'off the job' (away from the workplace) training.

● Training and development involves non-transferable skills (specific to the job being done) and transferable skills (which can be used in other jobs). Government schemes such as Labour's New Deal exist to help people to acquire a range of transferable skills.

● A number of different methods are used to train and develop employees including mentoring, coaching, in house and external courses and open learning.

● Induction training is the process of introducing new employees to the organisation and its culture.

● Multi-skilling training ensures that employees are trained to do several jobs rather than just one.

● Employers need to develop employees who have potential. Methods include job rotation, job enlargement, job enrichment and understudying, mentoring, coaching and sending employees on courses.

● Appraisals should be used on a regular basis to assess employee performance and to encourage employees to work more effectively

● Employees will not work effectively if they do not have the right environment to work in. This includes consideration of hours, wages, providing leave and Health & Safety at work.

● Employers need to understand the relationship between the main motivation theories and the way in which they manage their own organisations. The main theories include:

- Frederick Taylor and scientific management

- Abraham Maslow and the hierarchy of needs

- Douglas McGregor and theory X and Y

- Frederick Herzberg and the Two Factor Theory

KEY TERMS

training	the acquisition of knowledge and skills in order to do a job properly
development	providing opportunities for employees to widen and deepen their skills and knowledge so that they are more motivated and of more use to the organisation
mentoring	where a more senior employee provides advice and counselling to junior staff on their development inside the organisation
coaching	where a member of staff receives specialist training in particular aspects of their job
transferable skills	skills that can be used in a wide variety of jobs and working environments
non-transferable skills	skills for which there is little use outside the job and organisation where the employee presently works
appraisal	the regular assessment of an employee's progress by that employee's manager
360 degree appraisal	where a number of people appraise an employee to give them a better picture of their progress
scientific management	Taylor's definition for the accurate measurement of the main elements of a job so that the employee can then be trained to do it efficiently
hierarchy of needs	Maslow described this as a pyramid of needs which motivate employees throughout their working lives
theory X and Y	MacGregor said that all workplaces fell under one or other of these two headings – Theory X means that employees are lazy and must be forced to work hard, Theory Y takes a more positive view and assumes that employees will naturally work hard and are highly motivated
the two factor theory	Herzberg argued that certain factors called 'satisfiers' motivate people to work hard whereas others called 'hygiene' factors create the basic environment in which they work

Financial recording and financial documents

introduction

Every business has its stakeholders – its owners, its employees, customers, suppliers, lenders and other people and bodies who have an interest in what the business is doing. Stakeholders will want to know about the financial state of the business – whether the business is making a profit, can pay its wages, settle its bills, whether it is worth investing in. A business therefore needs to keep accurate financial records so that it can supply reliable information to these stakeholders.

In this chapter we take an overview of the way a business organises and uses financial information. We also look in detail at financial documents and see how they are completed and used to carry out financial transactions.

what you will learn from this chapter

● the stakeholders of a business between them need to know about the sales, profit and value of a business

● this financial information is available in the financial statements of a business, which are taken from the business accounting system; it is essential that this information is accurate

● the starting point of the accounting system of a business is the documentation generated by financial transactions

● when a business buys or sells goods and services a number of documents 'flow' between the buyer and seller; these can vary depending on whether the payment is to be made straightaway or later (on credit)

● when a business deals with these financial documents it is essential that it is accurate and that it checks them carefully

the need for financial recording

If anyone asks you how much you yourself are worth at any particular time, or how much you have spent within a particular period, you will probably be unable to give an accurate figure because you are unlikely to have kept a full record of every financial transaction you have carried out.

A business, on the other hand, must keep books to record its financial transactions. It will carry out the process of financial record keeping to provide information for a number of interested parties – its stakeholders. Look at the diagram below and read the text carefully . . .

STAKEHOLDERS	WHAT ARE THEY INTERESTED IN?	WHY ARE THEY INTERESTED?
Owners/shareholders/ managers	• Has the business made a profit? • Can the business pay its way? • Are the sales figures increasing?	• To see how much profit can be paid by the business to the owners/shareholders. • To assess if the business will continue in the foreseeable future. • To see if the business is growing.
Inland Revenue	• Has the business made a profit?	• To calculate the tax due on profit.
H M Customs and Excise	• What were the figures for sales and VAT charged on sales?	• To ensure that VAT charged on products is paid to H M Customs and Excise.
Bank manager/lender	• Has the business made a profit? • What is the bank balance or overdraft? • What is the value of the business?	• To check if the business can afford to make loan repayments. • To decide how much the bank can lend to the business.
Employees and trade unions	• Has the business made a profit? • Can the business continue to pay its way?	• To see if the business can afford pay rises. • To assess if the business will continue to provide jobs in the foreseeable future.
Customers	• Is the business reliable and will it continue to trade?	• To see if the business has the financial stability to carry out work for its customers.
Suppliers (people to whom the business owes money)	• Is the business trading profitably? • Are the bills being paid on time?	• To assess if the business is able to pay its bills on the due date.
Competitors	• What are the sales figures?	• To see if the business is expanding or declining and to consider whether the business is worth taking over.

the stakeholders

The stakeholders are:

- people inside the business – the owners, employees and managers
- people the business deals with – its customers and suppliers
- people who want to invest in the business or lend money to it
- bodies that want to tax the business – the Inland Revenue (taxation of profits) and H M Customs & Excise (collecting VAT charged on products)

The diagram on the previous page shows that different stakeholders need to know different types of financial information, including:

- sales figures and profit
- the value of the business

These figures are available in the 'financial statements' of the business.

When you have finished studying this unit you will see that the financial statements ('final accounts') are drawn up as the last part of a process in which data from financial documents is entered in the 'books' of the business, which in turn are used to provide figures for the final accounts. These then provide the information needed by the stakeholders.

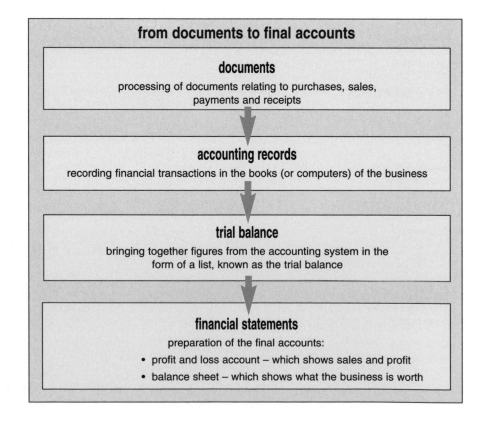

from documents to final accounts

documents
processing of documents relating to purchases, sales, payments and receipts

accounting records
recording financial transactions in the books (or computers) of the business

trial balance
bringing together figures from the accounting system in the form of a list, known as the trial balance

financial statements
preparation of the final accounts:
- profit and loss account – which shows sales and profit
- balance sheet – which shows what the business is worth

the need for accurate financial records

It may sound like stating the obvious to say that financial records must be accurate, but a business which does not have accurate financial records may run into serious problems.

Think about the following examples . . .

- a business that makes mistakes loses the confidence of its customers
- a business that overcharges loses its customers
- a business that overstates its sales figures overstates its profit and pays too much tax
- a business that overstates its sales figures and overstates its profit gives a false impression of its performance to its owners and shareholders
- a business that understates its sales figures understates its profit and pays too little tax
- a business that pays too little tax can get into trouble with the Inland Revenue
- a business that understates its sales figures and its profit can lose the confidence of its managers, shareholders and lenders.

You should be able to think of other examples.

Aclivily 18.1

Stakeholders and financial records

1   Identify four different stakeholders of a business and state why each of the stakeholders will be interested in what the financial records of the business have to say about the financial 'health' of the business. Try to supplement what it says in textbooks with information you can gather from people working in business and dealing with businesses on a day-to-day basis.

2   State why you think it is important that the financial records of a business are accurate.

What are the implications of the following problems, all caused by inaccurate record keeping?

(a) A business receives a part payment of £1,000 from its customer in settlement of debts totalling £10,000 but records it in its books as a payment for £10,000?

(b) Somebody thinking of investing in a company is told that the profit figure is £65,000 when in fact it is £95,000?

(c) The Inland Revenue discovers that the business in (b) has underestimated its profit figure by £30,000?

financial documents

In the next few chapters we will be dealing in a practical way with the processing of the figures through the accounting system of a business and the production of the final accounts – the profit and loss statement and the balance sheet.

In this chapter, however, we will concentrate on the first stage in the accounting process – the completion and use of financial documents. As we will see, different types of document are used in different types of transaction. The main distinction to be drawn is between cash transactions and credit transactions.

cash transactions and credit transactions

When a business sells goods or services it will either ask for payment to be made straightaway or at a later date:

- a *cash sale* is when payment is made straightaway, for example when you buy goods in a shop
- a *credit sale* is when payment is made at a later date, for example when a business orders supplies and pays later 'on account'

The words 'cash sale' used in this way do not mean that just cash (in the form of notes and coins) is used – a 'cash sale' can be made using cash or a cheque. 'Cash' here means 'on the nail', ie immediate payment.

documents used in cash transactions

Take for example an employee of a business going out into the town and buying some coloured photocopying paper needed urgently in the office or paying an engineer for repairs carried out. The transaction is very simple: payment is made by cash or cheque and a receipt is issued by the seller.

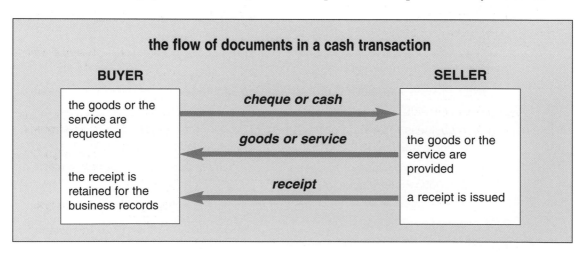

the flow of documents in a cash transaction

BUYER   **SELLER**

the goods or the service are requested	*cheque or cash* →
	goods or service ← the goods or the service are provided
the receipt is retained for the business records	*receipt* ← a receipt is issued

till receipt

When someone makes a cash purchase for a business – for example going out to buy some stationery – it is important that they obtain a receipt because the business needs to record the fact that money has been spent on stationery – it is a running expense of the business

When the purchase is made cash tills show on the screen the money amount of the purchase and also the change to be given. The till will also issue a receipt for all purchases when cash, a cheque, a debit card or a credit card is used. In the example below a customer has bought a pack of coloured paper and some disks from Everest Stationery. A till receipt has been issued.

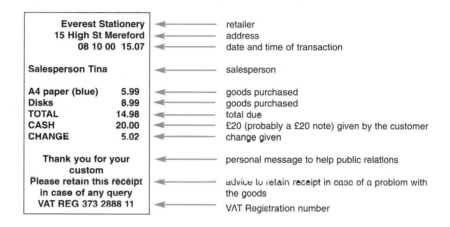

written receipt

Some businesses will write out a receipt on request, particularly if VAT needs to be shown (see the next page for an explanation of this). The example below is for the supply of more photocopier paper.

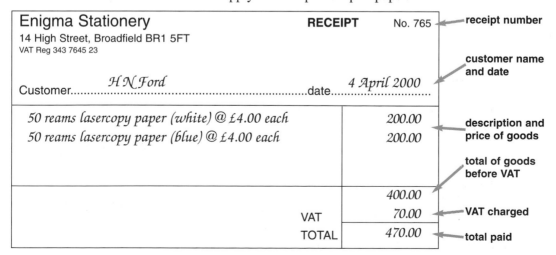

some notes on Value Added Tax (VAT)

You will see that the till receipt shown on the previous page quotes a VAT (Value Added Tax) number but no VAT amount. Receipts and invoices for purchases under £100 do not have to show the VAT amount separately – it is included in the final amount. If you think about it, most till receipts you get from shops do not show the VAT amount, but you still pay it!

VAT is quoted on a number of the financial documents you will be studying and you will need to know what it is and how it works:

- VAT (Value Added Tax) is a government tax on the selling price charged for most goods and services.

- There are some exceptions – eg VAT is not charged on books or food.

- Most businesses with sales above a certain amount must register for VAT.

A business which is registered for VAT charges VAT at the standard rate (currently 17.5 per cent) on the money value of the goods or services it sells. The formula for working out the VAT charged on a sale is:

$$\text{VAT charged} = \text{Sales amount} \times \frac{17.5}{100}$$

For example, if the business sells goods or services for £200 it has to add on 17.5% of the £200 to the amount charged, ie

$$\text{VAT} = £200 \times \frac{17.5}{100} = £35.00$$

The total amount the business receives will be:

$$£200 \text{ plus } £35.00 \text{ (VAT)} = £235.00$$

The business will keep the £200 but will have to pay the £35 to HM Customs & Excise, the government department which administers VAT.

Activity 18.2

Completing receipts

You work in 'Helios' – a lighting shop. During the course of a day you write out three receipts to customers:

1 2 flexilamps @ £13.99, plus 2 candlelight bulbs @85p each sold to George Meredith.

2 1 standard lamp @ £149.95, plus one 100 watt bulb @ 99p, sold to Alex Bell.

3 2 Georgian lamps @ £35.99 sold to Miss S Fox.

What will you charge each customer? You will add VAT to all three purchases and use the current rate of VAT. If you can, complete three blank receipts with the details.

the cheque

Cheques are provided by the banks for their customers so that they can pay people specific sums of money. Cheques are used both for cash transactions and also for settling accounts for credit transactions (where payment is made later). The cheque shown below is the cheque used for the cash sale which produced the receipt at the bottom of page 419. Cheques are normally provided by the banks for their customers in books with counterfoils. When the cheque is written out the details (amount, date and person being paid) are recorded on the counterfoil and the cheque is torn out and given or posted to the person being paid. See pages 433 and 434 for more on cheques.

tear off cheque here

Date 4/4/00	**Albion Bank PLC**	Date	*4 April 2000*	90 47 17
	7 The Avenue			
Pay	Broadfield BR1 2AJ			
Enigma Stationery	Pay *Enigma Stationery*			
	Four hundred and seventy pounds only			£ 470.00 —
				HARRIS N FORD
£ 470.00				*Harris N Ford*
083772	083772 90 47 17 11719881			

counterfoil   *cheque*

what happens to the cheque?

The cheque shown above is paid into the bank account of Enigma Stationery on a paying-in slip (see page 435) and will be cleared through the bank clearing system to Harris N Ford's bank. The cheque will then appear on Harris N Ford's bank statement (see page 437 for an example) as a deduction of £470 from the bank account. This process is shown in the diagram below.

Harris N Ford writes out a cheque for £470, dates it and signs it

▼

the cheque is given to Enigma Stationery for the paper supplied

▼

the cheque is paid in on a paying-in slip at Enigma Stationery's bank

▼

£470 will be added to the bank account of Enigma Stationery

▼

the cheque will be sent through a bank clearing system to Harris N Ford's bank – Albion Bank – and the £470 will be deducted from his account – and show on his bank statement

making a purchase on credit

financial documents for transaction 'on credit'

When a business buys goods or services *on credit* it orders the goods first and then pays later. During this process a number of different financial documents will be issued by the seller and the buyer. We will look in this chapter at a whole range of financial documents by means of a Case Study involving the purchase of fashion clothes.

You must bear in mind that not all purchases involve all the documents listed below. Many purchases are for services, eg office cleaning, and do not involve goods being sent. It is important for your studies, however, that

- you can recognise each of the documents
- you know what they are for
- you can complete a number of them

The financial documents shown here include:

- **purchase order**, which the buyer sends to the seller

- **delivery note**, which goes with the goods from the seller to the buyer

- **goods received note**, which is sometimes completed by the buyer to record the actual amount of goods received

- **invoice**, which lists the goods and tells the buyer what is owed

- **credit note**, which is sent to the buyer if any refund is due

- **statement of account**, sent by the seller to remind the buyer what is owed

- **remittance advice**, sent by the buyer when the goods are paid for

- **cheque**, which is completed by the buyer to pay for the goods

- **paying-in slip**, used for paying a cheque into a bank account

- **bank statement**, which records payments in and out of the bank account

the flow of documents

Before you read the Case Study, examine the diagram set out on the next page. Down the columns representing the buyer and the seller are various activities which lead to transactions, which in turn generate documents.

As we have just seen, you should appreciate that not all the activities happen all the time. Mostly, however, things run smoothly and the invoice is paid following receipt of a statement of account.

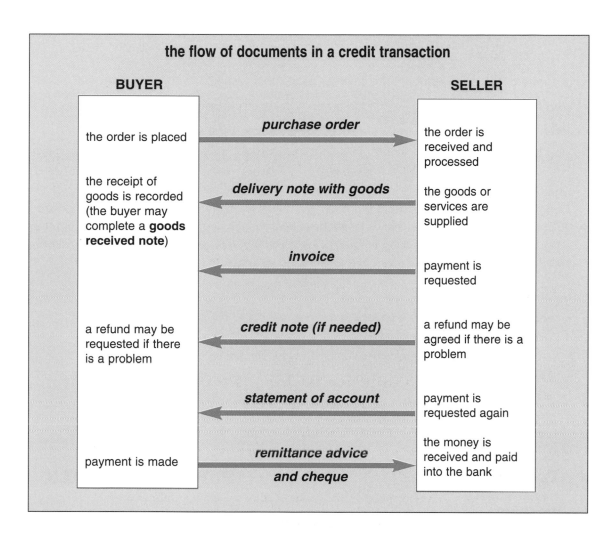

the flow of documents in a credit transaction

BUYER		SELLER
the order is placed	*purchase order* →	the order is received and processed
the receipt of goods is recorded (the buyer may complete a **goods received note**)	← *delivery note with goods*	the goods or services are supplied
	← *invoice*	payment is requested
a refund may be requested if there is a problem	← *credit note (if needed)*	a refund may be agreed if there is a problem
	← *statement of account*	payment is requested again
payment is made	*remittance advice and cheque* →	the money is received and paid into the bank

Case Study

Cool Socks
buying on credit

Cool Socks Limited manufactures fashion socks in a variety of colours. It supplies a number of different customers, including Trends, a fashion store in Broadfield.

In this Case Study we see an order for 100 pairs of socks placed by Trends with Cool Socks. The socks are delivered, but some are found to be faulty, so a refund has to be made. Finally, payment has to be made for the socks.

The Case Study looks in detail at the purchase and sales documents involved. Now read on.

PURCHASE ORDER – *the buyer orders the goods*

purpose of the document	to order goods or services
who completes it?	the buyer of the goods or services
what happens to it?	it is sent by the buyer to the seller
why must it be accurate?	if it is not completed accurately the wrong products may be ordered

what happens in this case?

Trends orders some socks from Cool Socks. The buyer at Trends will post or fax the authorised purchase order shown below. The order will have been written or printed out in the office, or produced on a computer accounting program. The details of the socks will have been obtained from Cool Socks' catalogue, or possibly by means of a written or telephoned enquiry.

points to note:

- each purchase order has a specific reference number – this is useful for filing and quoting on later documents such as invoices and statements

- the product code of the goods required is stated in the product code column

- the quantity of the goods required is stated in the quantity column – socks are obviously supplied in pairs!

- the purchase order is signed and dated by the person in charge of purchasing – without this authorisation the supplier is unlikely to supply the goods (the order will probably be returned)

Trends
4 Friar Street
Broadfield
BR1 3RF
Tel 01908 761234 Fax 01908 761987
VAT REG GB 0745 8383 56

PURCHASE ORDER

Cool Socks Limited, Unit 45 Elgar Estate, Broadfield, BR7 4ER	purchase order no 47609 date 25 09 00

product code	quantity	description
45B	100 pairs	Blue Toebar socks

AUTHORISED   signature............*D Signer*..date........*25/09/00*

---

see page 441 for an activity involving this document

DELIVERY NOTE – *the goods are delivered*

purpose of the document	it states what goods are being delivered
who completes it?	the seller of the goods
what happens to it?	it is sent by the seller to the buyer
why must it be accurate?	if the goods delivered do not tally with the description on the delivery note, the goods may be refused

what happens in this case?

The delivery note is despatched with the goods when the order is ready. It is normally printed out in the office, often by a computer accounting program. In this case, the delivery note travels with the socks, and a copy will be signed by Trends on receipt.

points to note:

- the delivery note has a numerical reference, useful for filing and later reference if there is a query
- the delivery note quotes the purchase order number – this enables the buyer to 'tie up' the delivery with the original order
- the details of the goods supplied – the quantity and the description – will be checked against the goods themselves
- the delivery note will be signed and dated by the person receiving the goods

---

DELIVERY NOTE

COOL SOCKS LIMITED

Unit 45 Elgar Estate, Broadfield, BR7 4ER
Tel 01908 765314 Fax 01908 765951
VAT REG GB 0745 4672 76

Trends	delivery note no	68873
4 Friar Street	delivery method	Lynx Parcels
Broadfield	your order	47609
BR1 3RF	date	02 10 00

product code	quantity	description
45B	100 pairs	Blue Toebar socks

Received

signature...... *V Williams* ......name (capitals). *V WILLIAMS* ......date. *5/10/00* ......

---

see page 441 for an activity involving this document

GOODS RECEIVED NOTE – *the buyer records receipt of the goods*

purpose of the document   it records what goods have been delivered

who completes it?   the buyer of the goods

what happens to it?   it is kept by the buyer

why must it be accurate?   a mistake may result in a problem with the delivery not being picked up

what happens in this case?

The goods received note (GRN) will be completed by the person in Trends who looks after the stock. In the case of this delivery, ten pairs of the socks have been received damaged – Trends will want a refund.

points to note:

- details of the goods are noted on the form
- the condition of the goods – the damage to the socks – is recorded and this fact will be notified on separate copies to the buyer, to Accounts and to the stockroom
- a goods received note is not used by all businesses

Trends   GOODS RECEIVED NOTE

Supplier

Cool Socks Limited,	GRN no	1871
Unit 45 Elgar Estate,	date	05 10 00
Broadfield,		
BR7 4ER		

quantity	description	order number
100 pairs	Blue Toebar socks	47609

carrier   Lynx Parcels   consignment no   8479347

received by   *V Williams*   checked by   *R Patel*

| **condition of goods** (please tick and comment) | good condition
damaged ✓ (10 pairs)
shortages | **copies to**
Buyer ✓
Accounts ✓
Stockroom ✓ |

see page 444 for an activity involving this document

INVOICE – *payment is requested by the seller (see next page)*

purpose of the document	it tells the buyer how much is owed and when it has to be paid
who completes it?	the seller of the goods
what happens to it?	it is sent by the seller to the buyer, who checks it carefully and keeps it on file for reference
why must it be accurate?	a mistake could result in the wrong amount being paid

what happens in this case?

The invoice, like the delivery note, is prepared in the seller's office, and is written out or produced on a computer accounting program. Invoices produced by different organisations will vary to some extent in terms of detail, but their basic layout will always be the same.

The invoice prepared by Cool Socks Ltd – illustrated on the next page – is typical of a modern computer-printed document.

points to note:

addresses

The invoice shows the address:

- of the seller/supplier of the goods – Cool Socks Limited
- the place where the invoice should be sent – to Trends
- where the goods are to be sent – it may not always be the same as the invoice address; for example a supermarket ordering a container load of bananas will ask them to be delivered to a distribution warehouse, not to the Accounts Department!

references

There are a number of important references on the invoice:

- the numerical reference of the invoice itself – 787923
- the account number allocated to Trends by the seller – 3993 – for use in the seller's and the purchaser's financial records for reference purposes
- the original reference number on the purchase order sent by Trends – 47609 – which will enable the shop to 'tie up' the invoice with the original order

Now look at the document and the explanations on the next two pages to find out what you have to check when you receive an invoice.

see pages 441 to 443 for activities involving this document

INVOICE – *payment is requested by the seller*

INVOICE
COOL SOCKS LIMITED
Unit 45 Elgar Estate, Broadfield, BR7 4ER
Tel 01908 765314 Fax 01908 765951
VAT REG GB 0745 4672 76

invoice to

Trends
4 Friar Street
Broadfield
BR1 3RF

invoice no	787923
account	3993
your reference	47609
date/tax point	02 10 00

product code	description	quantity	price	unit	total	discount %	net
45B	Blue Toebar socks	100	2.36	pair	236.00	0.00	236.00

GOODS TOTAL	236.00
VAT	41.30
TOTAL	277.30

terms
30 days

points to note and check on the invoice

You will need to check that the reference number quoted here ties up with your purchase order number.

The date here is normally the date on which the goods have been sent. It is known as the 'invoice date'. The date is important for calculating when the invoice is due to be paid. In this case the 'terms' (see the bottom left-hand corner of the invoice) are 30 days. This means the invoice is due to be paid within 30 days after the invoice date (2 October), so it is due to be paid by 31 October.

The arithmetic and details in this line must be checked very carefully to make sure that you pay the correct amount for what you have ordered:

- *product code* – this is the catalogue number which appeared on the original purchase order and on the delivery note
- *description* – this must agree with the description on the purchase order
- *quantity* – this should agree with the quantity ordered
- *price* – this is the price of each unit shown in the next column
- *unit* is the way in which the unit is counted up and charged for, eg units (single items), pairs (as here), or 10s,100s and so on
- *total* is the unit price multiplied by the number of units
- *discount %* is the percentage allowance (known as trade discount) given to trusted customers who regularly deal with the supplier, ie they receive a certain percentage (eg 10%) deducted from their bill

  – note that *cash discount* is also sometimes allowed – this is a percentage (eg 2.5%) deducted from the net amount before VAT is added on

- *net* is the amount due to the seller after deduction of trade discount, and before VAT is added on

The Goods Total is the total of the column above it. It is the final amount due to the seller before VAT is added on.

Value Added Tax (VAT) is calculated and added on – here it is 17.5% of the Goods Total, ie £236.00 x 17.5% = £41.30. The VAT is then added to the Goods Total to produce the actual amount owing: £236.00 + £41.30 = £277.30
Note that if a cash discount is taken, the VAT is calculated on the Goods Total after the discount has been deducted.

The 'terms' explain the conditions on which the goods are supplied. '30 days' means that payment has to be made within 30 days of the invoice date. Any cash discount is also noted here, eg '2.5% for settlement within 7 days of invoice'

CREDIT NOTE – *the seller gives a refund*

purpose of the document	A credit note is a 'refund' document which reduces the amount owed by the buyer. The format of a credit note is very similar to that of an invoice.
who completes it?	the seller of the goods
what happens to it?	it is sent by the seller to the buyer, who checks it carefully and keeps it on file with the invoice
why must it be accurate?	a mistake could result in the wrong amount eventually being paid

what happens in this case?

Trends has received 10 damaged pairs of socks. These will be sent back with a document known as a Returns Note to Cool Socks with a request for *credit* – ie a reduction in the bill for the 10 faulty pairs. Cool Socks will have to issue the credit note for £27.73 shown below.

points to note:

- a credit note can be issued for faulty goods, missing goods, or goods which are not needed
- the credit note quotes the invoice number and states why the credit (refund) is being given

---

———— CREDIT NOTE ————

COOL SOCKS LIMITED

Unit 45 Elgar Estate, Broadfield, BR7 4ER
Tel 01908 765314 Fax 01908 765951
VAT REG GB 0745 4672 76

to

Trends	
4 Friar Street	
Broadfield	
BR1 3RF	

credit note no	12157
account	3993
your reference	47609
our invoice	787923
date/tax point	10 10 00

product code	description	quantity	price	unit	total	discount %	net
45B	Blue Toebar socks	10	2.36	pair	23.60	0.00	23.60

Reason for credit
10 pairs of socks received damaged
(Your returns note no. R/N 2384)

GOODS TOTAL	23.60
VAT	4.13
TOTAL	27.73

see pages 445 to 446 for activities involving this document

STATEMENT OF ACCOUNT – *the seller requests payment*

purpose of the document a statement of account – which is normally issued at the end of every month – tells the buyer how much is owed

who completes it? the seller of the goods

what happens to it? it is sent by the seller to the buyer who checks it against the invoices and credit notes on file

why must it be accurate? a mistake could result in the wrong amount being paid

what happens in this case?

A seller will not normally expect a buyer to pay each individual invoice as soon as it is received. Instead, a statement of account showing what is owed is sent by the seller to the buyer *at the end of the month.* It shows:

- invoices issued for goods supplied – the full amount due, including VAT
- refunds made on credit notes – including VAT
- payments received from the buyer (if any)

The statement issued by Cool Socks to Trends for the period covering the sale (the invoice) and refund (the credit note) is shown below. Trends now has to pay the £249.57 owing.

STATEMENT OF ACCOUNT
COOL SOCKS LIMITED
Unit 45 Elgar Estate, Broadfield, BR7 4ER
Tel 01908 765314 Fax 01908 765951
VAT REG GB 0745 4672 76

TO

Trends
4 Friar Street
Broadfield
BR1 3RF

account 3993

date 31 10 00

date	details	debit £	credit £	balance £
02 10 00	Invoice 787923	277.30		277.30
10 10 00	Credit note 12157		27.73	249.57
			AMOUNT NOW DUE	249.57

see pages 446 to 447 for activities involving this document

REMITTANCE ADVICE — *the buyer sends a payment advice*

purpose of the document	a remittance advice is a document sent by the buyer to the seller stating that payment is being made
who completes it?	the buyer
what happens to it?	it is sent by the buyer to the seller
why must it be accurate?	a mistake could result in the wrong amount being paid

what happens in this case?

Trends have completed a remittance advice listing the invoice that is being paid and the credit note which is being deducted from the amount owing. Trends will make out a cheque for the total amount of the remittance advice. This is shown on the next page. It will be attached to the remittance advice and will be posted to Cool Socks in November.

points to note:

- the remittance advice quotes the account number (3993) allocated to Trends by Cool Socks – this will help Cool Socks to update their records when the payment is received
- the documents are listed in the columns provided: 'your reference' describes the documents issued by Cool Socks and quotes their numbers; 'our reference' quotes the number of the Purchase Order originally issued by Trends
- the amounts of the invoice and the credit note are entered in the right-hand column – note that the credit note amount is negative, so it is shown in brackets; the total payment amount is shown in the box at the bottom of the form – this will be the amount of the cheque issued
- payment can alternatively be made by computer transfer between bank accounts (BACS); in this case a remittance advice is still sent, but no cheque
- a 'tear-off' printed remittance advice listing all the items is sometimes attached to the statement sent by the seller; all the buyer has to do is to tick the items being paid, and pay!

TO   **REMITTANCE ADVICE**   FROM

Cool Socks Limited
Unit 45 Elgar Estate,
Broadfield, BR7 4ER

Trends
4 Friar Street
Broadfield
BR1 3RF
Tel 01908 761234 Fax 01908 761987
VAT REG GB 0745 8383 56

Account 3993   6 November 2000

date	your reference	our reference	payment amount
01 10 00	INVOICE 787923	47609	277.30
10 10 00	CREDIT NOTE 12157	47609	(27.73)
	CHEQUE TOTAL		249.57

see page 448 for an activity involving this document

CHEQUE – *the buyer sends a payment*

purpose of the document	a payment document which, when completed, can be paid into a bank account; it enables people to settle debts, for example a buyer paying money to a seller
who completes it?	the person who owes the money signs the cheque and writes the amount in words and figures, the name of the person who is to receive the money (the payee) and the date
what happens to it?	it is passed or posted by the buyer to the seller
why must it be accurate?	if the amount is wrong the seller could end up being underpaid or overpaid; also, any mistake on the cheque could result in the banks refusing to let it through the clearing system

what happens in this case?

Trends complete the details on the cheque – including the date, amount and signature – and send it to Cool Socks with the remittance advice.

points to note:

- If a cheque is not completed correctly, it could be refused by the banks. Particular points to note are:
    - the cheque should be signed – it is completely invalid without a signature
    - the amount in words and figures must be the same
    - lines should be drawn after the name of the payee and the amount to prevent fraud
    - the current date should be written in – cheques become invalid after six months

- The lines across the cheque are known as the 'crossing'. The words 'a/c payee only' are an important security measure because they mean that the cheque can only be paid into the account of the person named on the 'pay' line of the cheque.

Albion Bank PLC

7 The Avenue
Broadfield BR1 2AJ

Date *6 November 2000*   90 47 17

Pay *Cool Socks Limited* ——————————

Two hundred and forty nine pounds 57p   A/c payee only

£ *249.57* ——

TRENDS

V Williams

238628   90 47 17   11719512

---

see pages 448 to 450 for activities involving this document

paying the cheque into the bank

The flow of documents between buyer and seller is now complete.

The seller and buyer now have further financial documents to deal with because the cheque has to be banked by the seller and deducted from the bank account of the buyer:

- the seller pays the cheque into the bank on a **paying-in slip**
- the seller's bank will in due course send a **bank statement** to the seller showing the amount of the paying-in slip being added to the account
- the buyer's bank will in due course send a **bank statement** to the buyer showing the amount of the cheque deducted from the bank account

The process looks like this:

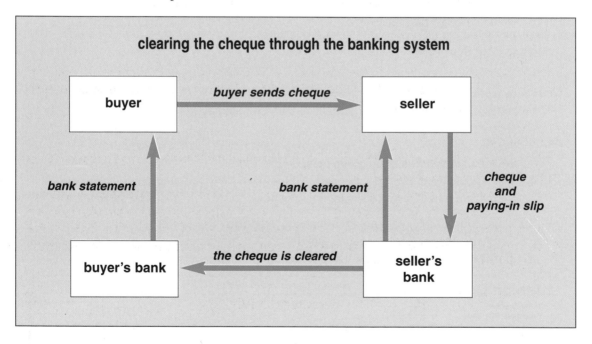

paying-in slip

The cheque will be paid into the bank on a paying-in slip, normally with other cheques and any cash that needs paying in. Paying-in slips are provided by the bank in books with counterfoils or carbon copies. They are usually printed with the name and bank account number of the business which will be paying in.

The paying-in slip used by Cool Socks to pay in the cheque sent by Trends is shown on the next page. In this case just the one cheque is paid in.

PAYING-IN SLIP – *the seller pays the cheque into the bank*

purpose of the document	to pay cheques and cash into a bank account
who completes it?	the business paying the money into the bank
what happens to it?	it is processed by the bank to place the money on the bank account of the business
why must it be accurate?	if the figures are incorrect on the paying-in slip and the bank does not pick up the error, the wrong amount may be placed on the bank account and shown on the bank statement (see page 437)

what happens in this case?

Cool Socks completes the paying-in slip and the counterfoil with details of
• the amount of money being paid in
• the signature of the person paying in the money
• the date that the money is paid in

The paying-in slip will be taken to the bank with the cheque and paid in over the counter. The money will normally go onto the account of Cool Socks the same day and taken off Trends' account three working days later.

points to note:
• If the business is also paying in cash, it is listed and totalled in the appropriate boxes on the paying-in slip and counterfoil.
• If the business is also paying in other cheques they are all listed on the back of the paying-in slip or on a tally roll and the total of the cheques is shown on the front of the paying-in slip
• If the paying-in slip is not preprinted with the business details the name of the account, the account number and the bank details (branch name and sort code number) will have to be inserted. This is very rare nowadays.

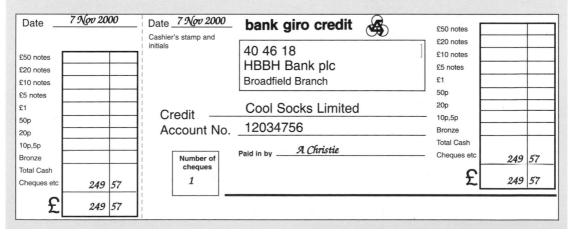

see page 452 for an activity involving this document

BANK STATEMENT – *a list of transactions on the bank account*

purpose of the document	to tell the business about payments in and out of the bank account and the bank balance
who completes it?	it is sent by the bank to the business
what happens to it?	the business receiving it will check all the items on it against its own records – normally kept in a 'cash book' to make sure that there are no errors
why must it be accurate?	if the bank makes a mistake (as banks sometimes do) the bank statement will differ from the records kept by the business and the bank will need to be told about any error; if the business has made an error in its financial records the bank statement will reveal this error to the business

what happens in this case?

At the end of November Albion Bank sends a bank statement to Trends. Trends will check off each item in its records to pick up any errors and will write in its cash book any item it has not recorded, eg bank charges.

points to note:

- The bank statement is set out in columns for:

  - the date

  - columns for payments made and receipts (money received)

  - details of each transaction:
    - 'Credit' means a paying-in slip paying in money
    - The six digit numbers are cheques
    - The receipts described as 'BACS' are payments received via the banks' computers
    - The payments described as DD are payments made via the banks' computers

  - a running balance of the bank balance; the letters 'CR' are short for 'Credit'. They indicate that the bank balance is 'in credit', in other words, it has money in it. If the bank balance was overdrawn – ie the bank customer is borrowing – it would have the letters 'DR' which are short for 'Debit'.

- The cheque for £249.57 written out to Cool Socks appears on the statement on 9 November (3 days after it was paid in).

- When Trends checks the bank statement it is unlikely that its final balance will agree with the final bank balance in Trends' financial records. The reason for this is that there will be timing differences – for example cheques written out by Trends and posted off but not yet paid in and deducted from the account.

BANK STATEMENT

Albion Bank plc
7 The Avenue, Broadfield, BR1 2AJ

Account title	Trends	
Account number	11719512	
Statement	85	

Date	Details	Payments	Receipts	Balance
20-0				
1 Nov	Balance brought down			1,678.90 CR
9 Nov	Credit		1,427.85	3106.75 CR
9 Nov	238628	249.57		2,857.18 CR
10 Nov	238629	50.00		2,807.18 CR
13 Nov	Credit		67.45	2,874.63 CR
16 Nov	Credit		100.00	2,974.63 CR
16 Nov	BACS HMRST 25453		500.00	3,474.63 CR
22 Nov	238630	783.90		2,690.73 CR
23 Nov	238626	127.00		2,563.73 CR
23 Nov	Credit		1,006.70	3,570.43 CR
23 Nov	BACS ORLANDO 37646		162.30	3,732.73 CR
24 Nov	DD Westmid Gas	167.50		3,565.23 CR
27 Nov	238634	421.80		3,143.43 CR
27 Nov	DD RT Telecom	96.50		3,046.93 CR
30 Nov	Bank charges	87.50		2,959.43 CR

transaction date | transaction details | cheque to Cool Socks | payments out of the account | payments into the account | running balance of the account

see page 452 for an activity involving this document

CHAPTER SUMMARY

- The stakeholders of a business need to know about the financial state of the business; this information can be found in the financial statements. The stakeholders include:
  - owners
  - managers
  - employees
  - customers
  - suppliers
  - lenders
  - investors
  - the tax authorities

- It is therefore important that the financial statements and the accounting system from which they are drawn are maintained accurately.

- The starting point of the accounting system of a business is the documentation generated by financial transactions.

- The accounting system then takes the information generated by the financial transactions through the books of the business, finally presenting it in the form of financial statements: the profit and loss statement and the balance sheet.

- A cash purchase is when someone buys something and payment is made straightaway. A credit purchase is when payment for a purchase is made at a later date. Both processes involves the issue of a number of different financial documents which 'flow' in a specific order. They are listed in the Key Terms opposite. The flow for a credit transaction can involve, for example:
  - purchase order sent by buyer
  - invoice and delivery note sent by seller
  - credit note sent by seller
  - statement of account sent by seller
  - cheque and remittance advice sent by buyer

- Financial documents must be completed accurately and checked on receipt to avoid problems such as the wrong goods being supplied or the wrong amount being charged.

- When money is received by the seller it must be paid promptly into the bank account on a paying-in slip and then checked on the bank statement when it is received.

KEY TERMS

stakeholders	people or bodies who have an interest in the business

Make sure that you are familiar with and can define the following financial documents described in this chapter:

receipt	a record of a purchase when payment is made straightaway – a document given by the seller
purchase order	sent by the buyer – the document orders the products
delivery note	sent by the seller with the goods, often signed as proof of receipt by the buyer
goods received note	an internal document completed by the buyer as a record that the goods have been received and checked
invoice	sent by the seller to the buyer advising how much is owed, for what, and when payment is due
credit note	sent by the seller to the buyer advising any deduction to be made from the amount owing
statement of account	sent by the seller to the buyer stating how much is owed, listing all invoices, credit notes and payments
remittance advice	sent by the buyer to the seller advising that payment is being made
cheque	a payment document which can be paid into a bank account
paying-in slip	a slip which lists cash and cheques being paid into the bank
bank statement	a list of payments in and out of the bank account

Make sure that you are familiar with the following terms:

cash purchase	a purchase where payment is made straightaway
credit purchase	a purchase where payment is made at a later date
Value Added Tax (VAT)	a tax charged by businesses on the sale of goods and services
trade discount	a percentage amount deducted from the invoice total before any VAT is added on
cash discount	a discount deducted from the invoice total after trade discount has been deducted and before VAT is added

19

Financial documents – practical exercises

Unit 5 Business finance
Recording financial information

in-tray exercise

In this chapter you will practise completing and checking the financial documents explained in the last chapter. The documents used here are those used in a credit purchase and when paying money into the bank. If you need blank documents they are available on the Osborne Books website: www.osbornebooks.co.uk in the Resources section. To remind you of the 'flow' of documents that normally takes place, study the diagram shown below.

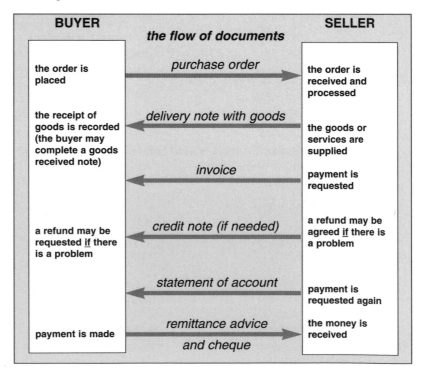

BUYER	the flow of documents	SELLER
the order is placed	purchase order →	the order is received and processed
the receipt of goods is recorded (the buyer may complete a goods received note)	← delivery note with goods	the goods or services are supplied
	← invoice	payment is requested
a refund may be requested <u>if</u> there is a problem	← credit note (if needed)	a refund may be agreed <u>if</u> there is a problem
	← statement of account	payment is requested again
payment is made	remittance advice → and cheque	the money is received

Activity 19.1

Making the purchase

Blank financial documents are available from the Resources section of the Osborne Books website: www.osbornebooks.co.uk

task 1

Work in pairs and play the roles of buyer and seller. The buyer is a clothes shop Oasis, 5 High Street, Mereford MR1 3GF and the seller a clothes importer, Fashions Imports Limited, Unit 4 Beech Industrial Estate, Salebury, Manchester, M62 5FG. You will need copies of blank purchase orders and invoices (see note above). You should use today's date and the current VAT rate, but will need to make up the following details:

- catalogue numbers
- order numbers and invoice numbers

The buyer is to complete two separate purchase orders and the seller is to complete an invoice and a delivery note for each order. The orders are as follows:

(a)   100 pairs of tights (black) at £1.50 each
25 sweatshirts (green) at £8 each
50 T shirts (black) at £3.50 each

(b)   25 fleeces (red) at £15 each
30 pairs of jeans (black) at £17.50 each
50 pairs of tights (black) at £1.50 each

There is no trade discount available to the buyer. Add VAT at the current rate and round it down to the nearest pence.

task 2

You work for Deansway Trading Company, a wholesaler of office stationery, which trades from The Modern Office, 79 Deansway, Stourminster WR1 2EJ. A customer, The Card Shop of 126 The Crescent, Marshall Green, WR4 5TX, orders the following on order number 9516:

(a)   50 boxes of assorted rubbers at 50p per box, catalogue no 26537

(b)   1000 shorthand notebooks at £4 for a pack of 10, catalogue no 72625

(c)   250 ring binders (red) at £2.50 each, catalogue no 72698

VAT is to be charged at the current rate on all items, and a 5% trade discount is given to The Card Shop. Prepare invoice number 8234, under today's date, to be sent to the customer. When the invoice is complete, calculate the amount due if a 2.5% cash discount is allowed for early settlement.

Checking invoices

task 1

A colleague in the Accounts Department of Cool Socks has prepared this sales invoice. You are to check it and state what is wrong with it. You are then to draw up a new invoice with the same reference number and today's date. Assume the price quoted is correct.

INVOICE

COOL SOCKS LIMITED

Unit 45 Elgar Estate, Broadfield, BR7 4ER
Tel 01908 765314 Fax 01908 765951
VAT REG GB 0745 4672 76

invoice to

Oasis
5 High Street
Mereford
MR1 3GF

invoice no	876512
account	3461
your reference	87541

date/tax point

product code	description	quantity	price	unit	total	discount %	net
45R	Red Toebar socks	100	2.45	pair	254.00	10.00	279.40

GOODS TOTAL	279.40
VAT	48.89
TOTAL	230.51

terms: 30 days

task 2

You work in the Oasis clothes shop and have received this invoice in the post. You check it against your Purchase Order, the details of which are:

Order No 98372 for 50 pairs of dark blue Country trousers @ £12.45 a pair (code 234DB). You are normally given 10% trade discount.

The jeans were received, as ordered, on the same day as the invoice.

Check the invoice against the purchase order and if there are any problems contact the Sales Ledger Department of The Jeans Company by e-mail, fax or letter. Draft out the text of your e-mail, fax or letter on a word processing file.

INVOICE

The Jeans Company

Unit 6 Parry Trading Estate, Southfield, SF1 5LR
Tel 01901 333391 Fax 01901 333462 email Jeansco@goblin.com
VAT REG GB 8762 54 27

invoice to

Oasis	
5 High Street	
Mereford	
MR1 3GF	

invoice no	942394
account	2141
your reference	98372
date/tax point	01 12 00

product code	description	quantity	price	unit	total	discount %	net
234B	Country trousers (black)	50	12.45	pair	622.50	5.00	591.38

GOODS TOTAL	591.38
VAT	103.49
TOTAL	694.87

terms: 30 days

Activity 19.3

A goods received note is completed

You work in an insurance broker's office and have just received a consignment of 50 reams of photocopy paper from Wintergreen Stationers. A ream is a packet of 500 sheets. The reams are packed in boxes of five. One of the boxes is badly dented at one end. The 5 reams of paper in this box are unusable as they will jam any photocopier or printer. The delivery note for the paper is shown below.

DELIVERY NOTE

WINTERGREEN STATIONERS

75 Holmes Street, Broadfield, BR2 6TF
Tel 01908 342281 Fax 01908 342538 Email WGreen@newserve.com
VAT REG GB 0822 2422 75

Uplands Insurance Brokers 8 Friar Street Broadfield BR1 3RF	delivery note no 68673 delivery method Parcelexpress your order 23423 date 02 10 00

product code	quantity	description
A4PPW	50 reams	A4 photocopier paper, white, 80gsm

Received
signature................*J Rutter*................name (capitals)...*J RUTTER*................date *5/10/00*

---

1   You are to complete a Goods Received Note. See the Osborne website: www.osbornebooks.co.uk for copies of blank documents.

The goods arrived by Parcelexpress, consignment number 7429472

2   Why is it important that a Goods Received Note is completed? What might happen if the brokers buying the goods just sent back the damaged paper by carrier and relied solely on the delivery note for its financial records?

The following day the invoice for the goods arrives by post. This will be dealt with in the next Activity.

Activity 19.4

A credit note is requested

The invoice for the photocopy paper delivered in the last Activity is shown below. It should be checked carefully for errors. Uplands Insurance Brokers normally receives a 10% discount on goods supplied.

You are to write the text of a letter (or fax or email) to the Accounts Department requesting a credit note for the returned paper. The text should include the money amount (including VAT) of the credit that is due.

INVOICE

WINTERGREEN STATIONERS

75 Holmes Street, Broadfield, BR2 6TF
Tel 01908 342281 Fax 01908 342538 Email WGreen@newserve.com
VAT REG GB 0822 2422 75

invoice to

Uplands Insurance Brokers
8 Friar Street
Broadfield
BR1 3RF

invoice no	9384
account	3455
your reference	23423
date/tax point	02 10 00

product code	description	quantity	price	unit	total	discount %	net
A4PPW	A4 photocopy paper white, 80gsm	50	1.70	ream	85.00	10.00	76.50

GOODS TOTAL	76.50
VAT	13.38
TOTAL	89.88

terms: 30 days

Activity 19.5

A credit note is issued

When you have had your answer to Activity 6.4 checked you should complete the credit note issued by Wintergreen Stationers, the suppliers of the damaged paper. Do not forget the discount!

You will find a blank credit note in the Resources section of the Osborne Books website: www.osbornebooks.co.uk

Activity 19.6

Sending statements

It is the end of the month of October in the Accounts Department of Wintergreen Stationers. You have been asked to prepare the statements for two of your customers. Their statements for last month (issued on 29 September) are illustrated on the next page – they will be needed for the starting balance for October. You will see how the starting balance (Balance b/f) is shown on the September statements.

The transactions on the two accounts for October are shown below.

Tiny Toys Limited

Date	Transaction	Amount (£)
10 10 00	Payment received	105.00
13 10 00	Invoice 9410	560.00
20 10 00	Invoice 9488	3450.50
26 10 00	Credit note 12180	230.50

R Patel Associates

Date	Transaction	Amount (£)
10 10 00	Payment received	4999.83
16 10 00	Invoice 9433	1098.50
23 10 00	Invoice 9501	678.35
26 10 00	Credit note 12183	670.00

You will find a blank statement in the Resources section of the Osborne Books website: www.osbornebooks.co.uk

STATEMENT OF ACCOUNT

WINTERGREEN STATIONERS

75 Holmes Street, Broadfield, BR2 6TF
Tel 01908 342281 Fax 01908 342538 Email WGreen@newserve.com
VAT REG GB 0822 2422 75

TO

Tiny Toys Limited
56 Broad Avenue
Brocknell
BK7 6CV

account   3001

date   29 09 00

date	details	debit £	credit £	balance £
01 09 00	Balance b/f			139.67
05 09 00	Payment received		139.67	nil
19 09 00	Invoice 9276	150.00		150.00
25 09 00	Credit note 12157		45.00	105.00

AMOUNT NOW DUE   105.00

STATEMENT OF ACCOUNT

WINTERGREEN STATIONERS

75 Holmes Street, Broadfield, BR2 6TF
Tel 01908 342281 Fax 01908 342538 Email WGreen@newserve.com
VAT REG GB 0822 2422 75

TO

R Patel Associates
78 Greenford Mansions
Mereford
MR3 8KJ

account   3067

date   29 09 00

date	details	debit £	credit £	balance £
01 09 00	Balance b/f			679.05
06 09 00	Payment received		679.05	nil
21 09 00	Invoice 9303	5345.50		5345.50
25 09 00	Credit note 12162		345.67	4999.83

AMOUNT NOW DUE   4999.83

Activity 19.7

Remittance advices and cheques

It is now the first week of November in the Accounts Department of Wintergreen Stationers. The October statements from suppliers are arriving in the post. Two are shown on the opposite page.

You are asked to make out a remittance advice and a cheque (ready for signing) to settle both accounts. Make up purchase order numbers. A sample cheque is shown at the bottom of this page. Blank remittance advices and cheques can be found on the Osborne Books website: www.osbornebooks.co.uk

You find the following note attached to the paperwork relating to the Hilliard & Brown Account.

NOTE TO FILE
19 October 2000

Hilliard & Brown - disputed invoice

Please note that we should not pay their invoice
3213 for £1,256.90 because the goods on the invoice
have not been delivered. Please check each month
when paying against their statement.

R Otter

Accounts Supervisor, Purchase Ledger

You check to see if the goods have arrived and find that they have not.

Albion Bank PLC
7 The Avenue
Broadfield BR1 2AJ

Date _____   90 47 17

Pay _____

_____ A/c payee only   £

_____   WINTERGREEN STATIONERY

123238   90 47 17   45195234

STATEMENT OF ACCOUNT
PRONTO SUPPLIES

Unit 17, Blakefield Estate, Broadfield, BR4 9TG
Tel 01908 482111 Fax 01908 482471 Email Pronto@imp.com
VAT REG GB4452 2411 21

TO

| Wintergreen Stationers
75 Holmes Street
Broadfield
BK2 6TF | account | 2343 |
| | date | 31 10 00 |

date	details	debit £	credit £	balance £
02 10 00	Balance b/f			234.75
05 10 00	Payment received		234.75	nil
19 10 00	Invoice 8717	290.75		290.75
23 10 00	Invoice 8734	654.10		944.85
25 10 00	Invoice 8766	125.00		1069.85

	AMOUNT NOW DUE	1069.85

STATEMENT
HILLIARD & BROWN

99 Caxton Street, Norwich, NR2 7VB
Tel 01603 342281 Fax 01603 342538 Email Hillibrown@newserve.com
VAT REG GB 4532 1121 06

TO

| Wintergreen Stationers
75 Holmes Street
Broadfield
BK2 6TF | account | 2234 |
| | date | 31 10 00 |

date	details	debit £	credit £	balance £
02 10 00	Balance b/f			560.00
05 10 00	Payment received		560.00	nil
19 10 00	Invoice 3213	1256.90		1256.90
23 10 00	Invoice 3244	987.60		2244.50
25 10 00	Credit note 4501		135.00	2109.50

	AMOUNT NOW DUE	2109.50

Activity 19.8

Checking cheques

You work in the accounts department of Morton Components Limited. The cheques on the opposite page have been received in this morning's post.

The date is 10 November 2000.

The following notice to staff is kept in the accounts office.

CHECK THE CHEQUES!

If you receive a cheque with a mistake or something missing, it may not be accepted by the banks. If this should happen you will need to get the missing item filled in or the mistake corrected and any correction initialled by the person writing out the cheque. If the person has posted the cheque to us this means in most cases posting the cheque back again with a covering letter asking for the mistake to be corrected. Look out for these mistakes:

mistake	what you do to correct it
there is no signature	send it back asking for a signature
the amount in words and figures differs	send it back asking for it to be corrected and the correction initialled
the name on the 'pay' line is wrong	send it back asking for it to be corrected and the correction initialled
the date is more than six months ago	send it back and ask for the date to be changed and the correction initialled
the date is missing	you can write it in! – this is the one situation where you do not have to send it back

---

1 Examine the cheques on the opposite page and write down what is wrong with them.

2 State in each case what you would do to put matters right.

3 Explain what the consequences would be if you failed to take action on any of the cheques – what would happen to the cheque? What effect might this have on the financial situation of your business?

(a)

Albion Bank PLC
7 The Avenue
Broadfield BR1 2AJ

Date _6 November 2000_

90 47 17

Pay _Marton Computers Limited_

Two hundred and forty nine pounds 87p — A/c payee only

£ _249.87_

K J PLASTOW

K J Plastow

083772 90 47 17 11719881

(b)

WESTSIDE BANK PLC
22 Cornbury Street
Shelford SL1 2DC

Date _1 November 2000_

78 37 17

Pay _Morton Components Limited_

One hundred and sixty five pounds only — A/c payee only

£ _160.00_

BACCHUS LIMITED

072628 78 37 17 23487611

(c)

Britannia Bank PLC
89 High Street
Broadfield BR1 8GH

Date

33 44 07

Pay _Morton Components Limited_

Thirty five pounds 95p — A/c payee only

£ _35.95_

DAVIES MEDIA

H Purcell

987482 33 44 07 24221913

Activity 19.9

Paying-in slips and bank statements

You work in the Accounts Department of Cool Socks. It is 23 November and you have to pay some cash and a cheque in at the bank today. The details of the items you have to pay in are:

Cheque (1 only)	£209.80
£50 notes	£550.00
£20 notes	£160.00
£5 notes	£80.00
£1 coins	£6.00
50p	£0.50
20p	£0.40

You are to complete a paying-in slip. A Cool Socks slip is shown below. Alternatively you can download a paying-in slip from the Resources section of the Osborne website www.osbornebooks.co.uk.

At the beginning of December you receive the bank statement shown on the next page. As part of your checking routine you would normally tally up (reconcile) the bank statement with your financial records. The records in this case are contained in the cash book which keeps a running total of items paid in and out of the bank account. The checking process involves ticking off and checking the amounts of the items that appear in both cash book and bank statement. You will also update your cash book for any items which appear in the bank statement but have not yet been entered in the cash book.

Answer the following:

1   Is the amount of the credit you paid in on 23 November correct?

2   What do the letters 'CR' in the right-hand column mean? What other letters could you see there?

3   The bank statement shows an item for bank charges on 30 November. This does not appear in your records. Why is this and what do you think you should do about it?

4   Two cheques – for £1,245.00 and £50.75 – do not appear on the bank statement. You wrote them out on 27 November when you were settling up the bills, entered them in your records and posted them off on that day. Why are they not on the bank statement? Are they likely to make the bank account go overdrawn?

Albion Bank plc
7 The Avenue, Broadfield, BR1 2AJ

Account title	Trends
Account number	11719512
Statement	85

Date	Details	Payments	Receipts	Balance
1 Nov	Balance brought down			1,678.90 CR
9 Nov	Credit		1,427.85	3,106.75 CR
9 Nov	238628	249.57		2,857.18 CR
10 Nov	238629	50.00		2,807.18 CR
13 Nov	Credit		67.45	2,874.63 CR
16 Nov	Credit		100.00	2,974.63 CR
16 Nov	BACS HMRST 25453		500.00	3,474.63 CR
22 Nov	238630	783.90		2,690.73 CR
23 Nov	238626	127.00		2,563.73 CR
23 Nov	Credit		1,006.70	3,570.43 CR
23 Nov	BACS ORLANDO 37646		162.30	3,732.73 CR
24 Nov	DD Westmid Gas	167.50		3,565.23 CR
27 Nov	238634	421.80		3,143.43 CR
27 Nov	DD RT Telecom	96.50		3,046.93 CR
30 Nov	Bank charges	87.50		2,959.43 CR

From documents to accounts

introduction

In the last two chapters we have seen what happens to the financial documents processed by a business. They form a 'flow' starting with the order and finishing with the payment. In this chapter we see how these transactions are recorded in the accounting system of the business. This system involves a 'flow' of financial data, starting with the documents, passing through the 'books' of the business and finishing up with financial statements which provide valuable information about the financial state of the business.

what you will learn from this chapter

● financial documents such as invoices, credit notes and cheques represent sales, purchases and payments which are recorded in the first instance in 'books of original entry' such as the sales day book, purchases day book and the cash book

● financial transactions recorded in the 'books of original entry' are then in most accounting systems transferred to accounts in the double-entry book-keeping system, eg sales account, purchases account, bank account; each transaction is normally recorded in two separate accounts

● the balances of the double-entry accounts are regularly listed in a checking procedure known as the trial balance; this picks up errors in the accounting system and also forms a basis for the production of the financial statements

● the financial statements are constructed from the double-entry accounts and comprise the profit and loss account and the balance sheet

● business accounts can be operated in a paper-based system (the 'books of the business') or increasingly commonly by computer

the accounting system

The accounting system of a business records information from documents such as invoices into the accounting records, checking that the information has been recorded correctly, and then presenting the information in financial statements which enable the owners and managers of the business to review progress.

In this chapter we look closely at the way this financial information is processed. Your external assessment may ask you to show the process in the form of a flow chart, or it may ask you to complete a flow chart. We show a summary flow chart below and will then explain the stages in more detail.

the accounting system of a business

financial documents
processing of documents relating to purchases, sales, payments and receipts, eg invoices, credit notes, cheques

books of original entry
initial recording of financial transactions in the books (or computers) of the business, eg sales day book, purchases day book, returns day books

double-entry book-keeping accounts
entering each transaction from the books of original entry (daybooks) into double-entry accounts contained in the ledgers

trial balance
bringing together figures from the double-entry accounts in the ledgers in the form of a list, known as the trial balance

financial statements
preparation of the final accounts:

• profit and loss account – which shows sales and profit

• balance sheet – which shows what the business is worth

books of original entry

The books of original entry (or 'prime entry') comprise a number of *day books* which list money amounts and other details taken from financial documents. For example the day books used for sales and purchases made on credit and involving invoices are:

sales day book – compiled from sales invoices issued

purchases day book – compiled from purchases invoices received

If any returns and credit notes are involved, two further day books are involved:

sales returns day book – compiled from credit notes issued

purchases returns day book – compiled from credit notes received

The day books are lists of transactions which form the basis for the double-entry accounting system. A typical sales day book is shown below. As you can see it lists invoices issued by the business. The arrows explain what the items are and show how the figures are transferred to the accounts.

Sales Day Book					
Date	Customer	Invoice No	Gross	VAT	Net
2000			£	£	£
17 Jan	R S Williams & Co	1101	141.00	21.00	120.00
18 Jan	R Singh	1102	188.00	28.00	160.00
20 Jan	R S Computers	1103	94.00	14.00	80.00
20 Jan	K L Pitching	1104	235.00	35.00	200.00
21 Jan	R S Thomas	1105	141.00	21.00	120.00
31 Jan	Totals		799.00	119.00	680.00

entered in a Sales account

entered in a VAT account

the amounts entered in the customer account

the reference number of the invoice

the customer (debtor) to whom the invoice was issued

the date on which the invoice was issued

double-entry accounts

the accounts

The accounting system of a business is organised on the basis of a number of *accounts* which record the money amounts of financial transactions. These accounts are kept in a series of ledgers (books), either in paper-based systems or on computer. There are accounts . . .

- in the names of customers and of suppliers of the business
- for total sales and total purchases
- for VAT charged and paid out
- recording various expenses
- for items owned by the business
- for items owed by the business

You will not need to set up accounts yourself or make entries in the accounts for the purposes of this Unit, but it is useful to know what an account looks like. A typical double-entry account for a customer you are selling to on credit looks like this in a paper-based system:

Debit			R S Thomas		Credit
Date	Details	£	Date	Details	£
2000			2000		
6 Jan	Invoice 1007	100.00	13 Jan	Credit Note 445	10.00
14 Jan	Invoice 1080	200.00	20 Jan	Cheque payment	90.00
21 Jan	Invoice 1105	141.00			

Note the following points:

- the name of the account is at the top – here it is the customer R S Thomas you are selling to
- the account has two sides: a debit side on the left and a credit side on the right; there are transactions in both
- the invoices issued to the customer are listed on the left-hand side – this is what the customer owes the business (he is a 'debtor' of the business)
- payments and any credit notes are listed on the right – these will reduce the amount owed by the customer
- the numerical difference between the two sides is what the customer owes in total – what is it? . . . use your calculator or your head   Answer £341

double-entry – debits and credits

The principle of double-entry book-keeping is that two entries are made for every financial transaction in two separate accounts:

*   one entry is made on the debit (left-hand) side of one account
*   the other entry is made on the credit (right-hand) side of the other account

For example, if a business pays wages, it has two accounts in which it makes entries:

*   wages account – to record the amount of wages
*   bank account – to record the amount of money paid out of the bank

The entries will look like this in a paper based system (the account layout has been simplified here):

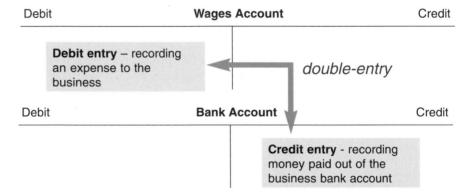

If the business was using a computer accounting program the double-entry would be carried out by entering the payment on one screen (eg the 'Bank Payments' screen) and indicating the other account on the screen by entering an account code in a required field. In simple terms, you do the entry in one account and the computer automatically does the entry in the other account.

account balances

You will see from this double-entry process and from the account on the previous page that every account has a balance – the amount of money in it. This will obviously either be a debit balance or a credit balance.

If you study accounting (as you may do in your Options) you will practise the debit and credit entries and learn the rules for which entry goes where. For this Unit you do not need to do this, but what you do need to know is:

*   that two entries (debit and credit) are needed for each transaction
*   two accounts are needed for each transaction
*   accounts will have either debit or credit balances, because they need to be listed in a trial balance (see later in the chapter, page 465)

the ledger – organisation of accounts

A 'ledger' is a book in which the accounts are written up.

The term 'ledger' describes the books which are used in paper-based accounting systems. The word 'ledger' is also used in computer programs, although, of course no books are involved here – all the data is held on computer file. The major advantage of computer accounting is that it is a very accurate method of recording business transactions; the disadvantage is that it is costly to set up because it requires investment in equipment, training and back-up facilities.

division of the ledger

Book-keepers and accountants confusingly refer to 'the ledger' when in fact they are talking about more than one book. 'The ledger' is in fact divided into a number of different ledgers. You need to know about this because each double-entry transaction may well involve two different ledgers and you will need to be able to identify in which ledgers each transaction is recorded.

The ledgers and the accounts they contain are shown in the diagram below. On the next page is an extract from a screen from a Sage computer accounting program showing how the ledgers are structured in the computer. The arrows and explanations have been added.

the 'Ledger' in a paper-based accounts system

SALES LEDGER
contains the personal accounts of customers to whom the business has sold on credit (the 'debtors').
It records information such as:
• invoices issued
• credit notes issued
• payments received

PURCHASES LEDGER
contains the personal accounts of suppliers from whom the business has bought on credit (the 'creditors').
It records information such as:
• invoices received
• credit notes received
• payments sent

GENERAL (NOMINAL) LEDGER
contains most of the other accounts not in the Sales or Purchases Ledger. The accounts include:
• sales and purchases
• expenses and income items
• items owned (assets)
• money owed (liabilities)

CASH BOOK
contains:
• cash account for cash held by the business
• bank account for payments in and out of the bank account
Entries are often made in the cash book without going through a day book.

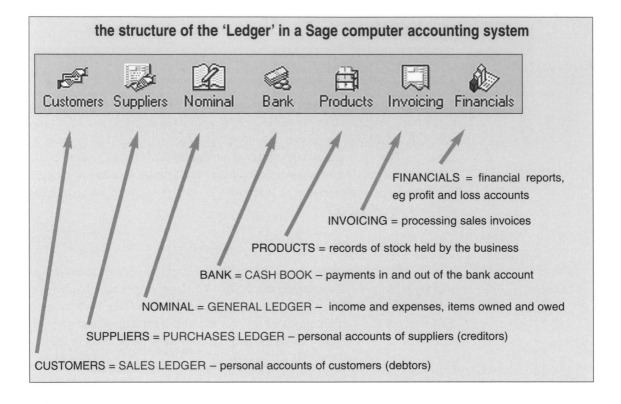

the structure of the 'Ledger' in a Sage computer accounting system

Customers Suppliers Nominal Bank Products Invoicing Financials

FINANCIALS = financial reports, eg profit and loss accounts

INVOICING = processing sales invoices

PRODUCTS = records of stock held by the business

BANK = CASH BOOK – payments in and out of the bank account

NOMINAL = GENERAL LEDGER – income and expenses, items owned and owed

SUPPLIERS = PURCHASES LEDGER – personal accounts of suppliers (creditors)

CUSTOMERS = SALES LEDGER – personal accounts of customers (debtors)

Activity 20.1

The accounting system

1   Where would you list sales invoices issued?

2   Where would you list purchases invoices received?

3   Where would you list credit notes issued?

4   Where would you list credit notes received?

5   Why is a double-entry accounting system called 'double-entry'?

What double entry accounts will you use for each of the transactions listed below? Ignore VAT. The accounts you have set up in your system include:

bank account, telephone account, computer equipment account, wages account, marketing account, sales account

6   You pay the wages for the month through the BACS.

7   You buy a new computer printer using a cheque.

8   You sell goods to a new customer who pays you straightaway by cheque.

9   You pay for an advert in the local newspaper by cheque.

10 You pay a Vodaphone bill by cheque.

Case Study

The accounting system at work

You have been asked to explain by means of flow charts how financial information 'flows' from the financial transaction involving a document, its listing in the book of original entry and its entry in two double-entry accounts in the ledgers. You can ignore VAT in your explanation. Remember that customers who owe you money are 'debtors' and suppliers to whom you owe money are 'creditors'. The accounts that you keep for them in the ledgers are 'personal accounts'.

You issue a sales invoice for goods sold on credit to a customer

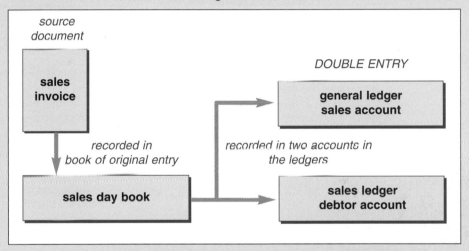

You receive a sales invoice for goods supplied by a supplier

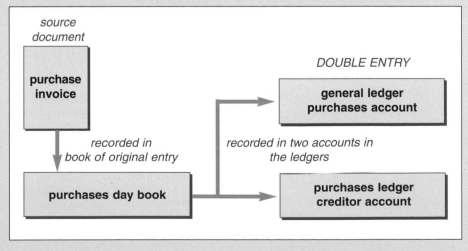

You issue a credit note for goods returned by a customer

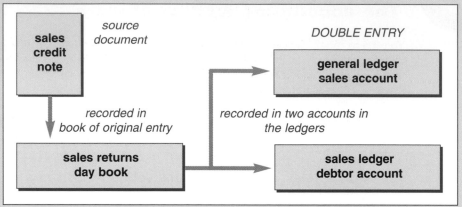

using the cash book

This is the one exception to the rule of document ➤ book of original entry ➤ double entry accounts. The cash book, into which you enter cheques and other payments acts both as book of original entry and also as ledger. As a result any payment made or received will miss out the middle stage. Look at the following examples:

a debtor settles up an account

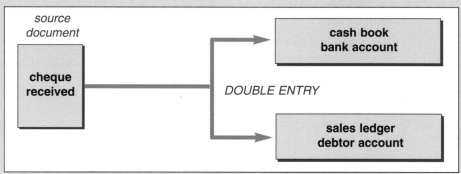

the business pays a telephone bill

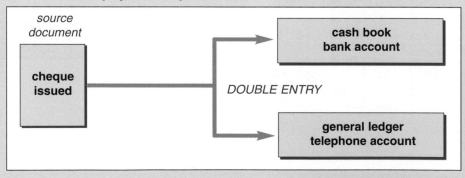

Activity 20.2

The accounting system

The flow diagrams shown below represent a number of financial transactions which are generated by financial documents and are eventually recorded in the double-entry accounting system. Some of the boxes have the descriptions missing.

You are to fill in the missing details, using the following:

Sales ledger (debtor account); purchases ledger (creditor account); sales day book; general ledger (sales account); general ledger (purchases account); purchases returns day book; cash book (bank account); purchase invoice; sales ledger (debtor account).

1

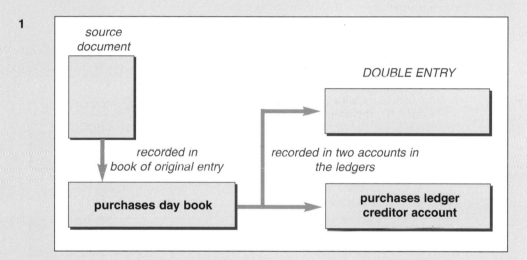

2

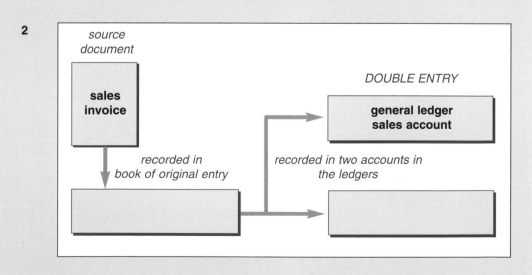

3

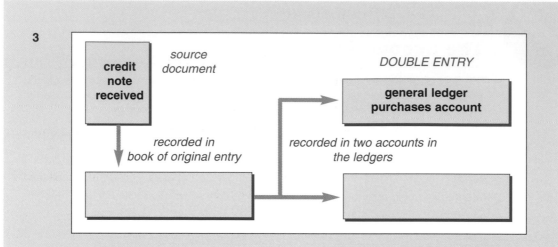

4

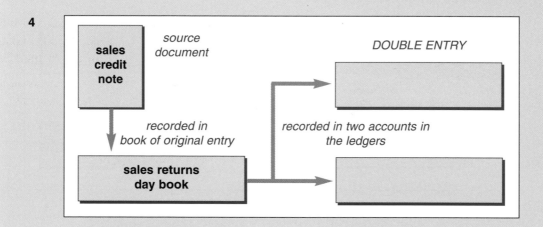

5

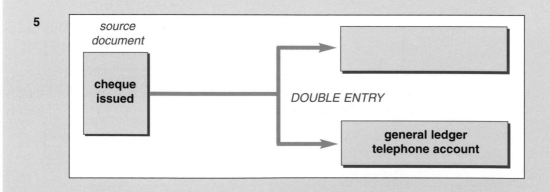

the trial balance

A trial balance is a list of the balances of all the accounts in an accounting system. An example is shown on the next page.

The trial balance is set out in two columns (see next page for an example).

Debit balances are listed on the left and credit balances on the right; the totals of the two columns should be the same.

A trial balance lists the balance of each account in order to check the arithmetical accuracy of the accounting system.

If you think about it, if the double-entry system is worked correctly, each debit entry in an account is matched by a corresponding credit entry, so total debit entries should equal total credit entries.

balances of accounts

The trial balance uses the balance from each double-entry account in the accounting system. By the balance of the account we mean the difference between the debit side and the credit side. (See page 457 for an account.)

You should note that certain accounts in a double-entry accounting system normally have debit balances, while others normally have credit balances.

balances which are normally debit

These are assets (items owned) and expenses; they include:

- cash account

- purchases account (stock bought)

- fixed asset accounts, eg premises, machinery

- expense accounts, eg overheads such as power, advertising, insurance

- drawings account (which records the amount of money taken out of the business by the owner for his/her own use)

- debtors' (customers) accounts; for the purposes of a trial balance the balances of individual customer's accounts are added up, and this total is entered in the trial balance as 'debtors' – it is the total owed by customers

- stock – this represents any raw materials and items that will be sold

balances which are normally credit

These represent liabilities (items owed by the business) and income:

- sales account

- capital account (the amount invested in the business by the owner)

- loans to the business by banks and other lenders

- creditors' (suppliers) accounts; as with debtors the total of all the personal accounts is entered in the trial balance, not the individual balances of each account

bank accounts – debit or credit

The bank account can either have a debit or credit balance – it will be debit when the business has money in the bank (an asset), and credit when it is overdrawn (a liability).

example of a sole trader's trial balance

Trial balance of Rashid Singh as at 31 December 2003		
	Debit	*Credit*
Name of account	£	£
Stock at 1 January 2003	12,500	
Purchases	105,000	
Sales		155,000
Administration	6,200	
Wages	20,500	
Rent paid	3,750	
Telephone	500	
Interest paid	4,500	
Travel expenses	550	
Premises	100,000	
Machinery	20,000	
Debtors	15,500	
Bank	450	
Cash	50	
Capital		75,000
Drawings	7,000	
Loan from bank		50,000
Creditors		16,500
	296,500	296,500

notes on the trial balance

- The heading for a trial balance gives the name of the business whose accounts have been listed and the date to which it relates.

- The debit and credit columns have been totalled and the totals are the same amount. The trial balance proves that the accounts are arithmetically correct, ie debit balances equal credit balances.

- The trial balance does not, however, prove complete accuracy – for example, an item could have been recorded on the correct side, ie debit or credit, but in the wrong account. Errors like this normally surface in time: for instance, a customer (debtor) may be charged for goods sold to someone else; the customer will soon let the business know!

- A trial balance is prepared at regular intervals – often at the end of each month. The reason for this is that, if an error is found, there will be, at most, one month's book-keeping entries to check back.

- The figure for debtors has been shown as a total amount, £15,500, rather than showing the individual amounts owing by each debtor. This is quite usual and is done in order to cut down on the number of balances listed in the trial balance. The figure for creditors is shown in a similar way – as a total of the personal accounts of creditors.

if the trial balance doesn't balance ...

If the trial balance does not balance, ie the two totals are different, there is an error (or errors):

- either in the addition of the trial balance
- and/or in the double-entry book-keeping

It will be the job of the book-keeper or accounts clerk to find the error (or errors).

from trial balance to financial statements

As well as being a check on the arithmetical accuracy of the book-keeping the trial balance is also a starting point for the preparation of the financial statements:

- profit and loss account
- balance sheet

We will deal with this process in the next chapter.

Now carry out the Student Activities which follow in order to give you practice in extracting a trial balance.

Activity 20.3

Extracting trial balances

You have been given lists of account balances from two accounting systems.

You are to prepare trial balances for the two businesses, using a spreadsheet if possible.

Make sure that both trial balances are headed up with the name of the business and the date.

When you have completed them both, make sure that the totals of the columns agree.

Then answer the questions at the end of the Activity.

Business 1: Betty Booth

Betty Booth keeps a designer clothes shop in the town.

Her account balances as at 31 March 2003 were:

	£
Stock	10000
Purchases	127500
Sales	248610
Advertising	4900
Wages	45000
Rent paid	7000
Telephone	1200
Directors salary	31000
Insurance	4000
Premises	145000
Equipment	3950
Debtors	5120
Bank (money in the account)	5430
Cash	150
Creditors	23400
Bank loan	5000
Capital	113240

Business 2: Colin Cox

Colin Cox runs a mail order CD business.

His account balances as at 31 March 2003 were:

	£
Stock	8500
Purchases	96250
Sales	146390
Advertising	10240
Wages	28980
Rent paid	6500
Telephone	1680
Interest paid	350
Travel expenses	1045
Postage	6500
Debtors	10390
Bank overdraft	1050
Cash	150
Creditors	28950
Drawings	29450
Capital	23645

tasks

1   Produce trial balances with columns for debit and credit balances, preferably on a computer spreadsheet (see the text at the beginning of the Activity for detailed instructions).

2   In the case of Betty Booth, explain what the Debtors and Creditors figures represent, where the totals have come from and what source documents were used to compile the figures. What aspect of her business do you think makes the Debtors figure much lower than the Creditors figure?

3   How does Colin Cox's bank account balance compare with Betty Booth's bank balance? Is there any other evidence from his figures which tell you about the state of his bank balance?

CHAPTER SUMMARY

- The accounting system of a business originates from financial transactions and the documents they generate.

- The flow of accounting information starts with the documents which are recorded in books of original entry; the data is then transfered to double - entry accounts and then to the trial balance. The information forms the basis of the financial statements of the business.

- The books of original entry – which are essentially lists of transactions – include the sales day book, purchases day book and the cash book. There are also day books for returns.

- The financial transactions recorded in the books of original entry are transferred to accounts in the double-entry book-keeping system, eg sales account, purchases account; each transaction is recorded in two separate accounts.

- The double entry accounts are constructed with a debit side (on the left) and a credit side (on the right). Each account will have a total (a 'balance') which can be calculated.

- The double entry accounts are organised in 'the Ledger'. The main ledgers are:
  - Sales Ledger, which contains the personal accounts of debtors
  - Purchases Ledger, which contains the personal accounts of creditors
  - Cash Book, which contains cash account and bank account
  - General Ledger, which contains all the other accounts, eg expenses

- An accounting system can be operated in a paper-based system or by computer. Computers tend to be more accurate and will automatically calculate account balances.

- The balances of the double-entry accounts are regularly listed in a checking procedure known as the trial balance; this picks up errors in the accounting system and also forms a basis for the production of the financial statements.

- The financial statements are constructed from the double-entry accounts and comprise the profit and loss account and the balance sheet.

KEY TERMS

day book	a book in which details of financial documents are listed, eg sales day book listing sales invoices issued
cash book	a book of account containing bank account and cash account; it also forms part of the Ledger (see below)
double-entry	a method of accounting in which two entries are made in the accounts for each financial transaction
debit	the left-hand side of a double-entry account
debtor	a person who owes the business money
credit	the right-hand side of a double-entry account
creditor	a person to whom the business owes money
account balance	the numerical difference between the two sides of a double-entry account
ledger	a book in which the double entry accounts are entered (the term can equally apply to a set of records held on a computer accounting program)
sales ledger	the personal accounts of customers ('debtors') who owe money to the business
purchases ledger	the personal accounts of suppliers ('creditors') who are owed money by the business
general ledger	also called 'Nominal' Ledger – contains the remaining accounts, eg expenses, income, items owned and owed
trial balance	a two-column listing of the balances of all the double-entry accounts; one column lists debit balances, the other column lists credit balances
financial statements	these are compiled regularly from the double-entry accounts and comprise:
	– a profit and loss account
	– a balance sheet

21 Financial statements

introduction

When a business has extracted a trial balance from its accounting records and verified that the accounts are accurate it can then draw up its financial statements – the profit and loss account and the balance sheet. The profit and loss account shows how profitable the business is and the balance sheet gives a picture of its financial 'health' and value.

what you will learn from this chapter

- the trial balance is the starting point for the construction of the financial statements of a business

- the profit and loss account summarises the revenues and expenses of a business and shows whether the business has made a profit or a loss over a specific period of time

- the gross profit in the profit and loss account shows the trading profit achieved; the net profit shows the profit after overheads have been deducted

- the balance sheet shows the assets (items owned), liabilities (items owed) and capital of a business at a particular date

- the assets in a balance sheet are either short-term current assets such as stock or long-term fixed assets such as machinery

- the liabilities in a balance sheet are either current liabilities (due within a year) or long-term liabilities such as bank loans

- working capital is the difference between current assets and current liabilities, capital is the investment of the owner(s)

- businesses often reduce the value of their fixed assets over time – a process known as depreciation

the trial balance and the final accounts

As we saw in the previous chapter, the trial balance is prepared from a list of the balances on all accounts in the ledger. The trial balance proves the arithmetical accuracy of the accounting data. It also forms the basis for the preparation of financial statements from the double-entry accounts. The statements are the profit and loss account and balance sheet.

This is the trial balance from the last chapter, plus a note about stock.

Trial balance of Rashid Singh as at 31 December 2003		
	Debit	Credit
Name of account	£	£
Stock at 1 January 2003	12,500	
Purchases	105,000	
Sales		155,000
Administration	6,200	
Wages	20,500	
Rent paid	3,750	
Telephone	500	
Interest paid	4,500	
Travel expenses	550	
Premises	100,000	
Machinery	20,000	
Debtors	15,500	
Bank	450	
Cash	50	
Capital		75,000
Drawings	7,000	
Loan from bank		50,000
Creditors		16,500
	296,500	296,500

Note: stock at 31 December 2003 was valued at £10,500

In order to prepare the financial statements of a business using a trial balance, we need to decide where all the figures will be used. For example we need to identify the assets and liabilities, and the expenses and revenue amounts. These are shown in the trial balance as either debit or credit balances.

debit balances

These comprise assets of the business (items owned), and expenses representing the total of purchases made and the cost of overheads for the year. The debit money column indicates that this business has made purchases of goods at a cost of £105,000 during the year, while wages is an overhead, a cost to the business of £20,500. The balances for premises, machinery, stock, debtors, cash and bank indicate, in money terms, an asset of the business. The debtors' figure includes the individual balances of all the firm's debtors, ie those customers who owe money to the firm.

credit balances

These comprise liabilities of the business (items owed), and revenue (income) amounts, including the total of sales made. For example, the sales figure shows the total amount of goods that has been sold by the business during the year. The figures for owner's capital, loan from the bank and the creditors shows the amount of the liability at the trial balance date. The creditors figure includes all the individual balances of the business' creditors, ie those suppliers to whom the business owes money.

treatment of stock

Stock means the materials and items which the business holds which it intends to sell. Stock obviously has a money value for the business. The question is, how is it recorded in the accounting records? You will see that the trial balance debit column includes an item for the stock value at the start of the year, while the end-of-year valuation is noted after the trial balance. For the purposes of financial statements, the stock of goods is valued by the business (and often verified by the auditor) at the end of each financial year. The year-end stock value is noted at the end of the trial balance because it does not, at this stage, form part of the accounting records – it is just stock that has been counted and valued. The valuation is entered into the accounting system when the final accounts are prepared.

the trial balance and final accounts

We can now indicate against each figure from the trial balance, in a column to the right, which financial statement it will appear in:

- expenses and revenue appear in the profit and loss account (abbreviated to 'P&L')
- assets and liabilities appear in the balance sheet (abbreviated to 'BS')

If this routine is carried out with the trial balance of Rashid Singh, it will then appear as follows:

Trial balance of Rashid Singh as at 31 December 2003			
	Debit	*Credit*	
Name of account	£	£	
Stock at 1 January 2003	12,500		P&L
Purchases	105,000		P&L
Sales		155,000	P&L
Administration	6,200		P&L
Wages	20,500		P&L
Rent paid	3,750		P&L
Telephone	500		P&L
Interest paid	4,500		P&L
Travel expenses	550		P&L
Premises	100,000		BS
Machinery	20,000		BS
Debtors	15,500		BS
Bank	450		BS
Cash	50		BS
Capital		75,000	BS
Drawings	7,000		BS
Loan from bank		50,000	BS
Creditors		16,500	BS
	296,500	296,500	

Stock at 31 December 2003 was valued at £10,500 P&L *and* BS

Note: P&L = profit and loss account; BS = balance sheet

a note on the stock figures

It is only the stock at the end of the year (the closing stock) that is shown as an asset in the balance sheet.

As you will see in the next section, we use the value of the stock at the start of the year (the opening stock) from the trial balance, and the closing stock to help us calculate a figure called cost of sales, which is used in the profit and loss account.

Thus the closing stock at the end of a year appears twice in the financial statements – firstly in the profit and loss account, and secondly in the balance sheet.

Activity 21.1

Linking the trial balance to financial statements

The following trial balance has been extracted from the accounting records of Guy Wainright at 31 December 2003:

Trial balance of Guy Wainright as at 31 December 2003

Name of account	Debit £	Credit £
Stock at 1 January 2003	25,000	
Purchases	210,000	
Sales		310,000
Administration costs	12,400	
Wages	47,000	
Rent paid	1,500	
Telephone	1,000	
Interest paid	9,000	
Travel expenses	1,100	
Premises	200,000	
Machinery	40,000	
Debtors	31,000	
Bank	900	
Cash	100	
Capital		150,000
Drawings	14,000	
Loan from bank		100,000
Creditors		33,000
	593,000	593,000

Note: Stock at 31 December 2003 was valued at £21,000

task

Mark against each figure from the trial balance (and also the closing stock) the financial statement – profit and loss account, balance sheet – in which it will appear.

This information will be used in the next Student Activity to construct the financial statements of Guy Wainright.

profit and loss account

a definition

A profit and loss account is a financial statement which summarises the revenue and expenses of a business for an accounting period and shows the overall profit or loss.

The profit and loss account – also known as the profit statement – uses information from the accounting records as shown by the trial balance:

- the sales (or turnover) of the business
- the purchases made by the business
- the overheads of running the business, such as administration, wages, rent paid, telephone, interest paid, travel expenses

The amount of sales is the revenue of the business, while the amounts of purchases and overheads are the expenses of the business. Look at the layout of the example of a profit and loss account on the next page.

the accounting period

The profit and loss account covers a set period of time – an accounting period – frequently a year of business activity. Businesses produce annual accounts as a matter of course, and as you will know from your investigations, the annual accounts of public limited companies are widely available. Often the financial year-end is the same as the calendar year-end, ie 31 December. You will also encounter other year-end dates. Sole traders sometimes choose 31 March because the tax year ends on 5 April.

Businesses may also produce financial statements such as the profit and loss account at regular intervals during the year as an aid to financial management. If a computer accounting program is used, it is a simple matter of printing it out from the financial reports menu (or icon).

The important point to remember is that the accounting period must be stated in the heading of the profit and loss account.

layout of a profit and loss account

In broad terms, the profit and loss account consists of a calculation:

REVENUE less EXPENSES = PROFIT or LOSS

If revenue is greater than expenses, then the business has made a profit; if expenses are greater than revenue, then a loss has been made.

**Profit and loss account
of Rashid Singh for the year ended 31 December 2003**

	£	£
Sales		155,000
Opening stock (1 January 2003)	12,500	
Purchases	105,000	
	117,500	
Less Closing stock (31 December 2003)	10,500	
Cost of Sales		107,000
Gross profit		48,000
Less overheads:		
Administration	6,200	
Wages	20,500	
Rent paid	3,750	
Telephone	500	
Interest paid	4,500	
Travel expenses	550	
		36,000
Net profit		12,000

format

The account is presented in a vertical format, ie it runs down the page. Two columns are used for money amounts: the right-hand column contains sub-totals and totals, while the left-hand column is used for listing individual amounts (eg overheads) which are then totalled and carried to the right-hand column.

cost of sales calculation

Cost of Sales represents the cost to the business of the goods which have been sold in this financial year. Cost of sales is:

> opening stock   (stock bought previously)
>
> + purchases   (purchased during the year)
>
> − closing stock   (stock left unsold at the end of the year)
>
> = cost of sales   (cost of what has actually been sold)

purchases and sales

The amounts for sales and purchases include only items in which the business trades. For example, a shoe shop buying shoes from the manufacturers records what it pays the manufacturers for shoes in its purchases account. The 'purchases' amount in the trial balance is the balance of the purchases account. When the shoes are sold the amount is recorded in the sales account and shown on the trial balance as 'sales'. By contrast, items bought for use in the business, such as a new till for the shop, are not included with purchases but are shown as assets on the other financial statement, the balance sheet.

gross profit and net profit

As this is a trading business which buys and sells goods, the statement shows two levels of profit: gross profit and net profit. If it were a service sector business, such as a secretarial agency, or an accountancy firm, it will show only a net profit or loss, because it does not buy and sell goods but provides a service.

Gross profit is calculated as:

SALES minus COST OF SALES = GROSS PROFIT

If cost of sales is greater than sales, the business has made a gross loss. This would be rather unusual!

Net profit is calculated as:

GROSS PROFIT minus OVERHEADS = NET PROFIT

If overheads are more than gross profit, the business has made a net loss.

overheads

The overheads are the running costs of the business, for example administration, wages, rent paid, telephone, interest paid, travel expenses.

what happens to net profit?

The net profit is the amount the business has earned for the owner(s) during the year, and is subject to taxation. The owner(s) can draw some or all of the net profit for personal use – the accounting term for this is drawings. However, it might be that part of the profit will be left in the business in order to help build up the business for the future.

The example profit and loss account shown opposite is for a sole trader, ie one person in business. For other business units, such as partnerships and limited companies, the profit and loss account will show how the net profit is shared amongst the owners of the business – an agreed share of profits to each partner or dividends to shareholders.

balance sheet

A balance sheet is a financial statement which shows the assets, liabilities and capital of a business at a particular date.

Balance sheets are different from profit and loss accounts which show profits for a time period such as a year. Balance sheets show the state of the business at one moment in time – things could be somewhat different tomorrow. A balance sheet is often described as a 'snapshot' of a business at one moment in time.

The money amounts of these assets, liabilities, and capital are taken from the accounting records of the business.

The balance sheet lists:

assets

Assets are amounts owned by the business, such as premises, vehicles, stock for resale, debtors (amounts owed by customers), cash, money in the bank.

liabilities

Liabilities are amounts owed by the business, such as creditors (amounts owed by the business to suppliers), any bank overdraft and loans.

capital

The capital is the amount of the owner's finance put into the business and profits built up over the years.

layout of the balance sheet

The balance sheet shows the value of the assets used by the business to make profits and how they have been financed. This concept may be expressed as follows:

ASSETS minus LIABILITIES = CAPITAL

The balance sheet shows the asset strength of the business, in contrast to the profit and loss account, which shows the profits from the trading activities.

A more detailed example of a balance sheet, using the figures from Rashid Singh's trial balance (page 475) is shown on the next page. Note that it is presented in a vertical format, and assets and liabilities are listed under the headings of fixed assets, current assets, current liabilities, long-term liabilities, and capital: these terms are explained in detail after the balance sheet.

Balance sheet of Rashid Singh as at 31 December 2003		
	£	£
Fixed assets		
Premises		100,000
Machinery		20,000
		120,000
Current assets		
Stock	10,500	
Debtors	15,500	
Bank	450	
Cash	50	
	26,500	
Less Current liabilities		
Creditors	16,500	
Working capital		10,000
		130,000
Less Long-term liabilities		
Loan from bank		50,000
NET ASSETS		80,000
FINANCED BY		
Capital		
Opening capital		75,000
Add net profit		12,000
		87,000
Less drawings		7,000
		80,000

We will now explain each of the main headings, starting from the top of the balance sheet.

fixed assets

These comprise the long-term items owned by a business which are not bought with the intention of selling them off in the near future, eg premises, machinery, vehicles, office equipment, furniture, etc. When a business buys new fixed assets, such expenditure is called capital expenditure (in contrast to revenue expenditure which is the cost of the business' overheads shown in the profit and loss account).

current assets

These comprise short-term assets which change regularly, eg stocks of goods for resale, debtors (amounts owed to the business by customers), bank balances and cash. These items will alter as the business trades, eg stocks will be sold, or more will be bought; debtors will make payment to the business, or sales on credit will be made; the cash and bank balances will alter with the flow of money paid into the bank account, or as withdrawals are made.

By tradition, fixed and current assets are listed from the top, starting with the most permanent, ie premises, and working through to the most liquid, ie nearest to cash: either cash itself, or the balance at the bank.

current liabilities

These are liabilities (items owed) which are due for repayment within twelve months of the date of the balance sheet, eg creditors (amounts owed by the business to suppliers), and bank overdraft.

working capital

This is the excess of current assets over current liabilities, ie current assets minus current liabilities = working capital. Without adequate working capital, a business will find it difficult to continue to operate (see Chapter 24 on page 540) as it may find it cannot pay its bills.

long-term liabilities

These liabilities represent loans to the business where repayment is due in more than one year from the date of the balance sheet; they are often described as 'bank loan', 'long-term loan', or 'mortgage'.

net assets

This section shows the actual amount of assets used by the business, ie fixed and current assets minus current and long-term liabilities. The net assets are financed by the owner(s) of the business, in the form of capital. The total of the net assets therefore equals the total of the 'financed by' section – the balance sheet 'balances'.

capital

Capital is the owner's investment, and is a liability of a business, ie it is what the business owes the owner. It is important to realise that the assets and liabilities of a business are treated separately from the personal assets and liabilities of the owner of the business. For example, if a group of people decided to set up in business they would each agree to put in a certain amount of capital to start the business. As individuals they regard their capital as an investment, ie an asset which may, at some time, be repaid to them. From the point of view of the business, the capital is a liability, because it is owed to the owner or owners. In practice, it is unlikely to be repaid as it is the permanent capital of the business.

To the owner's capital is added net profit for the year, while drawings, the amount withdrawn by the owner during the year, are deducted, ie:

	owner's capital	(from the trial balance)
plus	net profit for the year	(from the profit & loss account)
minus	owner's drawings for the year	(from the trial balance)
equals	closing capital	

This calculation leaves a closing capital at the balance sheet date which balances (agrees) with the net assets figure – the balance sheet balances. (Please note that drawings must not be included amongst the overheads in the profit and loss account).

In partnership balance sheets the same details, ie capital, net profit, and drawings, are shown for each partner, together with other items which relate specifically to the way in which the partners have agreed to share profits and losses.

In limited company balance sheets (see later in the chapter), details of the share capital issued by the company are shown, together with retained profits for the year, ie profit after payment of dividends to the shareholders.

production of financial statements

In the last few pages we have looked at the layout of the profit and loss account and the balance sheet. We now need to see how these financial statements are produced, using the trial balance as the starting point.

Against each figure from the trial balance we indicate whether it will appear in the profit and loss account ('P&L') or the balance sheet ('BS'). Look at the trial balance of Rashid Singh page 475 to see how this has been done. Note that the stock at the end of the year (which appears as a note to the trial balance) is marked to appear in both 'P&L' and 'BS'.

profit and loss account

The figures from the trial balance that have been marked 'P&L' (see page 475) are now entered onto the profit and loss account. The procedure is as follows:

- enter the sales figures in the right-hand money column
- now calculate the cost of sales in the left-hand money column, taking care to add the opening stock and to deduct the closing stock; work out the total (for Rashid Singh, it is £107,000), and carry it into the right-hand column
- deduct cost of sales from sales to give the figure for gross profit
- in the left-hand money column list the overheads of the business, work out the total (for Rashid Singh, it is £36,000), and carry it into the right-hand column
- deduct the total of overheads from gross profit to give the figure for net profit

As we have seen earlier, the right-hand money column contains sub-totals and totals, while the left-hand column is used for listing individual amounts.

balance sheet

For the balance sheet, all figures are entered in the right-hand money column, unless we want to calculate some intermediate figures – see the example of Rashid Singh's balance sheet on page 481. Using the items from the trial balance marked 'BS', work as follows:

- list the fixed assets and sub-total
- list the current assets in the left-hand money column and sub-total in the same column (for Rashid Singh, the figure is £26,500)
- write down the current liabilities and, if there is more than one, sub-total in the left-hand money column
- deduct current liabilities from current assets to give the working capital figure (£10,000 for Rashid Singh) and carry it into the right-hand column
- in the right-hand money column, add together the sub-total of fixed assets and working capital (to give £130,000 for Rashid Singh); from this figure deduct long-term liabilities (if any), to give a final 'net assets' figure (£80,000 for Rashid Singh)

Now complete the balance sheet by filling in the figures for the 'financed by' section:

- opening capital is from the trial balance
- net profit is the figure from the profit and loss account; it is added to opening capital and sub-totalled (£87,000 for Rashid Singh)
- deduct the figure for owner's drawings to give the total of the 'financed by' section, which balances with 'net assets' (£80,000 for Rashid Singh)

Spend a little time reading through and understanding the example of Rashid Singh's business, and then move on to the Student Activity which follows.

Production of financial statements
Guy Wainright & Jane Hayes

task 1

Please refer back to Activity 21.1 You should have already marked up the items from the trial balance of Guy Wainright according to whether they will appear in the profit and loss account or balance sheet. The trial balance is shown below for reference.

When your workings have been checked by your tutor, prepare the financial statements (profit and loss account and balance sheet) of Guy Wainright's business for the year ended 31 December 2003.

Trial balance of Guy Wainright as at 31 December 2003

Name of account	Debit £	Credit £
Stock at 1 January 2003	25,000	
Purchases	210,000	
Sales		310,000
Administration costs	12,400	
Wages	47,000	
Rent paid	1,500	
Telephone	1,000	
Interest paid	9,000	
Travel expenses	1,100	
Premises	200,000	
Machinery	40,000	
Debtors	31,000	
Bank	900	
Cash	100	
Capital		150,000
Drawings	14,000	
Loan from bank		100,000
Creditors		33,000
	593,000	593,000

Note: Stock at 31 December 2003 was valued at £21,000

see next page

task 2
The trial balance of Jane Hayes, who runs a bookshop, has been extracted at the end of her financial year on 30 June 2003, as follows:

Name of account	Debit £	Credit £
Stock at 1 July 2002	13,250	
Capital		70,000
Premises	65,000	
Motor vehicle	5,250	
Purchases	55,000	
Sales		85,500
Administration	850	
Wages	9,220	
Rent paid	1,200	
Telephone	680	
Interest paid	120	
Travel expenses	330	
Debtors	1,350	
Creditors		7,550
Bank	2,100	
Cash	600	
Drawings	8,100	
	163,050	163,050

Note: Stock at 30 June 2003 was valued at £18,100

(a) Using the trial balance, you are to prepare the financial statements (profit and loss account and balance sheet) of Jane Hayes' business for the year ended 30 June 2003.

(b) You are to provide an explanation to Jane of what each financial statement represents and write a note on each of the following terms:

- cost of sales
- net profit
- fixed assets
- current liabilities
- capital
- drawings

depreciation of fixed assets

In your investigations into final accounts (financial statements) of businesses you may come across references to 'depreciation', either among the overheads in the profit and loss account or in the fixed asset section of the balance sheet. Your course does not require you to study depreciation in depth, but you do need to know what the term means when it appears in the final accounts.

Depreciation is the estimate of the amount of the loss in value of fixed assets over a specified time period.

Fixed assets, for example vehicles and computers, reduce in value – or depreciate – as time goes by for a number of reasons:

- **passage of time** – as they get older, their value drops
- **wear and tear** – they get old and things go wrong with them, particularly if there is a lack of maintenance
- **obsolescence** – equipment can get out of date, for example computers and communications equipment

If you buy a new car on Thursday you will not be able to sell it for the same price the following Thursday; it will have dropped in value – depreciated – by a substantial amount in that time.

recording depreciation in financial statements

To provide a more accurate view of the financial state of a business, depreciation of fixed assets is recorded in the financial statements as follows:

- include the amount of depreciation for the year as an overhead in profit and loss account; the effect of this is to reduce the net profit
- the value of fixed assets shown in the balance sheet is reduced to reflect the amount that they have depreciated since the assets were bought

The reason for making these adjustments for depreciation is that the business has had the use of the fixed assets during the year: the estimated fall in value of the assets is recorded in profit and loss account, which now shows a more accurate profit figure while, in the balance sheet, fixed assets are reduced in value to indicate their approximate 'true' value.

an example of depreciation in financial statements

Rashid Singh tells you that he wishes you to show £2,000 for depreciation of machinery in his financial statements for 2003. As a result he will include an overhead for 'depreciation' of £2,000 in his profit and loss account. In the balance sheet the £2,000 will reduce the value of the machinery . . .

Balance sheet of Rashid Singh as at 31 December 2003 (extract)

Fixed Assets	Cost £	Depreciation to date £	Net £
Premises	100,000	–	100,000
Machinery	20,000	2,000	18,000
	120,000	2,000	118,000

---

calculating depreciation

Rashid has said that he wants depreciation for the year of £2,000. How is this figure arrived at? There are two main ways of calculating depreciation: straight line (fixed amount each year) and reducing balance (reduced amount each year):

straight line depreciation

This reduces the value of the asset by the same fixed amount each year. It is easily calculated:

$$\text{annual depreciation} = \frac{\text{the cost of the asset}}{\text{the number of years the asset is expected to last}}$$

Rashid has used this method. He expects his machinery, which cost £20,000, to last for 10 years. His calculation is:

$$\frac{\text{the cost of the asset (£20,000)}}{\text{10 years}} = \text{annual depreciation of £2,000}$$

reducing balance depreciation

If you buy an asset such as a car you will find that it depreciates more in the first year than in the second year. First year depreciation on a car can be as much as 40% of its value! In order to reflect this type of depreciation in the accounts a 'reducing balance' method is used. This applies a set percentage reduction to the value of the asset (the 'reduced' value) at the end of each year. With this method the depreciation amount itself goes down – reduces – each year.

If you buy an asset for £10,000 and reduce its value by 20% a year the depreciation calculation for the first two years would be:

Year 1	£10,000 x 20%	=	£2,000
Year 2	£8,000 (this is £10,000 minus the Year 1 £2,000 depreciation) x 20%	=	£1,600

You can see that in the second year the depreciation is only £1,600 compared with £2,000 in the first year.

Activity 21.3

Calculating depreciation

John Silver is starting up an antiques business. He is buying a new estate car for £20,000 to carry his antiques around in and a new computer and printer for £2,000.

These are his only fixed assets. His accountant has advised him to depreciate these assets using the following methods:

- depreciate the vehicle using 25% reducing balance depreciation
- depreciate the computer equipment using 25% straight line depreciation

You are to:

1 Calculate the depreciation amounts for the first two years, using the figures given and the methods stated.

2 Draw up the fixed assets section of his balance sheet for the two years, assuming he has not bought any further fixed assets.

Use the following format as a guide. The question marks represent the missing figures.

Fixed Assets	£ Cost	£ Depreciation to date	£ Net
Vehicle	20,000	??	??
Computer equipment	2,000	??	??
	22,000	??	??

using the financial statements

In this chapter we have concentrated on constructing the financial statements. In the next chapter we turn to the interpretation of financial statements by the various stakeholders of the business.

CHAPTER SUMMARY

- The profit and loss account and the balance sheet are the principal financial statements of a business.

- The trial balance with its debit and credit columns contains all the figures, apart from the year-end stock valuation, for the construction of the financial statements of a business. The figures are mixed together and so will need to be identified for use in either statement.

- The business will need to value its stock at the end of the financial period because the figure will be needed in the balance sheet.

- The profit and loss account shows the profit or loss made by a business over an accounting period (normally a year).

- The gross profit in the profit and loss account of a business which sells a manufactured product shows the trading profit achieved. This is the sales figure minus the cost of sales total (the cost of the goods which have actually been sold in the accounting period).

- The net profit shows the profit after overheads have been deducted. In the case of a trading company it is calculated as gross profit less overheads.

- The net profit is the profit earned by the owner of the business, and is taxable. The owner can take it out of the business or use it in the business.

- The balance sheet shows the assets (items owned), liabilities (items owed) and capital of a business at a particular date in time. The formula is:

  Assets minus Liabilities equals Capital.

- The assets in a balance sheet are either short-term current assets such as stock, debtors, cash and money in the bank, or long-term fixed assets such as machinery.

- Depreciation is the process by which a business reduces the value of its fixed assets over time; depreciation can be straight-line or reducing balance.

- The liabilities in a balance sheet are either current liabilities (due within a year) or long-term liabilities such as bank loans.

- Working capital is the difference between current assets and current liabilities and is the funding which enables the business to carry on its day-to-day operations.

- Capital is the investment of the owner in the business and can include profits which have built up over time.

KEY TERMS

profit and loss account	a financial statement which measures the profit made by a business over an accounting period
balance sheet	a financial statement which shows at any one time how a business is financed, its working capital position and the owner's capital
closing stock	a calculation of the valuation of stock at the end of the accounting period
cost of sales	the cost to a trading business of the value of the stock actually sold during the accounting period, calculated as opening stock plus purchases minus closing stock
gross profit	trading profit: sales minus cost of sales
net profit	owner's profit: gross profit less overheads
overheads	the running costs of the business
current assets	Items owned by a business for the short term
fixed assets	items owned by a business over the long term
current liabilities	items owed by a business and due for repayment within twelve months
long-term liabilities	items owed by a business and not due for repayment within twelve months
working capital	short-term funds used to finance the day-to-day operations of the business: current assets minus current liabilities
net assets	total assets less current liabilities – what the business is worth – equal to capital
capital	the investment by the owner in a business
depreciation	the estimated fall in value of fixed assets over time as a result of wear and tear, obsolescence and the passage of time, calculated as: - straight line depreciation: a fixed amount each year - reducing balance depreciation: a percentage of the value at the end of each year

22 Interpreting financial information

introduction

Stakeholders in a business need to assess – for a variety of different reasons – the financial performance of a business. This is carried out by examining the figures in the financial statements of the business and calculating and analysing ratios derived from the figures. The main areas of interest to stakeholders are the profitability of a business, its ability to pays its debts and the way it works on a day-to-day basis.

what you will learn from this chapter

- many different stakeholders have an interest in the financial performance of a business

- the main documents for providing financial information to stakeholders are the profit and loss account and the balance sheet

- the accounting ratios that measure solvency (the ability of a business to repay its debts) analyse the working capital position on the balance sheet

- profitability ratios analyse the relationship of various measures of profit against figures including sales and capital

- performance ratios examine areas such as the length of time for which stock is held and the period of time customers take to pay their invoices

- investors in public limited companies will also be interested in financial indicators such as the share price and the return on investment received in the form of dividends

financial information for stakeholders

As we saw at the start of Chapter 18 all businesses have stakeholders who have an interest in that business. These stakeholders include:

• people inside the business – owners, managers and employees

• people the business deals with on a day-to day business – its customers and its suppliers

• people who want to lend money to the business

• investors who want to put their money into the business

• the general public

• organisations that want to ensure that the business is being run correctly and according to the regulations laid down in law

We will now look at the users of accounting information in more detail and explain what sort of financial information stakeholders are asking for.

the owners

Whether the business is a small sole trader enterprise or a public limited company (where the owners are its shareholders), the owners will want to know how the business is performing in terms of sales and profitability, and whether it is solvent, in other words whether it can repay its debts.

the managers

The management of a business will want to know the financial state of the business as they will have to take day-to-day decisions on the basis of the information. Managers will therefore look at:

• performance against forecast targets – sales, expenses, profit

• ways in which they can improve that performance

• control of the money coming in and out of the business – paying debts and getting customers to pay

employees

The employer will want to motivate the employee and instill loyalty and provide job stability by showing that the business is profitable.

customers and suppliers

Customers that buy from a business will want to be reassured that the business is financially stable so that the product will be of good quality and that the business will still be trading if a repeat purchase needs to be made. Obviously the level of concern will depend on the purchase: someone buying a stapler will not be too interested in profit levels, but a tour company ordering a cruise ship will need to make stringent checks on the financial viability of the shipbuilder as shown in its financial statements and forward projections of sales and profits.

Businesses that supply goods and services will obviously want to be confident that the business that is buying will be able to pay for the products. If the customer is a new one, the seller may well insist on a reference from the buyer's bank or may be able to obtain a financial report from an agency such as Dunn & Bradstreet.

providers of finance

Lenders such as banks will want to be reassured that any money lent to the business will be repaid when due. They will be particularly interested in:

- profitability – can borrowing be repaid in the future?
- liquidity (the amount of money available to the business in the short term) – can that overdraft be repaid now?

the public

The public will be interested in the financial performance of a business, either as investors looking for dividends in that business, or for political or ethical reasons – is the business making too much profit? The public is not only interested in financial information about the business, it is also interested in questions such as is it polluting the environment? Is it exploiting the labour force in developing countries? Is it experimenting on animals for research purposes? Is it involved in genetic engineering of plants used in food manufacture? As we will see, businesses such as public limited companies that publish financial information for the public are increasingly including this type of information as well.

the tax authorities

The tax authorities will need to have financial information so that they can assess or check on how much tax will have to be paid. For example:

- VAT due to HM Customs & Excise is based on VAT charged on sales
- income tax for individuals in business (and corporation tax for limited companies) due to the Inland Revenue is based on business profit

types of financial information available

We will now look at the types of financial information used by the stakeholders of a business in order to monitor its performance.

financial statements

You will already have studied the main financial statements drawn up by a business. They are:

- the profit and loss account – showing sales levels and business profitability, income and expenses
- the balance sheet – showing the size of the business, how it is financed and how solvent the business is (what resources it has for repaying its debts)

Financial statements for smaller businesses are hard to come by: unlike limited company accounts, partnership and sole trader accounts are not publicly available. You may find partnerships and sole traders unwilling to release this type of information, and understandably so!

The financial statements of plc's are publicly available from the companies themselves and in abbreviated form from educational websites such as www.bized.ac.uk. The published Report and Accounts of plc's offer a interesting variety of methods of presentation of accounting information. They also provide information about issues such as environmental and social policy, which are becoming increasingly important. There are, of course other organisations which will present financial information to the public and employees: local authorities and public sector businesses, for example.

published Annual Reports and Accounts

Public limited companies whose shares are publicly traded publish each year:

- Annual Report and Accounts – a formal report in the form of a booklet containing a profit and loss account and balance sheet (both with detailed notes) plus other information required by company law. This is sent to the shareholders unless a Summary Statement (see below) is sent instead.
- Summary Financial Statement sent to all shareholders – this is less formal and less detailed than the Report and Accounts and is intended to be easier to read and understand.

If you look at an Annual Report and Accounts you will see that it also includes a Cash Flow Statement – which is not covered by your studies. This is only required of larger companies, and sets out how money has been received and spent during a financial year. It should not under any circumstances be confused with the Cash Flow *Forecast* which is an internal budget (see Chapter 23), quite different in format, and not published with the other financial statements. Extracts from the Report & Accounts of Tesco Plc are reproduced with kind permission on pages 511 and 512.

interpreting the financial statements

accounting ratios

Financial statements of businesses are analysed by means of accounting ratios which indicate to the business owner and lenders how the business is performing in financial terms. The term 'accounting ratio' can be misleading because it can include percentages and straight figures as well as the normal ratio (1 : 1 for example).

The accounting ratios are normally divided into three categories:

* **solvency** – these ratios give an indication of the ability of a business to pay off its short-term debt
* **profitability** – these ratios look in a number of different ways at the profit made by a business
* **performance** – these ratios give an indication of how efficiently the business is preforming in areas such as stock holding and chasing up customer debts

solvency

A business is solvent when it can pay its debts when they fall due.

As we have seen when looking at balance sheets a business needs cash or the ability to realise cash (eg from selling stock or being owed money by customers) as working capital. This is what the business will use to pay bills, wages, and other pressing expenses.

who is interested in solvency?

The owner(s) of a business will want to be reassured that the business is solvent. If the owner is a sole trader or partner and the business becomes insolvent (bankrupt), their possessions may have to be sold off to pay people to whom they owe money. Lenders, too, will want to know how solvent a business is; if there are problems they will want their money back.

measuring solvency: the current ratio

current ratio = current assets : current liabilities

Using figures from the balance sheet, this ratio measures the relationship between current assets and current liabilities. As we have seen, working capital (calculated as current assets minus current liabilities) is needed by all businesses in order to finance day-to-day trading activities. Sufficient working capital enables a business to hold adequate stocks, allow a measure of credit to its customers (debtors), and to pay its suppliers (creditors).

Although there is no ideal working capital ratio, an often accepted ratio is about 2:1, ie £2 of current assets to every £1 of current liabilities. However, a business in the retail trade may be able to work with a lower ratio, eg 1.5:1 or even less, because it deals mainly in sales for cash and so does not have a large figure for debtors.

The current ratio may also be expressed as a percentage:

$$\frac{\text{current assets}}{\text{current liabilities}} \quad \text{x} \quad 100$$

A current ratio of 1.5 : 1 becomes 150%

measuring solvency: acid test ratio

acid test ratio = current assets minus stock : current liabilities

One of the problems with the current ratio is that it includes stock in the current assets as a possible source of cash. Stock, of course, may be unsaleable or obsolete – out-of-date cans of beans, for example. The acid test ratio (also known as the quick ratio or liquid capital ratio) includes the current assets and current liabilities from the balance sheet, but stock is omitted. This is because stock is the least liquid current asset: it has to be sold first, turned into debtors, and then eventually into cash.

The balance between liquid assets, that is debtors and cash/bank, and current liabilities should, ideally, be about 1:1, ie £1 of liquid assets to each £1 of current liabilities. At this ratio a business is expected to be able to pay its current liabilities from its liquid assets; a figure below 1:1, eg 0.75:1, indicates that the business would have difficulty in meeting pressing demands from creditors. However, as with the working capital ratio, certain types of business are able to operate with a lower liquid capital ratio than others.

The acid test ratio may also be expressed as a percentage:

$$\frac{\text{current assets minus stock}}{\text{current liabilities}} \quad \text{x} \quad 100$$

An acid test ratio of 1 : 1 then becomes 100%

how are the ratios used?

With both the current and the acid test ratios, trends from one year to the next need to be considered, or comparisons made with similar organisations.

Activity 22.1

Solvency ratios

The following figures have been extracted from the balance sheets of Businesses A, B & C:

Business	Total Current Assets	Stock	Current Liabilities
A	£20,000	£5,000	£10,000
B	£20,000	£15,000	£10,000
C	£20,000	£15,000	£15,000

1 Calculate the current and acid test ratio for all three businesses.

2 Comment on how solvent the businesses are.

3 Why would it be misleading to rely on just the current ratio for one of the businesses?

profitability ratios

profitability

Most people dealing with businesses will want to know how profitable they are:

- owners – because it will affect the share of profits that they will get
- managers – because they will see how close to target they are
- lenders – they will know that money is being generated to repay them
- the tax authorities – they will be able to assess the amount of tax due
- the public – they will want to know if they are getting 'value for money'
- employees – they will be reassured that their jobs are safe

a large profit or a small profit?

Is it good policy to be seen to be making a large profit? Generally speaking, the answer is 'yes'. There are, however, one or two exceptions. A business is taxed on its profits, and many businesses will try to bring the profit figure (and the tax bill!) down by deducting as many expenses as possible from profit.

Also, the public do not like businesses making big profits at their expense. You may be able to think of businesses such as BT which dominate the market and have actually reduced their prices following large profits.

measuring profitability – gross profit percentage

You will know from your study of the profit and loss account that the gross profit of a business is the profit made after deducting from the sales figure the cost of making a product, the 'cost of sales'. The gross profit percentage is calculated using the formula:

$$\frac{\textbf{gross profit}}{\textbf{sales}} \quad \textbf{x} \quad \textbf{100} \quad = \quad \textbf{gross profit percentage}$$

This percentage relates the gross profit to sales. For example, a gross profit percentage of 50 per cent means that for every £100 of sales made, the gross profit is £50. The gross profit percentage should be similar from year-to-year for the same business. It will vary between organisations in different areas of business, eg the gross profit percentage on jewellery is considerably higher than that on baked beans. This is because jewellers sell fewer items of jewellery a week than a supermarket sells tins of baked beans.

measuring profitability – net profit percentage

You will know from your study of the profit and loss account that the net profit of a business is the profit made after deducting all the expenses, ie the cost of sales and overheads such as insurance, advertising, business rates, fuel, and so on. The formula is:

$$\frac{\textbf{net profit}}{\textbf{sales}} \quad \textbf{x} \quad \textbf{100} \quad = \quad \textbf{net profit percentage}$$

As with gross profit percentage, the net profit percentage (or 'margin') should be similar from year-to-year for the same business, and should also be comparable with other firms in the same line of business. Any significant fall should be investigated to see if it has been caused by an increase in one particular expense, eg wages and salaries or advertising.

measuring profitability – return on capital employed

This indicator compares the net profit of a business to the owner's capital. It gives a percentage figure which is a basic indicator of the return the owner is achieving on the capital invested in the company. The formula is:

$$\frac{\textbf{net profit}}{\textbf{owner's capital}} \quad \textbf{x} \quad \textbf{100} \quad = \quad \textbf{return on capital employed (ROCE)}$$

The owner's capital is to be found on the balance sheet in the 'Financed by' section and normally consists of capital invested plus reserves (including profit and loss) which have built up. You may find that some limited companies include long-term loans as part of capital. For the purposes of this book and external assessments you should keep to the formula quoted above.

Activity 22.2

Profitability ratios

The following figures have been extracted from the accounts of Businesses A, B & C:

Business	Capital Employed	Sales	Cost of sales	Other expenses
A	£500,000	£500,000	£250,000	£200,000
B	£800,000	£800,000	£600,000	£160,000
C	£500,000	£600,000	£480,000	£100,000

Calculate the gross and net profit figures and then the Gross Profit Percentage, Net Profit Percentage and Return on Capital Employed, for all three businesses.

Comment on your findings, assuming that the businesses all manufacture the same type of product.

performance ratios

We have seen that the solvency and profitability indicators are of particular interest to outside bodies. The owners and managers of a business, on the other hand, will be anxious to know how a business is performing. They are responsible for its level of performance:

"Is the stock moving as quickly as it should?"

"Are our customers paying up on time?"

"Are we making the most efficient use of our assets?"

There are a number of performance ratios which will provide answers to these questions.

stock turnover

Stock turnover measures the speed with which stock 'moves' (ie is replaced because it has been sold). Clearly the more quickly it moves the better. Stock turnover can vary with the type of business. For example, a market trader selling fresh fish who finishes each day when sold out will have a stock turnover of one day. On the other hand a furniture shop may have a stock turnover of 90 days, the average length of time for which an item of furniture is held in the shop before being sold. The lower the stock turnover figure, the more efficient the organisation, for the same type of business. Stock turnover can be measured using figures from the profit and loss account:

sales for the year = **stock turnover (ie number of times stock is replaced)**

stock

Some businesses measure stock turnover in days, using the formula:

average stock x 365 days = **stock turnover (in days)**

cost of sales

The danger signs for a business are when the stock turnover period gets longer: it indicates that stock is not selling, and this in turn will hold up cash flow. Average stock is: (opening stock + closing stock) divided by 2.

debtors' collection period

The debtors collection period shows how long, on average, debtors (ie the customers of a business) take to pay for goods sold to them on credit terms. The formula is:

debtors x 365 days = **debtors' collection period (in days)**

sales for year

The sales figure is taken from the profit and loss account and the debtors figure from the balance sheet. The debtors collection period can be compared with that for the previous year, or with that of a similar business. In the UK, most debtors should make payment within 30 to 60 days. A comparison from year-to-year of the collection period is a measure of the business' efficiency.

asset turnover

A business may want to know the value of sales generated from each £1 of net assets. This is calculated by the formula:

sales (£) = **value of sales generated by £1 of net assets**

net assets (£)

This figure will give an indication of how efficiently the net assets are being used. Remember: net assets are total assets less external liabilities. Clearly if the figure increases from year to year, the business is becoming more efficient: each £1 of net assets is producing more sales.

It is important with this ratio that like businesses are compared with like. Some businesses, eg internet service providers, achieve high sales on low net assets, so their asset turnover figure will be high. Other businesses, eg car manufacturers have high levels of net assets; their figure will be much lower.

Activity 22.3

Performance ratios

The figures shown below have been extracted from the balance sheets and profit and loss accounts of a business for two years' trading. The owner is rather concerned about the situation.

Examine the figures and then answer the questions set out below.

	Year 1 (£)	Year 2 (£)
Balance sheet extract		
Net assets	150,000	150,000
Debtors	12,500	25,000
Profit and loss account extract		
Sales	100,000	95,000
Purchases	50,000	60,000
Opening stock	15,000	17,500
Closing stock	17,500	30,000
Cost of sales	47,500	47,500
Overheads	22,000	25,000

1   Calculate the following performance indicators for both years of trading:

   (a) stock turnover (days) – assume average stock for Year 1 is the closing stock

   (b) debtor collection period (days)

   (c) asset turnover (£)

2   Comment on the significance of the figures you have produced (do not just say they have 'gone up' or 'gone down'). Identify any problems you can see and suggest possible solutions.

the use of accounting ratios

It is important to appreciate that accounting ratios should not be listed in a mechanical way but should be used for a purpose. They should be analysed and presented in a meaningful way to people in the business such as owners and managers or people outside the business.

The process of financial analysis is like a doctor examining a patient: it is a a process of observation, measurement (pulse, temperature and blood pressure), combined with experience and judgement.

shortcomings of accounting ratios

Accounting ratios do have shortcomings: they are not the complete answer to financial analysis. These shortcomings include:

- they only look back at financial statements in the past; they may not be valid for forward projections
- inflation can affect the figures: a small percentage increase in sales, for example, may be a fall in real terms
- an over-reliance on formulas can be misleading, eg saying that any current ratio less than 1.5 : 1 shows a weakness in working capital

In the Case Study which follows we will take two years' figures from Classy Foods Limited, a manufacturer of quality cakes, and interpret them for the benefit of the bank that is being asked to lend money.

Case Study

Classy Foods Limited
using accounting ratios

Classy Foods Limited makes cakes and pastries for the catering trade. The company needs to raise a £50,000 bank loan to finance the expansion of its premises and the purchase of freezers for its perishable products. The management have called in an accountant to help them draft a business plan.

The management needs to convince the bank that the business is flourishing, and they will achieve this by presenting the bank with a business plan containing the last two years' financial statements and key accounting ratios . . .

CLASSY FOODS LIMITED

SUMMARY PROFIT AND loss accountS

	£	£
	Year 20-1	*Year 20-2*
Purchases (all on credit)	72,000	95,000
Sales (all on credit)	225,000	278,000
Cost of Sales	70,000	93,000
GROSS PROFIT	155,000	185,000
NET PROFIT	45,000	68,000

CLASSY FOODS LIMITED
BALANCE SHEETS

	£	£
	31 Dec 20-1	*31 Dec 20-2*
FIXED ASSETS	205,500	265,700
CURRENT ASSETS		
Stock	3,500	5,500
Debtors	30,000	31,300
	33,500	36,800
CURRENT LIABILITIES		
Creditors	10,000	12,000
Bank Overdraft	14,000	10,000
	24,000	22,000
WORKING CAPITAL	9,500	14,800
	215,000	280,500
LESS LONG-TERM LIABILITIES		
Long-term loan	35,000	32,500
NET ASSETS	180,000	248,000
FINANCED BY		
AUTHORISED AND ISSUED SHARE CAPITAL		
100,000 shares £1 each fully paid	100,000	100,000
Reserves	80,000	148,000
SHAREHOLDERS' FUNDS	180,000	248,000

CLASSY FOODS LIMITED

KEY ACCOUNTING RATIOS FOR THE YEARS 20-1 AND 20-2

solvency	*20-1*	*20-2*
Current Ratio	1.40 : 1	1.67 : 1
Acid Test Ratio	1.25 : 1	1.42 : 1

profitability	*20-1*	*20-2*
Gross Profit Percentage	69%	67%
Net Profit Percentage	20%	24%
Return on Capital Employed	21%	24%

performance	*20-1*	*20-2*
Stock Turnover Period	18 days	18 days
Debtor Collection Period	49 days	41 days
Asset Turnover	£1.25 per £1	£1.12 per £1

comments on financial performance

The accountant is likely to make the comments along the lines of the following to the management of the company:

solvency

This business, which deals with perishable goods, keeps a low stock level, which reduces the liquidity ratios of the company. The current ratio increased from 1.40 : 1 to 1.67 : 1, indicating a rise in working capital to a very acceptable level, taking into consideration the low stock holding, and the guideline 2 : 1 ratio.

The acid test ratio, which excludes stock, is therefore of less significance for this company. It has increased over the year from 1.25 : 1 to a comfortable 1.42 : 1. Both figures are better than the guideline of 1 : 1.

profitability

Sales have increased by 24% over the year, which is encouraging.

Gross profit percentage remains steady, the slight drop of 2% probably representing a rise in raw material costs, notably dairy products.

Net profit percentage increased by 4% to 24%, reflecting increased efficiency and trimming of overhead expenses.

Return on capital employed rose from 21% to 24%, showing a healthy return on capital invested.

performance

Stock turnover period has remained unchanged at 18 days, a high figure, as would be expected with a company dealing with perishable goods. If the company did not have the freezers in which it keeps some of its stock, the figure would be even higher.

The debtor collection period has shortened from 49 to 41 days, improving the cash flow of the company.

Asset turnover has reduced slightly from £1.25 of sales per £1 of Net Assets to £1.12 of sales per £1 of Net Assets. The reason for this is not that sales have declined (they have gone up by 24% over the year) but because Net Assets have increased by 38%, reflecting the healthy net profit made during the year (net profit is added into the Reserves).

The bank, which has staff skilled in the interpretation of financial statements, will undoubtedly come to the same conclusion. They will be happy to lend the company the money it needs, as long as its Cash Flow Forecast shows that it can afford the repayments.

Activity 22.4

Interpreting the accounts

You are a clerk at the Greenham branch of the National Bank plc. Your present job involves assessing lending applications from your customers and writing analytical notes for your manager, Lionel Stirling. This process of financial analysis requires you to examine sets of final accounts and to extract relevant accounting ratios. During the course of a day's work you are requested to undertake a number of tasks.

Task One: Becker Packaging Limited

Becker Packaging Limited is the holding company of a group of companies whose account you hold at the bank. It owns two subsidiary companies, Cardbox Limited and Easywrap Limited. You have recently received the final accounts of these two companies.

You are to extract relevant accounting ratios for both companies and set them out in a table for comparison purposes. Write notes covering profitability, solvency and performance for the guidance of Mr Stirling. You are given the following extracts from trading and profit and loss accounts for the year ended 31 March 20-4 and the balance sheets as at that date:

	Cardbox Ltd	Easywrap Ltd
	£	£
Sales	175,000	200,000
Cost of sales	120,000	150,000
Gross profit	55,000	50,000
Net profit	25,000	35,000
Fixed assets	100,000	120,000
Stock	45,000	50,000
Debtors	17,500	25,000
Creditors	15,000	21,500
Bank overdraft	9,200	8,500
Share capital and reserves	118,300	130,000
Long term loan	20,000	35,000

Assume for your calculations that all sales are credit sales and the closing stock figure is an average for the year.

Task Two: Connors Sportsware Limited

Connors Sportsware Limited is a good customer of your bank and has recently been given a long term loan of £20,000 to refit and expand the business premises. The directors have recently approached your bank with a request for an overdraft of £10,000 for new stock. The cash flow forecast shows that the company can repay this amount over six months, after which time the situation can be reviewed. Mr Stirling hands you the final accounts for the last two years and asks you to work out ratios to show if the company is as sound as he thinks it is.

You are to work out relevant ratios for the two years and then write notes comparing the two years in respect of profitability, solvency, and performance for the guidance of Mr Stirling.

Extracts from trading and profit and loss accounts for the years ended 30 June 20-3 and 20-4, and the balance sheets at that date:

	20-3 £	20-4 £
Sales	240,000	400,000
Cost of sales	160,000	300,000
Purchases	160,000	318,000
Gross profit	80,000	100,000
Net profit	60,000	70,000
Fixed assets	70,000	75,000
Stock	14,000	32,000
Debtors	24,000	40,000
Bank	2,000	3,000
Creditors	20,000	40,000
Share capital and reserves	70,000	90,000
Long term loan	20,000	20,000

Assume for your calculations that all sales are credit sales, and average stock for 20-3 is closing stock.

Task Three: MacInrays Mints Limited

MacInrays Mints Limited manufactures confectionery. The Finance Director, John MacInray has recently approached Mr Stirling to ask for a overdraft of £25,000 for expansion of trading. John MacInray has brought in the latest set of accounts for the year ended 30 June 20-4, and Mr Stirling has asked you to analyse them.

You are to extract accounting ratios and write comments for Mr Stirling on the financial strength or otherwise of the company.

	£
Sales	175,000
Cost of sales	145,000
Gross profit	30,000
Net profit	1,500
Fixed assets	25,000
Stock	70,000
Debtors	10,000
Creditors	65,000
Bank overdraft	12,000
Share capital and reserves	13,000
Medium term loan	15,000

Assume for your calculations that all sales are credit sales and that the closing stock figure is an average for the year.

performance of public limited companies

The number of people investing their money in public limited companies has increased significantly in recent years, particularly since investors have been able to buy and sell shares on the internet. Investors in public limited companies will be interested in a number of financial indicators.

financial indicators of shares

The price paid for a share in a 'quoted' company traded on the stock markets will vary from day to day. If there is confidence in that company and confidence in the stock market as a whole, the price should go up over time. If the company is not doing so well (for instance if its profits go down) or if investors lose confidence in the stock market, the price is likely to go down.

The movement of prices in the stock market is tracked by a variety of different indices, including the FTSE 100 index and the FTSE Allshare index. These relate the level of share prices to a numerical base.

how to profit from investing in shares

Investors hope to make money from two sources:

- a rise in the price of the shares held – the idea is to 'buy low, sell high'
- the dividends paid by the company each year - the 'yield' of the shares

There are many different sources of information about share prices and dividends paid, including the financial pages of the press and financial data on the internet (eg Yahoo stock price pages). The financial pages of a newspaper such as The Times will show share prices and yields like this.

High	Low	Company	Price (p)	+/–	Yield	Price/ Earnings
304	160	Safeway	200	+ 2	6.3	9.3
480	286	Sainsbury J	340	+ 10	4.2	24.4
201	152	Tesco	162	+ 11	2.6	18.3

These need some explanation:

high/low

These are the highest and lowest price of the share over the last twelve months. As you can see from the figures shown above, the variation (and the potential to make money) is substantial.

company

The name of the public limited company. Companies are normally classified into sectors according to what they do. The companies here are all in the 'Retailers and Food' sector.

price

If you look in a newspaper this is the price in pence of the share the previous day. If you access the internet or teletext you can get same day prices.

+/–

This is the rise or fall in the price of the share over the previous day. The rise or fall is quoted in pence.

yield

This is short for 'dividend yield'. The dividend is the payment made to shareholders, normally out of the profits of a company. It relates the dividend to the market price of the share and is quoted as a percentage. It basically says how many pence you are likely to get per £1 invested. The higher the figure, the more money the investor will receive. The formula is:

$$\frac{\text{share dividend (in pence)}}{\text{market price of share}} \times 100 = \text{dividend yield}$$

price/earnings

The 'earnings' of a share is the amount of profit made by a company for every share issued. This is not the same as the dividend because not all profits are paid out in dividends. Companies keep and invest ('retain') a proportion of profits. The price/earnings ratio links the market price of the share and the profitability of the company. The formula is:

$$\frac{\text{market price of share (in pence)}}{\text{earnings per share (in pence)}} = \text{price/earnings ratio}$$

The higher the ratio the more 'expensive' the share is seen to be.

Activity 22.5

Who wants to be a millionaire?

This Activity will enable each student to choose and invest in shares on a competitive basis, and hopefully see a gain in 'capital' value. Each member of the class has £10,000 to invest over a time period, for example a term. The tasks listed below are a guideline only and may be varied by the teacher/lecturer to suit the situation.

1 Each student should invest a notional £10,000 in the shares of three companies chosen from the pages of the financial press or on-line financial sites.

2 The number of shares purchased, their price and reasons for the choice should be written down. Reference should be made to investor indicators such as dividend yield, price/earnings ratio, current pricing in the market and any articles and 'tips' in the press or on financial sites and bulletin boards on the internet

3 The written records should be given to the teacher/lecturer to keep in a file.

4 While the shares are held students should look out for articles about the companies in the press, or on the individual company websites and add them to their pages in the file.

5 At the end of the period each student should calculate the total value of the shares, and write a short summary, pointing out the reasons for the success or failure of their investments. They should then between them draw up a class league table.

financial information in published accounts

Public limited companies whose shares are traded on the stock markets publish each year an Annual Report and Accounts. This is a formal report in the form of a booklet containing the financial statements and other financial details required by law. Traded public limited companies also publish an Annual Summary which is sent to all shareholders; this is a less formal, less detailed and more 'glossy' document than the Report and Accounts and is intended to be easier to read and more suitable for investors.

As part of your studies you should obtain both the formal Annual Report and Accounts and the Annual Summary of the public limited companies you are investigating. Your external assessment may contain extracts from these types of document and you should be familiar with them and prepared to answer questions on the figures they contain.

Shown below are extracts from the Annual Summary of Tesco Plc. Study them and carry out the Activity on page 513.

Profit and loss account	1999 52 weeks £m	1998* 52 weeks (proforma) £m	1998 53 weeks (restated) £m
Sales at net selling price	18,546	17,447	17,779
Turnover excluding value added tax	17,158	16,142	16,452
Operating expenses	(16,155)	(15,212)	(15,505)
Employee profit-sharing	(38)	(35)	(35)
Operating profit	965	895	912
Profit/(loss) from joint ventures	6	(6)	(6)
Interest	(90)	(72)	(74)
Underlying pre-tax profit	881	817	832
Loss on disposal of fixed assets/operations	(8)	(9)	(9)
Integration costs	(26)	(63)	(63)
Goodwill amortisation	(5)	–	–
Profit before tax	842	745	760
Tax	(237)	(223)	(228)
Minority interest	1	–	–
Profit for the financial year	606	522	532
Dividends	(277)	(255)	(255)
Retained profit	329	267	277
Adjusted diluted earnings per share [†]	9.37p	8.70p	8.84p
Dividend per share	4.12p	3.87p	3.87p

[†] Excluding goodwill amortisation, integration costs, net losses on disposal of fixed assets and discontinued operations.
* 1998/99 was a 52 week year compared to 53 weeks for 1997/98. A proforma 52 week profit and loss account for 1998 has been used for comparison.

Profit and loss account from the Tesco Plc Annual Summary

Balance sheet

	1999 £m	1998 (restated) £m
Fixed assets	**7,553**	6,496
Current assets	**1,146**	942
Short term creditors	**(3,075)**	(2,713)
Net current liabilities	**(1,929)**	(1,771)
Total assets less current liabilities	**5,624**	4,725
Long term creditors	**(1,230)**	(812)
Provisions	**(17)**	(10)
Total net assets	**4,377**	3,903

Terry Leahy
Andrew Higginson
Directors

The summary financial statement was approved by the Board on 12 April 1999.

Balance sheet from the Tesco Plc Annual Summary

extract from Chairman's statement

"We have made good progress with our strategy of growing the UK business and developing the foundations for additional future growth from international markets"

investor information

summary five year record

Year ended February	1995 £m	1996 £m	1997 £m	1998 52 weeks (proforma) £m	1999 £m
Turnover excluding VAT					
UK	9,655	11,560	13,118	14,677	**15,835**
Rest of Europe	446	534	769	1,465	**1,167**
Thailand	–	–	–	–	**156**
	10,101	12,094	13,887	16,142	**17,158**
Operating profit (pre-integration costs and goodwill amortisation)					
UK	600	713	760	859	**919**
Rest of Europe	17	11	14	36	**48**
Thailand	–	–	–	–	**(2)**
	617	724	774	895	**965**
Underlying profit	595	681	750	817	**881**
Profit before tax	551	675	750	745	**842**
Adjusted diluted earnings per share	6.70p	7.30p	7.83p	8.70p	**9.37p**
Dividend per share	2.87p	3.20p	3.45p	3.87p	**4.12p**
UK food retailing productivity					
Turnover per employee (£)	140,842	143,335	146,326	139,770	**146,236**
Weekly sales per sq ft (£)	17.00	18.31	19.74	20.48	**21.05**
UK food retail statistics					
Market share in food and drink shops	12.0%	13.7%	14.6%	15.2%	**15.8%**
Number of stores	519	545	568	618	**639**
Total sales area (000 sq ft)	12,641	13,397	14,036	15,215	**15,975**
Full-time equivalent employees	68,552	80,650	89,649	105,008	**108,284**

Investor information from the Tesco Plc Annual Summary

Activity 22.6

Interpreting published accounts
Tesco PLC

Study the financial information from Tesco's Annual Summary shown on the previous two pages. Note that:

- money amounts are quoted in £millions
- minus figures are shown in brackets

Answer the following questions

1   What is the percentage increase in total Turnover (sales) over the five years?

   Produce a line graph or bar chart showing the trend. If possible, using a charting facility on your computer to do this (most spreadsheets provide this function).

   Comment on the trend shown.

2   What is the percentage increase in Profit before Tax over the same period?

   How does this trend affect the amount of money paid to shareholders in the form of dividends?

3   Comment on the earnings per share shown in the Profit and Loss account.

   Is this indicator the same as the price/earnings ratio? If not, how is it different?

4   What is the main aim of Tesco PLC? Why do you think the company has adopted this policy?

   What evidence can you see from the figures shown in these statements that this aim has been successful in recent years?

5   Many of the figures in the Profit and Loss Account represent the interests of various stakeholders in the company.

   Identify these stakeholders and explain what figures in particular will apply to them.

6   Comment on the working capital (net current liabilities) of the business as it is shown on the balance sheet.

   Is there a problem here?

   What does this tell you about the interpretation of accounting ratios?

CHAPTER SUMMARY

- Many different stakeholders have an interest in the financial performance of a business; they include:

  - owners, managers and employees

  - customers and suppliers

  - lenders

  - investors

  - the public

  - regulatory bodies

- The main documents for providing financial information to stakeholders are the profit and loss account and the balance sheet.

- Public limited companies publish their financial statements in two forms: the detailed Report and Accounts (as required by law) and a summarised version known as a Summary Financial Statement or Annual Review produced mainly for investors in the company.

- Accounting ratios can be extracted from the financial statements to provide stakeholders with indicators of the financial 'health' of a business.

- Solvency ratios measure the ability of a business to repay its debts. They analyse the working capital position on the balance sheet; they include the current ratio and the acid test ratio.

- Profitability ratios analyse the relationship of various measures of profit against figures including sales (gross profit percentage and net profit percentage) and owner's capital (return on capital employed).

- Performance ratios are useful for managers. They examine areas such as the length of time for which stock is held (stock turnover), the period of time customers take to pay their bills (debtor collection period) and the amount of sales generated from assets (asset turnover).

- Accounting ratios should be treated with a certain amount of caution: they only look back over past financial periods, they can be affected by inflation and they need to be interpreted carefully according to the type of business involved.

- Investors in public limited companies whose shares are traded on the stock markets are able to assess the company on a number of different financial indicators including:

  - the share price as it fluctuates over time

  - dividend yield as it relates to the market price of the shares

  - price/earnings ratio which relates profit to market price

KEY TERMS

profit and loss account
a financial statement which measures the profit made by a business over a financial period

balance sheet
a financial statement which shows at any one time how a business is financed, its working capital position and the owner's capital

cash flow statement
a financial statement which measures the flow of money in and out of a business over a financial period (not assessed in this unit)

accounting ratio
a financial indicator, which can be a ratio, a percentage or a time period, extracted from the financial statements of a business to provide stakeholders with a means of assessing its financial state

current ratio
current assets : current liabilities

acid test ratio
current assets minus stock : current liabilities

gross profit %
$$\frac{\text{gross profit} \times 100}{\text{sales}}$$

net profit %
$$\frac{\text{net profit} \times 100}{\text{sales}}$$

return on capital employed
$$\frac{\text{net profit} \times 100}{\text{owners capital}}$$

stock turnover (days)
$$\frac{\text{average stock} \times 365 \text{ days}}{\text{cost of sales}}$$

debtors collection period
$$\frac{\text{debtors} \times 365 \text{ days}}{\text{sales for year}}$$

asset turnover
$$\frac{\text{sales (£)}}{\text{net assets (£)}}$$

share price
the price (in pence) of a traded share

dividend yield
$$\frac{\text{share dividend (in pence)}}{\text{market price of share (in pence)}} \times 100$$

price/earnings ratio
$$\frac{\text{market price of share (in pence)}}{\text{earnings (ie profit earned) per share (in pence)}}$$

23 Budgeting in business

Unit 5 Business finance
Budgeting

introduction

The management of a business needs to plan for the future, both for the short term and for the long term. Short-term plans involve the drawing up of budgets which set annual targets for different functions within the business. As the year passes the budget targets are compared with the actual figures and discrepancies are picked up and action is taken as appropriate. Budgets therefore help management to keep its 'fingers on the pulse' of the business and thereby control it.

what you will learn from this chapter

● business planning can be long-term (the five year 'corporate plan') or short-term (the one year 'operational plan')

● an important part of the business planning process is the setting of budgets which help management to measure performance and to make decisions

● budgets can be function budgets (which set targets for functional areas within the business), and departmental budgets (which cover the performance of individual departments)

● the individual budgets combine into the cash budget (which forecasts the flow of money in and out of the business bank account) and the master budget (which sets out a forecast profit and loss account and a forecast balance sheet)

● budgets can be income budgets (eg sales budget) or expenditure budgets (eg staffing budget); they are normally expressed in money terms, but can be expressed in units (eg production budget)

● during the course of the year the budget projections will be compared with the actual figures and any difference ('variance') will be reported and acted upon

introduction to business planning

business planning and business plans

What is business planning? It is an ongoing process involving the setting of objectives and the monitoring of progress. It is important not to confuse the business planning process with the 'business plan' document you will encounter if you study Unit 6 'Business Planning'. This 'business plan' is a formal written document compiled normally when a business wants to raise finance. It is presented to a lender or major investor and sets out in a persuasive way why lending to the business (or investing in the business) is a feasible proposition. The business plan is the way a business 'sells itself' to a provider of finance, such as a bank.

the planning and monitoring cycle

Businesses should constantly be planning ahead. They may be planning specific projects, or they may be looking at the year ahead in order to calculate staffing and estimate sales. Whatever the situation, there are four distinct stages in the planning process:

1 set objectives – for example to increase sales by 25%

2 collect information – assess the situation – can the business produce 25% more goods? how much will it cost? can it sell them?

3 make specific plans – expand production, take on more staff

4 see how the business is getting on – the business can look at its sales figures each month, see if it is achieving its target, and try to do something about it if it is not

Now see how these four stages form the planning cycle shown in the diagram below. As we will see later, they all involve budgeting.

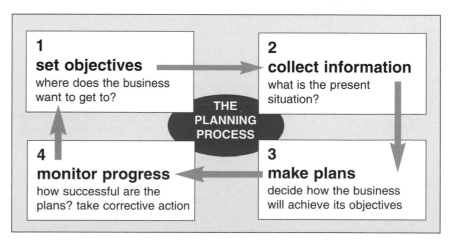

types of plans

Planning by a business can be divided into three distinct areas:

mission statement and vision statement

A mission statement is a public statement by the business setting out in general terms what the business does, what it aims to achieve, its values and standards. A vision statement is a more general statement of how the business sees itself developing in the future – a 'vision' of what it wants to be.

corporate plan

This contains the long-term objectives of the business (up to five years, for example) and involves all areas of business activity, eg profitability, market share, product range, staffing, environmental policy. The Corporate Plan is the responsibility of the highest levels of management of the business.

operational plans and budgets

The operational planning process follows the setting of objectives, ie the Corporate Plan and the gathering of internal and external information. Operational plans are normally for one year in functional areas such as sales, marketing, production, finance, human resources and administration. Operational plans set out the detail dictated by the objectives of the business, eg the number of products produced, pay rates, the amount of finance to be raised, the introduction of new technology. These plans will set specific targets for the business – and will require budgets (see below).

Operational plans are normally set by individual departments within the business – eg sales and marketing, production, finance – and will be the responsibility of the departmental manager. Operational plans are normally set for one financial year at a time. Plans are constantly reviewed and monitored by the people responsible for them. Towards the end of each year, new plans will be drawn up for the following year, taking into account all the developments during the current year.

budget setting

Operational plans involve the setting of budgets by departments and also by function. What exactly is a budget?

A budget is a table setting out projected figures for specific areas of business activity such as sales and production.

A budget is a method of planning, monitoring and controlling business activity.

A budget is based on information – past and current – and forecasts. It covers a set period of time, normally a year. A budget can deal with:

- income – eg from sales

- expenditure – eg production, staffing

A budget is commonly set in financial terms, eg a sales revenue budget, but it can also be expressed in terms of units, eg items produced, workers employed, items sold.

timescale of budgets

Most budgets are prepared for the financial year, and are usually broken down into shorter time periods, usually monthly. As time passes the actual figures achieved by the business can be compared with the budgeted figures and the differences between the two – the'variances' – can be entered on a report and investigated if necessary.

benefits of budgets

Budgets provide benefits both for the business and also for its managers:

assisting decision making

Budgets help the management of businesses to see the outcome of different courses of action and to make decisions accordingly.

motivating staff

Budgets motivate staff by setting targets which have to be met. This can, of course, only take place if the targets are realistic!

measuring performance

Budgets enable businesses to see how successful they are in meeting targets, eg sales, production, staff costs.

types of budget

There are two main types of budget: the function budget and the departmental budget.

function budget

The function budget is a plan for a specific function within a business, eg:

- sales budget – which covers sales income to be received by the business

- production budget – which covers the number and cost of items produced

- staffing budget – which plans the workforce's wages and salaries costs

departmental budget

The costs of running a business set out in the function budgets are also included by its operating departments in departmental budgets, eg sales department budget, administration department budget. The object here is to make each department run efficiently: its managers – known as the budget holders – will be set specific targets for spending and productivity in terms of staffing and spending, for example.

the master budget

The end result of the budgeting process is the production of a cash budget and a master budget which takes the form of forecast financial statements – an estimated profit and loss account and balance sheet at the end of the budget period. The master budget is the 'master plan' which shows how all the budgets 'work together'. Look at the diagram on the next page, which shows how all the budgets are related to each other.

limiting factors

A limiting factor is an aspect of the business which prevents it from expanding its operations any further – for example the volume of its products that it can sell. Other limiting factors include the availability of raw materials, skilled labour, factory and office space, or finance.

It is essential to identify these limiting factors. For most businesses the main limiting factor is sales – how much of its product range can a business sell? The starting point for the budgeting process is therefore normally the sales budget. The order in which the budgets are drafted will often be:

- **sales budget** – what can the business sell in the next twelve months?
- **production budget** – how can the business make all the items which it plans to sell?
- **staffing**, **purchases** and **overheads budgets** – what resources in terms of labour and raw materials will the business need to produce the items? – what other expenses will be incurred?
- **departmental budgets** – what resources will be needed by individual departments?
- **capital budget** – what fixed assets (eg machinery, vehicles) need to be purchased over the next twelve months?
- **cash budget** – what money will be flowing in and out of the bank account?
- **master budget** – a summary of all the budgets to provide projected financial statements, ie a profit and loss account and balance sheet

Study the diagram on the next page. It shows this process in action . . .

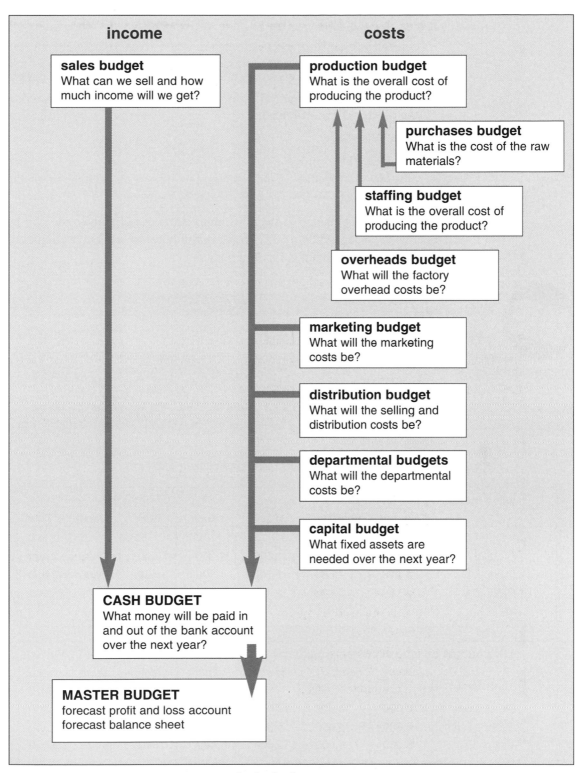

income

costs

sales budget
What can we sell and how much income will we get?

production budget
What is the overall cost of producing the product?

purchases budget
What is the cost of the raw materials?

staffing budget
What is the overall cost of producing the product?

overheads budget
What will the factory overhead costs be?

marketing budget
What will the marketing costs be?

distribution budget
What will the selling and distribution costs be?

departmental budgets
What will the departmental costs be?

capital budget
What fixed assets are needed over the next year?

CASH BUDGET
What money will be paid in and out of the bank account over the next year?

MASTER BUDGET
forecast profit and loss account
forecast balance sheet

the budgeting process

how budgets 'work'

This Unit does not require you to construct all the different types of budget 'from scratch', but rather to appreciate:

- the different types of budget
- what they are for
- how they work
- how they 'fit together' in the planning process – as in the diagram on the previous page

The Cash Budget is one of the most important types of budget and will be dealt with on pages 529 to 537. The Case Study below sets out examples of some of the most common types of budget.

Case Study

Osborne Giftware Ltd
setting the budgets

Osborne Giftware Limited imports novelty goods and sells them in the UK through shops, agency sales and mail order. It also manufactures a limited number of games in its factory near Bolton.

sales budgets

Set out below are two of its sales budgets for the coming year.

sales budget by product (extract)	January	February	March	April	May	June	Total
	£	£	£	£	£	£	£
Product A	1,000	1,000	1,000	1,000	1,000	1,000	6,000
Product B	1,500	1,500	1,500	1,500	1,500	1,500	9,000
Product C	2,500	2,500	2,500	2,500	2,500	2,500	15,000
etc . . .							

sales budget by type of customer (extract)	January	February	March	April	May	June	Total
	£	£	£	£	£	£	£
Direct sales	10,000	10,000	10,000	12,000	12,000	12,000	66,000
Agency sales	5,000	5,000	5,000	5,000	5,000	5,000	30,000
Mail order	5,000	5,000	6,000	5,000	6,000	6,000	33,000
etc . . .							

Certain aspects of the structure of the sales budget (and any budget) will stay constant, whether they are income budgets or expenditure budgets. For example, the budget is subdivided into 'budget periods': either months or four-weekly periods (the 52 week year is conveniently divided into 13 four-weekly periods). The extracts from the sales budgets on the previous page show six of the usual twelve monthly periods.

production budget

When Osborne Giftware has established its sales budget ('How many of each product can we sell?') it is then in a position to work out its production budget for the items it manufactures ('How can we make those products on time?'). It must be stressed that a production budget applies to a manufacturing business; a business providing a service will carry out a similar process using an 'operating budget.'

The production budget will take into account when in the year the manufactured items (games) will be needed and when they are likely to be sold. The budget therefore shows:
- the projected monthly sales figures
- the finished products in stock at the beginning and end of each month

production budget

UNITS	Jan	Feb	Mar	Apr	May	Jun	Jul	Aug	Sep	Oct	Nov	Dec
Opening stock	100	275	450	600	550	500	450	300	175	325	475	125
add Units produced	325	325	350	350	350	350	350	175	350	350	350	400
less Units sold	150	150	200	400	400	400	500	300	200	200	700	425
Closing stock	275	450	600	550	500	450	300	175	325	475	125	100

You will see from the production budget that it shows units of production. When the monthly production of units has been calculated, the budget can then be expressed in money terms – it will become a production cost budget. This will be made possible by applying a standard cost worked out by the business from the raw materials cost, the labour cost and the overheads (other expenses) which were needed to manufacture a single unit of production.

staffing budget

The staffing budget is a function budget which covers the staffing costs of all the departments within the business. It includes the pay before deductions, the employer's National Insurance and pension contributions. Six months' figures are shown here.

staffing budget (extract)

	January £	February £	March £	April £	May £	June £
Gross pay	40,000	40,000	40,000	40,000	40,000	40,000
National Insurance	4,080	4,080	4,080	4,080	4,080	4,080
Pension payments	2,000	2,000	2,000	2,000	2,000	2,000

budget reports – variances

The budget, once it is set for the financial year, is monitored by comparing actual results with the targeted figures. Any differences between the two are known as **variances**.

budgeted figures – actual figures = variances

Departmental managers in a business (in charge of 'budget centres') will base their decisions on departmental **budget reports**, normally produced by the finance department. Less significant variances will be dealt with by the manager and his supervisors; significant variances will need to be referred to a higher management level. Many variances, if they are very small, will not need acting on at all.

The illustration below sets out the format of a typical budget report for a sales department. The details shown are:

- the budget centre (sales department) and the budget holder responsible (the manager)
- budget, actual and variance figures for the current period (October here)
- year-to-date figures (these are optional)
- the variance trends: 'FAV' is short for 'favourable', ie better than budget, 'ADV' is short for 'adverse', ie worse than budget
- comments – the column here would be enough to record the reasons for smaller variances, but the manager would expect to receive a more detailed report for significant variances

BUDGET REPORT

Budget Centre Sales Department   **Budget Holder** T Hussain

Period October 2001   **Date** 7 November 2001

	current period				year-to-date				comments
	budget £000	actual £000	variance £000	trend	budget £000	actual £000	variance £000	trend	
Product A	200	250	+ 50	FAV	2,750	3,125	+ 375	FAV	
Product B	225	200	- 25	ADV	1,275	1,150	- 125	ADV	
Product C	425	450	+ 25	FAV	4,025	4,475	+ 450	FAV	

factors that cause variances

You may be asked in your assessment to:

- identify different types of variance
- comment on the factors that cause those variances

sales variance

sales variance = actual sales minus budgeted sales

A **favourable** (positive) variance will result when sales are better than budgeted. This might be the result of the price going up when demand for the product is strong, or special promotional offers for the product.

An **adverse** (negative) variance will result when sales are worse than budgeted. A *fall* in sales income from a particular product might be the result of overpricing or ineffective marketing.

Whatever the cause, if the variance is significant, management will need to take action. If sales are better than budget, management will make sure the success is continued through pushing up production and ensuring the marketing effort is continued. If sales are down, management will want to know why. Is the price right? Can marketing be improved? Is the product going out of fashion? Should the business be switching to other products?

The sales variance relates to **income**. Materials, labour and overhead variances, on the other hand, relate to **expenses**.

materials variance

materials variance = standard (budgeted) cost of materials minus actual cost

Note here that the budgeted cost is referred to as the 'standard cost'. This is the cost of the quantity of materials a manufacturing business expects to use.

A **favourable** (positive) variance will result when costs are lower than budgeted: the cost of the materials may have gone down, or the quantity of materials used may have gone down.

An **adverse** (negative) variance will result when costs are higher than budgeted: the cost of the materials may have gone up, or the quantity of materials used may have increased.

labour variance

labour variance = standard (budgeted) cost of labour minus actual cost

Here standard cost is the budgeted total labour cost: the expected number of hours worked multiplied by the appropriate wage rate.

A **favourable** (positive) variance will result when labour costs are lower than budgeted: the wage rate may have gone down (unlikely!), or the number of hours worked may be fewer – the business may have become more efficient.

An **adverse** (negative) variance will result when labour costs are higher than budgeted: there may have been an unexpected wage rise, or the number of hours worked may have increased more than was expected (the machinery or the computer systems may have broken down a lot, leaving people idle).

overhead variance

The overheads are the running costs of the business.

overhead variance = standard (budgeted) cost of overheads minus actual cost

Here standard cost is the budgeted overhead cost: the expected cost of the running expenses of the business.

A **favourable** (positive) variance will result when running costs are lower than budgeted: the business may have switched to a cheaper power company or telephone provider; it may have moved to offices with lower rental.

An **adverse** (negative) variance will result when running costs are higher than budgeted: rates and office rental may have gone up unexpectedly, or the telephone bill may have risen after a telesales campaign.

Note that overheads are either **fixed** and do not vary with the number of items produced (eg office rental) – or **variable** (eg electricity bill) and vary with the volume of items produced. Sometimes a business may calculate separate variances for fixed overheads and variable overheads (see below).

Activity 23.1

Investigating variances – costs

	standard (budgeted) cost £	actual cost £
materials	30,000	27,000
labour	60,000	75,000
overheads:		
fixed	30,000	27,500
variable	10,000	11,000
TOTAL COST	130,000	140,500

You have been presented with the above cost figures for a manufacturing company.

1 Calculate the variances for the four types of cost.
2 Identify whether they are adverse or favourable.
3 Suggest some factors which might have caused each of the variances.
4 If you were a manager of this business what would you want to investigate?

Activity 23.2

Commenting on the sales budget report
Premium Soft Drinks

Premium Soft Drinks manufacturers a range of drinks which it distributes throughout the UK.

You are given the following information about Premium's three main brands:

Sunzest is a healthy, additive free juice drink based on orange and lemon extracts aimed at the adult market.

Tingle is a brightly-coloured fizzy drink, aimed at the children's market.

Zing is a carbonated drink, sold in a fashionable can mainly to the teens market.

During the year the following events have occurred:

- all brands have been heavily advertised
- the summer was exceptionally hot
- early in the year there was a health scare over food dyes in children's food and drink
- in the summer a competitor launched a new competitively priced, additive free, children's drink which proved very popular

You are to:

1   Write comments on the performance of the three brands shown in the budget report. Explain in each case the factors that have made the variance favourable or adverse, adding any further points which you think might be relevant.

2   State what course of action the manufacturer might take to reverse any adverse trend.

BUDGET REPORT: Premium Soft Drinks

Budget Centre Sales Department   **Budget Holder** R Bolt
Period October 2001   **Date** 7 November 2001

	current period			year-to-date			trend	comments
	budget £000	actual £000	variance £000	budget £000	actual £000	variance £000		
Sunzest	200	250	+ 50	2,750	3,125	+ 375	FAV	
Tingle	225	200	- 25	1,275	1,150	- 125	ADV	
Zing	425	450	+ 25	4,025	4,475	+ 450	FAV	

Completing the sales budget report
Paradise Travel

Paradise Travel is a holiday company which sells UK and foreign holidays largely by telephone, mail order and from its website. During the last few years it has seen considerable growth in foreign holidays, largely because of the poor UK weather and the strength of the pound sterling against other currencies.

The budget for the current year is as follows:

holiday type	budgeted sales	actual sales	variance	FAV or ADV
	£	£	£	
UK	540,000			
European Ski	450,000			
European Sun	670,000			
USA Florida Sun	375,000			
USA Ski	230,000			
TOTAL	2,265,000			

The sales figures for the present year are shown on the right.

You have been told that a number of factors have affected sales of holidays during the year. These include: a strong pound sterling, bad summer weather in the UK, scare reports about avalanches in the Alps, the popularity

holiday type	actual sales
UK	496,000
European Ski	396,000
European Sun	801,000
USA Florida Sun	453,000
USA Ski	286,000

of TV 'holiday rep' programmes set in the Mediterranean area, the popularity of Disney theme parks, good snow conditions in the US mountains, cheap US flights.

You are to:

1 Draw up a budget report based on the format shown above, enter the actual sales figures and total, work out the variances and state whether they are 'FAV' or 'ADV'.

2 Take each of the types of holiday in turn and link them to the factors listed above.

3 Suggest ways in which any adverse trends, given the same conditions, could be reversed in the coming year.

4 State what could happen to sales in the coming year if the pound sterling fell in value against the US dollar and European currencies before the holiday prices had been fixed.

the cash budget

If you look at the diagram on page 521 you will see that all the main budgets contribute to the cash budget, which in turn provides the data for the master budget – the forecast financial statements. The cash budget is therefore central to every business: it projects the amounts of money received into and paid out of the bank account each month. A typical cash budget sets out:

- the expected bank account receipts and payments
- on a month-by-month basis
- for a twelve month period

The cash budget (also known as the cash flow forecast) shows projections of all money received and money spent over the year (including VAT), eg sales income, running expenses, payment of tax and purchase of capital items. The 'bottom line' of each monthly column shows the forecast bank balance at the end of that month.

format of the cash budget

A simplified format of a cash budget, with sample figures, is set out below. Study it carefully and read the explanation which follows.

Name ....Cash Flow Forecast for the .... months ending ....

	Jan £000	Feb £000	Mar £000	etc... £000
Receipts				
sales receipts	150	150	161	170
other receipts (loans, capital, VAT recovered)	70	80	75	80
Total receipts for month (A)	220	230	236	250
Payments				
to suppliers for raw materials or stock (creditors)	160	165	170	170
other payments (eg expenses, loans repaid, VAT paid)	50	50	50	60
fixed assets purchased		50		
Total payments for month (B)	210	265	220	230
Opening bank balance at beginning of month	10	20	(15)	1
add total receipts (A)	220	230	236	250
less total payments (B)	210	265	220	230
Bank balance (overdraft) at end of month	20	(15)	1	21

receipts

These are analysed for each month to show the amount that is expected to be received from sources such as cash sales, receipts from customers supplied on credit, sale of fixed assets, loans, capital introduced, any interest or other income received. Any refund of VAT received from H M Customs & Excise will also appear in this section.

payments

This section will show how much is expected to be paid each month for cash purchases, to creditors (suppliers), running expenses, purchases of fixed assets, repayment of capital and loans, and interest paid. If the business is VAT registered, VAT due to H M Customs & Excise will also appear here. (Businesses have to send off the VAT that they charge on invoices).

bank

The bank summary at the bottom of the budget shows the bank balance at the beginning of the month, to which all receipts are added (A) and payments deducted (B) resulting in the estimated closing bank balance at the end of the month. An overdrawn bank balance is shown in brackets, or by a minus sign.

timing and the cash budget

The important thing to remember when preparing cash budgets is that receipts and payments are entered in the column for the month in which they are received and paid. This may sound an obvious statement, but if you take into account products sold on credit and products bought on credit you will see that the money often changes hands months after the sale or purchase. Therefore great care must be taken in the following areas:

credit periods

The cash budget must take into consideration credit periods given on invoices issued and received. For example, if you are told that a business allows two months credit for the products it sells, it means that a sale invoiced in January will be paid for in March and entered as a sales receipt in the cash budget in the March column. In short there is a two month timing lag between sales and sales receipts.

In the same way, if you are told that a business is given one month credit for purchases made (eg stock) it means that a purchase made and invoiced in January will be paid for in February and entered in the cash budget in the February column. Here there is a one month timing lag.

Bills, too, (eg phone and power bills) are entered in the month in which they are paid, even if they apply to periods before or after the payment date.

constructing the cash budget

We will now explain the various headings which appear in the Receipts and Payments sections of the cash budget by means of a Case Study. This shows how the forecast is constructed and where the figures come from. Note that all figures include VAT where it is charged.

Case Study

Merry-go-round Limited
drawing up the cash budget

Merry-go-round Limited is a small private limited company. It is a family business which makes outdoor toys for children – slides, swings, climbing frames, trampolines and so on. It operates in a leased factory unit on an industrial estate in Broadfield. It supplies stores throughout the UK and also operates a successful factory shop which has the benefit of a cash sales income.

Tom Merry, the Managing Director, is looking to expand the company by purchasing in January new machinery which will enable the business to manufacture its own moulded plastic products. The machinery will cost £50,000 and will be financed partly by a bank loan for £25,000 and partly by new capital of £25,000 introduced by the shareholders (the Merry family). Tom realises that the expansion will also mean that extra working capital is required, and will probably need to be financed by a bank overdraft. The question is, how much cash will the company need?

With the help of his accountant he draws up:

• a capital budget showing the purchase of the new machinery in January of the following year

• a sales budget and a production budget showing the increased sales and costs for the year

He now needs to construct a cash budget to include in the Business Plan which he will take to the bank when he applies for finance. He uses a computer spreadsheet to set out the forecast, with a number of different headings in the receipts and payments sections.

As you read the following descriptions, refer to the cash budget shown on pages 534 and 535

receipts

cash sales   The factory shop is likely to take £8,000 per month in January and February, and then £9,000 a month when the new products are introduced (figures include VAT).

credit sales	Money received from credit sales is normally received in the month following issue of the invoice. Tom reckons he will receive £18,000 a month in January, February and March, and £25,000 a month for the rest of the year, following the introduction of the new products.
capital	The shareholders (the Merry family) will introduce £25,000 in January to help finance the new machinery.
loans	The bank is being asked for a £25,000 business loan to help finance the new machinery in January.

payments

raw materials	These are paid for a month after the invoice date. It is estimated they will cost £15,000 a month for the first four months of the year and £17,000 a month after that.
capital assets	The new machinery costing £50,000 will be bought and paid for in January.
wages	The wages bill for the company averages £10,000 a month.
water rates	Water rates for the year have to be paid for in advance in April. The company's water rates are £1,457.
telephone	Telephone bills, on the other hand, are paid for quarterly in arrears. On the basis of the previous year's bills they are likely to average £565 a quarter, paid in January, April, July and October.
heat and light	Gas and electricity bills are also paid for in arrears. They will average in total £650 a quarter, paid in January, April, July and October.
insurance	The company's comprehensive insurance premium of £7,500 is due in advance in June.
other costs	Other costs such as office expenses and advertising average £615 a month, paid monthly.
interest costs	Tom calculates that interest on his borrowing, including any overdraft will be £680 (March), £720 (June), £650 (September), £630 (December).
Loan repayments	Repayments on bank borrowing are £4,000 a quarter (March, June, September, December).
VAT	The company is registered for VAT and will have to send a cheque off with the VAT return every quarter. The amount each time will be VAT charged on sales less VAT paid on expenses over the previous three months.

totalling up the forecast

When the figures have been entered in the appropriate columns (see the next two pages), the following totals will be calculated by Tom's computer spreadsheet in the far right-hand column and the bank summary at the bottom of the forecast. If a computer spreadsheet is not used, these totals will have to be calculated manually – which is hard work! The figures are:

- totals for each category of receipt or expense in the far right-hand 'total' column (total across each row)

- total receipts for each month, and the far right-hand 'total' column, ie work down the columns

- total payments for each month, and the far right-hand column, ie work down the columns

- cross check the totals for both receipts and payments – ie the total of the monthly columns and the totals in the (far right) total column

- lastly, total monthly receipts and total monthly payments should be entered in the bank position on the appropriate line at the bottom of the forecast

the bank position

The bank position can now be calculated. Refer to the cash budget on the next two pages as you read this section.

opening bank balance Insert the bank balance at the beginning of January in the row marked 'Opening bank', the figure is £125 in this case.

add receipts Add total receipts for the month.

deduct payments Subtract total payments for the month.

closing bank This is the projected month-end bank balance of the business. It is an overdraft of £4,455 in January. This figure should then also be written in as February's 'Opening Bank' balance. The process is then repeated for February, and so on.

The bottom line of the cash budget shows the all-important figure of the closing bank balance (the expected balance at the end of each month).

A minus figure (or a figure in brackets) indicates an overdraft – ie the business will be borrowing from the bank on its current account.

A positive figure means there is money in the bank account. In this case Merry-go-round Limited will be borrowing on overdraft for most months until August when the borrowing will be repaid.

Now look again at the spreadsheet of the cash budget on the next two pages.

Cash Budget for Merry-go-round Limited, produced on a spreadsheet

	A	B	C	D	E	F	G
1	CASH BUDGET						
2	Name: Merry-go-round Limited						
3	Period: January - December 2000						
4							
5		Jan	Feb	Mar	Apr	May	Jun
6		£	£	£	£	£	£
7	RECEIPTS						
8	Cash sales	8000	8000	9000	9000	9000	9000
9	Credit sales	18000	18000	18000	25000	25000	25000
10	Capital	25000					
11	Loans	25000					
12	VAT receipts						
13	Interest						
14	Other income						
15	TOTAL RECEIPTS	76000	26000	27000	34000	34000	34000
16							
17	PAYMENTS						
18	Raw materials	15000	15000	15000	15000	17000	17000
19	Capital assets	50000					
20	Wages	10000	10000	10000	10000	10000	10000
21	Water rates				1457		
22	Telephone	565			565		
23	Heat & light	650			650		
24	Insurance						7500
25	Other costs	615	615	615	615	615	615
26	Interest costs			680			720
27	Loan repayments			4000			4000
28	VAT payments	3750			3885		
29	TOTAL PAYMENTS	80580	25615	30295	32172	27615	39835
30							
31	Opening Bank	125	-4455	-4070	-7365	-5537	848
32	Add Receipts	76000	26000	27000	34000	34000	34000
33	Less Payments	80580	25615	30295	32172	27615	39835
34	Closing Bank	-4455	-4070	-7365	-5537	848	-4987
35							

H	I	J	K	L	M	N
Jul	Aug	Sep	Oct	Nov	Dec	TOTAL
£	£	£	£	£	£	£
9000	9000	9000	9000	9000	9000	106000
25000	25000	25000	25000	25000	25000	279000
						25000
						25000
						0
						0
						0
34000	34000	34000	34000	34000	34000	435000
17000	17000	17000	17000	17000	17000	196000
						50000
10000	10000	10000	10000	10000	10000	120000
						1457
565				565		2260
650				650		2600
						7500
615	615	615	615	615	615	7380
	650				630	2680
		4000			4000	16000
4150				4150		15935
32980	27615	32265	32980	27615	32245	421812
-4987	-3967	2418	4153	5173	11558	125
34000	34000	34000	34000	34000	34000	435000
32980	27615	32265	32980	27615	32245	421812
-3967	2418	4153	5173	11558	13313	13313

the cash budget on a computer spreadsheet

the benefits of a spreadsheet program

The calculations on a cash flow forecast are not particularly difficult, but they do take a long time if you are tackling the task with only pencil, paper and calculator. The task is, of course, made simple when you have input the worksheet onto a computer spreadsheet program. You will be able to change any figure, and the computer will do all the recalculations automatically, for example:

- projections of different levels of sales – optimistic, realistic and pessimistic
- projections of different levels of expenditure
- the effect of buying an asset at different times

In each case you will be able to see the effect on the critical figure of the closing bank balance which indicates the amount of money the business may have to borrow.

use of formulas in the spreadsheet – column C

Extensive use is made in cash flow forecasts of the adding together of a range of cells. You will need to check your computer manual to find the formula to use for your own program. The formula used here is =Sum(C8:C14) where all the cells between C8 and C14 are added together. The formulas for column C are as follows:

- Rows 15 and 32 – Total Receipts   =Sum(C8:C14)

- Rows 29 and 33 – Total Payments   =Sum(C18:C28)

- Row 31 – Opening Bank   =B34

  – ie the closing bank balance of the previous month. Note that B31 is a value cell into which is entered the opening bank balance for the period.

- Row 34 – Closing Bank   =C31+C32–C33

- Column N – Total column

  Each row is totalled, eg cell N8 is =Sum(B8:M8) and N29 is =Sum(N18:N28). Column N is also totalled vertically, in the same way as the other columns, except that cell N31 is =B31 and cell N34 is =M34. N32 is =Sum(B32:M32) and N33 is =Sum(B33:M33).

Activity 23.4

Merry-go-round Limited
cash budget on the computer

The tasks in this Activity should be carried out using a computer spreadsheet program. If you are unable to gain access to a suitable system, you should set up the budgets using pencil, paper and calculator, but bear in mind that this will be a more laborious and less flexible alternative.

If you have the time and the opportunity, show the Case Study and completed spreadsheets to a bank lending officer to find out how a lender would react to the proposal.

1   Set up a computer spreadsheet for Merry-go-round Limited and input the figures from the source data in the Case Study. Try to avoid using the finished cash budget! Print out the forecast and check the figures against those shown in the Case Study.

2   The accountant of Merry-go-round Limited is unhappy about presenting a single cash budget to the bank and asks that a "best view" and "worst view" scenario are forecast on the following basis:

   (a) The best view assumes that:

   •   cash sales receipts increase to £11,000 per month from March

   •   credit sales receipts increase to £28,000 per month from April

   (b) The worst view assumes that the new machine fails to work and that the monthly sales receipts for the year stay at their January level.

   You are to set up two new spreadsheet files based on (a) and (b). Amend the sales receipts figures only. For the sake of simplicity do not attempt to adjust any other figures. Print out the two new files.

3   (a) What do the three forecasts show, and what would be the likely reaction of a lender such as a bank? How would the "best view" and "worst view" alternatives affect the proposed bank loan?

   (b) In the case of the "best view" and "worst view" scenarios, discuss the effect the increase and decrease in sales might have on raw materials purchases, VAT payable and interest payable.

CHAPTER SUMMARY

- Business planning involves setting objectives for a business.

- The planning process involves four stages:
    - setting the objectives – where the business wants to get to
    - collecting information which will enable the business to assess the present situation
    - making plans which state how the objectives can be achieved
    - monitoring progress, picking up on any problems and taking corrective action

- Objectives can be set out:
    - simply, as in a mission statement for public consumption
    - in a long-term 'corporate plan' which typically runs for five years
    - in a twelve month 'operational plan'

- Operational plans include the setting of budgets by functions within a business (eg sales, production, staffing) and by individual departments.

- Budgets can be income budgets (eg sales budget) or expenditure budgets (eg staffing budget); they are normally expressed in money terms, but can be expressed in units (eg a production budget).

- The budgeting process is determined by 'limiting factors' which are areas which limit the expansion of the business. For example, the amount of the product range which a business can sell will determine the figures that go into the sales budget, which will be the starting point of the planning process.

- The individual budgets combine into the cash budget (which forecasts the flow of money in and out of the business bank account) and the master budget (which sets out a forecast profit and loss account and a forecast balance sheet).

- Budgets must be monitored during the year – often four weekly or monthly. The budget projections will be compared with the actual figures in a budget report and any difference ('variance') will be reported and acted upon. If the actual figures are better than budgeted the variance will be favourable (FAV), if they are worse the variance is adverse (ADV). Managers must look carefully at the causes of any variance and take action accordingly.

- The cash budget shows the flow of money in and out of the bank account and forecasts the bank balance at the end of each month. It is an important budget, not only for management for internal monitoring, but also as a way of presenting the future financial state of the business to a lender such as a bank.

KEY TERMS

mission statement	a public statement made by a business setting out the activities, aims and values of the business
corporate plan	a long-term (typically five year) plan which sets out the overall long-term 'strategic' objectives of the business
operational plan	a short-term (one year) plan setting targets for specific functional areas within a business; an operational plan will normally contain a budget
budget	a table setting out performance targets for a specific area within a business
functional budget	a budget for a specific function within a business, eg sales, production, staffing
departmental budget	a budget for a specific department within a business
capital budget	a budget for the purchase of fixed assets
cash budget	a budget projecting the flow of money in and out of the bank account and forecasting the bank balance at the end of each month, also known as the 'cash flow forecast'
master budget	the forecast profit and loss account for the year, together with a balance sheet as at the year end
limiting factor	an aspect of the business which prevents it from expanding any further
favourable variance	the difference between the budgeted figure and the actual figure when the actual figure is better than the forecast figure – often written as 'FAV'
adverse variance	the difference between the budgeted figure and the actual figure when the actual figure is not as good as the forecast figure – often written as 'ADV'

Control of cash and working capital

introduction

We saw in the last chapter that the cash budget is a vital management tool in the planning and control of the finance of a business. In this chapter we look more closely at the control of cash and working capital in a business. We examine techniques for improving levels of cash and working capital and avoiding some of the dangers brought about by neglecting the principles of financial control.

what you will learn from this chapter

- cash passes through a business in a 'money cycle' which involves payments in and out of the bank account, as projected in the cash budget seen in the last chapter

- if the supply of cash coming into the business is restricted the bank account will come under pressure and become overdrawn; if the situation becomes very serious, the business could run out of cash and 'go bust' because it is unable to meet its commitments

- a business also relies on sufficient levels of working capital – this includes cash and also items such as stock and debtors which can be turned into cash; it is calculated as current assets minus current liabilities and measured through performance indicators such as the current and acid test ratios

- a business is able to control and improve its levels of cash and working capital through management of current assets and current liabilities, for example:

  – controlling stock levels to a minimum (stock ties up cash)

  – ensuring debtors pay up on time (releasing the cash needed)

  – paying suppliers as late as possible (hanging onto the cash)

the cash cycle

the importance of cash

It is often said that cash is the 'lifeblood' of any business. When the supply of cash dries up, the business fails. In this section we look in detail at how cash circulates in the business. As a first step, study the diagram below which shows the cash flowing in and out of a manufacturing business.

Then read the notes on the next page.

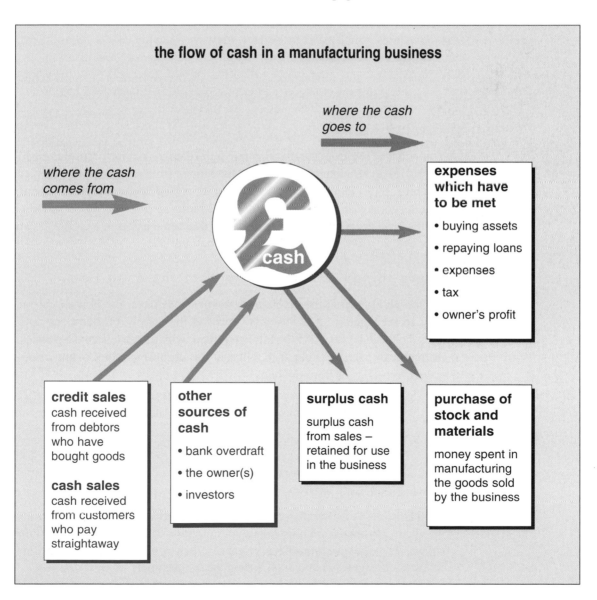

the flow of cash in a manufacturing business

where the cash goes to

where the cash comes from

£ cash

expenses which have to be met

• buying assets

• repaying loans

• expenses

• tax

• owner's profit

credit sales
cash received from debtors who have bought goods

cash sales
cash received from customers who pay straightaway

other sources of cash

• bank overdraft

• the owner(s)

• investors

surplus cash

surplus cash from sales – retained for use in the business

purchase of stock and materials

money spent in manufacturing the goods sold by the business

where the cash comes from

As you will see from the left-hand side of the diagram on the previous page, there are two main sources of cash:

- cash from the sale of the products of the business – the more the business sells, the more cash it will receive
- cash received from other sources, for example the bank overdraft, cash introduced by the owner(s) or other investors

where the cash goes

As you will see from the right-hand side of the diagram on the previous page, there are two main 'drains' on the supply of cash:

- expenses which have to be met anyway – buying assets (equipment), repaying loans, paying the owner(s), running expenses and taxation
- paying for the product being sold – in the case of a manufacturing business this will be stocks of raw materials and related expenses

surplus cash

You will also see from the diagram that a third arrow points to 'surplus cash'. If a business is trading profitably, and the money from sales is being received promptly, the amount of cash over time will exceed the amount being spent. As a result, a cash surplus or residue will build up, possibly in an interest-paying bank account. The business can be described as being 'liquid' – it can afford to pay off the amounts it owes as they fall due.

where things can go wrong with the cash flow

As you will see from the diagram on the previous page, the flow of cash is vital to the running of a business. Just as the supply of electricity to a household can be cut off if the bill is not paid, with disastrous consequences, the owner of a business can face failure if the 'cash flow' is not maintained – either from sales or from the bank!

This cycle of money coming in and out of the business can be very precariously balanced. For example:

- what if sales fall well below the targets set?
- what if a big customer who owes money goes 'bust'?
- what if the bank will not lend any more money on overdraft?

In all these cases the supply of cash will be reduced and the business may not be able to pay important bills or pay its suppliers. Look at the danger points shown on the diagram on the next page. Then read the Case Study which follows – it shows what can go wrong when the supply of cash dries up.

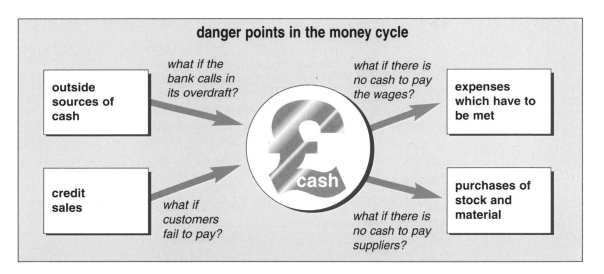

danger points in the money cycle

outside sources of cash

what if the bank calls in its overdraft?

what if there is no cash to pay the wages?

expenses which have to be met

credit sales

what if customers fail to pay?

what if there is no cash to pay suppliers?

purchases of stock and material

cash

Case Study

John Spender
cash flow problems

situation

John Spender has started up in business making novelty clocks. He buys quartz clock mechanisms from a wholesaler whom he pays 30 days after he has received the goods and the invoice. He makes the casings from wood and plastic in his workshop. He employs two production workers and does all the marketing, selling and administration himself.

He is very pleased that he has been able to secure contracts to supply a major department store chain and a catalogue mail order company with his clocks. They agree to pay him 60 days after he has supplied and invoiced the goods. He has a £5,000 overdraft with the Albion Bank to provide 'cash flow' for the period after he has paid for his materials, but before he receives payment from his two big customers.

this is what happens:

November

He and his production workers start to work flat out to supply the orders received – which are larger than expected. He has had to order more materials than expected, and his wages bill is bigger.

December

He has to pay for his first month's supplies. He has to borrow from the bank on overdraft to pay for them. The bank manager is reasonably happy about this, although he says the amount of £6,000 is larger than he was expecting from John's forecast (his Cash Budget).

January

Disaster strikes. The department store's buyer telephones to say that some of the clocks have been returned by their customers complaining that they are faulty. The department store is returning the faulty ones, and will not pay for the remainder until they have been sold. The mail order company, on the other hand, have had no problems, and he receives his first cheque from them. John is so busy that he fails to tell the bank what is happening.

February

John issues a cheque to the supplier of the quartz mechanisms, but the bank refuse to pay it, saying that the overdraft is too high – he has borrowed too much already. The supplier refuses to send any more mechanisms. John only has three weeks' supply left in stock.

March

John finds that he has to lay off his production workers – he cannot make any more clocks, and he cannot supply orders received. He has no money to pay the workers.

April

The bank makes formal demand for its overdraft, which now stands at £8,500; the bank wants its money back. It has a mortgage over John's house, and can sell it if John cannot repay the borrowing.

May

John's business fails. He is insolvent – he owes more than he has got.

Activity 24.1

Cash flow problems

Read through the John Spender Case Study and answer the following questions:

1 What is the document John has shown to the bank, telling them how much money he is going to need to borrow from them?

2 How much did John think he was going to need to borrow?

3 Why was he going to need this money?

4 Why did the amount of cash needed exceed his initial forecasts (ie before he sent out any goods)?

5 What technical problem occurred which meant that his supply of cash began to run out?

6 Was it a good idea just to sell to two customers? How could John have solved this problem?

7 Why did the supplier of quartz mechanisms refuse to supply any more?

8 Why did John lay off his production workers? What would have happened if he had kept them on?

9 What was the final 'death blow' to John's business. What could happen to him and his family?

10 What could John have done to avoid his business failing? Discuss this in class.

avoiding insolvency

what is Insolvency?

Insolvency is owing more than you have got and being unable to pay debts as they fall due. If the people who are owed money – the creditors – consider they can get their money back through the courts they can do so by:

- making an individual (sole trader or partner) 'bankrupt'
- 'winding up' a company or asking for a company 'administration order'

The end-result of these legal processes is that the assets (belongings) of the individual or company will be sold under court supervision to pay off the creditors.

As you will see from the John Spender Case Study, business failure is often a result of cash flow failure. It is not always entirely the fault of the business owner(s) – bad luck can occur – but good financial management can help.

how to avoid cash flow failure

Problems caused by cash flow drying up can normally be pinpointed to certain areas. Good management of these areas can help avoid this situation:

- management of debtors – getting them to pay up in good time
- management of creditors – paying suppliers as late as possible (but within the agreed terms!)
- management of stock – not holding onto too much stock

All these items form part of working capital. It is the wider issue of working capital management which we will look at next.

working capital cycle

definition of working capital

In the last section we looked at the circulation of cash in a business and the importance of making sure there is enough to meet bills and pay suppliers. Cash is just part of the working capital:

working capital = current assets *minus* current liabilities

The liquidity of a business – its ability to repay its debts as they fall due – is measured in terms of its ability to raise cash from its current assets, eg by selling stock, by getting its debtors to pay up.

the working capital cycle

Working capital must keep circulating for a business to survive. The diagram below, which is based on a trading business, shows a series of stages:

1 creditors sell goods to the business on credit

2 stock is sold to customers (debtors) on credit, or for cash (cash sales)

3 debtors make payment and the money is paid into the bank

4 the business pays the creditors from the bank account

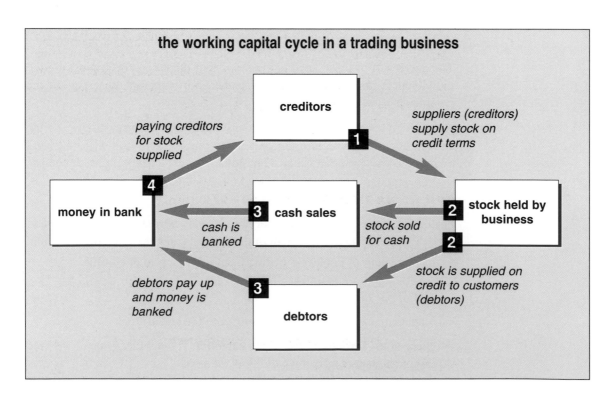

the working capital cycle in a trading business

The bank account will of course also see other payments in (eg loans raised) and payments out (purchase of fixed assets such as computers) which will affect the bank balance. The important point is that the business controls the cycle, as we will see shortly.

measuring working capital

accounting ratios

As we saw in Chapter 22, 'Interpreting Financial Information', the current ratio measures the relationship between current assets and current liabilities:

current ratio = current assets : current liabilities

The acid test ratio shows the same relationship but deducts stock from the current assets, taking the view that the stock may be out of date or unsaleable:

acid test ratio = current assets minus stock : current liabilities

Chapter 22 also showed that setting a standard for these ratios has to be viewed with great caution. For example, the normal recommended current ratio of 1.5 : 1 can be thrown out of the window when you look at a shop which sells for cash (and so has no debtors) but buys on credit. Tesco PLC (see page 512) actually has a negative working capital!

working capital cycle

A useful measure of the turn-round of working capital is the working capital cycle measured in days. This is the time lag between the date a business pays for goods it is going to sell and the date it actually gets payment for those goods. Obviously the shorter the time the better from the cash flow point of view. The calculation (with example figures) is:

working capital cycle	days
Time period that goods are in stock on average (nb this is the stock turnover figure - see page 500)	40
plus	
average number of days it takes debtors to pay up (nb this is the debtor collection period - see page 501)	35
equals	75
less	
average number of days it takes to pay creditors	30
WORKING CAPITAL CYCLE	45

Activity 24.2

Working capital cycle

A farming co-operative grows asparagus in its own farms and supplies a big supermarket chain with fresh asparagus in season. The working capital time periods of the two businesses are:

	farmers	supermarket
Period asparagus in stock (growing and harvesting)	120 days	5 days
Time period for payment from debtors	60 days	zero (cash sales)
Time taken to pay creditors	30 days	60 days

You are to:

1   Calculate and explain the working capital cycles of the two businesses.

2   Comment on the differences, explaining why there is a difference and suggesting what you would think about the situation if you were a farmer.

managing working capital

Good working capital management involves:

- **management of debtors** – vetting them in the first place and getting them to pay up in good time

- **management of creditors** – negotiating good prices and discounts, paying suppliers as late as possible, but within the agreed terms

- **management of stock** – not holding onto too much stock, but ensuring that you have enough

These three guidelines clearly apply to manufacturing or retailing businesses which hold stock. The same principles – apart from stock management – apply equally to service industries.

We will now consider each of the principles in turn.

management of debtors

checking out the buyer – 'creditworthiness'

When a business sells on credit to a business it has not dealt with before, it needs to make sure that the buyer is likely to be able to pay for the goods or services sold. The buyer must be creditworthy. It is all very well being able to clinch a sale for your product, but if the buyer goes bankrupt after you have delivered the goods, not only will you lose your money, you may well lose the goods as well! There are various ways in which you can 'check out' the buyer's creditworthiness:

- ask for a trade reference from another business which supplies the buyer
- ask for a reference from the buyer's bank

It is normal commercial practice for a buyer to supply these names and addresses to the seller.

If you are selling to a business you can obtain a credit report, for a fee, from a credit reference agency such as Dun & Bradstreet which collects useful business information. Many credit reference agencies nowadays are on-line.

payment terms

When a business sells goods or services, as we have seen earlier in this chapter, it needs to get the money in as soon as possible. It will have to arrange the most advantageous payment terms. The best terms are a cash sale – the money is received immediately and can be used in the business straightaway.

Normally a business will issue a sales invoice stating the period of time given to the buyer to pay up. The most common period is 30 days. This does not mean, however, that payment will be received then. Businesses often pay on a statement issued at the end of the month. An invoice issued in October will therefore normally be paid after the end of November when the statement is issued. Statistics show that the average payment period in the UK is approximately 45 days.

Some businesses offer a cash discount to buyers: this is a percentage reduction in the bill (often 2.5%) for quick settlement, eg within seven days. Clearly these businesses consider it is better to receive less money straightaway (it costs them 2.5%) rather than wait a month or so and possibly have to borrow that money from a bank and pay bank interest.

You should note that it is an unfortunate fact of business life that large buyers can demand very long payment terms from small sellers who may have to wait up to three months to be paid.

credit control

An efficient business will keep an eye on its sales ledger (which contains all the debtor accounts), making sure that it receives the money that is owed by sending out reminders, and taking stronger measures if necessary, a process known as credit control. The measures a business might take include:

- statement of account – a document setting out what is owed and when it has to be paid, normally sent out monthly – many businesses pay up on receiving a statement (see page 431 for an example)
- telephone call – some businesses which owe money ignore statements and may need reminding by telephone
- chaser letter – for example "we shall be grateful if you will settle up as soon as possible" or "kindly send your cheque by return of post"
- solicitor's letter – you put the matter in the hands of a solicitor or debt collecting agency who will write to the debtor threatening legal action
- court action – if the amount is large, you can take the matter to the civil courts – but only if you think the debtor has got the money

Good credit control means money in the bank for the business; poor credit control means that the business can lose money – people will tend to pay as late as they can, or in some cases not at all, if they can get away with it! If a debt is not paid it is known as a bad debt and will need to be 'written off'.

aged debtors analysis

As part of its credit control procedures a business will regularly draw up an aged debtors analysis. This is often done on a monthly basis when the statements are sent out. The aged debtors analysis sets out a list of debtor account balances with a breakdown of how long each debt has been outstanding, eg current (up to 30 days), 30 days (30 to 60 days), 60 days (60 to 90 days) and so on. The person dealing with credit control can therefore easily identify amounts that need to be chased up in various ways. The longer the period the stronger the remedy. Look at the example shown below.

HELICON LIMITED	AGED DEBTORS ANALYSIS						30 June 2000
Account	**Turnover**	**Credit Limit**	**Balance**	**Current**	**30 days**	**60 days**	**Older**
Hedley Turner & Co	370.00	1000.00	164.50	164.50	0.00	0.00	0.00
Hinchcliff & Co	320.00	750.00	376.00	376.00	0.00	0.00	0.00
Maxwell Nurseries	1730.00	1000.00	1632.75	799.00	833.75	0.00	0.00
Henry James Trading	2025.00	1500.00	1926.88	880.00	46.88	1000.00	0.00
R Patel	425.00	750.00	499.38	499.38	0.00	0.00	0.00
TOTALS	4870.00	5000.00	4599.51	2718.88	880.63	1000.00	0.00

Activity 24.3

Chasing the debtors

Study the aged debtor analysis shown on the previous page and answer the questions set out below. The standard payment terms for customers is 30 days.

1   Which two accounts might give the credit controller cause for concern, and why?

2   If you were the credit controller what would you do to deal with these accounts?

managing the suppliers

long credit

Businesses should always try to obtain as long a credit period as possible (ie pay as late as possible). This will help the flow of working capital. If it is possible, for example, to pay a supplier after sixty days rather than thirty, the amount owed will be available for use in the buyer's business as cash. Alternatively, if the buyer is borrowing from the bank on overdraft, a delay in settling a bill will mean borrowing less, and paying less interest. A business should, however, beware of taking liberties and making a habit of paying later than the due date – the seller may cut off credit altogether!

negotiating terms

It is possible to haggle over prices. It may also be possible to get one supplier to match the price of another (just as many electrical retailers will 'match' the price of another). The less a business has to pay for its supplies, the more working capital will be available.

managing stock

Holding stock costs money and is a drain on working capital, so businesses must steer a middle course between holding too much stock and holding too little stock.

If a business has a high level of stock, cash will have been paid out to finance it – cash which could have been put to better use in the business.

Also, a high level of stock may need a larger warehouse or premises than is necessary, and stockholding costs will be higher.

If on the other hand too little stock is held, sales will be lost if an item is out of stock because the customer will go elsewhere. Some businesses, particularly those in the manufacturing sector, operate a *just-in-time (JIT)* method which, as the name suggests, replaces stock just before it will be needed. This works well until the supply unexpectedly comes to a halt, for example when a natural disaster halts the supply of microchips for computers.

A business therefore needs efficient stock control which will strike the balance between holding too much stock and too little stock. This can be achieved by setting maximum and minimum stockholding quantities for each item of stock and deciding on appropriate re-order quantities.

Activity 24.4

Rally Bats Limited
working capital management

Ben Dawes is the managing director of Rally Bats Limited, a company which makes table tennis bats which he sells to wholesalers and also by mail order.

The company's balance sheet has just been prepared by the accountant. Ben says to you that he never seems to have much cash to take out for his salary.

He says that he has been asked to meet the bank manager next week because the bank account seems to be permanently overdrawn.

Ben shows you the working capital figures, his latest year-end aged debtors summary and the performance figures for debtors collection, stock turnover and creditor payment.

	last year	this year
	£	£
Stock	6,500	8,910
Debtors	15,250	25,800
Bank account	1,270	(7,810)
Creditors	5,685	14,780

RALLY BATS LIMITED	AGED DEBTORS ANALYSIS					
Account	Credit Limit	Balance	Current	30-60 days	61-90 days	older
LLB Sports	1000.00	2100.00	100.00	500.00	1000.00	500.00
Baylis Trading	5000.00	5050.00	2500.00	0.00	0.00	2550.00
R&S Wholesale	10000.00	12560.00	00.00	10590.00	1970.00	0.00
P J Smith Ltd	5500.00	4,575.00	880.00	2695.00	1000.00	0.00
Antonio Supplies	2000.00	1515.00	500.00	650.00	365.00	0.00
TOTALS	23500.00	25,800.00	3980.00	14435.00	4335.00	3050.00

	last year	this year
Stock turnover (days)	50	79
Debtor collection (days)	40	65
Creditors payments (days)	42	60

You are to

1 Calculate his working capital for the two years.

2 Calculate his current ratio for the two years.

3 Calculate his acid test ratio for the two years.

4 Calculate his working capital cycle (in days) for the two years.

5 Comment on the performance indicators you have calculated in 1-4 above.

6 Suggest ways in which he could improve his working capital management.

CHAPTER SUMMARY

- The availability of cash in a business is essential to its continuing operation. It passes through a business in a 'cash cycle' which involves payments in and out of the bank account, as projected in the cash budget.

- Sources of cash include income from the sale of its products or from other sources such as loans and the owner investing capital.

- The cash flows out to pay for essential purchases such as stock, running expenses and other assets which the business buys from time to time.

- Problems can arise with the flow of cash if sales decline, if customers fail to pay and loans are refused. In the worst case the business can go 'bust'.

- Cash is one of the elements of working capital which also includes debtors and stock among its assets as sources of cash.

- The working capital cycle expands on the idea of the cash cycle. In the case of a trading business it involves four stages:
  - creditors sell goods to the business on credit
  - the goods are sold to customers on credit, or for cash
  - debtors make payment and the money is paid into the bank
  - the business pays the creditors from the bank account

- The working capital cycle can be measured (in days) by adding the average time stock is held to the average time it takes debtors to pay up, and then deducting the average time it takes to pay creditors. This is the time lag between the date a business pays for goods it is going to sell and the date on which it gets payment.

- Careful management of the main elements of working capital – debtors, creditors and stock – is essential to the efficient working of the business.

- Debtors are a source of cash, so it is critical that they are not allowed to get away with delaying payment. Debtor management – known as credit control – involves 'vetting' customers in the first place and then monitoring payments through the sales ledger by means of an aged debtors summary.

- Creditors are a drain on cash, so it is useful if a business can pay as late as it can (without jeopardising the trading relationship). Creditor management therefore involves making sure that the business gets the best deal from its suppliers in terms of pricing and being able to pay as late as possible.

- Stock costs money to hold, so stock management – known as stock control – has as its main aim to hold just enough stock, and not too much or too little.

KEY TERMS

cash cycle   the flow of cash in and out of a business bank account

cash budget   a budget projecting the flow of money in and out of the bank account and forecasting the bank balance at the end of each month

insolvency   being unable to pay debts as and when they fall due

working capital   current assets minus current liabilities – the funds available to finance the day-to-day working of a business

working capital cycle   the time lag between the date a business pays for goods it is going to sell and receiving payment for those goods

creditworthiness   the ability of a debtor to pay for products supplied

credit control   the management of the sales ledger (debtor accounts) to ensure prompt payment of sales invoices issued

aged debtor summary   a list of debtor account balances with a breakdown of how long each debt has been outstanding

long credit   the negotiation of payment terms as late as possible

stock control   management of the levels of stock within a business, ensuring that:
                        - stock is ordered when necessary
                        - high stock levels are avoided

Just-In-Time (JIT) the policy of replacing stock just before it will be needed, and not before

The business plan – marketing and sales

introduction

A business plan is a document which is designed to 'sell' the business idea to a lender or investor. It summarises in a number of sections the research and planning undertaken by the business owners. The starting point of any business is the idea for the product – whether it is a manufactured item, a retail operation or a service. The business plan should convince the lender or investor – and the owner – that the idea will be viable. In order to do this, the business must research the market to make sure that there will be a demand for the product.

what you will learn from this chapter

- the business plan contains a number of sections:
    - the business idea and the type of business to be set up
    - market analysis – the competitors and their pricing
    - marketing planning – how the product will be promoted and sold
    - production/operations planning – premises, equipment, staffing, quality systems
    - financial planning – sources of finance, budgeting, forecasts for cash flow and profit and loss accounts
    note: production and financial planning will be dealt with in the next two chapters

- the viability of a business idea will depend on whether it will sell

- marketing analysis includes the use of primary (field) research and secondary (desk) research into demand for the product and trends affecting demand; it also looks at the competition and its pricing

- once a business establishes from its research that a product should sell, it should draw up a formal plan for the promotion, sale and distribution of the product; it should also evaluate its performance once it starts trading

structure of a business plan

useful sources of information about planning

Information about business plans is available from a number of sources. A number of the banks issue 'starter packs' which include 'proforma' business plans – ie documents you can fill in to form the business plan. Some of these packs contain software disks (PC format) which set out the necessary forms for you to fill in. You are encouraged to use IT (page set-up and spreadsheets applications) for the business plan, both for presentation and also for 'number crunching', so these disks will be very useful.

Important note: consult with your teacher/lecturer before approaching a bank for this type of material. The number of packs may be limited!

Another source of information is the Young Enterprise scheme. You may be combining your study of this Unit with a Young Enterprise project.

format

Study the diagram below. It is a structure plan of a typical business plan. There is no set formula for the document, but the structure of most plans is broadly similar, as you will see if you look at starter packs provided by the banks.

---

business plan format

the business idea   -   the product or service and the legal status of the business

the market   -   your customers, competitors, how you can be better
       -   their pricing, your pricing

promotion and sales   -   what do your competitors do to promote and sell their products?
       -   how will you promote, sell and distribute yours?
       -   how much will it all cost? sales and selling budgets?

production/operations   -   production planning for making a product, operations planning for providing a service
       -   the need for premises, equipment, staff, quality systems, insurance, compliance with the law (eg Health & Safety)
       -   what are the time schedules involved?
       -   how much will it cost? overheads? start-up costs? budgets?

financial planning   -   sources and uses of finance, budgets, break-even calculations, cash flow and profit and loss forecasts, start-up balance sheets
       -   monitoring of financial results

Note: a complete business plan is set out in Chapter 28 on pages 618 to 631.

the purpose of a business plan

definition

A business plan could be defined as:

> *A plan presented to a bank or other provider of finance, describing what the business intends to do, explaining what its costs will be, what it expects to earn, how it will repay money it has borrowed, and how soon it will make a profit.*

In other words it is a confident statement to a lender or investor describing the business, stating where it plans to go, and how much money it needs to get there.

A business plan can be prepared either when a business starts up for the first time, when it is expanding or when it is developing new products – in all cases it will need finance.

the purposes of the plan

The writing of a business plan is a very useful exercise . . .

for providers of finance

A business plan will help to persuade a lender such as a bank or venture capital company to lend money. Providers of finance need financial information about the business – a break-even analysis, cash flow and profit forecast – set out in a clear and detailed way.

for the management of the business

A business plan will help the management of a business to see clearly where the business is going or is likely to go. All too often a person running or starting a business does not have time to see further than the next week; a business plan will make the business owner sit down and think through business objectives and financial requirements.

for monitoring the business

Once a business is up and running, the regular writing (or re-writing) of a business plan will enable the management of a business to monitor its progress; it will also enable a provider of finance to see that repayment of loans and overdrafts will take place on schedule.

Activity 25.1

Finding the business idea

This Activity should help you to get some ideas for a product for your business. It can be used for the Portfolio work for this Unit and for helping you formulate ideas for a Young Enterprise or mini-business scheme.

- Divide up the whole class into smaller groups of approximately four students.

- Elect a secretary and a spokesperson for each small group.

- Conduct a 'brainstorming session' for ideas for products or services which the eventual mini-business could provide.

- The secretary should record the suggestions, and the group should select up to five ideas.

When the groups have come to the end of their discussions (or arguments!) the class should re-assemble and the spokesperson from each small group should present the ideas. The class as a whole can then debate the suggestions and add further ideas which emerge.

Activity 25.2

Defining the business objectives

If you are setting up a business in your school or college or planning a business as part of your Portfolio work . . .

1   discuss in your class the objectives of your business

2   produce a written statement of your business objectives

3   draft a Mission Statement for your business – bear in mind that it may have to be amended when you have produced the final version of your business plan

Note: you should be familiar with Mission Statements; if you need reminding, turn to page14.

marketing research for the plan

If you are starting a business you will need to collect marketing information which will help in your decision-making.

The subject of marketing research is covered fully in Chapter 11 (page 226). You should have studied this chapter before reading any further. You should be aware that marketing research can be either:

- primary 'field' research – interviewing samples of people, issuing questionnaires to find out at first hand what the 'market' thinks and wants
- secondary 'desk' research – making use of published resources and websites to study market statistics and trends

If you are considering manufacturing a product or providing a service you will therefore need to look at a number of critical questions . . .

is there a demand for the product?

There is no point in launching a new product for which there is no demand, or for which you cannot create a demand. Fashion clothes, for example, are notoriously subject to changes in demand. Many new businesses founder because their owners think they have a good idea but fail to carry out sufficient research to see if consumers are equally enthusiastic.

who are your customers?

Another aspect of marketing policy is to decide which group(s) of customers your business is going to target. This will in turn enable you to calculate how many customers you will be selling to, and whether you think they will be repeat customers who will buy from you again.

what is the competition doing?

If you are going to market a product you will need to research the competition, examining its products and its pricing. As you will know from your marketing studies, it is always more difficult to launch a new product in a market which is already congested with existing products.

what should you charge?

Pricing is notoriously difficult to get right. You need to know:

- what the competition are charging
- what the market will bear
- what your costs are

You can then set a price. There are a number of different pricing strategies.

market-led pricing

Pricing your product at the same level as your competitors; this is the price consumers expect to pay.

penetration pricing and destruction pricing

Penetration pricing is cutting the price as low as you are able below that of your competitors in order to penetrate the market with a new product. If you are intending to start a price war with with the object of knocking the competition out of the market entirely, this is known as 'destruction pricing'.

skimming

Charging a high price for an innovative product (normally a high technology product) – there is no competition and you need to recover the cost of developing the product.

added value pricing

You may be able to charge more than competitors by providing some 'added value' to the product in terms of extra quality or additional features.

what are the financial implications of this?

When you have worked out the number of customers to whom you will be selling and have assessed the market, you can then:

- fix a price for your product
- estimate the number of items you will be able to sell in a year
- estimate your annual sales figure (turnover)

Activity 25.3

Healthy Foods Catering

Read through the marketing and sales Case Study on the next four pages and answer the following questions:

1   What is 'the product'?
2   Who are the customers of the business?
3   What is the planned sales target for the first year?
4   How is the product to be priced?
5   How is the product to be promoted?
6   How is the product to be distributed?
7   What is the total marketing and sales budget for the first year? Is this a fixed or a variable cost for the business?

Case Study

Healthy Foods Catering
marketing and sales plan

Sarah and Louise Osborne are two sisters in partnership. They are starting a new catering business 'Healthy Foods Catering'. The business is to start trading in November.

They are preparing a business plan for the bank and ask the help of their brother Robert who is a marketing executive.

His first step is to draw up a marketing and sales plan.

the plan

The business will commence trading in November, manufacturing and selling a specialised range of healthy and vegetarian dishes (main and snack meals). Meals will be produced in the firm's own production kitchens, and will be sealed, vacuum-wrapped and chilled. Trial production of meals will commence early in October. Note that the term 'meal' refers to an individual course.

Initially orders will be processed as they are received and then delivered to individual customers. The consumer (private customer) market will be developed during the first three months of trading, but it is part of this plan to introduce and develop a range of meals and dishes to meet the commercial market, ie food wholesalers and distributors.

Production of meals will be undertaken by one of the partners and a member of the partner's family. The other partner will undertake the day-to-day sales and distribution. Both partners will be involved in promotional events.

objectives

1   To develop sales to the consumer and commercial markets to the value of £120,000 and provide a net profit return on sales of 10%.

2   To be selling on a regular basis (at least 2 orders per month) to five frozen food wholesale distributors.

3   To employ a salesperson/delivery person during the last three months of the first year of trading.

sales forecast

Consumer Sales

Sales target £90,000. Target customers 300.

The average unit price of a meal at sales price is £5.00 and therefore there is a need to sell at least 18,000 units during Year 1.

Research indicates that the average order value to be delivered will be £20 and a customer will purchase 15 times in a year. We will therefore need to build up a base of 300 regular customers to provide the turnover required.

Commercial Sales

Sales target £30,000. Target customers 5.

Average order value is expected to build up to £300 per order. Commercial customers will only be available to the company for approximately eight months of the first year of trading. Initial annual sales target will be as above.

the product

A range of 28 dishes (main and snack meals) of which 10 dishes will be available from the start of trading in November. The other 18 dishes will be gradually introduced into the range as the year progresses on the basis of 'the dish of the week'.

geographical area of market

Consumer Sales

Initial promotion will be within the boundaries of the area covered by Airedale Borough Council and the circulation area of the 'Airedale Courier'.

Commercial Sales

Following research during the early part of the year (January) to identify potential buying/decision-making personnel, the commercial market will be developed.

It is proposed to develop as customers a number of outlets which supply pubs, hotels, restaurants and other catering establishments, together with delicatessen and health food retailers. It is the firm's policy to develop a commercial base of customers in an area within a 30 mile radius of the production unit and by the end of Year 1 at least five suppliers will be purchasing at least twice a month.

market research - segmentation

Consumer market

Research has indicated that the potential market is as follows:

Age   20-45 years

Occupation   Professional people/middle class

Income   £18,000 and above

Commercial market

Sources of potential customer sectors identified:
- cash and carry wholesalers
- delicatessen wholesalers/retailers
- health food wholesalers /retailers
- frozen food wholesalers/retailers
- public house chains
- restaurants and cafes
- hotels and guest houses
- institutional caterers

pricing

Consumer Sales

Production costs will be identified and a margin of 65% (minimum) will be added in order to cover overheads and profit. A comparison with competitor prices should take place. Consumer prices should be finalised by October. There will be a need for monthly reviews of costs of fresh ingredients and a quarterly review for other ingredients.

Commercial Sales

Once initial costings have been identified and appropriate margins (see above) added, a discount structure for bulk purchase will be required. This needs to be prepared by the end of January next year. A comparison with competitor prices should take place, and final decisions made by the end of December. Competitors' price lists must be obtained on a regular basis.

distribution

Consumer Sales

Orders will be delivered direct to the customer's home in the firm's own transport – delivery to take place 2 days after receipt of order – evening delivery will be available. As the business develops, a planned delivery schedule will be introduced and customers will be notified of its delivery times.

Commercial Sales

Central bulk deliveries will be made to identified distribution outlets which can then sell on to individual small (retail) outlets. In the case of contracts with groups (eg breweries), distribution will have to be agreed with them at the time of negotiation. It is planned to deliver to distribution warehouses as far as possible.

promotion

Consumer Market

Three tasting sessions to be organised for the end of October and early November for approximately 35 to 40 people already identified as potential customers during initial research.

A promotional leaflet to be delivered to identified areas in Airedale – enclosing the leaflet with the 'Airedale Courier' during the first week of November.

Press release to be sent from mid-October onwards to five local newspapers.

Commercial Market

Mailing – identified commercial/group buyers to be sent a personally addressed letter introducing Healthy Foods Catering, together with details of menus/dishes. The letter will state that a follow-up telephone call will be made to arrange an appointment and a full presentation.

Advertising/Promotion – research to be undertaken with regard to a small advertising and press release campaign in appropriate local business journals.

Brochure/Leaflet – a simple cost-effective leaflet initially which can be used in both consumer and commercial markets. It will give brief details, including ingredients of dishes. The price list will be on a separate sheet for ease of reproduction, and to allow for price changes.

sales policy

Consumer Sales

A telephone selling approach will be developed in order to contact customers on a regular basis and at the same time build up deliveries in planned areas. Initially this work will be undertaken by the partners; if it is successful, a part-time evening telesales person could be employed.

Commercial Sales

Initial sales contact is to be undertaken by the partners. When sales have developed to a level which cannot be managed by them, an agent will be recruited to sell the range to appropriate outlets. There will then also be a need to appoint a telephone salesperson, who could take calls from both commercial and consumer customers and also ring specific customers to encourage them to place an order.

marketing budget

Sales Income: £120,000

Units produced: Consumer market 18,000 at an average price of £5.00

Commercial market 10,000 at an average price of £3.00

For Year 1 the company will have an initial budget of £10,800 (9% of turnover) which will be reviewed on a quarterly basis.

Allocation of budget	£
Press Advertising	500
Printing - Menus/price lists	850
Printing - Leaflets	1,850
Leaflet distribution	500
Food sampling at cost price	1,250
Sales folders	150
Direct Mailing campaign	2,250
Brochure	2,950
Miscellaneous/Reserve	500
TOTAL BUDGET	10,800

Activity 25.4

Marketing research and planning

Now that you have read the Case Study you should be well prepared for working out your own marketing and sales plan. You should write notes for your Portfolio on the topics listed below. Consult the checklist on the next page for further guidance.

topics . . .

1   who your competitors are

2   who your customers are

3   the features of your product which will make your customers prefer it to the products of your competitors

4   approximately how many items (product or service) you can sell in a year

5   what price you could charge for the product – and what your pricing policy is

6   what your approximate annual sales income should be

7   the methods you would use to promote your products

8   the ways in which your product will be distributed to customers

marketing and sales in the business plan

You do not have to write a marketing and sales plan the same length as the Case Study on the previous four pages. This plan is based on a full business marketing and sales plan and is included to show the level of planning a business would need to carry out. A briefer version would be acceptable in the business plan, which is a summary prepared for a prospective lender.

The checklist on the next page suggests a format you could adopt for the sales and marketing section of the business plan in your Portfolio. You will find similar guidance material in the bank business 'starter packs'.

on-going evaluation of the business plan

The business plan should not be forgotten once a business starts to trade. The targets set out in the plan should be regularly monitored and the plan should be modified if they are not being met. The budgeting process (see Chapter 23) will pick up variances: for example if sales are not up to target the situation will be investigated and action taken. Targets or prices may have to be adjusted. The business will also monitor figures such as market share. It needs to ask questions if it is not performing to target. Business planning is an on-going process and one of the major responsibilities of management.

BUSINESS PLAN CHECKLIST – MARKETING AND SALES

product

- who are your customers? which market segment do they belong to?

- who are your main competitors?

- what are their strengths and weaknesses?

- what do they charge?

- is the product price sensitive (ie will people not buy if the price rises a little, or will they buy more if the price drops)

- why is your product better or different from that of your competitors?

pricing

- what price will you charge?

- is this price different from that charged by your main competitors?

- if the price is different, why is it different?

- what do you expect to sell (in £) in each month?

- what will your annual sales turnover be for the first year of trading?

- what period of credit will you give?

promotion

- how do your competitors promote their product?

- how are you going to promote your product?

- what will it cost?

- how are you going to get feedback from your customers?

place

- how do your competitors distribute their product to their customers?

- how do you plan to distribute your product (or service) to your customers?

- will this offer a better service than your competitors?

CHAPTER SUMMARY

● A business plan is a written document presented to a bank or other provider of finance, describing what the business intends to do, explaining what its costs will be, what it expects to earn, how it will repay money it has borrowed, and how soon it will make a profit.

● The format of a business plan is not bound by a specific format, but it will normally contain:
  – the business idea and legal status of the business
  – a marketing and sales plan – customers, competitors, pricing decisions
  – details of the way the product will be promoted and sold
  – a production plan and a plan for quality systems
  – a financial plan – sources and uses of finance, budgets, break-even, cash flow and profit and loss forecasts, start-up balance sheets

● The business plan will help to support an application for finance and will also form a planning tool for the management of the business.

● Marketing research is important in the business planning process; it established whether there is a demand for the product, who the customers are and what the competition is doing.

● The business must make sure its pricing is set at the right level. There are a number of different ways of pricing a product. Pricing can be market-led, penetration pricing, skimming or added value.

● The main sections in the marketing and sales section of a business plan are:
  – a product description
  – an analysis of the market – the type of customers who will buy
  – an analysis of the competition and its pricing
  – the sales target for the year
  – your pricing decision
  – the methods you would use to promote the product
  – the ways in which the product will be distributed
  – a marketing and sales budget – the cost of marketing and sales

● The marketing and sales targets in the plan will need to be monitored on a regular basis in order to evaluate the success of the business and the plan.

KEY TERMS

business plan	a written plan presented to a bank or investor describing the objectives of the business, the product, its market, production and quality plans and financial plans
marketing plan	a plan which analyses the market for the product, its pricing, promotion and distribution – often summarised for inclusion in the business plan
market-led pricing	pricing at the same level as your competitors
penetration pricing	pricing below the level of your competitors in order to penetrate the market
destruction pricing	pricing in a 'price wars' strategy which aims to destroy the competition – to put it out of business
skimming	charging a high price for a new product in order to recover the cost of development
added value pricing	being able to charge more for a product because you are adding value to it in the form of extra quality or extra features
promotion	the process of drawing the consumer's attention to the product – by advertising and publicity
sales policy	the means of selling the product to the customer
distribution	the process of delivering the product or service to the customer
marketing budget	an estimate of the amount which will be spent by the business in the marketing process

26

The business plan – production and resources

introduction

In the last chapter we saw that the business plan should 'sell' the product idea and show that there is a market for it. The business plan should also show that the business has planned and costed the processes of producing the product or providing the service. This involves a consideration of the resources that the business will need – premises, equipment, people and the time to carry out the project.

what you will learn from this chapter

● starting a new business or expanding an existing business requires planning and timing so that the appropriate resources are obtained at the right time and at the right cost

● money is probably the most vital resource of all; the next chapter explains the processes of financial planning, including the critically important break-even calculation

● the costs of premises from which the business produces its product – a manufactured item, retail stock to sell or a service to provide – must be calculated carefully and the legal implications understood

● the business will need to plan for the equipment it is going to use: machinery used in production, computers, communications systems, mobile phones – the list will vary according to what the business does

● the business will need to plan for staffing requirements – the employees it will recruit, the wages it will have to pay, the legal implications of employing staff

● the business will need to implement some form of quality system

● all these processes involve careful timing – a business will have to know how to carry out some basic time scheduling

business premises

premises – work from home?

Many small businesses operate very successfully from home. These businesses are mainly sole traders who either provide a service to the public by travelling from home, or who deal with the public on the telephone or on the Internet. Examples include electricians, photographers, designers, and insurance sales representatives. Business owners who use the home as a base can charge a proportion of their expenses (telephone, electricity, heating) to their business – ie the business will pay rather than the expense falling on the household budget. A major disadvantage is keeping the business and private life separate: the problems of confidentiality and keeping small children at bay!

the e-commerce dimension

In an age where many service businesses are trading on-line, 'premises' can become virtual – in other words, a website on a computer server can replace commercial premises. The 'shop-front' is being replaced by the website home page. This enables the services business owner to work wherever he or she can get on-line, including from home. The practicalities of selling by e-commerce still require, however, that the product is stored and despatched – so premises will still be needed for handling the goods.

should I buy or rent premises?

If the business manufactures a product or needs to deal with the public face-to-face as part of its everyday operations, it needs premises – commercial property. Information about premises can be obtained from:

- local Chambers of Commerce (some produce registers of vacant premises)
- the commercial property offices of estate agents
- the commercial property pages in the local press

You will see when you look at this information that premises can be classified in terms of office space and warehousing and production space. This distinction is self-explanatory: certain businesses will only need offices, others will need a combination of office space and warehousing.

The principal concern when choosing premises will be whether you wish to buy or rent the property. If you have the capital you may wish to buy the premises, possibly with the help of a commercial mortgage. If, as is more likely, you do not have much spare money to invest, you will plan to rent a property and pay a regular 'rental' to the owner of the property.

Activity 26.1

Investigating premises

You run a business which is looking for a 2,500 square feet warehouse with office facilities. Obtain through your tutor details of up to five suitable vacant premises in your locality. Assess each of them in terms of

• price per square foot, *or*

• annual rental per square foot

• accessibility and parking facilities

• the annual Non Domestic Rate (if you can find this out from the Local Authority)

Write a brief report comparing the alternatives and giving your recommendation – with reasons (including location) – as to which warehouse is the best.

alternative task

Carry out the same exercise as above, but this time looking for an office of 1,500 square feet for an insurance broker.

what does the law say about premises?

If a business plans to operate from premises, there are a number of legal obligations that the owner(s) of the business must consider. These include:

planning permission

There must be planning permission for the type of business carried on at the premises – for example, you could not open up a retail outlet on an industrial estate, or set up a 'heavy' industrial process in a unit given planning permission for 'light' industrial usage. If you are using your own house for your business, planning permission may be required, depending on the use.

licences

Certain types of business need a licence to trade; these include: restaurants, food manufacturers, ice cream and mobile food stalls, sellers of alcohol and tobacco, nursing homes, child nurseries and scrap metal dealers.

checking the lease

If you are taking on a lease (ie buying the right to the property for a set period of time rather than buying it outright), have you checked any restrictive terms and conditions in the lease? Have you checked how long the lease has to run and how often the lease payments can be reviewed (ie increased), eg every five or seven years?

environmental restrictions

The law places strict controls on the emissions which a business can make into the atmosphere, into drainage systems, and into rivers and streams. Offenders can (and are) prosecuted for breaking these regulations.

Activity 26.2

Legal implications of premises

What legal implications relating to premises are involved for:

1   a graphic design consultancy operating from home – a sole trader who designs publicity leaflets, brochures, packaging, book jackets and so on, using a computer and a drawing board in a spare bedroom?

2   a car mechanic who decides to operate an engine tuning service from the garage in his house?

3   an ice cream salesman who plans to operate a 'Mr Creamy' van in the main shopping street in the town?

4   a skip rental firm which wants to take over an old quarry in which it plans to dump waste?

insuring premises and their contents

fire cover

This type of cover insures premises and its contents against damage by fire and other disasters such as lightning, explosions, aircraft, riots, vandalism, earthquake, storms and floods. The premises are normally insured for their rebuilding cost.

theft

This insurance covers the removable assets of the business, eg machinery, computers, office machines, stock and money. The cover is normally for assets both on the premises and also off the premises, eg goods in transit, and money being taken to the bank. These assets are normally insured for their replacement value and not their value in the books of the business.

business interruption

Another form of cover related to asset insurance is business interruption cover. This reimburses financial loss which happens as a result of the business coming to a halt following a fire or any of the other disasters covered under fire insurance. This cover can be extended to insure against problems caused by a failure of the utilities, eg a long-term power cut, or contamination of the water supply.

details of premises to go in the business plan

The checklist shown below gives an idea of the type of detail about premises you will need to write in the business plan. Compare this list with checklists from the bank business plan starter packs.

BUSINESS PLAN CHECKLIST – PREMISES

working from home

• are you intending to work from home?

• if so, do you need any planning permission for your business? – if in doubt consult a solicitor

• can you claim any business expenses from your domestic bills? – if in doubt consult an accountant

working from premises

• how much space do you need?

• will you be renting or buying?

• if you are buying 'leasehold' property, how long has the lease to run? (see note below)

• what will the rental cost or loan repayments be per month?

• what are your rates?

• what is the cost of insuring the premises and its contents?

• are there any legal restrictions on the premises – environmental? type of use?

timing for premises

• when will the premises be available?

• when do you need to move in?

• how long will it take you to get the premises ready for use?

Note: property for sale is normally either 'freehold' (which means you have full rights over the property – with no time restriction) or 'leasehold' (which means you buy rights to use the property, but for an extended period of years, eg 15 years).

planning for machinery and equipment

When a business plans to acquire machinery or equipment or vehicles a number of critical decisions will have to be made, including:

- should they be acquired now?
- should they be bought or leased?

Other factors affecting the choice will be the supplier chosen; this will be determined by quality, payment terms (ie when payment can be made), technical back-up and after-sales service.

The equipment which a business may need includes a wide range of items including telephones, computers and photocopiers, vehicles, and machinery used when producing a product or providing a service. We will now look at the ways in which the equipment can be acquired.

should the equipment be acquired now?

When a business starts up for the first time, it is easy to fall into the trap of making a 'shopping list' for resources, assuming that they all have to be acquired at once. This is not always the case, and great care should be taken in the planning process. A business will have to list all the items it wants to acquire, cost them, and compare them with the available financial resources. It can then decide which items have to be acquired immediately (telephones, delivery van) and which items can wait (the MD's new car).

should the items be bought or leased?

Equipment can be bought outright or rented (leased). This choice exists for a wide range of business assets – computers, photocopiers, machinery, cars and vans for example – buy now and pay up front, or pay regularly over a period of time. The term 'lease' is often used when a piece of equipment is rented: ownership remains with the firm 'leasing' it out. Occasionally the business has the option of buying the item at the end of the lease period.

There are a number of factors which will be involved in the decision to buy or to lease. The most crucial of these is the availability of capital or finance. If neither of these is available, the business cannot buy the asset, and the decision to lease will be made. If capital is available, the choice is normally based partly on financial considerations (how much tax can be saved) and also how soon the equipment will get out of date. There is little point buying an expensive piece of new technology if next year the price will have fallen, or the technology will have been superseded. For example, current thinking says that computer equipment used in business will only last for an average of two years before it needs upgrading.

Activity 26.3

The cost of equipment

You are setting up in business and know that your sales manager needs a mobile telephone paid for by the business. Investigate the various methods and costs of obtaining a mobile telephone and write a brief report concluding with a shortlist of two models together with the cost of the various alternatives.

details of equipment to go in the business plan

The checklist shown below gives an idea of the information about equipment that you will need to write in the business plan. The total cost of all the items will be an essential part of your financial plan (see next chapter).

BUSINESS PLAN CHECKLIST – EQUIPMENT

list the items that you will need . . .

description of item	
cost per year if leased	
purchase cost if bought	
expected life of item	
supplier chosen	

description of item	
cost per year if leased	
purchase cost if bought	
expected life of item	
supplier chosen	

and so on . . .

purchasing stock and materials

If the business you are planning is manufacturing a product or buying in goods which you are going to sell, you are going to need stock and materials. The price you pay and the terms you negotiate are critical for the profitability of the business. Purchasing has traditionally been defined as:

buying goods and services of the right quality, in the right quantity, at the right time, from the right supplier, at the right price

This may seem all very well in theory, but as most people in business will tell you, purchasing often gets a low priority in comparison, say, with selling.

getting the right price – efficient purchasing

The price of materials and stock purchased is an important factor for a business which wants to make a profit. Achieving a price cut for raw materials and stock can have a dramatic effect on profitability: 'a penny saved is a profit made' as the saying goes. Look at this example taken from a business which is already trading:

A manufacturing company makes garden gnomes. The financial details are as follows:

Annual sales	£500,000
Annual spending on materials	£250,000
Other expenses	£200,000
Net profit	£50,000

The management want to increase profit by £5,000. How can they achieve this? There are two alternatives:

1 Increase sales by £50,000 – the business makes £5,000 profit from £50,000 of sales.

2 Reduce material costs by £5,000 – this will bring about an increase in profit without the need for an increase in sales.

The second alternative appears by far the more attractive. If they spend £250,000 a year on materials, a saving of £5,000 is only a 2% reduction in material costs. To achieve the same increase in profit by increasing sales will require a 10% increase in sales. An increase in profitability is clearly more easily achieved by 'shopping around' for cheaper materials (a cut of only 2%) than by trying to increase sales of gnomes by 10%. £5,000 saved by efficient purchasing is a £50,000 increase in profit!

methods of obtaining lower prices

How are these lower prices to be found? Various suppliers must be approached, and prices obtained from price lists, telephone enquiries and written requests for prices. If suppliers realise that a business is 'shopping around' it may be prepared to drop a price to gain a customer. Businesses must also be aware of discounts offered for:

- early payment (cash discount), often 2.5% of the purchase price
- large quantity orders
- trade customers (trade discount) – this is discount given to customers 'in the trade' who are likely to give repeat orders

A new business must 'shop around' as a matter of course, and existing businesses should do so on a regular basis; it is all too easy for an established business to fall into a state of inertia when buying, and always buy from the same supplier, regardless of price.

timing of purchases

A supplier must be able to keep to specified schedules. Any unreliability in supply could lose valuable sales for the buyer: for example, a shop which is let down by a wholesaler and runs out of a popular item, or a manufacturer who is unable to obtain a vital component because the supplier has failed to deliver. A buyer must take careful note of the time it takes for an order to be processed by the supplier and the delivery time quoted.

quality and purchasing

The quality of an item means in very basic terms 'how good is it for the job?' As far as a business is concerned, purchasing for quality means balancing cost and performance: the item must do the job well, but at the lowest obtainable cost (see above). But there is no point compromising quality for price. If the car or the holiday produced by a car manufacturer or holiday company is defective, the consumer will go elsewhere for the next purchase.

Activity 26.4

Efficient purchasing

Why is it so much more efficient to 'shop around' for suppliers and get the best deal that you can rather than concentrating solely on your sales drive to improve your profitability? Illustrate your answer with a practical example involving revenues and costs (see the example on the previous page).

Is the price you can negotiate from suppliers the most important factor when purchasing? If not, why not?

BUSINESS PLAN CHECKLIST – PURCHASING STOCK

your stock

- a list of your needs for stock

- the cost of each stock item

your suppliers

- a list of suppliers for those items

- the terms given by those suppliers – eg cash terms or number of days credit

- an estimate of the monthly cost of stock

- an estimate of the annual cost of stock

the legal implications of production

For the purposes of business planning you should appreciate that manufacturing and selling a product (or in some circumstances providing a service) brings with it three basic legal obligations:

faulty products

If a product is faulty a customer will have a legal right to a refund or a replacement. There are no grounds for a manufacturer or a retailer disclaiming responsibility or putting up a notice stating 'no refunds'.

products as described

Products and services must be sold as described in advertising material, and must as far as is reasonably possible fulfil the claims made for them. A 'waterproof jacket' should withstand a shower of rain, but the manufacturer could dispute a claim, if, for example the jacket were worn in a tropical storm and let in water.

safety standards

Products must meet with safety standards. The children's toys market, for example, is subject each Christmas to the usual influx of highly dangerous cheap foreign imports: teddy's eyes which come off and are swallowed, poisonous paint, and so on. Products which do not meet with the safety standards can result in prosecution for the business concerned.

the insurance implications of production

public liability insurance

This type of cover insures against claims from members of the public who may be injured as a result of something which happens in connection with the business, eg a person who visits a workshop and is injured by a machine which topples over. The cover also extends to assets of the public, eg a parked car which is damaged by a falling roof tile from the business premises. If you have access to your home insurance policy, you will see that household insurance also normally includes public liability cover.

product liability insurance

An extension of public liability cover is insurance against claims arising from people who have suffered injury or damage from faulty products which they have purchased. This type of insurance will cover legal costs in defending claims made under consumer protection law.

planning for human resources

objectives of human resource planning

A business will need to choose and employ people so that
- the productivity and output of the business is efficient
- the profit is maximised
- people working in the business are motivated and satisfied

These objectives will inevitably result in a compromise!

the skills that will be needed

A business start-up will involve one or more entrepreneurs (people who get businesses going) who have to provide skills in a number of areas:
- administration and management
- marketing and selling
- finance/book-keeping/payroll
- production and operations
- research and development – the 'ideas' person

It may be that the sole trader has all these talents, or the partners/directors share these abilities between them. It is more likely, however, that the business starting up will have to 'buy in' help in one or more of these areas.

This can be done by:

- bringing in a new partner/director with a particular skill who may be willing also to put in capital and share in the success of the business
- using self-employed specialists (eg for accountancy services or marketing) on a contract basis
- employing temporary staff from an agency
- employing one or more general assistants who can be on the permanent payroll of the business

The first option (new partner/director) can be a risky proposition. There may be personality clashes between the people involved: can the new director get on with the existing management? Employing self-employed specialists or agency staff can be expensive, but it is also flexible: a business only pays for what it wants done. A general assistant may cost less in terms of £'s per hour, but there is little flexibility in terms of hours worked, and the employee(s) may need training.

the practicalities of human resources planning

As far as business planning is concerned, the owner(s) of a new or expanding business ought to bear in mind:

- Manpower planning – what are the staffing requirements likely to be?
- What training provision needs to be made?
- What facilities will need to be made available for staff welfare?
- Have the wages levels been fixed?
- Have Health and Safety requirements been planned out?

legal aspects of human resources planning

The Human Resources unit covers this area in detail. To summarise, the law places a burden of responsibility on the employer to

- abide by the age limits for employment
- pay at least the Minimum Wage
- issue written terms and conditions of employment
- avoid discrimination on the grounds of sex, age, race and religion
- abide by the Health & Safety at Work regulations
- maintain appropriate payroll records

employer's liability insurance

This type of cover insures the employer against claims from employees who have been injured at work. 'Employees' can include outside consultants and even students on work experience (you may have come across this problem!)

Activity 26.5

Planning for people

You are starting up a new business as a sole trader making picture frames. You are giving some thought to human resource planning:

1   What would be your main objectives in human resource planning?

2   You are very good at making picture frames but have had less experience in financial matters and in selling. What options are open to you in solving this problem? State what option you would choose, and why.

3   You are moving into a small workshop owned and subsidised by the local authority. What practical human resource planning will be necessary, bearing in mind that you may be employing other people to work at the premises?

BUSINESS PLAN CHECKLIST – HUMAN RESOURCES

the key people

- list the key people – owners/partners/directors

- state what their role in the business is

- state what they will be paid (estimate the annual gross income)

the employees

- the number of employees required

- their role (eg sales, production, administration)

- an estimate of the monthly wages and salary bill

- an estimate of the annual wages and salary bill

planning for quality

We have examined the issue of quality in detail in Chapter 5 (pages 110 to 119). When a business is planning sales, purchasing, production and staffing it will need to make sure that there are sound quality systems in place. Remember that quality involves not just production and the product, it should be instilled in all processes in the business, eg sales and after-sales.

quality control and quality assurance

These two terms means very different things.

- **Quality control** is an inspection process in the production function which attempts to reduce the risk of defective products leaving the factory in the first place.

- **Quality assurance** is based on the concept that quality is the responsibility of everyone working in the business; the objective is to ensure that defects do not occur in the first place.

A business plan should state what quality control and quality assurance policies are being adopted by the business. They are summarised below . . .

means of achieving quality assurance

TQM, team working and Quality Circles

Total Quality Management (TQM) involves the business being managed so that every individual has a responsibility to fellow employees for maintaining quality – it is particularly effective in team working. Quality circles involve regular meetings of employees to discuss quality problems and to suggest solutions for areas such as production, safety, design and cost.

training and development – Investors in People

A well trained and focused workforce help to maintain quality systems. The Government recognises good practice in its Investors in People award.

benchmarking

Benchmarking involves comparing the business with another business which is well-known for its excellent quality.

Quality Certification – BS EN ISO 9000

Businesses can apply for certification through a set of international quality standards – BS EN ISO 9000. This is a rigorous procedure but a business which successfully achieves these standards can use the BSI kitemark, which stands for very high standards of quality throughout the business.

planning for time

We will now look at some specific techniques used when a business is undertaking a project which involves planning to acquire physical resources – for example fixed assets such as premises, plant and machinery and current assets such as stock and materials. Examples of this type of situation are the business start-up, relocation of a business, and expansion of an existing business. These techniques are based on two types of flow chart:

- critical path analysis
- bar charts known as Gannt charts

The results obtained from the planning process – for example how long it will take to complete a project – will contribute to the business plan.

critical path analysis

Critical path analysis is a technique for working out the minimum time a project is likely to take. It is a form of what is termed 'network analysis'. Critical path analysis operates by examining all the individual actions which contribute to the project, eg ordering, constructing, testing, and determining the minimum time the project will take. The process can be very complex, and may be introduced by looking at a simple operation such as making a cup of instant coffee, eg 'take the kettle, fill it up, plug it in, take a cup' … and so on. This form of analysis is presented in visual form by a network of arrows. Each arrow represents an individual activity, and is normally labelled with the activity and the time it takes (in, say, weeks) to carry out the activity, for example:

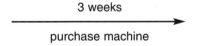

Arrows start and finish in circles known as *events* or *nodes*. Activities shown by arrows pointing into a circle (event) must be completed before any activity shown on an arrow coming out of an event can be started. For example:

It is common for a number of activities to take place simultaneously. If you are making a cup of instant coffee, the kettle will be boiling while you are getting a spoon and putting the instant coffee in the cup. In this case there will be arrows denoting these parallel activities, and these arrows will converge on the event which marks the pouring of the water into the cup. It is important to note that all activities on the converging arrows must be completed before any activity on any arrow leaving the circle can be started.

the critical path

You will know that if you are making a cup of coffee that you will have to wait for the kettle to boil while you get the cup and spoon out the coffee granules. You therefore have to wait the longest time of the two alternative activities (presumably boiling the water!) before completing the event and getting your steaming cupful of coffee. In critical path analysis the activities which take the longest time to complete are known as critical activities, and are shown with a thicker arrow.

In an analysis of a complex project, the quickest time the project will take to complete will be the sum of the time taken for the critical activities in sequence. In visual terms there will be a thick black line running through the network of activities: this will be the critical path, shown in the illustration below.

labelling the network

In critical path analysis, there are certain labelling conventions:

* The circle (event) is often annotated with numbers to show the stage in the project which has been reached. The number is the event number.

* The arrows (activities) are also given abbreviated labels:
    - the time taken for the activity is shown as a simple number which could stand for minutes, days, weeks as appropriate
    - the activity itself may be given a letter which is explained in a separate list (this would give clarity to the network when the activity descriptions are long and involved)

A critical path analysis is illustrated below. Note how the sum of the numbers on the critical path (the thicker arrows) indicates the activities which take the longest time – a total of 13 as opposed to the other route, which totals 8.

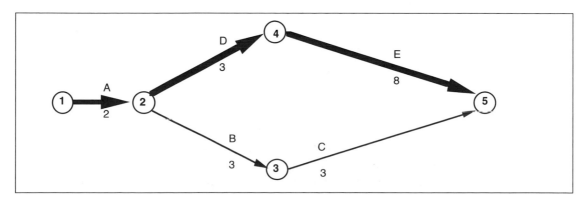

using a Gannt chart

It is also possible to set out the planning process on a bar chart known as a Gannt chart (illustrated on the next page). This form of time planning is commonly used in the production process (see the chapter on Production, pages 107 and 109) and is often computerised.

The Case Study that follows shows how a Gannt chart is constructed when a computer bureau wants to relocate its premises.

Case Study

Hermes Bureau
using a Gannt chart for time planning

You run a computer bureau – Hermes Bureau – which provides accounting, payroll and other computer services to a wide range of commercial customers. You are planning to invest in new premises shortly, and have purchased the lease of an office in the town, and will be able to move in six months' time.

You are taking the opportunity when moving to update your computer hardware and software systems. There are a number of important tasks to carry out before you move, and after consultation with your colleagues you have made the list set out below. Your software needs updating and customising for your bureau by programmers, and this will be the task which will take the most time. You see that all the tasks will have to be completed before you can become operational, and the obvious fact that the ordering of software and hardware can only take place after full assessment. You allow yourself a clear two week planning period before starting the process. You are very busy at the moment. When should you start planning?

Task A	time available for detailed planning	2 weeks
Task B	assessment of computer hardware	2 weeks
Task C	ordering new computers	2 weeks
Task D	assessment of new software	4 weeks
Task E	ordering software	10 weeks
Task F	obtaining quotes from removal firm	3 weeks
Task G	ordering the removal van	3 weeks

The Gannt chart drawn up by Hermes Bureau shows:

- the activities on a weekly schedule (the weeks are numbered across the top)

- the critical activities as black bars

- the activities which are not on the critical path as shaded bars

- float times for non-critical activities – ie times during which a delay can occur which will not hold up the project – as white bars

A Gannt chart is useful because each week it can be consulted to see what is due to start, to finish or to continue. Note that the chart shows the activity letters allocated to the critical activities.

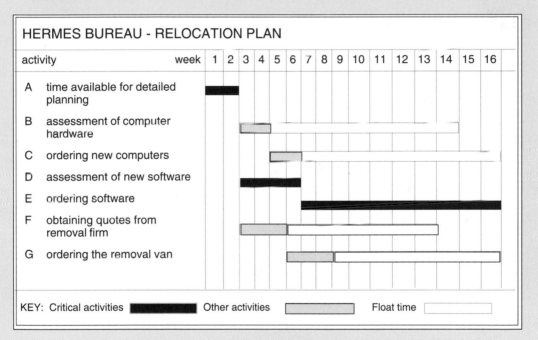

If Hermes Bureau had decided to use critical path analysis instead, the diagram would have looked like this:

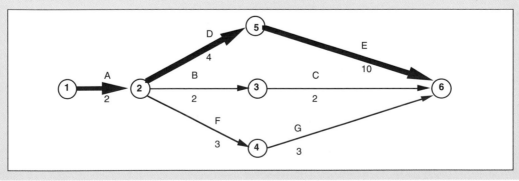

CHAPTER SUMMARY

- The choice of business premises is very important when planning a new business venture. The alternatives include:

  - to work from home or away from home?

  - to buy or to lease the property?

  The decision will depend on the nature of the business and the amount of funding available for the project. The decision will be reflected in the business plan.

- The business owner will have to plan carefully for any machinery and equipment which will have to be acquired. Again the decision will have to be made whether to purchase or to lease, and set out in the business plan.

- The business plan will also contain details of the stock or materials which will have to be bought for the production process (or to be sold, if the business is a retail one). The plan should show evidence that the owner has 'shopped around' for the best price and also taken note of factors such as terms offered and quality.

- The production process (for a manufacturer, retailer or service provider) has legal implications in terms of faulty products and safety standards. The process also needs adequate insurance against possible claims from the public.

- The business plan must also contain details of the planned staffing and its costs. A business needs to comply with the complexities of employment law and should ensure that it is insured against claims from employees for injury at work.

- Quality is an important factor in production. A business should declare in the business plan its policy on quality, covering areas such as quality control and quality assurance through schemes such as:

  - Total Quality Management

  - Benchmarking

  - Quality Certification

- The owner should show evidence in the business plan of his or her ability to deal with time planning, either through critical path analysis or through the construction of a Gannt planning chart.

KEY TERMS

lease	an agreement to allow someone to use property (such as premises or equipment) for a set period of time
Non-domestic rate	rates payable for business premises, collected by the Local Authority
public liability insurance	insurance which protects a business against claims from members of the public who may be injured on or near the business premises
product liability insurance	insurance which protects a business against claims from members of the public who may be harmed by one of the products of the business
employer's liability Insurance	insurance which protects a business against claims from employees who have been injured at work.
quality control	an inspection process which helps prevent faulty products from reaching the consumer
quality assurance	a quality system within the business which prevents faulty products from being produced in the first place
Total Quality Management	a management system within the business which ensures that every employee has responsibility for maintaining quality
benchmarking	comparing a business with another business well-known for its excellent quality
critical path analysis	a technique for working out the minimum time it will take to complete a project
Gannt chart	a horizontal bar chart which plans out the different activities which contribute to the completion of a project

Financial analysis and planning

Unit 6 Business planning
Financial analysis and planning

introduction

One of the most important parts of the business plan is the financial section. This sets out the sources of finance and shows how the planned product will be financially viable. It does this by means of financial forecasts and a calculation analysing when sales of the product will break-even and costs will be covered.

what you will learn from this chapter

- there are a number of different sources of finance for a business: some are internal (such as personal savings) and others are external (such as bank loans)

- when a business raises finance it will normally match the repayment period of the finance to the life of the asset, for example using an overdraft for working capital and a ten year loan for machinery

- the financial section of a business plan should contain six sections:

    1 the sources of finance – where the money is coming from

    2 estimates of the money needed, both for start-up costs and also for running costs

    3 a break-even calculation

    4 a cash flow forecast over a twelve month period

    5 a forecast operating budget (profit statement) over a twelve month period

    6 a start-up balance sheet

- a business will need to extract performance ratios on a regular basis in order to evaluate its success

sources of finance

Finance is normally needed for starting a business, buying a business, or expanding a business. Finance can be internal (from the owner's savings and capital or from profits), or external (from a bank, for example).

matching the finance to the assets

Lenders will normally want to match the period of any lending to the expected life of the asset financed. There are three generally accepted timescales for finance, although you may find definitions which will vary from these:

short-term	1 to 2 years	short-term requirements, ie working capital
medium-term	3 to 10 years	purchase of fixed assets, eg machinery
long-term	11 to 25 years	purchase of land and premises

As you will see, the longer the life of the asset purchased, the longer the loan that will be made available.

borrowing from the bank

types and sources of finance

We will now consider the various types and sources of finance. It should be noted that some of the sources listed here only provide finance to limited companies: this will be made clear in the text.

The banks are the largest providers of finance to all types of businesses. Forms of lending vary from bank to bank, and you should investigate the various schemes available and when they have to be repaid. A bank will be able to arrange, by itself, or through specialised companies which it owns:

- overdrafts
- factoring services
- short and medium-term loans ('business loans')
- leasing for equipment purchase and hire purchase
- commercial mortgages
- venture capital

interest on borrowing

Interest is paid on money borrowed and is calculated as a percentage of the amount borrowed. Banks normally set their interest rates at a set percentage (which varies according to the risk element in the lending) above the prevailing Base Rate. Base Rate is varied periodically at the direction of the Bank of England in order to 'fine-tune' the amount of borrowing in the economy. The reason for this is that interest is a cost to the business, and when interest rates are high they can restrict the amount a business can afford to borrow.

bank working capital finance

overdraft

An overdraft is short-term borrowing on a bank current account. It is relatively cheap because you only pay interest on what you actually borrow. You normally pay an arrangement fee when an overdraft is set up.

A 'limit' up to which you can borrow will be granted by the bank, and reviewed annually, when it can be increased, decreased or renewed at the same level. A renewal fee is payable for this service.

An overdraft is the most common form of finance for working capital. It provides the finance when a business needs to pay creditors or meet other short-term bills.

finance arranged through bank-owned companies

Finance houses, which are specialist companies owned in the main by the major banks, offer alternative ways of obtaining fixed assets:

hire purchase

An HP agreement from a finance house enables a business to acquire an asset on the payment of a deposit and to pay back the cost plus interest over a set period, at the end of which ownership of the asset passes to the borrower. Hire purchase is often used to finance vehicles and machinery.

leasing

Leasing arrangements are also provided by finance houses. With a leasing agreement, the business has use of assets such as cars and computers bought by the finance house. The business pays a regular 'rental' payment, normally over a lease period of two to seven years. Ownership of the asset does not normally pass to the business because the asset (the car, the computer) will have become out-of-date and will need renewing at the end of the lease period. Clearly a lease is not a loan, but it can substantially reduce the financial requirements of a business when it needs to acquire assets such as computer equipment and fleets of company cars.

factoring – working capital finance

Many banks also provide factoring services through specialist factoring companies. A business may have valuable financial resources tied up because its customers owe it money and have not yet paid. A factoring company will effectively 'buy' these debts by providing a number of services:

- it will lend up to 80% of outstanding customer debts
- it will deal with all the paperwork of collecting customer debts
- it can in some instances insure against non-payment of debts

Factoring frees money due to the business and allows the business to use it in its general operations and expansion plans. It is therefore a valuable source of short-term finance.

bank fixed asset finance

business loan

This is a fixed medium-term loan, typically for between 3 and 10 years, to cover the purchase of capital items such as machinery or equipment. Interest is normally 2% to 3% over base rate, and repayments are by installments.

commercial mortgage

If you are buying premises for your business you can arrange to borrow long-term by means of a commercial mortgage, typically up to 80% of the value of the property, repayable over a period of up to 25 years. Your premises will be taken as security for the loan: if the business fails, the premises will be sold to repay the bank.

finance for companies: venture capital

There are many specialist banks – 'merchant banks' – and investment companies which offer advice and financial assistance to limited companies looking for capital. This financial assistance takes the form of loans and venture capital which provides finance for fixed assets and for working capital. Venture capital companies will view these companies as investment opportunities and will put in money in the form of loans or purchase of shares, or both. In return, they may expect an element of control over the company and will possibly insist on having a director on the board of the company. A venture capital company considering investing will look for a business with a good sales and profit record – or potential.

financial assistance from the Government

The UK Government provides financial help – Regional Selective Assistance – to businesses setting up in areas which have traditionally had higher levels of unemployment and low earnings. This assistance – grants, cheap rents, free and subsidised advice – is administered through the Department of Trade and Industry, which is often referred to as the DTI. The areas given assistance are known as the Assisted Areas. They are shown as shaded areas on the map shown below. They are divided into three 'tiers':

Tier 1 (dark shading)

These are the areas of greatest need and include Cornwall, Merseyside, South Yorkshire, West Wales, the Welsh Valleys and all of Northern Ireland (not shown on the map).

Tier 2 (light shading)

These are local areas of need. They do not qualify for grants as high as those in Tier 1.

Tier 3 (not shown on the map)

This applies to businesses employing up to 250 people in certain areas of the UK.

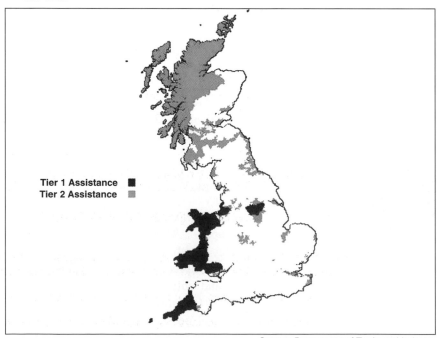

Source: Department of Trade and Industry

The Assisted Areas (provisional map published in 2000)

a financial needs schedule

A business plan will often summarise in a schedule (see below):

- the need for fixed assets and working capital (such as stock and money in the bank)
- the sources of finance used to pay for them – these could include bank finance, grants and money invested by the owner(s)

financial needs	
Item needed	*£*
office premises	125,000
computers	45,000
office equipment	12,500
vehicle	12,500
working capital	40,000
TOTAL COST OF PROJECT	235,000
to be provided by	*£*
own resources	125,000
bank finance:	
commercial mortgage for office	50,000
business loan for computers	20,000
overdraft for working capital	40,000
TOTAL OF FINANCING	235,000

Activity 27.1

Investigating types of finance

What alternative forms of financing could you suggest for the business shown in the above schedule for the following needs? Assume that the business is a limited company.

1   Working capital – bearing in mind that the business sells on credit.

2   Computers – the business may need to replace them every two or three years.

3   Share capital – the owner says he may be looking for outside investors.

budgeting for income and costs

the need for budgets

In Chapter 23 we looked at the need for businesses to budget – to estimate – for income and spending in different areas of a business. If the business is starting up for the first time or expanding its product line it will need to budget for sales income and for costs in areas such as marketing, production (or operations if it is a service business), and human resources (staffing).

It is clear that pricing must take into account the costs which the business will incur. These will include variable costs and fixed costs (overheads).

budgeting for variable costs and gross profit

Certain costs will be directly related to the number of items – a manufactured item or a service – produced by the business. These are known as **variable costs** or **cost of sales**. They might include costs such as:

- raw materials and components (for a manufacturer)
- stocks of items to sell in a shop (for a retailer)
- sales commission paid to sales reps

The business will need to make sure that it makes a profit when fixing its price. The first measure of profit is gross profit:

$$\text{GROSS PROFIT} = \text{SALES} - \text{VARIABLE COSTS}$$

As we saw in Chapter 22, gross profit is measured in percentage terms as gross profit margin:

$$\text{GROSS PROFIT MARGIN} = \frac{\text{GROSS PROFIT} \times 100\%}{\text{SALES}}$$

If, therefore, a business has budgeted sales income of £200,000 and variable costs (cost of sales) of £120,000, it will have a gross profit of £200,000 minus £120,000 = £80,000 gross profit. Its gross profit margin will be:

$$\frac{\text{£80,000 (gross profit)} \times 100\%}{\text{£200,000 (sales)}} = 40\%$$

This means that for every £10 of sales, £4 is profit once variable costs (cost of sales) have been paid off.

The business then has to pay off its fixed costs, known as overheads.

budgeting for fixed costs and net profit

There will be certain costs a business will have to pay, even if it produces no product or service at all. These are fixed costs, also known as overheads. If you are budgeting for a new business or product you should allow for fixed costs such as:

- premises – rent or loan repayments, insurance, security, rates
- services such as electricity, gas, telephone
- wages and salaries of permanent staff
- marketing and advertising, travel, postage, stationery
- depreciation – wear and tear on equipment

The business will want to make sure that the gross profit it has made (sales less the variable costs) will cover the fixed costs, or it will make a loss. Let us assume that the yearly total of all the fixed costs listed above is £60,000.

The second measure of profit is net profit:

NET PROFIT = GROSS PROFIT − FIXED COSTS (OVERHEADS)

As we saw in Chapter 22, net profit is measured in percentage terms as net profit margin:

$$\text{NET PROFIT MARGIN} = \frac{\text{NET PROFIT} \times 100\%}{\text{SALES}}$$

If we look again at the business illustrated on the previous page, it will have a net profit of £80,000 (the gross profit) minus £60,000 (the fixed costs) = £20,000 net profit. Its net profit margin will be:

$$\frac{£20,000 \text{ (net profit)} \times 100\%}{£200,000 \text{ (sales)}} = 10\%$$

This means that for every £10 of sales, £1 is profit once all the costs (both variable and fixed costs) have been paid off.

Activity 27.2

Measuring profitability

You have drawn up budgets for two different business ideas. The first will manufacture garden tools, the second will run two hairdressing salons. Which is more profitable? Work out the gross and net profit margins. Which business idea seems better, and why?

1   Annual sales £400,000, variable costs £280,000, fixed costs £80,000.

2   Annual sales £200,000, variable costs £80,000, fixed costs £80,000.

financial forecasts in the business plan

Budgeting involves drawing up estimates of:

- sales income for the year
- variable costs for the year
- fixed costs for the year

Once these figures have been established – and remember that they are only estimates – the business plan can move forwards with the production of three important forecasts:

the break-even calculation

This will enable the business to know exactly how much sales income it needs to cover its costs. Obviously if the business cannot cover its costs it needs to re-think the proposition.

the operating budget (forecast profit and loss account)

This projects the level of profits expected on a year's trading. It lists the sales income and both variable and fixed costs.

the cash flow forecast (cash budget)

This has already been explained in detail in Chapter 23. It projects the flows of money in and out of the bank account of the business during the year. It will pick up any times when the business will be short of cash – a dangerous occurrence in any business, but particularly so in a start-up situation.

We will look at these three projections in turn.

will the business break-even?

the concept of break-even

A business planning a new project is only likely to go ahead if it is eventually going to make a profit on that project. It will make a profit after it has broken even – as soon as its sales income covers its running costs. Note that break-even is only concerned with running costs – not start-up costs.

Break-even is therefore the point at which running costs are covered by the income received. After that point you are making a profit. A definition is:

break-even is the point at which sales income is equal to running costs

two ways of calculating break-even

There are two ways of calculating break-even:

by formula

These are basic calculations which use budgeted figures such as the gross profit margin percentage, variable costs and fixed costs.

by graph

This is a more sophisticated method which takes more time, but which provides the business with a great deal more information.

break-even by formula

1. to find out the level of sales in £ needed to break-even

The information you will need for the first calculation is the fixed costs (overheads) and the gross profit margin percentage. If you do not have the gross profit margin percentage, it can be calculated by dividing the gross profit by the sales and multiplying by 100. The break-even formula is:

$$\frac{\text{FIXED COSTS}}{\text{GROSS PROFIT MARGIN}} \times 100 = \text{BREAK-EVEN LEVEL OF SALES}$$

So taking the business we looked at on page 596, if gross profit margin is 40% and fixed costs are £60,000, the calculation is:

$$\frac{£60,000}{40} \times 100 = £150,000 \text{ OF SALES NEEDED TO BREAK-EVEN}$$

Projected sales for the period are £200,000, so the business has to achieve 75% of its target before it covers its running costs.

2. to find out the number of units to sell to break-even

When the business has worked out the number of units (items or services) it plans to sell over the first year of trading, it can use the following formula to work out the number of items it will need to sell to break-even:

$$\frac{\text{FIXED COSTS}}{\text{SELLING PRICE PER UNIT minus VARIABLE COST PER UNIT}}$$

$$= \text{NUMBER OF UNITS NEEDED TO BREAK-EVEN}$$

the break-even graph

A business is likely to find the calculation by formula on the previous page useful, but will point out its limitations. The management might ask questions like:

"How much profit will we make if we sell 200 more units per month than the break-even amount?"

"How much loss will we make if production is short of the break-even point by 100 units."

The answer is to be found in the construction of a break-even graph which plots units of production on the horizontal axis and sales and costs on the vertical axis. This graph shows:

• a total cost line which is the sum of fixed and variable costs

• a sales revenue line which rises from zero

Case Study

Prontoys Limited
drawing a break-even graph

Prontoys Limited is launching a new cuddly toy know as 'Wuffles'. It has decided to draw a break-even graph to check the feasibility of the scheme. Before a break-even graph can be constructed, a table will be drawn up setting out the income and costs for different numbers of units. A table for Wuffles is shown below. The data used is: selling price per unit £20, variable cost per unit £10, fixed costs per month £5,000. Some of the figures from the table are then used to plot straight lines on the graph. These are:

• the total cost line (Column C)

• the sales income line (Column D)

units of production	fixed costs	variable costs	total cost	sales income	profit/(loss)
	A	B	C	D	E
			A + B		D – C
	£	£	£	£	£
100	5,000	1,000	6,000	2,000	(4,000)
200	5,000	2,000	7,000	4,000	(3,000)
300	5,000	3,000	8,000	6,000	(2 000)
400	5,000	4,000	9,000	8,000	(1,000)
500	5,000	5,000	10,000	10,000	nil
600	5,000	6,000	11,000	12,000	1,000
700	5,000	7,000	12,000	14,000	2,000

notes on the break-even table

- the units of production here are at intervals of 100
- fixed costs (Column A) are fixed at £5,000 for every level of production
- fixed costs (Column A) and variable costs (Column B) are added together to produce the total cost figure (Column C)
- total cost (Column C) is deducted from the sales income figure (Column D) to produce either a positive figure (a profit) or a loss (a negative figure, in brackets) in Column E

As you can see, break-even occurs at 500 units.

construction of the break-even graph

The graph is constructed as follows:

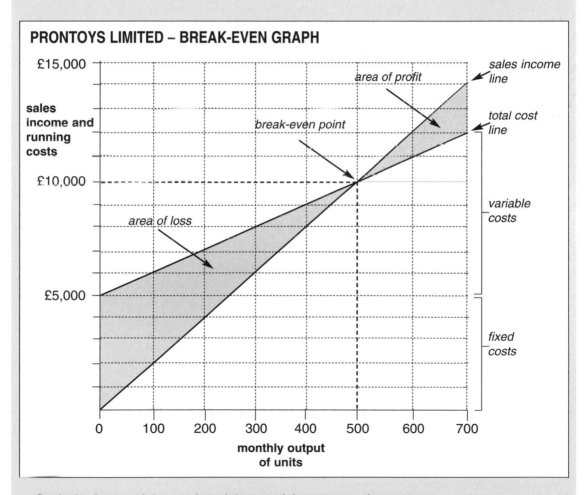

Study the format of the graph and then read the notes on the next page.

notes on the break even graph

- The vertical axis shows money amounts – the total cost and the sales income for different levels of production are plotted on this axis.

- The horizontal axis shows units of output at intervals of 100.

- The fixed costs of £5,000 are the same at all levels of output.

- Total cost is made up of fixed costs and variable costs.

- The total costs line starts, not at zero, but at £5,000. This is because if the output is zero, the business still has to pay the £5,000 fixed costs.

- The point at which the total costs and sales income lines cross is the break-even point.

- From the graph you can read off the break-even point both in terms of units of output (500 units on the horizontal axis) and also in sales income value (£10,000 on the vertical axis).

working out profit and loss from the graph

If you look at the graph on the previous page you will see two shaded areas. On the left of the break-even point is an 'area of loss' and on the right of the break-even point is an 'area of profit'. This means that for levels of output to the left of the break-even point (ie fewer than 500 units) the business will make a loss and for levels of output to the right of the break-even point, the business will make a profit.

If you read off the vertical distance (in £) between the sales income line and the total cost line (ie down the shaded area) you will find the exact amount of profit and loss for any level of output on the graph. Note that each dotted 'box' on the graph represents £1,000 from top to bottom. For example, at an output level of zero you will make a loss of £5,000 (this is the fixed costs figure) and at an output level of 700 units you will make a profit of £2,000.

If you refer back to the table of figures from which the graph was plotted (page 600) you will be able to check these figures taken from the graph against the expected profit and loss totals in the far right-hand column.

how the graph helps Prontoys Limited

The questions asked by the management were:

"How much profit will we make if we sell 200 more Wuffles per month than the break-even amount?"

"How much loss will we make if production is short of the break-even point by 100 units."

By reading the difference between the total cost line and the total income line, the answer to the first question is £2,000 and the answer to the second is a loss of £1,000.

Activity 27.3

Reading a break-even graph

You have been given a break-even graph for Insight Limited. Study the graph and answer the questions at the bottom of the page.

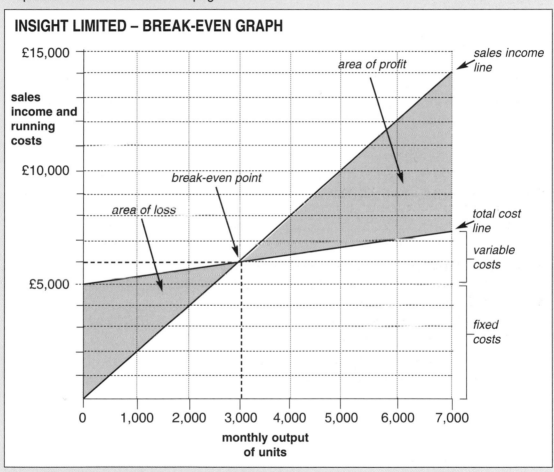

INSIGHT LIMITED – BREAK-EVEN GRAPH

1   How many units does Insight Limited have to produce to break even?

2   What are the fixed costs at the break-even point?

3   What are the variable costs at the break-even point?

4   What loss does Insight Limited make when output is zero units?

5   Why is this loss made?

6   What profit is made by Insight Limited when the output is 6,000 units?

Activity 27.4

Drawing a break-even graph

You have been given the projected monthly figures for two businesses and have been asked to construct break-even graphs for both of them. You have also been given a sheet of paper with hints for drawing break-even graphs.

---

hints for drawing break-even graphs

1   Use graph paper and a sharp pencil.

2.   You only need to plot two points for each line, one at zero output and one at maximum output. The lines will always be straight.

3.   Allow enough space on the vertical axis for the highest of the sales income figures.

4.   Allow enough space on the horizontal axis for the highest of the units of production figures.

5.   Make sure that your graph is correctly labelled.

---

business 1: Framers Limited

Framers Limited makes and sells framed Pop Art Posters. The selling price is £20 per framed poster, the variable cost is £10 per poster and the monthly fixed costs total £3,000.

units of production	fixed costs	variable costs	total cost	sales income	profit/(loss)
	A	B	C	D	E
			A + B		D – C
	£	£	£	£	£
0	3,000	0	3,000	0	(3,000)
100	3,000	1,000	4,000	2,000	(2,000)
200	3,000	2,000	5,000	4,000	(1,000)
300	3,000	3,000	6,000	6,000	nil
400	3000	4,000	7,000	8,000	1,000
500	3,000	5,000	8,000	10,000	2,000
600	3,000	6,000	9,000	12,000	3,000
700	3,000	7,000	10,000	14,000	4,000
800	3,000	8,000	11,000	16,000	5,000

tasks

1   Calculate the break-even point using the formula method to check the accuracy of the table on the previous page. The formula for the break-even quantity of output is:

$$\frac{\text{fixed costs (£)}}{\text{selling price per unit (£) less variable cost per unit (£)}}$$

2   Draw up a break-even graph, using the hints set out on the previous page.

3   Read off the graph the profit or loss if 100 posters are produced and sold each month.

4   Read off the graph the profit or loss if 600 posters are produced and sold each month.

5   Check the answers to 3 & 4 against the figures in the table on the previous page.

business 2: Winthrop Furniture

Winthrop Furniture makes and sells a wooden garden seat known as the 'Eden'. The figures for this business have not yet been set out in the form of a table. All you have been given are the following monthly figures:

Cost of timber and labour for making seat	£20 per seat
Selling price	£45 per seat
Monthly fixed costs	£15,000

tasks

1   Draw up a table showing fixed costs, variable costs, total costs, sales income, and profit or loss for production of seats in multiples of 100 from zero up to 1,000.

2   Calculate the break-even point using the formula method to check your workings. The formula for the break-even quantity of output is:

$$\frac{\text{fixed costs (£)}}{\text{selling price per unit (£) less variable cost per unit (£)}}$$

3   Draw up a break-even graph, using the hints set out on the previous page.

4   Read off the graph the profit or loss if 200 seats are produced and sold each month.

5   Read off the graph the profit or loss if 1,000 seats are produced and sold each month.

6   Check the answers to 4 & 5 against the figures in the table produced in question 1.

the cash flow forecast

This financial forecast is explained in full in Chapter 23, pages 528 to 537. You should read these pages again to remind yourself how a cash flow forecast works. Also study the format of the forecast shown below and read the revision notes that follow.

The cash flow forecast (also known as cash budget) shows projections of all money received and money spent over the year, for example sales income, running expenses, start-up costs. In short, everything that passes through the bank account is shown in the cash flow forecast. The 'bottom line' of each monthly column shows the forecast bank balance at the end of that month.

its place in the business plan

The cash budget is possibly the most important financial statement in the Business Plan which is presented to a prospective lender in an application for finance. It shows what amount needs to be borrowed and when. If the figures show that the bank balance will move into credit, it provides the lender with confidence that borrowing can be repaid, and also gives the owner confidence that targets can be met.

Name ....Cash Flow Forecast for the .... months ending ....

	Jan £000	Feb £000	Mar £000	etc... £000
Receipts				
sales receipts	150	150	161	170
other receipts (loans, capital, VAT recovered)	70	80	75	80
Total receipts for month (A)	220	230	236	250
Payments				
to suppliers for raw materials or stock (creditors)	160	165	170	170
other payments (eg expenses, loans repaid, VAT paid)	50	50	50	60
fixed assets purchased		50		
Total payments for month (B)	210	265	220	230
Opening bank balance at beginning of month	10	20	(15)	1
add total receipts (A)	220	230	236	250
less total payments (B)	210	265	220	230
Bank balance (overdraft) at end of month	20	(15)	1	21

receipts

These are analysed for each month to show the amount that is expected to be received from sources such as cash sales, receipts from customers supplied on credit, sale of fixed assets, loans, capital introduced, VAT recovered, and any interest or other income received.

payments

This section will show how much is expected to be paid each month for cash purchases, to creditors (suppliers), running expenses, purchases of fixed assets, repayment of capital and loans, interest paid and tax paid.

bank

The Bank summary at the bottom of the budget shows the bank balance at the beginning of the month, to which all receipts are added (A) and payments deducted (B) resulting in the estimated closing bank balance at the end of the month. An overdrawn bank balance is shown in brackets, or by a minus sign.

The Case Study Business Plan (pages 618 - 631) shows a typical cash flow forecast. Always remember that the figures included and calculated are always estimates. It is important to be realistic for these estimates.

the forecast profit and loss account

Another important forecast which is included in the Business Plan is the forecast profit and loss account. Whereas the cash flow forecast shows all receipts and all payments (including start-up costs, loans received, and owner's capital introduced) the profit and loss forecast is restricted to regular income items such as sales revenue and to running expenses. If you are not confident about the format of a profit and loss account, turn to page 478 for a reminder.

The profit and loss account forecast in the Case Study Business Plan (page 628) uses estimates for the first year of trading and so shows the profit for the year. You will find that the 'business starter packs' that you can get from the banks often set up a template for a monthly profit and loss account forecast, with comparative columns for estimated figures and also actual figures when they are known (see next page). This is a typical budget format; in fact the profit and loss account forecast is sometimes known as the 'operating budget'. For the purposes of your assessment, however, we recommend that you produce a profit and loss account forecast for the period of a year.

A typical bank 'proforma' profit and loss account forecast and also the Case Study profit and loss forecast are compared on the next two pages.

profit forecast

	month 1		month 2		month 3	
	budget	actual	budget	actual	budget	actual
SALES INCOME						
cash sales						
credit sales						
TOTAL SALES INCOME A						
DIRECT COSTS						
stock/raw materials						
sales commission						
other direct costs						
TOTAL DIRECT COSTS B						
GROSS PROFIT (A-B) C						
VARIABLE COSTS/OVERHEADS						
wages and salaries						
rent						
rates						
insurance						
heat/power						
telephone						
vehicle expenses						
stationery						
postages						
marketing/advertising						
travel						
bank charges						
interest and bank charges						
depreciation						
TOTAL VARIABLE COSTS D						
NET PROFIT (C-D)						

This form would be extended to show budgeted figures (and actual figures when available) for a twelve month period.

The figures from this forecast would in practice be summarised in the projection for the whole year shown on the next page.

FINANCIAL DATA – PROJECTED YEAR-END PROFIT STATEMENT

	£	£
Sales		480,000
Purchases	288,000	
Less closing stock	10,000	
Cost of Goods Sold		278,000
Gross Profit		202,000
Wages	43,750	
Directors salaries	48,000	
Rates	2,900	
Insurance	1,500	
Services	2,400	
Telephone	1,200	
Vehicle expenses	2,400	
Stationery	600	
Postages	1,800	
Marketing & advertising	12,000	
Office expenses	6,000	
Bank charges	600	
Interest	7,500	
Depreciation	14,625	
		145,275
Net profit		56,725

evaluation of the financial plan - profitability

It is essential that a business should monitor its financial results when it starts trading so that it can evaluate the success of its planning. This is in part taken care of by the budgeting process. A business can also extract performance indicators on a regular basis. For example it can examine the periodic profit statements and balance sheets it draws up in order to calculate indicators such as gross and net profit percentages and return on capital employed. If the business has outside investors it will need to calculate investment ratios to reassure the investors that their money is providing a satisfactory return.

projected opening balance sheet

The last essential document in the financial section of the Business Plan is the projected balance sheet of the business at the beginning of the first month of trading. Some business plans also include a projected balance sheet showing the position at the end of the year. The figures for the opening balance sheet will be available in the schedule of financial needs which is reproduced below. The numbers show where the figures in the balance sheet come from.

The only difference in figures is the working capital. The schedule below shows that the business can borrow up to £40,000 on overdraft to finance its day-to-day spending. When the business initially starts trading it has purchased stock for £24,000 (net of VAT) which is included as a current asset; this stock is financed by the overdraft for the same amount. As the business continues trading it will incur further costs during the month and so the overdraft will increase to cover this need.

---

financial needs

Item needed	£	
office premises	125,000	1
computers	45,000	2
vehicle	12,500	3
office equipment	12,500	4
working capital	40,000	
TOTAL COST OF PROJECT	235,000	

to be provided by	£	
own resources	125,000	5
bank finance:		
commercial mortgage for office	50,000	6
business loan for computers	20,000	
overdraft for working capital	40,000	7
TOTAL OF FINANCING	235,000	

FINANCIAL DATA – PROJECTED START-UP BALANCE SHEET

	Cost £	Dep'n £	Net £
FIXED ASSETS			
Premises	[1] 125,000	0	125,000
Computers	[2] 45,000	0	45,000
Vehicle	[3] 12,500	0	12,500
Office equipment	[4] 12,500	0	12,500
	195,000	0	195,000
CURRENT ASSETS			
Stock		24,000	
CURRENT LIABILITIES			
Overdraft		[7] 24,000*	
WORKING CAPITAL			0
			195,000
LONG-TERM LIABILITIES			
Bank Loans		[6]	70,000
NET ASSETS			125,000
FINANCED BY			
Authorised Share Capital			
125,000 ordinary shares of £1 each		125,000	
ISSUED SHARE CAPITAL			
125,000 ordinary shares of £1 each, fully paid		[5]	125,000

*note

Only £24,000 of the £40,000 overdraft was needed when trading started. It was required to pay for stock. The business still has a further £16,000 it can draw on to meet its future trading needs.

Remember that a balance sheet shows a 'snapshot' of the business on a particular day. In this case, on the following day the balance sheet will be probably be different – the bank account may change, stock may change, it may show amounts owed by customers (debtors).

CHAPTER SUMMARY

- Finance for a business can be internal (such as personal savings) or external (such as bank loans and grants).

- Finance for business can be classified according to the time for which it is required:
  - short-term: 1 to 2 years
  - medium term: 3 to 10 years
  - long-term: 11 to 25 years

- When a business raises finance from a bank it will normally match the repayment period of the finance to the life of the asset, for example using an overdraft for working capital, and a ten year business loan for machinery, a commercial mortgage for premises.

- Financing is also provided from outside the banking sector: for example hire purchase and leasing from a finance house, venture capital from a merchant bank.

- The financial section of a business plan will contain a number of separate sections which explain how and why the business project is viable.

- A schedule of financial needs will summarise the sources of finance – where the money is coming from and how it will be spent.

- Budgets will estimate the amount of income that will be received from sales and also the money needed, both for start-up costs and also for running costs.

- A break-even calculation will work out at what level of sales the business will have covered its costs. The calculation can be carried out either by applying a formula, or by drawing a graph. The graph will provide more information for management than the simple calculation.

- A cash flow forecast will project the inflows and outflows of money through the bank account over a twelve month period. It is a useful forecast in that it highlights the months in which the business may need to borrow from the bank on overdraft. It also helps to prove the viability of the project.

- The profit and loss forecast (operating budget) projects profitability over a twelve month period. Like the cash flow forecast it helps to prove the viability of the project.

- The start-up balance sheet can largely be taken from the schedule of financial needs. It shows what the business is investing in and how the investment will be financed.

- The financial plan will need to be monitored on a regular basis by the extraction of performance ratios in order to evaluate the success of the plan.

KEY TERMS

business loan	normally a three to ten-year loan offered by the banks to finance purchase of assets such as equipment
commercial mortgage	a long-term loan – typically twenty five years – offered by the banks to finance the purchase of property
overdraft	short-term borrowing on a bank current account
hire purchase (HP)	an arrangement in which an asset is financed by a Finance House and will eventually pass into the ownership of the borrower
leasing	an arrangement in which an asset is financed by a Finance House but ownership of the asset normally remains with the Finance House
factoring	the purchase of the debts of a business by a specialist factoring company – it turns the working capital of the business into cash
venture capital	financing of a company by means of share purchase or loans by a specialist investment company
Assisted Areas	defined areas of the UK which are eligible for Government grants – Regional Selective Assistance
variable costs	costs which vary in line with the level of production
fixed costs	costs which a business will have to pay even if it does not produce any product
break-even	the point at which sales income equals running costs
gross profit margin	gross profit divided by sales and multiplied by 100
cash flow forecast	a month-by-month projection of all the inflows and outflows of money through the bank account, normally over the period of a year
profit and loss forecast	a month-by-month projection of the profit of a business often with a summary projection of profit at the year-end; it is also known as an 'operating budget', containing comparative monthly columns for budgeted and actual income and expenses

28 Writing the business plan

introduction

This chapter looks at the practicalities of writing a business plan. In this book so far we have looked at the preparatory work in terms of defining objectives, market research and marketing planning, resource and production planning and financial planning. All these processes culminate in the business plan, a written document – often in ring binder or similar format – which will be presented to any potential lender of money or investor in the business. The object of the plan is to convince the reader, who may know nothing about the business, that the proposition is viable and that money invested in it will be safe and will enable the business to grow.

There is no set format for a business plan. The structure and contents of a plan may vary widely from business to business, depending on the nature and size of the project and the expertise of the writer. If you are undertaking a Young Enterprise or mini-business scheme, there may well be a specified format for you to follow.

Sonic Deco case study

To help you in the writing of your own plan we will set out the format and an example of a typical structure. The business is Sonic Deco Limited, a loudspeaker manufacturer. The sections of the plan are as follows:
- the business and its objectives
- personnel plan
- marketing plan
- production plan
- quality policy
- resource requirements
- financial support data
- monitoring and evaluation of results

getting help with the plan

A business plan, as we will see in this chapter, is a highly technical document, calling for the combined expertise of a marketing executive, an accountant and a production or operations manager. If the business owner is confident in all these aspects, there are books on the market and starter packs from the banks which will give guidance. If the business owner needs assistance, an accountant or management consultant will be able to help, although, of course, at a price. If you are undertaking a Young Enterprise or mini business scheme, you should consult your documentation. It is recommended that the plan be produced on a word processor so that it can be printed out in a presentable format. You should use a spreadsheet for the Cash Flow forecast and possibly also for presenting and calculating other financial data such as performance indicators.

Remember that a business plan is about selling a business idea. The effective use of communication skills is vital to the plan's success.

Case Study

Sonic Deco Limited
writing the business plan

In this Case Study we set out the business plan compiled by John Elliot and Edward Gardiner, the owners of Sonic Deco. They are forming a limited company to manufacture hi-fi loudspeakers. The product, the "Presence" loudspeaker, has already been successfully launched on the market by John Elliot working as a a sole trader; he is now being joined by Edward Gardiner. A large increase in production is planned, and the two directors need to approach the bank for finance of £110,000.

You should now read the notes set out below and study the relevant sections of the business plan which follows.

INTRODUCTORY PAGE

A business plan, like any complex document, needs careful thought about the order in which material is arranged. The first page is critical. It should include:

- the name and address of the business
- a summary setting out the business idea positively and clearly, quoting appropriate detail
- a list of contents – so that the reader can find the information he or she wants without having to thumb through pages of material

THE BUSINESS AND ITS OBJECTIVES

The nature of the business and its legal status (here a limited company) should be set out, together with the objectives of the business. The short-term (12 months) objectives should state:

- the type of product – whether it be a manufactured item or a service
- the expected sales volume (number of items sold)
- the sales value (the amount of income to be received from sales)
- the projected market share
- the profit target, eg net profit figure

It is common practice to summarise these objectives in a clearly-expressed sentence known as a 'Mission Statement'.

PERSONNEL PLAN

An important determining factor of the success of a business is the people that it employs. It is customary to list in a separate section the management of the business, showing their qualifications and experience. If necessary their CVs can be attached as an Appendix. The details of the other staff of the business should also be listed, although in rather less detail.

MARKETING PLAN

As we have seen in the marketing section of this book, a successful business should invest time and money in marketing. The business plan should convince the reader that the product or service will fulfil a specific need. The plan should set out details of:

- the product and its price (sales brochures could be included in the Appendix)
- the present market and the expected market share
- the competition, and why the proposed product is better
- promotion plans – showing timings
- distribution and sales
- the marketing budget (brief details)
- break-even calculations (note that this could also appear in the financial data section)

Note that the marketing plan which appears in the business plan is an abbreviated version of the internal marketing plan of the business (see Chapter 25 for an example).

PRODUCTION PLAN

The production plan will set out details of the physical resources needed for the production of the manufactured item. It will contain:

- a summary of the production method
- the premises used, showing full details of cost, valuation, whether freehold or leasehold
- the machinery and vehicles required, with details of cost, valuation and expected life
- raw materials needed, stating cost, supplier details and expected stock levels
- labour and training requirement

QUALITY POLICY

This will set out details of:
- quality control inspections
- quality assurance policies
- any plans for quality certification

RESOURCE REQUIREMENTS

This section summarises in financial terms:
- the resources that will be needed
- the amount of money being contributed by the owner(s)
- the amount of finance required
- the assets available for security

This section summarises for a potential lender the essential questions of:
- how much finance is being requested in proportion to the capital sum being invested by the owner(s)?
- what assets are available for security?

FINANCIAL DATA

This section contains:
- a twelve month cashflow forecast
- the balance sheet at the beginning of the twelve months
- projected profit and loss account for the first twelve months
- projected balance sheet at the end of twelve months

If the business is already trading, the financial data should also include past financial statements, normally over a three year period.

Remember that the cashflow forecast will include VAT, and the profit and loss account will not.

MONITORING AND EVALUATION OF RESULTS

The financial projections contained in the plan will enable the business to monitor and review performance during the course of the year.
The business will need to look at:

- **cashflow** – the business can compare the projected cash flow forecast figures with the actual figures on a monthly basis; if the figures are going widely adrift, the cashflow forecast can be redrafted

- **monthly profit and loss account** – often in the form of an operating budget

- **performance indicators** – profitability and liquidity percentages

It will be useful for the business each month to produce cumulative (year-to-date) figures for the profit and loss account. This will show any adverse or positive trend much more accurately.

BUSINESS PLAN

NAME	Sonic Deco Limited
ADDRESS	Unit 1b Severnside Industrial Estate
	Link Road
	Stourminster
	ST2 4RT
	www.sonic-deco.co.uk

SUMMARY

Sonic Deco Limited is a hi-fi loudspeaker manufacturing business founded by John Elliot and Edward Gardiner in 2000. John Elliot has fifteen years experience of loudspeaker design and has pioneered as a sole trader a new Deco 'Presence' speaker which is now in production in rented premises, and has already sold 500 units in six months to hi-fi dealers in London and the West Midlands. There is proven market demand for an estimated 5,000 units a year.

The new company proposes to takeover and expand the sole trader business. It will purchase an industrial unit, machinery and delivery vehicle. Total cost of assets will be £219,000. The owners are contributing £125,000 of capital, and the company seeks a further £110,000 from the bank: £50,000 by way of commercial mortgage on the premises, £20,000 by way of business loan for the machinery, and £40,000 by way of overdraft for working capital purposes.

CONTENTS

BUSINESS AND OBJECTIVES

NAME	Sonic Deco Limited
ADDRESS	Unit 1b Severnside Industrial Estate Link Road Stourminster ST2 4RT Tel 01605 577455 Fax 01605 577498 Email sonicd@goblin.com
LEGAL STATUS	Private limited company Shareholders: John Elliot 50% Edward Gardiner 50%
BUSINESS	Hi-fi loudspeaker manufacturer
START DATE	1 January 2000

MISSION STATEMENT

'Sonic Deco Limited will become a leading manufacturer of quality loudspeaker systems and a household name.'

SHORT-TERM OBJECTIVES

Sonic Deco will within the first twelve months of trading:

- produce and sell 4,800 units (pairs) of loudspeakers
- achieve sales turnover of £480,000
- achieve a pre-tax profit of over £45,000
- supply over 50 major hi-fi retailers throughout the UK
- take 10% of UK market in similar units

LONG-TERM OBJECTIVES

Sonic Deco will within the first three years of trading:

- increase the product lines to six loudspeaker models
- increase annual turnover to £1,000,000
- establish sales through agents in the EU, USA and Japan

PERSONNEL PLAN

KEY PERSONNEL

name	age	qualifications	position	annual salary
John Elliot*	35	BSc. MSc	Managing Director —responsible for production, sales and R & D	£24,000
Edward Gardiner*	45	BA.MBA.ACCA	Finance Director Company Secretary – responsible for finance and administration	£24,000

* CVs attached

OTHER PERSONNEL

job description	number	expected weekly wage
production line workers	3	£175
despatch clerk/driver*	1	£150
part-time packer*	1	£50
clerical assistant	1	£150

*to be recruited

MARKETING PLAN

PRODUCT

Sonic Deco 'Presence' loudspeakers (sold in pairs):

*   matched pairs in high density chipboard laminate with moulded fascia
*   attractive modern styling
*   two colourways – black ash and light oak finish
*   price £100 per pair (excluding VAT)

The product specifications and price have been arrived at following market research among existing customers:

*   questionnaires sent with products and mailings
*   customer comments made during telephone conversations

A copy of the brochure for the 'Presence' loudspeaker is included in Appendix 1.

THE MARKET

*   domestic use, supplied by hi-fi retailers and mail order houses
*   total UK sales in 1999 of £45m for similar units
*   expanding market (10% in 2000) – especially B, C1, C2 social groupings
*   further growth in market (forecast 7% p.a. to 2005) stimulated by demand from consumers for home entertainment systems

Sonic Deco Limited realistically expect to take 10% of the UK market in 2000.

THE COMPETITORS

Major names in the market are BEF, Rosedale, Session, M&W who take 80% of current total UK sales. Their weaknesses are:

*   staid image
*   high unit price – an average of £115 for similar units
*   slow delivery

We can gain market share by

*   our bright 'modern' image
*   price-cutting to £100 per unit
*   rapid delivery to suppliers
*   responsive after-sales service

We also have the advantage of being a small company which is able to offer a more 'personal' service to our customers.

– 4 –

MARKETING PLAN (CONTINUED)

PROMOTION

Promotion is by way of:

- monthly advertising in the hi-fi magazines
- mailshots to existing suppliers (quarterly from January 2000)
- purchase of product-related mailing lists (January)
- John Elliot visiting retailers and mail order houses
- sending the speakers for review to the hi-fi magazines

DISTRIBUTION AND SALES

Distribution of the speaker units is in sealed cartons direct to hi-fi retailers and mail order outlets. No wholesaler is involved.

Sonic Deco Limited is purchasing a van for local and urgent deliveries. It also has a contract with a carrier, SpeedDirect, which offers a 24 hour and three day delivery service within the UK.

MARKETING BUDGET

In the first twelve months the marketing budget has been estimated at £12,000. This will cover:

- advertising costs in magazines
- mailings
- purchase of mailing lists
- postages related to mailings

In addition, £1,800 has been budgeted for postage and delivery costs.

SALES PROJECTIONS

Expected turnover for the first 12 months, based on the sale of 4,800 units: £480,000

sales break-even figures:

$$\frac{£145,275 \text{ (total overheads)}}{42\% \text{ (gross profit margin\%)}} \times 100 = £345,892$$

Sale of units needed for break-even = 3,459

Sonic Deco Limited is confident of achieving this level of sales (72% of annual projected sales) in view of the existing good name of the speakers and the current demand shown in the order books.

PRODUCTION PLAN

PRODUCTION

Sonic Deco Limited will manufacture pairs of 'Presence' speaker units on a power saw and welding production line set up in their freehold premises. Three production line workers will produce 400 pairs of speakers per month.

The units will be packed on site in double-walled cartons with high-density moulded filling pads.

The units will be despatched from the premises either in the company van or collected by carrier.

The business will be administered from the premises by the two directors and a clerical assistant. An office will be set up on the premises.

All Health and Safety at Work conditions will be met.

PREMISES
freehold factory
Sonic Deco Limited will operate from:

> Unit 1b Severnside Industrial Estate
> Link Road
> Stourminster ST2 4RT

Freehold premises of 2,500 square feet
Purchase price £125,000
Professional valuation £127,500 (November 1999)
Business rates £2,900 p.a.
No mortgage currently outstanding
Financed by capital and proposed £50K bank commercial mortgage

MACHINERY
production line
Sonic Deco Limited will purchase power saws and other production machinery:
Cost: £45,000
Expected life: 5 years (20% straight line depreciation)
Financing: from capital and proposed £20k bank business loan

office machines
Sonic Deco Limited will purchase a PC and other office machines:
Cost: £12,500
Expected life: 5 years (20% straight line depreciation)
Financing: from capital

PRODUCTION PLAN (CONTINUED)

VEHICLE
Sonic Deco Limited will purchase a delivery van:
Cost: £12,500
Expected life: 4 years (25% straight line depreciation)
Financing: from capital

RAW MATERIALS

speaker units
Sonic Deco Limited purchase high quality bextrene cone individual speaker units for building into the 'Presence' cabinets.
Supplier is R & T of Cambridge.
Cost of the individual units is £20 (£40 per pair).
At present terms are cash, but from February 2000 terms will be 30 days credit.

speaker cabinets
Sonic Deco Limited purchase high quality chipboard laminates, internal bracing and filling from two suppliers.
Total cost of materials per pair of speakers is £20.
At present terms are cash, but from February 2000 terms will be 30 days credit.
Total materials cost per pair of speakers: £60
Average stock to be held is £10,000

LABOUR COSTS
The total annual labour budget is £43,750, calculated on the basis of employing the following for a 50 week year:
3 production line workers @ £175 per week
1 part-time packer @ £50 per week
1 despatch clerk/driver @ £150 per week
1 clerical assistant @ £150 per week

QUALITY POLICY

Strict quality control procedures are at present in operation for materials purchased and for finished products in respect of physical finish and sound reproduction.
Quality assurance includes a benchmarking exercise against BEF Plc and regular team meetings. Sonic Deco is at present investigating its overall systems with a view to application for Quality Assurance registration through BS EN ISO 9000 in late 2001.

RESOURCES REQUIREMENTS

RESOURCES REQUIRED

item	cost (£)
freehold premises	125,000
production machinery	45,000
office equipment	12,500
vehicle	12,500
materials and working capital	40,000
TOTAL	235,000

FINANCIAL REQUIREMENTS

item	finance(£)	
freehold premises	50,000	commercial mortgage*
production machinery	20,000	business loan**
stock/working capital	40,000	overdraft
TOTAL FINANCE REQUIRED	110,000	
CONTRIBUTION FROM OWN RESOURCES	125,000	
TOTAL	235,000	

*   commercial mortgage with annual repayments of capital and interest requested

**   business loan with first year interest only repayments requested

ASSETS AVAILABLE FOR SECURITY

security	value (£)	
freehold premises	£127,500	(valuation Nov. 1999)
other fixed assets	£70,000	(at cost)

FINANCIAL DATA – CASHFLOW FORECAST

Name of Business:	Sonic Deco Limited							
Period: January - Dec 2000								
	Jan	Feb	Mar	Apl	May	Jun	July	Aug
	£	£	£	£	£	£	£	£
RECEIPTS								
Cash sales								
Cash from debtors		47000	47000	47000	47000	47000	47000	47000
Capital	125000							
Loans	70000							
Interest								
TOTAL RECEIPTS	195000	47000	47000	47000	47000	47000	47000	47000
PAYMENTS								
Cash purchases	28200							
Credit purchases			28200	28200	28200	28200	28200	28200
Capital items	195000							
Wages	7645	7645	7645	7645	7645	7645	7645	7645
Rent/rates			290	290	290	290	290	290
Insurance	1500							
Services	200	200	200	200	200	200	200	200
Telephone				300			300	
VAT				7000			7000	
Vehicle expenses	200	200	200	200	200	200	200	200
Stationery	50	50	50	50	50	50	50	50
Postages	150	150	150	150	150	150	150	150
Bank charges			150			150		
Interest			500					
Loan repayments								
Advertising	1000	1000	1000	1000	1000	1000	1000	1000
Packaging	500	500	500	500	500	500	500	500
TOTAL PAYMENTS	234445	9745	38885	45535	38235	38385	45535	38235
NET CASHFLOW	-39445	37255	8115	1465	8765	8615	1465	8765
OPENING BANK	0	-39445	-2190	5925	7390	16155	24770	26235
CLOSING BANK	-39445	-2190	5925	7390	16155	24770	26235	35000

FINANCIAL DATA – CASHFLOW FORECAST

Sept £	Oct £	Nov £	Dec £	TOTAL £		
47000	47000	47000	47000	517000		
				125000		
				70000		
				0		
47000	47000	47000	47000	712000		
				28200		
28200	28200	28200	28200	282000		
				195000		
7645	7645	7645	7655	91750		
290	290	290	290	2900		
				1500		
200	200	200	200	2400		
	300			900		
	7000			21000		
200	200	200	200	2400		
50	50	50	50	600		
150	150	150	150	1800		
150			150	600		
			7000	7500		
			2000	2000		
1000	1000	1000	1000	12000		
500	500	500	500	6000		
				0		
				0		
38385	45535	38235	47395	658550		
8615	1465	8765	-395	53450		
35000	43615	45080	53845	0		
43615	45080	53845	53450	53450		

FINANCIAL DATA – PROJECTED PROFIT STATEMENT

PROJECTED TRADING AND PROFIT LOSS ACCOUNT OF SONIC DECO LIMITED FOR YEAR ENDING 31 DECEMBER 2000

	£	£
Sales		480,000
Purchases	288,000	
Less closing stock	10,000	
Cost of Goods Sold		278,000
Gross Profit		202,000
Wages	43,750	
Directors salaries	48,000	
Rates	2,900	
Insurance	1,500	
Services	2,400	
Telephone	1,200	
Vehicle expenses	2,400	
Stationery	600	
Postages	1,800	
Advertising	12,000	
Packing	6,000	
Bank charges	600	
Interest	7,500	
Depreciation	14,625	
		145,275
Net profit		56,725

Note:
The figures for purchases and sales on the cash flow forecast differ from those quoted above because the figures here *exclude* VAT.

FINANCIAL DATA – OPENING BALANCE SHEET

PROJECTED BALANCE SHEET OF SONIC DECO LIMITED AS AT 1 JANUARY 2000

	Cost £	Dep'n £	Net £
Fixed Assets			
Premises	125,000	0	125,000
Machinery	45,000	0	45,000
Vehicle	12,500	0	12,500
Office equipment	12,500	0	12,500
	195,000	0	195,000
Current Assets			
Stock		24,000	
Less Current Liabilities			
Overdraft		24,000*	
Working Capital			0
			195,000
Less Long-term Liabilities			
Bank Loans			70,000
NET ASSETS			125,000
FINANCED BY			
Authorised Share Capital			
125,000 ordinary shares of £1 each			125,000
Issued Share Capital			
125,000 ordinary shares of £1 each, fully paid			125,000

*Note that the overdraft of £24,000 results from the initial stock purchase of £24,000. The full overdraft requirement of £40,000 shown in the Resources Requirement section will not be utilised until the end of the first month of trading.

– 12 –

FINANCIAL DATA – YEAR-END BALANCE SHEET

BALANCE SHEET OF SONIC DECO LIMITED AS AT 31 DECEMBER 2000

	Cost £	Dep'n £	Net £
Fixed Assets			
Premises	125,000	0	125,000
Machinery	45,000	9,000	36,000
Vehicle	12,500	3,125	9,375
Office equipment	12,500	2,500	10,000
	195,000	14,625	180,375
Current Assets			
Stock		10,000	
Debtors		40,000	
Bank		53,450	
		103,450	
Less Current Liabilities			
Creditors		34,100	
Working Capital			69,350
			249,725
Less Long-term Liabilities			
Bank Loans			68,000
NET ASSETS			181,725

FINANCED BY
Authorised Share Capital

125,000 ordinary shares of £1 each	125,000

Issued Share Capital

125,000 ordinary shares of £1 each, fully paid	125,000
Profit and loss	56,725
	181,725

MONITORING AND EVALUATION OF RESULTS

SALES

Sales figures will be critical in the first year of trading. Sales figures will be reported to the directors on a weekly basis for discussion. The monthly sales budget will be completed promptly and any variances investigated and action taken accordingly.

Competitors' sales and national trends will be monitored and market share calculations for Sonic Deco completed six monthly.

CASH FLOW FORECAST

Monthly figures will be recorded and compared with forecast figures and inspected by the directors.

If the results fluctuate significantly the situation will be investigated and the forecast redrafted.

The cash flow forecast will be spreadsheet based.

OPERATING BUDGET

An operating budget will be set up on a computer spreadsheet.

Monthly figures will be extracted from the computer system and compared with the projected monthly equivalent from the forecast.

Year-to-date figures will also be calculated and compared with the forecast. The directors will investigate significant adverse and positive trends and take action accordingly.

All monitored figures will be supplied to a lender on request.

PERFORMANCE INDICATORS

Figures will be taken from the forecast financial statements on the computer to calculate:

- gross profit percentage
- net profit percentage
- return on capital employed
- current ratio (as %)
- liquid ratio (as %)

Note:
The appendices
are not illustrated

index